FIGURE 14

EASTWARD OAKLAND AND ALAMEDA TRAINS

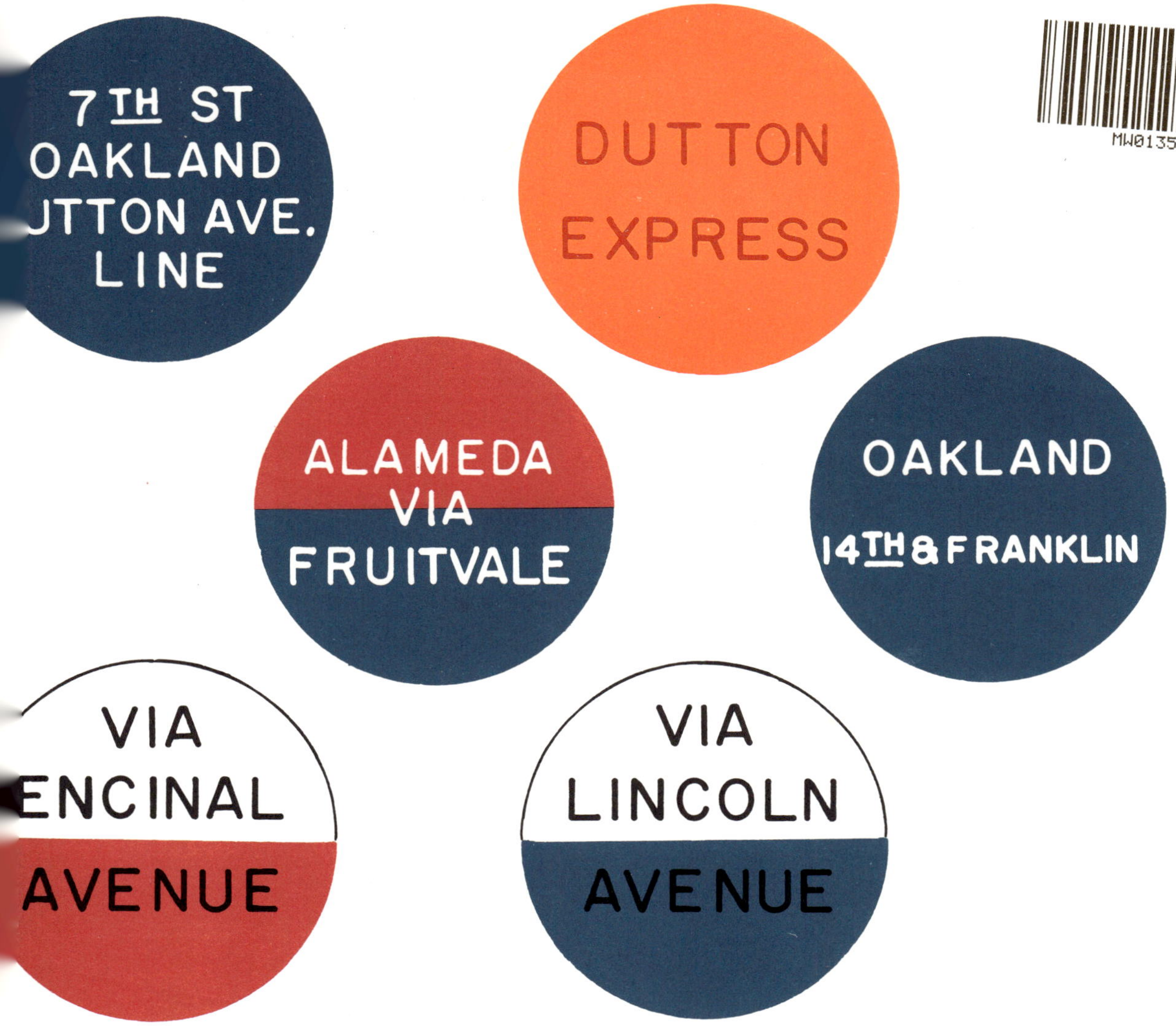

- 7TH ST OAKLAND DUTTON AVE. LINE
- DUTTON EXPRESS
- ALAMEDA VIA FRUITVALE
- OAKLAND 14TH & FRANKLIN
- VIA ENCINAL AVENUE
- VIA LINCOLN AVENUE
- OAKLAND 14TH & FRANKLIN STS. S.P. 16TH ST. STATION
- TO 14TH & FRANKLIN STS. ONLY

NOTE - Disc signs on trains are 22 inches in diameter; disc signs on street cars are 16 inches in diameter.

DISC SIGNS

Red Trains In The East Bay

**The History Of The
Southern Pacific
Transbay Train And Ferry System**

Robert S. Ford

INTERURBANS SPECIAL 65

Interurbans

PO Box 6444
Glendale, California 91205

Publisher . . . . Mac Sebree
Editor . . . . Jim Walker

© 1977 Interurbans Publications
a California Corporation

All rights reserved. This book may not be reproduced in part or in whole without written permission from the Publisher, except in the case of brief quotations used in reviews.

Library of Congress Catalog Number 77-78246
ISBN: 0-916374-27-0

First Printing: Summer 1977

Graphic Design by Mac Sebree
Cartography and Scale Drawings by the Author
Cover Painting by Harlan Hiney

To
MARJORIE

Dust Jacket Painting

FRONT COVER AND TITLE PAGE: Framed by signal bridges indicative of a first-class, heavy-duty railroad, a two-car Shattuck Ave. train accelerates away from Oakland Pier on a midday run to Berkeley.
Painting by Harlan Hiney

Back Dust Jacket Photos

STEAMING SOFTLY, the S.P. ferry *Eureka* awaits routine departure from Oakland Pier on a fine, sunny day in the early 1950s. She was representative of the scores of S.P. boats which faithfully plied the waters of San Francisco Bay over the decades, but by the time this photo was taken, her duties were few. Inset above is a closeup of the classic S.P. emblem done in stained glass, above the boat on the trainshed wall. A small touch for such a vast transportation facility, but more than fitting.
Both Donald Duke

Endsheets

FRONT DASH disc signs used by the O.A. & B. trains over the years were colorful in themselves. Each line had a different color combination, and an example of each has been preserved by author Bob Ford.

Table of Contents

INTRODUCTION 13

CHAPTER 1 **The Contra Costa Ferry** 17
The First Ferries—Enter Charles Minturn—The RANGER Tragedy—The Opposition Line—A Race Across the Bay

CHAPTER 2 **Rodman Gibbons' Railroad** 23
The San Antonio Extension—The 1868 Earthquake—Merger With the Central Pacific

CHAPTER 3 **Rails Through the Encinal** 29
The Extension to Hayward—The Hayward Earthquake

CHAPTER 4 **Arrival of the Overland Trains** 35
The First Train to Alameda—Oakland's Gigantic Celebration—The Wreck at Simpson's—Oakland Long Wharf

| CHAPTER 5 | **North to Berkeley** | 47 |

Hiram Graves' Ferry—The Berkeley Branch

| CHAPTER 6 | **Jim Fair and Hog Davis** | 51 |

The Line from Newark—A Gala Excursion—The $15,000 Franchise Scandal—The Webster Street Fracas—The Narrow Gauge Arrives in Oakland—Alameda Improvements—The Lease of 1887

| CHAPTER 7 | **Broad Gauge Locals** | 61 |

The First Ferry Building—The Creek Route—A Foggy Afternoon—Oakland Pier

| CHAPTER 8 | **After the Merger of 1885** | 69 |

The Decoration Day Disaster—The Nickel Ferry—The Railroad Strike of 1894—A New Ferry Building—The Alameda Pier Fire

| CHAPTER 9 | **End of the Steam Era** | 85 |

The San Francisco Earthquake—The Turkey That Crossed the Bay—The First Auto Ferry—The Great White Fleet—Wrecks and Other Misfortunes—A Bad Day on the Bay—The New System Takes Shape

| CHAPTER 10 | **Electricization** | 101 |

Reconstruction of the Alameda Lines—Seventh Street and the Melrose Extension—The Berkeley Loop Lines—The Richmond Line—Streetcars—A Tale of Four Stations

| CHAPTER 11 | **Ferry Tales** | 131 |

The Troublesome BAY CITY—Additions to the Ferry Fleet—Zone Day at the Fair—Fog on the Bay

| CHAPTER 12 | **The Big Red Trains** | 141 |

The Havenscourt Rate War—Dissolution—Sightseeing Trains—Composite Equivalent—Bridges . . . Bridges—Collisions and Wrecks

| CHAPTER 13 | **A Bridge of Ferries** | 159 |

Stormy Crossing—The Richmond Ferry—The Electric Ferries—Fog—The Great Merger

| CHAPTER 14 | **The O.A. & B. Lines** | 181 |

The 21-Cent Fare—East Bay Improvements—Flying Glass

CHAPTER 15 **In the Shadow of the Bridge** **195**
The Red Spot—Fog Schedules—Battling the Bridge—
A Ferry Christmas—The Death of an Institution—
The Last Auto Ferry

CHAPTER 16 **Last Trains to the Pier** **219**
The Non-Competitive Era—The Franklin Street Bus—
Difficulties With Alameda—End of S.P. Operations

CHAPTER 17 **The Interurban Electric** **239**
The Bridge Railway—Test Trains Across the Bridge—
Bridge Railway Opens—The Beginning of the End—
The Last Red Trains

CHAPTER 18 **Finished With Engines** **283**
Shipyard Ferries—The Last Ferry Tale—
Aftermath and Rebirth

APPENDIX A **Electric Railway Equipment** **293**
Final Disposition of Equipment—Big Red Comes Home

APPENDIX B **Railway Operations** **321**
Mail Trains—Freight Operations—Storage Yards—
Interlocking Facilities—Crossing Watchmen—Trackage
Ownership—Automatic Block Signal System—
Line Descriptions

APPENDIX C **Ferry Steamer Operations** **340**
New Life for the Auto Ferries

Bibliography **349**

Index **350**

Plates

Plate 1: Map of Oakland and Vicinity (1868) 25
Plate 2: Oakland Long Wharf (1906) 43
Plate 3: Oakland, Alameda and Berkeley Suburban Lines (1902) .... After 80
Plate 4: Fruitvale Power House 104

Plate 5:	West Alameda Shops (1923)	107
Plate 6:	14th & Franklin Station (1923)	111
Plate 7:	Alameda Pier (1923)	112
Plate 8:	Oakland Pier (1916)	116
Plate 9:	Oakland, Alameda and Berkeley Electric Lines (1913)	After 128
Plate 10:	Detail of Service—Downtown Oakland	225
Plate 11:	San Francisco Terminal (1940)	242
Plate 12:	Pole E-1 to 26th St. Junction and Bridge Yard Detail (1940)	246
Plate 13:	Interurban Electric Railway Company (1940)	After 256
Plate 14:	Car Diagrams—Classes 58-EMC-1, 58-EMC-4, 58-ETC-1, and 58-ECTC-1	296
Plate 15:	Car Diagrams—Class 58-EMC-2	298
Plate 16:	Car Diagrams—Class 58-EMC-3	300
Plate 17:	Car Diagrams—Class 58-EMCB-1	304
Plate 18:	Car Diagrams—Class 58-EMCB-2	307
Plate 19:	Car Diagrams—Class 58-EMB-1	309
Plate 20:	Car Diagrams—Class 45-ES-1	311
Plate 21:	Car Diagrams—Class ES-36½	314

Figures

Figure 1:	Contra Costa Ferry Schedules, 1852-1859	21
Figure 2:	East Bay Ferry and Train Schedules, 1864-1875	31
Figure 3:	Western Pacific, San Francisco & Oakland Railroads Time Table No. 2, December 6, 1869	40
Figure 4:	East Bay Schedules and Tickets, 1877-1893	58
Figure 5:	East Bay Suburban Schedules and Tickets, 1908-1916	148
Figure 6:	Richmond Ferry Inauguration, January 15, 1925	167
Figure 7:	S.P.-Golden Gate Ferries Schedules, 1937-1939	204
Figure 8:	Farewell to the Ferries	211
Figure 9:	S.P. Schedules and Tickets, 1926-1938	228
Figure 10:	Bridge Railway Inauguration	259
Figure 11:	Interurban Electric Time Tables	262
Figure 12:	Interurban Electric Transportation	266
Figure 13:	Interurban Electric Abandonment	277
Figure 14:	O.A. & B. Lines Disc Signs	Endsheets

Tables

Table 1:	Oakland Ferry Tariff, August 6, 1858	19
Table 2:	Population of East Bay Cities, 1860 to 1910	85
Table 3:	Operating Statistics, 1919	151
Table 4:	Comparative Labor Conditions for Platform Men, May 1, 1920	152
Table 5:	Passenger Traffic, 1927 and 1928	190
Table 6:	Auto Ferry Tariff, November 12, 1936	200
Table 7:	Bridge Railway Route Designations	250
Table 8:	Station Schedule of Train Movements, San Francisco Terminal, Tuesday, February 7, 1939, 4:00 p.m. to 6:00 p.m.	268
Table 9:	Annual Passenger Traffic, 1919 to 1940	273
Table 10:	Bridge Railway Daily Passenger Traffic, April 24, 1940	273
Table 11:	Electric Railway Numbering Series	293
Table 12:	General Specifications of Electric Railway Equipment	312
Table 13:	Final Disposition of Streetcars	315
Table 14:	Equipment Histories: O.A. & B. Lines—Pacific Electric—Los Angeles Metropolitan Transit Authority	316
Table 15:	Disc, Dome, and Whistle Signals	321
Table 16:	Storage Yards	322
Table 17:	Interlocking Facilities	324
Table 18:	Specifications of Ferry Steamers	343

THE *BERKELEY* leaves Alameda Pier. Southern Pacific's Alameda Pier facility was far more ornate than the busier Oakland Pier. **Southern Pacific**

Introduction

For nearly three generations, Southern Pacific played a vital role in the lives of countless thousands of commuters who lived in the cities of Oakland, Berkeley, Alameda, Albany, and San Leandro and worked across the bay in San Francisco. The trains which helped to shape the development of the East Bay communities first were drawn by steam engines and were called "locals" to differentiate them from mainline trains to distant points. Years later, when electric trains were running, this tradition lived on, used by many who commuted to and from the City on the Southern Pacific.

During the decades that the trains met the ferries, many plans were formulated to run trains across the bay and into downtown San Francisco. In fact, one of the very first plans suggested a type of underwater tube similar to that constructed nearly a century later. The account of this very early tube plan was reported in the *London Times* on December 27, 1872, and said in part:

> "A SUBMARINE RAILWAY: The American papers state that a railroad bridge which is to extend across the harbour of San Francisco to the mainland and to which the citizens have been opposed is to be somewhat of an architectural novelty. It is to run through an immense tube of boiler iron, which supports itself by its buoyancy, and is held 30 feet below the surface by a complicated system of cables, anchors, and buoys. The tube is 20 feet in diameter and is strengthened by an internal framework of iron beams. The principal problem was to have the buoyancy of the tube equal to the weight of a train of cars so as to require the minimum of anchorage support."

Ultimately, a great bridge was built spanning the waters of San Francisco Bay, and Southern Pacific's electric trains were able to run directly into downtown San Francisco. The bridge, however, also made it possible to drive an automobile or take a bus from the East Bay to San Francisco. This fact only served to accelerate the downward trend in ridership which dropped from a peak of nearly 30 million riders in 1919 to slightly less than nine million in 1940.

This history chronicles the development of the West Coast's first rapid transit system. It includes not only "nuts and bolts" data typical of many railroad histories, but more importantly, it is an account of the people who made the system what it was. It is a story of conductors, engineers, ferry captains, gatemen, and news butchers; it is also a story of a now-gone, slower-paced lifestyle when the world was a little more innocent. For instance, do you recall (or can you imagine),

- the sight of a knot of commuters standing by a typically Victorian station as a "San Francisco Express" train rumbles to a stop?

- the motion and sway of a crowded train as the conductor makes his way down the aisle, ringing up fares on the overhead register?

- taking a quick meal on the ferry where coffee was five cents per cup and a bottle of western beer sold for 15 cents?

- crossing the bay during a storm, as rain slashed the ferry's windows and as whitecaps marched before the wind?

- emerging from the darkness of the Ferry Building into the sunlight of lower Market Street where a parade of streetcars clumped around the three-tracked loop and newsboys hawked the *San Francisco News* and *Call-Bulletin* for a nickel, while the *Oakland Tribune* could be bought for only three cents?

- looking down on ships from the seven seas as the train came off the Bay Bridge, went past the Hills Brothers coffee plant, and entered the terminal, all to the accompaniment of the aroma of roasting coffee?

Through the many years of preparation of this book, a great many persons and organizations have provided valuable assistance. Without their kind and generous help, it would not have been possible to sort out the wealth of material on this vast and interesting subject. Foremost among those who have been helpful has been Vernon J. Sappers, who generously made his collection of photos and data available and also reviewed the manuscript for accuracy and thoroughness. Others who provided valuable assistance were Addison H. Laflin, Jr., Robert A. Burrowes, Louis L. Stein, Jr., Charles D. Savage, John C. Plytnick, Wilbur C. Whittaker, B.H. Ward, Robert P. Townley, Leo L. Mitchell, Robert W. Parkinson, Jack C. Gutte, Ken Kidder, Tom Gray, Paul Spenger, and N.B. Eddlestone. A note of appreciation also is given for assistance received from George Kraus of the Southern Pacific Transportation Company and the respective staffs of the Bancroft and newspaper libraries of the University of California at Berkeley and the California and microfilm sections of the California State Library in Sacramento. A special note of thanks is also given to the late Roy D. Graves, whom the author visited on a number of occasions to gather information about the early days of the steam locals. To Dudley Westler goes a special word of appreciation for providing editorial assistance during the preparation of the manuscript.

Finally, an extra special word of appreciation goes to my wife, Marjorie. During the preparation of this work, she had to put up with much more than do most wives. Countless times she would look at me and seeing a faraway expression on my face, would know that I was removed from the real world and was agonizing over a part of the book. When this happened, with patience and just a hint of laughter, she would say, "Hey, stop writing!"

SACRAMENTO, CALIFORNIA
February 1, 1977

A RED TRAIN for Dutton Avenue picks up speed after leaving East Oakland in Bridge Railway days. Today, trains of the Bay Area Transit District run along a nearly parallel alignment adjacent to Western Pacific tracks, left.
Charles D. Savage

THE STEAMER *Contra Costa* was the second boat of Charles Minturn's Contra Costa Steam Navigation Co. She is shown, right, at the Davis Street Wharf in San Francisco. River Packets *Capital* and *Helen Hensley* in background.
Roy D. Graves Collection

CHAPTER 1

The Contra Costa Ferry

SAN FRANCISCO! The name stirs excitement today just as it did a century ago. Then as now, San Francisco was a great port, a mecca for westward-bound travelers.

During the Gold Rush, all routes to California were hazardous to the extreme. Of those that journeyed overland, hostile Indians took their toll, and countless others died while crossing desert wastelands or perished in the deep snows of the almost insurmountable Sierra Nevada. Many more died on the longer and often perilous sea voyage. Every available ship, safe or unsafe, was pressed into service. Some foundered and sank, caught fire, or crashed with great loss of life on uncharted reefs and rocks. But still the Argonauts came, swarming in by one means or another from all parts of the globe.

For those who arrived by sea, the first glimpse of San Francisco was from a sailing ship entering through the Golden Gate. To the right, in Yerba Buena Cove, was an assortment of ships of every description. Schooners, brigs, barks, and full rigged ships; all types of sailing vessels, presenting a forest of masts. Interspersed here and there were elegant side-wheelers which had come around Cape Horn and steam-driven propeller boats.

These vessels were clustered around the piers and wharves which jutted out into the cove from East Street. Piers made of skeletons of abandoned ships and an odd assemblage of shacks perched precariously on rough pilings. As the ship drew closer, one could see that the waterfront was alive with humanity. Gamblers, touts, prostitutes, and more, hawking their wares and services to all comers.

Looking to the left, out over San Francisco Bay, one could see scores of craft of all sizes, coming and going up-river, down-bay, and all directions. Hay scows from Alviso, stern-wheelers from river landings, and the elegant white river boats down from Sacramento. As a backdrop to this melange of activity were the oak-studded hills of Contra Costa, across the Bay.

On landing in San Francisco, many of the immigrants sought immediate passage up-river to Sacramento and the gold fields. The city was but a brief stopover, as their real destination was the diggings. Places such as You Bet, Red Dog, and Toadtown lured the miner-to-be onward. Each was certain that the phrase, "There's gold in them thar hills," meant that fabulous quantities of the yellow metal were waiting just for him.

There were others who sensed that fortunes could be made an easier or a quicker way. These individuals preferred to remain by the Bay and pursue their particular capabilities, be it financier, merchant or gambler. Most who decided to settle by the Bay became residents of the fast-growing City of San Francisco. With all of the excitement and hubbub of the downtown area, with its talk of gold, gold, and more gold, some settlers decided that there would be advantages to living on the yet undeveloped eastern shore of the Bay. In response to advertisements carried in the *Daily Alta California*, San Francisco's foremost early newspaper, they purchased lots in the area called Contra Costa, which is Spanish for "Opposite Shore."

Soon, six communities evolved. The most prominent was Contra Costa, destined to become the city of Oakland. To the east were the towns of San Antonio and Clinton, later to be combined into Brooklyn and still later to become absorbed into Oakland. All three of these towns were located along the north bank of San Antonio Creek, the original name of the waterway which is now called the Oakland Estuary. Across the creek was the little town of Encinal, taking in the area now occupied by the main business district of Alameda. To the east of Encinal was the town of Alameda, located along the western shore of San Leandro Bay. The smallest of the settlements was the village of Woodstock, located to the west of Encinal near what is now the foot of Pacific Avenue.

The river packets working out of San Francisco did not make calls at these little East Bay communities as they were neither located along established routes nor were they of sufficient economic importance to have exclusive service. Consequently, the early settlers of the East Bay had to be content with crossing the Bay by whaleboat whenever a journey to San Francisco was necessary. A crossing of this sort could be long and arduous during times of choppy water. Furthermore, crossings were impossible during the not infrequent periods of dense fog for which the Bay is famous.

The First Ferries

Early in 1851, Rodman Gibbons, one of the original settlers of Contra Costa, proposed that some form of regular ferry service should be run across the Bay to San Francisco. Gibbons, who at that time was an agent for the DuPont Powder Company, provided funds to begin construction of a pier at Oakland Point, located west of the town of Contra Costa. He proposed to connect the pier with the towns of Contra Costa and San Antonio by way of a wagon road. Local wags, scoffing at the idea of a regular transbay ferry, dubbed the project "Gibbons' Folly" when the venture was suspended for lack of capital after only a short row of pilings had been driven.

Not being one to give up a project, Gibbons, in the company of several other East Bay citizens, journeyed by whaleboat to San Francisco to meet with Captain Thomas Gray, owner and master of the stern-wheeled river packet *General Sutter*. Gibbons was intent on persuading Captain Gray to operate his packet each Sunday from San Francisco to a landing on San Antonio Creek. He pointed out to the Captain that the venture should be profitable as it would give residents of San Francisco a chance to see the beautiful East Bay as well as give residents of the latter area some sort of connection with the rest of the world.

Captain Gray was agreeable to the proposal but had some misgivings as to the navigability of San Antonio Creek. He had heard of the treacherous sand bar near the mouth of the creek and did not know if there was an adequate depth of water at low tide. To determine if such an operation was feasible, Gibbons and Captain Gray decided to make a trip across the Bay in a small boat, making soundings at various locations.

A few weeks later, Gibbons, accompanied by Postmaster George M. Yard, again journeyed to San Francisco where the two met Captain Gray. The party then steamed back across the Bay in a small iron propeller boat which had been borrowed from financier Montgomery Blair. Gibbons, who acted as pilot, provided Captain Gray with soundings across the sand bar and up the channel of San Antonio Creek. When the little boat arrived at Moon and Adams Landing at the foot of Main Street (now Broadway) in Contra Costa, Captain Gray announced that the route appeared satisfactory and that he would begin operating the *General Sutter* on the route the following Sunday.

After several Sundays of operation, Captain Gray augmented the service with another of his boats, the little iron ferry *Kangaroo*. This boat, skippered by Captain John R. Fouratt, the first of a long line of Bay ferry masters of that surname, began making one trip each day between San Francisco and Moon and Adams Landing.

After operating through the winter of 1851-52, it became evident to Captain Gray that neither the *General Sutter* nor the *Kangaroo* were adequate for the job. In the spring of 1852, he placed the river packet *Jenny Lind* on the Sunday run and the *Hector*, a small ferry not much bigger than a yawl, on the daily run. The *Hector* was unique among Bay craft in that she was powered by a system of gears and cogs originally designed for use in a sawmill. When this ferry was retired a few years later, she was dismantled and her machinery moved to a redwood sawmill that operated in the vicinity of what is now upper Park Boulevard.

It soon was found that the *Hector* was grossly inadequate as a transbay ferry, and as a replacement, the river packet *Boston* was placed in daily service. The *Boston* did not stay on the run very long as she was replaced by the luxurious *Caleb Cope* early in March 1852. Offered for sale and moored at Contra Costa, the *Boston* burned to the water line on April 12, a fate fairly common to early day steamboats.

After operating the *Caleb Cope* for but a few months, Captain Gray sold his interests in the transbay service to William N. Brown, owner of the river packet *Erastus Corning*. This boat, which previously had been on the run up the San Joaquin River to Stockton, began making two round trips across the Bay on July 1, 1852, with Captain B.H. Ramsdall at the helm.

Enter Charles Minturn

During that same month, Charles Minturn, who had been operating bay and river routes out of Cunningham's Wharf in San Francisco, expressed an interest in transbay operations. On July 27, 1852, he placed his river packet, the *Red Jacket,* on the East Bay run, replacing the *Erastus Corning.* Minturn's boat, which originally had been named the *Empire,* and later named the *Kate Hayes,* had been especially outfitted for transbay service. When Minturn took over the ferry operation, he established a fare of $1.00 per person each way and $5.00 per ton of freight, which was not much of a transportation bargain considering the value of the dollar a century ago!

During 1852 and 1853, the *Red Jacket* usually was the regular boat on the East Bay run. During the summer months, three daily crossings were made. This was reduced to two daily crossings and an extra Sunday trip during the winter months. On special holidays, such as the Fourth of July, an extra boat, usually the *Erastus Corning,* was added, providing a departure every two hours from each side of the bay.

In San Francisco, Minturn's Contra Costa Ferry used the Pacific Wharf at the foot of Drumm Street until August 21, 1853, after which date, landings were made at the Jackson Wharf. In the East Bay, the ferry used Moon and Adams Landing at Contra Costa and the wharf at the foot of Commerce Street (now 14th Avenue) in San Antonio.

Because the wharf at Moon and Adams Landing was far from adequate to serve as a ferry terminal, E.R. Carpentier, an East Bay promoter, constructed a large U-shaped pier at that location during December 1852. This structure extended 40 feet south from the foot of Broadway and from the foot of Washington Street. A connection was built between the two legs where the water was three feet deep at low tide, making it more than adequate for the shallow draft ferries of those days.

Growth of the now incorporated city of Oakland and completion of Carpentier's Wharf prompted Minturn to add one daily crossing, bringing service to four crossings daily, with five on Sunday. This was a far cry from the one trip per week provided by the *General Sutter* just a little over one year previously.

Even with improved docking facilities in the East Bay, a major obstacle continued to plague the ferry operation. This was the notorious Oakland Bar, located at the mouth of San Antonio Creek. At that time, the creek did not run directly west into the Bay as the Oakland Estuary now does. Instead, the creek had a bend to the southwest near the foot of Market Street. To the north and west of this bend was a broad expanse of mudflats, while at the mouth of the creek was the infamous sand bar. At low tide, there was less than a foot of water covering the bar. This was one of the reasons that Captain Gray was skeptical of running the *General Sutter* up San Antonio Creek. The presence of the bar also had bearing on Gibbons proposing a pier at Oakland Point.

The bar continued to hamper traffic in and out of the creek, and on occasion caused an unwary pilot to become stranded. When this happened, there was little to do until the incoming tide lifted the craft off the bar. Time spent hung up on the bar was undoubtedly eased if one of the crew said, "Come on, boys, let's have a little game of poker until the tide comes in." A solution to the bar problem was not achieved until 1876, when the channel of San Antonio Creek was deepened and straightened by the U.S. Corps of Engineers.

Early in 1853, it became apparent to Carpentier that a ferry franchise would be financially advantageous. Consequently, in association with his brother Horace, he filed a proposal with the trustees of the city of Oakland seeking such a franchise. As a guarantee of performance, the Carpentier brothers accompanied their proposal with $10 in gold and a bond for $1,000. The trustees granted the Carpentiers an exclusive franchise for the operation of ferry service from Oakland to any other wharf or landing on San Francisco Bay. The franchise stipulated that the City of Oakland would receive a royalty of seven per cent of the gross revenue for the first five years and five per cent thereafter.

After receiving the franchise, the Carpentier brothers sublet it to their business associate, Charles Minturn. In turn, Minturn formed the Contra Costa Steam Navigation Company and contracted with John G. North for the construction of a new ferry designed expressly for the transbay trade. This boat, the *Clinton,* was built at the North Boat Works, located at Steamboat Point in San Francisco. She was placed in operation December 26, 1853, under the command of Captain John Minturn.

Soon after the *Clinton* was placed in service, fares across the bay were halved. Monthly commute fares dropped from $40 to $20 on January 1, 1854, and the single crossing fare went from $1 to 50 cents on the following March first.

As the cities of Oakland and San Antonio continued to grow and prosper, traffic gradually increased to a point where

TABLE 1 -- *Oakland Ferry Tariff, August 6, 1858*

Horses, each	50¢	Reapers, each	$3.00 to $7.00
Cattle, each	50¢	Threshers, each	$5.00 to $8.00
Calves, each	25¢	Ploughs, each	25¢ to 50¢
Hogs, each	20¢	One horse with buggy	75¢
Sheep, each	12½¢	Two horses with buggy	$1.00
Vegetables, sack	10¢	Stage coach	$2.00
Grain, ton	$1.50	Lumber wagon	$1.00
Hay, baled, ton	$2.00	Commute, per month	$5.00
Freight, ton	$2.00	Single passage	25¢

a second ferry became a necessity. During this period, whenever the *Clinton* was laid up, one of Minturn's other boats, such as the *Red Jacket,* was taken off a river run and pressed into service.

So, in mid-1857, Minturn again called on the skills of the North Boat Works to construct a ferry. This second ferry, the *Contra Costa,* was placed in operation September 15, 1857.

The bay ferries in the 1850s transported a great variety of freight in addition to the passenger traffic. This mode of operation was in marked contrast to operations of later years when only passengers and motor vehicles were transported across the bay. The following tariff, published in the August 6, 1858, issue of the *Alameda County Gazette* will give an idea of the diversity of transbay traffic carried by the *Clinton, Contra Costa,* and their contemporaries.

The Ranger Tragedy

Through the years, the Contra Costa Steam Navigation Company experienced several periods of competition. The earliest was operated by Messrs. Chipman and Aughinbaugh, owners of the high-pressure steamer *Ranger.* This vessel, commanded by Captain George W. Webster, began operating between the Long Wharf in San Francisco and Peralta Landing, west of Encinal, on August 22, 1853. Advertisements carried in the *California Chronicle* stated that the *Ranger* was "Warranted not to get aground," referring to the fact that it operated directly to the town of Encinal and did not go by way of San Antonio Creek with its treacherous sand bar.

Published schedules show that the *Ranger* departed from San Francisco at 10:30 a.m. and 4:00 p.m.; westbound crossings departed from near what is now the foot of Park Street at 8:00 a.m. and 1:30 p.m. In an effort to secure travelers bound for other towns, the schedules carried the note: "A hack runs daily between Alameda, San Antonio, and Oakland."

Service on this route was abruptly terminated on the morning of January 8, 1854, when the *Ranger* blew up just as she was leaving Peralta Landing. The *Alta California* reported the next day that the story of the explosion had been brought to them by two Frenchmen who had been on board the *Ranger* when she blew up. Making their way to shore, the two men walked to Oakland and caught the Contra Costa Ferry for San Francisco. They reported that the ferry had been about 300 feet from the wharf when the crown sheet in the boiler blew out. The blast sent the entire boiler sailing 100 yards out into the bay. The captain, who was in the pilot house, was thrown overboard, and the engineer, who was standing only four feet from the boiler, was blown across the stern post and severely injured. It was reported by the *Alta* that at least three people were killed and many were injured.

A brief revival of service on this route took place three years later, during the months of January and February 1857. This latter service was performed by a rebuilt paddle-wheel ferry, the *Peralta,* the first of two Bay ferries to be so named. Schedules published in the *Alameda County Gazette* showed departures from the Jackson Street Wharf in San Francisco at 9:00 a.m., 12:30 p.m., and 4:30 p.m. San Francisco-bound trips left Peralta Landing at 8:00 a.m., 11:00 a.m., and 3:30 p.m. As this service apparently was not profitable, it was withdrawn shortly after March 1, 1857.

The Opposition Line

Another more successful competitor to the Contra Costa Ferry was in the person of Captain Carlisle P. Patterson, a relatively successful river packet operator. Captain Patterson, in association with Fred Billings, a local businessman, formed the San Antonio Steam Navigation Company for the express purpose of operating a competing ferry service from San Francisco to Oakland and San Antonio. Under the presidency of James B. Larue, the San Antonio company acquired the river packet *Confidence* from the California Steam Navigation Company, and had her rebuilt for Bay service. As the *Confidence,* the boat had seen service on the Sacramento River, and was famous as the winner of a race with the *Queen City*. Renamed the *San Antonio,* the steamer entered service on April 18, 1858, bringing to a close Charles Minturn's monopoly of the route up San Antonio Creek.

Minturn, firmly believing in his rights under the exclusive franchise granted by the city of Oakland, sought a court injunction to prevent the non-franchised "Opposition Line" from serving Oakland. After passing through the lower courts, the case finally reached the State Supreme Court, which ruled that the trustees of the city of Oakland did not possess the right to grant such an exclusive franchise, and thus the injunction was denied.

Buoyed up by the court decision, Larue contracted for the construction of a second boat in the fall of 1858. Completed before the end of the year, the ferry *Oakland*—the first of two Bay ferries to be so named—entered service, alternating with the *San Antonio.*

Service by the two companies was hotly competitive, as each offered three round trips daily across the bay. Departures often were within a few minutes of each other, and often the race was on to see who would be first across the Oakland Bar.

Boats of both companies shared berthing facilities at Oakland and San Antonio. In San Francisco, the Contra Costa Ferry landed at the Jackson Street Wharf and later at the Davis Street Wharf. The Opposition Line used the nearby Pacific Wharf.

The bitter rivalry ultimately led to a rate war. Initially, transbay fares were 50 cents per crossing for both companies. Monthly commute tickets were $10, with purchasers usually paying with a "Single Eagle" gold piece. The Opposition Line soon halved its fares to 25 cents per crossing and $5 for a monthly ticket. Not to be outdone, Minturn lowered his fare to 12½ cents crossing and $2.50 for monthly tickets. Larue did not choose to meet this fare structure, and even with a higher fare was able to compete profitably because of public preference for his faster, more luxurious boats.

A Race Across the Bay

The keen spirit of competition was the probable cause of one of the most tragic ferry disasters on San Francisco Bay. This occurred on the morning of April 4, 1859, when the ferry *Contra Costa* blew up while en route to Oakland. The circumstances, as related by the *San Francisco Bulletin* were as follows:

The *Contra Costa* was scheduled to depart from the Davis Street Wharf at 9:00 a.m., as was the Opposition Line ferry *Oakland,* from the Pacific Wharf. At departure time, both ferries sounded their final bells and cast off their main hawsers. The two boats were then held only by their stern lines, and each was waiting for the other to start first. On board the *Oakland* were about 300 passengers, while the *Contra Costa* had about 150 passengers on board.

The *Contra Costa* cast off first, and to the enjoyment of everyone on board the two boats, the race was on! Soon the *Contra Costa* was about two lengths ahead of the *Oakland,* and this position was retained even though the *Oakland* was known to be the faster boat.

On reaching the Oakland Bar, the *Contra Costa* attempted a burst of speed. Suddenly, her starboard boiler blew up with a roar heard clear across the bay. Fortunately, most of the passengers on the *Contra Costa* were aft, watching the trailing *Oakland,* and the explosion caused only six fatalities. On seeing the boiler blow up, the *Oakland* hove to and came to the stern of the *Contra Costa,* where the passengers and crew of the *Oakland* rendered as much aid as possible. After picking up the passengers who had jumped overboard and transferring those still on board the stricken ferry, the *Oakland* resumed its journey to the East Bay.

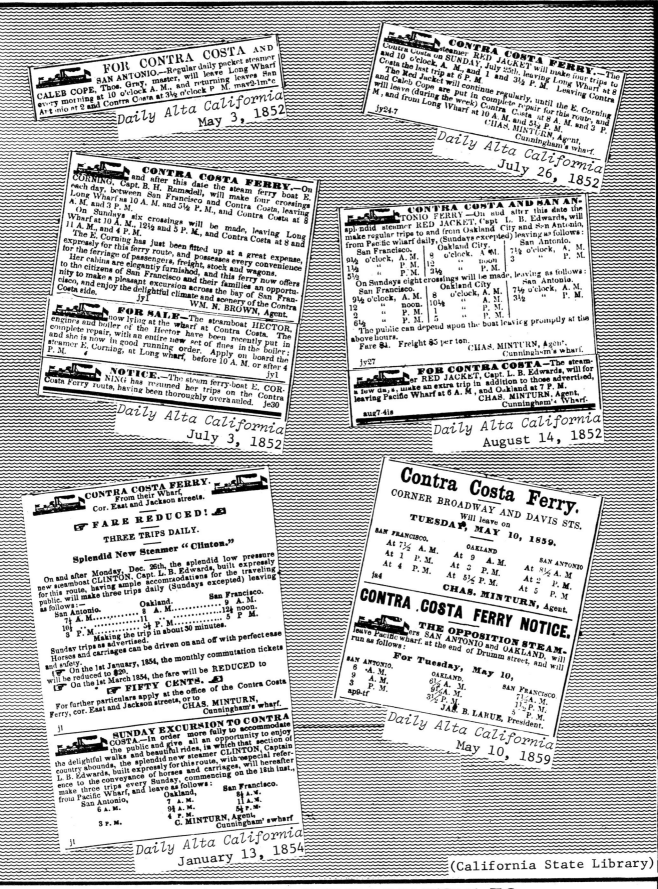

CONTRA COSTA FERRY SCHEDULES 1852-1859

Unofficial races between Minturn's boats and the Opposition Line ferries were not totally unknown. John Kelly, owner of a store on the Davis Street Wharf was watching this particular race through a spyglass when the *Contra Costa* blew up. He quickly got word to Charles Minturn, who ran down to the wharf and commandeered the steamer *Goliah*. With two physicians on board, Minturn took the *Goliah* over to the wrecked ferry. On arriving, he saw that there was an enormous hole in the foredeck, made by the boiler on its journey aloft. The explosion wrecked the hurricane deck, dropped the pilot house into the hold, and tipped the stack over onto the portside paddle box. On board, Minturn found that Captain John Lewis and pilot Nicholas "Knobby" Knowlton, both badly scalded, lay trapped in the demolished pilot house. He also found that the explosion tore through a partition into the adjacent saloon, blowing bartender Mitchell G. "Sixpence" Smith to kingdom come. No trace of Smith was ever found.

Minturn decided to tow the *Contra Costa* back to San Francisco, but because the *Goliah* drew too much water, he used the shallow draft *San Antonio* to tow the *Contra Costa* into deeper water. By the time the *Goliah* had put a line on board, news of the explosion had spread throughout San Francisco. Everyone who could make his way down to the wharf did so, and the crowds became so great that the police had trouble keeping control. When the *Goliah* dropped anchor just off the Vallejo Street Wharf, coroner McNulty, accompanied by several policemen, rowed out to the *Contra Costa*. After boarding, they arrested Captain Lewis and engineer Wyatt "Put" Birdsall and whisked them to the city jail, where each was held in lieu of $2,500 bail.

The next day, a coroner's inquest was held, during which testimony revealed some interesting facts about the *Contra Costa*. Charles Minturn testified that the ferry contained two low-pressure boilers which had been built in New York by Cunningham and Belknap in 1851. The boilers originally had been purchased for another boat. When they were not utilized, they had been stored in a vacant lot until bought for the *Contra Costa* in 1857. Engineer Birdsall testified that he needed a steam pressure of 44 pounds per square inch to get across the Oakland Bar. Although the boilers had never been inspected, he thought that they should have been able to stand about 60 pounds per square inch.

After taking this and other testimony under submission, the members of the coroner's jury concluded that the explosion was due to carelessness on the part of engineer Birdsall, and was occasioned by the rapid accumulation of steam which should have been relieved by the release of the safety valve by the engineer. Because there was no evidence of any laws being broken or of any willfully negligent acts being committed by either Captain Lewis or engineer Birdsall, both men were released and the case was closed. To the verdict should be added this footnote: "Even while racing, one should not take liberties with steam."

When the boiler of the *Contra Costa* exploded, it took off like a rocket and landed in the bay about 250 feet away. It was retrieved a week later and taken over to Shaw's Wharf, where an inspection revealed that there was a gaping hole located at the lower end of the fire chamber. After all the excitement of the explosion had died down, the *Contra Costa* was towed over to the North Boat Works, where she was rebuilt, reboilered, and then returned to service.

The adverse publicity caused by the explosion prompted Minturn and Larue to inform their respective employees that there were to be no more races between ferries. But, even after that, more than one captain was heard to tell his crew, "We ain't supposed to race anymore, but if that other ferry ever gets ahead of us...."

Races and explosions were not the only causes for excitement during the early days of ferry operations. When the fog came in and visibility dropped to zero, it was not uncommon for a ferry to get lost. Thus, because there was no form of transbay communications, whenever a boat became overdue during a thick fog, no one knew for sure just what had happened.

This was the situation with the ferry *Oakland* one foggy night in 1859. While tied up in San Francisco, the fog became so thick that the captain did not think it prudent to try to make the 9:00 p.m. crossing. So, he canceled the run and with the crew spent the night in the city.

Over in San Antonio, as the hour got later and later, consternation grew and imaginations ran rampant. All along the wharf were dire predictions that the *Oakland* had run aground, had lost her way, or even worse yet, had somehow been swept out to sea. The next morning, at first light, steam was raised in the *San Antonio*, which would have to make the first morning run. At the same time, a crew of men prepared a small boat to go in search of the *Oakland* once the fog lifted. Just then, through the mist, the melodious whistle of the *Oakland* was heard, and out of the fog loomed the shape of the errant ferry, much to the relief of everyone on the wharf.

In August 1859, Minturn and Larue agreed that competition on the ferry lanes was not mutually beneficial. An agreement was reached whereby the two lines were merged into one operation under the aegis of the Contra Costa Steam Navigation Company, with Larue as president.

The combined operation had four boats, the aging *Clinton* and *San Antonio*, and the newer and faster *Contra Costa* and *Oakland*. Effective with the merger, transbay fares were stabilized at 25 cents per crossing. To all appearances, it would seem that the Minturn-Larue combine would be in control of the transbay trade for quite a few years to come. However, the monopoly was to last for only another two years, for already a new version of "Gibbons' Folly" was being discussed in Oakland.

CHAPTER 2

Rodman Gibbons' Railroad

DURING the latter part of the 1850s, Rodman Gibbons, who was instrumental in the start of the first transbay ferry service, continually talked of his plan to build a pier at Oakland Point and operate ferries from there to San Francisco. Little came of this talk because of reminders of "Gibbons' Folly" and the operation of ferries down San Antonio Creek. Early in 1861, two significant developments occurred that ultimately led to the realization of Gibbons' dream. First, important local backing was achieved when George Goss, Charles W. Stevens and W. Hillegass joined with Gibbons to promote the project. Second, and more important, the original idea of connecting the pier to Oakland by means of a wagon road was modified to include a railroad.

As envisioned, a steam train would travel through Oakland, making stops at several stations, and then go out to the pier, where patrons would transfer to a swift ferry for the balance of the trip to San Francisco. This certainly would provide a most up-to-date transportation system and would be one that would operate more frequently and be quicker than the existing San Antonio Creek ferries. There also was the advantage of operating a ferry from a pier on the bay which obviated the necessity of traversing the sand bar at the mouth of San Antonio Creek.

In the spring of 1861, Gibbons and his associates sought approval of the railroad from the California state legislature. Formal application to the legislature undoubtedly was due to the recollection of the adverse court decision regarding Charles Minturn's so-called exclusive franchise granted by the city of Oakland several years previously. Approval of the railroad proposal subsequently was granted in a bill passed during the 1861 legislative session which authorized Gibbons and his associates to build a railroad:

> "... from a point at or near the westerly end of the bridge leading from the City of Oakland to the Town of Clinton, to a point on the Bay of San Francisco, where the Alameda County shore approaches nearest to Goat Island."

On October 21, 1861, after Governor John G. Downey had signed the bill, Gibbons and the others incorporated the San Francisco and Oakland Railroad and Ferry Co. John B. Felton, who later became mayor of Oakland, was named president of the new company.

As a vital first order of business, the railroad applied to the city council of Oakland for a franchise to operate a line from the eastern city limits, then near Fallon Street, westward along Seventh Street to Market Street and thence along what was later called Railroad Avenue (now West Seventh Street) to the western city limits near Peralta Street. From that point, the railroad would run west to Oakland Point, where a pier was to be built near the short row of pilings that marked the site of "Gibbons' Folly."

On November 20, 1861, the city council granted the franchise, and construction began immediately, the necessary capital having been secured from French interests. In contrast to the years of engineering study and design leading to the construction of any one of today's modern railroads, the con-

THE *LIBERTY* of the San Francisco & Oakland R.R. in the 1860s. This ornate specimen was the regular engine for early-day commute trains. **Roy D. Graves Collection**

struction of a railroad and a pier 100 years ago was a rather casual affair. For example, one morning early in 1862, Alex McBoyle and M.T. Dusenbury, having discussed the project with Gibbons, took a wagon load of timbers out to Oakland Point. After arriving, McBoyle walked to the water's edge, and gazing across the bay, said, "The pier will run out that way, so here's where we'll put the first piling." With that the two men set about boring holes with a large auger so that the first timbers for the three-quarter-mile-long structure could be erected.

Pine timbers for the pier were shipped down the coast from Oregon and were stored on Goat Island (now Yerba Buena Island) near the present site of the Coast Guard station. Each morning during construction, Dusenbury and a crew of men would row over to the island to get enough timbers for the day's work.

During the time the pier was being built, the railroad contracted with Vulcan Iron Works in San Francisco for two locomotives. One was a diminutive 2-2-0 type with a detached 4-wheel tender. The other, named the *Liberty,* was a larger 4-4-4 type. The smaller engine, which apparently bore no name, was shipped across the bay in ready-to-run condition. The larger *Liberty* was dismantled at the Vulcan shops and sent across the bay in pieces for reassembly at Oakland Point under the direction of Andrew J. Stevens, master mechanic of the railroad.

In the spring and summer of 1862, track progressed eastward toward the center of Oakland, where a station was built on the north side of Seventh Street at Broadway. On the morning of Wednesday, September 2, 1862, Dusenbury donned a conductor's cap and with engineer James Batchelder took the first passenger train from Oakland Point to downtown Oakland. The return trip connected with the ferry *Contra Costa,* which had been leased by the railroad from Minturn. The service which began that day consisted of six daily trips in each direction, leaving downtown Oakland about every two hours from 6:00 a.m. until 5:40 p.m. The eastbound ferry left the Davis Street Wharf at like intervals from 7:00 a.m. until 6:30 p.m. The new service provided by the railroad was a great improvement over that offered by the San Antonio Creek ferries and was enthusiastically accepted by the townspeople of Oakland.

During 1863, traffic on the line increased to the level where additional motive power was required. To meet the need, the railroad purchased a 2-2-4 type combination locomotive and express car from the Market Street Railroad in San Francisco. Years later, when describing this most unusual piece of equipment, Dusenbury recalled that "... it was not much more than a locomotive with a box car attached. We called her *Old Betsy,* and she was used as a relief engine whenever the *Liberty* was laid up."

The San Antonio Extension

The following summer, the lease on the ferry *Contra Costa* was terminated and the company's own boat, the *Louise,* was placed in service. During that summer, work was commenced on the extension to San Antonio. This extension began at the Oakland station and ran east along Seventh Street to Indian Creek Slough, the tidal canal connecting what is now Lake Merritt with San Antonio Creek. Here, a bridge was built, carrying the tracks across the slough and into San Antonio. Track then continued eastward along the north bank of San Antonio Creek to a terminal at the Commerce Street Wharf, where a station was built a short distance from the ferry landing.

With the opening of rail service into San Antonio on September 28, 1864, travel across the bay again became the object of bitter rivalry. To meet the challenge of competition, fares on the Larue boats were lowered for both passengers and freight. In spite of this, the Seventh Street trains soon were carrying the bulk of the traffic, due mostly to the fact that the trains were faster and provided six daily departures as compared to only three by the ferries.

The completed route of the railroad is shown on Plate 1, a reproduction of an 1868 map of Oakland and vicinity. Also shown are such contemporary features as Carpentier's Wharf, the Commerce Street Wharf, and Hibbard's Encinal Wharf, as

THE FIRST Oakland Station was at Seventh and Broadway; this view looks west. Oak trees in background gave Oakland its name. **Southern Pacific**

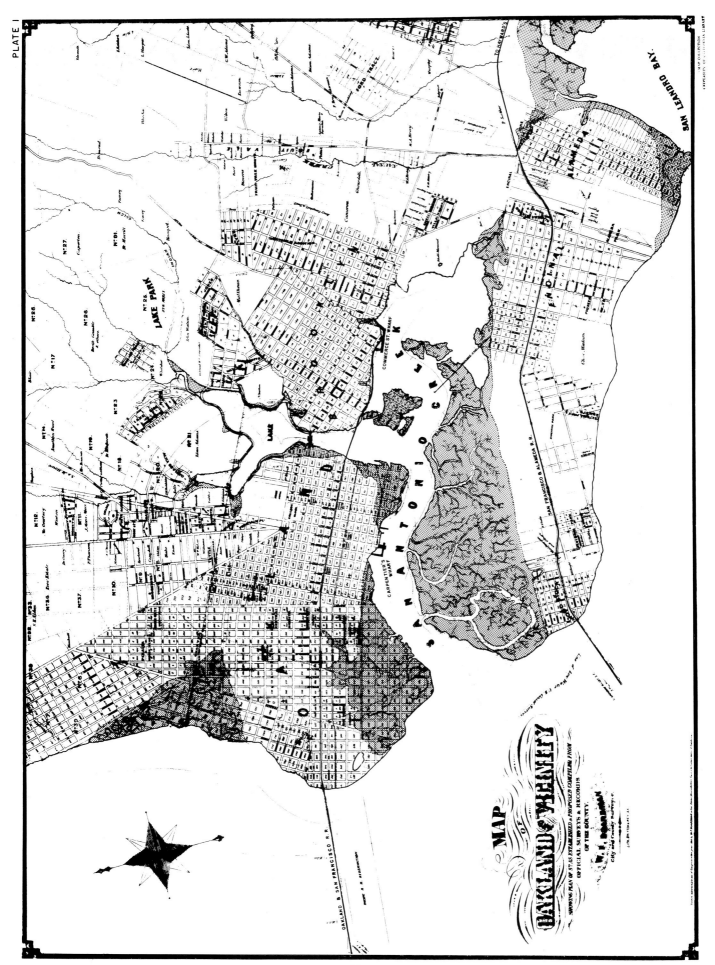

THE *WASHOE* steams toward Davis Street wharf. The words OAKLAND FERRY on the pilot house tell patrons that this craft is not bound for river ports as is the *Chrysopolis* to left.
Roy D. Graves Collection

well as the route of the San Francisco and Alameda Railroad. A projected rail route along Fifth Street is also shown. This route, which was taken from a preliminary survey of the Central Pacific Railroad, would have used the S.F. & A track as far as the "Encinal Line" (Centerfold Pl. 1), and then would have passed through the "Shell Mound" to the Commerce Street Wharf. The line would have then used Fifth Street to a pier to be built in the area identified as the "Pacific R.R. Reservation."

All during the summer of 1864, passenger traffic on the S.F. & O. continued to increase. It soon became evident that the ferry *Louise* was not a big enough boat. As a replacement, the hulk of the river packet *Washoe* was purchased and rebuilt for Bay service. This latter boat, which had been one of Captain G.W. Kidd's Opposition Line steamers on the San Francisco-Sacramento run, had blown up while running up river near Rio Vista on the night of September 5, 1864. After spending the necessary time at the shipyards, the refurbished *Washoe* became the mainstay of the S.F. & O. ferry fleet. Thereafter, the smaller *Louise* was used only as a relief and excursion boat.

Unfortunately, the cost of the extension into San Antonio and the expense of rebuilding the *Washoe* brought the railroad into a financial crisis which forced Gibbons, Goss, and the others to relinquish their interests in the company. After reorganization, A.A. Cohen, of the San Francisco and Alameda Railroad, became the new superintendent of the S.F. & O. One of Cohen's first acts was to promote the merger of the railroad with the Contra Costa Steam Navigation Company. The merger was accomplished on March 19, 1865, and the *Daily Alta California* noted,

> "The Oakland Railroad Company has purchased the ferries *Oakland* and *San Antonio,* known as the Larue line. The ferries will now run from the Company's wharf in Oakland instead of from Larue's wharf in San Antonio."

With an idea of further improving service, Cohen and his associates filed a Declaration of Intent with the Alameda County Recorder on January 22, 1866, proposing to extend the Oakland Point Pier to Goat Island, where a large ferry terminal would be built. Although the proposal ostensibly came from the S.F. & O., the Central Pacific, which had been quietly moving in the background, was the actual author. In order to implement the plan, the C.P. sought approval from Congress for permission to build the ferry terminal on the federally owned island. Congress did not grant the requested approval, and the proposal was dropped.

It was revived some years later, however, after the Central Pacific had absorbed the East Bay local lines. The revived plan called for a trestle and ferry terminal to be located on the shoal area north of Goat Island. As the floor of San Francisco Bay is owned by the State of California, approval for this new plan was sought from the State Legislature. This was accomplished without much difficulty, due mostly to the very close association between Collis P. Huntington and Leland Stanford of the Central Pacific (the latter also being a former governor of California) and those in the legislative and executive levels of State government. In approving the proposal, the Legislature granted the C.P. a 200-foot-wide right-of-way extending nearly four miles from Oakland Point to a mid-bay location north of Goat Island, and encompassing 150 acres of tide and submerged lands. Like the earlier plan, this proposal was never acted upon by the railroad, and the property thus granted was never fully utilized.

The 1868 Earthquake

The morning of Wednesday, October 21, 1868, dawned warm and clear, and at 7:54 a.m., the earth began to shake and tremble as a sharp earthquake occurred in the vicinity of Hayward, about five miles south of Oakland. Seven major aftershocks were felt during the next four hours. It was reported in the press that all of the shocks were of a "slow, rolling motion," and that with each shock, the earth shook violently for from seven to ten seconds.

Damage to the Oakland area was not as severe as it was farther south. Local damage consisted mostly in chimneys and brick walls being thrown down and windows being broken. The *Oakland Daily Transcript* reported that a portion of Carpentier's Wharf collapsed dropping 70 tons of coal into San Antonio Creek. Nearby, at Taylor's Wharf, 200,000 board feet of lumber went into the water and began floating down the creek.

The San Francisco and Oakland Railroad sustained major damage only at the Indian Creek Slough bridge, which was knocked eight inches out of alignment. Because the *Liberty*, with the only passenger train on the line, had tied up at San Antonio the night before, it was marooned. All early morning runs were canceled, though interim service was provided by mid-morning when a stand-by locomotive, probably *Old Betsy*, was coupled to two box cars and operated from the Point as far as Broadway. By the next day, the bridge had been repaired and regular schedules were resumed.

The *Transcript* noted that Broadway was crowded with people all morning seeking news of the earthquake, and that the telegraph office at Seventh and Broadway did a brisk business. Also reported was the fact that more than the usual number of people chose to go over to San Francisco that day. The crowds were so great that the *Louise* was used in addition to the regular ferry *Washoe*.

That same year, the Central Pacific, which had been acquiring a controlling interest in the local line, began a plan of modernizing the ferry fleet in anticipation of the completion of the transcontinental railroad. During the early part of the year, a shipyard had been built at Oakland Point, where the magnificent ferry *El Capitan* was constructed.

Launched in the first week in June 1868, this ferry was the largest on the Bay at that time. To celebrate the maiden trip of the new ferry, a gala morning excursion was held on June 21. Leaving San Francisco at 7:00 a.m., the ferry, with a contingent of state and city officials, bankers, lawyers, businessmen, and their wives, went over to the Oakland Point Pier to pick up a delegation of East Bay officials. The ferry then went up-bay toward Vallejo, and during this leg of the journey, a sumptuous breakfast was served in the saloon to the accompaniment of a string ensemble. After stopping briefly at Mare Island, the ferry returned to San Francisco by way of Raccoon Strait and Sausalito.

At the same time that the *El Capitan* was being built, the Oakland Point Pier was being reconstructed with expanded facilities. Most evident in the reconstruction was the lengthening of the pier from three-quarters of a mile to 6,450 feet. The new pier facilities were completed and in use before the end of 1868.

Merger With the Central Pacific

On November 8, 1869, the S.F. & O. became a part of the growing nationwide network of railroads. This event was signaled by the driving of the last spike connecting the local road with the rails of the Western Pacific Railroad, a Central Pacific subsidiary. On that date, Overland trains began operating in and out of Oakland Point Pier, using the Seventh Street route through town, and the citizens of Oakland could board a Silver Palace sleeping car for such faraway places as Ogden, Omaha, and even Chicago. The city of Oakland was the terminus of the transcontinental railroad; progress and wealth were at hand.

Also during the year 1869, the need developed for a new and larger locomotive to handle the increasingly longer local trains along Seventh Street. An order was placed with Danforth-Cooke for an engine of the 4-4-0 wheel arrangement. This engine was delivered later in the year, and was named the *Oakland*. It was the last locomotive purchased by the S.F. & O., as by that time the Central Pacific had a controlling interest in the local road. This control was manifested on June 29, 1870, when the C.P. consolidated the S.F. & O. and the San Francisco and Alameda into the San Francisco, Oakland and Alameda Railroad. This short-lived entity was absorbed into the parent company a brief two months later when, on August 22, all operations were taken over by the Central Pacific.

After the merger of August 22, local trains began to be operated by regular Central Pacific engines. Soon the original S.F. & O. engines were reassigned to other duties. The *Liberty* was operated for a while as C.P. 178, but in 1872 it was rebuilt from a 4-4-4 type to a 4-4-0 type and sold to the Stockton and Copperopolis Railroad where it became their No. 3. This engine later became Southern Pacific No. 1101 and was retired in 1892. Both the *Oakland* and *Old Betsy* were sent to the Central Pacific shops in Sacramento. The *Oakland* became a shop switcher until retired in 1877. The mechanical works from *Old Betsy* were used as part of a stationary engine.

On November 9, 1869, the *Oakland Daily Transcript* editorialized on the local transportation picture from 1851 to that date. In closing, the paper paid tribute to the one man who, more than any other, foresaw the development of a dependable transportation system:

> "To Rodman Gibbons, Esq. belongs the honor of being one of the few men who at an early date appreciated the possibilities of Oakland. The piles driven by Mr. Gibbons, and then styled 'Gibbons' Folly' still stand on our waterfront, but the long wharf, stretching out into deep water with trains of cars thundering over it, vindicate the farsightedness of the man who years ago saw what Oakland might and would be. 'Gibbons' Folly' was not such utter foolishness after all, as doubtless many who then laughed now think."

IN THE PHOTO, opposite, artist Joseph Lee captured the pastoral beauty of the Woodstock area that is now West Alameda. Buildings to the right are the shops of the San Francisco & Alameda R.R. Same buildings are shown in lower photo. **Roy D. Graves Collection**

CHAPTER 3

Rails Through the Encinal

CHARLES MINTURN, operator of the San Antonio Creek ferries, was one who recognized the advantages of developing trans-bay transportation routes. He owned considerable acreage in what is now the south-central portion of Alameda. After observing the success of the San Francisco and Oakland Railroad, he began making plans for a similar railroad-ferry operation to serve the growing towns of Encinal and Alameda. Minturn's plans undoubtedly were influenced by a bill which had been introduced in the 1863 session of the California State Legislature. This bill authorized the County of Alameda to subscribe $220,000 for a proposed Alameda Valley Railroad. This proposed line would connect the S.F. & O. at San Antonio with the San Jose and Stockton Railroad, then being built toward Vallejo's Mills, now known as the Niles District of the city of Fremont.

Capitalizing on this idea, Minturn, in association with Alfred E. Cohen and E.B. Mastick, organized the San Francisco and Alameda Railroad on March 25, 1863. Minturn allowed that the new S.F. & A. would serve essentially the same purpose as the proposed Alameda Valley Railroad, but that its western terminus would not be San Antonio, but rather a ferry terminal located at the western tip of the Alameda peninsula.

After organizing the railroad, Minturn and his associates selected a site in the town of Woodstock for the location of the company shops. From Woodstock, a pier would be built into the bay, where a ferry terminal was to be located. East from Woodstock, the line would run along what soon would be called Railroad Avenue (now Lincoln Avenue) through the town of Encinal to a temporary terminal in the northwestern part of Alameda, near what is now Pearl Street and Fernside Boulevard. After the necessary financing, franchises, and rights-of-way were secured, construction began at the foot of Pacific Avenue and proceeded easterly, reaching the Alameda terminal during the summer of 1864.

During the construction of the railroad, a 3,130-foot-long pier was built into the bay from the Point. Also during this period, the railroad placed an order with Vulcan Iron Works in San Francisco for two 2-2-0 type locomotives similar to the one previously delivered to the San Francisco and Oakland Railroad. The two engines were delivered to Alameda Point during the summer of 1864. One was named the *E.B. Mastick;* the name of the other has been lost, but it probably was named either for Cohen or Minturn. Cars for the line were built at the company shops during this period of construction.

THE FIRST FERRY operated by the San Francisco & Alameda Railroad was the *Sophie MacLane,* here seen heading across the Bay in the era of sailing ships.
Roy D. Graves Collection

In order to have a ferry available on opening day, Charles Minturn leased one of his own river packets, the *Sophie MacLane,* to the railroad. The first revenue train, pulled by the little *E.B. Mastick,* was run on the morning of Thursday, August 25, 1864. The *Daily Alta California* duly noted this event:

> "The San Francisco and Alameda Railroad which runs from the long wharf on the southwest point of the Encinal, up through the pleasant village of Alameda and up toward the head of the Valley of Alameda, will be opened for travel as far as High Street, about 5 miles, this morning. The elegant passenger boat *Sophie MacLane* will leave the corner of Vallejo and Davis Streets at 9 a.m., with regular trips scheduled thereafter. Fare from Davis Street to High Street is 25 cents. The track is graded as far as San Leandro, with the iron to be laid as soon as it arrives from the east."

Soon after the opening of service, a new 4-4-0 type locomotive, the *J.G. Kellogg,* was built at the company shops at Woodstock. This engine soon became the regular locomotive, and the *E.B. Mastick* was relegated to standby service. The other 2-2-0 type locomotive apparently was sold to the Los Angeles and San Pedro Railroad, where it became their *San Gabriel.* This latter locomotive was operated for only a few months in Southern California, as it blew up early in 1869.

THE *J.G. KELLOGG,* one of the first locomotives in Alameda, was built locally by the road's own shop forces.
Roy D. Graves Collection

The *Sophie MacLane* was the regular S.F. & A. ferry for only a short time, as it soon was decided that the larger *Contra Costa* would be better suited for the job. The *Contra Costa* was transferred from its San Antonio Creek duties to the run from Alameda Point, and the *Sophie MacLane* was then put on one of Minturn's up-river runs, resulting in a bit of good fortune for the transbay riders because a month later, on the morning of October 26, she blew up while moored at Benicia, killing four people and seriously injuring eight others.

The Extension to Hayward

With the opening of service as far as Alameda, attention was directed to the extension to San Leandro and Hayward (known at that time as Hayward's). Because the tidal canal connecting San Leandro Bay with the Oakland Estuary had not yet been excavated, the Alameda area was not an island as it is today, but rather was a long peninsula. It was a fairly easy task to push track across the open land east of the town of Alameda. After crossing Sausal Creek, the track cut diagonally across a large tract of land owned by Peter Sather, and then turned southward at Simpson's Station to run cross-country to San Leandro, where a small station was built at the corner of Ward Street (now Estudillo Avenue) and the County Road (now East 14th Street). Service as far as San Leandro began the morning of March 1, 1865, and a schedule of four trips daily in each direction was advertised.

The extension to San Leandro got off to a very slow start, somewhat to the disappointment of the owners of the railroad. The very first train, which arrived at the San Leandro depot shortly before 9:00 a.m. that morning had only a couple of passengers on board. It was also reported that the first westbound trip, which departed at 9:00 a.m. sharp, had only a very few more. Because of soft track conditions, the little train had to run slowly as far as Alameda. West of there, the train picked up speed and arrived at the Point in time to connect with the ferry *Contra Costa,* which put in at the Davis Street Wharf at 10:15. The *Alameda County Gazette* commented that the hour and one-quarter journey should be pared down to about an hour once the track had time to settle.

FIGURE 2

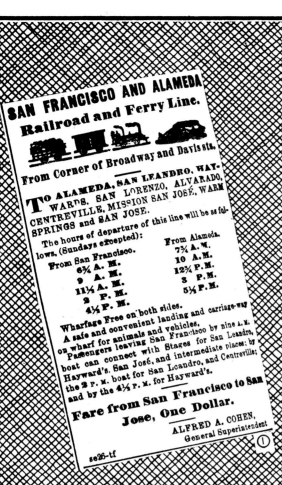

① *Daily Alta California*
   October 5, 1864
   (California State Library)

② Berkeley *Advocate*
   April 14, 1875
   (Bancroft Library)

EAST BAY FERRY AND TRAIN SCHEDULES 1864-1875

As an inducement to the further extension of the S.F. & A., a bill was proposed during the 1865 session of the Legislature which restated some of the provisions of the Alameda Valley Railroad bonding act passed two years previously. This new bill proposed that for each five miles of line built by the S.F. & A., starting at San Antonio, Alameda County would be authorized to issue $25,000 in seven per cent gold bonds, with the proceeds of the bond sale going to the railroad. The bill further stipulated that the initial five miles from San Antonio must be completed within ten months of passage of the bill and that the entire line as far as Vallejo's Mills must be completed within two years.

Because Cohen already had made his own plans for just such a line connecting San Antonio with Vallejo's Mills and had secured the necessary financing, he informed Governor Frederick F. Low that county bond money would not be needed. Consequently, Governor Low allowed the bill to die without signature.

Cohen's plan for the connecting railroad crystallized on March 22, 1865, when he and his associates formed the Contra Costa Railroad Company. Plans were immediately announced for the construction of a line by the C.C.R.R. from a connection with the S.F. & A. at Simpson's to a junction with the San Francisco and Oakland at San Antonio. In spite of the proposals, plans, and postponements, actual construction of this link did not materialize until several years later after both local lines had come under the control of the Central Pacific.

All during the time that the Contra Costa Railroad was being proposed, construction of the San Francisco and Alameda was progressing steadily southward toward Hayward along a route paralleling and just east of the County Road. When the track reached what is now the intersection of Watkins and D Streets, a small station was built to serve this little community of but 30 houses. The interest in the extension to Hayward was not so much for the potential passenger traffic but for the more important freight traffic hoped to be derived from such trackside sources as the Brighton Cattle Market and Mape's Flouring Mill. Until the coming of the railroad, these and other businesses in the Hayward area were completely dependent on the irregular service offered by the hay scows which used Mount Eden Slough. When the S.F. & A. entered the area demonstrating the advantages of scheduled train service, the volume of traffic carried by the scows dropped significantly.

On Friday, August 25, 1865, a free excursion train ran from Alameda Point to Hayward to commemorate the completion of the railroad. The *Contra Costa* left the Davis Street Wharf at 9:00 a.m. with a large contingent of excursionists on board. The connecting excursion train left the Point at 9:30, and after picking up additional passengers along the way, arrived at the end of track at 10:30. Here, the crowd was invited to join a promenade held in J.T. Edmonson's spacious warehouse. At noon, the guests were treated to a lavish lunch served in a specially prepared wing of the warehouse. During the meal, speeches of welcome and those which painted glowing predictions of success for both the community and the railroad were given by Cohen, Henry Robinson, Dr. Henry Gibbons, and other dignitaries. With the lunch consumed and the speeches digested, the excursionists returned to the cars and the train puffed back to Alameda Point, arriving there in time for the passengers to catch the 2:30 ferry to San Francisco.

Regular service to Hayward began the next day with four trips daily. The fare to the end of the line, which to urbane San Franciscans seemed a long way out in the country, was 75 cents each way or five tickets for $2.50.

From the time service first began, passenger traffic all along the line steadily increased as more and more people flocked to the Alameda area to make their homes. It soon became apparent to Cohen that the leased ferry *Contra Costa* was far from adequate for the service performed. Being one to desire the very best for his line, he arranged for the construction of the ferry *Alameda,* the first of two Bay ferries to be so named. This *Alameda* was the first double-end beam ferryboat built expressly for San Francisco Bay service. Launched in 1866, the new ferry was an immediate success. After the *Alameda* entered service, the lease on the *Contra Costa* was terminated and she was returned to Minturn.

Traffic on the S.F. & A., which now extended from Woodstock all the way to Hayward, a distance of about 17 miles, continued to increase. Early in 1868, an order was placed with Grant Locomotive Works for a locomotive having a 4-4-0 wheel arrangement. This engine, named the *F.D. Atherton,* was delivered that summer and proved to be a valuable relief for the little *E.B. Mastick* and the larger *J.G. Kellogg.*

The Hayward Earthquake

The Hayward earthquake of October 21, 1868, although severe, caused less damage to the San Francisco and Alameda than it did to its neighboring road, the San Francisco and Oakland. This was most likely due to there being very few structures on the Alameda road which were susceptible to damage.

In contrast to the railroad, brick and frame structures in Hayward (erroneously carried in some press reports as Haywood or Haywood's) were almost totally destroyed. The press of that day carried many accounts of collapsed buildings and other destruction which took place during the main shock, which occurred at 7:54 a.m., and the aftershocks which came at 8:26, 8:40, 8:44, 8:47, 9:11, 10:25, and 11:40.

The next day, the *Daily Alta California* carried the following account of what had happened in the Hayward area:

> "One of the most alarming and destructive earthquakes ever felt since its settlement by whites occurred this morning at about ten minutes before 8 o'clock. The direction of shock seemed to be from southwest to northeast and so severe was it that in a number of places the ground opened from 6 inches to 2 feet, through which water and quicksand, in considerable quantities, were forced to a height of from one to three feet.
>
> "Edmonson's large warehouse is a complete wreck, not a beam or board remaining in its original position.
>
> "Mape's Flouring Mill is turned topsy turvy. Machinery, stones, etc. were pitched out in a very unceremonial manner, and now lie promiscuously around."

San Leandro also sustained heavy damage, and the court house at that locality was destroyed. The *Alta* reported that the County Clerk had been trapped inside the crumbling building and had been killed. The prisoners which had been lodged in the basement jail also had become buried in the rubble and it was not known how many had died. Then as now, earthquakes were major disasters, disrupting the community for days and even weeks.

During that same year, the Central Pacific began acquisition of the Alameda road with the intention of incorporating it and the S.F. & O. into the ever-expanding C.P. system. Working through its subsidiary the Western Pacific, the C.P. pushed north from Vallejo's Mills (now the Niles district of Fremont)

THE FERRY *Alameda* was the pride of the S.F. & A. Launched in 1866, she was the first double end, vertical beam ferry on the Bay.
Roy D. Graves Collection

in 1869 and made a track connection with the S.F. & A. at San Leandro in August of that year. Thereafter, Overland trains, and those from Sacramento, used the S.F. & A. track from San Leandro to Alameda Point, where passengers transferred to the ferry *Alameda* for the balance of the trip to San Francisco.

Formal integration of the S.F. & A. into the Central Pacific system was accomplished on June 29, 1870, when the Alameda road, together with the S.F. & O., were combined to form the San Francisco, Oakland and Alameda Railroad, a Central Pacific subsidiary. This subsidiary was absorbed into the parent organization on the following August 22, and thereafter, all service along the route of the S.F. & A. was operated by the Central Pacific.

Former S.F. & A. runs were soon taken over by engines and cars lettered for the Central Pacific. The locomotive *E.B. Mastick* was transferred to the Oakland roundhouse, where it was used for a few years as a shop switcher until scrapped in 1874. The *J.G. Kellogg* became Central Pacific No. 176, and later was sent to the Central Pacific shops in Sacramento for rebuilding. It subsequently was sold to the Stockton and Copperopolis Railroad, where it became their No. 2. Still later, the engine became Southern Pacific No. 1100; it was scrapped in 1891. The *F.D. Atherton* had been almost totally demolished in the wreck at Simpson's in November 1869. It is reported that the few salvageable parts were used in the erection of Central Pacific No. 177, which was built at the C.P. shops in Sacramento in 1873.

THE *F.D. ATHERTON* stands amid the wreckage caused by the Hayward earthquake of 1868.
Roy D. Graves Collection

A FREIGHT TRAIN rumbles off the ferry *Thoroughfare* and into the Oakland Long Wharf yard. Passenger terminal is at left.
R.S. Ford Collection

CHAPTER 4

Arrival of the Overland Trains

THE CENTRAL PACIFIC Railroad was the outgrowth of a dream of destiny by Leland Stanford, Collis P. Huntington, Charles Crocker, and Mark Hopkins, the "Big Four" of railroad legend. Their first task was to push the rails east from Sacramento, up and over the snowy summit of the Sierra Nevada, and across the burning deserts of Nevada to a meeting with the Union Pacific at Promontory, Utah. Once the connection had been made and the Overland trains began operating as far as Sacramento, Stanford and his associates turned to the problem of getting rails to San Francisco Bay.

Various routes were considered for the extension of the Central Pacific to tidewater. Most were cloaked in secrecy so as not to give any advantage to potential competitors such as the California Pacific Railroad, which had just recently opened a line from Sacramento to Vallejo. After considering routes through Walnut Grove and Antioch, a selection was made which involved the financially troubled Western Pacific Railroad. The Western Pacific of this period bears no relationship to the present railroad of the same name; it went out of existence many years before the present-day Western Pacific was formed.

The early-day Western Pacific had been formed on December 13, 1863, by Peter Donahue of the North Pacific Coast Railroad. As formed, the W.P. was an outgrowth of a still earlier line, the San Jose and Stockton Railroad. Donahue's route for the W.P. was from San Jose north to Vallejo's Mills, and then east along the canyon of Alameda Creek to Amador Valley (now Livermore Valley) and then over Livermore's Pass (now called Altamont Pass) to Stockton and ultimately Sacramento.

The building of the Western Pacific began at San Jose, and track had reached Vallejo's Mills when a lack of funds forced a cessation of construction. Because the line had been surveyed nearly all of the way to Sacramento, and as it appeared to be an advantageous route to San Francisco Bay, it was more than just a coincidence that the Construction and Finance Company, a Central Pacific subsidiary, stepped forward with an offer of funds to complete the line.

Construction of the Western Pacific began anew in the spring of 1867, with crews laying track south from Sacramento and east from Vallejo's Mills. During this renewed period of construction, an agreement was reached between Donahue and the men of the Central Pacific transferring all Western Pacific stock to the Central Pacific. On May 15, 1869, the W.P. became a wholly owned C.P. subsidiary; on June 23 of the following year, it was merged into the parent company.

To bridge the gap between Vallejo's Mills and the San Francisco and Alameda tracks at San Leandro, the Central Pacific formed the San Francisco Bay Railroad on September 28, 1868. After building a connection at Vallejo's Mills, construction progressed northward at a fairly rapid rate, reaching the S.F. & A. rails at San Leandro in early summer 1869.

During construction of the San Francisco Bay Railroad, the track of the S.F. & A., from San Leandro west, was rebuilt with heavier rail to bring it up to C.P. standards. In commenting on this rebuilding, the *San Francisco Bulletin* noted that 120 tons of rail had been delivered along the line of the S.F. & A. one morning between daybreak and 9:00 a.m.

In building north from Vallejo's Mills, the route of the new railroad lay about a mile west of the settlement of Hayward. To serve this little community, a station named Marion was established at a point where Davis Street crossed the track.

Because the ultimate goal of the Central Pacific was Oakland rather than Alameda, a switch was installed at Simpson's Station, and a new line built north therefrom essentially along the route of Alfred Cohen's projected Contra Costa Railroad.

The First Train to Alameda

In Sacramento, the California State Agricultural Society opened its annual fair on Monday, September 6, 1869. In commemoration of that event, that day's Overland train was routed by way of the newly completed Western Pacific from Sacramento to Alameda. The 16-car train, which left Sacramento at 10:00 a.m., was hauled by three locomotives. On board were former Governor Leland Stanford, S.F. & A. President Alfred A. Cohen, many dignitaries and excursionists, and eleven Overland passengers. After being delayed at Stockton so that work trains could clear the line, the train arrived at the San Joaquin River Bridge at Mossdale. Here, the train was further delayed as crews were still spiking down the rails on the bridge. When the train arrived at Vallejo's Mills, there was yet another delay, as one engine and a number of cars were cut off so that they could go down to San Jose.

When the train finally arrived at Alameda at 7:30 p.m., it was met by a large crowd of cheering people. At the depot, a large arch had been built over the track. Across the top of the arch was spelled out WELCOME; the pillars of the arch were decorated with roses, evergreens, and flags. After a brief stop to acknowledge the greetings, the train continued west, arriving at the Alameda Point Pier at a little before 8 p.m. Here, the train's contingent boarded the ferry *Alameda* for the remainder of the trip to San Francisco. Thus marked the arrival of the first Overland train, a pattern which was to continue with minor variations for the next 89 years.

At 7:30 the next morning, the first train bound for Sacramento and points east left Alameda Point with 80 passengers on board. Advertised schedules beginning that day showed the ferry leaving San Francisco at 7:00 a.m. and 3:30 p.m., with the train departing from the Alameda Pier just thirty minutes later. The trains from the east arrived at the pier at 10:30 a.m. and 7:00 p.m.

With service established to San Francisco by way of Alameda, the Central Pacific, working through its subsidiary the San Francisco Bay Railroad, continued construction toward the San Francisco and Oakland Railroad at San Antonio. On September 9, the *Oakland Transcript* ran the following account of the construction of the new line:

> "The new road runs straight from Swett's Stables in San Antonio to Vallejo's Mills. The grading is complete from San Leandro as far as Fruit Vale Avenue, and all that is needed on this part are two small bridges. From Fruit Vale Avenue to Swett's Stables, the line will be mostly on trestle through the property of Larue and Swett. There are many tent camps spread along the line, and the work force consists of 30 carpenters, 110 laborers, and 140 horses and mules."

THE *ALAMEDA* nears the Davis Street Wharf in schooner days.
Roy D. Graves Collection

OAKLAND LONG WHARF (above, right) as it looked shortly after completion in 1870. At left the *El Capitan* departs under a cloud of coal smoke. View (right) shows facility in the 1880s after Oakland Pier had been placed in operation.
Both Roy D. Graves Collection

A BUNCH OF THE BOYS pose near the Yard Office at Oakland Long Wharf in the days of full-rigged sailing ships. **Southern Pacific**

Completion of the trestles leading to Swett's Stables was accomplished by the end of October, and on Wednesday, November 8, 1869, the Overland trains began operating by way of the Seventh Street route to and from the ferry terminal at Oakland Point. Thereafter, the route through Alameda reverted back to strictly local status, being served only by the S.F. & A. local trains.

The first eastbound train left Oakland Point at 8:00 a.m. on November 8, and went up Seventh Street between lines of cheering people. As this was the day that Oakland was to become the western terminus of the transcontinental railroad, all business in town was suspended and the schools were let out.

Oakland's Gigantic Celebration

A gigantic celebration was planned by Oakland's civic leaders to coincide with the arrival of the first Overland train from the east. In order to generate enthusiasm for the event, the following circular was distributed throughout the city:

> "A Finance Committee, consisting of Messrs. Henry Durant, E. Bigelow, and G.W. Dam, will solicit subscriptions from the citizens in order to defray the expenses to be necessarily incurred for Music, Fireworks, and Decorations. The citizens of Oakland are earnestly requested to illuminate their houses and decorate them with flags in commemoration of the great event that is of such incalculable importance to the City of Oakland."

Many days of effort went into the preparation for the celebration. Flags and streamers were hung from housetops and buildings along Seventh Street and along Broadway. Spanning Broadway from First to Ninth Streets were flags representing nations and famous steamboats. At Seventh and Broadway, a huge arch, standing 19 feet over the tracks was built. The crown of the arch was decorated with the Temple of Liberty, above which was a large American flag. The pillars of the arch were decorated with evergreens and flags and carried a number of mottos, among which were:

> "Governor Stanford—The more railing he does, the better we like him."

> "Hail to the enterprise which makes steam shout defiance to the desert."

> "The Emigrant Train—Once drawn by oxen, now by locomotive."

> "Oakland bears one end of the longest rails in the world."

Also displayed prominently on the arch was a life-sized portrait of General Winfield Scott, beneath which was printed, "The Union, it must be and shall be saved."

All of the decorations were in anticipation of the first Overland train, which was due to arrive at Seventh and Broadway at 6:00 p.m. It was hoped that there would be several thousand people on hand to greet it on its arrival. The train, which consisted of the locomotive *Mariposa,* two baggage cars, and six coaches, with 260 passengers on board, arrived at 5:05 p.m. After only a brief stop, the train proceeded down Seventh Street to the Oakland Point Pier, where a large crowd had gathered. Arriving at the pier, the passengers boarded the ferry *El Capitan* and debarked in San Francisco just a few minutes past six o'clock.

Even though the train had been early, Oaklanders by the hundreds turned out for the celebration. Piles of pitch and cordwood had been placed at street corners along Seventh Street, from Oak to Market Streets, and along Broadway from First Street to Telegraph Road. At dusk, the wood was ignited to give both a festive air to the celebration and to provide warmth during the chill November evening. To add to the festivities, young boys were given red, blue, and green roman candles, which they shot off into the air. The cannon *Live Oak* had been placed near the station, and was fired rapidly for over an hour, shattering many nearby windows. To all of this noise was added music by the Oakland Brass Band, which was lined up at the station and played while McClure's Cadets entertained the crowd by marching in formation back and forth along Seventh Street.

After about 5,000 people had gathered at the station, Mayor John B. Felton and former Mayor Dr. Samuel Merritt addressed the crowd. Mayor Felton noted that Oakland could now take its place as a great city in California. After the speeches, the Honorable Edward Ingam read an appropriate poem from the pen of Bret Harte:

WHAT THE ENGINES SAID
—*Opening of the Pacific Railroad*—

What was it the Engines said,
   Pilots touching—head to head,
Facing on the single track,
   Half a world behind each back?
This is what the Engines said,
   Unreported and unread!

With a prefatory screech,
   In a florid Western speech,
Said the Engine from the West:
   "I am from Sierra's crest;
And, if altitude's a test,
   Why, I reckon, it's confessed,
That I've done my level best."

Said the Engine from the East:
   "They who work best talk the least.
S'pose you whistle down your brakes;
   What you've done is no great shakes,
Pretty fair,—but let your meeting
   Be a different kind of greeting.
Let these folks with champagne stuffing,
   Not their Engines, do the puffing.

"Listen! When Atlantic beats
   Shores of snow and summer heats;
Where the Indian autumn skies
   Paint the woods with wampum dies,
I have chased the flying sun,
   Seeing all he looked upon,
Blessing all that he has blest,
   Nursing in my iron breast
All his vivifying heat,
   All his clouds about my crest;
And before my flying feet
   Every shadow must retreat."

Said the Western Engine, "Phew!"
   And a long, low whistle blew.
"Come now, really that's the oddest
   Talk from one so modest,
You brag of your East! You do?
   Why *I* bring the East to *you*!
All the Orient, all Cathay,
   Find through me the shortest way,
And the sun you follow here
   Rises in my hemisphere.
Really,—if one must be rude,
   Length, my friend, ain't longitude."

Said the Union, "Don't reflect, or
    I'll run over some Director."
Said the Central, "I'm Pacific,
    But, when riled, I'm quite terrific.
Yet today we shall not quarrel,
    Just to show these folks this moral,
How two Engines—in their vision—
    Once have met without collision."

This is what the Engines said,
    Unreported and unread;
Spoken slightly through the nose,
    With a whistle at the close.

The ceremonies were concluded with Colonel John Scott, Marshal of the Celebration, leading the crowd in three hearty cheers for the railroad.

The Wreck at Simpson's

The excitement generated by the arrival of the first Overland train into Oakland was marred six days later, when on Sunday, November 14, 1869, the first major railroad accident in California history occurred. The accident took place along the jointly operated Western Pacific-San Francisco and Alameda track between Simpson's and San Leandro. One hundred years ago, this was open country, pasture land with only an occasional farmhouse. In terms of today's landscape, it would be near the foot of 66th Avenue, just north of the Oakland-Alameda County Coliseum.

At the Oakland Point ferry terminal that fateful morning in 1869, the *El Capitan* had delivered its passengers to the waiting Overland Limited, Western Pacific Train No. 1. The locomotive on the train that day was the elegant Mason-built engine *Sonoma,* on board which were Engineer Edward Anderson, Fireman Peter McManus, and a student fireman named George Thompson. Leaving the pier at 8:30 in hazy sunlight, the six-car train rumbled up Seventh Street and made an unscheduled stop for water at San Antonio. The train then ran south along newly built track at about 25 miles per hour. Slowing to about 10 miles per hour, the train approached the switch at Simpson's. The time was 9:00 a.m., and the Overland train was just five minutes late.

At Simpson's, the weather was getting foggy, and visibility was down to about 300 feet and getting worse. Because of the fog, Engineer Anderson asked Thompson to stand in the gangway and ask Switchman Bernard Kane if the Alameda-bound local, due through Simpson's at 8:55 had come by. Thompson shouted to Kane and received a nod and a gesture he interpreted to mean "All clear, go ahead." Thereupon, Anderson eased his train through the switch and picked up speed along the joint track. Soon, the Overland train had completely vanished into the thickening fog.

That same morning, a six-car westbound Alameda local, S.F. & A. Train No. 16, pulled by the *F.D. Atherton,* left its eastern terminus of Hayward at 8:15 a.m. After making a stop at San Leandro, the train approached the eastern junction of the joint track section. Engineer Henry A. Williamson noted that although the sun was out, the weather ahead looked foggy. Because it was then 8:45, he knew that he had but ten minutes to get to Simpson's. In order to be on time, he ran his train at a good clip along the nearly level, straight track. At Jones' Station, near what is now 98th Avenue, the train entered a dense fog.

According to E.J. Van Bleek, a farmer who resided near the track, the fog had come in that morning and was so thick that he could no longer see his barn from the house. Going out to check his stock, he heard a train passing over the trestle at Damon's (now Seminary Avenue), but he could not see it. Suddenly, while standing outside his barn, he heard two whistles simultaneously signaling "Brakes down!" Then, through the fog, came the loudest crash and explosion that he had ever heard. Running across the fields and through the fog, he came upon the wreck and did all he could to aid the victims.

The next morning, all of the newspapers carried front-page stories of the disaster, and details of the wreck were sent by telegraph to all parts of the nation. Because the art of photography was still in its infancy, the newspapers had to rely solely on the flowery words of their reporters. The press carried many columns of details of the wreck scene, interviews with survivors, and lurid descriptions of the killed and injured. An example of this style of journalism is given below, excerpted from the November 15, 1869 issue of the *Daily Alta California:*

TERRELE CATASTROPHE

TERRIBLE CATASTROPHE

FRIGHTFUL RAILROAD ACCIDENT

Collision Near Alameda Between The Western Pacific And Alameda Trains

----

FIFTEEN PERSONS KILLED AND TWENTY WOUNDED

Two Locomotives Smashed To Pieces

ONE PASSENGER CAR TELESCOPED INTO ANOTHER

Dreadful Sufferings Of The Survivors

We have occasion to record to-day the first serious railroad accident which has occurred upon this coast. The community was startled, yesterday forenoon, by the announcement of a fearful accident which had taken place on the Western Pacific Railroad. The report soon got abroad, and there was considerable excitement upon the streets. Of course at first the most exaggerated rumors prevailed—according to the accounts, some thirty or forty persons being killed. A general rush was made for the Oakland boats by parties having friends on board the morning train East, by persons actuated by curiosity, and by newspaper reporters. During the entire day, the wharves were crowded by people anxiously awaiting the arrival of the boat in order to receive the first intelligence.

No single occurrence since the last earthquake has excited so much interest and attention as the accident yesterday. A gloom seemed to spread over the city. Everyone appeared to forget pleasure and were only anxious to learn the particulars. The Telegraph office and the offices of the different newspapers were thronged throughout the day by inquiries as to the latest news. Everyone who arrived in the city from the scene was interviewed repeatedly.

It appears that at about 9 o'clock yesterday morning, the regular morning train of the Western Pacific Railroad Company collided with the train from Hayward's when about one and one-half miles from Brooklyn Station. Both trains were running at a high rate of speed, and the collision was most terrible. The engines of both were completely demolished by the shock, and the scene which ensued beggars description.

The Western Pacific express train was made up as follows: The locomotive "Sonoma" and tender, then the express and

FIGURE 3

Western Pacific, San Francisco & Alameda & Oakland Railroads.

JOINT TIME TABLE, No. 2,

BY WHICH ALL TRAINS ARE TO BE RUN WEST OF SAN LEANDRO.

To take effect Monday, December 6th, 1869, at 12:05 o'clock A.M.

For the Government and Information of Employees only, and is not intended for the information of the public. The Company reserve the right to vary the same as circumstances may require.

☞ Read Rules Carefully.   Important Changes have been made.   ☞ See back of Card.

EASTWARD.

31	29	27	25	23	21	19	17	15	13	11	9	7	5	3	1
Pass'gr	Pass'gr	Pass'gr	Pass'gr	Pass'gr	Pass'gr	Pass'gr	Pass'gr	Pass'gr	Pass'gr	Pass'gr	Freight	Pass'gr	Pass'gr	Pac. Ex	Pass'gr
B	A	A	B	B	A	A	A	A	E	B	B	B	B	C	A
P M	P M	P M	P M	P M	P M	P M	P M	A M	A M	A M	A M	P M	P M	P M	P M
	6.20	6.15	5.10	5.10	4.00	1.30	11.30	10.30	9.00	7.15					
	7.10	6.40	6.00	6.00	4.35	2.10	12.05	10.05	9.25	7.50	9.00	10.00			
	7.20	6.55	6.20	6.20	4.52	2.25	12.23	10.20	9.35	8.05	9.20	10.22			
	7.35	7.00	6.34	6.34	5.00	2.32	12.30	10.26	10.02	8.28	6.28	10.28			
11.30			6.36	6.54	5.00	2.43	12.45	10.48	10.16	8.25	6.50	10.50	5.00	12.30	8.00
11.40			7.15	7.15	5.25	3.05	1.00	11.05	10.35	8.45			4.45	1.05	8.55
11.55					3.45	2.45									
12.15															

WESTWARD.

2	4	6	8	10	12	14	16	18	20	22	24	26	28	30	32
Pass'gr	Pac. Ex	Pass'gr	Freight	Freight	Pass'gr	Pass'gr	Pass'gr	Pass'gr	Pass'gr	Pass'gr	Pass'gr	Pass'gr	Pass'gr	Pass'gr	Pass'gr
A	D	B	B	B	B	E	B	B	A	A	A	A	A	A	B
A M	A M	P M	A M	A M	A M	A M	A M	A M	A M	A M	P M	P M	P M	P M	P M
					6.30	8.30	10.00	10.30	12.30	2.30	5.00			7.30	
7.30	1.25	12.40	6.15	7.30	8.40	9.40	10.30	11.40	12.40	2.40	5.40	4.40	6.00	7.80	8.00
7.40	1.35	12.10	5.85	7.10	8.20	9.20	10.15	11.20	12.20	2.20	5.20	4.20	5.40	7.05	7.50
6.45	12.40	11.51	5.40	6.55	8.00	9.00	10.00	11.00	12.06	2.00	5.00	4.00	5.10	6.40	7.40
6.30	12.30	11.45	5.30	6.45	7.50	8.50	9.50	10.50	11.55	1.55	2.50		5.00	6.40	7.40
6.22	12.20	11.30													

STATIONS.
Lv .....SAN FRANCISCO..... Arr
.....ALAMEDA WHARF.....
.....ALAMEDA STATION.....
.....SIMPSON'S.....
.....SAN LEANDRO.....
Arr.....HAYWARDS..... Lv

STATIONS.
Lv .....SAN FRANCISCO..... Arr
.....OAKLAND WHARF.....
.....OAKLAND.....
.....SAN ANTONIO.....
.....SIMPSON'S.....
Arr .....SAN LEANDRO..... Lv

*Trains will not stop.

A—Daily. B—Daily, except Sundays. C—Wednesdays only. D—Mondays only. E—Sundays only.

☞ In case No. 17, Oakland Road (due at San Antonio at 11.45 A. M.,) is behind time, they will have right of track as against No. 6, until 12 o'clock noon.

Trains meet and pass at Stations marked by full faced figures.

☞ All Trains will approach the Switches at San Leandro and Simpson's with great care, and know that all is right before passing.

A. J. STEVENS, Master of Transportation.

JOSIAH JOHNSON, Superintendent.

JOHN CORNING, Ass't Gen. Supt.

A. N. TOWNE, Gen'l Supt.

Collection of Vernon J. Sappers

mail car, baggage car, next following the smoking car, and three passenger cars, the latter being a palace sleeping car. The train left Oakland Point on time, at half-past eight o'clock, going at the usual speed. As the train arrived at the switch at Alameda Junction, the engineer enquired of the switchman whether all was clear, and received an answer that all was right. There was a dense fog, it being impossible to see more than a few feet. The train went on, and when it reached a point about a mile beyond the junction, going at full speed, the Alameda train was noticed. As soon as they saw each other, both engineers signalled "Brakes down," by blowing their whistles, but it was too late. The locomotive "F.D. Atherton" of the Alameda train, coming with full force, the two engines struck each other with a terrible crash.

It is almost impossible to describe the scene of the disaster. The one engine was driven into the other, and both were smashed to pieces. The boilers were thrown to the right side, the smoke stacks being thrown to the left. The Alameda train consisted of six cars, including the baggage car, which was thrown up almost perpendicularly.

By the sudden crash, the smoking car of the Western Pacific train was driven back with such momentum that it was telescoped in the passenger car to the rear, nearly filling it. Of the six cars on the Alameda train, only one was uninjured, and only two of the Western Pacific cars escaped with but little injury.

As soon as the collision had occurred, messengers were sent in all directions, to Oakland, San Leandro, and other stations. The place was one of confusion for hours. Many of the people who had come to render assistance became helpless, and knew not how to lend a helping hand, so awe stricken were they at the sight before them.

Killed in the accident were Engineer Anderson, Student Fireman Thompson, and Brakeman Frank B. Milliken, all on board the Western Pacific train. Also killed were Fireman Charles Martin of the Alameda train and 11 passengers, most notable among whom were J.B. McDonald, Roadmaster of the Sacramento Valley Railroad, and Alexander Baldwin, U.S. District Judge of the State of Nevada. In addition to those killed, 21 passengers were injured, some very seriously.

Within a short time of the accident, officials of the Western Pacific were at the scene, and a crew of Chinese laborers was at work building a shoofly around the wreck. By that afternoon, the line was reopened, and the uninjured Overland passengers were put on a special train to complete their journey east. Local S.F. & A. service was not resumed until late that afternoon.

The evening following the accident, a coroner's jury was convened at the Alameda Station to hear from witnesses and to fix the blame for the accident. The jury, composed of F.M. Campbell, C.F. Wood, H.D. Bacon, Francis K. Shattuck, Rodman Gibbons, and Charles Wood, subpoenaed many witnesses, and the deliberations took several meetings, spread over four days.

Surviving crew members of the Western Pacific train testified that Switchman Kane had given them the "go-ahead" signal. Kane, a slight man in his early 50s, was then called to testify. He stated that he had been employed by the railroad since the previous May. Most of his employment had been spent as an engine wiper, but for the previous two weeks he had been a switchman at Simpson's. He stated that he was familiar with the weekday timetable, and recited from memory the times and destinations of all trains due through Simpson's. However, he stated that he was not familiar with the schedules of Sunday trains, and consequently he did not expect that there would be a westbound Alameda train due when the eastbound Overland train arrived. In further explanation, he said that a "donkey train" of a couple of freight cars had passed through Simpson's while he was in the switchman's house having breakfast, and that he had mistaken this latter train for an Alameda local. He thus assumed that there would be no other locals for quite a while.

Kane was then asked about the times shown for Sunday trains on the timetable. He replied that he did not know how to read, but said that when he had reported to work, someone had read the timetable to him. He further stated that he had never found it necessary to learn how to read. When asked to point out Simpson's on the timetable, he was unable to do so. Further testimony by Cohen, president of the S.F. & A., W.H. Mills, master mechanic of the W.P., and G.W. Adams, roadmaster of the W.P., brought out the fact that it had not occurred to anyone to ask Kane if he knew how to read.

At noon on November 18, the verdict of the coroner's jury was made public. It was stated that the blame was attached to the "ignorance and illiteracy of Switchman Bernard Kane." The verdict concluded with the observation that ignorance is not in itself a crime, nor is it a criminal offense to make a false pretense of ability to read.

After the verdict of the coroner's jury was announced, Kane was arraigned before the grand jury on a charge of manslaughter. When the case came to trial before Justice Smith in San Leandro, it was dismissed on the grounds that there was insufficient evidence to prosecute him for an act of willful negligence. In publishing the final outcome of the case, the *Alta California* commented:

> "The point is beyond remedy, yet something can be done to prevent such disasters in the future. No man should be employed as a switchman until he has shown by trial that he can read print and manuscript."

Sentiment against the railroad ran fairly high immediately after the wreck, as the public felt that there was decided room for improvement in the safety record. A number of unique ideas were proposed, one of the more interesting of which was published by the *Daily Alta California,* which suggested that a large spring be placed between the tender and first coach on all passenger trains. The idea was that the spring would act like a buffer and protect the coaches from being wrecked in case the locomotive stopped suddenly.

Acute awareness of accidents also was evident among employees of the railroad; as witness a minor accident at Oakland Point nearly becoming a serious brawl. It seemed that a couple of days after the wreck at Simpson's, a cut of freight cars was mistakenly shunted onto a siding containing a number of Silver Palace sleeping cars. When the freight cars crashed into the coaches, the crew on board jumped off with fists flying and gave the hapless switchman an unmerciful pounding. Of course, the locomotive crew, on seeing the fight develop, came to the defense of the switchman, and a real rhubarb erupted. Tempers were finally calmed only after officials from the yard office arrived on the scene.

When the Western Pacific began operating into Oakland over the rails of the San Francisco and Oakland, it was recognized by the management that mainline passenger trains might delay the local trains while making their station stop at Seventh and Broadway. To overcome this possible congestion, it was decided to construct a separate mainline station, located two blocks west of Broadway, at Clay Street. To serve this station, a special siding was installed, extending from Market to Clay Streets. Construction of these facilities was begun on November 10, 1869, and completed by the end of the month.

Other improvements made to the S.F. & O. included the replacement of all of the old rail with heavier iron. As a memento of this track replacement, a rusty spike, reputedly the last S.F. & O. spike pulled, remained on display at Wilson's Saloon on Seventh Street for many years after all traces of the

A BUSY PLACE was Oakland Long Wharf, even after passenger operations had been changed to Oakland Pier. Freight kept Engine 1051 at work (above) while below it can be seen that lumber was a very important commodity. **Both Roy D. Graves Collection**

S.F. & O. had vanished from sight. During the track replacement program, a work train, usually pulled by the locomotive *Reindeer,* could be seen busily puffing along Seventh Street, trying all the while to keep out of the way of the local and mainline passenger trains. There also was much activity going on down at the Point, where an enlarged 15-stall roundhouse was being built along with other facilities for a greatly expanded railroad yard.

Because the traffic density along Seventh Street was steadily increasing, the Central Pacific decided that a special freight bypass would be necessary so that freight trains could have direct access to the new Oakland Point freight yards. This proposed route would branch from the main line at San Antonio, cross Indian Creek Slough to First Street, and use that thoroughfare to the Point. Construction of this route began on November 25, 1869, with the building of a trestle from Larue's Warehouse in San Antonio to Badger's Wharf in Oakland, and the placing of fill from that point to the end of First Street. The line was completed and placed in operation by the end of 1870, thereafter the Seventh Street route was used solely for passenger trains.

In order to consolidate the East Bay operations, the Central Pacific formed a subsidiary operating company, the San Francisco, Oakland, and Alameda Railroad Company on June 29, 1870. Shortly after the merger of the Western Pacific into the Central Pacific, the S.F.O. & A. also was merged with the parent organization. And with all operations under the direct control of the Central Pacific, the Oakland and Alameda operations lost their separate identities.

The loss of identity was most apparent in the engines used to pull the local trains. Gone were the little Vulcans, gone also were the *Liberty,* the *Oakland,* and the *E.B. Mastick.* In their places were newer and larger C.P. engines, magnificent locomotives from McKay & Aldus, William Mason, Rhode Island, and other famous manufacturers of that period. The only holdovers from the local operations were two of the ferries operated by Central Pacific's expanding "navy." Although now carrying the C.P. emblem, the *Alameda* and the *Oakland* were still in regular service and were reminders of the earlier days when Rodman Gibbons and Alfred Cohen each operated a purely local railroad.

Oakland Long Wharf

After the merger of the two local lines and the absorption of the Western Pacific, the Central Pacific was in complete control of the East Bay railroad system. During this period, the railroad continued its program of improving its facilities. The most notable improvement was the construction of the famous Oakland Long Wharf, a wooden pier which originally extended 11,000 feet into the bay from Oakland Point. Construction and enlargement of the Oakland Point facilities ultimately replaced the inner portion of the pier with rock fill. By 1906, the wooden outer portion was only 4,400 feet long.

The pier was designed and built under the direction of S.S. Montague, chief engineer, and Arthur Brown, bridge engineer, of the Central Pacific. It was a pine timber structure, with the bents being composed of 65-foot-long pilings, each having a butt diameter of from 12 to 18 inches. At the outer end of the wharf, where the depth of water at low tide was 24 feet, a complex of two freight piers on the north side, and three finger piers for passenger operations on the south side, was built.

A new double track main line was built from Oakland Point out to the end of the pier, which contained 19 diverging tracks to serve the various berths and piers. Also at the end of the wharf were warehouses, storage areas for 40,000 tons of grain, and pens for 550 head of livestock. The pier was designed for the transshipment from rail to ship of any commodity handled by the railroad, and the facilities were built to accommodate the largest ships then afloat.

PLATE 2

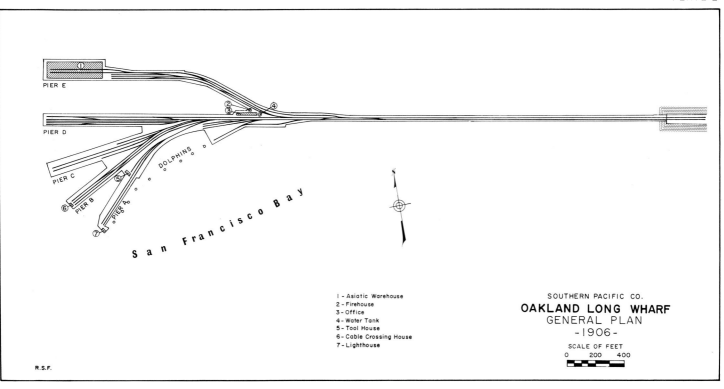

The pier was operated just like any railroad yard, even though it was located near the middle of San Francisco Bay. Present was a yard office, water tank supplied by a pipeline from wells onshore, and an all-important firehouse. Communication with the mainland was afforded by the Sunset Telephone and Telegraph Company, which constructed a pole line along the south side of the pier. Passenger service to and from the Long Wharf began on the morning of Monday, January 16, 1871, when the ferry *El Capitan,* with Captain Edward Hacket in command, began meeting trains at the new facility. On that same date, the adjacent S.F. & O. pier was abandoned and subsequently removed.

During construction of the Long Wharf, the large car ferry *Thoroughfare* was built at the Oakland Point shipyards. With the opening of the Long Wharf, the car ferry was placed in service, with Captain John Hackett in command, between that facility and the Second Street Freight Pier in San Francisco. The *Thoroughfare* was very unique on the Bay in that she was totally unlike any other ferry then operating. Tracks on board the ferry had a capacity of 16 loaded freight cars, and there also were holding pens for 300 head of cattle. With a capacity load of 1,280 tons, the ferry could make a one-way crossing in about 40 minutes.

A further consolidation of rail and ferry service took place in 1873, when a bridge was built across San Antonio Creek from the foot of Alice Street over to Alameda. Thereafter, all Alameda trains operated by way of this bridge, along Alice Street, through what is now Harrison Square, to a connection at 7th and Harrison Streets, and thence to Oakland Long Wharf. Concurrent with this rerouting, all service to Cohen's Wharf at Woodstock was abandoned.

By the year 1873, the Central Pacific had made capital in-

LOOKING EAST along Oakland Long Wharf; Oakland Pier in right distance. This 1893 view was taken to show pole line installed by Sunset Telephone & Telegraph Co. **Louis L. Stein Jr. Collection**

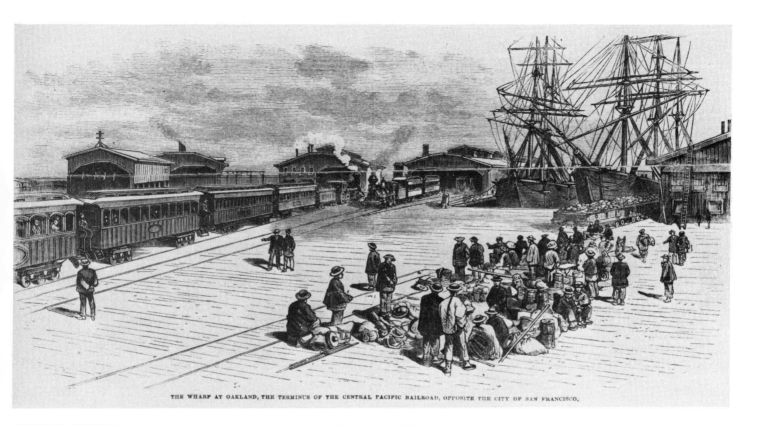

TRAIN OF ORNATE passenger coaches has just arrived at Oakland Long Wharf; in middle distance can be seen a two-car local train. The pigtailed Chinese immigrants in this engraving have undoubtedly just arrived from their native country. **Bancroft Library**

vestments to the East Bay system totaling over $875,000. All of the improvements reflected the phenomenal increase in passenger traffic in the decade since the opening of the original two local lines. This is best illustrated by noting that when the San Francisco and Oakland Railroad first began operating along Seventh Street, only six two-car trips per day were offered. Ten years later, service to Oakland had been increased some six-fold, as trains, many up to 10 cars in length, were operated at headways of 30 minutes during daylight hours and 40 minutes at night. With most trains being filled to capacity, even more service was needed. It was rumored by the *Oakland Daily Transcript* that 10-minute, or even 5-minute service was being contemplated by the railroad. A further increase in service was begun in 1893 with the creation of an Oak Street Local. This train left Oakland Pier one minute ahead of the Fruitvale train, making a stop only at 7th and Broadway. Fruitvale trains stopped at West Oakland and Market Street, and then ran non-stop until Clinton was reached.

A LOCAL FROM BERKELEY pauses at Oakland 16th Street Station in 1872. Horsecar is on the West 14th Street line.
Vernon J. Sappers Collection

CHAPTER 5

North to Berkeley

TO THE NORTH of Oakland in the 1860s, the grassy hill slopes stretched nearly unbroken all of the way to San Pablo Bay. Here and there were occasional farms, and down across the rolling hills meandered tree-lined creeks. In this pastoral setting had been located the then-new campus of the College of California, forerunner of the University of California. After the college had been opened for classes, land promoters moved into the area with the intent to establish a town near the campus, for at that time, the only nearby settlement was Oakland, a number of miles to the south. The first recorded proposal for the new town appeared in the November 3, 1868, issue of the *Alameda County Gazette,* which stated:

> "Berkeley is the name of a projected town near Oakland, laid out on the grounds of the College of California."

Like others of their day, the founders of Berkeley predicted that its success was dependent on the establishment of a de-

BERKELEY STATION in pastoral days. View looks north from Bancroft Way; short trestle denotes Strawberry Creek.
Bancroft Library

pendable railway to link their community with Oakland and San Francisco. Early transportation to the Berkeley area and the college was by way of a steam dummy which ran down Telegraph Road. Because the steam line did not go all of the way to Oakland, it was necessary to change to a horse car if one desired to go to downtown Oakland, then located along lower Broadway, below Seventh Street. The steam dummy and horse car trip also was required of those destined to San Francisco, as Seventh and Broadway was the closest train station to Berkeley.

Hiram Graves' Ferry

In order to provide a direct route from Berkeley to San Francisco, Hiram T. Graves and Henry Durant formed the Berkeley Railroad and Ferry Company in July 1874. They proposed to build a line which would run from a station located in the center of town, down Shattuck Avenue to the little bayside community of Ocean View. Here, at a place called Jacob's Landing, a pier would be built, where patrons could transfer to a ferry for San Francisco.

After raising a portion of the required funds, Graves and Durant began construction of the Jacob's Landing pier. By the middle of October, the pier had been completed, but construction of the connecting railroad had not yet begun. Desiring to inaugurate service as soon as possible, Graves leased the ferry *Clinton* from Charles Minturn and placed her in service between Ocean View and San Francisco on Friday, October 2, 1874. At the same time, arrangements were made for a stagecoach to operate between the ferry landing and the center of Berkeley. It was hoped that initiating service in this manner would spur additional subscriptions so that the railroad could be built as soon as possible.

A week later, on the afternoon of October 8, the *Clinton* made a special trip across San Francisco Bay with guests of the railroad and the Berkeley Land and Improvement Association. The purpose of the trip was to announce the opening of the new service and to stimulate interest in the sale of lots. No effort was spared to make the trip a festive affair, and the ferry was elegantly decorated and outfitted. During the trip across the bay, the guests were treated to music by Alper's Band, which played all of the popular tunes. On arrival at Jacob's Landing, the band struck up a quick step for the debarking passengers. After admiring the view, the guests were invited to a nearby grove of willows, where a large table, set up in the form of a cross, had been piled high with all forms of domestic and imported delicacies. To the left of the table, nestled in a bed of ice, were many bottles of fine champagne to slake the thirst of those interested. Amid the munching of food and the popping of champagne corks, Graves mounted a small podium and welcomed the crowd to the beautiful East Bay. After introducing the officials of the railroad company and those of the improvement association, Graves introduced J.W. Winans, a Regent of the College of California, who spoke at length on the success of the railroad which would ensure the growth of the city of Berkeley.

After the speeches had been completed, a large tarpaulin was spread in an adjacent area and the crowd was invited to dance to the music of Alper's Band until time for the ferry to sail. At dusk a sonorous blast from the *Clinton's* whistle told one and all that it was time to leave, and everyone trooped back on board the ferry which arrived in San Francisco after dark. It was agreed that Graves and Durant had "pulled out all of the stops" and had put on a grand excursion.

In spite of public acceptance of the Berkeley railroad scheme, sufficient money was not immediately forthcoming to

SMALL WOODEN station was the second at this downtown Berkeley site. **Roy D. Graves Collection**

build the desired rail connection, and this portion of the project had to be temporarily deferred. There was, however, enough money available for the company to buy its own ferry; hence when the Mare Island-Vallejo Ferry Company offered a little boat, the *Mare Island,* for sale during the spring of 1875, it was purchased by the Berkeley company.

With the purchase of the *Mare Island,* the lease of the *Clinton* was terminated and that ferry returned to Minturn. Thereafter, the *Mare Island* made the daily crossing between the wharf at the corner of Front and Green Streets, in San Francisco, and Jacob's Landing, connecting at that point with the stagecoach for the center of Berkeley. This service was increased to three daily crossings in 1876, at which level it remained until service was withdrawn the following year, after the inauguration of the West Berkeley local trains. The *Mare Island* subsequently was sold to Alaska interests, who used her for a time on the Yukon River. The pier at Jacob's Landing, no longer being needed for ferry service, was dismantled during March 1878.

The Berkeley Branch

With the apparent lack of ability of Graves to build a railroad into Berkeley, plans for such a line were proposed from a different quarter. This time, Leland Stanford, who had taken note of the activities at Ocean View, proposed a line into Berkeley as a part of his expanding East Bay network.

In order to construct the line, Stanford organized the Berkeley Branch Railroad on September 25, 1875, as a subsidiary of the Central Pacific. It was announced that the subsidiary would build a single track railroad into the center of Berkeley from a connection with the Northern Railway, another Central Pacific subsidiary then abuilding toward Martinez. The proposed route of the Berkeley Branch Railroad would leave the tracks of the Northern Railway at Emory's, the original name of Emeryville, go cross-country to Lorin, now known as South Berkeley, and continue to Dwight Way, where it would turn onto Shattuck Avenue for the remainder of the way to Berkeley.

Track was completed as far as University Avenue during July 1876, and a small station with a siding was built at Center Street. Service to Berkeley was inaugurated on Wednesday, August 16, with trains running from Berkeley only as far as West Oakland, where patrons had to change to a Seventh Street train for the balance of the trip to the Long Wharf and the ferry to San Francisco.

Two years later, in 1878, track was extended from University Avenue to Berryman's, a small community located at what is now the intersection of Shattuck Avenue and Vine Street. Service to this latter point was inaugurated on July 1, 1878, and through service between Berkeley and Oakland Pier was begun a short time later, obviating the transfer to and from Seventh Street trains at West Oakland.

Operation of the Berkeley Branch Railroad was handled under lease by the Central Pacific, as the subsidiary was only a construction company. Due to corporate reorganization, the lease of the Berkeley Branch was transferred from the Central Pacific to the Southern Pacific Company on April 1, 1885. Ownership of the trackage to Berkeley remained with the Berkeley Branch Railroad until it was merged into the Northern Railway on May 15, 1888. Ownership of the latter road was merged into the Southern Pacific Railroad on April 14, 1898, although Southern Pacific had taken over operation of the Berkeley trains on August 22 of the previous year. After the merger, all track in Berkeley was owned by the Southern Pacific *Railroad,* and trains were operated by a separate, although related organization, the Southern Pacific *Company.*

A second local line to the Berkeley area was operated along the tracks of the Northern Railway as far as Delaware Street, in West Berkeley. The Northern Railway, also a Central Pacific subsidiary, was formed on July 19, 1871, and built trackage north along the shore of the Bay from West Oakland through Emory's to Ocean View, West Berkeley, and Richmond. Local train service between Shellmound and Delaware Street, in West Berkeley, was inaugurated on March 1, 1877.

The first regularly assigned engine on the West Berkeley line was the *Theodore Judah,* an engine of 4-2-2 wheel arrangement. The engine was built in 1863 by Danforth-Cook. For use on the West Berkeley line, the engine was converted to double-end status through the installation of a pilot and headlight on the tender. In the latter part of the 1880s, the engine was replaced by heavier equipment. She subsequently was sold to the Union Colliery Company for use hauling coal trains on Vancouver Island, British Columbia. Renamed the *Queen Ann,* the engine was used in coal train service until retired and scrapped in 1912.

On May 15, 1888, the original Northern Railway was reorganized to form a new Northern Railway. As previously mentioned, on April 14, 1898, this second Northern Railway was merged into the Southern Pacific Railroad along with the Northern California Railway and the California Pacific Railroad. As with the Berkeley Branch Railroad, trains on the West Berkeley line were operated by the Central Pacific under lease arrangements until August 12, 1893, when the lease was transferred to the Southern Pacific, which operated the trains thereafter.

FIRST REGULARLY assigned engine to West Berkeley locals was Central Pacific No. 4, the *Theodore Judah,* outshopped by Danforth Cooke in 1864. **R.S. Ford Collection**

PRIDE AND JOY of Sen. Fair was the ferry *Newark*. Here she is seen with the original oversize paddle boxes during the days when full-rigged ships called at San Francisco.   **Southern Pacific**

CHAPTER 6

Jim Fair and Hog Davis

DURING the latter part of the 19th century, the nation experienced what has been called "narrow gauge fever." This was the result of sound logic which argued that if it took so many dollars to construct a broad gauge (i.e., standard gauge) railroad, then a narrow gauge railroad performing the same service could be built for less money. To the uninitiated, only the distance between the rails would appear to be the difference between broad gauge and narrow gauge lines. But, in fact, the savings on tie length was only a minor factor. Major savings on costs could be figured on the fact that locomotives and cars were smaller and thus weighed less. This, in turn, was reflected in savings on excavations, fills, tunnels, bridges, and nearly every facet of railroad construction. Because of these factors, and the fact that curves could be much sharper, the narrow gauge was ideally suited to mountainous terrain.

Such a rugged topography existed in the Santa Cruz Mountains, lying between the fertile Santa Clara Valley and the Monterey Bay area. Any railroad crossing this range by necessity had to climb canyon walls and push through numerous tunnels, a natural habitat for the narrow gauge railroad. That such a railroad eventually was proposed was purely logical.

The proponent of this particular manifestation of "narrow gauge fever" was Senator James G. Fair, a rather flamboyant San Francisco figure who had amassed a fortune in numerous successful mining ventures in Nevada. Fair, who surrounded himself with equally colorful associates, organized the South Pacific Coast Railroad on March 25, 1876. As conceived, this narrow gauge line was to run from San Francisco to San Jose and Los Gatos, and then over the mountains to Santa Cruz. Fair and his colleagues even let it be rumored about that the new railroad might eventually be extended as far as the Colorado River, some 600 miles away.

Because he preferred to operate in the background, manipulating finances and people, Senator Fair appointed A.E. Davis, better known as "Hog" Davis, as president of the new railroad. Davis had acquired his rather unusual nickname because of ownership of a hog ranch on Jersey Island, up in the Sacramento-San Joaquin Delta. To assist Davis, Fair named B.B. Minor as Secretary of the railroad and Thomas Carter, of the North Pacific Coast Railroad, as Superintendent.

One of the first problems besetting Fair and his associates was that of selecting a route from San Francisco down to Los Gatos. Because the Stanford-Huntington interests had the peninsula pretty well tied up, the only route available lay along the eastern shore of San Francisco Bay. Selecting the little town of Newark as the center of operations, Fair and Davis began construction of the South Pacific Coast from that point southward in May 1876. Track also was built west to Dumbarton Point, where a ferry connection was to be made for San Francisco. It is interesting to note that early surveys of the Newark area showed Dumbarton Point as being in San Mateo County, with the county line running along the western edge of the Coyote Hills. Resurveys in later years moved the county line to its present location in the center of Dumbarton Strait.

Within a short time, it was realized that a lengthy ferry trip between Dumbarton Point and San Francisco would defeat any hoped-for advantage that the narrow gauge might have over the established routes of the Central Pacific system, and a terminal site closer to San Francisco was deemed necessary. The site ultimately chosen was Alameda Point, not far from the old San Francisco and Alameda Railroad pier.

To connect Alameda Point with Newark, Senator Fair organized the Bay and Coast Railroad on May 1, 1877, as a subsidiary of the South Pacific Coast. Starting construction in Newark in 1877, the Bay and Coast built track northward toward Alameda, crossing San Leandro Bay by way of a trestle and drawbridge. Track was completed as far as Encinal Avenue and Park Street by early 1878, and train service between that point and Newark was inaugurated on March 20 of that year. In noting the new service, the *Oakland Times* reported:

> "On Wednesday, the first regular train of the Bay and Coast Railroad ran from Los Gatos to Alameda. Train No. 1 left Los Gatos at 6:30 a.m. and arrived at Park Street at 9:45 a.m., making the trip at about a speed of 30 miles per hour. Train No. 2 left Alameda bound for Newark at 10:15 a.m., arriving there at 11:30 a.m. Train No. 3 left Newark at 1:30 p.m. and arrived at Park Street at 2:45 p.m. At 4:15 p.m., train No. 4 left Park Street, arriving at Los Gatos at 7:35 p.m. Stations served by the new line are Park Street, San Leandro, San Lorenzo, Mount Eden, Alvarado, Newark, Alviso, Agnews, Santa Clara, San Jose, and Los Gatos. Service from Park Street is only temporary until the ferries to San Francisco begin running. Work on the ferry slips is progressing, with many piles being driven and 15,000 cubic yards of mud being dredged daily from the pier area."

During the time that the Bay and Coast was building toward Alameda, Senator Fair was preparing to carry his railroad across San Francisco Bay. To accomplish this, a ferryboat of sufficient capacity and speed would be required to handle the expected crowds. Late in 1876, Fair contracted with William E. Collyer, owner of a shipyard at the foot of Humboldt Street in San Francisco, for the construction of the ferry *Newark*. Launched on April 18, 1877, the *Newark* was placed under the able hand of Captain John Leale, and put on the run carrying supplies from San Francisco to Dumbarton Point.

By the end of May, the Bay and Coast had extended track along Encinal and Central Avenues as far as what is now Pacific Avenue. Here, the track turned north toward Alameda Point. At the point, a pier was under construction, and just to the north, facing San Antonio Creek, a group of freight wharves was built.

In anticipation of an increase in traffic, once the trains began running out of Alameda Pier, the South Pacific Coast contracted with William Collyer for a second ferry. This boat, the ***Bay City***, was launched on May 18, 1878, only two weeks prior to the inauguration of through service from Alameda Pier to Los Gatos.

On June 1, through train service from Los Gatos to Alameda was begun, and the ferry *Newark* was placed in operation on the run to Alameda. As Alameda Pier had not yet been completed, it was necessary to operate passenger ferry service from the San Antonio Creek freight pier until the following month. The announced schedule, effective June 1, showed the ferry leaving San Francisco at 5:00 a.m., 9:20 a.m., and 4:20 p.m., making connections at Alameda with trains for Park Street, San Jose, and Los Gatos. An additional boat left San Francisco at 6:20 p.m. and connected with a train that went only as far as Park Street. Regular hourly local service was not inaugurated until the following month, when the ferry terminal at Alameda Pier was completed. Also at that time, the ferry *Bay City* was placed in regular service, making alternate trips with the *Newark*.

With the opening of ferry service to Alameda and train service to Los Gatos, the absolute monopoly on Bay Area transportation enjoyed by the management of the Central Pacific had been broken. Jim Fair had accomplished the impossible . . . he had beaten the Central Pacific in its own backyard!

A Gala Excursion

To celebrate the opening of service, a gala excursion was held on Sunday, the second of June. On the morning of that day, the ferry *Newark*, elegantly outfitted for the occasion, pulled out of the Market Street slip at 9:20 a.m. with about 2,000 of San Francisco's finest on board. Present were gentlemen and their ladies representing the San Francisco Board of Supervisors, local and state officials, financiers, merchants, and many other notables from all walks of life. Senator Fair had seen to it that everyone of importance had received an invitation to the event.

At the San Antonio Creek freight piers, a train consisting of 11 brand new coaches and 21 flat cars equipped with benches stood waiting behind two highly polished locomotives. On an adjacent track stood a second train of 10 cars intended for the some 600 East Bay passengers to be picked up at Park Street and along the way.

After leaving the pier, the two trains made their way through Alameda and then through the countryside to San Jose and Los Gatos, arriving at the latter point at 1:40 p.m. On arrival, the guests were treated to a sumptuous lunch spread on tables beneath giant oaks near the narrow gauge depot. Nearby, a "beer spring" was in full operation, slaking the thirst of many a derby-hatted gentleman.

After lunch, Senator Fair, "Hog" Davis, and many other officials expounded at length on the future of the South Pacific Coast. They told how the line was sure to bring business to the fertile Santa Clara Valley, and take the products of agriculture to markets to the north. Touching on railroad construction, it was noted that the line had cost about $20,000 per mile so far, and it was estimated that it would cost about $35,000 per mile to push the slim gauge rails over the mountains to Santa Cruz.

Soon, a long whistle blast was heard from the lead engine, signaling that it was time to reboard the cars for the journey home. As soon as the train had cleared Los Gatos, the engineer "opened her up" for a fast, non-stop speed run all of the way back to Alameda. Arriving in San Francisco, on board the *Newark*, at 6:30 p.m., everyone agreed that the trip had been a grand success and that Jim Fair certainly knew how to build a railroad!

With the advent of the narrow gauge, the citizens of Alameda once again could enjoy direct service to San Francisco.

JOHN LEALE (center) and crew on lower deck of the *Newark*. Bartender, at left, was kept very busy by ferry patrons.
Vernon J. Sappers Collection

Fares on the new narrow gauge locals were competitive with those on the broad gauge, as the Central Pacific became known. A single trip to San Francisco was 10 cents, and a monthly commutation ticket cost but $3. The local fare within the city limits of Alameda was five cents on the narrow gauge trains in contrast to the free intra-city travel provided by the broad gauge locals over in Oakland.

The South Pacific Coast was off to a good start. Passenger and freight traffic was brisk and increasing. To meet the increasing demand for transbay service, a third ferry, the *Garden City*, was constructed by the Collyer shipyard; she was launched on June 20, 1879. This ferry was intended to carry both passengers and freight cars, and consequently narrow gauge track was laid on the main deck. As a car ferry, the *Garden City* would operate between the San Antonio Creek freight piers and the wharves along East Street, in San Francisco, which were served by dual gauge trackage. As a passenger ferry, she would operate as a relief boat for either the *Bay City* or the *Newark*.

The $15,000 Franchise Scandal

With the completion of mainline service as far as Los Gatos, and the establishment of local service to Alameda, ideas of expansion even further into Central Pacific territory were discussed at length among Fair, Davis, and the others associated with the narrow gauge. By the end of 1878, these ideas had crystallized into plans for a branch line to run from Alameda over to Oakland.

A proposal for just such a line was filed with the Clerk of the city of Oakland on January 20, 1879. At the February 14 meeting of the City Council Committee, A.C. Dietz, a prominent Oakland businessman, presented the Davis proposal for consideration. Dietz, who was accompanied by his attorney, Charles Travers, explained that he was acting as agent for the South Pacific Coast Railroad in the matter of a proposed branch from Alameda to Oakland. Travers then stood up, and addressing the committee, outlined the route of the proposed line:

> "The South Coast Railroad [sic] wants the privilege of coming across the Estuary, then striking a line east of Fallon Street, and skirting along the marsh, and finally running to Oak Street and then across [Lake Merritt] to Adam's Point."

He stated that the narrow gauge was seeking no subsidy nor aid and that the line would be built entirely on private right-of-way and would not utilize any city streets. Travers went on to say that the South Pacific Coast would build its own bridges across the Estuary and across one arm of Lake Merritt. Furthermore, Senator Fair was considering the possibility of extending the line north from Adam's Point across upper Webster Street (now Piedmont Avenue) at least as far as Te-

THE *BAY CITY*, tied up at Alameda Pier in narrow-gauge days.
Roy D. Graves Collection

THE *GARDEN CITY* churns eastward on the "Narrow Gauge" run over to Alameda. To the left is the *Oakland* on her way to Oakland Pier.
Roy D. Graves Collection

mescal and Berkeley. In conclusion, Travers stated that, if necessary, the railroad would post a performance bond of from $250,000 to $500,000, should the city so require.

On the evening of the following Monday, February 17, the regular meeting of the City Council was convened in the Oakland City Hall. Present was an unusually large number of spectators, as it was known that the matter of the Dietz franchise was on the agenda.

After dispensing with the minutes and other routine items, the main topic of interest was brought up. Dietz, Travers, and a number of others spoke at length extolling the virtues of the proposal, which was variously reported as the "Fallon Street Road" and "Dietz' Lake Merritt Railway." Most of those who spoke in opposition to the plan wanted to know precisely where the line would go, as no maps or other documents purporting to show the line had been presented. In the words of one spectator: "I won't be in favor of the line until I know which side of my barn the track will be on." Councilman W.E. Grinnell then addressed the Council on the similarities of the Dietz proposal and a prior one known as the Freeman Franchise.

It seems that two years previously, in 1877, three businessmen from the East Coast had come to Oakland to discuss possible capital investments, and the matter of building a new railroad line was brought up. These men felt that because the Central Pacific operated an east-west route through town, a north-south line would be extremely profitable. Subsequently, an engineer was employed to stake out a line up Fallon Street, which at that time was unimproved, as far as Lake Merritt. The City Council was then approached on the matter of a franchise, which was sought in the name of one of the businessmen, a Mr. Freeman. In conclusion, Councilman Grinnell noted that the franchise, which had been granted, had now lapsed and was available to Dietz or any other party.

In the ensuing discussion of the Dietz proposal, questions were asked of the bridge over to Adam's Point. It had not been made clear if it was to be only a railroad bridge, or if foot and wagon traffic would be allowed. To this, a spectator who owned a small dairy on Oak Street near 17th Street asked if it was to be a toll bridge and would he be allowed to drive his cows across the bridge to graze on the hills behind Adam's Point. In answer to some of the questions, Dietz stated that the expected cost of the Lake Merritt Bridge would be about $30,000 and that final design of the structure had not yet been worked out.

Before being voted upon, a second franchise proposal was introduced by Councilman S. Milbury. This proposal, known as the Elsey proposal, requested council permission for a nearly identical route up Fallon Street as far as Lake Merritt. After discussing the relative merits and shortcomings of both proposals, a vote was taken on the Dietz proposal, it being the first one on the agenda. Voting in favor of the franchise were Councilmen M.W. Fish, W.E. Grinnell, E. Hook, J.M. Miner, and W.A. Walter. Councilman Milbury glumly abstained from the voting and the ordinance was passed. The Elsey franchise was then routinely taken up and placed to a vote, with only Milbury voting in the affirmative. With his franchise in hand, Dietz smilingly announced to the city council that only that morning, A.E. Davis, of the narrow gauge, had promised him that trains would be running over the Fallon Street route before the year was out.

The next day's issue of the *Oakland Tribune* reported on a rumor that was circulating about town to the effect that some of the councilmen had received a payoff with regard to the Dietz franchise. On the following day, the city was shocked to read that the rumor was true and that there had in fact been a plot and a counter-plot prepared by backers of both the Dietz and Elsey franchises. What finally came to light can best be described as one of the most scandalous episodes of Oakland municipal government. "Bribery!" screamed the *Tribune*. "The Council is corrupt and graft ridden . . . franchises bought and sold like so much merchandise!"

In an interview by a reporter from the *Tribune*, C.M. Burleson, a local real estate broker, shed some light on the background to show how a well-intentioned scheme grew out of hand to become a major scandal. Burleson, who had been in-

BALDWIN-BUILT South Pacific Coast Engine No. 1 with a two-car train at 11th and Webster. Many homeowners along here fumed at the noisy, smoky trains. **Roy D. Graves Collection**

volved in the Freeman Franchise proposal, learned from Dietz of the South Pacific Coast interest in the Fallon Street route. He had also learned from other sources of the displeasure of the Central Pacific with the entry of the narrow gauge onto the East Bay scene. Thus, he could foresee the possibility of a real fight for a franchise along Fallon Street once Dietz' proposal was made public. Rather than have a major squabble in the council chambers, he had met with Councilmen Hook, Miner, Fish, and Milbury to work out an alternative proposition. The five men decided that the only answer would be to arrange for a third party to be awarded the franchise, which could then be sold to the highest bidder.

One of Burleson's acquaintances, Charles Elsey, was approached with the idea of applying for the Fallon Street franchise. Elsey was assured by the group that there would be no financial risk and that after he had received the franchise, he could sell it and the proceeds could then be divided amongst them. Elsey agreed to this, and it was decided that his proposal would be introduced at the council meeting of February 17 after Dietz had made his presentation.

In order to assure passage of the Elsey proposal, five council votes were needed. It was known that Councilman Walter was a narrow gauge man and that Councilman Fonda was a Central Pacific man. This left only Grinnell, who at that time was uncommitted. Grinnell was approached and agreed to the plan, and the Elsey franchise was as good as passed, or so the councilmen thought. During all this time, Burleson acted as agent for Elsey in his dealings with the "pool," as the group of councilmen called themselves. Everything appeared to be set for the next council meeting. But, as the saying goes, "The well-laid plans of mice o' men gang oft' agley."

Word of the "pool" and the Elsey arrangement had leaked out to Dietz, who contacted "Hog" Davis, telling him that it looked as if the council was rigged against them. Davis, through his intermediaries, then approached the Elsey backers, offering them $8,000 to withdraw their application. This, Elsey and his associates refused to do. The Davis emissaries then approached the men of the "pool" and told them that the sum of $15,000 would be made available for them to divide if they would vote in favor of the Dietz proposal. As time for the council meeting approached, a prominent, although unidentified Oakland attorney went to "see" Mayor W.R. Andrus to secure his backing of the Dietz proposal. The last attempt at coercion took place a scant two hours before the council meeting, when the Elsey people were again approached and offered the $8,000 to withdraw, but being confident of securing the franchise, they again declined. So, the matter went to a vote, and the $15,000 proffered to the "pool" bought "Hog" Davis his Fallon Street franchise.

In the days that followed, the *Tribune* carried emphatic denials from the councilmen who were implicated as receiving money from Davis. Mayor Andrus wrote at length decrying such slanderous talk, denying that neither he nor any of his councilmen would ever stoop so low as to be the recipient of bribes. Still the talk persisted, aided and abetted by Councilman Milbury, who had remained loyal to Elsey to the end. By the time the week was out, every man on the street knew that in addition to the councilmen, the mayor and even City Attorney Peter W. Byrne had been members of the "pool." Of course none of the principals admitted to receiving any money, and when interviewed on the subject, Councilman Grinnell just smiled and said that all he had ever received from either Dietz or Davis was a cigar and a glass of wine.

The upshot of the whole affair was that the city council resigned en masse, and a new council was elected at a special election held on March 10. In spite of all this, "Hog" Davis had the Fallon Street franchise in his hip pocket, but for reasons known only to himself and Fair, it was never exercised. Whether the narrow gauge actually had serious intentions for this route or whether all of this action was merely a smoke screen to obscure other dealings never was made clear.

The Webster Street Fracas

During the latter part of 1879, Davis applied to the Board of Supervisors of Alameda County for permission to utilize the county-owned Webster Street Bridge for a crossing of the Oakland Estuary. The Central Pacific rose to the challenge and attempted to block entry of the narrow gauge into Oakland by using Thomas Meetz, colorful owner-operator of the Alameda, Oakland and Piedmont Railroad, a horsecar line which had tracks on the bridge. Meetz, with generous assistance from C.P. attorneys, opposed the use of the bridge by the narrow gauge on the grounds that it was not strong enough to support the weight of a locomotive and train. Although not publicized, Meetz also acknowledged that he could not meet the challenge of competition between his slow, somewhat irregular horsecars and the more modern steam trains.

In the complaint of *Thomas Meetz v. The County of Alameda,* filed in the Twelfth Judicial District Court in and for the County of San Francisco on December 3, 1879, Meetz sought to enjoin the County Board of Supervisors from granting a right-of-way on the Webster Street Bridge to the South Pacific Coast Railroad. The basis of the complaint was that the county did not possess the authority to grant franchises or rights-of-way. Judge Dangerfield, in agreeing with the plaintiff, issued an injunction which forbade the county from granting permission to the narrow gauge to use the bridge. In spite of the ruling, the Board of Supervisors unanimously granted a 25-year use permit to Davis, allowing him use of the bridge for railroad purposes. The use permit stipulated that the railroad could be either single-tracked or double-tracked, and that motive power could be either steam locomotives or horses. In return for the use of the bridge, the South Pacific Coast was to strengthen and widen the bridge at its own expense, pay for the continued maintenance of the bridge, and pay up to $100 per month for the bridge tender's wages. This action of the Board of Supervisors resulted in Judge Dangerfield, on December 31, citing the board as being in contempt of court. Further sparring on the part of the county's legal staff, using arguments that a use permit had been issued, not a franchise nor a right-of-way, resulted in the injunction ultimately being lifted.

Not being able to stop the narrow gauge at the Webster Street Bridge, Meetz met Davis head-on at the Oakland City Council meeting of February 16, 1880. Desiring a franchise for a route up Webster Street, Davis purportedly had secured a petition favoring the narrow gauge and signed by over two-thirds of the property frontage owners on the street. Meetz also wanted to extend his horsecar line up Webster Street, and had prepared the necessary documents petitioning the city for just such a franchise.

After the necessary discussions, the question of the Meetz franchise was put to a vote of the city council; the result was four affirmative and three negative. The city clerk announced the vote and stated that it appeared that Mr. Meetz had obtained his franchise for the horsecar line. Dietz and Davis, who were present in the audience, apparently had been caught napping. They, and others, immediately objected to the vote. Because of the uproar, a second vote was taken on the measure; this time it was three affirmative and four negative. Councilman Babcock later admitted that he had not understood the question and had erroneously voted in the affirmative on the first ballot. He had then corrected himself and the Meetz proposal had been defeated. Councilman Babcock then presented another proposal for a franchise along Webster Street, this time in the name of Davis. This latter proposal was tabled, to be taken up at the next council meeting. After the meeting had adjourned, Babcock was seen earnestly talking to Davis and Dietz, who were undoubtedly telling him how he had just about blown the ball game.

The next day's issue of the *Oakland Tribune* carried an article exposing the reported crooked dealings on the part of Davis. The paper said the "Railroad Octopus," as the narrow gauge was now referred to, had not secured signatures of two-thirds of the bona-fide property owners, as it had claimed. Instead, included on the petition were names of owners of marshland near the foot of Webster Street, and in a number of cases where property was owned in joint tenancy, each co-owner had signed as being a single owner of property. Furthermore, it was reported that property owners had been paid as much as $500 to sign the petition.

On the evening of March 1, a hearing on Davis' petition was held in the council chambers. The hearing, which lasted until well after 11:00 p.m., was attended by a capacity crowd. During the proceedings, charges and counter-charges were hurled by both proponents and opponents of the scheme. One of the property owners along Webster Street claimed that "We're being railroaded just like we were with the Fallon Street Road," referring to the Dietz proposal which resulted in a city-wide scandal the previous year. Opponents of the scheme pointed out that Davis would have to have signatures from property owners representing at least 4,960 feet of frontage of the 7,440 feet along Webster Street from the Estuary to 14th Street. Although Davis claimed signatures from 5,577 feet of frontage, after deducting owners of marshland and duplication of signatures, only 4,502 feet actually were represented. It also was brought out that one of Davis' most vocal proponents was J.G. Eastland, owner of a large parcel of land in the block bounded by 14th, Franklin, 13th, and Webster Streets, upon whom Davis had called a short time previously to discuss the possibility of a terminal site at that location. It also was mentioned that $5,000 in cash passed between the two gentlemen, assuring Davis of Eastland's vigorous support for the narrow gauge.

After hearing all of the facts of Davis' petition, the city council committee adjourned for the evening and the matter was put over until the regular city council meeting two nights later. At that meeting, the city council heard the first reading of a franchise allowing the South Pacific Coast to construct and operate a narrow gauge railroad along Webster Street from the bridge north to the south line of 14th Street. The ordinance had a number of interesting features, among which was the requirement of free transportation of any local passengers carried wholly within the city limits of Oakland. The ordinance also stated that it would become null and void if: (1) the line along Webster Street was owned or operated by any railroad other than the South Pacific Coast; (2) the line was built to any gauge other than narrow gauge; and (3) the line was ever extended north of the south line of 14th Street without the railroad first securing written approval of at least two-thirds of the property owners along Webster Street from 14th Street north to the city limits. This last clause would come back to haunt the management of the narrow gauge during the years to come when rumors persisted that the road would push on through Oakland, cross the Berkeley Hills, and build into the Sacramento Valley.

Because it appeared that the Oakland City Council would routinely grant Davis his Webster Street franchise, an application was made on March 3 to Judge A.M. Crane of Department No. 1 of the Superior Court of Alameda County seeking a writ of prohibition preventing the city from granting the franchise. The application was made by Dr. E.W. Buck, owner of property along Webster Street between 10th and 11th Streets, on behalf of all of the Webster Street property owners who were in opposition to the franchise.

In answer to the application, Judge Crane ordered the city council to show cause why a temporary writ should not be made permanent. At the hearing, held on March 6, Dr. Buck claimed that Davis had not secured the support of owners of two-thirds of the property frontage, as required by law. City Councilman Glascock then took the stand and, after filing a demurrer agreeing with Dr. Buck, asked that the writ be quashed on the grounds that a writ cannot be used to restrain a legislative body, which a city council is by definition. As supporting evidence, he cited several cases from the 52nd and 53rd *California Reports*.

In ruling on the writ, Judge Crane agreed with Councilman Glascock, and stated that the California State Supreme Court had ruled that a writ of prohibition could apply only to judicial proceedings, and that since a city council is a legislative body, he was forbidden by statute from restraining, by writ, any municipal body from doing its work. Thus, he ordered the writ quashed.

At the City Council meeting on the evening of March 8, Davis' franchise application was read for the second and third time, and Judge Crane's order quashing the writ was read. The matter of the franchise was then put to a vote; the result was five affirmative and two against. In anticipation of the vote, Mayor Andrus was on hand in his office, and the ordinance was taken to him immediately after passage so that he could sign it. After affixing his signature, the mayor shook hands with Davis and everyone talked about how soon the dirt would fly along Webster Street.

Meanwhile, Thomas Meetz, who had been in the audience,

ENGINE 2 and three-car train at 14th & Webster, 1884. Engine was built by Baldwin in 1876, scrapped in 1902.
Roy D. Graves Collection

quietly left the city hall by way of a side door, a beaten man. A few days later, realizing that he could not compete with the narrow gauge trains, he withdrew his horsecar service, and put his horses out to pasture.

The Narrow Gauge Arrives

Construction of the Webster Street line was begun by the Bay and Coast Railroad early in 1880. From the Alameda Point freight piers, track was pushed across the marshland toward the south approach to the Webster Street Bridge, while at the bridge a pile driver was placing timber pilings along the west side of the bridge so that the deck could be widened for the narrow gauge rails. By the end of May, the new deck had been completed and rails spiked down upon it. Also, the track from Alameda Point had nearly reached the bridge. The only gap was a small parcel of land belonging to John Bird, who was adamant that no railroad would ever cross his property. After many heated exchanges, some punctuated by gunshots, an agreement finally was reached whereby the railroad was allowed to build across the Bird property.

North of the Estuary, the first earth was turned on June 2, 1880, when a group of Bay and Coast construction men showed up at Seventh and Webster and started digging around the Central Pacific tracks, preparatory to placing a crossing at that location. The construction plan called for the crew to work from Seventh Street down to the bridge, and then from Seventh up to 14th Street, where a depot would be built in the block bounded by Webster, 14th, Franklin, and 13th Streets.

Construction along Webster Street dragged on intermittently until that winter. On January 7, 1881, the Oakland Township Railroad was incorporated with the intent to finish construction of the line. This South Pacific Coast subsidiary

SOUTH PACIFIC COAST's new Alameda Pier depot shortly after it opened in 1884. Oakland Estuary is to the left, Oakland in left distance.
Roy D. Graves Collection

FIGURE 4

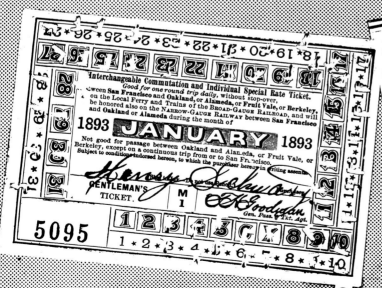

EAST BAY SCHEDULES AND TICKETS
1877-1893

had been incorporated in San Francisco with a capitalization of $500,000. The official announcement of the formation of the subsidiary stated that the O.T.R.R. would build a line,

> "... from the northerly line of the Township of Alameda along Webster Street to 14th Street, and thence by the most practical route to a point on the northerly and westerly boundary of the Township of Oakland."

It was announced that the line would be about 10 miles in length. Not mentioned, of course, was that the proposed line, if completed, would be in violation of the ordinance of March 3, 1880, allowing construction of the Webster Street line only as far as 14th Street.

By early May 1881 track had been built as far as the proposed downtown Oakland depot, and on Saturday, May 28, a special inaugural train was run from Alameda Point over to Oakland. The *Oakland Times* reported on the event the following Monday:

> "The South Pacific Coast arrived in Oakland last Saturday and may push on to Piedmont and Berkeley. The first train came up Webster Street and consisted of nine coaches pulled by Engine No. 4, Pete Wilson, engineer, W.B. Brown, fireman, J.J. Whitney, conductor, and brakemen Will Davis and George McMahon. The train left Alameda Point at 2:15 p.m. On board was railroad president A.E. Davis and others. The train stopped at First Street, Seventh Street, and Fourteenth Street. Regular service starts today with a 40-minute running time between Fourteenth and Webster and the Ferry Building."

The *Times* further stated that two new Baldwin locomotives had been purchased expressly for the new line as were 12 new passenger coaches, built by Carter Brothers in Newark. The new coaches were 40 feet long, 8½ feet wide, and elegantly finished in black walnut and primavera. Each coach was equipped with red plush seats, gas lamps, water closet, drinking water, coal stove, and represented the ultimate in the car builder's art.

The new service was an immediate success, and it was reported by the *Oakland Tribune* that the time from 14th and Franklin to San Francisco via the narrow gauge was only 27 minutes; this was eight minutes less than on the broad gauge locals of the Central Pacific. As an attempt to meet the challenge, the Central Pacific proposed to eliminate a number of their West Oakland stations in order to speed up service. Even with this competition, Jim Fair's narrow gauge trains continued to do a brisk business.

During the time the South Pacific Coast was under construction, all efforts were used to get the line and its branches into full operation. For as soon as the trains began running, the money would start coming in. Only a little effort went into nonessentials, as these could wait until a later date. By the year 1883, the railroad was grossing about $2,000 per mile of track, and the time had come for major improvements to the system.

One of the first improvements was the replacement of the Alameda Point pier with a more substantial structure. Planned was a 2½-mile-long rock-fill mole and timber trestle that would be wide enough for two tracks plus a wagon road. At the western end of the structure would be a multi-tracked train shed, a group of ferry slips, and a small yard. In order to construct this complex, Fair and Davis organized the San Francisco and Colorado River Railroad on January 16, 1883. Although this South Pacific Coast subsidiary was supposedly formed for the purpose of linking the two places named in its corporate title, actual construction was limited to the building of the mole, trestle, ferry terminal, and appurtenances.

A great deal of effort went into the construction of this structure. Required were great amounts of rock for the fill portion. Because much of the ferry terminal area was in an area of shallow water, a great deal of dredging of bay mud also was required. After taking over a year to construct, the new Alameda Mole was opened for service on March 15, 1884.

After completion of the new mole facilities, Fair and his railroad were in an excellent position to compete with the Central Pacific. Passenger and freight trains were rolling over the line, and the profits kept coming in, proving that the original premise of the soundness of the narrow gauge was true. All the while, Leland Stanford and his associates continued to stew over what to do about this little line that was making such a profit in the midst of their territory.

The Lease of 1887

In the summer of 1886, a seemingly unrelated incident in Nevada proved to be a fortuitous turn of events for Leland Stanford. It seems that Fair and three of his former mining associates, John Mackay, James Flood, and William O'Brien had formed the Nevada Bank. Because of a downturn in some financial dealings, the bank was on the verge of failure, and money was sorely needed. The banking trio turned to Fair as a source of capital, and he agreed to sell the narrow gauge to satisfy the bank's needs.

Knowing that Stanford wanted to gain control of the narrow gauge, Fair set up a meeting in the fall of 1886 to discuss the matter. The meeting, which took place on board a special train which ran from Alameda to Santa Cruz and return, was attended by Fair, Stanford, A.N. Towne, General Manager of the Southern Pacific, and A.C. Bassett, Superintendent of that railroad's Pacific Division. By the time the special train had arrived back at Alameda Mole, everyone in the party was in agreement to a lease of the narrow gauge, and all that had to be worked out were a few supposedly minor details.

Because of the impending lease, the Southern Pacific, which itself was a product of reorganization of the Central Pacific, took over most of the operations of the narrow gauge in the early part of 1887. In order to legally acquire the South Pacific Coast Railroad, Stanford and his associates formed a new corporation, the South Pacific Coast *Railway*, on May 23 of that year.

But still the lease negotiations dragged on. Finally, as summer approached, Stanford met Fair's price of $5,500,000, payable in the form of four-percent gold bonds. In late June, the legal documents were drawn up and signed, transferring ownership of the narrow gauge from James G. Fair to Leland Stanford effective July 1, 1887. On that same date, the South Pacific Coast Railway leased all of its facilities to the Southern Pacific Company for a period of 55 years, and once again, all Bay Area transportation facilities were under one flag.

In the years succeeding the lease of 1887, the narrow gauge gradually was assimilated into the vast Southern Pacific system. Within not too many years, narrow gauge tracks had been replaced by standard gauge rails, and years later, the route over the Santa Cruz Mountains was abandoned. By 1942, when the lease was due to expire, the original route of the narrow gauge had become an integral part of the Southern Pacific. With the expiration of the lease, the South Pacific Coast Railway was dissolved and all its assets and properties were taken over by the Southern Pacific.

ORIGINAL SAN FRANCISCO Ferry Building (opposite, above) with its hacks, drays and derby-hatted gents. Oakland Pier (opposite, below) as it looked before the turn of the century. **Both Roy D. Graves Collection**

CHAPTER 7

Broad Gauge Locals

ALL DURING the time that Hiram Graves was trying to promote a ferry and railroad line over to Berkeley and Jim Fair and "Hog" Davis were spiking down narrow gauge rails from Newark to Alameda, the Central Pacific was busily improving its own transbay transportation facilities. The improvements were brought about not only because the management of the Central Pacific sensed that their monopoly of service might be challenged, but also because the growth of the East Bay area was at a rate which generated an ever-increasing volume of traffic each year.

When the Oakland Long Wharf had been opened for service in 1871, it was the finest rail-ferry transfer facility to be found anywhere on the Pacific coast. As the frequency of passenger trains increased, this busy mid-bay terminal rapidly became overtaxed, and it soon became apparent that there must be a general improvement of the terminal facilities on both sides of the bay.

Ever since the days that Charles Minturn and James Larue bitterly fought for transbay traffic, the East Bay ferries used the Davis Street Wharf as their terminal in San Francisco. Although the wharf was antiquated, crowded, and generally inadequate to serve as a point of arrival and departure of transcontinental and transbay travel, it was located only a few blocks from the main business district of the city.

Discussing the matter at the headquarters of the Central Pacific, Leland Stanford and his associates decided that what San Francisco needed was a new and proper railroad terminal that would befit the business and commerce center of the west. They reasoned that because Market Street was being projected by Jasper O'Farrell to run as straight as a die all the way to Twin Peaks, the logical location of the terminal would be at the foot of that broad thoroughfare. Even though at that time lower Market Street was the site of warehouses, chandleries, and a myriad of other water-oriented businesses, it was hoped that the area might eventually become the center of business and trade.

After acquisition of the property and the demolition of some old wharves and piers, construction began along East Street (now The Embarcadero) of a timbered deck area which would extend nearly 100 feet into the bay. This area was designed to serve as a terminal area for six horsecar and cable car lines as well as a loading area for hacks, wagons, drays, and the like. Beyond the timbered deck, which had a frontage of about 500 feet along East Street, a huge wooden terminal building was built, flanked on the water side by six ferry slips. The terminal building consisted of a 25-foot-wide concourse, open to the timbered deck area, and a number of spacious waiting rooms designed for the comfort of passengers of the Central Pacific and other lines which would use the facility. Surmount-

THE *OAKLAND*, the second ferry to be so named, steams briskly across the Bay.

Southern Pacific

ing the building was a four-sided clock tower which could be seen up and down East Street as well as far up Market Street.

Construction of the Ferry Building was completed during the summer of 1875, and the Central Pacific began making ferry runs in and out of the new facility on the morning of Saturday, the fourth of September. In reporting on the opening of the new Ferry Building, the *San Francisco Chronicle* commented:

> "The Ferry Building is the first new structure in this part of town and will undoubtedly make Market Street a main artery."

Concurrent with the construction of the Ferry Building, the Central Pacific made plans to improve its fleet of ferries. Recognizing the fact that the aging *Oakland* was no longer adequate for transbay service, she was retired and converted into a freight car transfer barge. In her place, a new ferry, also named the *Oakland,* was to be constructed at the Oakland Point shipyard.

Rather than go to the time and expense of building a completely new ferry, it was decided to acquire the river packet *Chrysopolis,* which had been built by John G. North in 1860, and have her converted into a double-end ferry. Conversion of the *Chrissy,* as the packet was familiarly called, began in the early part of 1875, with crews stripping down the superstructure and lengthening the hull from 245 feet to 265 feet. Soon the frame of the new ferry rose, and by early summer, the second *Oakland,* which had been elegantly finished in polished hardwood and gleaming brass, was launched and made ready for service. In reporting on the new ferry, the *Oakland Tribune* commented that she had cost many thousands of dollars more than had been anticipated. In fact, it was rumored that if the *Oakland* had been built new from the keel up, she would have cost far less than the extensive rebuilding of the former river packet.

Being the newest boat on the Bay, the *Oakland* had the distinction of making the first revenue run from Oakland Long Wharf to the new Ferry Building on the morning of September 4, 1875. That trip also was the maiden revenue run for the new ferry.

That day's issue of the *Oakland Tribune,* in reporting on the new Ferry Building and the ferry *Oakland,* announced that the *El Capitan* soon would be withdrawn from service for a refurbishing which would place her on a par with the *Oakland.*

After the *El Capitan* had been returned to service, the *Alameda* would be withdrawn for a much-needed overhaul. Rebuilding of this older ferry would entail a lengthening of 14 feet and a complete rebuilding of the hurricane and texas decks. Furthermore, the hull was to be completely scaled to rid it of a massive growth of barnacles which not only impaired her speed, but made her sit a foot lower in the water than when she originally had been launched.

The Creek Route

With the improvements at San Francisco underway, the management of the Central Pacific concentrated on enlarging their grasp on East Bay transportation. Because of the substantial growth experienced in the city of Oakland since the coming of the transcontinental railroad, there came a renewed demand for the operation of a ferry from downtown Oakland directly to San Francisco. Such a ferry operation should be able to transport horses, livestock, wagons, and any other manner of cargo as well as passengers.

In order to inaugurate this type of service, the Central Pacific set about building a ferry slip at the foot of Broadway, in Oakland, near the site of Carpentier's Wharf. The boat chosen to operate this service was the *Capital*, a side-wheel packet of Sacramento River fame. The *Capital* had been built in 1866 by the John G. North shipyard for the California Steam Navigation Company, which had put her on the run from San Francisco to Sacramento. The *Capital* was 277 feet long and had been one of the largest and fastest boats on the Sacramento River. In 1871, ownership of this fine craft passed to the California Pacific Railroad, which had taken over the operations of the California Steam line. By 1875, the California Pacific had come under the control of the Stanford interests, and the *Capital* was transferred to the Central Pacific operations.

In the fall of 1875, the packet was sent to the Oakland Point shipyard to be rebuilt into a double end ferry for the San Antonio Creek service. According to the *San Francisco Bulletin* of September 5, 1875, she would be renamed the *Underwriter* and would be placed in service the following

OOPS. *El Capitan* churns a broad wake (right) as it passes Oakland Long Wharf, but comes to grief (below) on the mud after being hit by the *Alameda* (see page 64).
Roy D. Graves Collection; Vernon Sappers Collection

spring. When spring arrived, however, the ferry was outfitted for service still bearing her old Sacramento River name.

The first operating schedule of the Creek Route, as the new service was called, took effect on Saturday, July 1, 1876. This schedule was very unique in that arrivals and departures at the Broadway slip were dictated by the tidal stage at the Oakland Bar, located at the mouth of San Antonio Creek. In 1876, this notorious sand bar was still a navigation hazard and was the cause of much trouble to shipping, just as it had been years before in the days of the ferries *Contra Costa* and *San Antonio*. Initial schedules of the Creek Route, which showed departures at irregular intervals, called for three daily crossings, with an extra crossing added on Sundays. With the dredging and straightening of San Antonio Creek in 1877, a regular schedule of five daily crossings was begun on January 1, 1878.

All during the interval of time that the new Ferry Building was placed in operation and the Creek Route ferry service was inaugurated, the Central Pacific was experiencing a dramatic increase in freight tonnage moved in and out of Oakland Long Wharf. By the year 1875, this tonnage had increased to the point where the car ferry *Thoroughfare* was being operated at maximum capacity. Thus, it became apparent to the management of the railroad that in the event that the *Thoroughfare* should become laid up for any extended period, a severe jam of freight cars would develop on the east side of the bay. As a remedy to this situation, the Oakland Point shipyard was called upon to construct a second car ferry. This craft, the *Transit,* was launched during 1876 and provided a welcome relief for the overworked *Thoroughfare.*

A Foggy Afternoon

Ferry collisions, although never numerous, were always on the minds of skippers whenever the fog set in and reduced visibility to near zero. The afternoon of Wednesday, February 20, 1879, was no exception as a dense, wet fog settled down onto the surface of the bay. Everything disappeared from sight as the afternoon progressed, and soon visibility was down to only a few feet. At the Ferry Building, the *Alameda* was getting ready to make the 3:30 p.m. trip over to Oakland Long Wharf, while at that latter locality, the *El Capitan* was getting ready for a similar departure.

As departure time approached, the two captains entered their respective wheelhouses, peered into the thickening fog, which was so dense that they could scarcely see the water beyond the bow, and signaled their deckhands to make ready to cast off. Leaving the Ferry Building with some 400 passengers, the *Alameda* steamed cautiously into the fog. As it neared Goat Island, with only a short distance to go, the shape of the *El Capitan* suddenly loomed across the port bow. With engine bells clanging and calling for full astern, and paddles churning a foaming wake, the *Alameda* crashed into the *El Capitan*, whose captain was valiantly trying to turn his craft out of the way.

The impact of the *Alameda* tore a gaping 20-foot-wide hole in the hull of the *El Capitan* just forward of the port side paddle box. In moments, the stricken ferry started taking water, and it was evident that she would not stay afloat for long. The 150 or so passengers on board were quickly transferred to the *Alameda* as the *El Capitan* slowly began to sink in 25 feet of water. With everyone off, the *Alameda*, which had sustained little damage, backed off, and the *El Capitan* settled deeper into the water until the hurricane deck was awash.

On arrival at Oakland Long Wharf, the captain of the *Alameda* notified the Wharfinger, who in turn arranged for the steam tug *Anasha* to find the *El Capitan* and put a line on board. After a short search in the fog, the ferry was located and towed to a mud bank, where she was grounded for the night.

With the loss of the *El Capitan,* service on the Creek Route was temporarily discontinued and the *Capital* was brought over to the Long Wharf to make the *El Capitan's* runs. The next day, the *El Capitan* was towed over to the Oakland Point shipyard, where she spent a period on the ways before being returned to service.

Oakland Pier

With a fine new Ferry Building in San Francisco, and three dependable passenger ferries, the Central Pacific began the design of what was to become one of its most famous structures, the Oakland Pier. This facility, which was to be built along the south side of the Oakland Long Wharf, ultimately would be of a size to accommodate hundreds of trains per day, and the original structure, with its additions, was to survive as an East Bay landmark for over 75 years.

The main part of the pier was constructed as a rock-fill mole that was wide enough for four tracks plus a wagon road

OAKLAND PIER before 1900, looking east; Pier Tower at right, Long Wharf at left. Mainline and westward locals used middle pair of tracks; eastward locals used track at far left.
Roy D. Graves Collection

MAINLINE TRAIN (above) awaits its passengers inside the Oakland Pier train shed. Out on the line (left), engine 1222 and train at East Oakland Station. Locomotive was built by Rhode Island in 1868 and was scrapped in 1907. **Southern Pacific; Roy D. Graves Collection**

NINE CARS and suburban engine thunder eastward along the three-track right-of-way leading from Oakland Pier.
Roy D. Graves Collection

ENGINE 1503, two views. Upper view is along Seventh Street, lower at West Oakland roundhouse. This was a typical steam local prime mover. **Both Roy D. Graves Collection**

along its north side. At the western end there was built an enormous train shed, which spanned a total of 14 tracks intended for use by transcontinental and mainline passenger trains as well as the local steam trains. South of this Victorian-styled building was a coach yard of sufficient capacity to accommodate as many cars as might be needed during peak periods. Inside the cavernous train shed were offices, a large waiting room, and the multitude of other facilities that go with a busy train terminal.

The bay side of the building was home port for the Central Pacific "navy." Here was the main ferry slip, with other layover slips located on each side, and in an adjacent part of the building were located offices for the Wharfinger and the officers of the ferry fleet.

Construction of the rock-fill mole got underway early in 1880, with a steady stream of rock trains bringing fill on a nearly around-the-clock schedule. By the following year, the fill had been completed and erection of the buildings had begun. The entire facility was completed early in January 1882, and a formal inauguration party was scheduled for the evening of Friday, January 20.

Preparations for the Grand Ball were under the direction of Eli Dennison, general news agent and caterer of the railroad, and took the better part of a week. By the time the special trains began arriving at the Ball from Sacramento, Stockton, San Jose, and other communities, the pier terminal had taken on a festive look. Admission to the buffet supper, which started at 6:00 p.m., was by tickets, which had been on sale at all stations throughout the Bay Area at a price of 50 cents.

As each train pulled in, the guests alighted and were directed to the west end of the train shed, which had been partitioned off by huge canvases to form a dining area. On entering the area, guests moved along four tables, each 70 feet long, upon which all varieties of delectable food were displayed: Appetizers, crisp salads, hot vegetables, a mountain of snowy-white potatoes, and the most impressive item, a line of 100 roast turkeys, with white-clad chefs to carve and serve as much as anyone wanted.

During dinner, the guests were treated to music by the Oakland Brass Band, which played from a raised platform in one corner of the dining area. After the supper had been consumed, the doors of the waiting room were thrown open and the Brass Band led the crowd into the gaily decorated room, where a Grand Ball and Promenade soon was in progress. Dennison was especially pleased with the preparation of the waiting room, as several of his crew had spent many days on their hands and knees polishing the floor to an extremely high luster. So polished was the floor that it was reported that more than one gentleman lacking in sobriety barely made his way across the floor.

On Sunday, January 22, 1882, passenger trains began making their runs in and out of the new Oakland Pier. Thereafter, Oakland Long Wharf was used solely for freight trains and car storage.

Concurrent with the opening of service to Oakland Pier, Central Pacific instituted two changes which affected the local steam train operations. One of these changes involved the use of a group of seven engines built especially for the Seventh Street line. These engines had a distinctive Prairie, or 2-6-2 wheel arrangement. They were designed and constructed under the supervision of Andrew J. Stevens, master mechanic of the Sacramento Shops, during 1881 and 1882. Unlike any other engine used on the East Bay local lines, these engines were essentially double-ended, that is, they could operate equally well in either direction. Such a feature was desirable on the local lines as all engines were operated facing Oakland Pier, even on eastward trains. This operating procedure obviated the necessity of turning engines at terminals.

The second change, which also went into effect on January 22, was changing the double-tracked Seventh Street line from

CENTRAL PACIFIC's Prairie-type suburban engines were most unique. No. 233 later became S.P. 1903 and is now owned by the Castro Point Railway Museum, Richmond, Calif.
Roy D. Graves Collection

BENEATH A CLOUD of black coal smoke, the *Piedmont* approaches Oakland Pier. In right distance, billboards line the trestle portion of Oakland Long Wharf while Goat Island can be seen in left distance over buildings at end of Long Wharf. **Roy D. Graves Collection**

right-hand to left-hand operation. This change was made necessary by the construction of a third track for local trains between Oakland Pier Tower and West Oakland and also between East Oakland and Sather. On these three-track sections, the north track was for eastward local trains, the middle track for westward mainline and local trains, and the south track for eastward mainline trains. This mode of operation of the local trains continued throughout the period of the steam locals and was not changed to right-hand operation until some 30 years later during reconstruction of the Seventh Street line in anticipation of electric train service.

In the years following the opening of Oakland Pier, traffic increased steadily to the point that all three ferries, the *El Capitan, Oakland,* and *Alameda,* were needed to fill posted schedules. Thus, as there was no extra boat available, the Oakland Point shipyard was called upon to build a fourth ferry. This boat, the *Piedmont,* was launched in 1883, and represented a radical departure in design from previous boats.

Unlike other Bay ferries, the *Piedmont* had no walking beam. Instead of having a vertical cylinder with a piston attached to the walking beam, which in turn was attached to the crank rod which turned the paddle wheels, the *Piedmont* had a mammoth cylinder which was laid horizontally within the hull. The piston from this cylinder, which had a stroke of 166 inches, was connected directly to the paddle wheel crank. That this novel idea of a beamless paddle ferry apparently was not too successful can be noted by the fact that the design was never duplicated, and later ferries built at Oakland Point either had a walking beam or were equipped with compound engines.

Shortly after the *Piedmont* entered service, the Central Pacific acquired the river packet *Amador.* This single-end paddle wheel boat, which had been built by Patrick Tiernan in 1868, was modified to a double-end ferry design. On entering service, she was placed on the Oakland Pier to San Francisco run, bringing the number of ferries in that service to four: the *Amador, El Capitan, Oakland,* and *Piedmont.*

The era of Central Pacific operation of the East Bay local lines came to a close on April 1, 1885. On that date, the Southern Pacific Company, which had been formed in the state of Kentucky on March 17, 1884, leased all Central Pacific operations in California, Nevada, and Utah for a period of 99 years. The Southern Pacific, which was another corporation in the house of Leland Stanford, subsequently embarked on a long-term program of expansion and improvement of the East Bay suburban lines which actions ultimately led to the creation of the Bay Area's first electric rail rapid transit system.

AUTOS WERE STILL A DREAM when the new San Francisco Ferry Building was opened in 1898. Horsecars and cable cars carried the crowds. **Roy D. Graves Collection**

CHAPTER 8

After the Merger of 1885

WITH THE LEASE of the Central Pacific Railroad on April 1, 1885, the Southern Pacific embarked on a program to expand and improve the facilities at Oakland Pier. These improvements, which were reported to have cost about $100,000, consisted of the construction of an addition along the south side of the train shed. With the completion of this addition, which was designed expressly for use by suburban local trains, the main train shed was used solely by mainline trains.

Two years later, the Southern Pacific leased the narrow gauge properties of the South Pacific Coast Railroad, and once again all transbay traffic was under one banner. The lease of the narrow gauge included not only all of the operating properties, but also a ferry then under construction at White's Yard in North Beach, San Francisco. The keel of this boat, the *Encinal,* had been laid on December 20, 1886. She had been designed by Captain Austin Hills, and all construction was under the supervision of W.E. Collyer, who had recently sold his own shipyard south of Market Street. It has been reported that the ferry cost $160,000 to build, and that some 60 men worked on her all during 1887. Construction of this ferry consumed 500,000 board feet of prime Puget Sound fir and

PLANNED AS THE PRIDE of the South Pacific Coast, the *Encinal* was launched five months after the narrow gauge was absorbed by S.P.
Roy D. Graves Collection

75,000 board feet of California cedar. The machinery for the ferry was designed by Hinkley and Hayes and was built at the Fulton Iron Works.

On the morning of Wednesday, November 16, 1887, a large crowd assembled at White's Yard to witness the launching of the *Encinal*. At shortly after 11 a.m., Captain Hills gave the word to make the ferry ready for launching, and at 11:39, Mrs. J.E. Keller broke the traditional bottle of champagne across the ferry's bow proclaiming "I christen you, the *Encinal*!" Amid cheers, whistles, and the clanging of bells, the ferry slid gracefully into the waters of San Francisco Bay. On board the ferry on its trip down the ways was James G. Fair, Captain John Leale, and other dignitaries.

Once in the water, the tugs *Katy* and *Etna* put lines on board and towed the ferry over to Alameda Point for outfitting. After being tied up for nearly three months at Alameda Point, the *Encinal* was given a trial run on the morning of February 8, 1888. Departing from Alameda Point at 9 a.m., with Fair, "Hog" Davis, Captain Austin Hills, and other guests on board, the ferry made a tour of the bay. From Alameda Point, she went over to Hunters Point, and then turned north toward the Golden Gate. Nearing Alcatraz Island, the *Encinal* caught up and overtook the North Pacific Coast ferry *Tiburon*. After sailing up Raccoon Strait, the ferry rounded Angel Island and headed back to Alameda Point, returning to that location shortly after 11 o'clock. As the trial run was a success, the *Encinal* then moved to the main slip at Alameda Pier, where she received passengers for the noon departure for San Francisco.

With the *Encinal* in service, the *Newark* was sent to the Oakland Point shipyard for a much-needed refurbishing. At that same time, Superintendent W.W. Slater announced that all bay ferries soon would be thoroughly modernized and would be equipped with electric lights. The *Piedmont* was the first Southern Pacific ferry to be illuminated with incandescent lights. To provide the electric power, a small generator was installed in the engine room. On the *Piedmont's* upper deck, there was installed a row of 59 lamps of 16 candlepower each (about equal to 15-watt globes by today's standards). The main saloon received a row of 20 candlepower lights down the center, with clusters of 16-c.p. lights along each side. In addition, each stairwell received six 16-c.p. lamps and the main deck was illuminated by a string of 50 16-c.p. lamps. With the successful installation of electric lights on the *Piedmont*, the other ferries were withdrawn from service in turn and had similar electric systems installed. At the same time, to bring Alameda Pier up to the same level of illumination as Oakland Pier, electric lights were installed throughout in place of the oil lamps previously in use.

The Decoration Day Disaster

In the latter part of the nineteenth century, Memorial Day was a traditional day to make pilgrimages to the cemeteries to place flowers and wreaths on grave sites. In 1890, Decoration Day, as it was then called, fell on a Friday, giving promise to many of the possibility of a three-day weekend. The day dawned clear, with a slight breeze blowing across the bay. It was such a beautiful day that nearly everyone wanted to go somewhere. Those living in the East Bay were bound on going to the City to stroll up Market Street or take the steam car to the beaches. Conversely, those who resided in San Francisco were just as intent on going over to Oakland or Berkeley to visit relatives, enjoy a picnic, or go to one of the cemeteries to pay their respects to their departed loved ones.

By midday, crowds on both the narrow gauge and broad gauge locals had thinned somewhat, although the lines still were doing a brisk business. In San Francisco, the 1:15 p.m. "Narrow Gauge" ferry pulled out for Alameda Pier with a capacity crowd. On board were passengers headed not only for Oakland and Alameda, but also for San Jose and the Santa Cruz beaches, as this ferry connected with a mainline train for those distant points.

DECORATION DAY DISASTER happened here, at the Webster Street Bridge. Crews have fastened a cable around the body of the car that went into the water. Engine No. 3 (below), the "Hoodoo Engine," was still at the bottom of the Estuary when above photo was taken.
Roy D. Graves Collection; R.S. Ford Collection

Arriving at Alameda Pier at 1:40, the crowd debarked and moved into the train shed, where the waiting trains stood. On one of the tracks stood a Webster Street local, composed that day of narrow gauge engine No. 3, combination baggage-coach No. 77, and two commute coaches; the train crew consisted of Engineer Sam Dunn, Fireman Charles O'Brien, and Conductor Ed Rerath.

Pulling out of the pier at 1:45, Engineer Dunn took his train across the mudflats toward the Webster Street Bridge. Like all eastward local trains, the engine was running backwards as there were no facilities at Oakland-14th Street to turn engines. At about this same time, the yacht *Juanita,* which was cruising up the Estuary, whistled for the Webster Street Bridge to be opened. Hearing the yacht's whistle, Bridgetender J.N. Dunlap placed a red flag between the rails on the south approach to the bridge, as there were no railway signal lights on this particular bridge.

According to Captain Henry McIntyre of the yacht *Cosco,* which was tied up nearby, the bridge opened to allow the *Juanita* to pass through. As the bridge was slowly closing, the Webster Street local approached from the south at about five miles per hour. Much to McIntyre's horror, the train knocked the red flag off the track and continued on to plunge into the open draw. With a gigantic splash and roar, engine No. 3 disappeared from view beneath the murky waters of the Estuary. Fortunately, the train had broken in two, and only the first car followed the engine into the water; the other two cars remained on the track, although tottering at the brink.

Within moments, word of the catastrophe had spread and a crowd rushed to the scene to render aid. Some of the passengers in the submerged coach had been able to break windows and swim to safety, but it was feared that many women and children had been drowned. Soon, a number of men could be seen on the roof of the coach, wielding axes and chopping a large hole, through which the trapped passengers were pulled. It was not too long until all of the survivors had been rescued. It was later determined that 13 passengers had lost their lives due to drowning.

That afternoon, an engine was dispatched from Alameda Pier to retrieve the two coaches still on the track. The next day, the sunken coach was pulled from the Estuary and put back on the track and towed away for repairs. Engine No. 3 remained at the bottom of the Estuary.

By the next day, all passengers and crewmen, except Dunn, had been accounted for. According to Fireman O'Brien, Dunn had gone down with his engine. But had he? No one knew for sure. The *Oakland Tribune* reported that Dunn had surreptitiously showed up at his rooming house in West Alameda the afternoon of the disaster. Although still damp and visibly shaken, he had talked to no one, picked up his belongings, and disappeared.

The big question that set the Bay Area buzzing was: "Where is Sam Dunn?" Tight-mouthed officials of the railroad claimed at first that they had not seen him. But a few days later, an unidentified official admitted that Dunn had been in the company offices in San Francisco for the purpose of an official inquiry. At that time, he was so distraught over the disaster as to be almost completely irrational. About all that the company official would say was that Dunn had escaped from his engine, had swum ashore, and had hidden among some pilings for a while fearing he would be lynched.

Several days later, the local newspapers carried the report of the findings of the Board of Inquiry. The Board found that

IN GENTLER TIMES, local East Bay transit was handled by such as Engine 22 (above), used frequently on the narrow-gauge locals, while the customers waited at ornate depots like the Chestnut Street station on the Encinal Ave. line (below). The South Pacific Coast favored this delightfully Victorian Style.
Roy D. Graves Collection; Louis L. Stein Jr. Collection

SMOKY PASSAGE: Engine No. 3 and train leaves High Street bound for Alameda Pier (above); note three-rail track in foreground which allowed both standard and narrow-gauge trains to use Encinal Ave. Engine 21 (below) takes the crossover at 12th & Webster in Oakland; like other narrow-gauge engines, this one wound up in the Owens Valley where it labored until 1945. **Both Roy D. Graves Collection**

while Engineer Dunn was to blame for the accident, two factors also were present which had a direct bearing on the case. The first was the operating rule which specified that engines on eastward trains be run backwards. This meant that on the trip to Oakland, the tender was in front of the engine and may have obscured Dunn's vision of both the red warning flag and the opened drawbridge. The second, and more important factor, was that the Webster Street Bridge, unlike the broad-gauge Alice Street Bridge, was not equipped with derails and signal lights. The Board of Inquiry felt that if the bridge had been so equipped, the accident might not have happened.

With the publishing of the findings of the Board of Inquiry, a coroner's jury was empaneled in Alameda to try Dunn for manslaughter. The first action of the jury was to dispatch Sheriff Hale to find him, as he apparently was in hiding. He was variously reported as having been seen in Calistoga, Monterey, and other distant places. But Sheriff Hale was unable to find him, and the jury found Dunn guilty in absentia of the charge of manslaughter.

About a year later, Dunn came out of hiding in the Santa Cruz Mountains when he signed on as a fry cook at the Santa Cruz County Poor Farm. There he worked most of his remaining years, a totally broken man who never fully regained his sanity.

About a week after the accident, engine No. 3 was lifted from the Estuary and towed to Newark, where she was rebuilt and put back in service. Because of this accident, and one near Felton a number of years earlier which also had taken 13 lives, engine No. 3 became known as a "hoodoo" engine, and consequently was not too popular with the more superstitious crews.

The Nickel Ferry

PRIDE OF John L. Davie's Nickel Ferry was the *Rosalie*.
Roy D. Graves Collection

After the South Pacific Coast had been leased in 1887, the Southern Pacific enjoyed a monopoly of transbay traffic for the next six years. In 1893, the specter of competition again was raised. This time, it was in the form of John L. Davie, owner of the Davie Transportation Company, who operated the ferry *Rosalie* on the run from Vallejo to San Francisco. Davie, who later was to become Mayor of Oakland, reasoned that it should be a very profitable venture to operate his ferry in competition with the Southern Pacific Creek Route ferries. Subsequently, Davie's general manager, J.J. Ebert, made a public announcement that the *Rosalie* would begin operating between the foot of Franklin Street, in Oakland, and the foot of Mission Street, in San Francisco, on Wednesday, July 5, 1893. The announced fare was to be five cents per crossing.

The first trip for this new operation departed from San Francisco at 4:30 that morning. In spite of the pre-dawn foggy darkness, the trip was well patronized. As soon as the gangplank was lowered, a goodly sized crowd pushed on board the *Rosalie*. Frank C. Givens, on his way home to Elmhurst, had the distinction of being the first person to hand his nickel to the purser. The *Rosalie* arrived at the Franklin Street Wharf at a few minutes before 5:00 a.m., and after discharging the passengers from San Francisco, took on about 150 early-rising commuters for the first westbound trip. Approaching San Francisco a little before 6:00, everyone on board lined the rail and shouted: "Rah, rah, rah, zip, boom, bah, Davie Ferry, rah, rah, rah!" as the *Rosalie* berthed at Mission Street.

With a two-hour headway and a 30-minute crossing time, the *Rosalie* soon captured the fancy of potential Creek Route patrons. She soon was carrying capacity crowds, and on August 11, 1893, the service was augmented by the little ferry *Grace Barton*, owned by the Whitney Ferry and Transportation Company. During mid-August, the *San Francisco Bulletin* made a rough passenger count which showed that the *Rosalie* was averaging about 1,000 passengers per trip, the *Grace Barton* about 400, and the Southern Pacific ferry *Alameda*, which was being operated on the Creek Route, only about 40 passengers.

Getting off to a brisk start, traffic on the Davie Ferry, or Nickel Ferry as the line generally was known, gradually tapered off. By the end of summer, the *Grace Barton* had been withdrawn from service and placed on other runs. Sometime later, the *Rosalie* was replaced by the *Alvira*, another Davie boat, which continued to ply the route for the following two years. Finally, in mid-1895, without any public announcement, all service was withdrawn and the Southern Pacific again had a monopoly on transbay service.

Even though it was no longer operating, Davie's Nickel Ferry had made its impact on the Southern Pacific. To meet the competition, S.P. had been forced to lower its Creek Route fares to five cents per crossing, and for several decades after the *Rosalie* and *Alvira* had made their last crossing, the Creek Route ferries continued to offer a bargain rate for transbay travelers.

The Railroad Strike of 1894

One of the most violent strikes in the nation's history paralyzed the entire railroad industry during the summer of 1894. The strike developed out of a desire on the part of the American Railroad Union to be recognized as the sole bargaining agent for the employees of the Pullman Company. The Company, on the other hand, believed that its employees were not interested in having this or any other union represent them. Reaching an impasse in the late spring of 1894, the union adopted a different tactic in an attempt to force recognition. This involved an embargo on the movement of any train containing Pullman cars. With the embargo in effect, nearly all intercity trains were halted, as many passenger trains in those days carried at least one Pullman car.

Strike sanction by the A.R.U. officially began at noon on Wednesday, June 27, 1894. Because the Southern Pacific handled a great number of Pullman cars, train operations at Oakland and other points ground to a halt by 4:00 p.m. that day. With the strike in effect, mail and freight began to pile up in Oakland, and the railroad considered the hiring of strikebreakers in order to move the mail and freight and also to operate a few mainline passenger trains.

Unusual as it may seem, even though the A.R.U. was striking against the Pullman Company, most regular Pullman employees were not union members and thus were not on strike. Nearly all of these employees were willing to work their trains when and if they were operated. Because of this willingness of the Pullman employees to man their cars, the Southern Pacific decided to put the strike to a test and made an attempt to operate an Overland train. To assist the train crew in the case of trouble from strikers, the railroad hired 40 deputy sheriffs to assure law and order. At the last minute, the company decided against running the train as there were insufficient trainmen who could be persuaded to cross the picket lines.

By Friday, the newspapers reported that all mainline railroads west of Chicago were completely tied up. On the Southern Pacific, all broad gauge operations were closed down. The narrow gauge lines were still operating as usual, however, as the A.R.U. had decided not to interfere with those operations as there were no A.R.U. members on that division.

That same day, the following telegram was received in the Sacramento headquarters of the union:

H.A. KNOX, A.R.U., SACRAMENTO
ADOPT MEASURES TO TIE UP ENTIRE SOUTHERN PACIFIC SYSTEM WITHIN YOUR REACH.
EUGENE V. DEBS
PRESIDENT, A.R.U.

With this telegram, Debs had sounded a declaration of war against the Southern Pacific. What had started out as a secondary boycott served to make the railroad more insistent on getting its trains running. This caused feelings to run high and resulted in more and more non-A.R.U. employees coming over to the union camp.

One of the first direct confrontations between management and the employees took place in the Oakland yards that Friday morning. While making up a train of passenger coaches, three yardmen were asked to couple on a number of Pullman cars. This they refused to do, and all three men immediately were fired. This act only served to anger other employees, and it turned the A.R.U. strikers into an ugly mood.

At the same time, A.R.U. members were talking earnestly to narrow gauge crews, attempting to convince them that they should join their broad gauge brethren in the walkout. The opening wedge on the narrow gauge occurred at 12:45 p.m. that day, when the fireman from engine No. 19 walked off the job while his train was standing at the 14th and Franklin Depot. Although a member of the Brotherhood of Locomotive Firemen, he felt that the A.R.U. had a definite case against the railroad. Because the company was not held in very high esteem by many of the employees, other Brotherhood members on the narrow gauge soon joined the walkout. By that Friday evening, the A.R.U. jubilantly issued a statement that not a wheel was rolling anywhere on the vast Southern Pacific system. The only exception was a lone train, operated by C.F. Hall, Roundhouse Foreman at West Oakland, which chuffed up and down Seventh Street in order to hold the franchise.

The effect of the strike was felt everywhere on the Southern Pacific. The Oakland Point shops were closed and locked to prevent vandalism; Oakland Pier was closed and patrolled by special deputy sheriffs. Ferry service to Oakland Pier was annulled because the company feared that the boats might be damaged by strikers if they attempted to land at that facility.

That weekend, the only mainline train operated anywhere on the Southern Pacific system was a special operated for the convenience of Mrs. Leland Stanford, widow of one of the founders of the railroad. Mrs. Stanford's train had been stranded at Dunsmuir when the strike began. In deference to her, the union agreed to a special movement from Dunsmuir to Oakland. The train, composed of eight-wheeler No. 1648 and one coach, which had a large "A.R.U." painted on its sides, arrived in Oakland at 10:35 the morning of July 2 after an uneventful trip down the west side of the Sacramento Valley.

That same weekend, the railroad attempted to complete the runs of several trains which had been stranded along the way when the strike began. One of these, a mail and passenger train from the east, arrived at the Oakland 16th Street Station early in the morning of Sunday, July 3. The arrival of the train caught the strikers unawares, and seeing some Pullman cars on the rear, the strikers seized the train and cut all of the air hoses. This latest action by A.R.U. members prompted the company to notify all employees that anyone not back on the job by 1:00 p.m. Tuesday would be fired. When the announcement was read to the strikers gathered at Oakland Pier, it was met with jeers and catcalls, and resulted in the union becoming even more determined to see the strike through. Meanwhile, a nationwide call went out to all organized labor to come to the support of the striking union. In making this call for support, Debs urged that a nationwide general strike be called if necessary.

The regular and special editions of Bay Area newspapers for July 4, 1894, carried screaming headlines about the strike. Stories datelined Chicago described how the strikers were burning railroad depots and cars. The militia had been called out to restore order, and army troops, with rifles at the ready, were marching on hundreds of striking railroad men. Matters got completely out of hand in Chicago and the strikers could not be quelled until the army had been forced to fire on many of them, killing an undetermined number.

In the Bay Area, things were only a little better. All trains, both broad gauge and narrow gauge, were tied up, and all Southern Pacific facilities, with the exception of the Creek Route ferries, were either closed or rendered inoperative. The company had made an attempt to protect its property by hiring a great number of special deputies; however, the strikers overpowered them and broke into both the West Oakland

THE *NEWARK* sits in the slip at Oakland Pier. Twin towers housed water tanks for fire control.
Roy D. Graves Collection

shops and Oakland Pier and caused a great deal of damage by vandalism. In a number of cases, striking railroad men ran locomotives out of the yards and onto the main line, where the steam and water was bled from the engines, effectively blockading the track. At 16th Street Station, the strikers took seven box cars and by splitting switches, put all seven on the ground crossways to the tracks, further blocking the line at that point. In addition to all this, a number of signal towers were broken into and signal wires cut and equipment damaged or destroyed. In all, damage to the Southern Pacific facilities in the East Bay alone amounted to hundreds of thousands of dollars. With the passing of each day, the strikers grew more militant, and soon were in complete control of all railroad properties.

As ferries still were running on the Creek Route, and were also making occasional runs to Oakland Pier, the A.R.U. made a concerted effort to stop this last vestige of service. The strikers at Oakland Pier were instructed to board any ferry which attempted to land there and put her out of service in any way that they could. Later that day, much to the glee of the strikers, the *Alameda* made an attempt to land at Oakland Pier with a large load of mail and express. Nearing the slip, the captain saw the hostile strikers and hurriedly reversed engines and backed out into the bay. He then took the ferry to the foot of Broadway, and no further attempt was made to berth at Oakland Pier until the strike was settled.

The Creek Route, which in normal times was operated with the *Capital* had been augmented with the ferries *Oakland, Piedmont,* and *Newark*. But still there were thousands of people waiting to cross the bay, and the *El Capitan* and *Alameda* soon were added to the Creek Route. With six boats on the run, it became necessary for a ferry to wait at the mouth of the Estuary until the boat ahead had entered the bay on its westbound trip, as the channel was too narrow for two boats to pass. Even so, it was very difficult to navigate the big boats in the confines of the narrow waterway; hence the *Piedmont's* ingloriously becoming stuck in the mud was not totally unexpected. Unfortunately for the crew of the ferry, this misfortune did not go unnoticed by the strikers, who stood on the shore and hollered and jeered at the difficulty. It is reported that several of the more daring strikers found a rowboat and attempted to board the stranded ferry with the idea of capturing it for their union, but the boarders were put off in fast order by burly deckhands who threw them unceremoniously into the cold water.

The late evening edition of the *Tribune* carried an item about the further deepening of the labor troubles. It announced that the military was to be called to operate the trains and restore order. On the morning of July 10, the ferry *Alameda,* under command of Captain John Leale, was dispatched to the Presidio of San Francisco to pick up two cavalry troops, with 200 horses, and five battery companies composed of 600 officers and enlisted men. The ferry then proceeded to Mare Island, where a battalion of Marines boarded. Moving on to Benicia Arsenal, the ferry picked up a company of infantry. The ferry then steamed up the Sacramento River to the K Street Landing in Sacramento.

After discharging the troops and their equipment and mounts, which were used to quell a near insurrection in the capital, Captain Leale took his ferry back to San Francisco Bay. Leaving Sacramento at 4:30 p.m., the *Alameda* steamed back down the river, arriving at the Ferry Building at 3:30 the next morning. A few hours later, the *Alameda* again went to Mare Island and picked up 400 sailors and brought them to Oakland Pier. It had been planned to use Navy personnel to operate the ferries in case the strikers convinced the ferrymen

OVERSIZE PADDLE BOXES were a feature of the *Newark* before her 1903 rebuilding. **Vernon J. Sappers Collection**

INSIDE THE FERRY BUILDING, this large ticket concourse served Oakland, Alameda and transcontinental train passengers.

Roy D. Graves Collection

to walk off their boats. The *Alameda,* with her contingent of sailors on board, moored along the south side of Oakland Pier, staying there from July 12 to July 23, at which time she cast off and took the sailors back to Mare Island.

On July 12, with 350 Marines in full battle dress patroling the Oakland Pier and Alameda Pier areas, the massive job began of cleaning up the wreckage left by the strikers. At 11:00 a.m. that day, the *Bay City* connected with the first narrow gauge local to operate after a suspension of not quite two weeks. That same day, the leaders of the various A.R.U. locals throughout the country called on Debs to ask him to call off the strike. At 9:30 the following morning, Debs announced from his prison cell that the strike was terminated and that all A.R.U. members were to go back to work. With this announcement, service quickly was resumed on the narrow gauge lines as they had suffered little damage. Most broad gauge trains also soon were running, although evidence of damaged facilities were to be seen everywhere. In addition, troops were stationed everywhere throughout the system, at depots, roundhouses, on ferries, and riding on trains.

When the striking employees reported for work, the railroads informed them that only non-A.R.U. personnel would be eligible for employment. When told of this, the national headquarters of the union made a concerted plea to organized labor to support its members in a new strike call. In response, Samuel Gompers, President of the National Federation of Labor, stated that his union would support the A.R.U. in a nationwide general strike if one was called. By this time, however, nearly all railroad employees had tired of the strike and, because it was considered to be "someone else's fight," were most desirous to return to work. In support of their members, the various railroad brotherhoods announced that they would not support any new A.R.U. strike.

Still there were sporadic incidents during which A.R.U. members attempted to block the passage of trains. At one of these, a freight train from Mendota was stopped and captured at Seventh and Cedar Streets. The crew was pulled off the train, set upon, and badly beaten. In response to this action, the railroad once again called in army troops, who soon arrived on the scene with a Gatling gun, an early type of machine gun. Seeing themselves outnumbered, the A.R.U. members quickly dispersed and the train was allowed to go on its way.

By July 20, 1894, operations had returned to normal and all remaining military personnel were recalled. The great railroad strike was over, having cost the nation untold millions of dollars. The determined A.R.U. members came out losers, as all subsequently were blacklisted by the railroad industry and were forced to find employment elsewhere.

A New Ferry Building

During the latter part of the 1880s, transbay passenger traffic increased to the point that the Ferry Building that had been constructed only 10 years previously had become overcrowded and outmoded. What was needed was an imposing new Ferry Terminal which would serve not only the many lines on the bay but also the riverboat lines which radiated out from San Francisco. Because the facility would service many separate lines, it was logical that the owner should be the State of California, through its Board of Harbor Commissioners.

In the early 1890s, the Board appointed A. Page Brown as chief architect for the new Union Ferry Terminal. Brown was assisted by Howard C. Holmes, state engineer and chief engineer for the project, and Edward R. Swain, supervising architect. The design which was developed for the new structure called for a massive two-storied building faced with sandstone quarried from the Coast Ranges west of Willows. The building was to be surmounted with a clock tower designed after the

AN ALAMEDA LOOP train, headed by engine 2182, rumbles across the Harrison St. bridge (above). This Oakland Pier train, after traversing Alameda, will return to the same pier via the Fruitvale Ave. bridge. Engine 1221 and train (below) leave Harrison St. bridge for Oakland Pier.
Roy D. Graves Collection; Louis L. Stein Jr. Collection

Giralda Tower of the Cathedral of Seville in Spain. The tower, 235 feet in height, was to contain four clock dials, each 23½ feet in diameter and weighing 2,500 pounds. The clock mechanism was to include a pendulum which would be 14 feet long.

Construction of the new facility, which was to be located immediately east of the old Ferry Building, began in the early part of 1891. Prior to the closing of the old Ferry Building on June 25, 1891, an interim facility for Southern Pacific ferries was built near the foot of Mission Street, just south of the old structure.

With the old Ferry building closed and partly dismantled, construction of the new building was begun in earnest in the fall of 1891. Construction took longer than had been anticipated, however, and even though it was planned to have the new building ready for occupancy by 1896, an additional two years was required for completion. The new Ferry Building finally was completed in July 1898, although mostly obscured by the old Ferry Building still standing in front of it. Formal opening and dedication of the new $967,879 facility was set for 9:00 a.m., Wednesday, July 13, 1898.

The previous evening, Southern Pacific moved all of its ticket facilities from the interim ferry terminal to the new Union Ferry Terminal, which was the official name of the new building. Ferries continued to use the interim facility until noon that day, at which time operations were moved to the new Ferry Building. The last ferry into the interim facility was the *Bay City*, which after discharging her passengers, cast off and moved over to a slip at the new Ferry Building, where she made ready for a 12:15 departure. The first ferry into the new Ferry Building was the *Piedmont,* which arrived from Oakland Pier at 12:45 p.m. On hand on the main, or upper level, was State Engineer Holmes, who had the honor of lowering the apron onto the upper deck of the ferry so that the passengers could debark. After leaving the ferry, the crowd moved along a passageway and into the great concourse, with its vaulted glass clerestory. Across the gleaming mosaic floor were potted palms, standing against the marble walls. To one side, the Army band played, while in the other direction, the ladies of the Red Cross were serving light refreshments. The only somber note was the presence of members of the New York Regiment, on duty in San Francisco because of the Spanish-American war then raging in Cuba and the Philippine Islands.

(It may be recalled that this concourse later was the location of the world-famous California Panorama, which was an enormous plaster relief map of the Golden State. Representing three years of design and 14 months of labor by 25 artisans, the giant diorama stretched the entire 450-foot length of the concourse and was completed at a cost of $145,000. It was unveiled on the evening of November 19, 1924, before a party of over 1,000 guests. The sight that left them breathless was of how California would look—every stream, lake, and snow-capped mountain, every village, town, and city—if one flew at an altitude of 10,000 feet just off the coast all the way from the Mexican border north to Oregon. It was to become known far and wide as the most perfect and accurate topographic reproduction ever conceived.

TYPICALLY S.P. was Oakland's 16th Street Station in the 1890s (above). This structure, an example of "Huntington Standard" architecture, was replaced by the present station in 1911. Station serves as background for foot-powered parcel delivery vehicle, turn-of-the-century version (below).

Roy D. Graves Collection; Louis L. Stein Jr. Collection

(After attracting tens of thousands of viewers, the Great Map was dismantled in 1960 to make room for expanded State office facilities and the World Trade Center. Purchased by a land developer, the diorama was shipped to Redding in 300 crates, where it now rests with an uncertain future.)

With the new Ferry Building in use, the old Ferry Building, with its post office substation, was demolished. It had been proposed to fill in the old timbered deck area and the site of the wooden buildings and to turn the entire area into a Ferry Plaza, complete with several rows of palm trees. After filling in the area, however, most of it was turned to street use, including the famous three-track streetcar loop which was located immediately in front of the Ferry Building.

Concurrent with the opening of the Ferry Building, plans were drawn up for the replacement of both the narrow gauge Webster Street Bridge and the broad gauge Alice Street Bridge. Both of these structures would be replaced by a new dual-gauge crossing to be constructed at the foot of Harrison Street. During construction of the new bridge, a third running rail was laid along Webster Street which would allow standard gauge equipment to be operated along that route.

Construction of the Harrison Street Bridge was begun during the early part of 1898, with completion accomplished by late September. After the necessary track connections were made, the first train crossed the Estuary by way of this span shortly after 11:00 a.m. on Wednesday, September 28, 1898. At that same time, the two older bridges were taken out of service. The aging Webster Street Bridge subsequently was dismantled and removed, being replaced the following year by a new vehicular bridge built at the same location by the County of Alameda. As an interim measure, a plank deck was laid on the Alice Street Bridge so that horse and wagon traffic across the Estuary would not be interrupted. After the new Webster Street Bridge was opened to traffic, the Alice Street Bridge was removed.

On the evening of October 21, 1898, there was an accident at the north end of the Harrison Street Bridge which reminded many employees of the Decoration Day Disaster some eight years previously, and it was only a stroke of luck that kept a narrow gauge local from plunging into the Estuary. At the Oakland end of the bridge, Flagman John Sullivan, on hearing a train approaching, peered across the bridge in the gathering dusk. Thinking that it was a broad gauge Alameda loop train headed for Oakland Pier, he called to Switchtender F. Underwood to set the switch for the broad gauge First Street route.

THIS WAS BERKELEY in steam days, as a S.P. San Francisco local departs. Tracks at right are for the already electrified Key Route. Seventy years later, BART subway station was built here.
Roy D. Graves Collection

To Sullivan's surprise, a narrow gauge Webster Street train rumbled across the bridge. Before he could yell to the switchtender, the narrow gauge train had hit the switch and jumped the track. Fortunately, none of the three cars on the train fell off the approach to the bridge, even though all were off the track. The only casualty was Conductor Alexander Buchanan, who was standing on the platform of the rear coach and who lost his footing. He slipped and fell some 20 feet into the murky water below. He was quickly pulled from the water, sputtering and dripping, and had a few choice words for the negligent flagman.

The year 1898 also saw the launching of the first screw propeller ferry used on the bay. The keel for this boat, the *Berkeley,* was laid on January 25 of that year. The ferry was a radical departure from earlier boats in that she was of steel construction throughout and had a triple expansion engine instead of the usual walking-beam engine. The ferry was designed by Irving M. Scott after similar boats then in operation by the Pennsylvania Railroad in the New York area.

Launching of the *Berkeley* took place at 12:15 p.m. on Tuesday, October 18, 1898, at the Union Iron Works in San Francisco. The press estimated that there were about 2,000 persons in attendance at the launching. After a brief address by Martin Kellogg, President of the University of California, Miss Ruby Richards, daughter of the President of the Berkeley Board of Trustees, broke the ceremonial bottle of champagne across the bow. Miss Marion Huntington, daughter of Henry E. Huntington of the Southern Pacific, then pressed the button which released the dogs holding the ferry on the ways, and amid cheers and whistles, the *Berkeley* slid gracefully into the waters of San Francisco Bay.

The following Saturday morning, the *Berkeley* left the Union Iron Works on a trial cruise which took her around the bay. On completion of the trip, she was accepted by the Southern Pacific and taken to Oakland Pier, where she was placed in service within a few days. The new ferry was considered a great success by the railroad, as she could seat 1,800 passengers, more than any other boat then in use. With the addition of this large ferry, schedules from Oakland Pier were rearranged to provide for a 20-minute headway, with three boats being in use at all times.

The *Berkeley* was elegantly finished, with parquet floors, a stained-glass clerestory, and beautifully polished woodwork. She was truly a credit to the shipbuilder's art, but she also was known for her "round bottom," as some commuters still recollect. Her rounded hull, in contrast to the flat-bottomed hulls of the paddle-wheel boats, gave the ferry a decided tendency to roll, especially if the skipper brought her into the slip in a strongly moving riptide. In this situation, the ferry would slam into the fender on one side of the slip causing her to pitch and roll.

With the addition of the *Berkeley* to the bay fleet, the aging *Alameda* was retired. The older ferry was scrapped, and her hull reportedly was used as a part of the foundation of the Dumbarton Toll Bridge then under construction. At that same time, the *Amador* was transferred up-bay and placed on the run from Vallejo Junction (located one mile west of Crocket) to South Vallejo, where connection was made with trains of the Napa Valley Branch.

On the bay, the *Berkeley* was not the speedy ferry that had been hoped for. Although of adequate size, she was a plodder as she went back and forth across the bay. For a number of years, the Southern Pacific made various attempts to modify her in an effort to obtain some additional speed. One of the modifications tried during the early years was the installation of a new type of patented four-bladed propeller. The inventor of this propeller claimed that it would materially add to the speed of any ferry.

The *Berkeley* was taken to the Oakland Point shipyard, where a set of the new propellers was installed at no cost to the company. Back in the water, the ferry steamed slowly down the Estuary and around to Oakland Pier. Approaching the slip, the captain rang up "Full Astern," as was the custom to slow the boat prior to entering the slip. Suddenly the engines went wild, turning over at a terrific rate. The engine gang finally got things under control, and it was found that the ferry would not respond to any engine speed, but sat dead in the water. After being towed back to the shipyard, it was discovered that all of the blades of the new propellers had sheared off under the strain of the reversed engines. With that, the original propellers were reinstalled, and the *Berkeley* continued to plod her way back and forth across the bay for many years to come.

The Alameda Pier Fire

The year 1902 saw a major change take place on the narrow gauge Encinal Avenue line. Beginning in the spring of that year, a third running rail was placed to allow broad gauge trains to operate as far east as High Street. The new rail was of 62-pound weight and was obtained from a track rebuilding project near Brentwood, in eastern Contra Costa County. The *Alameda Daily Encinal* reported that new broad gauge cars, pulled by 4-6-0 type engines of the 2000 class, would be operating on the south side line by mid-September. The story also said the broad gauge cars had sliding gates (narrow gauge cars had no gates) and in all probability, the railroad would be charging local fares for rides between stations, even though the franchise prohibited the charging of any local fares. Ultimately, the change from narrow gauge local service on the Encinal Avenue line was set for December 15. It took a disastrous sequence of events to move this date forward by about four weeks.

Fire always was a dreaded word in areas of railroad piers and wharves because of their great expanse of timbers, much of which were soaked with oil dripped from engines and cars. At any of these facilities, there were the ubiquitous water barrels, possibly placed more for moral support than for actual benefit. Such facilities usually had elaborate fire control systems. Oakland Long Wharf had a complete fire station near the end of the pier, with water being supplied from wells onshore. These same wells provided the fire supply at Oakland Pier, with its enormous train shed and appurtenant buildings. At Alameda Pier, a similar fire protection system was in place, although not as elaborate as the one in Oakland.

In spite of precautions, a series of events sometimes occurs which singly would cause little concern, but in combination wreaks a great deal of havoc and destruction. This was the situation on the night of Wednesday, November 19, 1902. As reported in the *Oakland Tribune* the next day, the last narrow gauge train had left Alameda Pier at 12:05 a.m. At that same time, the ferry *Oakland,* with Captain John Leale at the helm, having made the last run over from San Francisco, was tied up taking on fuel oil. Because the ferry would be tied up all night, most of her crew had gone ashore and were preparing to bed down in the bunkhouse at the end of the pier.

It was a blustery night, and a strong wind was blowing in from the Golden Gate. Dark patches of scud blew overhead, and there was a smell of rain on the wind. Leaving the bunkhouse, one of the deckhands went out into the windy night, and glancing south along the tracks, saw orange tongues of fire licking at the walls of the train shed. Running back inside, he shouted, "Fire!", and then ran to alert the night crew at the pier and also the crew on board the ferry. By that time, one wall of the train shed was a mass of crackling flames. Within moments, the entire roof of the structure was ablaze and the interior was a roaring inferno. Jumping on board the *Oakland,* the deckhand helped the others to cast off. Because of low steam pressure, the big ferry could not move very fast and by

ALL THAT WAS LEFT after the November 19, 1902 Alameda Pier fire. Ferry slip to right served as interim facility until new Alameda Pier was built.
Roy D. Graves Collection

NEW ALAMEDA PIER was opened in 1903 and was certainly the most elaborate ferry terminal built by S.P. Alameda coaches in foreground are typical of those used on steam locals prior to 1910.
Roy D. Graves Collection

the time she had begun to make way, the slip was ablaze and the fire had jumped to the upper deck of the ferry.

As soon as they had been alerted, the night crew on the pier had tried to summon help, but the fire already had burned out the telephone and telegraph lines. So they ran over to the bunkhouse, and with the ferry crew, most of whom were in their underwear, jumped into the bay in an effort to save their lives.

Over in San Francisco, the blaze was spotted shortly after it broke out. Word immediately was sent to the San Francisco Fire Department, requesting that a fireboat be sent to the scene. Within moments, the fireboat *Governor Irwin* was underway, steaming at full speed across the bay. Approaching the *Oakland,* whose upper deck was now in flames, the fireboat came about, aimed its fire hoses at the burning ferry, and succeeded in extinguishing the blaze. But all was lost at Alameda Pier. There, the raging fire quickly consumed every piece of wood with an awful roar. The conflagration, visible for many miles around, was one of the most spectacular blazes in the history of the Bay Area.

The next morning, after the fire had burned itself out, Alameda Pier was a scene of total destruction. Only a few charred timbers and burned pilings were left to give mute evidence of the intensity of the conflagration. As soon as possible, the railroad sent a team of investigators to assess the damage and to try to determine the origin of the fire. It was never conclusively decided what had started the fire but it was surmised that the last train out that night had dropped some burning coals onto the oil-soaked ties, which after smoldering for a while had been fanned into flame by the gusty winds.

All but one of the men who had jumped into the bay were accounted for the next day. It appeared that there had been one fatality, Victor De La Santa, a night watchman on board a pile-driver scow which had been moored along the north side of the pier. It was thought that De La Santa had been drowned because the scow was found floating upside down in the bay the next morning. However, when the fog lifted, he was seen in a rowboat, stranded on a mud bar in the middle of the Estuary, wildly waving and yelling to be rescued.

The loss of Alameda Pier to the Southern Pacific was costly, but to the narrow gauge lines, it was nearly a fatal blow. The company estimated that the loss might be as high as $350,000. This figure included the pier and its entire facilities as well as 16 broad gauge cars and 31 narrow gauge cars. The cars had been in the yard at the end of the pier and had burned completely, with their steel parts dropping into the bay. One of the narrow gauge cars that had been destroyed was a parlor car, one of only two on the system.

In summing up the report on the fire, the *Oakland Enquirer* commented:

> "A very probable outcome of the fire will be the conversion of the narrow gauge as far as Los Gatos into the broad gauge system, for there is so little of the narrow gauge equipment remaining that it will be impossible to run more than the most meager service on the through line."

Work on the reconstruction of Alameda Pier got underway by the beginning of 1903, with the new facility being placed in service later that year. The new pier was a decided improvement, and was the most ornate ferry terminal built by the Southern Pacific. During the period of construction, interim terminal facilities were maintained at the freight ferry slip on the Estuary side of Alameda Mole.

The principal effect of the fire was the immediate switch to

NINE COLLECTORS pose for posterity at Oakland Pier. Clean-shaven chap in background was obviously a non-conformist.
R.S. Ford Collection

broad gauge equipment for all runs on the Encinal Avenue line. Although there were still a few mainline narrow gauge trains running through Alameda, they were becoming an anachronism. It was evident to both the railroad and the patrons that within a few years the little narrow gauge trains would be but a memory. Not so apparent was the fact that within the next 10 years, the broad gauge steam locals also would be gone, replaced by a more efficient form of rail transportation.

TIME OF TRANSITION: This pier-bound steam local approaches the Lorin Station. Shortly afterward, electric trains replaced the steam engines and their weary cars; even the station name was changed, to South Berkeley. **Louis L. Stein Jr. Collection**

CHAPTER 9

End of the Steam Era

DURING the last part of the 19th century, the cities of the East Bay increased in size at a phenomenal rate. What originally had been a group of small, separate towns in 1870 had developed into a sizable metropolitan area by 1900. The transportation system which had evolved during that 30-year period had become by 1905, not only inadequate, but also outmoded and uneconomical.

TABLE 2 - *Population of East Bay Cities, 1860 to 1910*

Year	Alameda	Berkeley	Hayward	Oakland	San Leandro	Total
1860	460	...	...	1,543	...	2,003
1870	1,557	...	504	10,500	426	12,987
1880	5,708	...	1,231	34,555	1,369	42,863
1890	11,165	5,101	1,419	48,682	1,811	68,178
1900	16,464	13,214	1,965	66,960	2,253	100,856
1910	23,383	40,434	2,746	150,174	3,471	200,208

Data from California Department of Finance.

Reflecting a post-1900 growth rate which exceeded a total of 10,000 persons per year, a competitive development took place which had far-reaching effects on the Southern Pacific suburban system. In 1902, Francis M. "Borax" Smith, of the Twenty-Mule Team Borax empire, founded the San Francisco, Oakland, and San Jose Railway. This operation, which was known as the Key Route, was built to capitalize on the transition of the East Bay from an area of separate cities and towns to one which would serve (to use the latter-day phrase) as a "bedroom community" for those who worked in San Francisco and lived in the East Bay.

ENGINE 1358, with its cab still lettered for the Oregon & California Ry., pauses on the West Berkeley line at Delaware St. so the crew can pose proudly with their two-car local.
R.S. Ford Collection

The Key Route constructed a long pier into San Francisco Bay some distance to the north of Oakland Pier. Operating onto this pier from five suburban lines were fast, clean electric trains. The trains connected with ferries for San Francisco, thus providing many East Bay patrons with an alternative route to the City. From the beginning, competition between the Southern Pacific and the Key Route was spirited. In Berkeley, Key Route's Berkeley line ran along Shattuck Avenue, only a few feet to the east of the Southern Pacific tracks. Here, passengers could choose which line they preferred, and it soon became apparent to the Southern Pacific that many of their former riders chose the Key Route trains. This was especially true for those who lived in Berryman, as they would take the S.P. train down to Berkeley, and then walk over to the waiting Key Route train for the balance of the trip to San Francisco.

It was due to this loss of patronage to the Key Route that the Southern Pacific announced that on April 11, 1904, a five-cent local fare would be collected on all trains in Berkeley. Since the beginning of service to Berkeley some 35 years previously, no local fares had been collected. All transbay fares were collected at the Ferry Building, and because the railroad did not employ gatemen, local passengers could get on and off trains at will. This free local service was particularly helpful to schoolchildren, as they could go to and from school without the need to pay a fare.

With the establishment of local fares, gatemen were placed on all vestibule platforms to operate the gates and to collect the local fares. At the same time, ticket stations were set up at Berryman and Dwight Way, in addition to one already in operation at the downtown Berkeley station. With the establishment of the ticket stations, all passengers were obliged to purchase tickets prior to boarding trains. Gatemen were instructed to accept cash local fares only at Ashby Avenue, where a ticket agency was not established due to the light population density of that area.

Four months later, on September 2, a much publicized engineering achievement was placed in operation along the mainline track from Oakland Pier to Port Costa. This was an automatic block signal system which was reported to be the longest of its type installed on any railroad on the Pacific Coast. The section of track protected by the system included that used by the Berkeley locals and the West Berkeley trains as well as mainline freight and passenger trains. The system included steel semaphore bridges spanning four tracks and placed at Oakland-16th Street Station, the Key Route crossing, Emeryville, and the West Berkeley station. Beyond this latter point, where the line was double tracked, 50 equally spaced semaphore poles were installed. The system was installed under the direction of E.M. Cutting, Superintendent of Block and Signal Systems for the railroad.

The following year saw continued improvement to the Oakland Pier area. Oakland Long Wharf and the old Peralta Street freight wharves rapidly were becoming overcrowded, and the railroad management decided that the construction of a new, larger facility south of Oakland Pier should serve the needs of the railroad for the foreseeable future. In September 1905, work began on filling in the bay along the outer half of the mole for a distance of 300 feet to the south. This would allow ample room for the construction of a new freight slip and a freight car yard capable of handling many more cars than at the two existing facilities. At the same time, it was announced that a hood would be constructed over the passenger slip at Oakland Pier to protect passengers during inclement weather. The design of the hood would be similar to that at the new Alameda Pier and at the Key Route pier.

On April 16, 1906, there was a major change in service which affected the broad gauge local trains on the Alameda loop line. At 2:00 p.m. that day, the Horseshoe Line was inaugurated to replace the service operated by the loop trains. Heretofore, loop trains had operated from Oakland Pier by way of First Street to the Fruitvale Avenue Bridge. The trains then returned to Oakland Pier by way of Alameda, Lincoln Avenue, and the Harrison Street Bridge. Trains on the new Horseshoe Line operated in both directions between Oakland Pier and Alameda Pier, crossing the Estuary at the Fruitvale Avenue Bridge. Using First Street through Oakland and Lincoln Avenue through Alameda, the line was heavily patronized. Headways were set at 20 minutes, the same as that on the Seventh Street line. Establishment of this route gave patrons in the Fruitvale-Alameda area several choices as to trains for San Francisco. For example, if one missed the Seventh Street train for Oakland Pier, he could easily take a Horseshoe train for Oakland Pier or one running in the opposite direction for Alameda Pier.

The San Francisco Earthquake

Early in 1906, the Southern Pacific announced plans to end all narrow gauge service. What once had been Jim Fair's main line to Santa Cruz would be converted to standard gauge and a new steel bridge would be built replacing the old wooden San Leandro Bay bridge. It was proposed to make Wednesday, April 18, 1906, the last full operating day for the narrow gauge. On the following morning, all narrow gauge equipment was to be taken from Alameda to San Jose for eventual disposal. It was expected that the line would be closed down for only a few days to allow the changing of gauge, and that by April 22 standard gauge trains would be operating through Alameda to San Jose and Santa Cruz by way of the former narrow gauge line. At 5:12 a.m. that final day, however, Mother Nature turned the tables on men's dreams and schemes: April 18 was the day of the Great San Francisco Earthquake.

In San Francisco before dawn that morning, the still, cool air gave promise of another beautiful day. Shortly after 5:00 a.m., as cable cars and streetcars were beginning their early morning runs as the street lights began to wink out and as the sun started its climb from behind the Berkeley Hills east of the bay, there suddenly was a sound which has been described as a "deep and terrible rumble" coming from the north in increasing loudness. It was just a few seconds past 5:12 a.m.

Police Sergeant Jesse Cook, who had been standing at the corner of Washington and Davis Streets, looked up the hill to the west and saw that "the entire street was undulating. It was as if the waves of the ocean were coming toward me." At the same time, while walls were crashing down with thunderous roars, the streets were quickly becoming choked with dust. Through it all, people by the thousands were running into the streets to escape certain death in the collapsing buildings.

The first shock lasted about 40 seconds, and after a respite of but 10 seconds, a second major shock of 25-second duration further shook the city. After this second shaking, a deathly silence hung over the city, as the multitude who had rushed into the streets stood in awe of the force of nature.

Down on the waterfront, many buildings built on filled ground had toppled or collapsed. The Ferry Building had withstood the shaking, and sustained only a few broken windows. The clock on the tower, which had been running about three minutes fast, had stopped at 5:15. The hands remained in this position for more than a year until the clock mechanism could be repaired.

In the East Bay, damage to Oakland and other cities was minimal, consisting principally of fallen chimneys and brickwork. The only reported damage to the Southern Pacific broad gauge system was the Harrison Street Bridge, which was temporarily out of service due to its being knocked askew. It was also reported that several coal bunkers at the end of Oakland Long Wharf had collapsed, sending their stored coal into the bay. In contrast, damage to the narrow gauge system was widespread and quite severe. In the Santa Cruz Mountains, tunnels caved, fills settled, and track buckled. In the East Bay, the San Leandro Bay Bridge was totally inoperative, having been knocked out of alignment. Because of the earthquake, all narrow gauge schedules immediately were annulled. The only narrow gauge trains to roll after the earthquake were those used in pulling up the narrow gauge rails.

By mid-morning, service on the East Bay system was nearly normal. Later that day, however, as the gravity of the situation in San Francisco became apparent, ferry service across the bay was curtailed. By the middle of the afternoon, the following notice had been sent to all East Bay stations, and after being read by employees, was posted in a conspicuous location.

> To: All Station Agents
> By Order of General Funston, Commanding Officer of San Francisco
>
> Do not furnish passage to a single person to San Francisco until further notice.
>
> W. R. SCOTT,
> Superintendent

In San Francisco, refugees by the thousands began streaming down Market Street toward the Ferry Building, bent on leaving the broken and burning city. As a measure of good will, the Southern Pacific announced that free transportation would be provided those desiring to cross over to the East Bay. The announcement was carried in the following notice which was posted in the Ferry Building:

> All sufferers of San Francisco who wish to leave town by our ferries may do so without an application to the gateman. For points outside of Oakland, apply to Depot Master at Oakland.
>
> W.S. PALMER
> S.P. Co.

So great was the number of people leaving San Francisco that it was impossible to make an accurate passenger count. It was estimated by ferry Captain John Leale that upwards of 70,000 persons were transported free of charge from San Francisco to Oakland on April 19. To this must be added a like number on the succeeding days while the city was in flames.

During the days while San Francisco burned with flames that could be seen for more than 50 miles, the Southern

HEADING towards Oakland Pier, Engine 2124 (above) and train drift into Ashby Ave. station. The 2124 was outshopped by Cooke in 1888. West Oakland Roundhouse (below) has Seventh St. engine 1902 on the ready track. To the right is shop switcher No. 7, a diminutive 0-4-0T built by Baldwin in 1882.
Both Louis L. Stein Jr. Collection

HORSES and wagons as well as people rode the *Thoroughfare*. This was the first of two Bay ferries to carry that name. (See page 90.)
Thomas Gray Collection

Pacific provided relief not only through free transportation to the East Bay, but also in the form of running special trains loaded with food, fire-fighting equipment, and medical supplies from points as far away as Los Angeles. At the height of the fire, when members of the San Francisco Fire Department were dropping from sheer exhaustion, several ferry loads of fire engines and men crossed the bay from Oakland to provide very welcome relief.

One of the casualties of the fire was the loss of the corporate headquarters of the railroad. When it became evident that the building housing the offices soon would be consumed by the flames, the Southern Pacific moved its offices over to Oakland, setting up business at temporary quarters in the Union Savings Bank Building, at the corner of 13th Street and Broadway. The stay in Oakland was brief, and within a month, the company had moved back to quarters in the Ferry Building. Permanent offices were not occupied until a move was made to the Flood Building on September 9, 1906.

The earthquake also severely damaged a number of slips at the Ferry Building, causing curtailment of ferry service to the East Bay. Affected most was the south side, or "narrow gauge" line to Alameda, on which all service was suspended until the middle of the following month. During the interim, Alameda patrons had to use the north side, or "broad gauge" line to Oakland Pier.

The Turkey That Crossed the Bay

One of the more interesting stories to come out of the San Francisco earthquake concerned a Mrs. Brennan, operator of a small lunch stand in the Ferry Building. It seems that Mrs. Brennan lived with her two daughters in a small apartment on McAllister Street just up from Market Street. On the morning of the earthquake, Mrs. Brennan and her daughters had been awakened by the terrible shaking. Running out into the street, they watched as columns of smoke soon began rising all around.

The Brennan apartment building had not been too heavily damaged by the quake, but as the fires ate their way slowly toward McAllister Street, it was evident that the building was doomed. By that afternoon, fires were burning briskly all along Market Street. The "Ham and Eggs" Fire, which had started near the intersection of Hayes and Gough Streets, was burning toward McAllister Street, and by nightfall, would consume all of the buildings along that street between Gough and Market Streets.

Realizing that they would have to get out, Mrs. Brennan and her daughters picked up what belongings they could carry and made their way down to the Ferry Building. Because of the fires, the trio had to use a circuitous route which took them past Nob Hill and Telegraph Hill. Arriving at the Ferry Building in the late evening, Mrs. Brennan opened her lunch stand to one and all. Assisted by her daughters, she started making hearty sandwiches and put coffee on to brew on her two-burner kerosene stove.

All that night, during which the city glowed from the flames then out of control, and all the next two days and nights, Mrs. Brennan and her daughters served sandwiches, poured coffee, and provided food for the hundreds of weary firefighters, all without accepting any money in payment.

With the fires finally out, the city faced a gigantic task of rebuilding. Mrs. Brennan was faced with an equally great task, that of finding a place to live in the burned-out city. With the good wishes of the management of the Ferry Building, she converted the back end of her lunch room into a makeshift bedroom, where she and her daughters lived for the following year.

In talking of their experiences, many of the firefighters spoke of Mrs. Brennan and the food she had served, causing many to ask if something could be done to repay her for the kindness that had been extended. By November of that year, a plan was laid which was quietly spread around. Soon, money began to come in from city firemen and all others she had served. On Thanksgiving morning, a delegation of men gathered at the Ferry Building with baskets of food. Placed at her doorstep were all types of fresh vegetables, pies, breads, and a magnificent 22-pound turkey ready for roasting.

On hearing the commotion out front, Mrs. Brennan came to her door. Seeing the gifts, she exclaimed at how thoughtful her many friends were. But, she asked, how can anyone roast a turkey on a kerosene stove? None of the men had thought of this, but they departed with promises that she was not to worry about this mere detail. Soon, there were offers from all around the city for the use of stoves and ranges, though these did not provide good answers as many of the locations were quite distant. The topic of what to do for Mrs. Brennan was discussed all along the waterfront as the morning wore on.

Near noon, when the ferry *Newark* landed at the Ferry Building, the First Officer went to see Mrs. Brennan offering her the use of that ferry's fine galley. The offer obviously was the answer to the problem, and soon a most curious procession left the coffee shop and boarded the ferry. First came an assortment of rough-looking wharfmen, each carrying a large basket crammed with vegetables, pies, or other food. Bringing up the rear was Mrs. Brennan, who carried the turkey which was covered by a large piece of cloth to protect it from the seagulls who swooped and dived overhead.

On board the ferry, the turkey was stuffed and the vegetables prepared. During the next five hours, while the *Newark* went back and forth across the bay, the turkey was roasting in one of the ovens, and soon the tantalizing aroma of roast turkey spread throughout the ferry. Many passengers were justifiably disappointed when they entered the dining room hoping to have some Thanksgiving turkey, only to find that there was no turkey on the menu.

By that evening, the turkey had become golden brown and all the other delicacies were piping hot. When the *Newark* arrived in San Francisco, the turkey and the trimmings again were placed in baskets. With all of her many friends, Mrs. Brennan trooped off the ferry and over to the lunch room, carrying the bountiful feast.

That evening was a most memorable one for Mrs. Brennan and her two daughters. With her many friends crowding into the confines of her lunchroom, she carved the turkey and served what was later described as a most delicious Thanksgiving dinner. Before eating, Mrs. Brennan told everyone how thankful she was to have such really fine friends. After dinner, brandy and whiskey livened their spirits, and one of the visitors brought out a concertina; soon, laughing and singing filled the corridors of the Ferry Building. The party, which lasted well into the night, was long remembered as one of the greatest ever to be thrown along the waterfront.

The First Auto Ferry

Shortly after the turn of the century, vehicular traffic on the Creek Route began to increase as more and more horse-drawn freight wagons carried goods for delivery across the bay, and by 1905 horseless carriages began making appearances at the landings, with drivers seeking passage for themselves and their machines to the other side. It soon became evident to the management of the Southern Pacific that an entirely different type of boat was needed on the Creek Route. Instead of a passenger-type ferry, a boat which could be capable of handling vehicles on an unobstructed lower deck and passengers on an upper deck was required. Thus was born the concept of the auto ferry. With this idea in mind, the company called on the shipwrights at the Peralta Street shipyard to build what was to be the first ferry used expressly for automobile traffic.

Taking the better part of a year to build, the new ferry, named the *Melrose,* slid down the ways and into the Estuary on the morning of Saturday, April 11, 1906. As the ferry was without engines at that time, she was towed across the bay to the Union Iron Works for final outfitting. The engines and boilers for the ferry were fabricated in the company shops in Sacramento and shipped to Union Iron Works, where the rest of the marine equipment was to be installed.

Installation of the machinery took nearly a year, as the job was interrupted by the San Francisco earthquake. Finally, on January 4, 1909, steam was brought up in the boilers, and the ferry was made ready for her maiden trip. Captain J. Curley mounted the ladder to the wheelhouse, and after signaling "Slow Ahead," took the new ferry out into San Francisco Bay. After a successful trial run around the bay, the *Melrose* was placed in service on the Creek Route, a run on which she was to serve for the next 20 years.

The *Melrose* was a unique-appearing boat, with her unusually tall stack and a texas deck devoid of the usual walking beam. Although a paddle-wheel ferry, she boasted two inclined tandem engines, obviating the need for the walking beam. This design had been selected in order to have as clear a lower deck as possible, with only a small area in the center part of the deck taken up by the fidley. The upper deck, although not as ornate as most of the passenger boats, seated 400 passengers.

During the same month that the *Melrose* was launched, the Bay lost one of its two freight car ferries. This venerable craft, the *Thoroughfare,* had ferried countless thousands of tons of cargo across the bay for nearly 38 years; she was now removed from service due to a decline in traffic. This left only the newer *Transit* in car ferry service between Oakland and San Francisco.

In reporting the retirement of the *Thoroughfare,* the *San Francisco Call* noted that the two car ferries had experienced more collisions than any other two ferries on the bay. It seemed that one or the other continually was crashing into this pier or that wharf. It was observed by the *Call* that the retirement of the ferry would be greeted with delight by the Navy and other users of the bay who would now be able to navigate without having to dodge both of these behemoths.

The *Call* also recounted what was probably the most memorable collision between the two car ferries. According to the story, some 10 years earlier, the *Thoroughfare* and the *Transit* had both left Oakland one afternoon, fully loaded with freight cars destined for China Basin, in San Francisco. As this was to be the last trip of the day for both ferries, the crews knew that the first one back to Oakland Long Wharf would get the earlier liberty.

The two ferries, sitting in adjacent slips, quickly unloaded their freight cars, and they both cast off for Oakland at about the same time. Soon the race was on! Like two prehistoric dinosaurs plodding across the bay, each ferry churned a foaming wake and headed for the single slip at the end of the Long Wharf. Drawing close to the slip, the ferries pushed on neck and neck. Each captain was sure that the other eventually would give way, and thus was intent on putting his boat into the slip first. Suddenly, when abreast of the entrance to the slip, the two ferries came together with a splintering of wood and a screeching of metal. Momentum carried the two boats forward until they stopped with a bone-jarring lurch, firmly wedged between the fenders of the slip.

Somewhat abashed at the result of the dead heat, the two captains, who for good reason, went unnamed in the story, went over to the Wharfinger's office to report the accident to Superintendent Mackenzie. After hearing their story, Mackenzie leaned back in his chair and stared at the ceiling for a full two minutes, during which time the silence was such that the ticking of a clock in the adjacent office could be clearly heard. Finally, he told the two captains:

"Your accident isn't quite as serious as it might seem, I guess, but I'll have to have a damned good reason to tell San Francisco why I didn't fire the both of you right now. Oh no . . . I wouldn't fire you for a little thing like this, but I want you two to get together and think up a good, reasonable explanation. So that you will have nothing to distract you, I'm giving both of you a furlough without pay until you get your explanation ready."

The *Call* concluded the story with the observation that even after all of these years, the two captains still were on vacation!

The Great White Fleet

San Francisco and the entire Bay Area hosted the greatest gathering of peaceful naval power ever seen on the West Coast when the famous "Great White Fleet" of the U.S. Navy entered the bay on the evening of May 5, 1908. Prior to that time, newspapers had been full of stories about the fleet and by late afternoon of the day of arrival, tens of thousands of people waited patiently from every vantage point around the bay. Not only were there throngs along the waterfront and crowding Telegraph Hill, but the Marin shore and mountains were crowded with people as were the East Bay shores and the Berkeley Hills.

Promptly at 9:00 p.m., the battleship *Connecticut*, flagship of Rear Admiral Robley "Fighting Bob" Evans, steamed through the Golden Gate. The flagship was followed by the entire Atlantic Fleet, consisting of 17 battleships and six torpedo destroyers. On the heels of the Atlantic Fleet came the Pacific Fleet, led by the armored cruiser *West Virginia*, flagship of Rear Admiral James H. Dayton. Following the cruiser were nine other cruisers, one gunboat, and five torpedo destroyers. The two fleets were followed by the usual complement of support ships, a supply ship, a hospital ship, a collier, a refrigerator ship, and a brig. The "Great White Fleet" represented essentially the entire U.S. Navy and consisted of 46 ships.

Because of the enormous crowds generated by the fleet, Southern Pacific scheduled 226 special mainline trains each day from surrounding towns. People came from far and near to view the spectacle, and trains arrived from Sacramento, Fresno, and even as far away as Salt Lake City. In San Francisco, where all schools were dismissed for the event, the United Railroads brought every streetcar out of the barn, some 500, to handle the crowds.

In the East Bay, the local suburban lines were expected to carry the brunt of the mass of people who wished to see the fleet. To handle the mass movement, Southern Pacific issued Special Time Table "A" on May 6, 1908. The timetable covered special operations on the lines operating out of Alameda Pier. Instead of the usual 30-minute headways, trains would operate every 20 minutes as did those from Oakland Pier. Even with this significant increase in service, which saw a total of eight boats an hour on three lines between the East Bay and San Francisco, ferries operated at or beyond rated passenger capacity on nearly all trips. So great were the crowds bent on seeing the fleet that the local press reported that upwards of 50,000 people were unable to cross the bay because of the overcrowded ferries.

The principal civic event honoring the fleet was a gala welcoming ceremony held in San Francisco during which Governor J.W. Gillett welcomed Admiral Evans and the fleet to California shores. The event was followed by a massive parade up Market Street which featured 15,000 sailors from the fleet. Two days later, a similar parade was held in Oakland in which 6,000 sailors and five bands marched through the business district and to Lake Merritt, where a city-sponsored picnic was held in honor of the fleet.

During all of this time, many thousands viewed the many great ships riding at anchor. So popular was the viewing of the fleet that the U.S. Government opened Goat Island to the public and chartered the Southern Pacific stern-wheelers *Fruto* and *Herald* to provide transportation between Oakland Pier and the island.

Finally, at 10:00 a.m. on May 18th, the flagship *Connecticut* raised anchor and got underway, and the fleet slowly steamed from the bay. One by one, the great white ships went through the Golden Gate, and one by one the countless thousands of spectators made their way home filled with memories of a spectacle that would never be duplicated.

THE VIOLENCE of the explosion which ripped open the boiler of Engine 2088 is evident from the mass of twisted tubing, and the missing headlight, bell and sand dome. (See page 92.)
Roy D. Graves Collection

MISFORTUNE at the Fruitvale Ave. Bridge on December 24, 1906, placed Engine 1488 squarely in the middle of things. Both 1488 and 1519, right, were heading Horseshoe Line trains. That blob above No. 1488's smokestack is the headlight, balancing delicately on the overhead wires where it came to rest after the impact.

Roy D. Graves Collection

Wrecks and Other Misfortunes

During the years of operation of the steam locals, many accidents were reported in the local newspapers. That accidents happened with a fair degree of regularity was due in part to a lack of adequate safety devices and to a relatively unrestrictive manner of operation of trains. One of the more notable accidents occurred on the Encinal Avenue line on Wednesday, July 15, 1903. That morning, broad-gauge engine No. 2088 left the High Street terminal shortly before 7:00 a.m. with a commute train bound for Alameda Pier. The consist of the train was combination baggage-smoker No. 3046, followed by commute coaches Nos. 1123, 1138, 1140, 1160, and 1134. After making stops at stations along Encinal Avenue and Central Avenue, the train slowed for the station stop at Webster Street. Suddenly, without warning, the engine blew up with an earthshaking roar. The blast, which was heard as far away as downtown Oakland, shattered windows all around, causing some $5,000 in property damage. According to Fireman Edward G. Gale,

> "The first that I knew something was wrong was when I saw steam in the water glass. However, before I could jump, everything let go."

Fortunately, the force of the blast was outward and upward, and neither he nor Engineer Willis E. Duncan was seriously injured.

After climbing down from their cab, the two enginemen appraised their locomotive. The engine appeared to be a total wreck, with boiler tubes fanning out in all directions. They also saw that the engine was off the track and that the sand dome, headlight, and bell were missing. The headlight later was found lying in the street about a block away. The bell had arced through the air and came crashing down through the roof of a house on an adjacent street. The sand dome never was recovered, and it was believed that it had sailed over the rooftops and come down in the bay some two blocks away.

With the engine off the track, the line was completely tied up, and after a relief train had picked up the passengers, the Alameda wrecker, pulled by engine No. 2057, arrived on the scene. After much tugging and pulling, No. 2088 was put back on the track and towed off to West Alameda. From her appearance, everyone agreed that she probably was heading for the scrap heap. Not so. She was rebuilt and was returned to the steam locals.

Two years later, on Thursday, August 31, 1905, there was a collision near Oakland-16th Street Station which proved the maxim that two trains cannot occupy the same track at the same time. One of the trains involved was the West Berkeley shuttle, which operated from Delaware Street only as far as 16th Street Station, where patrons were obliged to transfer to a Berkeley train to continue their trip to Oakland Pier and San Francisco. The West Berkeley train then would continue down the track a short distance to a siding where it would lay over until it was time to make the next trip to West Berkeley.

On eastward trips, the West Berkeley train normally waited until the Berkeley train had made its station stop at 16th Street. It would then move onto the main line and into the station to pick up its passengers. On this particular day, the West Berkeley train consisted of engine No. 1207, an eight-

HORSESHOE LINE train, headed by Engine 1388, charges off the Fruitvale Ave. bridge on the way to Oakland Pier (above). The Class E-4 engine was built by Rogers in 1884, scrapped in 1928. Another Horseshoe line train (below) crosses the marsh en route to Alameda Pier. The empty land in both photos is now heavily industrialized. **Both Roy D. Graves Collection**

wheeler operated by Engineer Charles A. Loring, and two coaches. Standing on the far side of his train, Loring heard a train go by on the main track and assumed that it was the Berkeley local. He climbed into his cab, and without looking back along the main track, moved off down the siding toward the main line.

At this same time, the Berkeley local, which was a couple of minutes late, came pounding down the main line toward 16th Street Station. Seeing the West Berkeley train moving toward the switch, the engineer of the Berkeley train, Walter D. Bruce, sounded four whistle blasts, and realizing that the shuttle train apparently was not stopping, he "big holed" his brakes. The momentum carried his train forward on skidding wheels allowing it to sideswipe the eight-wheeler, knocking it off the track. After both trains had come to a shuddering halt, Engineer Bruce was heard to shout in Loring's direction, "Hey, what in hell were you trying to do?" Loring, badly scalded by escaping steam, had to be lifted down from his engine and taken to a hospital.

An official inquiry was made of the accident the following week. Engineer Loring was asked why he had attempted to run his train directly into the path of the oncoming Berkeley train. He replied that he thought the Berkeley local already had gone by and also that he had not heard any warning whistles. However, in spite of his statements, the company found him guilty of operating a train without due caution.

An accident occurred on the Fruitvale Bridge on the morning of December 26, 1906. Normally the local train from Alameda Pier would meet its opposing train at Alameda-North Park Street at 8:47 a.m. On this particular morning, the local, in the charge of Conductor Roy Cummings, made its station stop on time and was given a green signal to proceed from the towerman at Fruitvale. At the same time, the opposing train from Oakland Pier was pounding down the line toward Fruitvale trying to make up time as it was running late and had missed its boat connection. Nearing Fruitvale, Engineer Curran saw that he had a green signal for the approach to Fruitvale Bridge. Both trains entered the single-tracked bridge at nearly the same time. Fortunately, they slowed to about five miles per hour while crossing the span. Just east of the center span, they collided with a crash heard for some distance around. Had the trains been moving faster, they might have tumbled into the water below with a great loss of life.

The Alameda-bound train was running tender-first, and the tender was crumpled and buckled up at an angle of about 35 degrees. The smoker of the Alameda-bound train was totally splintered. Blame for the accident was placed with the Fruitvale towerman, a man named Smith, who had been assigned to tower duty only a few days previously.

Engine 1488, which was on the Oakland-bound train, was involved in another accident nine months later. Running east from Alameda Pier, Engineer J.W. Aldrich noted a team of horses with a wagonload of gravel moving across the crossing at Webster Street. The teamster suddenly saw the approaching train and yelled and spurred his horses in an attempt to get off the tracks. Becoming startled, the horses reared and the load of gravel was dumped squarely in the path of the approaching train. Unable to stop, the train hit the pile of gravel at about 15 miles per hour and derailed. The engine dove off the embankment to the east, while the smoker car went off on the opposite side. Aldrich and Fireman E.B. Stone jumped to safety from the toppling engine.

One of the last major accidents on the steam local system took place just north of the Harrison Street Bridge on the evening of Saturday, July 4, 1908. The scene was not too far from the site of the Decoration Day Disaster of 1890.

On that particular night in 1908, a local from Alameda Pier clumped its way across the Harrison Street Bridge, bound for 14th and Franklin Streets. C.A. McCurdy, towerman at First and Harrison Streets, saw the approaching local, gave it the right-of-way, and set the signals to stop along the First Street route. At this same time, Train No. 57, a five-car Santa Cruz to Oakland train, was speeding along First Street at a fast clip trying to make up lost time, being due at First and Broadway at 6:49 p.m. and it was then past 7 o'clock. The train's engineer, Everett J. Barry, did not see the red block signals until it was too late. The derail being open, Barry's train shot from the track and skidded over the ties directly into the path of the oncoming local train.

Engineer William Marks of the local set his brakes in an attempt to stop his train, but because he was coming down a slight grade, he was unable to stop and crashed into the smoker coach of the Santa Cruz train, cutting it practically in two and burying the passengers under the debris. Of the 23 passengers on board the smoker, seven were killed instantly and 16 were injured. The line was tied up until 10 o'clock the next morning. After Engineer Marks and Towerman McCurdy had been cleared of responsibility, blame was placed with Engineer Barry, who was fired for his flagrant violation of signals.

A Bad Day on the Bay

Wrecks and other accidents were not happenings unique to only the steam locals; the bay ferries also had their share of grief. During the early part of this century, traffic on the bay was much greater than it is today. In addition to the three Southern Pacific ferry lines—which utilized from six to nine boats—there also were other ferry lines, as well as river packets, oceangoing ships, navy vessels, and the ubiquitous yawls, sloops, and steam schooners which plied back and forth taking cargo from wharf to wharf. During days when the weather was clear and the bay was calm, navigation, although fairly simple, occasionally was made difficult by the sheer number of craft in a given locality. At night, or in stormy weather, when the wind shrieked and the spray blew off the whitecaps, Bay skippers had their work cut out for them. The times in which the fog settled down and nothing could be seen except gray mist and gray water were the times that ferrymen dreaded the most. It was times like these that the unexpected usually happened.

Fog could develop at nearly any time of the year; hence, so did accidents, leaving many a story of collisions and near misses in the fog to be recounted whenever old bay hands reminisced. One such story concerned the time the *Oakland* crept across the bay in an unusually thick fog. When abeam with Goat Island, Captain Hendrickson heard a whistle off the starboard bow. Because he could not tell where the whistle came from, he stopped his ferry just in time to get rammed in the starboard paddle box by the lumber schooner *Phoenix*. Another time, on a foggy evening in 1906, the *Bay City* was slowly nearing Alameda Pier with about 500 passengers. Without warning, the lumber schooner *Tampico,* bound for the Estuary, came out of the fog and crashed into the port bow of the ferry. Reversing her engines, the *Tampico* backed off, only to come crashing into the ferry a second time. It later turned

HOT-AIR BALLOON ascension drew some 6,000 to S.P.'s 14th and Franklin station on August 14, 1909. The 80-foot diameter gas balloon, the *City of Oakland,* was built by Capt. R.A. Van Tassell. In right distance is the original Oakland City Hall.

Louis L. Stein Jr. Collection

out that the *Tampico* was out of control as her ship's telegraph was totally inoperative.

Most of the collisions and near misses, however, were with other ferries, as pilots attempted to keep to their schedules in spite of wind, fog, or tides. The *Berkeley,* perhaps, was the most unmanageable ferry on the bay, and on more than one occasion she was involved in collisions with other boats. In fact, on one memorable journey across the bay in 1905, she not only had a near miss with the *Newark,* but also nearly ran down the Key Route ferry *San Jose.*

Usually on very foggy nights, ferry service would be annulled or curtailed. There were times, though, when the boats ran mostly because the skippers hated to be tied up and felt that they could "make it across the bay one more time." One of the worst periods of fog on record occurred during the month of December 1908. During all of that month, there was hardly a day that remained clear enough for good transbay navigation. On the fourth of that month, a thick, pea-soup fog had settled down to the water by nightfall, and when the *Berkeley* pulled out of the Ferry Building at 6:20 p.m., Captain E.A. Jones, who had been skipper of the ferry since she was launched, knew that he would have to steer carefully.

Steaming cautiously across the bay, the *Berkeley* approached Oakland Pier. Ringing up "Slow Ahead," Captain Johnson steered toward the entrance to the slip. Suddenly, there was a crash as the ferry grazed the fender on the north side of the slip. The rebound, coupled with a flood tide, swung the boat in such a way that she slammed against the south side fender. With the first crash, some of the passengers panicked and they rushed toward the lifeboats on the starboard side. This shift caused the ferry to list which in turn caused more panic. By the time the crew had restored order, it was found that an elderly woman had been crushed and fatally injured. Three men also had been injured while desperately trying to lower a lifeboat. With order restored, the *Berkeley* moved into the slip and made fast.

Three days later, the fog was thicker than before. On that day, visibility was down to zero by 3:30 p.m., forcing the annulment of all ferry schedules. By 5:00, it appeared that the fog had lifted somewhat and that it might be possible to resume ferry service. With a capacity crowd on board, the *Piedmont* cast off on what was to be a rather lengthy trip across the bay. Steaming ever so slowly, it seemed to the passengers that it was taking an eternity to get to the Ferry Build-

TRAIN TIME in downtown Oakland: Schenectady-built 2034 (right), on a Webster Street local, blocks traffic (or was there any?) at 13th and Webster. Engine 2084 and train (below) are tucked into the downtown Oakland depot. Electrification of the line already is in progress.
**Louis L. Stein Jr. Collection;
Roy D. Graves Collection**

ing. On all sides, foghorns and diaphones could be heard; the ferry's own whistle was blasting every few moments. With Oakland Pier out of sight in the fog, it seemed that the ferry was not even moving. Some passengers began to show concern as the hour grew later and later. Others passed the time with seeming unconcern in the bar and restaurant. Finally, at about half past eight, the lights of the Ferry Building could be seen dimly ahead, and at 8:45, the *Piedmont* berthed in what turned out to be one of the Key Route slips. The crossing had taken nearly four hours, a record.

At about the same time that the *Piedmont* had left Oakland Pier, the *Yerba Buena,* which had been leased from the Key Route, set out to try to make it across from San Francisco to Alameda Pier. Casting off from the Ferry Building at 5:30, the ferry moved ever so slowly across the bay. Nearing Alameda Pier about an hour later, Captain Charles H. Blaker misjudged the location of one of the foghorns and missed the entrance to the slip by about 100 feet. With a sudden shudder, the *Yerba Buena* became firmly grounded on a mud bar at the mouth of the Estuary.

With engines running full astern, the ferry shook and pitched, but she was held fast and unable to move. Captain Blaker knew that high tide was due in about an hour and that only then would there be enough water to float the ferry off the bar. So he announced to the passengers that there would be a slight delay and invited everyone to enjoy the facilities of the restaurant while waiting for the tide to come in.

At about 7:30, with engines running full astern, the *Yerba*

WITH BAGGAGE CAR on rear, eastbound Berkeley local pulls out of Lorin (later South Berkeley) Station.
Louis L. Stein Jr. Collection

Buena backed off the mud bar and again attempted to make port. The trip, however, was not yet over. On entering the slip, with zero visibility, the ferry somehow swung around so that she became wedged crosswise in the slip. With assistance from shore, and much churning of the water, it took about half an hour to get the ferry turned so that she could move to the apron and discharge her passengers.

In spite of the adventures of the *Piedmont* and the *Yerba Buena,* the fog still was to get in one last lick before finally lifting. Later that night, the *Oakland* arrived in San Francisco on what normally would have been her last trip before tying up. At the Ferry Building were 38 automobiles which had been waiting for passage across the bay for several hours. After loading the cars on the lower deck, the *Oakland* cast off at 10:10 p.m. for a special run back to Oakland Pier. Over at Oakland Pier, the *Newark,* with Captain John Leale in command, took on board about 2,000 passengers and cast off for San Francisco at 10:22 p.m. Captain Leale had been informed of the special trip of the *Oakland,* and he instructed his lookouts to keep their eyes sharp. Steaming cautiously through the fog, Captain Leale expected the *Oakland* to approach and pass on the port bow.

Suddenly there was a yell from one of the lookouts, and the *Oakland* broke out of the fog, steaming toward the *Newark* dead amidships on the port side. With a splintering crash, the *Oakland* hit the *Newark* just forward of the port side paddle box.

Seeing a large hole just above the water line, many of the passengers on board the *Newark* panicked and many women fainted. With reassurances from the crew, calm was restored in a short time. The *Oakland,* which had sustained damage only to her jackstaffs, rails, and bow rudder, backed off and continued on her way to Oakland Pier. Captain Leale took the *Newark* across the bay at reduced speed, as there was some water coming into the engine room. As they neared the Ferry Building, a deckhand brought word to the captain that souvenir hunters were trying to make off with life preservers and anything else that they could detach. Stopping the ferry a few hundred yards from the slip, Captain Leale went down to the main deck to address the passengers. Standing before them, he announced, "When you people drop those life preservers, I'll land this ferry!" Since he was a captain who was known for taking no nonsense from anyone, the crowd laughingly tossed the life preservers and other mementos into a pile at his feet.

The *Newark* was towed across the bay the next morning by a Red Stack tug to the Oakland Point shipyard, where she was repaired and returned to service.

The *Berkeley* starred again in a collision on the morning of April 15, 1909, when a tule fog developed quickly on part of the bay. On that morning, both Oakland Pier and the Ferry Building basked in brilliant sunlight. Looking east from the Ferry Building, one could see the Berkeley Hills rising above a fog bank which lay between San Francisco and Goat Island. This patch of fog, which at most was only about a mile across, was right down to the water.

Leaving the Ferry Building at 7:00 a.m., Captain James Blaker took the *Berkeley* out of the slip and then turned her over to Chief Officer Nicolaus Nelson, while he went below for breakfast. Cautiously entering the fog bank, Nelson steered the ferry for Oakland Pier, knowing that another ferry soon was due to pass him going toward San Francisco. Suddenly, out of the mist came the *Encinal,* almost directly in front of the *Berkeley.* Nelson rang up "Full Astern," and the big ferry slowed somewhat, with water churning and boiling from the bow propeller. Before she could be stopped, the ferry struck a glancing blow to the *Encinal* amidships, ripping out 50 feet of sheathing on the port side. Damage to the *Berkeley* was confined to the port side of the lower deck, which was crushed and stove in.

Within moments after the collision, the fog lifted and put the entire collision scene in plain view from the Ferry Building. Both ferries were removed from service after completing their runs. Repairs to the *Berkeley* cost about $450 and she was back in service within the week. It took somewhat longer to repair the *Encinal,* as the damage ran to about $2,500. A few days after the accident, the company made an official inquiry into the accident. The blame was placed on Captain William Murphy, of the *Encinal,* who was cited for not operating his ferry with due caution in foggy weather.

The New System Takes Shape

Shortly after the Key Route began operating, rumors began to circulate that the Southern Pacific would scrap its steam suburban trains in favor of a new electric system to be built along the lines of some of the more successful suburban electrifications in the east. Though the rumors persisted, the home office in San Francisco remained silent on the issue, neither confirming nor denying the stories. It appeared that the rumors may have been started by personnel of the railroad's own engineering department, who had been called on to look into the design of rights-of-way, fixed plant, and rolling stock for just such a modernized system.

By late 1905, all of the cost estimates and engineering details had been worked out for a modern system which encompassed not only the reconstruction of most of the existing lines, but also expansion of the system into areas not yet served. However, the San Francisco earthquake forced the temporary postponement of the project, as the railroad found that it had to concentrate on more urgent matters connected with the aftermath of the earthquake.

There appeared in the local newspapers on August 15, 1906, an item which set to rest the rumors and put the Southern Pacific squarely on the path toward a new system. Front-page stories carried a statement that E.H. Harriman, President of the railroad, had given his personal sanction to the electricization project, as it was called, and that it would be carried to completion as soon as possible.

The plan of the electricization as outlined in the articles, stated that Alameda Pier would be completely converted to use by suburban electric trains. This facility was to be the center of all electric train service in the East Bay, while Oakland Pier would remain solely a facility for steam trains. The reason given for not including Oakland Pier in the new suburban system was that there were too many technological difficulties connected with operating both steam and electric trains out of one terminal. In the new plan, Alameda Pier would be served by the two Alameda lines, the Webster Street line and the Seventh Street line, which would use the Webster Street line to Alameda Pier. Additionally, the Webster Street line would be

DURING RECONSTRUCTION of Seventh Street, it was necessary to keep the trackway clear as the steam locals operated on 20-minute headways. **Louis L. Stein Jr. Collection**

extended north of its 14th Street terminal in an attempt to recapture some of the patronage lost to Key Route's 22nd Street line, which at that time terminated at Broadway.

The plan also stated that for the time being neither the Berkeley nor the West Berkeley lines would be electrified as it was impractical to route them over to Alameda Pier. No mention was made in the plan of what was to become of service along Seventh Street west of Webster nor of the fate of the Horseshoe line. However, rumors had it that steam locals still would serve Seventh Street from Broadway west and that the Horseshoe line probably would be abandoned.

The electricization proposals were further amplified by Julius Kruitschnitt, director of maintenance and operations, who, on July 8, 1907, outlined the principal reconstruction work to be undertaken. He commented,

> "The biggest job we have before us, at present, is to convert the Alameda, Oakland and Berkeley suburban services into electric lines."

Within two months, Southern Pacific (and its subsidiary, South Pacific Coast) applied to the councils of the various cities it served for a series of new franchises providing for the complete replacement of the steam lines with a modern electric system. The company also applied for franchises for new routes in Berkeley, Oakland, and Alameda. The Berkeley routes included new service to Thousand Oaks as well as to the university campus. New service in Oakland called for an extension of the Melrose line through East Oakland to San Leandro and Hayward. The new routes for Alameda envisioned a thorough coverage of the Island City. Not only would the north and south side lines be connected by way of new track through the Cohen Tract, but track also would be laid along Lincoln Avenue west from Mastick to a connection with the south side line near the Pacific Borax Works. Crosstown service would be provided between the north side and south side lines along 8th Street and also along Pearl Street. Of all the proposed routes in Alameda, only the Pearl Street trackage was not built.

With the applications for new franchises filed, contracts were let for new trackwork, cars, power generation facilities, and a host of items which make up a brand new railroad. Southern Pacific was determined that the new system would not be merely an electrification of an existing system, but rather it would be truly a new railroad from the ground up.

With the completion of construction and the delivery of new rolling stock, a new era of East Bay transportation was ushered in. Out of this change came the first rapid transit system seen on the Pacific Coast.

PREVIEW OF coming attractions: Prior to inauguration of electric service, Southern Pacific lined up this massive display on the tracks leading to Oakland Pier. Steam local equipment is at left, the new electrics on the right. **Southern Pacific**

CHAPTER 10

Electricization

THE SEVEN-YEAR period, from 1905 to 1912, saw the design and construction of what was described in contemporary technical journals as an outstanding example of a suburban railway electrification. Originally estimated to cost about $4 million, the project had consumed $10,600,000 by the time it was completed in 1912.

Included in this figure, in addition to charges for seven years of preliminary and final design, were the costs for completely rebuilding 29.3 miles of existing suburban lines and for building 21.1 miles of lines into new areas. Most of the system total of 50.4 miles was laid with new 75-pound to 120-pound rail placed on redwood ties, under which was a layer of crushed rock eight inches thick. The track along Seventh Street was laid with 141-pound girder rail, the only section of track so constructed.

The overhead electrical system consisted of catenary trolley wire which was suspended from steel bridges placed on 240-foot centers and spanning two or four tracks along sections of private right-of-way. For street operation, steel poles with crossarms were placed every 120 feet along the centerline of the street. In some cases, such as along Seventh Street, Webster and Franklin streets, and some lines in Berkeley, steel poles with span wires were placed along the curb line. All steel bridges and poles were numbered for use as reference markers in the same manner that mileposts are used on mainline operations.

Rather than rely on commercial power, the Southern Pacific decided to erect its own power generation facilities along the north bank of the Estuary near Fruitvale. The powerhouse, which cost $900,000 to build and equip, was a familiar East

Bay landmark for many years, particularly to commuters using trains which crossed the Fruitvale Avenue Bridge.

At the time of its construction, the Fruitvale Powerhouse was recognized by the American Institute of Electrical Engineers as an outstanding achievement in the field of power generation, and on the evening of May 19, 1911, the San Francisco Section of the AIEE held its monthly meeting at the nearly completed facility. The meeting featured a dinner served in the great turbine room and catered from one of the railroad's dining cars.

The meal was followed by a program presented by A.H. Babcock, chief electrical engineer, who had the overall responsibility during construction of the plant. Also on the program were D.J. Patterson, architect of the plant, J.J. Ferrier, office engineer, and H.Y. Hall, electrical engineer. Babcock was certain electrification was going to spread to other parts of the S.P. system, and observed:

> "In the first place, it may be well to state the general purposes of the plant. The electrification of all the lines around San Francisco Bay, generally speaking, is the ultimate purpose—that is to say, all of the lines on both sides of the Bay. The first step is being made now; the other steps will follow as fast as the service conditions will warrant the expenditure of the necessary money."

Babcock said the location of the plant was determined by the presence of large quantities of low-temperature cooling water and adequate low-cost land. Babcock and his associates then described the plant in great detail:

The north wing of the powerhouse contained 12 oil-fired water-tube boilers, rated at 645 horsepower each and manufactured by the Parker Boiler Company at a total cost of $137,000. To the west of the boilers, plant designers had allowed space for the installation of four additional boilers should the need ever arise for additional capacity. The building also was designed so that automatic coal and ash-handling apparatus could be installed if it was found desirable to do so. Steam from the boilers was piped to the south wing where it was fed into two double-flow turbogenerators, each of 5,000 kilowatt (kw) rated capacity and 7,500 kw two-hour load capacity. The turbogenerators were built by Westinghouse Manufacturing Company at a cost of $95,000 each and provided 3-phase 25-cycle alternating current at 13,200 volts when operating at 1,500 revolutions per minute.

There was additional floor space in the south wing for the installation of two more turbogenerators, and the west wall of this wing was designed for easy removal in connection with the construction of an annex to house yet two additional units. Thus, the powerhouse had an operating capacity of 15,000 kw and an ultimate capacity of 45,000 kw. Connected to the underside of each turbine was a pair of surface condensers designed to maintain 28 inches of vacuum and containing 24,000 square feet of cooling surface. The condensers were built by Henry R. Worthington Company at a total cost of $47,000. Also present were two Worthington high-speed turbine circulating pumps, each with a capacity of 10,000 gallons per minute and driven by Terry steam turbines.

Rising above the powerhouse as a landmark was an unlined steel stack 14½ feet in diameter and whose total height was 139 feet above ground. Completion details of the plant included a 60-ton Shaw electric traveling crane with 15-ton auxiliary hoist in the turbine room, a machine shop, two 460-foot deep water wells, a 5,000 gallon rooftop water tank, a 55,000-barrel fuel oil storage tank, a fireproof vault in the basement for company records, exterior space for coal handling and storage, and finally, an 11,000 emergency power tie with Great Western Power Company.

Construction of the powerhouse got underway in the early part of 1909. The structural steelwork was designed by J.C. Lathrop, fabricated by the American Bridge Company, and erected by the Southern Pacific Bridge Department. Steelwork was completed in June 1909, and the Parker boilers were installed shortly thereafter. After most of the remaining equipment had been installed, the exterior shell of the building was completed. The exterior consisted of red brick with window and corner trim of lighter-colored sand-lined brick. Taking an additional year and one-half to complete, the powerhouse with its appurtenant substation was ready for service by the end of May 1911.

Operation of the powerhouse was divided into three 8-hour shifts. Each shift had a watch engineer, a fireman and two oilers. In addition, the day and evening shifts each had a water tender, and the day shift had a time and materials clerk. The first superintendent of the powerhouse was William Redford, who had been an inspector during construction of the facility.

Because of its engineering importance, the *Journal of Electricity, Power, and Gas* published the following editorial on completion of the powerhouse:

> "The Fruitvale Powerhouse of the Southern Pacific Company is unique . . . and should serve as a far-reaching example of the possibilities of inexpensive but effective treatment of form and finish, adding to the city a quasi-public building which will enhance the general appearance of the district, rather than introduce an eye-sore of the so-called mill or factory type (of powerhouse). . . . To build such a plant without a mistake in fabrication, without unforseen delays, or a change from the completed drawings is most remarkable.
>
> "Here, alternating current is generated at 25 cycles and is distributed to be converted to direct current by means of rotary converters. In view of the fact that 60 cycles has become the standard . . . and that the plant has been equipped to receive an auxilliary (supply) at this frequency, necessitating extra machinery in the form of frequency converters, the question arises as to the advisability of using this extra apparatus and generating at a low frequency rather than at the prevailing frequency and converting to direct current through motor-generators."

Electricity generated at the powerhouse was distributed to three substations, one located in the south wing of the powerhouse and the others at West Oakland and North Berkeley, respectively. The Oakland feeder left the powerhose in two conduits, each carrying three 4/0 lead-sheathed copper cables. After passing Fruitvale Station, the feeder went to aerial construction, consisting of six 4/0 bare copper wires, along the Seventh Street line as far as Lake Merritt. Here, the feeder was again placed in conduit which ran along First Street to the West Oakland Substation.

The Alameda feeder served as a second power tie to the West Oakland Substation. This latter feeder went by way of three submarine cables across the Estuary and used aerial construction along Lincoln Avenue and Webster Junction to West Alameda, where a high-level Estuary crossing was made. The crossing, supported on two towers, each 250-feet high, consisted of six high-voltage lines and four 1,200-volt lines, each 1,250 feet in length.

North of the crossing, the Alameda feeder went directly to the West Oakland Substation. From this latter location, the Berkeley feeder followed the Ninth Street line to North Berkeley Substation. The entire route of this feeder consisted of aerial construction with four 4/0 bare copper wires except for a short stretch of conduit construction near Emeryville.

All three substations converted the 13,200-volt power to 1,200 volts for placement on the trolley system. Substation No. 1 (at Fruitvale Powerhouse) served all lines east of Webster Street (both in Oakland and in Alameda). Direct current

ERECTION OF the steel framework of the Fruitvale Powerhouse was finished by June 1909 (right) and the entire structure completed by the spring of 1911 (center).
Bancroft Library

TWIN TOWERS supporting high voltage lines crossing the Estuary frame the *Garden City*, working the Creek Route. **Bancroft Library**

PLATE 4

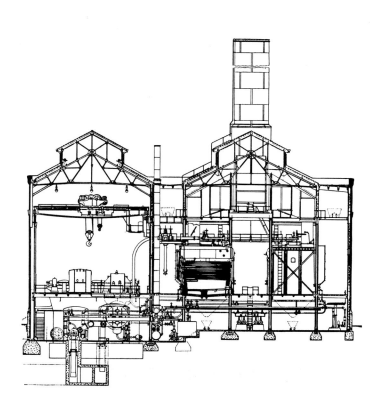

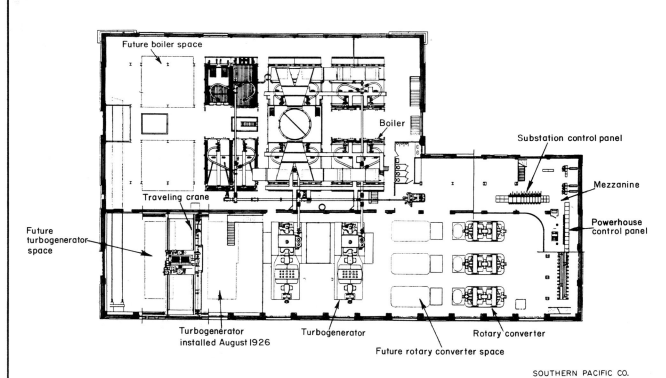

Adapted from
Journal of Electricity Power and Gas v.26, no.22 June 3, 1911

SOUTHERN PACIFIC CO.
FRUITVALE POWERHOUSE
PLAN AND SECTION
1911

feeder lines followed all tracks except for the Fernside loop; the feeder went directly from Lincoln Avenue to Encinal Avenue by way of Park Street. Substation No. 2 (at West Oakland) served all lines between Webster Street and Shellmound, including West Alameda, Alameda Pier, and Oakland Pier. Substation No. 3 (at North Berkeley) provided power for lines north of Shellmound; there was no feeder along the Ellsworth Street line. In addition to power for the trolley system, all substations provided power for a 2,300-volt signal system and direct current for a private telephone system.

Substation No. 1 was located at the east end of the south wing of the Fruitvale Powerhouse. Present were three General Electric 1,500-kw, 1,200-volt rotary units and transformers; space was allowed for three additional units should the need arise. Each rotary unit consisted of two 750-kw, 600-volt rotaries connected in series. Power to each rotary unit was supplied through a General Electric 1,500-kw 3- to 6-phase transformer. Transformers were forced-oil, water-cooled 13,200-volt to 440-volt type and were located in a fireproof room in the basement of the powerhouse.

The substation also provided power to a 125-250 direct current system for the generating excitation circuits, station lighting, overhead crane, and other power requirements. The substation switchboard was located on a gallery on the east end of the turbine room adjacent to the main powerhouse switchboards.

Substation No. 2 contained four rotary units for power for the trolley system. The substation also provided power for a 4,000/2,300-volt 62.5-cycle 3-phase alternating current system serving the company shipyard, the West Oakland main line shops, Oakland Pier, and 16th Street Station. A branch of this system followed the Seventh Street and Webster Street lines to the Harrison Street Bridge, crossed the Estuary in a submarine cable, and then went by aerial line to West Alameda and Alameda Pier. A second service from the West Oakland Substation was for arc lights at West Oakland, Oakland Pier, and along 18th Street, Franklin Street, and Webster Street. Substation No. 3 contained three rotary units in addition to transformers for the signal system.

Early in the planning of the new system, it had been decided that the proper design of rolling stock was most critical. What would be needed was a car that would have ample seating capacity, relatively good acceleration and high speed, and yet have low initial and maintenance costs. Personnel of the engineering department took critical looks at equipment then being operated not only by the Key Route, but also on the Pacific Electric and more distant systems.

One of the earliest designs considered was for a short platform wooden car which would be built along lines similar to cars then being operated by the Key Route. Also proposed were steel cars of a design similar to those then being operated by the Columbus, Delaware and Marion Railway in Ohio. These, and other designs ultimately were discarded in favor of one for longer cars having double-length platforms for quicker loading and unloading.

An order for equipment of this type was placed with American Car and Foundry Company in 1910, with the first delivery scheduled from the St. Charles, Mo., plant in the early part of 1911. Included in the initial order were specifications for 20 motorized coaches, 30 nonmotorized coaches, and 10 motorized combination baggage-coaches. This first order subsequently was increased to a total of 125 cars at a total cost of just over $1 million.

The cars were built entirely of steel and were 72 feet 10½ inches long over buffers. In order to provide maximum seating,

WEST OAKLAND substation in 1911, exterior (top) and inside (center) with rotary converters on main floor and control panels on gallery. **Vernon J. Sappers Collection**

NORTH BERKELEY substation is shown in this 1912 view which looks east along Solano Avenue. **R.S. Ford Collection**

the cars were designed with a width of 10 feet 4 inches. This permitted the use of "3 and 2" seating in addition to a 25¾-inch-wide aisle. The coaches all seated 116 passengers, while the combination cars seated 88 passengers; the combination cars had a 15-foot-long baggage compartment at one end. No lavatories were provided in the coaches, but the combination cars originally were outfitted with single lavatories with a dry hopper.

Crowd-swallowers these cars were, but of a most utilitarian design, with sides, ends, and roofs being framed with members pressed from 1/16-inch steel plate. To these were riveted 7/64-inch plate on the sides, 3/32-inch plate on the ends, and 1/16-inch plate on the roofs. Platforms on all cars were 6 feet 3 inches long, with 4-foot, 4-inch-wide divided step openings. These openings were closed by sliding wire-mesh gates which were operated by levers mounted on the outside of the vestibule doorposts. The gate opening mechanism was manufactured by Pitt Car Gate Company.

All cars originally had steel window sashes provided by Forsythe Brothers Company, but these subsequently were replaced by wooden sashes made of ash. Interiors of the cars were equipped with Hale and Kilburn rattan walkover seats.

The exteriors of the cars originally were painted dark olive, which was the standard for all passenger cars on the Southern Pacific. The exterior of each car received a number of coats of paint followed by three coats of varnish. Interior walls were painted dark bronze and the headlining was beige; all interior surfaces were varnished to a high gloss.

Trucks for the cars were of the two-bar equalizer type and were manufactured by Baldwin Locomotive Works. Wheels on the motor cars were 36½ inches in diameter and were of steel-tired type with cast steel spokes. Wheels on trailer trucks were of rolled steel variety and were 33 inches in diameter. The motor cars, when fully equipped, weighed 109,400 pounds; trailers weighed 67,200 pounds.

All cars were equipped with Westinghouse pneumatic train signals and schedule AML automatic air brakes. Each motor car was equipped with four GE-207A motors of 125 horsepower each. The two motors on each truck were series connected. Car controls were of G.E. Type M. Current at 600 volts for the control and lighting circuits was provided by a dynamotor mounted on each car.

Motor cars originally were provided with one General Electric US-121-A pantograph. Due to major maintenance problems with these pantographs, they subsequently were replaced with Westinghouse S522-type pantographs. Motor cars also originally had clarion whistles which later were replaced by the well-known trombone type.

After delivery, the cars were thoroughly tested and were proclaimed by officials to be of excellent design. However, near the end of the one-year warranty period, rumors were heard that the operating department would recommend that the entire order of cars be returned to the manufacturer. Mentioned was the substantial wear and maintenance costs while being operated under normal conditions, and the fact that the cars had suffered severely in accidents with wagons and autos.

Complaints from commuters were heard with regard to the lack of heat in the winter and the lack of ventilation on warm days. In response to all of the charges, the railroad stated that all parts of the system—wires, cars, method of construction—were still under trial and had not yet been accepted. Ultimately, all of the system was accepted and the maintenance and operating problems were ironed out.

Reconstruction in Alameda

The first suburban line to be rebuilt was the Encinal Avenue line. Reconstruction of this line began at High Street in April 1908, and proceeded westerly toward Alameda Pier. The work consisted of removing the existing tracks and relaying them with entirely new materials along an alignment that was four feet wider between tracks. The new alignment was necessary to allow room for the line of center poles between the tracks. One of the major difficulties experienced during reconstruction was that of keeping one track clear at all times so that the steam locals could maintain their schedules.

By the latter part of 1909, the new track was completed along Encinal Avenue, and in October of that year, Southern Pacific awarded a contract with Hutchinson and Company for the grading of the new Fernside loop, which would connect the Encinal Avenue line at High Street with the Lincoln Avenue line near the Fruitvale Avenue Bridge. Erection of the center poles along Encinal began at High Street in September 1908. The stringing of the catenary trolley wire was not begun until the following February when a test section was installed near High Street; feeder cable was installed a month later.

Work on the new track from Mastick west to Pacific Junction began in January 1910 after completion of the reconstruction of the northside line east of that point. Work on the Fernside loop continued intermittently during that period due to delays in right-of-way acquisition and the presence of squatters. One squatter, George Hilton, had built a shack surrounded by fences squarely in the middle of the proposed trackway. It was not until February 5, 1910, that a platoon of local police was able to tear down the shack and fences and force Hilton to move from the land that he claimed was his.

In January 1910, work began on the reclamation of the marshland surrounding the existing yards and roundhouse at West Alameda. This area had been designated as the site of the general shops for the new system. Included in the plans was the removal of the old roundhouse and other facilities and the construction of a six-track electrified yard as well as a modern shop building for the repair and servicing of suburban electric equipment.

The shop building, constructed of reinforced concrete, was 460 feet long and 200 feet wide. The north side of the building housed a three-track inspection bay running its entire length and had a capacity of 18 cars. Each inspection track had a pit 38 inches deep running its entire length; the rails of the inspection tracks were raised 14 inches above the shop floor allowing an equivalent pit depth of 52 inches. Each pit was equipped with compressed air lines, 600-volt DC testing lines and 220-volt AC lighting circuits.

The overhead trolley wire ran through the shop building. The section of wire over each pit was controlled by a switch that normally was in the "off" position, indicating the trolley wire was deenergized and grounded. In order to move equipment, it was necessary to manually hold the switch in the "on" position to keep the trolley wire energized.

The west part of the central bay was the site of the repair shop. Served by two stub tracks and one through track, the repair shop had a capacity of nine cars. Each track had a pit 24 inches deep running one-half the length of the shop. The east part of the central bay was the machine shop, through which

PLATE 5

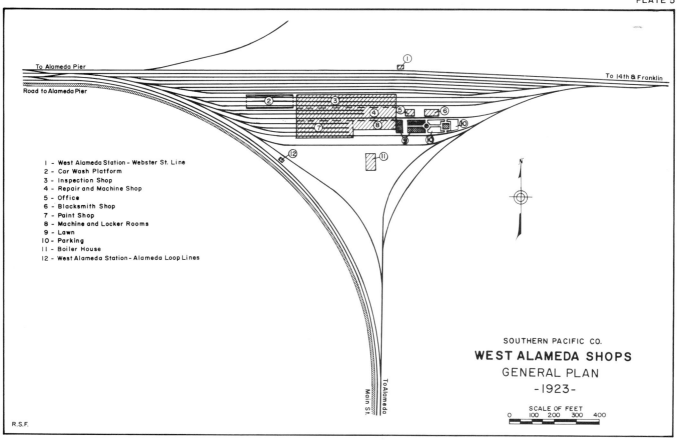

1 - West Alameda Station - Webster St. Line
2 - Car Wash Platform
3 - Inspection Shop
4 - Repair and Machine Shop
5 - Office
6 - Blacksmith Shop
7 - Paint Shop
8 - Machine and Locker Rooms
9 - Lawn
10 - Parking
11 - Boiler House
12 - West Alameda Station - Alameda Loop Lines

SOUTHERN PACIFIC CO.
WEST ALAMEDA SHOPS
GENERAL PLAN
-1923-

ONLY A FEW CARS had been received at West Alameda when this photo was taken in April 1911. View looks east toward newly completed shop building. Trolley wire was not yet energized.
Bancroft Library

WEST ALAMEDA worked furiously to prepare the brand-new green cars for service in 1911. Car 320 on middle track (above) lasted (in U.S. Maritime service) until 1947. Machine Shop at West Alameda Shops (below) was equipped with this traveling crane which easily lifted heavy truck high over men and machinery. **Both Vernon J. Sappers Collection**

ran one track from the repair shop. Here was a wheel lathe, boring mill, and wheel press. A 20-ton traveling crane ran the entire length of the repair and machine shop bay. The crane runway was of sufficient height to permit trucks to be lifted and moved over the tops of car bodies.

The west half of the south part of the shop building housed the paint bay and had four tracks with a total capacity of 12 cars. East of the paint bay were rooms for paint storage and mixing, brass dipping, seat and sash washing, stores, and lockers for employees.

There also was a substation in this part of the building which received power at 13,200 volts from Fruitvale Power House. The substation contained three 100-kw transformers to provide 220 volts AC for lighting and shop equipment, two 50-kw motor-generators to provide 220 volts DC for shop equipment, one 26-kw 600-1,200-volt dynamotor to provide 600 volts DC to the pits, one 50-kw frequency changer to convert 2,300-volt, 62.5-cycle, 3-phase AC to 220-volt, 25-cycle AC for yard lighting, and two 25-kw, 13,200-2,300-volt transformers to supply current to the interlocking and block signal system.

Adjacent to the substation was a special room for air brake and armature repair. The mezzanine level above this room contained space for the offices of the chief clerk and superintendent of the West Alameda Shops.

In addition to the main shop building, there also was a boiler house containing a 100-horsepower marine boiler, a 500-gallon capacity fire pump, and a 250-cfm capacity air compressor. East of the shop building was a blacksmith shop containing a 1,000-pound steamhammer, punch, shears, and two forges. Nearby was a two-story building housing the inspection foreman's office and motormen's headquarters.

In February 1911, the first shipment of the new cars arrived at West Oakland. The cars were received from the manufacturer minus pilots, pantographs, controls, car lights, and other equipment.

The first cars to be prepared for operation were examples of each basic type: a motorized coach, a trailer coach, and a motorized baggage-coach. As these were the first cars through the shops, they were numbered, respectively, 300, 400, and 600. The three cars subsequently were made up into a single test train for trial operation.

On the morning of Thursday, April 7, 1911, a steam locomotive was coupled to the three-car test train, and, with a number of company officials on board, a run was made from West Oakland to the powerhouse. Here, with officials of the railroad and representatives of the various contractors and manufacturers looking on, valves were opened which allowed the steam into the big turbo-generators, bringing them to life. The high-voltage power was put on the line into the adjacent substation, where the motor-generators came to life, changing the high-voltage alternating current to 1,200-volt direct current, and with a final throw of a switch, the trolley wire outside the powerhouse was energized. For this test, the "hot wire" section extended only from the powerhouse around the Fernside loop to High Street. The remaining portion of the system in Alameda was not yet ready for power as many of the wiring details still had not yet been completed.

Moving outside the substation, the group stood beside the test train, knowing that the Moment of Truth finally had arrived. They watched as trainmen raised the pantographs of the two motor cars. With a hiss and a throb, the compressors of the cars started up. Climbing on board, the group crowded toward the cab of the 600, where a representative of the General Electric Company took the controls. Releasing the air brakes, he inched the controller to the first notch. Effortlessly, the big train began to move slowly down the track toward the bridge.

After crossing the Estuary, the train was switched onto the new Fernside loop track, where the three-car train was run back and forth and a number of tests were made. The 300 and the 600 were then run singly for speed tests and attained speeds of up to 40 miles per hour. After posing for a number of official photographs, the train was run back to the powerhouse and the power was cut off.

The steam engine then was brought down from Fruitvale and coupled onto the train to take it back to West Oakland. With the outstanding success of the test runs, it was announced that the Encinal Avenue line would be rushed to completion so that electric service could begin on May 11, 1911. As the date approached, however, it was realized that the required number of cars had not yet been completely outfitted, and that the opening date would have to be postponed until June 1.

During the third week in May, two two-car trains were assigned to the Fernside loop for instruction purposes. Whenever a steam local on the Lincoln or Encinal Avenue lines arrived at its terminal, the trainmen received instruction on a waiting electric train during their layover time.

On the morning of Saturday, May 20, 1911, a test train was run in Alameda under the control of Conductor J.C. "Pop" Fielding and Engineer Dan Quille, both veteran trainmen. Quille was wearing his usual engineer's garb, and just before he boarded the train, he was handed a cap which bore the title *MOTORMAN*. This title proclaimed a new company policy, that of identifying the operators of the new electric trains as motormen rather than as engineers. This new designation, however, was not well received by the employees, and in 1914 the company reverted back to the original designation of engineer.

With Quille at the controls, "Pop" Fielding gave the highball, and the gleaming new train rolled out of the yard and onto the main line, headed for Alameda Pier. At the pier was a contingent of company officials, among whom were Trainmaster P.H. Speakman, Roadmaster E.O. Corrigan, Assistant Superintendent W.A. Norton, and Western Division Superintendent W.A. Whitney. On the tracks at the pier terminal were grimy wooden coaches and panting steam engines, waiting for their runs to begin. Soon, the gleaming dark green train hove into view and came to a stop on the extra track.

VERY FIRST S.P. electric train to be operated in the East Bay was this one, on April 7, 1911. Behind baggage-coach 600 is trailer 400 and motorized coach 300. **Thomas Gray Collection**

PASSENGER MOTORS were frequently used to reconstruct the Alameda lines. Car 312 works here with home-made tower car built from old box car. **Louis L. Stein Jr. Collection**

With the officials on board, the train went all of the way out the Encinal Avenue line to South High Street. The train then was run back to Alameda Pier, where officials met with members of the local press and expounded on how great the new service would be.

Early on the morning of Thursday, June 1, two two-car trains left West Alameda, bound for South High Street, to begin revenue service on the Encinal Avenue line. The first revenue train left South High Street for the pier at 8 o'clock, with veteran engineer John Macauley at the controls. For the balance of that week, electric trains were operated only in base service, from 8:00 a.m. to 5:00 p.m. The steam locals continued to be operated on this line during morning and evening commute periods as well as late-night service.

On the following Sunday, the single early morning steam local was operated as usual until 8:00 a.m. After that time, it alternated with two electric trains until 11:40 a.m. when after arriving at South High Street and discharging its passengers, it continued around the Fernside loop and on to West Oakland, bringing to a close some 39 years of steam train operation along Encinal Avenue. Thereafter, all schedules were operated with electric equipment.

With full electric service on the Encinal Avenue line, the railroad instituted a major change in the vending of tickets along that line. Heretofore, agency stations were operated at many locations. The company announced that all of these stations would close at the end of the business day on Friday, June 16, and that the closing of agency stations would be spread to the other lines as soon as they were fully operational with electric equipment. With the closing of the agency stations, cash fares would be accepted by trainmen, who also would sell the monthly commutation tickets.

In an effort to simplify the fare structure, the railroad announced that after June 16, the old intra-city 2½-cent ticket

THIS SPINDLY wooden contraption, complete with pantograph, was used to string catenary at Alameda Pier. **Louis L. Stein Jr. Collection**

110

no longer would be accepted on the Encinal Avenue line. Instead, there would be a new 5-cent ticket which would be good anywhere in Alameda. This change in fares caused a storm of protest, with Alameda city councilmen and various civic groups protesting to the railroad and pointing out certain franchise provisions calling for low intra-city fares. The railroad gave in and reinstituted the 2½-cent local fare on the Encinal Avenue line on September 14, but this new ticket carried the restriction that it was not valid east of High Street.

On June 10, 1911, the final shipment of new cars was received from the manufacturer, and the shop forces at West Alameda rushed these cars through the shops as fast as possible. At that same time, the work of electrifying the Webster Street and Lincoln Avenue lines was nearing completion. During the rebuilding of the Webster Street line, Southern Pacific proposed two modifications to the existing service.

One of the proposals involved the single-tracked Harrison Street Bridge, long a bottleneck to cross-Estuary traffic. Southern Pacific proposed to use this bridge only for the Oakland-bound trains; pier-bound trains would be routed over the tracks of the San Francisco-Oakland Terminal Railways, which crossed the Estuary on the adjacent Webster Street Bridge.

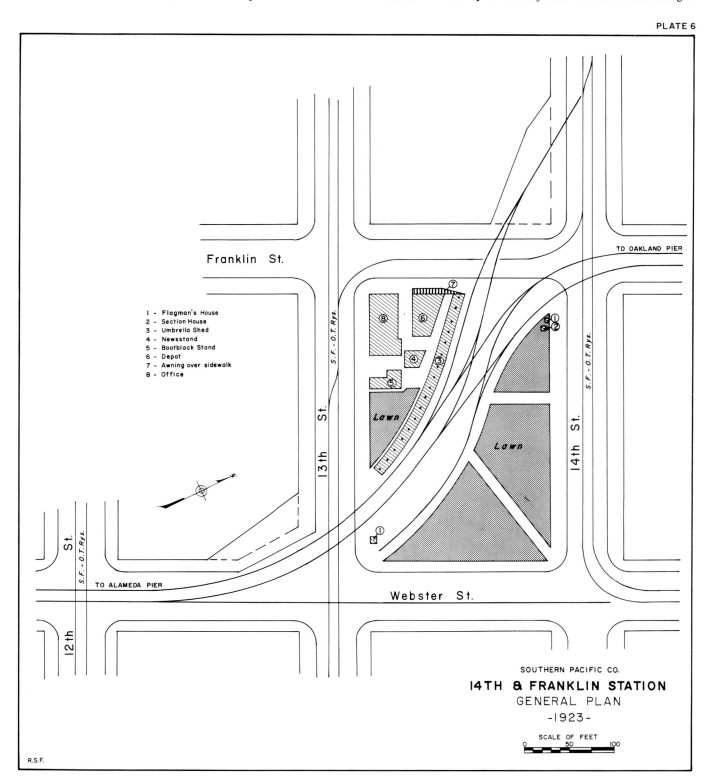

PLATE 7

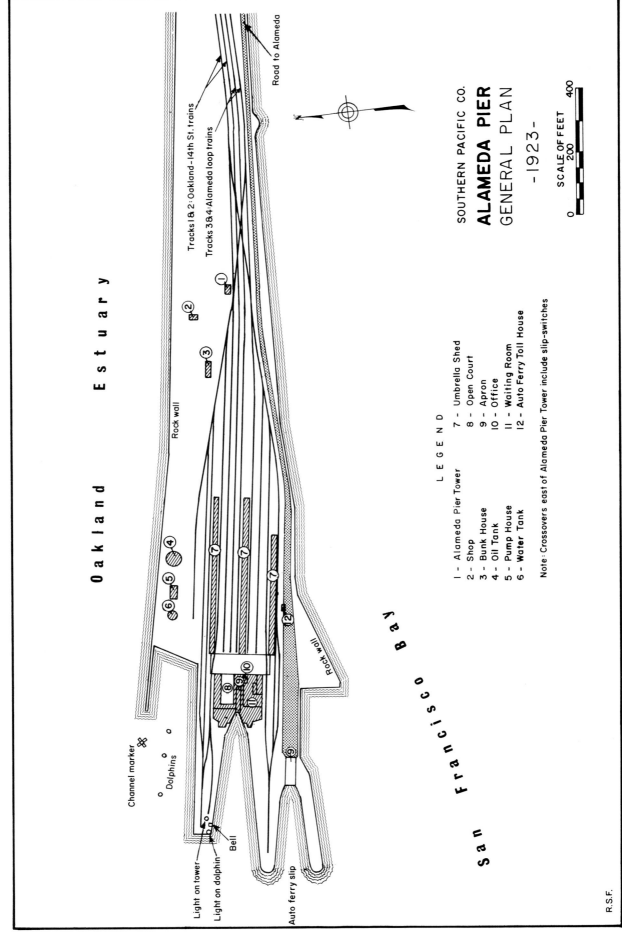

ELECTRIFICATION meant much more than stringing wire: tracks were rebuilt, too, as at here on busy Seventh Street. Steam locals are still operating. Many of the Victorian buildings survive in the 1970s.
Vernon J. Sappers Collection

The second proposal involved the location of the downtown Oakland terminal at 14th and Franklin Streets. As there was much agitation on the part of the City of Oakland and numerous merchants to get the railroad either to improve or remove the old depot, the Southern Pacific proposed to abandon the property and make use of the "Five Block Law."

Under the provisions of this statute, any railroad could obtain rights along the tracks of another railroad for a distance not to exceed five blocks provided not more than 500 feet of trackwork was necessary to make the connection. Southern Pacific intended to use this statute to take its trains up Webster Street on the rails of the San Francisco-Oakland Terminal Railways as far as 19th Street. This would put the S.P. in a better competitive position with regards to the S.F.-O.T. Railway's own Key Route 22nd Street line. However, neither this proposal nor that utilizing the Webster Street Bridge went beyond the talking stage, and ultimately, the old narrow gauge depot was electrified and made ready for the new service.

On the morning of June 19, 1911, a two-car train was taken from West Alameda all of the way up the Webster Street line to 14th and Franklin Streets. This marked the first entry of a Southern Pacific electric train into downtown Oakland, long considered a stronghold of the Key Route. From 14th and Franklin, the train then went back down the Webster Street line as far as San Antonio Junction, where it ran out the Lincoln Avenue line to North Park Street before returning to West Alameda.

On the morning of Tuesday, June 27, electric train service was begun on the Webster Street line. The first of a pair of trains began the revenue service with the 8:30 a.m. departure from Oakland. As with the Encinal Avenue line, steam local service was resumed that afternoon at 4 o'clock. The next morning, however, all runs were made by electric trains, and the steam trains no longer chuffed up and down Webster Street.

A second trial run was made on the Lincoln Avenue line on June 29, 1911. On this date, the test train was run from West Alameda to North Park Street and then around the Fernside loop to the Encinal Avenue line, returning to West Alameda by that latter route. Service on the Lincoln Avenue line was begun on August 1, with trains running from North Park Street to the pier by way of Webster Junction. On that same date, the Alameda loop line, which continued to be operated with steam equipment, was rerouted so that it no longer served Alameda Pier.

The new routing of the loop trains was similar to that of the old Alameda broad gauge line of previous years. Instead of running from Oakland Pier to Alameda Pier and return, all schedules started and terminated at Oakland Pier. During the morning hours, trains on this line operated from Oakland Pier via First Street and the Harrison Street Bridge to Lincoln Avenue and North Park Street.

The return to Oakland Pier was by way of the Fruitvale Avenue Bridge. In midmorning, the routing was reversed, so that the steam locals traveled west along Lincoln Avenue. This routing of the loop trains continued in effect until the line was changed to electric operation several months later.

The Melrose Extension

Reconstruction of the lines out of Oakland Pier began with the rebuilding of the Seventh Street line. From the pier east to the foot of Seventh Street, it was a fairly easy task to construct a four-track main line across the open marshland, but the situation along Seventh Street, from Bay to Fallon Streets, was an entirely different matter. The franchise for this route had expired several years earlier, and the railroad was operating only on a temporary permit. When the company approached the Oakland City Council on the matter of a new franchise, it found the council ready to drive a hard bargain.

During the franchise hearings, which lasted much of January 1911, B.H. Pendleton, President of the Oakland City Council, proposed that a 50-year franchise be granted containing conditions called the "Oakland Plan of Revenue Sharing." In this plan, the railroad would pay for the rebuilding of all of the pavement along Seventh Street in addition to the normal track work required. This effort would result in a newly paved thoroughfare which would be a fitting route for the new electric trains.

The financial stipulations of the plan called for the railroad to receive seven per cent per year interest on its investment in the street. In addition, 70 per cent of the gross receipts of the line would be allowed to the railroad for the expenses of operation and maintenance. One-third of the remaining would go to the city with the balance going to the railroad as profit. It was estimated by the city that their share for the first full year of operation would be about $19,000.

Understandably, the railroad had its own idea as to what constituted a proper franchise. The railroad plan envisaged simply a 50-year franchise with no profit-sharing provisions and no responsibility for street paving other than the usual distance beyond the outside running rails.

The question was resolved on March 21, 1911, when the Oakland City Council granted approval of a 35-year franchise along Seventh Street. The S.P. agreed to a schedule of annual payments to the city of $5,000 for the first 15 years and $8,500 thereafter. Also included was the stipulation that the railroad would pay for the repaving of Seventh Street, estimated to cost about $200,000, and pay for the installation, operation, and maintenance of street lights for the life of the franchise.

Work on the rebuilding of Seventh Street was begun by the Oakland Paving Company on May 9, 1911. The order of work consisted of removing all paving from the trackway and replacing the old rail with new 141-pound girder rail. Then, working only on one side of the street at a time, the remainder of the pavement and curbstones was removed and the street regraded. Finally, the street lights, curbs, gutters, and pavement were placed.

A major task in the project was the coordination of work with the heavy vehicular traffic which used Seventh Street and street railway lines crossing at Washington Street and Broadway. Furthermore, the steam locals continued to pass by every 20 minutes, even though Seventh Street was temporarily single-tracked between Henry and Fallon streets.

East of Fallon Street, most of the line was along private right-of-way, and, like the section near the pier, presented a fairly easy task to upgrade the track and install trolley wire. By November 1911, the entire line from Oakland Pier out to Melrose had been converted to electricity. In mid-November, in anticipation of the opening of service, six of the new cars were brought over from West Alameda to West Oakland. At the same time, finishing touches and last-minute tests were being made at the West Oakland substation preparatory to its being placed on line.

On the morning of Thursday, November 30, 1911, the operator at the West Oakland substation energized the trolley wire from Oakland Pier eastward along Seventh Street. At the same time, the trolley wire westward from the Fruitvale Powerhouse was cut in. With power in the wires and with a knot of officials looking on, the pantograph was raised on one of the new cars and it was made ready for a test run out to Melrose.

After waiting for the 11 o'clock local to run by, the four-car train moved onto the main line. Rolling up Seventh Street on the tail of the local, the train of dark green cars evoked stares from passers-by along the street. At Broadway, a brief stop was made so that the local could get some distance ahead. While stopped, the train was thronged by many people fascinated by the new equipment.

Leaving Broadway, the train ran at a good clip past East Oakland and Fruitvale stations, arriving at Melrose at 11:32. After changing ends and again allowing the steam local to get some distance ahead, the electric train made a nonstop run back to West Oakland. On arriving, it was decided that the line was ready for revenue service and that the electric trains would begin running the next day.

The next morning, December 1, two two-car electric trains entered revenue service on the Seventh Street line, alternating with two steam trains. This level of service was maintained until December 12, when it was decided to phase out all steam trains on the line.

On the morning of the twelfth, the two electric trains and two steam trains began their runs as usual. Shortly after noon, when one of the steam locals arrived at Oakland Pier, its departing run was taken over by an electric train. A short while later, the final steam local on the Seventh Street line pulled into Oakland Pier on a track adjacent to a waiting electric train. On hand to greet this train were W.A. Whitney, Superintendent of the Western Division, E.E. Calvin, General Manager of the Southern Pacific, and a number of other civic and company officials.

After the arrival of the steam train, Calvin gave a hand signal to the motorman in the cab of the electric train. The pantograph on the train was raised and the car lights came on, indicating that the electric train was ready for boarding and bringing to a close 51 years of steam train service along Seventh Street.

One week later, on the morning of Tuesday, December 19, the steam loop line was changed to electric operation. Whereas the steam trains had used the First Street route through Oakland, the new electric service utilized Seventh Street, ending most local train service to Oakland-First and Broadway station. Furthermore, service was reinaugurated between Oakland Pier and Alameda Pier, with trains using a section of new track along Lincoln Avenue between Mastick and Pacific Junction. This new track closely followed the route of the long-abandoned San Francisco and Alameda Railroad.

During the period of reconstruction of the Seventh Street

OAKLAND PIER as viewed from the east; Oakland Pier Tower to right.

Southern Pacific

line, plans and surveys were made for the construction of a large loop line east of Melrose. This proposed loop would enclose much of the area newly annexed to the City of Oakland. It initially was proposed to build through the newly developing subdivisions bearing names that are now nearly forgotten, names such as Melrose Heights, Iveywood, Hillsdale, and Broadmoor. Near San Leandro, the track would divide. One section would swing down toward the bay and connect with the Stonehurst Branch. It would then follow this line back to Sather station, where the loop would be closed. The other track would continue southward to San Leandro.

Grading for the Melrose Extension was begun at both Melrose and Dutton Avenue on the morning of April 12, 1910, by Peter Hoare, a contractor from Hayward. The first major obstacle to be met at Melrose consisted of the moving of a number of houses which were purchased by the railroad and moved to the south of East 14th Street where they were used as rental property. By the spring of 1912, the tracks had reached 55th Avenue, and service was extended to this station on Thursday, April 11.

For the short time that this station was the terminus, only every other train operated that far; alternate trains continued to turn at Melrose. Operation was further extended to Hillsdale on December 29, 1912, with the establishment of regular 20-minute service to that point. Hillsdale served as the end of the line for the next year and one-half, at which time the eastern terminus was moved to Havenscourt, 1.4 miles distant from Melrose.

As part of the Melrose Extension plan, a two-story concrete and steel substation was proposed for the area immediately west of the station. The substation, which was never built, was to have served all of the lines east of Melrose. Also proposed but not done was the electrification of the main line from Fruitvale south through San Leandro, Hayward, Decoto, and to Niles.

Track finally reached Dutton Avenue, in San Leandro, during the summer of 1913, with service to this point being inaugurated on Tuesday, September 30. For many years, service on the sparsely populated portion of the line east of Havenscourt was operated as a separate connecting line. On this outer line, a single car ran on a 40-minute headway, connecting with every other pier train at Havenscourt. It was not until the mid-1920s that the area had become sufficiently developed to warrant through service between Dutton Avenue and Oakland Pier.

With the tracks now at Dutton Avenue, the announcement was made that the line soon would be extended across San Leandro Creek on a concrete bridge and then along Santa Clara Avenue (now called Bancroft Avenue) to a station at Estudillo Avenue. It was rumored that the line ultimately would be extended to Hayward which would become a transfer point between the trains of the Southern Pacific and those of the Peninsular Railway, an S.P. subsidiary then planning to build north from San Jose. However, due to increased right-of-way costs and the considerable expense of bridging San Leandro Creek, the extension from Dutton Avenue to San Leandro at first was deferred and finally forgotten.

In celebration of the inauguration of the new electric train service along Seventh Street, the Seventh Street Improvement Club sponsored a gala New Year's Eve parade and celebration on Saturday, December 30, 1911. The event was described by the *Oakland Tribune* as one of the most colorful in the history of that city:

> "Oakland, the City Electric, vibrated with currents of joy last night, with Seventh Street as its magnetic core, charged with the full hum and energy of the municipality's brilliant life. The street flashed and gleamed from Fallon Street to the Bay in three miles of effulgent light and color. Seventh Street, long the home of the smoking, smashing, grumbling, and wearisome steam engine, with its soot and smoke and noise, has been converted into a clean thoroughfare with light, clean electric trains."

Since the day after Christmas, merchants and homeowners had been busily decorating storefronts and houses all along Seventh Street from Bay to Fallon Streets with bunting, flags, greens, and holly. The city and the railroad jointly entered into the spirit by stringing decorations along the span wires which supported the trolley wires.

The night of the celebration was clear and not too cold. With the approaching darkness, the entire street was bathed in an incandescent glory as street lights and illuminated decorations were turned on. At Fallon Street, an immense parade gathered and prepared to march toward the bay. Along the route, thousands of people gathered, many arriving by local train or streetcar.

Shortly after 7:00, the parade got underway. It was a pageant of color, music, and action, as 12 divisions marched all the way down Seventh Street from Fallon to Bay Streets, and then countermarched all the way back to Fallon Street.

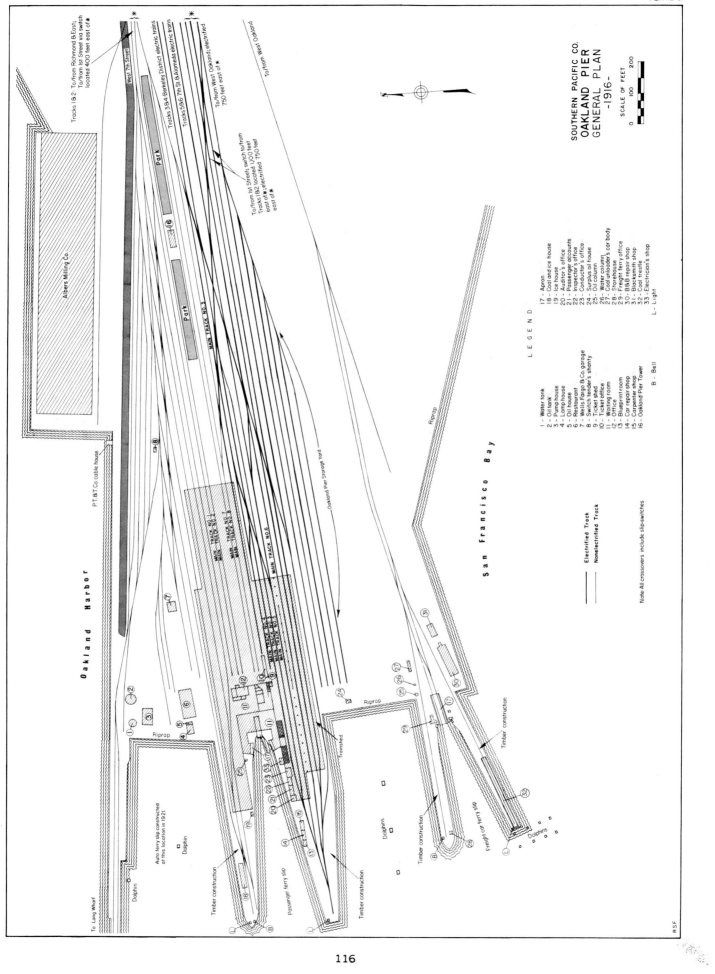

ONE OF THE FIRST revenue electric trains to reach Hillsdale in December, 1911. Looks like there's no shortage of uniformed help on this five-car consist.
R.S. Ford Collection

In the vanguard was an entourage of decorated automobiles carrying various city and county dignitaries. The first vehicle of this group was that of the Grand Marshal of the parade, Col. Louis Schaffer of the California National Guard. Following close behind was a car carrying Chief Adelbert Wilson and Capt. J.F. Lynch of the Oakland Police Department. Marching behind these cars were Companies A and F of the California National Guard, behind which came Scott's Military Band, outdoing all with snappy march music.

Next came a two-car steam local, drawn by locomotive 1905 carrying a banner proclaiming *23 FOR ME*, signifying its last run. The engineer was dressed to represent Father Time and had a white robe and a long, flowing beard. Behind this train was a pair of three-car electric trains which were brilliantly illuminated with more than 3,000 light globes. At the front end of the lead car (a combination baggage-coach) was a large, five-pointed star outlined in lights. Behind this star and strung out along the roofs of the three cars was the name *SOUTHERN PACIFIC COMPANY* spelled out in lights. The following train, which was also brightly illuminated, carried the phrase *CIVIC CO-OPERATION RESULTS IN EFFICIENCY,* also spelled out in lights along the roofs of the cars.

The second division of the parade consisted of another group of decorated automobiles. Dignitaries in this group consisted of Mayors Frank K. Mott of Oakland, J. Stitt Wilson of Berkeley, plus Harold W. Clapp and B.C. Edgars of the Southern Pacific, and George Yager, president of the Seventh Street Improvement Club. Other automobiles of this group carried the members of the Oakland City Council and other civic and business figures. The autos were followed by the well-known Valegra's and Silva's Concert Band.

Division three was headed by an elaborate float sponsored by the Seventh Street Improvement Club. Behind this float were three autos carrying officials of the Oakland Paving Company. Following the cars and marching to the music of George Williams' Band were all of the employes who worked on the rebuilding of Seventh Street. The next division was an equestrian patrol entered by Piedmont Parlor of the Native Sons of the Golden West. They were followed by a unit of the Native Daughters of the Golden West, a float entered by the Oakland Floral Depot, and marching units from the various improvement clubs located along the Seventh Street line.

Division five of the parade consisted of uniformed marching units of the Irish-American League, League of the Cross Ca-

To Berkeley... and Beyond

THE NEW BERKELEY LOOP line tapped new markets for S.P. To connect Thousand Oaks with Berkeley it was necessary to build the Northbrae tunnel, shown during excavation (upper left). Dirt is filled in over the top of the concrete structure (center left). The three photos along bottom show the first electric train through the bore on December 22, 1911. Naturally, civic leaders made speeches. The train was under the command of veteran conductor Samuel W. Bones (lower right), who certainly looked the part. North portal of tunnel is shown (upper right) after housing boom got underway. Right center photo (looking toward Solano Ave.) shows there was still plenty of room left for new development.

**Louis L. Stein Jr. Collection, three photos;
Addison H. Laflin Jr. Collection, two photos;
Vernon J. Sappers Collection, two photos.**

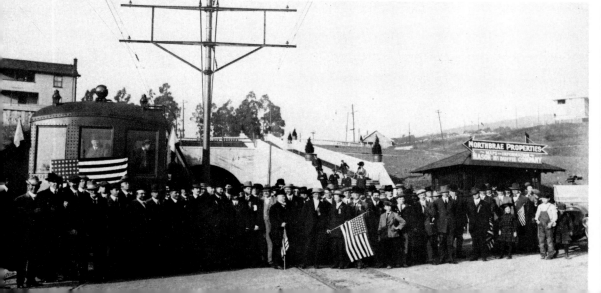

dets, and the Businessmens League, all marching to McBain's Fifth Regimental Band, which played some of the newer marches composed by John Phillip Souza.

The Oriental Division, which the *Oakland Tribune* described as one of the most beautiful parts of the parade, was next. Included was the band and marching unit of the Chinese Native Sons of the Golden West, several many-legged Chinese dragons that turned and twisted along the street, and mounted units of the Chinese Merchants Association. Bringing up the rear of this division was an elaborate float depicting a Chinese tea garden which contained a number of ladies dressed in luxurious silken gowns.

The next division was headed by Sheriff Frank Barnett, riding a magnificent horse whose bridle and saddle gleamed with polished silver. Behind him came marching units of the Benevolent and Protective Order of Elks and the Loyal Order of Moose. Following close behind was Division Eight, which consisted of marching units of the Red Caps Association, Knights of Pythias, American Order of Foresters, and the Afro-American League. The next division consisted of uniformed marching units of the Boy Scouts, each carrying troop and patrol flags, and units of the various Congregational Cadets.

Another spectacle was Division Ten, the Japanese Division. This division consisted of a special Japanese marching unit which carried more than 300 illuminated lanterns and was sponsored by the Japanese Merchants Association. The final division of the parade was headed by Gray's Military Band and consisted of a vast cavalcade of floats. The prize-winning float, which was by far the most impressive, was that entered by the Golden West Brewery. This float depicted the ancient art of brewing and included an enormous highly polished copper kettle manufactured by Thomas Booth Company which had been used for years by the local brewery.

After the last of the floats had passed by and the traditional squad of street sweepers had disappeared down the way, the crowd moved toward the Broadway station, where a program, street dance, and carnival had been scheduled. After the usual opening remarks by various civic leaders, Mayor Mott took the podium and addressed the crowd on the great future of the new thoroughfare. After the introduction of officials of the railroad and the Seventh Street Improvement Club, the program was ended with a rendition by C. Patrick Hildsley of the song, "Oakland," composed especially for the event by Fred Campbell and Mrs. Waldo S. Rucker.

After the program, the area in front of the station was cleared, the assembled musicians struck up a waltz, and soon couples, many in costume, began dancing. The celebration and revelry lasted well after midnight and would be remembered for years to come.

The Berkeley Loop Lines

All during 1910 and 1911, the newspapers carried accounts of electric railway construction taking place in the East Bay. Not only was the Southern Pacific building its system, but also the San Francisco, Oakland & San Jose Railway, operating under the aegis of the Key Route, was actively expanding its own system into new areas. Ultimately, it developed that Berkeley became the arena where the two systems chose to compete most actively.

Southern Pacific was the first line into downtown Berkeley as it operated the original steam line into town, but Key Route drew the first blood when it built its own Berkeley line, laying tracks just a few feet from the Southen Pacific line. From the start, the two lines fought vigorously for the patronage of the commuter.

At that time, what is now North Berkeley was just beginning to emerge as a desirable residential area, and subdivisions developed by the Mason-McDuffy Company and the Newell-Hendrichs Company attracted many potential home buyers. It was here, north of the main business district, that the stage was set for the inevitable confrontation between the two growing systems. The local press gleefully reported that both the Southern Pacific and the Key Route were racing toward the Thousand Oaks district in an effort to get there first.

On the one hand, Southern Pacific was extending its Shattuck Avenue line north to Northbrae and Thousand Oaks. On the other hand, Key Route was busily laying tracks along Sacramento Street with plans to tap the new Northbrae district and establish a station only a few feet from the proposed Southern Pacific station.

In answer to the Key Route Sacramento Street line, Southern Pacific started construction of a line along California Street, which runs parallel and only one block to the east. The California Street line would be built north to a connection with the Shattuck Avenue line at Thousand Oaks, thus forming the Berkeley loop. When completed, the California Street line would compete directly with Key's Sacramento Street line. Stations on both lines would be only a block apart, with trains operating at similar times on both lines.

The plans for extending the Shattuck Avenue line north from Berryman to Thousand Oaks called for a section of private right-of-way paralleling Henry Street, thence along Sutter Street to Hopkins Street, where Northbrae station would be established. North of this point was a 60-foot-high hill, along the top of which was Marin Avenue. Rather than cut through this hill, Southern Pacific proposed to run its tracks parallel to El Dorado Avenue and over to Marin Avenue and The Alameda.

From this point, it would be necessary to construct track along The Alameda in order to get to Thousand Oaks. Because The Alameda already contained a double-tracked streetcar line, it was proposed that a third and fourth track be built along this street for Southern Pacific trains.

The Berkeley Board of Trustees was not enthusiastic about the prospect of having four electrified tracks running along a Berkeley street. Local residents also were opposed to the scheme and suggested that the line run only as far as Northbrae station.

The impasse finally was resolved when Mason-McDuffee Company granted the railroad a right-of-way running from Northbrae 2,000 feet northwesterly to Solano Avenue and The Alameda. Because this right-of-way lay across the 60-foot-high hill, its use would necessitate the excavation of a deep cut at least 1,000 feet long. In addition, the cut would have to be spanned by two bridges carrying Marin and Los Angeles Avenues over it. Because of protests by adjacent property owners over the unsightly nature of such a large cut, it finally was decided to convert the open cut into a tunnel. The double-tracked Northbrae Tunnel was 465 feet long and was the only tunnel on the system.

Using the cut-and-cover method of construction, the tunnel alignment was fully excavated. The walls and crown of the tunnel then were formed with reinforced concrete and the

BEAUTIFUL BERKELEY station served both steam and electrics. Steam local awaits departure time (above) shortly after structure was completed in 1908. Scene in 1912 (below) shows S.P. electric in foreground while, behind the station, can be seen a Key Route train which had arrived at its terminal at about the same time. The two lines were vigorous competitors. Local streetcar completes the transit scene.
Roy D. Graves Collection; Thomas Gray Collection

overlying area backfilled and sloped to conform to the original ground level.

It is interesting to note that this tunnel, which was built in 1910, served for 31 years as the Southern Pacific's principal entry into the Thousand Oaks district. After the withdrawal of S.P. service, the tunnel was boarded up, only to be reopened a short while later for use by Key System trains which operated over former Southern Pacific tracks into Thousand Oaks. With the cessation of Key System rail service in 1958, the tunnel again was boarded up. Eventually, it was acquired by the city of Berkeley and converted into a two-lane vehicular tunnel that is still in use today.

The track reconstruction along Shattuck Avenue and the extension through the Northbrae Tunnel were completed early in December 1911. On the morning of Friday, December 22, a two-car train made a trial run over the new line. On arrival back at Oakland Pier, it was reported that the line was in excellent shape and was ready for service.

That afternoon, a number of company officials took the ferry over to Oakland Pier, where they were joined by a group of Berkeley civic officials who had come down to the pier for the purpose of riding the first electric train into Berkeley. Prior to boarding the three-car train, everyone was handed a large yellow badge that was inscribed: *BERKELEY—FIRST ELECTRIC TRAIN OF THE SOUTHERN PACIFIC—DECEMBER 22, 1911*. The train, which left Oakland Pier promptly at 2:00 p.m., was operated by four veteran employees: Samuel W. Bones, conductor, George Randall, motorman, and E.C. Moisan and E.E. Clark, brakemen.

Running nonstop out Shattuck Avenue, the train arrived at Berkeley Station at 2:20, greeted by a large group of spectators. After the passengers had detrained, B.J. Bither, President of the Berkeley Chamber of Commerce, mounted a small platform and greeted the train on behalf of the merchants of Berkeley. He then made a brief speech congratulating the railroad on having completed the elaborate and costly system. Bither then introduced F.J. Atherton, Chief of the Bureau of Economics of the Southern Pacific, who spoke at length on the development of the system and commented on how Berkeley would prosper when the system became fully operational. Mayor Wilson stepped forward to express regret at the passing of the colorful steam locals which had become such a Berkeley tradition, and to prophesy that the citizens of the East Bay would one day acquire the system and operate it as public property. After speaking, the mayor led the crowd back on board the waiting train for an inspection trip to North Berkeley and the Thousand Oaks District.

Leaving Berkeley Station, the train ran nonstop past Berryman, still the end of the steam line, and onto the new trackage of the Berryman Extension. After passing through the Northbrae Tunnel, the train ran down Solano Avenue to the Thousand Oaks station. Here, a stop was made so that the passengers could inspect the North Berkeley substation. On the return trip to downtown Berkeley, all of the passengers were treated to cold punch served through the courtesy of G.R. Bartlett, one of Berkeley's leading confectioners.

The following morning, electric service was begun on the Shattuck Avenue line as far as Berryman beginning at 9 o'clock. Electric service was withdrawn at 4 o'clock that afternoon and replaced by steam locals. This mode of operation continued all during the succeeding week, as crews received instruction on the operation of the electric equipment.

The following Saturday, December 30, the steam locals began their early morning runs as usual. With the 9:00 a.m. conversion to electric service, it was announced that there would be no more steam operation on this line, closing out 36 years of steam train service in downtown Berkeley. When the last pier-bound steam local made its station stop at Berkeley, a number of well-wishers were on hand to bid it good-bye.

A reporter from the *Berkeley Daily Gazette* was at the station and interviewed John Boyd, a G.A.R. veteran who was then in his 70s. Boyd had lived in Berkeley for over 40 years and vividly remembered the arrival of the first Central Pacific train into town. He recalled,

> "Back in those days, the locals ran only hourly. And even then, the ferry for the last train to Berkeley left the City at 8 p.m., because after that hour, no one would want to come over here anyhow!"

Another old-timer interviewed was Professor Meyer Jaffa, instructor of nutrition at the University of California. Professor Jaffa was among those present on the first steam train into Berkeley in 1876. He well remembered the dirt streets, crude station, and the cluster of oak trees that stood along what is now the center of Shattuck Avenue. He also mentioned that he was on board the first train into Oakland Pier in 1882 and also was an invited guest on the first electric train into town the previous week.

He was at the station that day as he planned to ride the last steam train down Shattuck Avenue. With the last "All aboard!", Professor Jaffa boarded the train just before it pulled out, and soon the train was just a tail of smoke disappearing down Shattuck Avenue.

Full electric service to Thousand Oaks was begun January 1, 1912, and emphasis now was placed on rushing the California Street line to completion, thus finishing the first phase of the Berkeley loop. Three days after the new service had begun on the Shattuck Avenue line, a test run was made out California Street to Thousand Oaks. Two days later, on January 4, 1912, revenue service was inaugurated on this line, with trains being through-routed with those of the Shattuck Avenue line. Initially, service on the California Street line was operated on an 80-minute headway. With the issuance of the January 11 time card, the headway was changed to the customary 20 minutes, and California Street trains were no longer through-routed with those of the Shattuck Avenue line.

The second phase of the Berkeley loop involved a line along Ninth Street, passing through Albany, and then proceeding easterly along private right-of-way through open country to Thousand Oaks. The latter part of this line was routed along Solano Avenue when that street was laid out. Construction of the Ninth Street line commenced near Shellmound Park in 1910 and proceeded northerly, with the final rail being laid in the latter part of January 1912, only a few weeks after the completion of the California Street line.

A trial run was made with a two-car train over the Ninth Street line on Friday the second of February. The special operation left Oakland Pier at 2:00 p.m. and ran nonstop to Thousand Oaks by way of the Shattuck Avenue line. The return trip was made by way of the new line, with everyone on board being in agreement that the line was ready for revenue service.

On the following morning, February 3, a minimum-level service was inaugurated on the Ninth Street line. Service consisted of only two trains per day. One of these, a morning commute run, originated as a Shattuck Avenue train which operated through Thousand Oaks and returned to the pier via the Ninth Street line. The second train was an evening run which ran on the reverse of the morning run. This level of service was continued until February 19, when 20-minute service was instituted on the line, with trains being through-routed with those of the California Street line.

The arrival of the Southern Pacific into Albany was of great civic importance as it gave that city its first direct link with San Francisco. Heretofore, persons desiring to go across the bay were obliged to take the streetcar down San Pablo Avenue and either catch the local at Stanford Avenue or continue on to 40th Street to catch the Key Route train.

All during the construction of the Berkeley loop lines, Southern Pacific was busily engaged in the construction of the Ellsworth Street line into what had formerly been exclusive territory of the Key Route. S.P.'s aim was to tap the campus area of the University of California. The necessary permission to build the line had been received from the Berkeley Board of Trustees in 1909 with the only proviso being that the line must be in full operation prior to January 1, 1912.

Of course, the campus area already was well served with rail lines. Local streetcar service was being performed along College Avenue, Telegraph Avenue, and Bancroft Way. In addition, Key Route had announced plans to operate trains from the Key Route pier to the campus by way of Alcatraz and College Avenues. Thus, in order to get to the campus, Southern Pacific was forced to choose the inferior Ellsworth Street route.

Surveying and grading of the new line was begun in December 1909 at Woolsey and Adeline Streets, which point was named Woolsey Junction. Track work was begun at the junction and was completed to just beyond Bancroft Way by the end of November 1911. Several test runs were made during December, with full service scheduled to begin Sunday, December 31, just one day short of the expiration of the time limit set by the Berkeley Board of Trustees. The opening of this never-successful line was anything but auspicious.

At 5:51 on the morning following the inauguration of 20-minute service on the Ellsworth Street line, a loud crash was heard. The cause was a fast-running westbound train that had snagged the trolley wire at the Key Route crossing near Woolsey Junction. Fortunately, the Southern Pacific wires were not badly damaged, and the train was able to continue on its way to Oakland Pier, but the Key Route wires were brought down and lay sputtering on the ground until a line crew arrived at the scene some time later.

Service on the Ellsworth Street line and on Key Route's Berkeley line was disrupted for several hours. However, as it was the morning of New Year's Day, there were no commuter trains scheduled, and service was restored before any great number of people were about.

The Richmond Line

At the Berkeley franchise hearings of November 1908, the representatives of the Southern Pacific stated that the company was considering an electrification of the West Berkeley line and extending it northward to Richmond, and possibly even to Martinez.

Three years later, in October 1911, the Southern Pacific applied to the California State Railroad Commission for permission to acquire a street railway franchise along Cutting Boulevard in Richmond. In the application, it was stated that H.G. Cutting, holder of the franchise, desired to dispose of it and sought no compensation. The franchise was duly transferred to the Southern Pacific with the stipulation that passenger service along Cutting Boulevard must commence within the next four years.

At the same time, Southern Pacific received a franchise from the City of Richmond which stipulated: (1) the railroad must provide illumination of all streets over which it operated; (2) the local fare was to be 5 cents; (3) the city will designate the location of all stations; (4) the railroad will pay the City two per cent of the annual gross income; (5) the railroad may operate freight trains on city streets only between the hours of 10 p.m. and 6 a.m.; and (6) passenger service must be started by March 1, 1913.

The route ultimately selected for the Richmond line was to leave the Ninth Street line at Richmond Junction, to be located at Solano Avenue and Adams Street in downtown Albany. Following Adams Street, the double-tracked line would cross Cerrito Creek and after traversing Panhandle Boulevard (now named Carlson Boulevard) for a distance of two miles, the line would cross the main line tracks on a viaduct and continue north along the west side of these tracks to Cutting Boulevard. From this point, the Richmond line would go west along Cutting Boulevard to Tenth Street, where it would turn north to the downtown Richmond Terminal at MacDonald Street. The line also would have a branch which would continue west along Cutting Boulevard to the Standard Oil Refinery at Point Richmond.

After the line had been surveyed, detailed design and cost estimates were made for the 16.58-mile-long route. Modifications to the original design eliminated the viaduct over Stege. A $1,035,000 contract was let to B.W. Perrin Company in August 1912 for construction of the line, to be completed by June 1, 1913.

During the period of design, the railroad made a traffic count and prepared population projections for the Richmond area. The survey found that there was an average of 550 daily riders on the East Shore and Suburban Railway streetcars between Richmond and Oakland. There were also about 125 daily passengers riding between Richmond and San Francisco. Of these, 75 used mainline S.P. trains from Richmond station, and 50 used the Santa Fe ferry from Point Richmond. The analysis of the traffic and population data indicated that Richmond never would become a city of consequence, and thus never could support an electric suburban line.

The decision, then, was made to abandon the entire project even though 1,265 feet of single track had already been constructed at the outer end of the line near the Standard Oil Refinery at Point Richmond. The Richmond extension was officially dead when the franchises were allowed to lapse on February 16, 1916.

Streetcars

In 1910, if one were to appraise the Southern Pacific East Bay suburban system then in various stages of construction, one would see that there were areas of exclusive operation such as Alameda and East Oakland. In other areas such as Berkeley and downtown Oakland, Southern Pacific was actively matching Key Route on a nearly line-for-line basis.

Only in Piedmont and Claremont was Key Route without

direct competition, and it was physically impractical for Southern Pacific to attempt to put service into these areas. Key Route did not experience any direct competition with its 22nd Street line and with the inauguration of service along this line, some of the patronage of S.P.'s Webster Street line was siphoned off. Hence, Southern Pacific reasoned that Key's 22nd Street line would be "fair game" for some form of competing service.

Instead of approaching the Oakland City Council for a franchise for a line to compete with the 22nd Street line, Southern Pacific chose to operate through its San Jose-based subsidiary, the Peninsular Railway. This latter company sought a franchise for a line to run between the 14th and Franklin Streets station and the main line station at 16th Street.

Railroad officials blandly explained that the proposed line was to be the northern end of a Peninsular line which was to run up the east side of the Bay, from San Jose to Oakland.

The Oakland City Council was agreeable to the Peninsular proposal as it welcomed any company to Oakland who might give some competition to Key Route and Southern Pacific. To further its image with the landowners along Franklin Street, the Peninsular Railway offered to pay half of the costs of the new sewer line then being built along that street from 14th to 22nd Streets.

The only major opposition to the new line came from the Oakland Chamber of Commerce, which passed a resolution directed to the Oakland City Council agreeing that the new line was necessary but questioning the advisability of routing it along Franklin Street. The Chamber came up with the idea that the new line should be built along a private right-of-way located halfway between Franklin and Webster Streets. The Chamber also proposed that the line not be run along 18th Street to the 16th Street Station, but instead be extended across 22nd Street and terminate somewhere in the vicinity of Piedmont Avenue.

The Oakland City Council duly granted a franchise for a streetcar line running along Franklin Street, from 14th to 20th Street, and then west by way of 20th and 18th Streets to the 16th Street Station. With the franchise in hand, Peninsular Railway constructed the line without any great difficulty. On completion, it was leased to Southern Pacific for operation.

Service on this line, which proved to be the final track addition to the East Bay suburban system, was inaugurated on March 27, 1912. In the beginning, 10-minute service was operated with transbay cars between a stub-track terminal in front of the 16th Street Station and 14th and Franklin Streets. Because the line actually was a streetcar type of operation, Southern Pacific placed an order with Pullman Manufacturing Company for 20 center-entrance cars.

In preparation for operating the 18th Street line with streetcars, a balloon track was built in front of the 16th Street Station. A section of single track also had been built along 8th Street, in Alameda, between Lincoln and Central Avenues. The 8th Street trackage formed a second loop in the island city and was used exclusively by the streetcars of the Crosstown line, although franchise service with transbay cars of the Horseshoe line operated along 8th Street prior to inauguration of streetcar service.

The streetcars for the Crosstown line arrived at West Alameda in July 1912. They arrived without pantographs, fenders, or other equipment; they were painted cherry-red and were numbered CP800 to CP819. Southern Pacific planned to have the cars outfitted and ready for service within two months, and opening day for the Crosstown line was set for September 15. While being tested, it was found that the streetcars, called "dinkeys" by many, were much lighter in weight than the suburban cars. Because of this fact, they tended to ride up and over the heavy spring switches and become derailed. To remedy this problem, the railroad ordered heavier wheels and truck parts to add weight to the cars. The new truck parts did not arrive until late fall, and it was not until November 11 that the first car with rebuilt trucks was ready for a test run. That afternoon, the car, with many officials on board, made a complete circuit of Alameda, from the pier to Lincoln Park. A run also was made to 14th and Franklin Streets. No difficulties were encountered, and the other cars were similarly equipped and made ready for service.

Streetcars entered service on the new Crosstown line on August 1, 1913, providing 10-minute service between 16th Street Station and downtown Oakland; two of every three cars continued on to the new Alameda streetcar loop. Alameda streetcars alternated between Lincoln Avenue and Encinal Avenue; going by one route and returning by the other. With inauguration of service with streetcars, the larger transbay cars were withdrawn from service along 18th Street until a few years later when the 18th Street transbay line was begun.

Because of the leased status of the 18th Street trackage, operating timetables designated this route as the "Peninsular Railway." Furthermore, it had been proposed that the cars of the Crosstown line carry the Peninsular Railway emblem. For a short while, streetcar No. 809 was lettered *PENINSULAR RAILWAY,* but this designation soon was replaced with *SOUTHERN PACIFIC.*

With 10 lines in full operation, Southern Pacific proposed an eleventh, and final, line which was to run from Oakland Pier to 16th Street Station and thence by way of a track connection to the 18th Street line, terminating at 14th and Franklin Streets. With service on this line, it would be possible to go from 14th and Franklin Streets to San Francisco by way of either Oakland Pier or Alameda Pier. Regular service on the 18th Street transbay line was inaugurated on November 1, 1914. With this new line in operation, streetcar and train traffic was fairly heavy along 18th and Franklin Streets, as the trains ran at 20-minute intervals and streetcars of the Crosstown line were on 10-minute headways.

In anticipation of the opening of service of the 18th Street transbay line, Southern Pacific placed an order in the latter part of 1912 with Pullman Manufacturing Company for 17 additional cars of a design similar to the original transbay equipment. Included in the order were 10 motorized coaches, five motorized baggage-coaches and two baggage motors. In addition to being able to provide full baggage service, the latter two cars would do switching chores at West Alameda and would be used for mail train service between Oakland Pier and Berkeley.

The most notable feature of the new Pullman cars was the adoption of round end windows as a safety feature. It had been found during the first two years of operation that the large rectangular end windows, although providing good visibility, did not provide adequate protection in case of a wreck. All of the original equipment that had motorman's cabs and controls subsequently were rebuilt with the round, or porthole, end windows. Only one of the non-control trailer cars received this treatment, and the remainder retained their rectangular end windows.

STREETCAR 806 (opposite) at 14th and Franklin station. In background is new Oakland City Hall; note horse-drawn bakery wagon at left. **R.S. Ford Collection**

OAKLAND-16th STREET STATION was much changed after the advent of the electrics. In this view, car 330 lays over on new stub track in front of station.
Southern Pacific

A Tale of Four Stations

One of the characteristics of the Southern Pacific East Bay suburban system was the use of station buildings at principal points. Original structures dated back to the steam era and were wooden buildings designed in typical railroad fashion. In later years these structures were painted a dingy "Huntington Yellow." To small fry watching the local trains, these stations gave a flavor of mainline railroading not found on the competing Key Route.

The electrification of the suburban lines spurred a program of station building in the East Bay. The program included the replacement of the principal stations in Oakland and Berkeley as well as new construction at two other sites. The first of the four new stations was built in downtown Berkeley.

In the latter part of September 1906, an article appeared in the local newspapers announcing that the old wooden Berkeley station was to be replaced with a modern brick structure to be located a short distance to the north. It was further announced that the new building would be of substantial proportions, fitting for the principal railroad station of the city. The design of the new station would conform to the general architectural style of the new buildings on the University of California campus which had been designed by the world-renowned Paris architect, M. Benard.

The Southern Pacific Berkeley Station was designed by D.J. Patterson, Architect, and J.H. Wallace, Assistant Chief Engineer of the company. The facility was to be 188 feet long and 41 feet wide and would be composed of two rectangular sections separated by a small park. The southern section would contain the main waiting room, city ticket offices, and a separate waiting room for women. The northern section would be the location of the baggage room, boiler room, miscellaneous offices, and a combination men's smoking room and waiting room for students.

The exterior walls of the station were to be of dark red brick with a trim of light buff terra cotta. The north, west, and south sides of the building would have a covered arcade, the columns of which also would be of terra cotta. The same terra cotta was to be used on the pediment and the friezes and cornices making up the entablature. The interior of the building was to be floored with white marble, with the walls being paneled with polished oak. Both the main waiting room and the smoking room would have a large open fireplace. The station grounds were to be artfully landscaped with lawn areas, a fountain, several palm trees, and a pavement of decorative concrete. In all, the building and grounds would be pleasing to the eye and would become a landmark for years to come.

Construction of the station, which was to take up most of the railroad-owned property along the east side of Shattuck Avenue, began in the latter part of 1906. The facility was completed and opened to the public in January 1908, three years before the first electric trains entered Berkeley.

During the construction of the new Berkeley Station, the Southern Pacific announced that construction would begin shortly on a new station at First and Broadway in Oakland. Although not really a suburban station, as it was to be used primarily by trains running to Stockton, San Jose, and Los Angeles, the First and Broadway station was served for a few years by steam trains on the Horseshoe line as well as those on the Stonehurst line.

The new station, which was opened to the public in December 1907, cost about $25,000 to build and was architecturally similar to the new Berkeley Station. The First and Broadway station was composed of two separate buildings connected by a columned arcade that was 195 feet long running along the First Street side. The westerly portion of the station, that closest to Broadway, contained a general waiting room, ticket offices, women's waiting room, gentlemen's smoking room, and a newsstand. The other portion of the station contained the baggage room and the boiler and furnace room.

The exterior of the station was of red brick with mudsills, corners, and trim of gray cement brick; the roof was of blue slate. The interior of the waiting rooms were paneled with polished redwood and had ceilings of exposed redwood beams. A large, open fireplace dominated the general waiting room, which was floored with vitrified tile. Surrounding the station complex and extending from Broadway to Franklin Street, was a large, landscaped area consisting of lawns, shrubs, and decorative concrete paths.

With a new station at First and Broadway, it was proper that the antiquated station at 16th Street should be next in line for replacement. Southern Pacific was aware of its severe limitations for both mainline and suburban trains. All too frequently, mainline trains blocked the tracks while discharging or taking on crowds of people and large amounts of baggage and mail. This caused the locals to be delayed, and frequently put the Berkeley line off schedule.

As a solution, the railroad decided in 1910 to replace the old station with something more modern and up-to-date. James Hunt, a noted Chicago architect, was retained to design a spacious station having separate facilities for mainline and suburban trains. The design adopted was one having ground level platforms for mainline trains and an upper-level suburban concourse.

TRACKS of the 18th Street line curve toward the terminal loop in front of Oakland-16th Street Station (above); concrete ramp to right is for track connection to Oakland Pier lines. From 1911 to 1914, suburban electrics used ground level tracks behind station (below). To left is departing Shattuck Ave. train while, to right and following close behind, a California St. train arrives from Oakland Pier. **Roy D. Graves Collection; Louis L. Stein Jr. Collection**

MAINLINE BERKELEY station, at 3rd and University, also served some suburban patrons. This is a 1913 view.
Vernon J. Sappers Collection

Work on the new station began in October 1910 with the razing of the old structure to make room for the new $370,000 depot, which was built under the supervision of J.Q. Barlow, assistant chief engineer of the railroad. The new building, which began to take shape by the end of the year, was of ample proportions, being 273 feet long and 60 feet high. It was built entirely of reinforced concrete with an exterior facing of Sierran granite.

The interior dimensions were equally grand, having a main waiting room that was 116 feet long and 60 feet wide and having walls faced with California marble. The west side of the waiting room opened onto the loading area for the mainline trains. In addition, this side of the waiting room also contained a broad stairway leading to the upper level, or suburban elevation, where the new electric trains would arrive and depart.

The suburban elevation also was served by a baggage elevator for the transfer of baggage and parcels between mainline trains and suburban electric trains. The 16th Street Station was completed and formally dedicated on Thursday, August 1, 1912. However, as the suburban elevation track connections had not yet been completed, electric trains continued to use the ground level facilities for the next year and one-half.

With the completion of the 16th Street Station, work turned to the replacement of the infamous "Death Curve," located in West Oakland and the site of many grade crossing accidents. Along this portion of the line, the tracks ran southerly toward Ninth and Pine Streets, where they curved west to Seventh and Bay Streets. At this point, the tracks originally joined those of the Seventh Street line for the run out to Oakland Pier. It was this curved stretch of track, with its five grade crossings, that became called the "Death Curve."

After the reconstruction of the facilities at Oakland Pier, a six-track main line was constructed between the pier and West Oakland. Two of the tracks were for mainline steam trains and the other four were double tracks for the Berkeley lines and the Seventh Street line, respectively. At West Oakland, the tracks of the Berkeley lines joined those of the steam lines just before entering the "Death Curve." Realignment of the curved portion of the line involved the purchase of a new right-of-way from Dalton Iron Works and also from the Realty Syndicate, who owned what was then tidelands property.

The new alignment, which had only one grade crossing at Seventh Street, consisted of a pair of tracks for the steam trains and a second pair of tracks for the electric trains. The new route cost $750,000 and was opened for service as far as the foot of 11th Street on July 11, 1913.

North of 11th Street, the new route went by way of a four per-cent grade leading to a timber structure that took the tracks to the Suburban Elevation Station at 16th Street. Here, a steel-bent supported platform had been built over the open area between the station building and the mainline tracks. The platform was at the second-story level of the building and contained covered loading platforms on each side of the tracks. North of the Suburban Elevation Station, a timber structure carried the tracks back to ground level at the foot of 20th Street. The elevated structure, which cost nearly $500,000 to construct, was 3,844 feet in length. Service on the new elevated trackway through the Suburban Elevation Station was begun on the morning of February 19, 1914. After that date, the catenary trolley wire was removed from the ground level tracks.

The construction of the dual facilities proved to be a wise decision, as within a very few years, the ground level facilities were accommodating over 50 daily mainline trains. At this same time, the Suburban Elevation saw 488 electric trains pass through each day on five transbay lines. The crowds of people generated by this number of mainline and suburban trains was further augmented by the more than 200 daily arrivals and departures of streetcars on the Crosstown line which used the balloon track in front of the station. To round out the transit activity in front of the station, streetcars on several of the Key Route local lines terminated on West 16th Street, only one-half block away.

All during the time that a magnificent new station was being built in Oakland, the only mainline station in Berkeley was the antiquated Delaware Street facility. The Southern Pacific always considered its downtown station as the main Berkeley facility. Passengers destined for mainline points were

THE ONLY ELECTRIC freight locomotive to operate on the O.A. & B. lines was the CP 200, seen here shortly after delivery at West Alameda Shops.
Vernon J. Sappers Collection

encouraged to check their baggage at Berkeley Station and then board an electric train for a trip down to the Oakland 16th Street Station, where a transfer was made to mainline trains.

Periodically, the Berkeley City Council would approach the railroad with a proposal for a mainline station to be located at the foot of University Avenue. However, the railroad was adamant, insisting that it would take passengers longer and would be inconvenient for them to have to use a station far removed from downtown Berkeley. Finally, tired of fighting the railroad, the city took the matter to the California State Railroad Commission on August 15, 1912. A week later, on August 23, the Commission handed down a decision ordering the railroad to build a suitable mainline station at the foot of University Avenue and to modify its schedules so that intrastate trains would serve it.

The basis for the decision was twofold. First, only a few trains per day stopped at the Delaware Street station, with all of the more important trains passing it by. Second, on the average, Berkeley passengers were charged 35 cents more on intrastate tickets under existing ticketing arrangements than they would be if mainline service was available from the foot of University Avenue. The decision in favor of the city stipulated not only the location of the station, but also that it should be built of pressed brick in a modified Spanish style and would not cost less than $15,000. Finally, it was decreed that the architectural plans for the building be submitted to the commission for approval within 90 days.

Construction of the station began in January 1913, and it was completed and opened to the public on August 16. At that time, the Delaware Street station was closed and later torn down. The opening of Berkeley's new station was cause for a gala citywide celebration. The high point of the celebration was a caravan of automobiles, led by a large sight-seeing car driven by E.C. Platt, that left the Hotel Shattuck at 2:00 p.m. and drove around the city and then down to the new station. After the caravan had arrived and a sizable crowd had gathered, a special steam train from Oakland Pier pulled in, bringing a contingent of railroad officials.

Mayor Charles D. Heywood greeted the officials and then spoke to the assembled crowd. He noted that starting that day, 46 trains would stop at the station; this would "put Berkeley on the map." He also predicted that the station soon would be the center of a new and thriving business district as the city had plans to fill the expanse of mudflats to the west.

Although the only local trains to serve this station were those on the West Berkeley line, the Third and University station long outlived its downtown cousin. In later years, the station was an important stop for all mainline trains, as patrons from Berkeley, Oakland, and other neighboring areas used the facility in preference to the Oakland-16th Street Station. The station continued in use until 1971, when it was closed after Amtrak took over the mainline Southern Pacific passenger operations. The station building was sold and now serves as a restaurant.

NEATLY FRAMED by two other ferries, the *Garden City* enters the slip at the San Francisco Ferry Building on the Alameda run. *Piedmont* is to the right approaching from Oakland, while, to the left, the auto ferry *Yosemite* comes in from Richmond. **Vernon J. Sappers Collection**

CHAPTER 11

Ferry Tales

ONE OF THE regular columns appearing in the *San Francisco Call* during the years prior to World War I was one entitled "Ferry Tales." The column was widely read and presented the human interest side of that transportation institution unique to San Francisco and a few other privileged cities. It was here that many anecdotes and sidelights were reported about the ferries and the way they enriched the lives of countless thousands of commuters.

The average businessman who lived in the East Bay and worked in the City spent about an hour each day on board the ferries. As time went by, most commuters developed a sense of fondness for their usual boat. On board, they would head for a favorite seat. For some, the unending card games would be picked up where they were dropped on the previous trip. Others preferred to retire behind their newspapers to read of the affairs of the world. On morning trips, the restaurant would be crammed with commuters trying to gulp a quick breakfast during the short 20-minute crossing.

Many of the more hardy commuters considered the evening ferry trip an ideal decompression chamber, where they could lean on the rail and mull over the events of the day. Many enjoyed the tang of the salt air and the crisp breeze as the ferry churned eastward. Leaning on the rail, one could watch the screaming and diving gulls that followed the ferries back and forth across the Bay. To the west, across the water, was the skyline of San Francisco. At dusk, as the lights would come on, the City would stand in bold relief against the setting sun.

To the east, the lights of the East Bay, yet undimmed by smog, formed a sparkling blanket at the foot of the darkening Berkeley Hills.

For those who were veteran bay-watchers, there always were interest and excitement in the continual activity of ships, ferries, sloops, tugs, and other water craft that plied the bay. Perhaps a tramp freighter would be sighted coming in past Alcatraz Island, flying an unusual flag. Maybe the *Transit* would attract their interest as she plodded across the bay with an odd assortment of freight cars. On occasion, particularly on weekends, the attraction would be children filled with excitement as they tossed bread crumbs for the gulls to catch on the wing. With 26 boats arriving and leaving the Ferry Building each hour, it was the ferries themselves that often created the most exciting times on the bay.

The Troublesome 'Bay City'

The *Bay City* seemed to have a fetish for being involved in collisions or getting into lesser troubles. Three times in as many years, she found herself in a situation that resulted in a trip to the shipyard for repairs. The first occurrence, which also involved the *Berkeley,* was on the evening of April 5, 1911. At the Ferry Building, the *Berkeley* was taking on passengers for the 6:35 departure for Alameda Pier. Up in the wheelhouse, Captain E.A. Jones looked at his watch and peered across the Bay. He noted that there was a slight breeze and he could see the lights of the *Bay City,* getting ready to leave Alameda Pier.

What ordinarily would have been a routine trip across the Bay turned out to be anything but that. The events of the crossing subsequently were described by First Officer Albert Johnson of the *Berkeley:*

> "Soon after we left the Ferry Building, Captain Jones turned the wheel over to me. And, as I got abeam of Goat Island, I saw the *Bay City* rounding the island on course. I gave the usual whistle signal that I would pass her to starboard. This was acknowledged by the *Bay City*.
>
> "I kept on course and when we were about to pass, to my surprise, the *Bay City* turned and started to cross my bow! I turned the wheel sharply and whistled. But, instead of turning, the *Bay City* steamed directly in front of me. I turned as sharp as I could and would have missed her if she hadn't of also turned. It was then that her bow took me amidship on my starboard side."

The resulting collision badly damaged both ferries. Fearing the boats would sink, the passengers were in a state of panic. Women were screaming hysterically and men were trying valiantly to lower lifeboats and to help others don life jackets. After the panic had subsided and it had been determined that neither ferry would sink, each backed off and was able to limp to its respective destination.

At the subsequent investigation, Captain William Rogers of the *Bay City* stated unequivocally that neither he nor his First Officer had steered into the path of the *Berkeley.* Instead, he claimed that it was the *Berkeley* that had been off course and had not heeded his signals. To this accusation, Captain Jones reiterated what First Officer Johnson had said, closing with the statement that the *Bay City* was the ferry that was off course and had given the wrong signals. Because the identity of which boat actually was off course could not be determined, the guilt for the accident could not be placed.

Damage to the *Bay City* consisted of one sheared-off rudder, a broken apron, and a number of smashed lifeboats. The *Berkeley* suffered a four-foot hole amidships and several broken steam lines.

A little more than one year later, on the afternoon of July 8, 1912, the main shaft of the *Bay City* broke while she was in mid-Bay, rendering her paddle wheels useless. In the days before radio, there was no way to communicate her plight except by using whistle signals. On board other passing ferries, passengers noticed the idled ferry and must have commented one to another, "Hey, what's that ferry tooting for?", and "Wotinell's going on with the *Bay City*? She's just sitting there whistling!" Finally, after drifting for about a half hour, the tug *Collis* came to the rescue and put a line on board. The ferry then was towed to Alameda Pier so that her passengers could debark; she then was taken to the shipyard for some emergency repairs.

The *Bay City* again was involved in a collision on January 26, 1913. This time it was the *Melrose* that crossed her path, with the usual results. The *Bay City* was making the 9:30 a.m. crossing from Alameda Pier to San Francisco, and the *Melrose* was bound for the Creek Route. When both boats had left their terminals, the weather was clear although there was a bank of dense fog lying off Goat Island. On approaching the fog bank, Captain Peter Wall of the *Bay City* slowed his ferry and posted a deckhand at the bow as a lookout. Captain John Hickey of the *Melrose* did likewise. Both boats slowly entered the fog, and visibility quickly was reduced to zero. Suddenly, one of the lookouts shouted, "Ship dead ahead!", but it was too late. With a deafening, splintering crash, the two ferries came together with a shock that jolted them from bow to stern. There was immediate panic on board both boats, as people screamed and clawed at life jackets, fearing the ferries would sink.

After the crews had calmed the passengers, the damage was surveyed. The collision had sent the bow of the *Melrose* plowing into the main deck of the *Bay City*. Although there was a big hole ripped in the side of the *Bay City,* it was decided that she would not sink, so Captain Hickey backed the *Melrose* off, and, because of damage to her bow, turned the double-ended ferry around and steamed her slowly over to the Oakland side of the bay. Captain Wall took the *Bay City* over to the Ferry Building, going ever so slowly so as to take as little water as possible. The subsequent company investigation found that both captains had exercised the utmost caution in operating through the fog bank. Consequently, neither captain was blamed for the accident and the examiners decided to blame it entirely on the extremely dense fog.

Additions to the Ferry Fleet

Early in 1911, it became apparent to the Southern Pacific that automobile and wagon traffic on the Creek Route steadily was increasing. This resulted in the decision to build a second auto ferry to be designed after the highly successful *Melrose*. The new ferry was built at the S.P. shipyard and was christened the *Thoroughfare,* the second S.P. ferry to carry that name. The new ferry was launched on October 12, 1911. She cost $170,000 and had a vehicle capacity of 97 autos and 45 teams. After being outfitted, the vessel was taken for a trial run under the command of Captain William McKenzie on the

AFTER BEING REPLACED on the transbay runs by newer and faster boats, the *Bay City* was transferred to the Crockett-South Vallejo run. Here she is seen steaming up the Napa River past Mare Island Naval Shipyard. **Southern Pacific**

afternoon of March 30, 1912. After returning from the trial run, finishing touches were made on her, and she entered service on the Creek Route on May 1, 1912.

With the *Thoroughfare* in service, the Southern Pacific rearranged the Creek Route schedules so that boats operated at 30-minute intervals throughout the day and evening. It also was announced that automobiles and horse-drawn vehicles would no longer be accepted on the ferries running from Oakland Pier except during early morning or late evening hours when the Creek Route ferries were not running. Heretofore, it had been the custom to accept autos and wagons on the Oakland Pier boats whenever space was available. Even so, only a maximum of four vehicles per trip was allowed.

The *Thoroughfare* had been in service only a little more than a year when she was involved in an accident caused by a malfunction of her ship's telegraph. Steaming up the Estuary shortly past noon on August 14, 1913, Captain James McLean signaled to slow engines for the approach to the Broadway Wharf. Getting no response from the engine room, Captain McLean signaled to reverse engines. But still there was no response, and steaming full ahead, the ferry smashed into the slip with a crash that was heard up Broadway as far as Fifth Street.

The sound of the collision emptied saloons, barber shops, and stores in short order. The quickly gathering crowd saw what had been the wharf, now demolished. The bow of the ferry had cleaved the approach and now lay on the bank of the Estuary. On board, many of the autos had been damaged and passengers had been thrown to the deck. Fortunately (for the S.P.), the ferry sustained little damage, and after repairs had been made to the telegraph system, she resumed her runs on the Creek Route.

With the launching of the *Thoroughfare*, the Southern Pacific had nine ferries operating on three routes. The *Newark, Oakland,* and *Piedmont* usually were seen on the run to Oakland Pier. The Alameda Pier route, still called by many the "Narrow Gauge Ferry," was served by the *Bay City, Encinal,* and *Berkeley*. The two auto ferries, the *Melrose* and the *Thoroughfare* were assigned to the Creek Route, assisted by the *Garden City*. With the *Amador* having been retired a few years earlier and the *El Capitan* transferred to the Crockett-

South Vallejo run, there was need for still more boats on the bay to satisfy the ever-increasing traffic.

The engineering department of the railroad, always looking for design innovations, came up with plans for a new type of large-capacity ferry for use on the heavily traveled Oakland Pier run. The design, which was a modification of that used for the *Melrose* and *Thoroughfare*, envisioned a pair of two-cylinder compound engines, one located on each side of the hull. Each engine would be connected to one paddle wheel, and each would have its own controls and stack. This design had two distinct advantages: use of a two-cylinder engine would obviate the need of the walking beam which was required of all one-cylinder engines, and the ferry would have greater maneuverability as each paddle wheel could turn independently.

Construction of the first of an order for three ferries of this type was begun at the Southern Pacific shipyard in 1912, shortly after the launching of the *Thoroughfare*. This ferry,

CHURNING a white wake, the *Thoroughfare* leaves the Ferry Building in 1927. In right distance is the approaching *Melrose*; to left is the *Alameda*. **Vernon J. Sappers Collection**

WITH A CRUSH of commuters standing on the foredecks, the *Alameda* enters the slip at the Ferry Building on a typically overcast San Francisco morning. To the right, the *Piedmont* has just left to go back to Oakland to collect another boatload; to the far right is the *Melrose* on the Creek Route.
Vernon J. Sappers Collection

which was christened the *Alameda,* was the second bay ferry to be so named. In order to get the second boat of this class underway as soon as possible, a contract was let with the New Jersey Ship Building Company for $97,000 to cover the construction of the hull. This second ferry, christened the *Santa Clara,* was completed at the Southern Pacific shipyard after the *Alameda* had been launched. The third boat of this group never was built. She was to have been named the **San Mateo**, a name that was used on an auto ferry some 10 years later.

The *Alameda* was launched in the latter part of 1913, and after outfitting, was made ready for a trial run on February 18, 1914. On that day, the new ferry was run back and forth across the Bay. It was noted that she entered into a race with the ***Berkeley,*** considered by many to be the fastest ferry on the Bay, and beat her across the Bay by a good four minutes.

A formal christening party was scheduled for the *Alameda* on Monday, February 23, at Alameda Pier. The railroad sent out 1,400 invitations to the event, which included a tour of the Bay. The official party for the christening included Miss Jeanette Kilham, who would break the traditional bottle of champagne across the bow, Alameda Mayor Frank Otis, railroad officials, and members of the Alameda Chamber of Commerce. Unfortunately, the party got a little out of hand.

Arriving at the pier, the official party found that about 400 guests already had boarded the ferry, and the Coast Guard had decreed that because the ferry was not yet certified, no additional passengers could board. Even though there still were about 1,000 ticket holders at the pier, the Coast Guard stood firm. Not being able to persuade enough people on the ferry to debark so that the official party could board, the embarrassed railroad officials suggested that the party use the Southern Pacific tug *Ajax,* which was tied up nearby. The tug, however, was not licensed to carry passengers and the Coast Guard vetoed this suggestion.

Finally, the *Alameda* whistled off, and the 1,000 disappointed ticket holders watched her steam from the slip for a three and one-half hour trip around the Bay. The ferry, under the command of Captain P.F. Wold, formerly of the ***Bay City,*** steamed over to Hunters Point and then turned north past the Ferry Building. She continued past Alcatraz Island to Sausalito, where she turned east. After traversing Raccoon Strait, she went to San Quentin Point and then over to Point Richmond. From here, the ferry made a speed run at 20 knots back to Alameda Pier, passing the Key Route Pier and Oakland Pier en route. With the arrival back at Alameda Pier, a belated christening party was held for the 400 guests who had made the tour of the Bay and the handful of others still waiting at the pier.

The following year, the ***Santa Clara*** was launched and completed. Like previous Bay ferries, she had been designed under the supervision of J.G. Camp, superintendent of floating equipment. Camp declared that the ***Santa Clara*** was by far the finest ferry yet turned out by the Southern Pacific shipyard. He also confided that he thought that she was a better boat than her sister ferry, the *Alameda.*

Talking to a reporter from the *San Francisco Examiner,*

Camp noted that the ferry had cost the railroad more than $500,000 to build. Like the *Alameda,* she was of large capacity, having seats for 1,500 passengers and enough life preservers for 3,500 persons. Being of this capacity, she was scheduled to be operated principally on the heavily traveled run to Oakland Pier.

On Saturday, July 3, 1915, the *Santa Clara* was taken for a trial run around the Bay. On the morning of that day, the new ferry left the shipyard for a preliminary run over to San Francisco. She then returned to Oakland Pier, where at 2:00 p.m. a party of company officials boarded. Leaving the pier, the *Santa Clara* steamed by Alcatraz Island and over to Sausalito. She then crossed the Golden Gate and steamed past the site of the Panama-Pacific International Exposition, arriving back at Oakland Pier in the late afternoon. In the wheelhouse during the trial run were Captains Charles Carson and C.J. Anderson, two of the skippers who were to be assigned to the new ferry when she entered revenue service the following week.

A scant six weeks after entering service, the *Santa Clara* experienced her first mishap on the Bay. The ferry was approaching the Ferry Building from Oakland Pier. As she neared the slip, Captain T.E. Talbot signaled for "Slow Ahead." With paddle wheels turning slowly, the big ferry nudged her way into the slip until she was only a few tens of feet from the apron. The captain then signaled "Stop," but Chief Engineer George Corson, in the engine room, misunderstood the signal and gave full power to the engines. The ferry suddenly surged ahead and crashed into the apron. Luckily, only a few passengers were hurt, none seriously. The only damage to the ferry was a broken section of the deck railing.

The Creek Route was better known as the Nickel Ferry because of the traditional five-cent fare for foot passengers. Periodically, the Southern Pacific attempted to put the line on a paying basis, and each time the request for a fare increase was made, it was turned down.

One of the nearly annual requests for a fare increase was filed with the California State Railroad Commission on November 12, 1912. The railroad asked for a fare hike from five cents to 10 cents in order to put the line on a parity with the fare charged from Oakland Pier.

Evidence presented at the hearing in support of the request showed that during the period from August 1 to November 1, 1912, the Creek Route ferries carried 2,473 teams, 10,785 automobiles, 7,316 motorcycles, and 30,715 foot passengers. And even with this volume of traffic, operating expenses exceeded revenues by $1,299.12. The company estimated that with an increase in passenger fares from five cents to 10 cents, the line would just about break even. The request subsequently was denied on the grounds that the 10-cent fare from Oakland Pier included the suburban trains.

In a further effort to augment revenues on the Creek Route ferries, Southern Pacific announced that starting August 15, 1915, automobiles would not be accepted on passenger ferries running from Alameda Pier. In opposition to this plan, W.J. Hanford, of the State Railroad Commission, argued that the order was discriminatory and unwarranted. He pointed out that autos still would be accepted on the freight ferries at Alameda Pier, but these ran only at infrequent intervals and they did not have the speed nor comfort of the passenger boats. Hanford claimed the Creek Route offered grossly inferior service compared with the pier boats. Although it was not publicized, he said, the last Creek Route ferry each night took an extraordinarily long time to cross the Bay. This was because of a one and one-half hour layover at Oakland Pier to take on fuel oil.

During World War I, when the Southern Pacific was operated by the United States Railroad Administration, two temporary additions were made to the ferry fleet operating between Oakland Pier and San Francisco. In order to consolidate East Bay terminal operations, the U.S.R.A. operated Santa Fe passenger trains to Oakland Pier and discontinued the use of the Santa Fe Richmond Pier.

To augment service from Oakland Pier, the U.S.R.A. transferred the Santa Fe ferries *San Pablo* and *San Pedro* to the Southern Pacific transbay route. It is reported that these two ferries were used only infrequently and spent most of the war years tied up at Oakland Pier. After the federal government returned the railroad operations to the original owners, the two Santa Fe ferries returned to the San Francisco-Richmond run.

Zone Day at the Fair

The Panama-Pacific International Exposition has been described as one of the most lavish and beautiful spectacles ever to be witnessed in the Bay Area. The exposition was located in what is now the Aquatic Park area of San Francisco. It is here that the Palace of Fine Arts still stands as a lasting memento, more than six decades after the fair ended.

During the exposition, many "days" were celebrated, ranging from Colorado Day to Women's Day and Boy Scout Day. Because the fair was held to commemorate the opening of the Panama Canal, the most important of the special days was set aside to honor the Canal Zone. This day, Thursday, May 26, 1915, was designated "Zone Day," and was marked by many special events, not the least of which was a spectacular demonstration of underwater demolition.

Plans for the demonstration called for an abandoned ship to be moored in the Bay and blown up. On the Estuary, the hulk of the ferry *Amador* was found beached and rotting on the mudflats. This once proud craft had been a river packet and later had been rebuilt as a double-ended ferry. She plied the route from Oakland Pier to the Ferry Building for many years until relegated to the up-bay run from Vallejo Junction to South Vallejo. After being retired in 1904, she was stripped of all machinery and equipment and then beached on the Estuary. For a few years, she was used as a boathouse for the University of California Rowing Club. Now deserted and abandoned, she was the ideal candidate for the munitions demonstration.

Pulled off the mud, the old ferry was taken to a local shipyard where her superstructure was torn down. In its place rose the shape of a naval gunboat. Built of timber, canvas, and papier-mache, this new-old boat was christened the *Zone* and painted in a typical wartime camouflage pattern. Sporting fake guns, triple stacks and armored wheelhouse, the *Zone* was towed across the Bay and anchored several hundred yards off the California Building at the fair.

On the morning of Zone Day, naval divers attached three mines to the hull of the *Zone*. The mines each weighed 200 pounds and carried as much explosives as had been used by the German Navy in the sinking of the *Lusitania.* By 3 o'clock that afternoon, thousands of expectant onlookers had flocked to the shore. Peering over this mass of humanity, a reporter wrote that at least 10,000 pairs of eyes must have been riveted on the *Zone,* riding calmly at anchor.

NOTE THE MARKED similarity of the *Melrose* (above) and the *Thoroughfare* (below). Minor differences included placement of windows, types of engines.
Robert W. Parkinson Collection

A launch made a final inspection trip around the gunboat and then returned to shore. A hush fell on the crowd. Suddenly, the entire ship was enveloped in a gigantic black cloud as a tremendous roar split the air. Fragments of the *Zone* could be seen hurtling hundreds of feet in the air. Moments later, after the smoke had cleared, there was nothing left of the *Zone*, nee *Amador*. She had been blown to bits. In the demonstration, the old ferry had experienced one final moment of glory, which perhaps was better than to have rotted away ignominiously on the mudflats.

Collisions between ferries seemed to occur about once a year, and near misses seemed to occur at about the same frequency. Generally, Southern Pacific boats were outpaced by the faster Key Route ferries. But it was known that if the boat of one company were to cut off an opponent, nothing would be said to the captain if he was not caught by the Coast Guard. On occasion, a captain might cut it a little too close, and although there was no collision, there was some answering to do before a panel of Coast Guard inspectors.

This was the case on the bright, brisk morning of Thursday, June 3, 1915. That day had been designated as "Alameda City Day" at the World's Fair. All schools on the Island City had been closed so that pupils and their parents could attend the festivities at the fair. Hundreds of schoolchildren and their parents crowded on board early morning trains bound for Alameda Pier. At the pier, the kids ran on board the waiting *Bay City*, filled with excitement. By the time the ferry was ready for the 8:30 departure, both decks were crowded to capacity.

Whistling off, the ferry churned its way across the Bay. When abeam of Goat Island, people near the stern noticed the orange Key Route ferry *Fernwood* rapidly overtaking the *Bay City*. As they watched, the faster ferry caught up until the two ferries were side by side, only 20 feet apart. Many of the children on the *Bay City* thought that the two ferries were racing, and they ran back and forth along the deck, shouting encouragement. Many of the more seasoned Bay travelers knew the imminent danger if the two boats moved any closer together. As the *Fernwood* slowly drew ahead, the ferries were inexorably drawn together until there was but a scant four feet of foaming water separating them.

In the wheelhouse of the *Bay City*, veteran captain Donald McKechnie had seen the *Fernwood* coming up on his starboard side, and he had pulled to port in order to keep his distance. As the *Fernwood* drew closer and closer, he slowed his ferry and finally stopped and reversed engines to avoid certain collision. It was only after the *Fernwood* had pulled ahead that Captain McKechnie signaled for "Full Ahead" and got underway again toward San Francisco.

On arriving at the Ferry Building, a number of passengers from the two ferries headed for telephones to call in a complaint to the Coast Guard. Subsequently, the two captains were called to the office of the Inspector of Hulls and Boilers to explain their dangerous actions on the Bay. Captain McKechnie stated that it obviously was the fault of the Key Route ferry, as he had done everything he could to avert a collision. Captain John Lewis, of the *Fernwood*, claimed that he did not realize that he was so close to the *Bay City*. After hearing the statements, the inspecting officer, Captain Bulger of the Coast Guard, cited Captain Lewis for operating a ferry without due caution. Turning to Captain McKechnie, the Coast Guard officer noted that the *Bay City* was carrying an unusually large number of people on that particular trip. Because the number of passengers was in excess of the certified limit for the ferry, Captain McKechnie was cited for operating an overloaded ferry.

A little more than four months later, on Saturday, October 30, passengers on the *Oakland* were witnesses to a potentially dangerous accident. On this day, which had been one of beautiful fall weather, many people had gone to the World's Fair which soon was to close. Returning to the Ferry Building, many hundreds of people boarded the *Oakland* for the 6:30 p.m. departure for the East Bay. Shortly after leaving the ferry slip, there was a sudden crash that sounded like an explosion, followed by ripping and pounding noises. Without warning, the pin that held the shaft to the walking beam had snapped, sending the heavy steel shaft lurching forward and down through the cabin roof, narrowly missing a number of passengers.

Sitting helpless in the water several hundred yards off the Ferry Building, the *Oakland* waited to be rescued. Soon the faithful tug *Ajax* arrived from Oakland Pier to tow the big ferry across the Bay. The tug, with the ferry in tow, arrived at Oakland Pier at 8:10, about an hour late. After being nudged into the slip to discharge her passengers, the *Oakland* was taken to the shipyard for needed repairs.

Oakland Long Wharf was a landmark on the eastern side of San Francisco Bay. Built on tide and submerged lands leased from the City of Oakland, the facility became the subject of a dispute between the city and the S.P. On the one hand, the city claimed that the wharf was a menace to navigation and should be removed when the current lease expired on December 31, 1918. The railroad countered that the facility, although acknowledged to be inadequate, served a very definite purpose to Bay shipping. The railroad further announced that it had long-range plans to fill a large area of tidelands south of Oakland Pier. This filled ground would be the site of a modern freight yard and car ferry terminal. This announcement prompted the City of Oakland to renew its efforts to get a termination of the lease and the removal of the wharf. It was rumored that the city, while publicly claiming that the pier was unsafe and a hazard to navigation, actually wanted to gain control of the facility so that the municipal Harbor Department could operate it as part of the proposed Oakland Outer Harbor plan.

In the early part of 1918, the railroad petitioned the City for a five-year extension of the lease on the pier. The reason given was that this would allow the railroad sufficient time to complete the new facilities south of Oakland Pier. On March 17, the City reaffirmed its stand on the removal of the pier and denied the granting of any time extension on the lease. In reply to the City, William Sproule, President of the Southern Pacific, argued that the railroad did not have a sufficient work force to remove the pier after the termination of the lease. Furthermore, because the railroads had come under the wartime authority of the U.S. Railroad Administration, Sproule claimed that the dispute over the removal of the pier now lay between the City of Oakland and the federal government.

Finally, as 1918 drew to a close, agreement was reached between the railroad, the Railroad Administration, and the City with regard to the abandonment and removal of Oakland Long Wharf. On December 31 of that year, the old structure formally was abandoned, ending nearly 48 years of railroading in mid-bay. Demolition of the pier began in January 1919, and by the following April, all traces of it had disappeared. It is interesting to note that most of the 50-year-old pilings of the pier were in a remarkable state of preservation. So unusual was their condition that a research team from the American Wood Preserving Association examined them and could find only a few instances of damage by teredo worms or other marine borers.

WESTERN PACIFIC MOLE forms the background as the *Garden City* plies the Creek Route.   **Southern Pacific**

Fog on the Bay

Fog always has been a source of trouble on the Bay. As ferries and ships crept slowly through the gloom, whistles and bells sounding, lookouts were ever on the watch, hoping that nothing would cross the bow. It seemed that whenever the fog settled, the car ferry *Transit* would come to some sort of grief. Usually it was nothing more serious than an unintentional sideswipe or the splintering of some pilings. However, the car ferry experienced a potentially dangerous encounter on the morning of February 8, 1917, in a very dense fog.

The car ferry was heading slowly for China Cove with its usual load of freight cars, when suddenly off the port bow loomed the shape of a large ship. Turning the wheel sharply to avoid a direct collision, the captain of the *Transit* almost managed to steer clear, but momentum carried the heavily laden ferry crashing sideways into the ship, which was the Dutch freighter *Soerkarta* carrying more than 3,000 tons of high explosives. Fortunately, the collision did little damage to the freighter, which was riding at anchor, but it wrecked the portside paddle box and paddle wheel of the ferry. After limping to port and discharging her freight cars, the *Transit* had to be towed across the Bay for repairs.

That same year, the *Encinal* nearly was sunk in thick fog on the night of October 29, while steaming slowly down the Estuary. The ferry had made her last trip to Broadway Wharf and was on her way down to the S.P. shipyard to tie up for the night. At about the same time that she left Broadway Wharf, the brand new Western Fuel Company tug *Biddle* was making ready for her maiden departure from the Moore and Scott shipyard. On board the tug was Captain Andy Steele who was to take the tug across the Estuary to the home berth. Backing out into the water, Captain Steele failed to see the approaching *Encinal*. On board the ferry, Captain Nils A. Jacobsen was unaware of any other water traffic near him, and consequently he was startled when the tug backed into the slowly moving ferry.

After the collision, the 15 members of the ferry crew scurried around to survey the damage. Below decks, it was found that the ferry was taking large amounts of water through a hole on the starboard side. Informed of this, Captain Jacobsen decided to make a run for the shipyard before the ferry sank in the Estuary. However, with the added speed, water began to pour into the hull at an alarming rate, and the captain decided that it would be more prudent to try to beach the ferry than to have her sink in the middle of the Estuary.

Steering toward the shore, Captain Jacobsen grounded the ferry on a sand bar, where with a slight list, she sat. After assuring himself that the ferry was neither in danger of sinking nor floating off, the captain set up marker lights on the boat. With that, he and his crew lowered a lifeboat and rowed ashore, planning to return in the morning with help from the shipyard.

With the arrival of morning light, Coast Guard personnel arrived at the scene of the apparently abandoned ferry. After making their inspection, they summoned Captain Jacobsen and Captain Steele to the Coast Guard offices to inform them of their respective breaches of marine law. Captain Jacobsen was cited for abandoning a vessel in a navigable waterway, and Captain Steele was cited for improperly operating a vessel and for not posting lookouts to warn him of approaching ships.

Collisions were not the only newsworthy items to develop on the Bay. Occasionally, there was an incident that reflected human pathos. One such incident occurred on board the *Melrose* on July 9, 1917, just after the ferry had made its 6:20 p.m. departure from the Ferry Building. The ferry, bound for the Creek Route, had taken on board the usual number of autos and foot passengers. Just after the ferry had cleared the slip, a man jumped from the upper deck into the Bay.

Hearing the yell, "Man overboard!", Captain William Richter immediately stopped his ferry. A lifeboat, manned by two deckhands, quickly was launched from the aft port side of the ferry. As soon as the lifeboat was in the water, the *Melrose* unexpectedly began to back, sucking the foaming water into its paddle wheels. To the horror of the passengers leaning over the rail to watch the rescue, the lifeboat was sucked into the paddle wheel and crushed to matchsticks. With engines stopped, a second lifeboat was launched and the bodies of the two deckhands were retrieved from the water as well as the man who had nearly drowned in his attempt at suicide.

Returning to the slip, Captain Richter asked that he be relieved of his command for the rest of the day as he was very distraught over the deaths of his two deckhands. About a half hour later, the *Melrose* again left the slip with Captain Samuel Forsberg at the wheel.

At the ensuing investigation, Captain Richter insisted that his order to reverse engines had not caused the death of his deckhands. Instead, he claimed, the wake from the *Thoroughfare*, which was just entering the adjacent slip, had thrust the lifeboat under the churning paddle wheels of the *Melrose*. However, the investigators found the captain guilty of improperly operating a ferry as it was noted that a captain is fully responsible for whatever may occur during his command.

On the afternoon of December 23, 1919, the *Encinal* again was the victim of a fog-shrouded collision. This time, the Mexican freighter *Korrigan III* collided with the ferry with a crash that was heard throughout the Ferry Building. The *Encinal*, working the Creek Route, slowly was approaching the Ferry Building in a strong ebbtide; the freighter was moving up-bay at about two knots. The freighter crashed into the ferry just forward of the starboard paddle box, creating a deep gash that allowed torrents of water to pour into her hull.

On the main deck of the ferry were about 50 automobiles that were parked so close together that after the collision, the occupants of the cars could not open their doors and had to crawl out of the windows. Running to the life-preserver racks, the screaming passengers found tightly nailed slats holding the preservers in their racks. Being unable to pull them free, the passengers became panic-stricken, and the fear was heightened as the ferry slowly began to list to starboard. With the ferry crew trying to maintain order, Captain Charles Crowdace got the *Encinal* underway again and was able to make it the remaining 500 feet to the Ferry Building.

After tying up, the damage to the ferry was surveyed, and it was found that she had suffered some $2,000 worth of damage to her starboard side. In addition, some of the passengers had been injured and one of the automobiles had been badly damaged. There had been no apparent damage to the *Korrigan III*. The subsequent investigation of the collision revealed that Captain Crowdace had not been giving his required fog whistle signals, hence the skipper of the freighter had no way of knowing that the ferry was crossing his course. Furthermore, the tightly nailed slats on the life-preserver racks were noted and the Southern Pacific was reprimanded for not having the necessary safety equipment in a readily obtainable condition.

A FIRE which started in the engine room nearly destroyed the *Santa Clara* in 1915. The ferry is seen at the S.P. Shipyard in Oakland, a hulking ruin. She subsequently was rebuilt and steamed across the Bay for another quarter century. **Vernon J. Sappers Collection**

IN FIRM COMMAND of the roadway, this seven-car train, headed by car 312, makes the station stop at Morton Street on the Encinal Ave. line. Destination sign reads SAN FRANCISCO VIA ALAMEDA PIER; train will return to pier via Lincoln Ave. line. Line drawing made from this photo adorned early-day suburban timetables. Porthole front windows appeared later.

Southern Pacific

CHAPTER 12

The Big Red Trains

THE NEARLY 10 years from the completion of the electrification of the East Bay suburban lines until 1920 was a decade that demonstrated one inescapable fact: that the operations were far from profitable. This situation remained true in spite of swollen revenues brought by World War I and its dramatic rise in passenger traffic. All during this time, Southern Pacific continually sought fare increases and even proposed the sale of the entire ferry and rail system to any independent operator. There were no takers.

Perhaps the most striking development during this period so far as the average man on the street was concerned was the change of color of the trains in 1912 from the dull, drab green used on mainline equipment to a sprightly cherry red. This livery, which previously had been adopted on the Pacific Electric, was selected in the belief that a red car would be more visible during periods of inclement weather than would one that was painted the traditional green. This color, from which the terms "The Big Red Cars" and "The Red Trains" developed, was adopted on many Southern Pacific electric properties.

The first cars to appear in the new color were placed in service on August 19, 1912. Subsequently, all equipment was repainted as it was sent through the shops for servicing. Even so, it was a number of years before all cars were repainted, and it was not uncommon to see a mixture of red and green cars in one train.

On July 1, 1912, the Southern Pacific adopted a new type of commute ticket. The company had found that many commuters were lending their tickets to other members of their families, and thus, in the eyes of the railroad, they were cheating. In an attempt to curb this practice, the company required purchasers of July commute tickets to be identified by sex. Women's monthly tickets were printed on pink stock with the word *FEMALE* overprinted in red; the men's tickets were on blue stock and were overprinted with *MALE*.

At that same time, the railroad announced a new policy on car advertising. In the days of the steam locals, the interiors of cars were filled with advertisements ranging from clothing to patent medicines. Because the new electric cars had been tastefully designed, the railroad decided that they would not carry any of the unsightly signs. It was expected that the absence of advertising would attract new riders which would offset the loss of revenue from the advertisements.

Also in July, it was reported that the Brown News Company would continue to operate newsstands on the ferries and at the stations as before and would provide the ever-popular

EARLY-DAY MEET: A Shattuck Ave. and a California Street train meet at Thousand Oaks. Area today is a bustling suburban business district.
Vernon J. Sappers Collection

"news butchers" on the electric trains. The "news butcher" was an all-important person on most commute runs, where he could be seen going from car to car, hawking his papers, peanuts, and chewing gum. Although a holdover from the days of the steam locals, he was considered by many to be an essential service to the commuting public.

The press noted that the Brown News Company and the railroad mutually shared in a most profitable business. The news company paid the railroad 23 per cent of its gross sales on the trains and 12½ per cent of the gross sales on the ferries and at the stations. In 1911, total sales by the news company amounted to $471,400, of which the railroad received $103,000.

The Havenscourt Rate War

On July 29, 1913, the East Oakland Protective League requested the California Railroad Commission to find that the 15-cent single fare to stations east of Melrose was discriminatory. The League noted that while Seminary Avenue was only 11.8 miles from San Francisco, a passenger riding to that point had to pay the second-zone, 15-cent fare. In contrast, a passenger bound for Thousand Oaks, which was 12.1 miles from San Francisco, paid only the first-zone, 10-cent fare.

In answer to the charges, the representatives of the Southern Pacific pointed out two important facts. First, the lower fare to Thousand Oaks was due to competition with the Key Route. Second, because of the existing fare structure, the Oakland, Alameda and Berkeley lines were far from profitable. For the fiscal year ending June 30, 1913, the system showed a deficit of $383,982. This figure included only out-of-pocket costs; it did not include either interest on capital investments or payments to sinking funds. This deficit represented a loss of 17 cents for each passenger carried on the trains and ferries. Thus, instead of lowering second-zone fares, the railroad men insisted that the entire fare structure should be modified upward.

The S.P. published figures which showed operating revenues were $1,339,636, while expenses were $1,723,618. Also revealed was the fact that during June 1913, 24,780 trains were operated and 1,733,191 passengers were carried. Finally, valuation figures were presented which showed that the East Bay suburban system had a total valuation of $40,119,116. This figure included $32,387,138 worth of real estate, $2,756,345 worth of rolling stock, and $567,397 worth of floating equipment.

After hearing all of the testimony, the Railroad Commission denied the plea for reduced fares to points east of Melrose. The Commission also found that there was insufficient justification for a general increase in transbay fares at that time.

With the plea for reduced fares denied, the members of the East Oakland Protective League met and decided to take matters into their own hands. On the morning of October 1, 1913, a number of men gathered in an open field near the tracks of the Melrose Extension. Led by Walter Leimert of the Wickham-Havens Real Estate Company, the men erected a barricade across the tracks near the entrance to the Havens Court subdivision. The barricade consisted of ties, earth, and rail, all of which was tied together with strands of barbed wire, and was emplaced after the first three trains had gone by. When the fourth train arrived, it slowed to a stop, unable to proceed any further.

Getting off their train, the crew surveyed the situation under the watchful eyes of Leimert and his group. After talking the matter over, the crew began pulling timbers off the track and shoveling the earth out of the way. However, as soon as one tie was pulled free, another would be tossed onto the pile. This continued until it was time for the train to start its run for Oakland Pier. After the train had departed, the barricade was built up and further strengthened.

When the train arrived at Melrose, word was passed to the station agent of the difficulty at Havenscourt. This information was relayed to San Francisco and a call was made to the Oakland Police Department for assistance. Soon a police patrol arrived at the scene, but as there was no violence, the police merely stood by, claiming that this was not a police matter but rather was one for the State Railroad Commission to decide. That whole day, no trains got past the barricade, and passengers from the San Leandro shuttle car were forced to walk around the barricade in order to board the pier-bound trains.

The next day, the war of nerves was settled when a delegation from the East Oakland Protective League and the realty company called on the railroad management at the S.P.'s Flood Building offices. After a long discussion, the residents of the Havenscourt area agreed with the railroad point of view with regard to operating expenses and revenues. On their return to Havenscourt, the train stopped at the barricade. After alighting, the expeditionary party announced that the matter was settled and that the barricade was to be removed. With a certain amount of grumbling, the men joined the train crew in pulling down the barrier, and by midafternoon, trains were rolling again past the site of the skirmish.

Even after the outward effects of the Havenscourt rate war had died down, there was widespread disenchantment with the railroad on the part of many civic leaders in the East Bay. On October 3, 1913, a meeting was held at the Oakland City Hall to discuss the problems of local transportation. At the meeting, Mayors Frank K. Mott of Oakland, Charles D. Heywood of Berkeley, and Frank Otis of Alameda, and other civic dignitaries, discussed the possibility of the formation of a public utility district for the purpose of acquiring and operating the local and transbay properties of the Southern Pacific and the Key Route.

The initial meeting and its subsequent sessions produced general agreement in the area of the formation of such a district. Those present felt that the operators were providing inferior service at a fare that was excessively high, but when the matter of the cost of acquisition of the systems was discussed, it was realized that it would be extremely difficult to get the necessary financial backing. At this juncture, the matter rested and no further meetings were held. However, as the years went by, the germ of the idea of public ownership remained alive and reappeared periodically. This notion ulti-

STILL IN GREEN paint, and still sporting squared-off front windows, car 330 suns itself on the lead to the inspection bay at West Alameda Shops. **R.S. Ford Collection**

mately came into full bloom a half century later, long after the Southern Pacific had withdrawn from the local transportation field.

As it had done in previous years, the Southern Pacific approached the State Railroad Commission in 1914 with a concerted effort to win an across-the-board fare increase. Formal application was made on April 12, when a brief was filed seeking to raise the first-zone single fare from 10 cents to either 12½ cents or 15 cents. Formal hearings on the rate increase were held in the Commission chambers on June 16, 1914. The railroad was represented by its principal legal advisor, C.W. Durbrow. The opposition consisted of the County of Alameda as well as all of the incorporated cities served by the Oakland, Alameda and Berkeley lines. Legal counsel for the opposition was led by Benjamin E. Woolner, city attorney for Oakland, assisted by Frank V. Cornish, city attorney for Berkeley.

Durbrow presented testimony which showed that the 1912 expansion of the system had cost the railroad $4,314,378, and the total value of the electric system now was $26,553,667. He pointed out that with increased labor costs, the O.A. & B. lines were losing 11.7 cents for each 10-cent passenger. These losses amounted to a total of $58,000 per month during the year 1913. Obviously, Durbrow argued, the present fares were totally noncompensatory and were confiscatory as they did not reflect a fair return on the capital invested in the electric system.

Paul Shoup, Assistant to the President of the Southern Pacific, then was called to testify. He observed that the Southern Pacific system as a whole would be better off financially without the electric suburban system if the present deficits were allowed to continue. If the Commission authorized the railroad to increase its rates, he said, it should do so without any consideration to the traffic which would be diverted to the Key Route. Shoup went on to point out that the Southern Pacific would be willing to sell its East Bay suburban lines either to the Key Route or the Santa Fe. He added, however, that it was common knowledge that the Key Route had not been meeting its own operating expenses and had been for sale for the last two years. On its own, the Key Route had approached the Santa Fe with a purchase plan, but had been politely but firmly turned down. The Santa Fe was not interested in getting into the local transportation field.

After hearing all of the arguments showing that the Southern Pacific was losing money and hearing the representatives of the various cities argue against any fare increase, the Commission, on October 13, denied the railroad any fare increase at all. This announcement was not entirely unexpected, and after reading the decision, one of the attorneys for the railroad was heard to say, "Well, all right, we'll be back next year!"

Dissolution

In June 1913, the United States Government forced the dissolution of the Union Pacific and Southern Pacific railroads into two independent corporations. This edict ended what had been identified as the Harriman Lines, a railroad which stretched from San Francisco east to Chicago as well as north to Portland, south to Los Angeles, and southeast to New Orleans. The western portion of the former Harriman Lines consisted of the combined operations of the Central Pacific, Southern Pacific, and the Texas and New Orleans Railroads. These, along with certain subsidiaries, formed the nucleus of the new Southern Pacific.

In connection with the dissolution, the Southern Pacific announced that it would gather all of its electric properties under the corporate heading of the Pacific Electric Railway. Paul Shoup, formerly of the Pacific Electric, would be president of the new corporation, and William Norton, general manager of the Oakland, Alameda and Berkeley Lines was designated as vice president. It was proposed that one division of the new P.E. would include all existing operations in Southern California. Other divisions would include the Peninsular Railway, San Jose Railroads, Stockton Electric Railway, Monterey Electric Railway, and the Oakland, Alameda and Berkeley Lines. Ultimately, the enlarged Pacific Electric also would include the Southern Pacific interurban system then under construction from Portland south to Corvallis. It was announced that long-range plans for the further enlargement would include the electrification of the Coast Line, running from San Francisco to Los Angeles. Along this line would be operated deluxe high-speed interurban trains running between the two cities.

Also being considered was the electrification of the main line north to Portland, the Northwestern Pacific line from San Rafael to Eureka, and an extension of the Pacific Electric Santa Ana line south to San Diego. In all, this would create an electric interurban railroad stretching some 1,000 miles from Portland, on the north, to San Diego, on the south. In addition, there would be another 1,000 miles of branch and local lines, resulting in the largest interurban railway system in the world.

One of the first tasks in the implementation of this scheme would be to bring labor costs on the O.A. & B. under control. At that time, Pacific Electric employees were members of the local street railway union and received wages that were on a parity with workers of other street railways. In contrast, employees of the O.A. & B. were members of the Brotherhood of Railway Trainmen, and being railroad employees, they received higher wages. The S.P. felt that the O.A. & B. lines were interurban in character, and the idea was to make O.A. & B. wages conform to the lower P.E. rates.

When the Brotherhood of Railway Trainmen heard of this plan, the immediate reaction was to place a strike call against the railroad in the event that the plan was implemented. Representatives of the brotherhood called on E.E. Calvin, vice president of the railroad, to inform him that any attempt to place streetcar men on the suburban trains would be met with an immediate strike of the entire Southern Pacific system.

To this, Calvin stated that the new electric system would be operated by an entirely independent corporation which would operate with leased equipment over leased trackage. Because of its independence from the Southern Pacific, the new operator would be free to enter into any labor agreements that it chose. Calvin further stated that although the new company might use platform men on the Crosstown line, it tentatively planned to use only brotherhood employes on the pier trains. Inconclusively, the union and the railroad discontinued further negotiations. Left unanswered were a number of important questions: Would the employees of the O.A. & B. Lines be reclassified as streetcar men? What would the pay scale be when the Pacific Electric took over? How would Southern Pacific seniority be protected when the new operation began?

When negotiations broke off on July 27, 1913, the brotherhood polled its members on a strike vote. When the ballots were counted, the vote was found to be overwhelmingly in

INTERIOR of the Oakland Pier trainshed was immense and cavernous. From left (above) are trains for the 18th Street, Ellsworth and Shattuck Ave. lines; at right is Seventh Street train. View (below) taken from the platform of the Shattuck train looks west toward the Bay. California Street train is in distance; Seventh Street train to left. **Addison H. Laflin Jr. Collection**

favor of a walkout. At the same time, the Order of Railway Conductors voted in favor of supporting the B.R.T. walkout.

Because of the strike vote and the fact that neither the railroad nor the brotherhood could agree on the basic issues, both parties agreed to binding arbitration under the terms of the Newlands Arbitration Act, which had been passed by the Congress the previous year. The Board of Arbiters in the dispute consisted of M.E. Montgomery, Vice President of the Brotherhood of Railway Trainmen; W.R. Scott, General Manager of the Southern Pacific; and Judge John F. Davis. The board's findings, announced on October 18, 1913, scuttled the S.P. plan for good.

The Board held that the Oakland, Alameda and Berkeley lines were an integral part of the Southern Pacific and could neither be leased to another company nor be covered by any labor contract differing from that of the mainline operations. Thus, the expansion of the Pacific Electric Railway into Northern California never materialized.

With the forced separation of the Union Pacific Railroad and the Southern Pacific Company, the United States Government began action to force a similar separation of the Central Pacific from the Southern Pacific. On February 11, 1914, the Justice Department filed a petition for dissolution in the Federal Court for the District of Utah. The petition claimed that the union of the Southern Pacific and the Central Pacific violated both the Pacific Railroad Act of July 1, 1862 and the Sherman Anti-Trust Act.

In arguments heard before Circuit Judges Sanborn, Hook, and Carland, the government argued that a transcontinental route formed from a merger of the Central Pacific and Union Pacific would be a logical competitor for the Southern Pacific route which stretched from San Francisco to New Orleans. The Southern Pacific replied that the Central Pacific and the Southern Pacific were so closely tied that it would be impractical and damaging to try to sever them. Furthermore, the railroad stated that because the federal government previously had ordered the Southern Pacific to assume and pay the debts of the Central Pacific, the government could not now dissolve the union without paying substantial damages.

After three years of hearing testimony and analyzing briefs, the court handed down a decision on May 10, 1917, denying the petition for dissolution. The court noted that doubt had been cast on whether any antitrust law could affect proprietary relations established prior to passage of the law. The court concluded that the long history of the control of the Central Pacific by the Southern Pacific had shown in itself not to be injurious to shippers or to the general public.

The decision of the court was greeted with a great sigh of relief at Southern Pacific headquarters, for if the ruling had gone the other way, the transportation history of the Bay Area would have been drastically altered. All of the trackage then owned by the Central Pacific would have been divorced from the Southern Pacific. This action would have required the Seventh Street line to be operated by a separate company.

HEAVY-DUTY railroading and street running mixed on the S.P. This was the Seventh and Webster interlocking tower, perched like an eagle's roost above the intersection. In this mid-1910 era, there were 25 S.P. trains and streetcars crossing each hour.
Vernon J. Sappers Collection

Although the Southern Pacific would have retained control of the lines in Alameda, the Webster and 18th Street lines, and the lines to Berkeley east of Shellmound, Oakland Pier and the main line through 16th Street Station would have been the property of its principal competitor.

With the announcement of the court decision, it was rumored that Robert S. Lovett, President of the Union Pacific, had spurred the government into action because he was eagerly seeking an entrance into San Francisco Bay. It was further alleged that the Union Pacific would be willing to pay $100 million for the purchase of the entire trackage of the Central Pacific. As an alternative, the U.P. was said to be willing to buy control of the Western Pacific Railroad for $30 million. With the passage of time, neither of these proposals came to fruition, and never again was there a serious challenge on the home grounds of the Southern Pacific.

Sightseeing Trains

In order to capitalize on the expected tourist trade generated by the Panama-Pacific International Exposition in 1915, the Southern Pacific announced that it would operate a daily sight-seeing train during the Fair season. The proposal undoubtedly was derived from the profitable sight-seeing business provided by the Pacific Electric Railway in the Los Angeles area.

It was planned that a train of specially built observation cars, having oversized windows and manned by special attendants, would leave Alameda Pier each morning. This train would run along the Encinal Avenue line and the Fernside Loop to the Fruitvale Avenue Bridge and the powerhouse, where a brief stop would be made so that passengers could detrain and inspect this noteworthy facility. The sight-seeing train would then run down the Seventh Street line to Oakland Pier and out the Shattuck Avenue line to Berkeley Station. A motor bus would meet the train at this stop to take passengers on a side trip through the University of California campus.

After the passengers had returned, the train would continue out Shattuck Avenue to Thousand Oaks, Albany, and the Ninth Street line. Arriving back at 16th Street Station, the train would go by way of the 18th Street line to 14th and Franklin Streets. After a stop for lunch, the train would return to Alameda by way of the Webster Street line, arriving there in time for a midafternoon ferry for San Francisco.

After public announcements had been made that the service would be operated during the 1915 Fair season, the plan dropped from sight. A brief mention of it appeared in the fall of 1915, stating that the railroad still was contemplating running the service and that it might start some time in 1916. By the summer of 1916, however, the plan had been all but forgotten as the railroad by then was involved in more pressing matters.

In anticipation of additional passenger traffic from the World's Fair, the Southern Pacific streamlined its system of fare collection at the Ferry Building for eastbound trips. Heretofore, tickets were required prior to boarding the East Bay ferries, forcing cash fare riders to stand in line to buy a ticket before they could go through the turnstiles. On February 16, 1915, a new cash fare system was instituted. Coin boxes were installed at the turnstiles so that patrons could drop their dimes or commute tickets in while passing through.

SUBURBAN right-of-way was immaculate in early days. This view shows outer end of Seventh Street line on what is now Bancroft Ave.; dirt road crossing tracks is now 80th Ave.
Vernon J. Sappers Collection

The year 1915 also brought the announcement that the lease on the company offices in the Flood Building was due to expire. Rather than pay the $22,000 monthly rental, the railroad was considering constructing its own corporate headquarters. Three sites were under study: one in Oakland at the site of the 14th and Franklin Streets Station and two in downtown San Francisco.

On June 19, 1915, the Board of Directors of the railroad, while meeting in New York, approved the construction of a 12-story office building at the Oakland site. The proposal for the $1 million structure was enthusiastically received by the Oakland City Council, which felt that with the establishment of the main headquarters of the Southern Pacific in Oakland, that city was well on its way to becoming a business center to rival San Francisco. The Council allowed the railroad almost any latitude in the construction of the new building, and the only restriction that was placed on the plan was that construction must start by January 1, 1917.

After the announcement that the new building site had been chosen, a reporter from the *San Francisco Examiner* queried railroad president William Sproule as to when the company actually would move across the Bay. To this, he replied gruffly, "No comment." As it turned out, the proposal to go over to Oakland was merely a feint, as at that same time, the

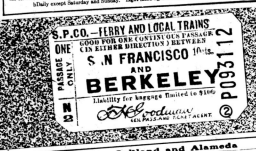

EAST BAY SUBURBAN 1908-

FIGURE 5

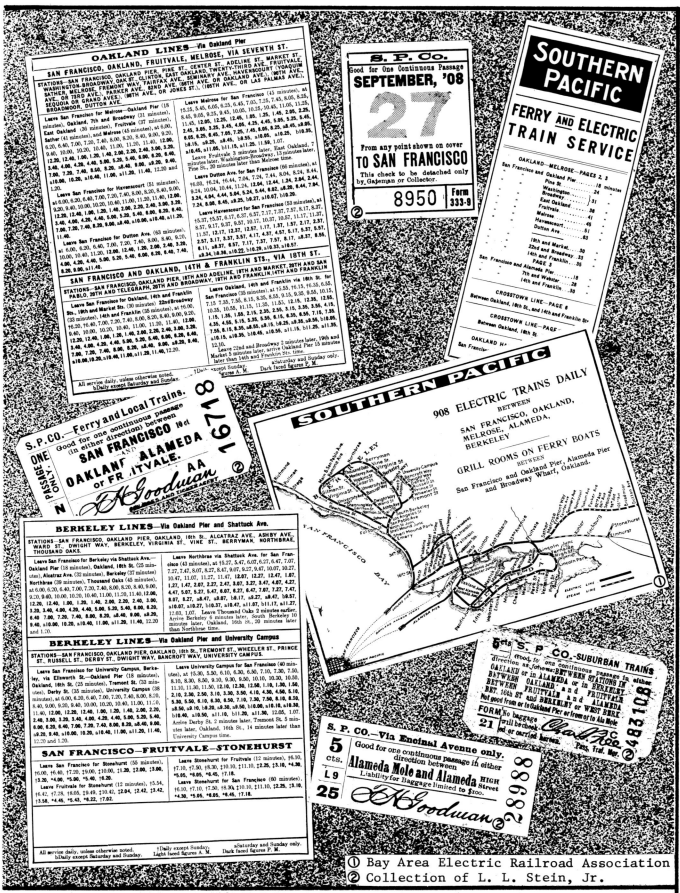

① Bay Area Electric Railroad Association
② Collection of L. L. Stein, Jr.

SCHEDULES & TICKETS
-1916

railroad quietly was buying up property near the foot of Market Street, where would rise the landmark known in later years simply as "65 Market Street."

In mid-1916, the S.P. announced that all electrified trackage it owned in the East Bay would be transferred to certain of its subsidiary companies. This was to be done in line with company policy that the Southern Pacific Company was to be an operating company only and was not directly to own any trackage. At that time, the former steam local lines already were owned by subsidiaries: the original line out Seventh Street as far as Melrose was owned by the Central Pacific Railway; the Berkeley main line as far as old Berryman Station was owned by the Southern Pacific Railroad; and the lines in Alameda as well as the Webster Street line all were owned by the South Pacific Coast Railway.

Of the newly constructed electric lines, which at that time were owned by the Southern Pacific Company, the tracks of the Melrose Extension were to be transferred to the Central Pacific for the sum of $567,738.58. In Berkeley, the Ellsworth Street, California Street, and Ninth Street lines as well as the Shattuck Avenue line east of old Berryman Station were to be transferred to the Southern Pacific Railroad for $1,774,790.66. The trackage of the 18th Street line would be transferred to the Peninsular Railway for $913,423.78. All of these amounts represented the actual costs of construction plus six per cent interest to June 30, 1916.

After the transfer of ownership, the subsidiary companies would lease the trackage to the Southern Pacific Company for a monthly rental fee. The fee would be of a similar magnitude as the rental of the Alameda trackage from the South Pacific Coast Railway, for which the Southern Pacific Company paid $26,360.22 per month. The only facilities to be retained by the Southern Pacific Company would be the Fruitvale Powerhouse and the two substations.

Composite Equivalent

As it had done nearly every year since 1914, the Southern Pacific applied to the California State Railroad Commission in 1917 for an across-the-board rate increase. A hearing was held on August 3 before Commissioners Frank Devlin, E.O. Edgerton, and Max Thielen; the railroad claimed that it had lost more than $500,000 on the East Bay suburban operations during 1916. This figure did not reflect any interest payments on the $26 million invested in the new system but represented only the losses due to operating costs. The representatives of the railroad noted that there had not been an increase in the basic commute rate of $3 in nearly 50 years. As background for the existing fare rate, a letter was introduced from James Horsborough, Jr., Assistant to the General Manager of the railroad and addressed to G.W. Weeks, President of the San Francisco-Oakland Terminal Railways. A portion of the letter quoted Leland Stanford, President of the railroad in 1869, as saying, "I want the monthly commute rate to be $3 because I want to do something for the average East Bay working man and his family."

Counsel for the railroad then presented data showing that in 1916, the operating costs of the East Bay electric lines were $2,333,276, while revenues were only $1,775,471, resulting in a deficit of $557,805. The lawyer then observed that the East Bay electric lines had been for sale for some time, but nobody was making any offers.

The commission then was presented with a proposed rate increase which the railroad felt reflected current operating expenses. Rather than rely on a flat 10-cent single fare and $3 monthly commutation rate to most East Bay stations, the railroad presented a fare schedule which scaled upward from a 10-cent single and $3 commute fare from San Francisco to Oakland Pier or Alameda Pier to a 35-cent single and $5.40 commute fare to Thousand Oaks and 35-cent single and $5.05 commute fare to High Street. The fare to Broadmoor and Dutton Avenue would go from a 20-cent single and $4 commute to a 50-cent single and $6.55 commute fare. Mayor Davies, of Oakland, called the rate proposal "ridiculous and uncalled for." He vowed that he would fight the increase with all of the powers granted to him by the Oakland city charter. Mayor Greene of Alameda agreed to support Davies. The Alameda mayor noted that the Key Route also was planning a similar increase, and urged the cities to present a united front against both of these companies. Soon, all of the civic groups in the East Bay were aligned against the two transit operators, and when hearings on the rate increase were resumed in November, they were well represented. At the hearings, the State Railroad Commission took note of the hue and cry of the commuter groups, civic organizations, municipal governments, and nearly everyone else. Ultimately, the Commission handed down a decision denying any rate increase at that time. As before, the railroad representatives vowed, "We'll be back next year!"

In a subsequent effort to reduce taxes on a part of the system, the Southern Pacific applied to the California State Board of Equalization to divorce the Creek Route from the balance of the system for taxation purposes. The railroad contended that the Creek Route was a purely local operation and was not a part of the intrastate railroad system. Thus, it was felt that there should be a lower tax rate on the Creek Route ferries than on the remainder of the system. On March 23, 1918, the Board of Equalization denied the claim of the railroad, reaffirming the contention that the Creek Route was part of the entire Southern Pacific system and should be taxed at the higher rate. With the announcement of this decision, the railroad filed suit against State Treasurer Friend W. Richardson, asking the court to reverse the decision of the Board of Equalization and also to refund $70,843.53 in excess taxes paid to the state. At the conclusion of the trial, Superior Court Judge Sturtevant found for the S.P. and ordered that the refund be paid.

In January 1918, the State Railroad Commission again held hearings on proposals by the Southern Pacific and Key Route to increase the basic transbay fare, this time from 10 cents to 15 cents for the first zone. As before, the various cities and civic groups mounted a concerted effort to block any such increase. After the railroads had presented their data showing that the transbay operations were continually losing money, the opponents unveiled to the Commission a bold plan that was called the "Composite Equivalent." As envisioned, this plan would eliminate some $10 million worth of duplicate facilities and would result in a simplified transbay operation run by only one railway. It was claimed that the proposal would result in annual savings in excess of $1 million due to greatly lowered costs. This, in turn, could result in a lower overall fare structure.

Under the "Composite Equivalent" plan, all lines offering duplicate service would be abandoned. For example, the Southern Pacific 18th Street line would be abandoned in favor of the Key Route 22nd Street line. In Berkeley, the Southern Pacific Ellsworth Street line would be discontinued in favor of the Key Route Alcatraz Avenue line, and the Key Route Berkeley-Shattuck Avenue line would be abandoned east of Alcatraz Avenue as it served the same area as the Southern Pacific Berkeley-Shattuck Avenue line. The plan also called for the combination of the Southern Pacific California Street line with the Key Route Sacramento Street line. Under the plan, trackage would be retained along Sacramento Street, from Stanford Avenue to Rose Tower, and along the California Street line from there to Thousand Oaks. The resulting line, to be known as the Sacramento Street-Thousand Oaks line would be operated by the Southern Pacific.

The "Composite Equivalent" plan also called for the abandonment of two of the three ferry terminals on the Bay. All ferries and electric trains would use the facilities at Oakland Pier. The Key Route pier either would be abandoned or turned over to the Santa Fe for use by its mainline trains. The Key Route trains would be switched onto the Southern Pacific tracks near the foot of 40th Street for the run to Oakland Pier. Alameda trains would use the Webster Street Bridge and Seventh Street for their access to Oakland Pier.

After the presentation of the "Composite Equivalent" plan, a number of technical problems emerged. First, there was the problem of operating voltages. While the Southern Pacific operated at 1,200 volts, Key Route operated at only 600 volts. Thus it would be impossible for the trains of one railroad to operate on the tracks of the other without extensive and costly modifications. Second, there was the question of the identity of the surviving railroad and its labor relations. The entire Southern Pacific operation was staffed with members of the various railway brotherhoods. Key Route employes all were streetcar men and were paid at a lower wage scale.

After hearing all the testimony, the Railroad Commission issued a report on April 18, 1918, that outlined three possible methods of achieving an economical operation of the transbay transportation facilities. The first of the alternatives was similar to the "Composite Equivalent" plan. The second plan divided the East Bay into a number of exclusive territories, with either Key Route or Southern Pacific being the sole operator in any given area. The third plan, which the Commission reported as being the most feasible, specified the lease of all Key Route transbay facilities by the Southern Pacific.

Both railroads agreed that a more economical operation of the lines in the East Bay was desirable. They claimed, however, that in order to pay for a merger of the two systems, it would be necessary to increase the transbay fares to at least 18 cents. Because the Commission felt that the existing fares would be adequate to finance a merger, all further talks on this subject were discontinued.

Now unable to obtain a fare increase through the State Railroad Commission, the Southern Pacific turned to the U.S. Railroad Administration, operators of the nation's railroads during World War I. The railroad requested permission to increase its East Bay suburban fares by 10 per cent. After a brief hearing on May 27, 1918, Director General William Gibbs McAdoo granted the railroad permission to increase its first zone fares from 10 to 11 cents and the monthly commute rate from $3 to $3.30. The date of the increase was set for June 7, at which time fares on the outer two zones also would be increased, from 15 and 20 cents, respectively, to 16 and 21 cents. Commute fares on the two outer zones would increase from $3.50 and $4 to $3.85 and $4.40. The increase also affected the Creek Route ferries and the Crosstown line streetcars; fares on these lines would go from five to six cents.

A year later, Southern Pacific applied to the Railroad Administration to raise the basic transbay fare an additional four cents in order to put it on a parity with the 15-cent fare then charged by the Key Route. In opposition to this increase, Oakland City Attorney H.L. Hagen claimed that if Southern Pacific increased its basic fare to more than 25 cents per round trip, it would be in violation of certain franchise clauses. If this occurred, Hagen commented, the lease of city-owned land upon which Oakland Pier was located might be put in jeopardy. Hagen further claimed that the U.S. Railroad Administration, as wartime operators of the railroad, did not have the authority to violate these franchise provisions.

When he was asked how the Key Route, which held similar franchises, was able to increase its fares above the 25-cent ceiling, Hagen answered that with the passage of the state constitutional amendment granting to the State Railroad Commission the right to set intrastate fares, the state had preempted that right from the city. He further pointed out that the Key Route had applied to that commission for the 15-cent fare and

TABLE 3 -- *Operating Statistics, 1919*

Passenger Traffic			
Line	Per day	Per month	Gross revenue, per month [1]
Seventh Street [2] . . .	24,450	733,500	$100,025
Lincoln Avenue	5,950	178,500	26,775
Encinal Avenue	5,529	165,870	24,880
18th Street	6,432	192,960	9,648
Shattuck Avenue . . .	5,952	178,560	26,784
Ellsworth Street . . .	4,265	127,950	19,192
California Street . .	3,121	93,630	14,044
Ninth Street	4,010	120,300	18,045
Webster Street	3,505	105,150	5,257
Horseshoe	2,824	85,260	4,263
Crosstown Street Car .	6,244	187,320	9,378
Total . . .	72,282	2,169,000	$258,291

Scheduled Headways						
Line	Base Service		Peak Service		Night & Sunday	
	Headway (min.)	Cars per train	Headway (min.)	Cars per train	Headway (min.)	Cars per train
Seventh Street . . .	20	2-3	20	4-7	40	2
Suburban Connection	40	1	20	1	40	1
Lincoln Avenue . . .	30	1	30	2-6	45	1
Encinal Avenue . . .	30	1	30	3-7	45	1
18th Street	20	1	20	2-4 [3]	40	1
Shattuck Avenue . .	20	2	20	3-5	40	2
Ellsworth Street . .	20	1	20	2-4	40	1
California Street .	20	1	20	2-3	40	1
Ninth Street	20	1	20	22	40	1
Webster Street . . .	30	1	30	2-3	45	1
Horseshoe	--	-	20	1-3	--	-
Crosstown Street Car	10	1	10	1	15	1

[1] Based on 15-cent transbay and 5-cent local fare.
[2] Includes Suburban Connection
[3] Franchise limit of two cars per train on 18th Street. Trains are operated in two or more sections when traffic requires three or more cars.

had received permission for the rate increase. In contrast, the Southern Pacific had elected to apply to the U.S. Railroad Administration, and had not received any sanction from the state commission. Hagen ventured to speculate that if the Southern Pacific was required to retain the 11-cent rate, Key Route might be forced to cut its fares by four cents in order not to lose patronage. In spite of this opposition by the City of Oakland, the regional director of the Railroad Administration, Hale Holden, announced that beginning Monday, September 1, 1919, the basic transbay fare on the Southern Pacific would be increased from 11 cents to 15 cents.

Even with the fare increase, the Oakland, Alameda and

TABLE 4 -- *Comparative Labor Conditions For Platform Men, May 1, 1920*

	Southern Pacific Company	San Francisco-Oakland Terminal Railways	San Francisco-Sacramento Railroad	United Railroads of San Francisco	Northwestern Pacific Railroad	Peninsular Railway
STREET RAILWAYS						
Hourly wages, 1st yr.	$0.4250	$0.550	...	$0.520	...	$0.510
2nd yr.	0.4375	0.590	...	0.540	...	0.520
3rd yr.	0.4525	0.590	...	0.560	...	0.530
4th yr.	0.4675	0.590	...	0.560	...	0.530
Hours in 1 day's work	9.5	10	...	10	...	9.3
Overtime rate	Straight time	1½	...	Straight time	...	Straight time
Vacation time	None	None	...	None	...	12 day's pay
Days off	1 in 12	1 in 7	...	Optional	...	Optional
INTERURBAN RAILWAYS						
Hourly wages, 1st yr.	...	$0.570 1/	...	$0.480	...	$0.520
2nd yr.	...	0.610 1/	...	0.500	...	0.540
3rd yr.	...	0.610 1/	...	0.520	...	0.550 2/
4th yr.	...	0.610 1/	...	0.520	...	0.550 2/
Conductor's wages	$180 per month	...	$0.56 per hour	...	$5.00 per 100 mi. 3/	...
Engineer's wages	$5.60 per 100 mi. 4/	...	0.56 per hour	...	5.00 per 100 mi. 3/	...
Brakemen's wages	$121.55 per month	...	0.45 per hour	...	$0.42 per hour	...
Gatemen's wages	105.75 per month	...	...	...	...	...
Hours in 1 day's work	8	10	11	10	8	10
Overtime rate: Conductors	$0.75 per hour	1½	Straight time	Straight time	Pro rata	Straight time
Engineers	0.86 per hour	...	...	...	...	...
Vacation time	None	None	None	None	None	12 day's pay
Days off	5/	1 in 8	None	Optional	None	Optional

Data from California Electric Railway Association : *Data Sheets Regarding Labor Conditions as of May 1, 1920*.

1/ Rate shown is for motormen and conductors; brakemen receive same rate as Street Railway platform men.
2/ Plus $5.00 per month.
3/ Minimum day is $6.00.
4/ Minimum day is $6.05.
5/ Days off rotate and are dependent on run number.

Oakland and Alameda to Benefit by $1,500,000 Bridge

PROPOSED Oakland-Alameda bridge would have carried trains, streetcars, autos. By the time a new crossing was finally achieved, S.P. had lost interest in running trains here.   **Bancroft Library**

Berkeley Lines continued to operate at a loss. In 1920, this loss amounted to more than $500,000, even though the annual passenger traffic total exceeded 25,000,000. During that year, it was reported that operational costs were $1.27 for each $1 in fares collected.

In order to save nearly $500,000 a year, a plan was implemented in the early part of 1920 to reduce the number of cars in each train to a bare minimum. This in turn reduced labor costs as fewer gatemen were required. In addition, three interlocking towers were closed and single-car trains on certain lines were operated with a two-man crew consisting of engineer and conductor rather than a three-man crew which included a gateman.

During the 1920s, labor and wage conditions were far from equalized throughout the electric railway industry. In many cases, railways serving the same localities had differing wage rates and benefits. This situation was particularly true in the East Bay area, where Southern Pacific and San Francisco-Oakland Terminal Railways (Key Route) competed not only for passengers but also for trainmen. One of the labor difficulties facing Southern Pacific was due to the low wage rate paid to platform men on the streetcars. When compared to four other street railway operations in this part of California, Southern Pacific had the lowest wage rate. Platform men working similar jobs for the Key Route earned about $25 per month more than did those on the S.P. In fact, a Southern Pacific platform man could leave his job and go to work for the United Railroads of San Francisco and earn about $40 per month more than what S.P. had paid him.

Brakemen on the suburban trains also earned less than their counterparts on the Key Route; in this case, the difference was about $37 per month. Of eight electric railways using brakemen in passenger service, only two, the Northwestern Pacific Railroad and the San Francisco, Napa and Calistoga Railway, paid their brakemen less than did Southern Pacific. Conductors and engineers on the Southern Pacific, however, made better than average wages. They earned about $15 per month more than did those working for the Key Route. Of the 10 interurban lines in this part of California, only the San Francisco-Sacramento Railroad, Sacramento Northern Railroad, and Central California Traction Company had a higher wage scale for passenger conductors and motormen than did S.P.

Bridges ... Bridges

One of the first concrete proposals for the construction of a bridge across San Francisco Bay was put forth in 1916, when three engineers, Wilbur J. Watson of Cleveland, Ohio, William R. Davis of Albany, New York, and Harlan D. Miller of New York City, outlined a plan for a bridge before the Oakland Chamber of Commerce. The plan envisioned a $20 million structure which would carry electric trains, autos, and trucks from the vicinity of Fifth and Adeline Streets in Oakland to Third and Market Streets in San Francisco, a distance of about six miles.

Because of differing operating voltages, it was proposed that the bridge have two sets of double electric railway tracks. One set would be for Southern Pacific suburban trains while the other would be for trains of both the Key Route and the Oakland, Antioch and Eastern, an interurban running from Oakland to Sacramento. Between these two sets of tracks would be a pair of two-lane roadways, one for autos and the other for trucks and buses. On the Oakland side of the bridge, the trains from the Oakland and Berkeley lines of the Southern Pacific would turn onto the structure at Seventh and Adeline Streets. Key Route and O.A. & E. trains would use tracks along Adeline Street to gain access to the bridge. From Fifth and Adeline streets, the bridge would parallel the Western Pacific tracks and cross over the Oakland Estuary near the Western Pacific mole. The tracks of the Alameda lines would join the bridge near the outer end of the Alameda mole.

In San Francisco, it was proposed to route vehicular traffic directly onto Market Street. Rail traffic would descend into a Market Street Subway and proceed to an underground East

Bay Transit Terminal, which would be located near the intersection of Market and Powell Streets. The bridge railway would be designed for high density operation, with trains operating on headways as close as 105 seconds. With a maximum speed of 45 miles per hour, it was estimated that the running time from downtown Oakland to downtown San Francisco could be reduced from 32 minutes to 12 minutes.

On August 17, 1916, the War Department held hearings on the Bay Bridge proposal. At the hearings, the Oakland Chamber of Commerce announced that it was enthusiastically in favor of a Bay bridge, and it was adopting as its 1916 slogan, the phrase, "We Want A Bridge!" Objection to the Bay Bridge proposal was voiced by Col. Robert A.L. von Falkenberg, a local design engineer, who outlined his own plans for a Bay bridge. The von Falkenberg plan consisted of a 140-foot-wide pontoon bridge which would cost about $19 million. This bridge would carry four lanes for auto, bus, and truck traffic, four tracks for electric trains, and two tracks for mainline steam trains. The alignment of the bridge was roughly the same as that proposed by the Watson-Davis-Miller interests.

After the hearings had been completed, the War Department gave provisional approval to the Watson-Davis-Miller plan, provided financial arrangements as well as backing by local governments could be obtained. As neither of these immediately were forthcoming, the plans for a Bay crossing were shelved for the next few years.

While interest was increasing for a Bay bridge, talk also was heard for an improvement to the bridges across the Oakland Estuary. Water traffic was on the increase as was vehicular and rail traffic on the bridges. More and more skippers were complaining about the delays caused by the slow-moving drawbridges which blocked the waterway. On land, it was recognized that the bridges were becoming bottlenecks to autos, streetcars, trains, and other traffic. For example, it was noted that the density of water traffic necessitated the opening of the Harrison Street Bridge about 10 times each hour; hence every other train or streetcar was delayed from one to four minutes. Because of this continuing disruption to schedules, the Webster Street trains were occasionally delayed and missed their ferry connection at Alameda Pier.

This difficult problem of water traffic versus bridge traffic finally was resolved when the U.S. War Department issued an order on October 30, 1916, directing the Southern Pacific, owner of the Harrison Street Bridge, and the County of Alameda, owner of the Webster Street Bridge, to make certain modifications. The order instructed the owners to:

> 1. Increase the clear height above mean high water to 28 feet under the draw span and its approaches.
> 2. Increase the clear width of the open draw to 200 feet, and
> 3. Allow for a clear height of 200 feet above mean high water when the draw is open.

In order to meet these specifications at a minimum of cost, the railroad and the county agreed on April 23, 1917, to construct a joint facility using a double-leaf bascule design. The cost for such a structure was estimated to be about $2 million.

The proposed bridge would contain a deck that would be 85 feet wide. The western 30 feet would contain a double track for Southern Pacific electric trains and streetcars. The east side of the bridge would have a 36-foot-wide roadway, along the center of which would be a double track for San Francisco-Oakland Terminal Railway streetcars. A ten-foot-wide sidewalk would flank the roadway along its eastern side. As planned, the bridge would have a minimum over-water clearance of 50 feet, alleviating the necessity of opening it for small craft.

The Oakland approach to the bridge would start at Fifth and Webster streets and would run toward the Estuary along an elevated alignment located 75 feet west of Webster Street. Locating the approach in this manner had three advantages. First, it would keep lower Webster Street clear for traffic to and from the existing Webster Street Bridge. Second, it would minimize right-of-way costs as the Southern Pacific owned much of the land along the west side of Webster Street, and third, the elevated alignment would carry traffic over the Western Pacific tracks on Third Street and the Southern Pacific tracks on First Street.

After crossing over First Street, the elevated alignment would make a reverse curve toward the east, crossing over the approach to the existing Webster Street Bridge and curving to cross the Estuary near the Harrison Street Bridge. On the Alameda side, the roadway would descend by way of a four per cent grade to the northern extension of Alameda's Webster Street, adjacent to the Breuner's Warehouse. The Southern Pacific tracks would continue south and cross over the roadway before descending to ground level and joining the existing tracks.

One of the problems created by the selection of a bridge of this design was the loss of the track connection at First and Harrison Streets. This junction, formerly used by the Alameda broad gauge steam locals, was used by all freight trains running between Oakland and Alameda. There was much discussion between railroad officials and officials of the City of Alameda with regard to the possible loss of entry of freight trains into Alameda because the existing franchises for operation across the Fruitvale Bridge and along Lincoln Avenue did not allow for freight trains. As the City of Alameda was greatly in favor of the new Webster Street Bridge, these franchises were modified to allow freight trains on both Lincoln Avenue and the Fruitvale Avenue Bridge.

State law allowed a county to enter into a joint bridge agreement provided the county pay for only one-half of the cost of the facility. In order to secure the necessary funds for the bridge, the County of Alameda proposed a bond issue of $900,000. Put to a vote, the bond issue was passed on August 14, 1917, and it appeared that construction of the new Webster Street Bridge could commence in the early part of 1918, with the entire structure being completed early in 1920. However, by the fall of 1917, the United States was deeply involved with World War I, and it became prudent to defer all new construction that was not absolutely necessary. Hence, plans and specifications for the new bridge had to be shelved for the duration. By the time the war was over and the economy had stabilized, the railroad no longer was interested in a joint bridge across the Estuary. Because the bond issue was insufficient to build a vehicular bridge, the County was forced to abandon its plans and design a less expensive Estuary crossing.

Collisions and Wrecks

The first major accident on the East Bay suburban lines involving the new electric equipment occurred during the evening of Sunday, February 4, 1912, at Alameda Pier. Passengers of the westbound 10 o'clock train of the Encinal Avenue line were given a scare when the pantograph caught the catenary trolley wire and brought it down onto the roof of the steel coaches. Fortunately, no one was seriously injured, although two men who were leaning against the steel door jambs had their coats badly burned. The accident tied up the line to Alameda Pier for the balance of the night. Passengers on two of the late boats were compelled to return to San Francisco and take the ferry to Oakland Pier and a train on the Horseshoe line. These trains could run only to Park Street, however, from where passengers either boarded streetcars or walked home.

A month later, on the night of March 5, a nearly identical accident happened to the 8:30 p.m. Lincoln Avenue train as it was running eastward from Alameda Pier. This time, nearly a mile of trolley wire was brought down. Many passengers on board the train were thrown into a panic as the wires smashed windows and sparked like lightning bolts. The passengers of the disabled train had to walk about a mile to Webster Street to catch streetcars for their various destinations. Traffic in and out of Alameda Pier was not restored until 11:00 p.m. During the tie-up, Alameda ferry traffic was diverted to Oakland Pier.

Three weeks later, on March 27, there was a serious accident on the Berkeley loop lines. The schedules then in effect called for eastbound trains to run only one minute apart on the four lines to Berkeley. The order of trains out of Oakland Pier was: Ellsworth Street, Shattuck Avenue, California Street, and Ninth Street. Where trains of several lines passed a given station, only one would be scheduled to stop. This was the case at San Pablo Avenue, which was a regular stop only for California Street trains, although certain eastward Shattuck Avenue trains also made a flag stop there.

On that particular morning, the four Berkeley trains made their 11:25 a.m. departure from Oakland Pier. The four trains ran in close succession as far as Ninth Street Junction, where the Ninth Street train branched off. The lead train, destined for Ellsworth Street, rolled through San Pablo Avenue without stopping. One minute later, the Shattuck Avenue train approached. The motorman noticed several people on the station platform, and he slowed his train to make a flag stop. However, right on the heels of this train was a California Street train piloted by Motorman J.F. Wilson. Not realizing that the Shattuck train had stopped, Wilson approached too fast and did not apply his brakes until too late. With a resounding crash, the California Street train slammed into the rear of the standing Shattuck Avenue train.

The collision caught most of the passengers on both trains unawares. Some were thrown to the floors of the cars and shaken up; nine were seriously hurt and had to be taken to a local hospital. The blame for the accident was placed with Wilson, who was cited for operating his train at excessive speed

AFTERMATH of the wreck at Oakland Pier on June 6, 1918. Motor car 300 (above) was heading an 18th Street train; trailer 448 (lower) was peeled open like a can of sardines.
Both Leo Mitchell Collection

THE DAY THE ROOF FELL IN: A California Street train split a switch on November 10, 1918, and brought the Oakland Pier trainshed roof down. To say that the mishap tied up transbay service that day is an understatement. Interior photo (below) shows car 302, the car that caused the havoc in the first place, pinned by the wreckage. Amazingly, the light steel car suffered only minor damage; the same could not be said for the structure.
Louis L. Stein Jr. Collection; R.S. Ford Collection

HORS DE COMBAT after a small confrontation, control trailer 439 awaits a tow to West Alameda for some corrective surgery.

R.S. Ford Collection

and without due caution. The rear brakeman of the Shattuck Avenue train, A.L. Webster, also was cited. He was charged with inadequately protecting the rear of his standing train.

Down at Oakland Pier, there were two collisions in 1918 that caused considerable damage to equipment and the pier trainshed. The first occurred early on the morning of June 6, while trains were being made up for the first runs of the day. Engineer C.A. McKenzie, on motor car No. 300, was guiding his 18th Street line train through the maze of switches leading to the pier trainshed. At the same time, another train was approaching on an adjacent track. For some undetermined reason, one of the slip switches had not been aligned properly, and McKenzie's train split the switch and sideswiped trailer car No. 448 on the next track.

Engineer McKenzie was seriously injured in the collision, suffering from a fractured skull. Less injured with contusions and bruises were Brakeman George L. Guess and Car Inspectors Howard L. King and Tom Balales.

Five months later, on the morning of Sunday, November 10, a single-car California Street train brought down the roof of the Oakland Pier trainshed. On this morning, which was the day before the signing of the Armistice of World War I, the train had come in from the Berkeley main line and was moving through the switches leading to track 5. The rear truck of the car split a switch and moved down the adjacent track 3, and before the engineer could get his train stopped, the front end of the car had swung out and hit the pillars supporting the roof of the trainshed. With a crash and roar, 75 feet of the roof came down on the heavy steel car. Fortunately, none of the seven passengers on board the car at the time of the accident was injured. The car sustained little damage other than some broken windows and a few dents in the roof.

Of necessity, all suburban rail traffic in and out of the trainshed at Oakland Pier was suspended for the day. As an interim measure, a temporary terminal was set up near Oakland Pier Tower. All that day, and most of the night, crews labored to restore the roof to its original shape, and by the next morning, new pillars had been emplaced and operation again was normal.

THIS WAS S.P.'s BRIDGE OF FERRIES, in 1927. The twin-stacked *Alameda* and *Santa Clara* are about to pass on the Oakland Pier run. The single-stacker to left is coming in from Alameda Pier. In the middle, the *El Paso* steams in from Oakland Pier. Auto ferry to the right is bound for Alameda Pier. In the foreground, tied up at the San Francisco Ferry Building, is Western Pacific's *Edward T. Jeffery.* The ferries were slow, but fun and relaxing and romantic.

Southern Pacific

CHAPTER 13

A Bridge of Ferries

WHEREAS THE YEARS 1910 to 1920 saw the creation and perfection of the East Bay electric railway system, the following decade witnessed the ultimate development of the Southern Pacific ferry fleet. During that period, the fleet had a net increase from 12 to 18 boats. In 1920 there were nine passenger ferries working three routes and only two auto ferries on one route. Ten years later, the automobile had made its presence felt and there were 11 auto ferries on four routes. With full service on all routes, one could look east from the Ferry Building and always see four to six S.P. ferries as well as those of other companies plying their way across the Bay.

The decade of the '20s began with a threat of a strike by the members of the Masters, Mates, and Pilots Association, the Marine Engineers Beneficial Association, and the Ferryboatmen's Union. These three organizations demanded a $30 per month increase in wages for their members. The union representatives promised that if these demands were not met, the men would walk off the boats on the morning of Monday, December 12, 1920.

As in hearings before the State Railroad Commission, the Southern Pacific argued that it was losing money on the transbay operations and that there could not be a wage increase without a consequent increase in fares. The deliberations wore

159

THE WEST'S MOST FAMOUS landmark, the San Francisco Ferry Building, sits astride the foot of Market Street; this mid 1920s view shows the looping streetcars which complete the chain of transport for hordes of transbay commuters. At left is the *Delta Queen*, just arrived from Sacramento River points. Photo (opposite page) is a bird's-eye view of the other end of the S.P. ferry route—Oakland Pier. Red electrics used the trainsheds to the right of the twin-stacked ferry; mainline trains were directly ahead with auto ferry slip at the bottom left.

Both Southern Pacific

OAKLAND PIER from the air, looking toward San Francisco. It was one of the busiest railroad terminals in the world, but it is all gone now, replaced by the Seventh Street Marine Terminal and the east portal of the BART subway tube to San Francisco.

Southern Pacific

on, but neither side backed down. By early December it looked like S.P. commuters would soon have to rely on the Key Route.

Finally, at an eleventh-hour meeting which was presided over by San Francisco Mayor James Rolph, Jr., the walkout was averted after both sides agreed to a compromise. Accepted was a more modest wage increase. In return for this, the unions agreed not to protest a proposed reduction in service so as to lower operating costs.

The Southern Pacific then approached the Railroad Commission with a petition to curtail early morning and late evening service across the Bay. At the hearing before the commission, Robert Adams, who was assistant auditor of the railroad, claimed that the passenger ferry operations were losing $38,000 per month. With the increase in the ferrymen's wages, Adams argued that the railroad must either raise fares or curtail service. Agreeing that certain savings could be effected with a slight reduction of service, the Commission granted the Southern Pacific permission to discontinue a few of the very early morning and late night ferry and electric train runs beginning July 17, 1921.

In contrast to the purported deficit operation of the passenger ferries, traffic and profits on the auto ferries was on the increase. On the Creek Route, this traffic had developed to the level that it was not uncommon for drivers to have to wait for two or three boats before boarding. Early in 1921, Southern Pacific began construction of an exclusive auto ferry facility at Oakland Pier. The slip and waiting area was built as an extension of Seventh Street and was located immediately north of the trainshed in the area formerly occupied by Oakland Long Wharf.

It was proposed to transfer auto ferry service from the Creek Route to the new Oakland Pier facility on the morning of July 1, 1921. On that Friday morning, the *Thoroughfare* made a trial trip over to the new slip, but because of strong tides, she crashed into the side of the slip, tearing out a dolphin and a number of pilings. Emergency repairs were made to the slip, and formal opening of service could not be made until the 1:10 p.m. departure from the Ferry Building.

At the Ferry Building, the new Oakland Pier auto ferries operated out of Slip 10, which formerly was the berth for the Creek Route ferries. Boats on this latter line were transferred to Slip 9. Auto ferry service to Oakland Pier initially was scheduled for a 30-minute headway from 6:10 a.m. until 6:40 p.m.; hourly service was performed thereafter until 12:40 a.m. At the start, the ferries *Thoroughfare* and *Melrose* were assigned to this service. At the same time, Creek Route service was limited to foot traffic, with the ferries *Garden City* and *Encinal* being used.

Auto ferry service to Oakland Pier was interrupted shortly after 7 p.m. on July 4, when the *Melrose*, attempting to land, tore out 25 feet of piling. Being unable to make the landing, the ferry backed out into the Bay and headed for the Broadway Wharf. There ensued a wild scramble as the waiting autos made U-turns and raced pell-mell down Seventh Street in order to try to be first in line at the Broadway Wharf. The drivers knew that the boats could hold just so many cars and that those last in line would have to wait for at least three boats. The race of drivers, all jockeying for position, became so hectic that the police had to be summoned to provide traffic control along lower Broadway.

All that evening and the following day, boats cast off from Broadway Wharf as soon as they were loaded and without regard to schedules. Still the line of waiting autos grew longer. To assist the *Melrose* and *Thoroughfare*, the ferries *Garden City* and *Encinal* were pressed into auto ferry service. There still were not enough boats as more and more autos lined up at the foot of Broadway. Finally, at 6 o'clock, the big ferry *Newark* appeared at Broadway Wharf, and she too was used as an auto ferry. Two days later, service was transferred back to

Oakland Pier, and the *Melrose* and *Thoroughfare* had the job of transporting autoists back and forth across the Bay.

All the following year, the two faithful auto ferries plied back and forth between Oakland Pier and the Ferry Building. Still the auto traffic increased, and it became readily apparent to the railroad that additional boats were needed if adequate service was to be maintained. At about this time, a seemingly unrelated series of events took place which ultimately provided the Southern Pacific with three badly needed auto ferries.

In the upper part of San Francisco Bay, at Carquinez Strait, was an auto ferry operation which called itself the Six Minute Ferry. This company operated an aging ferry between Crockett and Morrow Cove, near Vallejo. The route was right on the main highway between Oakland and Sacramento, and crossings took only about six minutes, hence the name. Experiencing a dramatic increase in traffic, the ferry company recognized the need for additional ferries. To satisfy this need, the company made arrangements with James Rolph and Company, a San Francisco-based shipping and coaling firm, for the construction of two steel ferries of 80-car capacity.

The keel for the first of the pair of ferries was laid on August 27, 1921, at the Union Plant of Bethlehem Shipbuilding Corporation. The keel of the second was laid on the adjacent way on February 20, 1922. Early in March of that year, disaster struck the Six Minute Ferry in the form of a landslide which completely destroyed the ferry facilities at Morrow Cove. The ferry company then abandoned service and went out of business. This left James Rolph and Company with two ferries on the ways and no one to operate them once they were completed.

Fortunately, Southern Pacific was in dire need of additional ferries and a lease of the two boats quickly was consummated. The first of these ferries, christened the *San Mateo*, was launched on May 9, 1922. After completion, this ferry was delivered to Southern Pacific on July 21 and placed on the run to Oakland Pier. Three days after the launching of the *San Mateo*, the keel for the third ferry of this group was laid, with the second and third ferries both being launched the following October. On the fifth day of that month, the *Shasta* was launched after a brief ceremony during which Miss Dorothy Gunn, daughter of A.S. Gunn, Assistant General Manager of Bethlehem Shipbuilding Corporation, christened the ferry. The last ferry of this group, the *Yosemite,* was launched two weeks later, on October 19. The *Shasta* was completed and delivered to the Southern Pacific on November 18, 1922, but the *Yosemite* was not delivered until January 25 of the following year. These new ferries afforded a great deal of relief to the overburdened Oakland Pier route. They were swift and soon became mainstays of this run, releasing older ferries such as the *Garden City* and *Encinal* for service on the passenger runs.

Stormy Crossing

The years 1920 and 1921 were fairly accident-free, with only a couple of minor incidents to create excitement. On November 9, 1920, the *Newark's* engines failed while she was in mid-bay en route to Alameda Pier. After the ferry had drifted for about an hour, three tugs arrived and towed her to her destination. The following July, the *Encinal* crashed into her slip at the Ferry Building when she was caught in a strong riptide. Captain Peter R. Crone later reported that one of her lifeboats had been smashed, and a portion of the deck rail had been carried away. In addition, the flagpole had sheared off and had come crashing down, narrowly missing some passengers standing on the main deck.

That following winter, the passengers of the *Garden City* experienced what must have been one of the most frightening

HIGH WINDS and heavy seas on Christmas Day, 1921, caused the Garden City to crash broadside into the Key Route pier, blocking eastbound track. The storm, one of the most severe in decades, forced the annulment of all transbay service on both S.P. and Key Route.
Vernon J. Sappers Collection

Bay crossings ever recorded. During the first weeks of December 1921, rain and wind whipped the Bay. Ferry crossings all were rough. The able ferrymen, however, kept their boats on course and on time in spite of the wind and the waves.

On Christmas morning, under threatening skies, the *Garden City* prepared for the 9:55 a.m. departure from the Ferry Building for Alameda Pier. Under the able command of Captain C.J. Anderson, the ferry pulled out of her slip into the teeth of a fierce south gale. Bucking strong winds, the ferry took an hour and one-half to make the normal 18-minute crossing. Approaching Alameda Pier, Captain Anderson saw that the Western Pacific ferry *Edward T. Jeffery* had taken refuge in the slip after being blown off course.

Standing off Alameda Pier, Captain Anderson waited for the *Jeffery* to leave so that he could make port. During this time, the strong south wind kept pushing his ferry northward and Captain Anderson had to turn into the wind and keep his paddle wheels turning so as to keep from drifting. Finally, the *Jeffery* cast off and left the slip in an attempt to make her own home port across the Estuary. Captain Anderson then tried to enter the slip at Alameda Pier, but due to the very strong winds, the ferry was blown to the north of the entrance dolphins. Backing off, the captain again attempted to put his ferry into the slip, but with the same result. After trying and failing the third time, Captain Anderson decided that the safest refuge from the storm would be back at the Ferry Building across the Bay.

With the wind shrieking and the spume blowing across the decks, the ferry could no longer stand the strain. With a sharp snap, the rudder and steering gear broke, rendering the ferry helpless in the wind. At the same time, the wind increased to full gale force and the ferry was blown sideways to the north. Seeing the plight of the *Garden City,* the crew of the tug *Ajax,* which was tied up at Oakland Pier, cast off in order to attempt a rescue. After getting a tow line on board, the tug began to pull the ferry to the shelter of Oakland Pier. On board the ferry, the mood lightened as the passengers sensed that safety was soon at hand.

Suddenly a huge wave broke over the ferry, tossing it like a cork. The tow line parted and before the tug could get turned, the *Garden City* was blown northward at about five knots. The parting of the line put the passengers into immediate panic. Women screamed and men rushed toward the life jackets. Sensing sure disaster stemming from the panic, Captain Anderson wisely ordered his crew to keep the passengers away from the life jackets. He feared that with life jackets many people might jump overboard only to be drowned in the heavy seas. Knowing that the ferry was not in imminent danger of sinking, he felt that it was the safest place for the passengers to be. Furthermore, he could see that the ferry was being blown toward the mudflats north of Oakland Pier and soon would be grounded.

Still being blown broadside, the *Garden City* moved past Oakland Pier and appeared to be headed toward shore near the 16th Street Station. Suddenly, as if a great hand was pushing it, the ferry began moving in a more northerly course toward the open water. Looking out of the spray and rain-drenched windows, the passengers could dimly see the Key Route pier looming out of the mist. Within moments, the ferry was at the trestle, and with a crash and a shudder, she crashed broadside into the pier, nearly severing it.

With great urgency, the passengers scrambled off the ferry, which was perched so that the lower deck overhung the eastbound track. With the winds buffeting them, the passengers clung to the pier. Feeling the vibrations from the crashing waves, which surged to within inches of the rails on the pier, the passengers crawled on hands and knees toward the safety of the Key Route mole, about one-half mile away. Once on the rock fill, they found the waves breaking 20 feet high and everyone became thoroughly drenched.

While the *Garden City* was being blown off course, all Southern Pacific ferry traffic was canceled. The Key Route had annulled all of its ferry crossings by midmorning, stranding about 1,000 people at its mid-bay ferry terminal. Because of the gale winds, those at the Key Route pier were marooned until it was safe to operate trains to the end of the pier. Standing in the shelter of the Key Route trainshed, the people were nearly in a state of panic as they could feel the building shake and shudder from the pounding waves. The drama was heightened when someone called attention to the drifting *Garden City,* which could dimly be seen through the blowing rain.

The wind subsided sufficiently by 2:15 so that a relief train could be sent to the Key Pier to rescue those stranded. Key Route passengers were then returned to their original boarding stations, frightened but dry. But the passengers from the *Garden City* were not so fortunate. After making the safety of the Key Route mole, they had to hike several miles through the rain and mud to San Pablo Avenue. Once there, looking more drowned than alive, they caught streetcars to continue their journey on this blustery Christmas Day of 1921.

After the wind had subsided, the Red Stack tug *Restless* was sent to rescue the *Garden City*. The ferry was towed to the Peralta Street shipyard for repairs. A week later, a Board of Inquiry was convened, headed by Captain Charles F. Heath, Superintendent of Steamers of the Southern Pacific. After hearing a full account of the storm and its effect on the *Garden City,* Captain Anderson was found guilty of poor judgment because of his attempt to return to San Francisco rather than to try to make port at Oakland Pier or to gain shelter in the Estuary. The Board also criticized First Officer N.A. Jacobsen for not dropping anchor as soon as the ferry lost her rudder and started to drift northward.

Two months after the *Garden City* incident, the *Melrose* starred in a near-miss situation. On February 4, 1922, the auto ferry left the Ferry Building on the 7 a.m. run to the Oakland-Broadway Wharf. Steering the ferry through the dense fog, Captain H.H. Holmes cautiously took the ferry across the Bay. Nearing the mouth of the Estuary, the captain sighted the shape of the freighter *K.J. Luckenback* dead ahead through the fog. Turning sharply, the captain steered clear of the impending collision, but in the act of turning, he lost his bearings. Being able to see but a few yards ahead, Captain Holmes steered for what he thought was the entrance to the Estuary. Suddenly, the ferry jolted and lurched as she ran aground on the Alameda side of the Estuary near the C.A. Smith lumberyard.

After trying to back off the mudbar, Captain Holmes began to whistle for help. Soon the reliable *Ajax* appeared out of the fog and took the 75 passengers off the ferry and over to Oakland Pier. Left on board were the crew members and 16 automobiles. With the *Melrose* effectively blocking the ferry lane in the Estuary, all Creek Route service was diverted to Oakland Pier. After the fog lifted, two Red Stack tugs were sent to the stranded ferry to pull her free of the mud. Once afloat, Captain Holmes started the engines and continued on his way to Broadway Wharf where the impatient drivers were waiting for their cars.

In June 1922, Southern Pacific announced that as the *Garden City* was slow and of limited capacity, she no longer was able to serve the needs of the rapidly growing transbay traffic.

THE *NEWARK* was a familiar sight on San Francisco Bay from the time she was launched in 1877 until 1923 when she was rebuilt as the *Sacramento*.
Roy D. Graves Collection

AFTER WORKING on the Bay for more than 40 years, the *Bay City* was stripped and beached, where the ravages of time and vandals destroyed what was left of her.
R.S. Ford Collection

TWIN-STACKED *Alameda* steams eastward toward her namesake city; Western Pacific pier is in right background.
Roy D. Graves Collection

Because the ferry was to be retired, a special ceremony was held on the morning of June 7 during one of the crossings from Alameda Pier to the Ferry Building. The guest of honor was Charles Pratt, who had been commuting from Alameda to San Francisco every day since 1880. During the ceremony, Pratt talked of riding on the *Garden City,* his favorite ferry. In mid-bay, a special last rite was said for the ferry and then Pratt cast a model of the ferry into the Bay. As the model sank out of sight, everyone on board was saddened at the prospect of the loss of an old friend.

When the *Garden City* left Alameda Pier for San Francisco at 1:15 the following morning, it was to be her last trip in revenue service. The following day, the railroad decided to keep the venerable ferry as an extra boat, as there was no immediate replacement for her. As it turned out, the "last rites" for the *Garden City* proved to be some seven years premature, as she continued to ply the ferry lanes until 1929.

With continuing pressure for larger and faster ferries, Southern Pacific began the design of what was to become the largest all-passenger ferry to be operated on the Bay. This ferry, the *Sacramento,* was the product of rebuilding the old South Pacific Coast ferry *Newark.* Rebuilding took place at the company shipyard during 1923 and the *Sacramento* was launched in January 1924. The ferry was designed under the supervision of Charles Green, assistant superintendent of steamers. She had a maximum speed of 14½ knots, had seats for 1,900 passengers, and had a maximum rated capacity of 4,000 persons. The railroad boasted that this was the largest possible size for a Bay ferry as she completely filled the slip at the Ferry Building.

The maiden voyage of the *Sacramento* took place on the morning of Saturday, February 9, 1924. Under the command of Captain George Fouratt, the ferry took her contingent of 1,000 guests for a three-hour cruise around the Bay. During the trip, live music was provided by orchestras on both main and upper decks. At noontime, a sumptuous buffet lunch was provided in the main salon by Allan Pollock, chief of the dining car department.

After the buffet lunch, a ceremony was held during which a large oil painting of the state Capitol was presented to the railroad by Murray Laidlaw on behalf of the Sacramento Chamber of Commerce. The painting was unveiled by Miss Margaret Spear and was accepted for the railroad by C.M. McFaul, assistant passenger traffic manager and F.L. Burkhalter, assistant general manager of the Southern Pacific. After the return to Oakland Pier, the *Sacramento* was prepared for regular service. On the following Monday, she entered service on the run to Oakland Pier, a run on which she served for many years.

With the addition of the *Sacramento,* time was running out for the older ferries. The first to go was the venerable *El Capitan,* the ferry that had initiated transbay ferry service from Oakland Long Wharf more than 50 years previously. In the early part of 1925, the *El Capitan* was retired from her upbay run between Vallejo Junction and South Vallejo. The old ferry was put up for sale on June 14, 1925, and purchased by Thomas Crowley for $750, a price reported to be well below her scrap value. The *San Francisco Chronicle* reported that Crowley planned to use the ferry in several motion pictures scheduled to be filmed in the Sacramento River area.

Toward the end of the decade, the three South Pacific Coast ferries were retired. The *Bay City* and the *Garden City* were the first to go in 1929. The *Bay City* subsequently was dismantled, and the *Garden City* was taken to Eckley, near Port Costa, where she was moored as a fishing resort. At this writing, the grand old ferry was still tied up, although in a somewhat dilapidated condition. The *Encinal* was retired in 1930 and five years later she was bought by Paul Spenger for $600. After her machinery was removed and she was converted to a restaurant, Spenger moored the *Encinal* at the mouth of San Rafael Creek, in Marin County. The ferry restaurant became widely known for its fine seafood and unique entrance, which was through the jawbones of a 70-ton whale. In 1942, Spenger moved the ferry to Benicia. The end of the *Encinal* came in 1959, when she was burned for scrap after Spenger had retired from the restaurant business and the ferry and adjacent property had been purchased by the California Department of Parks and Recreation as part of the new Southhampton Bay State Park.

The Richmond Ferry

With the outstanding success of the auto ferry service to Oakland Pier, Southern Pacific decided that the time had come to add a second auto ferry route to the East Bay. Reasoning that a direct line to Richmond and the Lincoln Highway might ease some of the traffic congestion on the Oakland Pier ferries, the railroad turned to the establishment of a ferry route to that point. Since an application for just such a route already had been made to the State Railroad Commission by the Richmond-San Francisco Transportation Company, the Southern Pacific quietly bought this fledgling line and its three ferries then under construction by Bethlehem Shipbuilding Corporation.

The keel of the first of the Richmond-San Francisco ferries was laid on June 19, 1924. On Navy Day of that year, October 27, this ferry was christened the *El Paso* by Bernice and Lurline Roth, four-year-old twin daughters of Lurline Matson Roth and William Roth, vice president of Matson Navigation Company. After five weeks of completion work, the *El Paso* was delivered to the Southern Pacific on December 8, 1924. The new ferry immediately was placed on the run to Oakland Pier to assist the three boats of the **San Mateo** class.

One week after the laying of the keel of the *El Paso,* the keel of the second of the three ferries was laid. This ferry, the *New Orleans,* was launched on the morning of December 10, 1924. During the launching ceremonies, Captain C.F. Heath, superintendent of steamers of the Southern Pacific, noted that the new ferry had cost $510,000. When in service, she would be able to carry 78 autos and would be one of the fastest ferries on the Bay.

After being handed a bottle of Spring Valley Water, Miss Ruth Burkhalter, daughter of F.L. Burkhalter of the Southern Pacific, christened the ferry. The ceremonies closed with the presentation of a platinum watch and a gold bracelet to Miss Burkhalter by Joseph J. Tynan, President of Bethlehem Shipbuilding Corporation.

The third ferry of this group had its keel laid on September 22, 1924. On the following December 27, this ferry was christened the *Klamath* by Miss Anna M.C. Parsons, daughter of J.H.R. Parsons, traffic manager of the Southern Pacific. During the launching ceremonies, H.F. Mortenson, President of the Klamath County Chamber of Commerce, spoke on how all of southern Oregon was honored and proud to be represented on the Bay by such a fine ferry. The *New Orleans* and *Klamath* were not completed for service until January 1925. The for-

**RICHMOND FERRY INAUGURATION
JANUARY 15, 1925**

IT'S 11:10 on a beautiful San Francisco Bay morning, and all boats are right on schedule. To the right, a sloop crosses the bow of the *Alameda*, steaming in to the Ferry Building from Oakland Pier; at left, the *Yosemite* arrives from Richmond. White tower at end of pier housed fog bell and served as marker for approching ferries. **Southern Pacific**

mer was delivered to the Southern Pacific on January 2, the latter on January 26.

With the *El Paso* and *New Orleans* added to the fleet, there were sufficient boats available to inaugurate service on the new line to Richmond. Service on this new route began on Thursday, January 15, 1925. At 10:30 that morning, the *New Orleans* docked at the new Richmond Ferry Terminal, which was located at the end of Garrard Boulevard adjacent to the Santa Fe ferry slip. Lined up to greet the ferry and to board for a trip to the City was a procession of about 100 automobiles and a large group of civic dignitaries.

That afternoon, when the *New Orleans* again docked at Richmond, a bizarre group of costumed people boarded for a much advertised Neptune Ceremony to be held while crossing the Bay. First on board was Father Neptune, played by Henry A. Johnston, followed by Miss Hazel Vickery who was dressed as Neptune's bride. The couple was followed by many costumed court attendants and a bevy of girls dressed in the latest bathing costumes. Father Neptune and his entourage made their way to the upper deck, where they held court. Nearing midbay, Father Neptune cried in a loud voice and raised his trident aloft. Gaining everyone's attention, the Old Man of the Sea and his bride then were joined in solemn aquatic matrimony. With the rites completed, Miss Mathilda Meyer led the court attendants in a series of hornpipe dances which lasted until the *New Orleans* docked at the Ferry Building.

After the festivities of opening day, the *New Orleans* plied back and forth between the Ferry Building and Richmond, making eight crossings daily in each direction. Sunday and holiday service was augmented by a second boat, usually the *El Paso* or *Klamath*, which made an additional seven crossings each way. The new boats remained on this run only a short while as they soon were transferred to the Oakland Pier run. The smaller *Yosemite* was assigned to the Richmond run, assisted on Sundays and holidays by either the *San Mateo* or *Shasta*. Fares on the Richmond ferry initially were set at $1.20 for car and driver and 50 cents for motorcycle and driver. The fare for foot passengers was 20 cents one-way or 35 cents for a round-trip ticket.

From the beginning, the service to Richmond was fairly successful. It was reported that during the first 10 days of operation, the *New Orleans* carried more than 3,000 passengers between Richmond and the Ferry Building. On the first Sunday of operation, with two boats working the line, 656 automobiles were carried. It was expected that this number would increase significantly as drivers became used to the new route and as the summer touring season approached.

With an eye to attracting regular commuters, Southern Pacific contracted with Key System Transit Company for the operation of a motor coach from downtown Richmond to the Ferry Terminal. The bus line, which was known as the Richmond Ferry Line, started at 23rd Street and MacDonald Avenue, ran west to Garrard Boulevard, and thence to the Ferry Terminal. As a further inducement for regular passengers, monthly commutation tickets were sold for $6.50 and were honored on both the buses and the ferries.

On the afternoon prior to the opening of the ferry service, Key System ran a free bus along the new motor coach route so that prospective patrons could inspect the ferry *New Orleans* which was tied up at the ferry landing. On the following day, this bus, a Fageol of 1920 vintage, made seven trips along the route, connecting with each ferry. Company records indicate that $8.40 in 6-cent fares was collected that first day. Thereafter, the bus, which was subsidized by the Southern Pacific, continued to meet each ferry until cessation of ferry service to San Francisco in 1939.

The S.P.'s new auto ferries were attracting attention in another quarter.

In the early part of 1925, A.C. Mott, transportation engineer with the State Railroad Commission, began an investigation into the earnings and valuation of the auto ferries. The railroad claimed that the total valuation of the system was $10,732,622, which included $3,025,422 for seven auto ferries. In contrast, Mott arrived at what he considered a fair valuation of the system of only $2,744,671. After auditing the railroad's books and finding net earnings of $952,157 for the year 1924, Mott reported to the Commission that the rate of return was 12.8 per cent. Turning to the books for the year 1925, Mott showed that the auto ferry properties had been overvalued by some $8 million in order to keep the rate of return at an inflated level. Using his own valuation figure, Mott reported that the Southern Pacific was earning a whopping 31.63 per cent on its auto ferry system!

In response to the claim by the state, the railroad used its own valuation figures and arrived at a more modest 10.83 per cent annual return. Furthermore, the railroad claimed that the auto ferry system was but one part of the entire transbay ferry system and could not be valued separately. As proof of this point, counsel from the railroad argued that when profits from the auto ferries were applied to offset losses from the passenger ferries, the net annual return on the entire transbay system was but 0.63 per cent. Instead of the auto ferry fares being unreasonably high, the railroad argued, both these and those on the passenger ferries should be raised sufficiently to bring the combined net return to at least seven per cent.

Discounting the claims of the railroad, the Railroad Commission ruled on June 30, 1925, that the auto ferry fares between Oakland Pier and San Francisco must be reduced on or before July 15.

Whereas the existing fare ranged from $1.05 for car and driver to $1.90 for a truck with trailer, the new reduced fare would range from 60 cents for car and driver to $1.50 for a truck with trailer. Similarly, the fare for foot passengers or extra auto passengers would be reduced from 8 cents to 5 cents.

The railroad replied that the rates would be confiscatory, and if allowed to go into effect, would result in a request for a general increase in all transbay fares. The Southern Pacific then turned to the United States District Court to seek an injunction preventing the State Railroad Commission from enforcing the new rates. In a brief filed with the court, railroad attorneys C.W. Durbrow and Guy V. Shoup, contended that while the Southern Pacific had the best ferry and interurban system in the world, the present fares were unjustly low and noncompensatory.

As proof, the court was shown that during the first half of 1925, a net loss of $456,140 was recorded for the entire transbay system. The brief concluded that the new rates would be below the cost of operation and that there would be losses to the ferry system of $2,000 per day. Federal Judge A.F. St. Sure and Circuit Judge W.H. Hunt subsequently ruled that the present fares could remain in effect but that refund coupons representing the difference between present and proposed fares must be issued pending the outcome of a new study to determine the validity of both fare structures.

The second study was completed by late December and it showed that the railroad was earning a net return on its auto ferry investment of 38.1 per cent. On reviewing the report, the Federal Court upheld the right of the state to view the auto

TOO LATE TO DO MUCH GOOD, West Oakland finally got its Seventh Street underpass. View looks west with special train posed for demonstration photo. Within a few short years, Oakland Pier was abandoned and few autos used the facility.   **R.S. Ford Collection**

ferry system as a separate operation. Thus, the injunction was allowed to lapse on the afternoon of December 5, 1925. At that time, ticket takers were instructed to start collecting the lower fares and no longer to issue refund coupons.

F.S. McGinnis, passenger traffic manager of the Southern Pacific, said the railroad was prepared to pay out $265,910 in refunds; starting on December 9, special windows would be available at the Ferry Building where persons holding refund coupons could get them redeemed.

When the refund coupon plan originally was announced, E.H. Logan of Alameda figured that this might be an easy way to turn a modest profit. Logan started buying up as many refund coupons as he could at a price of 10 cents each. Many drivers viewed his venture with skepticism as they felt that the railroad would win its case and the higher fares would persist. Thus, those that did not throw their refund coupons into the Bay were able to collect a dime from Logan. During the five months that the coupons were issued, Logan bought as many as possible. These purchases put him into a financial crisis that forced him to sell his car and many of his personal belongings.

Finally, by the first of December, Logan had purchased 8,400 coupons at a cost to him of $840. On the day that the refund coupons were redeemed, Logan took his bulging valise-full of tickets over to the Ferry Building. After the tickets were counted by the agent, Logan was solemnly paid $4,044.47, which represented a profit to him of more than $3,200.

Because of the reduction of fares on the auto ferry to Oakland Pier, the ferry to Richmond suffered an immediate loss in traffic. Drivers coming from Vallejo and Sacramento found that it was just as easy to drive all of the way down San Pablo Avenue and to the foot of Seventh Street, where the fare was 60 cents, than to take the somewhat more convenient Richmond ferry, where the fare still was $1.20. In an effort to equalize fares on the two lines, and also to undercut the Golden Gate Ferry Berkeley-Hyde Street line, the fares on the Richmond ferry were reduced to equal those on the Oakland Pier line on April 25, 1926. This brought an immediate upswing in traffic and soon the boats to Richmond again were doing a brisk business.

In an effort to provide improved auto ferry service to the East Bay, Southern Pacific inaugurated all-night service on the Oakland Pier route on February 11, 1926. With the new service, never again were drivers forced to race headlong down to the pier only to see the last boat churning out of the slip. Effective that day, daytime schedules used four boats on 15-minute headways from 6:30 a.m. until 8:00 p.m. Evening service, until 1:30 a.m., was operated on a 30-minute headway, with an hourly "Owl Boat" being operated thereafter.

The increased traffic which resulted in the "Owl Boat" and the 15-minute headways during the days helped to point out a major deficiency in the approach to the Seventh Street ferry landing. For many decades, Seventh Street had been a main artery through Oakland for those destined to San Francisco. With the opening of auto ferry service from Oakland Pier, drivers discovered that there was a major bottleneck where Seventh Street crossed the multiple steam and electric tracks forming the lines to the 16th Street Station and points east and north.

NEW GENERATION ferry—propelled by diesel engine—was the *Fresno*, steaming toward Oakland Pier trailing the usual diving, crying gulls. To the left, the twin-stacked *Santa Clara* approaches the Ferry Building.
Vernon Sappers Collection

On December 10, 1925, the *San Francisco Chronicle* editorialized on the problems stemming from this busy grade crossing:

> "Too much cannot be said in praise of the excellent auto ferry service now being rendered by the Southern Pacific. Since inauguration of the Oakland Pier service, with plenty of boats running on short schedules, thousands of cars can be handled.
>
> "But, there is one severe obstacle. This is the railway crossing at the foot of Seventh Street. Here the gates drop every 20 minutes to allow the speeding electric trains to go by. This results in cars being backed up for blocks during heavy traffic periods. For instance, last Sunday, traffic was so heavy and there were so many trains, that only about ten cars could get through each time the gates were raised. This resulted in the *New Orleans* leaving on one trip with only 28 cars on board, less than half of her capacity. Yet, there were nearly a hundred cars backed up on Seventh Street waiting to cross the tracks.
>
> "This bottleneck needs to be broken and should be done so as soon as possible with some sort of grade separation."

In spite of the bottleneck, about which everyone agreed something should be done, auto traffic to Oakland Pier continued to increase and drivers continued to fume as the gates went up and down with maddening regularity.

One of the first plans put forth as a solution was that of a viaduct to be built at the foot of Goss Street, one block north of Seventh Street. This plan drew little support and it soon dropped from sight. In the early part of November 1926, Mayor Davies put the matter of a separated crossing before the Oakland City Council. That body voted for an undercrossing at the foot of Seventh Street. As the mayor was in favor of a viaduct, he would not endorse the action of the council. Because of this stalemate, the California Railroad Commission was asked for an opinion on the relative merits of a subway crossing as opposed to a viaduct. The commission replied that a timber viaduct would cost about $300,000 less than a concrete subway crossing. It also was noted by the commission that the cheaper viaduct would be advisable as the construction of a Bay Bridge in the future would render the ferries obsolete.

On November 10, 1926, it was announced that W.H. Kirkbridge, maintenance engineer of the Southern Pacific, had completed the plans and specifications for a timber and steel viaduct at the foot of Seventh Street. The estimated cost of this structure was $285,409. Cost of construction would be shared equally by the railroad and the City of Oakland. On receipt of the plans, the Oakland City Council balked at the viaduct idea; the council still wanted a subway undercrossing and would not compromise. Thus, nothing was done and while the viaduct plans collected dust, drivers continued to swear and fume at the damnable railway crossing. Ultimately, the Oakland City Council had its way as a concrete-lined subway was constructed in the early part of the 1930s. Of course, the Railroad Commission's prediction on the crossing was correct; not too many years later, the opening of the Bay Bridge forced the abandonment of the auto ferries.

The Electric Ferries

With traffic continually increasing from Oakland Pier and the prospect of additional boats to be needed on other lines, Southern Pacific began in 1925 the design of what was to become the most modern group of auto ferries ever operated on the Bay. Whereas all existing Southern Pacific boats were powered by steam, the new ferries were to rely on diesel engines for power and were to have electric motors turning their screw propellers. A total of six ferries of this type were to be built; three would be assigned to the Southern Pacific for East Bay

MODERN IN EVERY respect, the *Stockton* (above) makes her run. Increasingly, the automobile traffic dominated the ferries. By 1926 (middle) this Oakland Pier scene had become typical. Tickets were purchased at toll booth in far distance, and surrendered to uniformed attendant before driving onto boat. *Yosemite* (bottom) crosses a bay that is unusually smooth and serene. In the background can be seen the long line of the Key Route Pier with Key's ferry terminal at far left.
**Thomas Gray Collection;
Vernon J. Sappers Collection (two)**

service and three to the Northwestern Pacific for service across the Golden Gate to Sausalito.

The keel of the first of the electric ferries was laid at the Bethlehem Shipbuilding Corporation Union Plant on November 8, 1926. On the morning of January 16, 1927, this ferry was christened the *Fresno* by Miss Shirley Harding, daughter of C.R. Harding, engineer of standards of the Southern Pacific. Present for the launching were Mayor A.E. Sunderland and 48 guests from the namesake city in the San Joaquin Valley. These guests had arrived at Oakland Pier that morning by special train and had been taken on a breakfast cruise around the Bay prior to landing at the Bethlehem Yard. During the launching ceremonies, F.S. McGinnis, passenger traffic manager of the railroad, remarked that the *Fresno* had cost $525,000. The ferry had a capacity of 100 automobiles and would be unique as she had an all-electric galley to serve her dining room. At the close of the ceremony, A.S. Gunn, vice president and general manager of Bethlehem Shipbuilding Corporation, presented Miss Harding with a diamond watch.

The keel for the second ferry of this group, the *Stockton*, was laid at the same yard on November 15, 1926. On the following fifth of March, Miss Louise Shoup, daughter of S.P. President Paul Shoup, broke a bottle of Stockton spring water across the bow of the ferry to christen it. In a manner similar to the launching of the *Fresno*, the City of Stockton was represented by Mayor R.J. Wheeler and about 100 civic dignitaries. The group had arrived at Oakland Pier that morning and had been taken for a breakfast cruise prior to the 1:15 p.m. launching.

The last of the Southern Pacific electric ferries was the *Lake Tahoe*, which was built by the Moore Dry Dock Company in Oakland. For this launching, which took place on the afternoon of March 23, 1927, an official party boarded the *Shasta* at the Ferry Building for a special trip across the Bay. At the launching, Miss Helen Dyer, daughter of J.H. Dyer, general manager of the railroad, wielded the traditional bottle of champagne. After the ferry had been launched, J. Albert Moore, President of Moore Dry Dock Company, presented Miss Dyer with a wristwatch and a bouquet of red roses. The official party then reboarded the *Shasta* for a celebration trip back to San Francisco.

The *Fresno* was the first of this trio of ferries to be ready for revenue service. On April 9, an official party from Fresno again journeyed to Oakland Pier, where the new auto ferry met them for a three-hour cruise around the Bay. Following an elaborate luncheon, the ferry was dedicated and then Mayor Sunderland presented a plaque from his city to the railroad honoring the occasion. On April 23, the new ferry was delivered to the Southern Pacific, and she was placed on the run to Oakland Pier shortly thereafter. The *Stockton* was completed and delivered to the railroad on May 21, with the *Lake Tahoe* being delivered the following month.

In addition to the three electric ferries built for the Southern Pacific, three boats of identical design were built for the Northwestern Pacific's proposed auto ferry route to Sausalito.

Of these ferries, the *Mendocino* was built by Bethlehem Shipbuilding Corporation, the *Redwood Empire* by Moore Drydock Company, and the *Santa Rosa* by General Engineering and Drydock Company. All three of these ferries were launched in the spring of 1927 and were completed in time for the inauguration of auto ferry service from the foot of Mission Street to Sausalito on July 1, 1927. In later years, the three N.W.P. boats joined their sister electric ferries on the heavily traveled auto ferry run to Oakland Pier.

Fog

For decades, fog plagued the captains of the Bay ferries. When visibility was reduced to zero, danger was an ever present passenger. For instance, on the afternoon of December 12, 1925, the *Oakland* was slowly groping her way toward the Ferry Building from Alameda Pier. Nearing San Francisco, the captain headed for Slip No. 6, the regular Alameda slip. As his vessel approached the entrance dolphin, the skipper dimly made out the outline of another ferry occupying the slip. This was the Alameda-bound ferry which had not yet departed because of the heavy fog. Stopping the *Oakland*, the captain began to back and turn his ferry so that he could enter the adjacent Slip No. 5.

Behind the *Oakland*, shrouded in the fog, was the Key Route ferry *San Leandro*, also steaming very slowly toward the Ferry Building. The Key Route captain saw the *Oakland* approaching her slip and planned to pass to her stern. Giving the appropriate whistle signals, the Key Route captain was startled when he realized that the *Oakland* was backing and turning. Fortunately, both ferries were moving very slowly, and they came together with only a slight bump. No damage was sustained and no one was injured. Both ferries subsequently docked and discharged their passengers.

A more serious accident occurred on a clear summer afternoon in July 1926. On this particular day, the *Melrose* cast off from the Ferry Building for the 4 o'clock Creek Route run. Under the command of Captain Samuel Forsberg, the ferry steamed east toward Goat Island. Suddenly, down in the engine room, there was a loud bang and a prolonged hiss as the valve stem on the engine broke. With steam hissing uncontrollably, the paddle wheels stopped turning and the ferry sat dead in the water. Fortunately, Captain Charles F. Heath, superintendent of the ferry fleet, was on board a nearby ferry bound for Oakland Pier. He saw the distressed *Melrose* and heard her whistle signals. Arriving at Oakland Pier, Captain Heath dispatched the faithful tug *Ajax* to rescue the ferry.

After casting off from Oakland Pier, Captain C.L. McNulty on board the *Ajax* steered for the *Melrose*. On nearing the ferry, he slowed his tug so that his crew could throw a line to the ferry crew. With a line on board, Captain McNulty placed his hand on the reversing lever and pushed it to "Full Astern," or so he thought. Instead, the tug leaped ahead with full power and crashed amidships into the *Melrose!*

The *Melrose* immediately began taking water at an alarming rate, and the passengers, in near panic, rushed for the life preservers and lifeboats. Seeing that the ferry was on the verge of sinking, Captain Forsberg ordered everyone to climb on board the *Ajax*, whose bow was sticking into the side of the *Melrose*.

Hearing the frantic whistle signals of both the *Melrose* and *Ajax*, the tug *Alcisco* came to the rescue, followed shortly by the Red Stack tug *Alert* and the Shell Oil Company tug *F.A. Douty*. With all of the ferry passengers on board the *Ajax* and *Alcisco*, the *F.A. Douty* got a line on board the foundering ferry and quickly towed her over to a mud bar south of Alameda Pier, where she was grounded.

The next day, the *Melrose* was patched up, floated off the mud bar and taken over to the company shipyard where she underwent $12,000 worth of repairs. Two days after the accident, Inspectors Frank Turner and Joseph Dolan, of the

Bureau of Navigation, held a hearing on the accident. After listening to an account given by Captain Forsberg, Captain McNulty was called to explain his actions. He claimed that he had been having trouble with the reversing lever and he thought that he had put it to "Full Astern" when he called for power. The inspectors decided that this was an inadequate excuse and they found him guilty of poor operation of a ship.

Fog again was responsible for a pair of accidents that occurred just off the Ferry Building just two hours apart on the morning of November 28, 1930. The day was especially foggy, with visibility near zero during the morning commute rush. Coming in from Alameda Pier, the *Santa Clara* cautiously approached the Ferry Building just after 8 o'clock. Captain John Souza was sounding his whistle signals when suddenly out of the gray mist came the freighter *Irisbank*. Realizing he was on a collision course, Captain Souza turned his ferry from the path of the oncoming freighter. The evasive action was not quick enough, however, as the ship struck the ferry a glancing blow.

A short two hours later, with the fog still lying low, the *Oakland* was involved in a similar collision at the same location. This time it was the freighter *Pennsylvanian* that caused the damage. She tore a gaping 12-foot-wide hole in the superstructure of the *Oakland*. Luckily, the hull of the ferry was not pierced and she was in no danger of sinking. Still, many passengers panicked, and when rope ladders were tossed down from the deck of the freighter, many clambered up. With order restored, the *Oakland* continued to the Ferry Building. Those who had climbed the ladder to the deck of the *Pennsylvanian* were put ashore at a pier just north of the Ferry Building.

Collisions and engine trouble, although cause for alarm, were taken in stride as "just part of a day's work" by the ferrymen. Suicide attempts, on the other hand, always were a constant worry to officers and deckhands alike. With the multitude of shipboard duties, it was not always possible to keep a lookout for the occasional passenger who might want to end it all. From the point of view of the potential victim, there almost always was some sort of an opportunity to jump overboard when no one was looking.

On a sunny afternoon in March 1928, the *Piedmont* pulled out from the Ferry Building for what ordinarily would be a routine crossing to Alameda Pier. Most passengers were intent on grabbing a bite to eat or enjoying the fresh air from the upper deck. The deckhands and officers were going about their many duties and nobody seemed to notice the middle-aged gentleman who slowly walked aft. As the boat neared the mouth of the Estuary, the man stood near the fantail as if to enjoy the view. He slowly removed his glasses and placed them carefully with his hat on a nearby bench. After glancing over his shoulder, he stepped off the back end of the ferry and into the cold waters of the Bay.

Hearing the yell, "Man overboard!" Captain W.J. Susan immediately stopped his ferry. Running aft, Second Officer Sigurd Hovda and two deckhands quickly got a lifeboat into the water in an attempt to save the drowning man.

Following close behind the *Piedmont* was the auto ferry *Melrose* on her way to Oakland Pier. Seeing the commotion on the *Piedmont*, Captain J.B. Chamberlin of the *Melrose* hove to and put one of his lifeboats in the water to help with the rescue. With the wakes from the two ferries increasing the choppiness of the Bay, a wave suddenly broke over the *Piedmont's* lifeboat, swamping and capsizing it. Hearing a yell, the boat from the *Melrose*, which had just picked up the would-be suicide victim, went over to rescue the men from the *Piedmont*. Hovda and one of the deckhands were pulled out of the water.

The second deckhand, George Roth, was nowhere to be seen. It later was confirmed that he had gone down when the boat had capsized and had drowned; he was unable to swim.

With the three survivors put back on board the *Piedmont*, both ferries continued to their destinations. The would-be suicide victim was placed in a hospital for observation.

The Great Ferry Merger

The auto ferry business in the 1920s not only was a lucrative enterprise for the Southern Pacific, but it caught the attention of others who desired to make a profit from transporting autos across the Bay. One of these was the Golden Gate Ferry Company, an independent firm which began operating between Sausalito and the foot of Hyde Street in San Francisco in 1922. Looking for new worlds to conquer, this company, which was headed by Harry E. Speas, announced in June 1925 that it was planning to spend $2 million in the establishment of auto ferry service from Hyde Street to Berkeley and also from Berkeley to Sausalito.

The Berkeley routes would involve a 50-year lease of City-owned tidelands, construction of a 4,400-foot-long timber pier, and the purchase of three new auto ferries. Also proposed was a bus line which would run from downtown Berkeley via the ferry to downtown San Francisco, forming a new commute line across the Bay. After the announcement of the proposed bus line, Southern Pacific and the Key Route joined forces in an attempt to prevent the Golden Gate Ferry from entering the transbay bus field. At first, the two railroads tried to block the bus plan by seeking a restraining order to prevent the City of Berkeley from leasing the tidelands to the ferry company. On July 15, 1925, however, the State Supreme Court denied the issuance of the restraining order on the grounds that the city was within its rights to lease its property to whomsoever it chose. Winning this point, the Golden Gate Ferry inaugurated its ferry line to Berkeley on November 11, 1927, but it deferred and ultimately abandoned the plan to operate buses from Berkeley to San Francisco.

With the firm prospect of the establishment of one line to the East Bay, the Golden Gate Ferry turned to the creation of a second East Bay line. Noting that Alameda was without direct auto ferry service to San Francisco, the ferry company approached the Alameda City Council for permission to construct a pier at the foot of Pacific Avenue. On June 15, 1926, the Alameda City Council endorsed the Golden Gate Ferry proposal for service from their city to Pier 36, at the foot of Townsend Street, in San Francisco.

During the time that the Golden Gate Ferry Company was making arrangements for auto ferry service to Alameda, the Southern Pacific was not idly standing by. Working quietly behind the scenes, the railroad made preparations to start its own auto ferry service from Alameda Pier to the Ferry Building. As there was no road at that time out to the pier, the railroad arranged with the Alameda City Street Department for the construction of such a road, with the railroad paying all costs. At that same time, work was commenced on an auto ferry slip to the south of the existing passenger ferry slip. When asked about the new service, F.S. McGinnis replied that the Southern Pacific always had contemplated auto ferry service to Alameda. With the completion of the Posey Tube (con-

necting Alameda with downtown Oakland) and the road across Bay Farm Island, such an auto ferry service now was justified.

In response to this statement, A.O. Stewart, President of the Golden Gate Ferry Company, made a biting observation:

> "It seems very strange that only after the Golden Gate Ferry has publicly given notice to inaugurate service to Alameda that the Southern Pacific comes along and announces its intention to install auto ferry service to Alameda. In my opinion, the Southern Pacific has only one object in view, namely to monopolize Bay transportation."

Stewart felt confident that his line soon would begin the new service to Alameda, as he had franchises from both Alameda and San Francisco and had filed an application for a Certificate of Public Convenience with the State Railroad Commission. It was common knowledge to Stewart and others that the Southern Pacific once had held a vehicular ferry franchise between Alameda and San Francisco, but most everyone was of the understanding that that franchise had lapsed.

The June 27, 1926, meeting of the Alameda City Council very nearly ended in a riot when the matter of the road to the pier came to a final vote. Presenting the case for the railroad were E.J. Foulds, of the railroad's legal staff, and former mayor E.K. Taylor. Taylor tried to tell how the new service would start within the month, but he was unable to speak because of the shouts, jeers, and catcalls. Opposition to the road to the pier was voiced by L.R. Weinman, spokesman for the Alameda Non-Partisan League. Weinman favored the Golden Gate Ferry and charged that the Alameda City Council had been aiding the Southern Pacific in its efforts to defeat competition.

The council's vote on the matter ended in a tie, and Mayor Frank Otis cast the tie-breaking vote, a "yes" vote in favor of the Southern Pacific. At this, the council chambers erupted into pandemonium. Those inside as well as some 1,000 spectators outside City Hall began to yell and hurl epithets at the council and the mayor. Things quickly got out of hand, and the police were called to restore order. During the commotion, it was necessary to escort Otis out a side door and down to his car, as it was felt that it would not be safe for him to remain in the building. In front of City Hall, one of the spectators

TRAVEL BY AUTO ferry meant either driving frantically to catch the departing ferry, or waiting patiently in line for the next boat. Auto ferry entrance (above) in San Francisco was at the foot of Mission Street; note Pickwick Stage waiting in line for the next Oakland boat. Richmond auto ferry slip (below) was more modest; *Yosemite* is about to cast off.

Robert W. Parkinson Collection

AWAITING ANOTHER commute run, the *Alameda* rests in the slip at Oakland Pier. To reach mainline trains, passengers would walk straight ahead; electric suburban trains could be found in trainsheds to right.
Southern Pacific

jumped onto a window ledge and loudly demanded the resignation of Otis and all of his "henchmen." The man quickly was arrested for disturbing the peace and the onlookers soon melted away as the police were seen going through the crowd swinging their billy clubs.

Rushed to completion in record time, the road from West Alameda to Alameda Pier was completed by August 10, 1926. It was proposed to start auto ferry service on the morning of August 14, just two days prior to the hearing for the Golden Gate Ferry's Certificate of Convenience, but the Golden Gate Ferry demonstrated that it was not afraid of the Southern Pacific. Working through San Francisco City Attorney John O'Toole, the ferry company arranged to have the San Francisco Board of Supervisors file a *quo warranto* suit in Superior Court against the railroad. The suit asked that the railroad be permanently restrained from starting auto ferry service between San Francisco and Alameda Pier on the grounds that the railroad did not possess a valid franchise for this service. With the signing of the injunction by Judge Trabucco, it appeared that the mighty Southern Pacific's new auto ferry service had been stopped in its tracks. Certainly stopped was the grand procession through Alameda to the pier by 80 decorated automobiles. The procession, which was to be headed by Mayor Otis and his City Council, was to have met the first auto ferry from San Francisco.

With its apparent victory at hand, the Golden Gate Ferry Company contracted with General Engineering Company of Alameda for the construction of three new ferries. The firm also went ahead with plans for the construction of a $250,000 pier and slip at the foot of Pacific Avenue. On August 16, in the chambers of the State Railroad Commission, the hearing on the application for a Certificate of Public Convenience by the Golden Gate Ferry was opened. Present was the legal staff of the ferry company and its many supporters. Opposite them was the formidable legal staff of the Southern Pacific. The proponents stated their case, asserting that only Golden Gate possessed a valid franchise. Further, the ferry company noted that the Southern Pacific was under court order not to provide auto ferry service to Alameda.

Attorneys E.J. Foulds and H.C. Booth of the Southern Pacific then spoke in opposition to the Golden Gate Ferry proposal. They closed their presentation with a petition to have the *quo warranto* suit transferred to the United States District Court on the grounds that the Southern Pacific was operating under the various federal railroad acts of 1861 and 1862, and hence the necessity of franchises was a federal question. As the motion was not contested by the ferry company, the commission ruled that the matter of the Certificate of Public Convenience be tabled until the suit was decided.

On August 27, 1926, in the court of Federal District Judge A.F. St. Sure, the Southern Pacific pleaded for auto ferry service to Alameda Pier. The railroad pinned its case on three main points:

- Auto ferry service had, in fact, been operated by the

Southern Pacific between San Francisco and Alameda Pier during the years 1894 and 1895, and thus a precedent already had been established.

- Alameda Pier may be construed to be but a "way station" on the Creek Route, a line already operated with auto ferries. Thus, auto ferry service to Alameda Pier should be considered as a part of the Creek Route operation.
- Because Southern Pacific was operating under the various federal railroad statutes of 1861 and 1862, franchises or permits from lesser governmental jurisdictions were unnecessary.

At noon on September 4, 1926, Judge St. Sure issued a ruling agreeing with the Southern Pacific and dissolving the injunction. Anticipating this decision, Southern Pacific had placed the *El Paso* in one of the auto ferry slips at the Ferry Building. As soon as the ruling was made known, the barricade at the apron was removed and the *El Paso* began receiving autos and passengers for Alameda Pier. Shortly after 1:00 p.m., the ferry cast off from San Francisco with the first revenue traffic for the auto ferry slip at Alameda Pier. The ferry arrived at that location just past 1:25, meeting Mayor Otis and his belated welcoming party.

But the suspense was not over. That same day, the State Railroad Commission ordered the Southern Pacific to appear to show cause why a Certificate of Public Convenience and Necessity was not needed for the new service. The commission also asked the railroad to answer why it should not cease and desist from performing the service until such time that a Certificate was issued. At the subsequent hearing before the commission, the S.P. attorneys argued that as the federal court had ruled that franchises were not necessary, and as the state statute which was enacted in 1923 requiring Certificates of Public Convenience and Necessity specifically exempted existing operations, the railroad felt that such a certificate was totally unnecessary. After deliberating several days, the commission agreed with the railroad and issued an order upholding the right of the Southern Pacific to operate without a Certificate of Public Convenience and Necessity.

Surely, it seemed that the Southern Pacific had won the last round and that the Golden Gate Ferry never would be allowed to serve Alameda. But not quite. In May of the following year, the ferry company filed with the State Supreme Court a request for a writ of review to set aside the commission's order. At the hearing before the court, all of the previous arguments pro and con for both sides were aired. In addition, Key System Transit Company appeared as a Friend in Court supporting the right of the Southern Pacific to operate its auto ferry to Alameda. On October 27, 1927, the Supreme Court handed down a ruling signed by Justice J.H. Richards which stated that Section 50d of the Public Utilities Code made it unnecessary for the Southern Pacific to secure a Certificate of Public Convenience and Necessity for its auto ferry service to Alameda.

The management of the Golden Gate Ferry was not one to give up easily, and when it was noted that the court's ruling was based on a 4 to 3 decision, they decided to apply for a rehearing in hopes that the court might reverse itself. With the granting of a new hearing, the company brought the entire matter of franchises, need for a Certificate of Public Convenience and Necessity, and the claim that the Alameda Pier service was a brand new operation.

Ultimately, this strategy bore fruit, as the court did reverse itself and on June 30, 1928, it issued a ruling that the Southern Pacific auto ferry service to Alameda Pier was a new operation and did not come under the provisions of Section 50d of the Public Utilities Code. Hence, the court pointed out, the railroad must possess a Certificate of Public Convenience and Necessity in order to perform this service. Anticipating a further appeal on the part of the railroad, the court concluded its ruling by stating that it would not entertain any motions for a third hearing on this matter.

With publication of the court's ruling, the Railroad Commission ordered the Southern Pacific to suspend the Alameda Pier auto ferry service on or before September 15, 1927, a deadline that subsequently was extended several times. The commission also ruled that a joint hearing would be scheduled on the matter of Certificates of Public Convenience and Necessity for both the Southern Pacific and the Golden Gate Ferry Company. It was implied that only one certificate would be issued as the commission was on record as opposing duplication of services.

It now appeared that the Southern Pacific and the Golden Gate Ferry were headed for a final showdown on the Alameda ferry. Both companies had expended a great deal of legal effort in trying to outdo the other. Neither side seemed willing to give in. Then, suddenly, a change in tempo occurred. Using the old adage, "If you can't beat 'em, join 'em," emissaries from the two companies met to explore the possibilities of merging the two auto ferry systems into one large operation. In November 1928, newspaper articles hinted at a proposed merger, but representatives of both companies made repeated denials.

The following month, application was made to the State Railroad Commission for approval of the merger proposal. In the subsequent public announcement, S.P. Eastman, a director of the Golden Gate Ferry Company, stated that approval should be received shortly, and after the merger, duplicate service would be eliminated and the new system should be able to handle half again as many autos due to a more efficient use of boats.

On February 18, 1929, articles of incorporation of the Southern Pacific-Golden Gate Company were filed with the California Secretary of State. Named as directors of the new company were A.O. Stewart, Milton Esberg, S.P. Eastman, and Benjamin Diblee, of the Golden Gate Ferry Company; Paul Shoup, E.H. Maggard, and F.S. McGinnis of the Southern Pacific; and E.J. Foulds of the Northwestern Pacific. Financing of the new company was to be by issuance of $10 million in first mortgage 5 per cent bonds and 419,000 shares of stock. The money thus raised would be used to purchase the auto ferries, facilities, and routes of the Golden Gate Ferry, Southern Pacific, and the Northwestern Pacific.

Of the stock of the new company, 156,750 shares would be designated "A" stock, with the remainder being "B" stock. Each stockholder of the Golden Gate Ferry Company would receive 1½ shares of "A" stock and ½ share of "B" stock for each share of Golden Gate Ferry stock. This would account for 209,000 shares of stock; the remaining 210,000 shares would be held by the Southern Pacific.

Stewart announced that with the sale of the auto ferry operations, the Golden Gate Ferry Company would be reorganized and would continue to operate its other subsidiaries. These included the Sears Point Toll Road Company, the Golden Gate Motor Transport Company, the American Toll Bridge Company, operators of the Dumbarton and Carquinez Bridges, and several local truck lines.

During the month of March 1929, W.C. Fankhauser, financial advisor of the Railroad Commission, held a series of hearings on the proposed merger at the conclusion of which official approval for the merger was granted. Because the Southern Pacific-Golden Gate Company was established to be

INSIDE STORY: Basic amenities could be found on all S.P. ferries including below-deck restaurant (above), refreshment stand (middle)—this one on the main deck of the *Oakland*—and, of course, places to sit (bottom). This view is of the *Berkeley,* whose gleaming parquet floor and stained glass clerestory windows lent a touch of elegance.
All Southern Pacific

only a holding company rather than an operating company, the Southern Pacific established a wholly-owned subsidiary to lease and operate the auto ferries. This operating company, Southern Pacific-Golden Gate Ferries, Limited, was formed at the same time as was the parent holding company. The operating company took over all auto ferry operations of the Golden Gate Ferry, Southern Pacific, and Northwestern Pacific on the morning of May 1, 1929. To call attention to the merged system, all employees on the auto ferries wore blue ribbons inscribed *ALL ABOARD–SERVICE THAT SERVES–LET'S START TODAY* on the first day of merged operations.

The great merger brought 28 boats under one house flag and nearly all auto ferry routes operated on San Francisco Bay. The only auto ferries which did not come under the control of the Southern Pacific-Golden Gate Ferries were those of the Richmond-San Rafael Ferry and the Martinez-Benicia Ferry.

Advertising for the new merged operations quickly appeared in newspapers and on billboards throughout northern California and showed that the new company operated boats from the Ferry Building to Alameda, Oakland, Sausalito, and Vallejo and also from the Hyde Street Wharf to both Berkeley and Sausalito.

Changes gradually occurred after the new system became operational. Gone were the "Golden Boats," as the Golden Gate Ferries were known. In place of their yellow paint, all were painted the traditional white. Boat assignments were shifted as boats of the **San Mateo** class were changed from the San Francisco-Richmond line to the Hyde Street-Berkeley line; in their place, the Richmond line received several of the "Golden" boats. The three steel electrics from the Northwestern Pacific and the newest electric ferries of the Golden Gate group were put on the heavily traveled Oakland Pier run augmenting the former Southern Pacific steel electric ferries. The *New Orleans,* after having her upper deck rebuilt, was placed in service on the long upbay run to Vallejo, displacing the former Monticello boats.

As a final note to the protracted battle for an auto ferry route to Alameda, the State Railroad Commission scheduled a hearing for May 31, 1929, on the application of the Golden Gate Ferry for a Certificate of Public Convenience and Necessity. The hearing was very brief, and after listening to a statement by the legal staff of the Southern Pacific, the commission dismissed the application on the grounds that because the companies had merged, the subject now was moot.

BERKELEY STATION was the architectural pride of the S.P. red electric system. Here, car 359 and train pause for northbound passengers. Sidewalk sign proclaims cut in Pullman fares; S.P. was fighting the depression and you could buy your long-distance tickets right here.
R.S. Ford Collection

CHAPTER 14

The O.A. & B. Lines

THROUGHOUT MUCH of its existence, the Southern Pacific East Bay suburban system operated semi-autonomously as the Oakland, Alameda and Berkeley Lines. Although the system had a close affiliation with the parent road's Oakland Division (which later became the Western Division), it always was operated as a separate entity. This fact was true even in later years when the O.A. & B. Lines were absorbed into the Western Division, whose main lines extended from Oakland eastward to Sacramento. At that time, the O.A. & B. Lines officially became known as the Western Division Electric Lines.

During the decade from 1920 to 1930, the O.A. & B. Lines continued to present a dismal picture of unprofitability. In spite of an increase in patronage, rapidly rising labor and other costs kept earnings near the vanishing point. During this period, Southern Pacific continually applied for fare increases and service reductions in order to keep the O.A. & B. Lines from descending into a flood of red ink.

This 10-year period saw the delivery in 1924 of the last cars added to the system. These six cars were built by St. Louis Car Company and were nearly identical to the original cars. The new cars were numbered 362 to 367 and originally were assigned to the 18th Street line. In later years, these cars were used almost exclusively in Alameda. During this decade also occurred the initial abandonments of service, as the number of

ONE-CAR TRAIN on the 18th Street line lays over at 14th and Franklin. Oakland was now quite a city with its imposing skyscrapers; City Hall is in distance. City fathers looked with disfavor on S.P.'s ramshackle structure, by now facing a shaky future.
Kenneth Kidder Collection

transbay lines was reduced from nine to eight and streetcar service was eliminated—all in the name of economy.

One of the major economic problems that had plagued the Southern Pacific for many years was that of the aging depot at 14th and Franklin streets. Everyone, including the railroad, agreed that the station was in disreputable condition, but with such a marginal operation, S.P. was reluctant to make any major improvements. Both the railroad and the city of Oakland hoped that the entire facility would be either replaced or abandoned. The citizens of Oakland were becoming tired of the eyesore that blighted the heart of the city; the city council was persistent in its requests to the railroad either to improve or raze the old depot.

Beginning in 1918, Southern Pacific promised the city that a new office building soon would be built on the depot site. This promise subsequently was proven to be merely a feint so that a corporate headquarters building could be built in downtown San Francisco without inflated land costs. In December 1920, the State Railroad Commission publicly criticized the railroad for not following through with plans for a new station in downtown Oakland. The Southern Pacific replied that it would be unable to build a station building at that time due to poor economic conditions, but promised that the land soon would be leased to an unnamed syndicate who would build a $1 million office building.

As part of its refusal to improve the depot property, the railroad claimed that 14th and Franklin was only a way station and could not be justified as the location of a large and costly terminal building. In arguing this point before the Oakland city council, railroad attorneys presented evidence that during the week of December 12 to 18, 1920, an average of 7,025 daily passengers boarded or alighted at the station. Of this number, only an average of 467 passengers per day used the station facilities. Because of this low number, the attorneys contended that the station was operated at a deficit and complete abandonment would be in the economic interests of the company.

On this point, the city's attorneys raised a legal question which proved somewhat vexing to the railroad. The S.P. had always held that the entire station area was operating property. If this was the case, city attorneys countered, why was not the station property fully developed to yield the greatest revenue? On the other hand, they said, if the property could not be fully developed, it should be reclassified as nonoperating property, in which case the city of Oakland would stand to collect some $15,000 in annual taxes for the portion of the station outside the right-of-way lines.

In order to avoid the reclassification of much of the property to nonoperating status, the Southern Pacific applied on February 16, 1921, to the State Railroad Commission for permission to construct a new station building at the 14th and Franklin site. This time, the building was planned to cost only $500,000 and would consist of six stories of office space with a ground floor station and arcade.

Included in the request for the new station building was a petition to abandon both the Webster Street transbay line and the Crosstown streetcar line. The petition stated that abandonment of these two lines, which were claimed to be only marginal operations at best, would relieve the railroad of any costs of a new Estuary crossing as the old Harrison Street Bridge was slated for removal in accordance to the War Department directive of 1916. Predictably, a new uproar ensued.

City Manager C.E. Hewes of Alameda said that loss of the Crosstown streetcar line would be a blow to the island city. He further remarked that although the railroad stated that the cars were losing money, they were well patronized most of the day.

The *San Francisco Chronicle* summed up the problems at 14th and Franklin streets in this editorial:

> "It is a self-evident proposition that Oakland is entitled to a proper modern station at the Southern Pacific terminal at 14th and Franklin Streets. The old shack, or rather combination of shacks, that for some decades has served the depot needs at that point would be a disgrace to a tank town in the desert.
>
> "The Railroad Commission's order some time ago directing the Southern Pacific to provide a proper depot was no more than a requirement that the company act decently toward the City of Oakland. Now the Southern Pacific comes forward with an offer to spend ten times as much money as the Commission specified provided it is allowed to make certain curtailments of service. How the railroad is justified in asking for the elimination of streetcar service to Alameda we do not know."

SEVEN-CAR train rumbles down Franklin Street approaching 14th; Key Route tracks in foreground.
Louia L. Stein Jr. Collection

The proposal to abandon the Webster Street and Crosstown lines subsequently was denied by the Railroad Commission. Claiming that both lines were a public necessity, the commission ruled that they should continue to be operated for the time being. The commission also ordered the railroad to tear down the aging facilities at 14th and Franklin and to erect in their place a modern station building to cost not less than $50,000.

But a new plan was afoot. The railroad quickly appealed this ruling to the State Supreme Court on the grounds that the property was to be sold to the Athens Athletic Club for construction of a combination office building, club headquarters, and railroad station. In support of the railroad, Oakland City Attorney Leon E. Gray petitioned the court to nullify the commission's ruling because the city was in possession of a joint application from Southern Pacific and the Athens Athletic Club for permission to construct just such a structure.

On October 14, 1922, the story of the proposed building was published in the local newspapers. Planned for a total cost of over $2 million was an 11-story building to be known as the Athens Terminal Building. The ground floor would consist of a terminal for trains of the 18th Street and Webster Street lines as well as streetcars of the Crosstown line. From the second to the eighth floor would be office space which would be available for lease. The top floors of the building would be devoted to club use and would include hotel accommodations, club rooms, gymnasium, and a salt water swimming pool.

It was proposed that the Athens Athletic Club purchase the

STREETCAR 809 at West Alameda awaiting repairs after a collision with a truck on the Crosstown line.
Louis L. Stein Jr. Collection

block-square property from the railroad for $1,250,000. The cost of the property and that of constructing the terminal building would be financed through the sale of bonds to the Pacific Mutual Life Insurance Company. With this proposal made public, the State Supreme Court set aside the ruling of the Railroad Commission, and by the close of 1922, it looked like the problem of the old depot at 14th and Franklin Streets finally had been resolved.

At the time of the proposal of the Athens Terminal Building, several major operational changes were planned for the lines that would use that facility. A new scheme called for the abandonment of streetcar service to Alameda. A further plan—never implemented—called for trains of the Seventh Street transbay line to terminate at Oak Street except for certain rush hour trains which would operate through to Dutton Avenue.

To compensate for the loss of direct train service to East Oakland, streetcar service would be inaugurated between 14th and Franklin Streets and Fruitvale, Melrose, and Dutton Avenue. Equipment for this service would be the cars released from the abandoned Crosstown line. Inauguration of this service to East Oakland would require the construction of a double-tracked curve at Seventh and Webster streets, and Southern Pacific actually acquired property on this corner in anticipation of this change.

With all of these plans under lively discussion, the War Department stepped in and pointedly reminded the railroad that the Harrison Street bridge had been cited as a hazard to navigation and was under order to be removed. This order revived the 1916 plan for a joint Southern Pacific-Alameda County rail and vehicular bridge. But, after making an economic study for a new bridge, the railroad concluded that continued operation of the Webster Street and Crosstown lines across a new bridge would result in increased annual operating costs of $135,000. Most of this increase would be due to underwriting one-half of the cost of the $1,750,000 bridge.

Hence, it was concluded that the most economical solution would be the abandonment of both lines concurrent with the removal of the Harrison Street Bridge. To compensate for the abandonment of the Webster Street line, additional service would be operated on both the 18th Street and Seventh Street lines. Local traffic on the Crosstown line would be diverted to the nearly parallel Santa Clara Street car line of the Key System Transit Company.

In order to ensure removal of the Harrison Street Bridge prior to the December 31, 1923, deadline, the last full day of operation of the Webster Street and Crosstown lines was set for Wednesday, December 26, 1923. The last Webster Street train for San Francisco left 14th and Franklin streets at 12:20 a.m. December 27. After this departure, late-night streetcars departed for Alameda at 15-minute intervals until the last car, which left at 1:25 a.m. This car crossed the Harrison Street Bridge at 1:28 and made its run around the Alameda loop. It then returned to 14th and Franklin streets, where it tied up at 2:17 a.m.

Shortly after the car had made its return trip across the bridge, men working under the glare of arc lights began dismantling the drawspan. By morning, when the tide was at ebb, pontoons and cribbing had been placed beneath the deck of the bridge preparatory to raising it off its center pin. As the tide came in, water was pumped from the pontoons, and by 10:40 that morning, the drawspan had been lifted 18 inches. The span then was floated over to the Oakland side of the Estuary where it was dismantled.

"DINKY" 804 and two-man crew at Oakland-16th Street Station. Although S.P. operated these streetcars for some 10 years, they are now all but forgotten.
R.S. Ford Collection

After the removal of the center span, the approaches to the bridge were dismantled. The last portion of the old bridge to be removed was the concrete center pier. This block was blown up with 1,400 pounds of dynamite on the morning of February 23. The blast, which shot water 50 feet into the air, rattled windows for several miles around.

With removal of the Harrison Street Bridge, the Oakland city council turned to the Southern Pacific and asked, "But what about the old eyesore at 14th and Franklin? What has happened to your grand plan for the Athens Terminal Building?" To this, the railroad replied that the plan had fallen through and that there were no immediate plans for the property. As the property still was for sale, the railroad did nothing to maintain it and as the years went by, it became even more shabby and rundown.

Streetcar service continued to be operated from 16th Street Station to the decrepit 14th and Franklin Streets Station, as did the trains of the 18th Street transbay line. With abandonment of service on Webster Street, the eastward track crossing 13th Street was removed from service. The westward track was retained, however, and was used once a day for a late-night franchise trip by an 18th Street train from 14th and Franklin down to 2nd and Webster and return.

On March 20, 1926, all streetcar service on the local 18th Street line was discontinued, leaving that route exclusively to the 20-minute service provided by the 18th Street transbay

WORKERS DISMANTLE the Harrison Street bridge (above): Webster Street bridge at far right. The tug is the *Ajax*, workhorse of the S.P. navy. Refugee from abandoned S.P. Portland, Ore., electric system (right) was trailer coach 470. S.P. wanted to use these cars on the 18th Street line.
**R.S. Ford Collection;
Vernon J. Sappers Collection**

COMPLETE WITH FENDERS, huge S.P. red electric rounds the corner from 20th Street and switches onto Key System Webster Street trackage. Trains of the 18th Street line were the only ones on the O.A. & B. lines to be equipped with fenders.

Louis L. Stein Jr. Collection

line. East Bay Street Railways bought all 12 streetcars for $2,000. Four were rebuilt for that company's local lines in North Oakland and Berkeley.

In an effort to improve the remaining operation on 18th Street, Southern Pacific applied to the Oakland City Council for permission to abandon the single track on 21st Street and replace the single track on 20th Street with a double track. The S.P. noted that while certain portions of 20th Street were too narrow for double track, the railroad would acquire sufficient property to widen the street. The S.P. also asked that the franchise requirement limiting trains to two cars be amended to allow three cars of a shorter, different type.

What the railroad had in mind was the utilization of cars of 56-foot length from the just-abandoned Southern Pacific electric lines in Oregon. As a demonstration, three of the Portland "Red Electrics" were put on public display at 14th and Franklin streets. Unlike the O.A. & B. cars, the Portland cars were equipped with green plush seats and art glass in the upper sashes of the windows. These features gave the cars a very elegant look when compared to the more spartan interiors of the East Bay cars.

The Oakland City Council, however, was opposed to any move which might delay the removal of the 14th and Franklin Streets Station. Opposition also was voiced by property owners along the route who feared that the Portland cars were too heavy and dangerous and would hamper auto traffic. Consequently, the council vetoed the request for a double track route along 20th Street and the use of the shorter cars.

At long last, on August 11, 1926, Southern Pacific consummated the sale of the entire block at 14th and Franklin streets to Charles Schlessinger for $2,250,000. The *Oakland Tribune* reported that this was the largest single real estate transaction in the history of the city. The *Tribune* also noted that Schlessinger wanted to build a combination office and terminal building along the lines of the ill-fated Athens Terminal. This plan also fell through, however, and the property eventually became the site of a block-square parking lot.

With the sale of the 14th and Franklin property, Southern Pacific proposed to reroute its 18th Street trains from Franklin Street one block east to Webster Street. This arrangement required the construction of new track eastward along 20th Street to the Key System Transit Company tracks at Webster Street. Here, the new route would use the Key System tracks as far as 14th Street, where a connection would be made with the Southern Pacific "franchise spur," a single track running on Webster Street from 14th to 13th Streets. This short stretch of single track, by necessity, would be rebuilt as double track.

Some modification also would be necessary along the stretch of Key System track so that Southern Pacific trains could be operated. The principal change here would be the replacement of the single-suspension trolley wire with catenary trolley wire built to Southern Pacific standards and height. The new routing also would result in a 600-volt territory being established for the 18th Street line and extending along Webster Street from 20th Street to 14th Street, the only use of the lower voltage on the S.P. lines.

In return for the granting of trackage rights to Southern Pacific, Key System Transit Company received trackage rights along Webster Street from 14th to Sixth Streets. These latter rights were never exercised, however, because of inability of Key System equipment to operate under 1,200-volt trolley wire. In order to operate cars on the rerouted 18th Street line, Southern Pacific installed electropneumatic dual voltage equipment on cars 362 to 367, making them the only cars on the system capable of being operated at 600 volts.

With all of the modifications to cars and track completed, S.P. abandoned service along Franklin Street and through the 14th and Franklin Station on November 7, 1926. The next morning, the track connections were completed, and for the first time in the history of East Bay transportation, red Southern Pacific trains could be seen sharing the same track with orange Key System streetcars.

During January and February of 1927, the tracks were removed from Franklin Street as were the buildings and tracks from the old depot site at 14th and Franklin streets. On February 26, while Dolan Brothers workers were razing the old buildings, foreman Owen Leonard spotted an old rusty can lying among the foundations of what once had been the newsstand. Picking up the can, he pried the lid off and poured out some 400 shiny $5 gold pieces. Checking with his boss, Leonard was told that the rule of "finders keepers" applied and the money was his to keep. That night, Owen Leonard went home a happy man, as not many workmen in those days could boast of making $2,000 in one day.

The 21-Cent Fare

It seemed that no matter what fares were charged on the O.A. & B. Lines, the railroad needed yet higher fares to offset rising costs of operation. All the while, some city or civic group was trying to roll the fares back to what some "expert" believed was a reasonable level. Alameda's complaint was a case in point. In 1919 the 10-cent fare was raised to 15 cents, an exorbitant increase in the city's view. Then, in 1923, the fare went to 18 cents and Alameda sued, on April 19, 1923, to force the railroad to roll back the 18-cent fare to the original 10 cents charged prior to 1919.

The suit was an outgrowth of two years of complaints to the commission by the city over the level of service offered by the Southern Pacific. Alameda City Attorney W.J. Locke stated that with the elimination of the 5:46 a.m. train and boat to San Francisco and the 1:15 a.m. ferry from the city, a severe hardship was placed on early morning and late night travelers to and from Alameda. As a compromise, the railroad agreed to add an extra early morning and late night run on the Horseshoe line, thus allowing Alameda patrons to make use of boats to and from Oakland Pier.

Pursuing the plea for higher fares, Southern Pacific and Key System jointly applied to the Railroad Commission in August 1925 to increase the one-way transbay fare from 18 cents to 25 cents. In addition, first zone monthly commute tickets would be increased from $4.30 to $6.50 and local fares from six to eight cents. At a hearing held on September 24 before the Railroad Commission, Oakland Trainmaster C.A. Veale testified that although the number of riders was increasing, so was the average length of each passenger trip. Veale also noted that the then valuation of the O.A. & B. Lines was $72,971,392; considering the revenues from the 18-cent transbay fare, Southern Pacific was enjoying only a 2½ percent annual return on its investment in the Red Electrics.

Appearing after Veale was J.E. Warren, chief clerk of the passenger traffic department. Warren showed that the net loss of the entire rail and ferry system during the first half of 1924 was $80,135. He said the losses would be much greater if the commission disallowed the use of profits from the auto ferries to offset losses from the passenger system.

Warren then compared the Southern Pacific operation to several commuter systems on the East Coast, stating that if the S.P. were allowed to charge comparable fares, the one-way fare from San Francisco to Oakland would be 42 cents. Finally, he argued that the proposed 25-cent fare was reasonable because Interstate Commerce Commission regulations permitted the Southern Pacific to charge up to 28 cents for a first zone one-way fare on its steam railroad lines.

The Railroad Commission postponed an immediate decision and scheduled another hearing for the following January. At the later hearings, the railroad reiterated its plea for a fare increase, which ranged from a first zone one-way fare of 25 cents to a one-way fare to San Leandro of 38 cents. Stating that the losses to the rail-ferry system during the first half of 1923 amounted to a staggering $664,405, the railroad claimed that the 25-cent fare would give it an annual return on its investment of only one-half of one per cent.

Finally, the Railroad Commission ruled on January 25, 1926, that Southern Pacific could increase its first zone one-way fare from 18 to 21 cents. At the same time, second and

A TWO-CAR Shattuck Ave. train picks up speed along the elevated track at Oakland-16th Street Station. In a few minutes she will tie up at Oakland Pier, in right distance. **W.C. Whittaker**

LAYING OVER at Alameda Pier is this seven-car Dutton Ave. Express. Second car is non-control trailer 404, the only car of this class to be equipped with porthole end windows.
Vernon J. Sappers Collection

third zone fares were raised to 25 cents and 28 cents respectively, while local fares were set at seven cents.

As a concession to school and university students, special student fares went into effect on October 1, 1926. Heretofore, students had to pay the regular seven-cent local fare. On that date, Southern Pacific began issuing special student commute books containing 20 tickets for 87 cents, the same as that charged by Key System.

With a 21-cent fare established, Southern Pacific and Key System returned to the Railroad Commission in the early part of 1928 seeking a further raise in transbay fares to 25 cents and a raise in local fares to 10 cents. After hearing that the two systems were still losing money, the commission denied the request for an increase in single-fare tickets, but an increase in commute rates was authorized to take effect on July 1, 1928. Under the new fare structure, first zone commute rates were raised from $5.20 to $6.50, second zone (Sequoyah Station) from $5.50 to $6.65, and third zone (Broadmoor and Dutton Avenue) from $6 to $7.

It is interesting to note that in the period from 1919 to 1926, the transbay fare increased from 10 cents to 21 cents. Yet, in the succeeding years from 1926 to the cessation of electric train service in 1941, the basic single-ticket fare remained at 21 cents.

Ever since the days of the Composite Equivalent Plan in 1916, Southern Pacific and Key System held periodic talks on merger of the two systems. Both companies felt a merger would be beneficial as it would eliminate duplicate lines and facilities, but the technical difficulties of merger such as different operating voltages precluded any action. After one of the meetings in 1926, William Sproule, President of the Southern Pacific, commented that the O.A. & B. Lines could not be directly merged with the Key System because of certain provisions of the First Mortgage held by the Southern Pacific. However, these provisions would not prevent the railroad from setting up a subsidiary operating company to take over the operations of both the O.A. & B. and the Key System.

On December 1, 1926, J.H. Dyer, general manager of the railroad, announced that the transportation department was undertaking a survey to determine the efficiencies of a merged system. The survey indicated that certain actions could be taken short of actual merger which would improve service and reduce operating costs.

One of the proposals dealt with the duplicate service provided to downtown Berkeley. Here, the tracks of both companies ran parallel and only a few feet apart. Key System and S.P. trains departed Berkeley at nearly identical times. The traffic survey showed that trains often ran at less than one-fourth capacity and predicted that if schedules could be staggered so as to give Berkeley a departure every 10 minutes, trains would run with more patrons. In addition, it was proposed that joint ticketing arrangements be made on these two lines, with commute tickets of either company honored on any train.

With the publicity given to the talks of merger, several of the East Bay cities argued in favor of such a plan on the grounds that a more economical operation would enable a rollback of fares to the old 15-cent level. However, at a hearing before the State Railroad Commission on June 30, 1927, Robert Adams, assistant auditor of the railroad, argued that instead of decreasing fares, a merger would require a fare increase to at least 25 cents to pay for modifications to track and equipment. Adams claimed that the O.A. & B. Lines never had been a paying proposition and had lost $1,048,163 in

OAKLAND PIER was a railfan's delight. Converging every 20 minutes were trains from the many lines. Above we see trains from Berkeley and the Seventh Street line bearing down on Oakland Pier Tower, at left. Farther out the Seventh Street line (below), a five-car train rumbles eastward between 23rd Ave. and Fruitvale. Combo on rear of train will be on front upon return from Dutton Ave.
Both W.C. Whittaker

1926. And, he added, passenger traffic was at the lowest level since 1917.

Again in February 1929, Southern Pacific approached the Railroad Commission for permission to raise fares to 25 cents in order to offset increasing losses. To support its plea for higher fares, the railroad presented passenger traffic figures for 1927 and 1928 (Table 5). Also presented, for comparison, were the figures for four other companies serving the East Bay.

TABLE 5 -- *Passenger Traffic, 1927 and 1928*

SOUTHERN PACIFIC COMPANY	1927	1928
Oakland Pier Lines	17,187,323	16,859,982
Alameda Pier Lines	4,919,880	4,859,434
Oakland Pier Auto Ferry	5,753,618	5,797,048
Alameda Pier Auto Ferry	281,524	300,904
Creek Route Auto Ferry	604,295	543,118
Richmond Auto Ferry	378,670	577,965
Total	29,125,310	28,938,451
OTHER SYSTEMS	**1927**	**1928**
Key System Transit Company	16,045,335	15,533,998
Western Pacific Railroad	74,436	73,470
Santa Fe Railway	146,280	106,561
Golden Gate Ferry Company	1,171,132	2,252,939
Total	17,437,183	17,966,968
TOTAL, ENTIRE EAST BAY	46,562,493	46,905,419

All during the time of discussions of merger and pleas for fare increases, another grand plan slowly was evolving that ultimately would affect both the ferries and the electric trains. Because the use of automobiles continued to grow, the need for a Bay Bridge became more and more evident. Back in 1921, a pair of noted bridge designers, Ralph Modjeski of Chicago and John Vipond of New York unveiled a plan for a Bay crossing extending from Alameda to Mission Rock.

Included in this plan was a 12,000-foot-long mole extending west from Alameda toward midbay. West of the mole would be an 11,500-foot-long truss bridge ending at a lighthouse structure located on the east side of the South Bay ship channel. Crossing under the ship channel would be a 3,500-foot-long underwater tube which would terminate near Third Street in San Francisco. This Bay crossing was designed with a 40-foot-wide roadway containing four vehicle lanes.

Flanking the roadway along the north side would be a double track for the interurban trains of Southern Pacific, Key System, and the San Francisco-Sacramento Railroad (the then current name of the interurban running to Sacramento). The estimated cost of this crossing was $40 million.

Unlike previous Bay crossing plans, the Modjeski and Vipond scheme remained viable over the succeeding years. Although greatly modified and shifted in location, it served as the stimulus for serious planning for the San Francisco-Oakland Bay Bridge. In 1929, the State Railroad Commission, together with the State Highway Commission, began to formulate definite plans for a Bay bridge. One of the first efforts was the creation of the San Francisco Bay Bridge Commission. This commission conducted a traffic survey on the needs of train-riding commuters on December 12, 1929. The object of the survey was to determine the points of origin and destinations of commuters who used the Southern Pacific and Key System ferries and trains. So that similar data could be developed for auto ferry users, a like survey was made the following day on all eastward auto ferries.

In those precomputer days, it took weeks to reduce the data and to develop a statistical pattern. Soon the expected pattern emerged showing that most riders who were commuters lived in the area from North Berkeley to San Leandro and worked in or near the financial district of San Francisco. The survey emphasized the fact that a Bay bridge must be easily accessible from the entire East Bay and must terminate near lower Market Street in San Francisco.

With these data at hand, talks of merger of the Southern Pacific and the Key System began again. This time, merger meetings were attended by the top brass—Paul Shoup, President of Southern Pacific and Alfred J. Lundberg, President of Key System. Both men agreed that the operation of the ferries would be ended once the bridge was completed and trains began running across it. Furthermore, plans for a bridge railway were formulated which called for a new operating company to take over all transbay operations of both the Southern Pacific and the Key System.

East Bay Improvements

During the period of controversy over the old depot site at 14th and Franklin streets, a number of changes and proposals materialized affecting other portions of the O.A. & B. Lines. What once had been open country east of Melrose had in the years since 1913 become dotted with subdivisions. By 1923 the population density of that area had reached the point where through service from Dutton Avenue to Oakland Pier was warranted. This service was inaugurated on Monday, February 18, 1924, replacing what was identified as the Suburban Connection.

Through service was a great boon to the area, as no longer did patrons have to take the shuttle car and transfer to pier-bound trains at Hillsdale. On that day, express train service to San Francisco also was inaugurated, and morning and evening commuters had a choice of routes. One express train ran down Seventh Street to Oakland Pier, while another was routed across the Fruitvale Avenue Bridge and Lincoln Avenue to Alameda Pier.

Also during this period, there were several street improvement projects in Berkeley. The first, in 1925, was the rebuilding and widening of Solano Avenue from San Pablo Avenue east to The Alameda. When Southern Pacific originally built its line along this street, most of the adjacent land was open country and there were very few automobiles about. In the intervening years, homes and businesses were built and auto traffic had reached the point where street improvement was required. As originally built, there was a double track with center poles for the catenary trolley wire.

With the rebuilding of the street, this arrangement was changed to a single track from Albany to Thousand Oaks, a distance of 0.9 mile and from Thousand Oaks to Contra Costa, a distance of 0.3 mile. At Thousand Oaks, the portion of the wye that was located on Solano Avenue was removed. The center poles along Solano Avenue also were removed and were replaced by poles located along the curb line. Movement along most of this single track, including movements into and out of

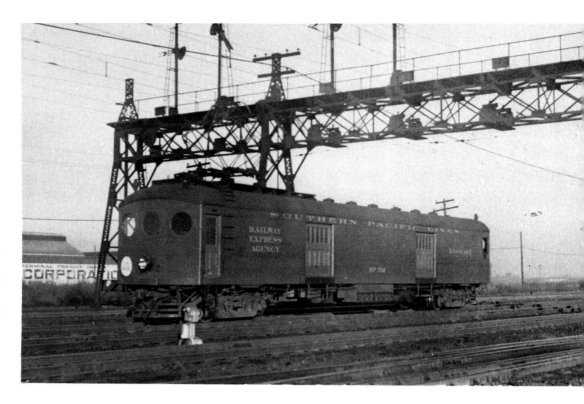

THREADING ITS WAY through Pier Yard, baggage motor 701 begins a trip to Berkeley.
Charles D. Savage

a siding at Ramona Avenue, were controlled by Masonic Tower, located at the Santa Fe Railway Crossing.

A similar program of street rebuilding took place along Shattuck Avenue, from University Avenue to Rose Street in 1927. Here, the double track was retained, but the center poles were removed, thus allowing the tracks to be moved closer together.

In 1926, the problem of multiple tracks and duplicate service along Shattuck Avenue, Berkeley's main thoroughfare, was discussed at a series of meetings of the Berkeley City Council. At that time, there were five tracks along Shattuck Avenue from Ward Street to Dwight Way and four tracks north from there to University Avenue. Occupying the center of the street was the double-tracked Southern Pacific Shattuck Avenue line, with catenary trolley wire supported by center poles. Immediately to the east was a single track for Key System trains, beyond which was a double track for Key System streetcars. The three Key System tracks merged to two tracks at Dwight Way. The single-suspension trolley wires over the Key System tracks were supported by a line of poles along the east curb of Shattuck Avenue and another row of poles located between the Key System and Southern Pacific tracks. With this maze of tracks, poles, and wires on Shattuck Avenue, it is little wonder that the members of the Berkeley City Council felt that the time had come for a simplification of the transit lines along Shattuck Avenue.

As a possible solution, a plan was proposed by Southern Pacific whereby it would voluntarily abandon its Ellsworth and California Street lines if, in turn, Key System would abandon its Shattuck Avenue train line and reroute its streetcar line. This would leave Shattuck Avenue with only two tracks running along the center of this broad thoroughfare. But Key System did not want to lose its important Shattuck Avenue route, and the S.P. plan was not looked upon with much favor by its East Bay competitor.

The City Council then tried to come up with some solutions. In time, four possibilities were developed with regard to the operation of the two train lines:

1. Key System trains could be switched onto Southern Pacific tracks at Ward Street and use the Berkeley Station as their Berkeley terminal. The principal problem with this alternative was that of rewiring the Key System trains for 1,200-volt operation, the cost of which was determined to be excessive.

2. A 600-volt territory could be established on the Southern Pacific from Ward Street to University Avenue. This would enable Key System to operate along this track without modification. However, the installation of dual-voltage equipment on the Southern Pacific cars, which was estimated to cost about $700 per car, was a major item. In addition, Southern Pacific was not in favor of this plan because of the operating difficulties that it presented.

3. A dual-voltage locomotive could be used to pull the Key System trains from Ward Street to Berkeley Station. This proposal presented difficulties in that car lights on the Key System trains could not be connected to the locomotive without modifications to the cars.

4. The most novel proposal was that of construction of gauntlet tracks from Ward Street to Berkeley Station. This proposal envisioned that each track would have three running rails and a pair of trolley wires, one for each voltage. Using gauntlet tracks, each train could be run at its own voltage without modification. A major problem would be that of crossovers and sidings at Berkeley Station.

All these proposals promised to be costly, and Southern Pacific, Key System, and the city of Berkeley all were unwilling to make the necessary capital outlays. So all four proposals ultimately were forgotten, leaving Berkeley still with four tracks running down the middle of its main street and orange Key System trains actively vying for passengers with the red Southern Pacific trains. The only aspect of the problem that was ever resolved during S.P.'s tenure was the removal of the fifth track between Ward Street and Dwight Way. This was done in 1930, and thereafter, Key System trains and streetcars shared common tracks all the way from Ward Street to University Avenue.

Flying Glass

The decade of the 1920s was one of improved safety records. In that 10-year period, there were only four accidents newsworthy enough to make the local newspapers. The first occurred shortly past noon on Monday, October 4, 1920, at the suburban elevation of the 16th Street station. During midday operations, trains of five lines passed the station in close succession every 20 minutes. Usually there was less than five minutes of elapsed time between the first and last train of each group. The order of eastward trains was Ellsworth Street, 18th Street, Shattuck Avenue, California Street, and Ninth Street.

On this day, the first two trains had cleared the station and the Shattuck Avenue train had made its station stop. As this train started to pull out, a fast-moving California Street train came rumbling in. Nearing the station platform, Engineer John Cooney of the California Street train applied his brakes in the usual manner. Finding no response, Cooney placed the brake lever into full emergency. Still unable to stop, the train slammed into the rear of the slowly moving Shattuck Avenue train.

The collision partly crumpled the front of the California Street train, trapping Cooney in his cab. It was not until one-half hour after the collision that workmen were able to free him from his cab. After being rushed to a hospital, it was found that Cooney had suffered a brain concussion. Conductor R.G. Stagg, although badly bruised, was not seriously injured, and none of the passengers on board either train was injured seriously enough to require hospitalization.

Two years later, on October 13, 1922, there was a sideswipe collision between cars 336 and 607 which was referred to for many years afterward as the "can-opener" wreck. Combination baggage-coach No. 607 and a coach had been made up as a train at Oakland Pier Yard. Moving from the yard toward the pier trainshed, the engineer guided his train through the slip switches, keeping a wary eye on signals and other moving trains.

As he approached one of the switches, the engineer noted a red signal and an approaching two-car train on the adjacent track. On the ground was Brakeman Ferini, who waved the pier-bound train past the red signal, thinking that the switch was aligned for a clear track. The switch, however, was aligned for the track occupied by the approaching train, and the two trains came together on their left front corners. The results were disastrous. The front end and entire left side of car 336 was completely wrecked as a corner of car 607 tore out all the window posts. At the same time, the left front corner of car 336 caught car 607 just above the letter board and, like a giant can opener, slit it open from end to end.

Fortunately, neither train was carrying passengers, and none of the crewmen was injured. The two cars, now almost totally wrecked, were towed to West Alameda where they underwent extensive rebuilding and several months later they both emerged as nonmotorized trailers 460 and 461. Many years later, both cars again were motorized and were renumbered 386 and 387.

In 1925, a minor accident occurred at Alameda Pier that jolted a few dozing early morning commuters into full awareness. The morning was cold and very foggy as the first train from Lincoln Avenue approached Alameda Pier Tower at about 6:15 a.m. Engineer W.O. Earnrish was running his train at reduced speed due to the very poor visibility. As he approached the pier terminal, he undoubtedly was hoping that the fog would be lifted by the time he made his next run out to the pier.

Suddenly, on the track ahead, illuminated in the fuzzy glare of his headlight, Earnrish made out the indistinct outline of a darkened car. Putting his brakes into full emergency, the two-car train slid on the wet rails and smashed into a standing train.

Except for some broken glass, neither car was extensively damaged. Furthermore, except for being shaken up, no one on board the Lincoln Avenue train was injured. Subsequent investigation revealed that the darkened train had been spotted on the wrong track by car hostlers the night before.

The last major accident to occur during the period from 1920 to 1930 occurred on Saturday, February 9, 1929. This wreck involved a Ninth Street train, and it tied up the line to Berkeley for several hours. The single-car train, carrying about 100 passengers, had stopped at the suburban elevation of 16th Street station, and on departing had received a green signal from 16th Street tower. Engineer F.A. Sugden accelerated his train downgrade to the ground level tracks and toward his next station stop at 34th Street.

AFTERMATH of collision is painfully evident. This is front end of California St. train after the rear-ender of October 4, 1920, in which Engineer John Cooney was trapped.
R.S. Ford Collection

Nearing 20th and Wood Streets, Sugden noticed a switch engine standing on a siding adjacent to his track. He paid it little attention as he had a green signal showing in the next block signal. Suddenly, almost too late, he saw that the switch ahead of him was aligned for the siding. Putting his brakes in full emergency, he attempted to stop his fast-moving train. With a lurch, a jolt, and a crash, the car careened through the switch and crashed into the tender of the standing steam engine.

The accident happened so suddenly that most of the passengers were caught unawares and were thrown to the floor of the car. Conductor E.P. Flanders, who was standing in the aisle near the rear of the car, was thrown down and knocked unconscious. Engineer Sugden, unable to protect himself, was lacerated by flying glass as the window of his cab literally exploded in his face. Jumping off their engine, the switching crew ran back to the car and rendered first aid to the two trainmen as well as to the some 20 injured passengers. Blame for the accident was placed with C.A. McCurdy, towerman at 16th Street Tower, who had given a green signal to the Ninth Street train but had failed to align the switch for the main line track.

Not all of the stories to come out of the "Roaring 20s" concerned wrecks. There also was a train robbery and numerous tales of students who earned their way through college "slinging gates" on the red trains. By working morning and evening commute runs, students could earn as much as $65 per month, which was good pay in those days. Thus, many men who eventually became doctors, lawyers, dentists, or other professionals, had much of their education made possible by the Southern Pacific.

Many of the students who attended college in San Francisco became proficient as quick-change artists at the beginning and end of their respective runs. While working a westward morning commute run, the college student would tally his tickets and cash while nearing Oakland Pier. Before the train even came to a halt in the trainshed, the student would be off and running toward the Gillie Room. Here, after turning in his receipts, he would scramble out of his uniform, stow it in his locker, put on his day clothes, and gather up his books. Running pell mell, he would leap onto the ferry just as it was casting off. All of this activity had to be accomplished during the three- or four-minute interval between the arrival of the train and the departure of the ferry. To miss the boat meant a 20-minute wait and possibly a tardy arrival at class.

One of the least-liked runs of the student-gatemen was what was known as the "drunk special." During weeknights, the 10:40 p.m. Seventh Street train would leave Oakland Pier with two cars and only a handful of passengers. On Saturday nights, however, this train ran with as many as six cars, with the extra cars being manned by the extra brakemen. To many, it must have seemed odd to see a six-car train leave the pier late at night with only a dozen or so passengers on board. The train left Dutton Avenue at 12:47 a.m., and it was the last run of the night to the pier.

This long train, with only a few passengers on board, would arrive at Seventh and Broadway at 1:20, where it would be met by hundreds of people, many of whom were in an advanced state of intoxication. During the ensuing 10-minute run to the pier, it was necessary to collect fares from everyone on board; this always proved to be a mighty task. With a winey and beery atmosphere and many bellicose passengers, more than one gateman wished that his passengers would either miss the ferry, or better yet, stagger off the end of the pier and drown.

The station of Nobel, on what formerly had been the West Berkeley-Richmond steam-era local line, was the site of an armed train robbery on the morning of Friday, November 7, 1930. On that morning, train No. 36, the steam-powered Stockton Passenger, had left Oakland Pier and after a brief stop at Berkeley, was running at a brisk pace toward the next stop at Richmond.

Two men, sitting in the lead coach, quietly left their seats and went out onto the forward vestibule. They climbed onto the roof of the next car forward, a baggage car, and then crawled along the roof until they could drop down onto the engine's tender. Climbing stealthily into the cab of the engine, they suddenly placed pistols at the heads of Engineer R.E. Lemery and Fireman F.E. O'Brien and shouted, "Stop this train!"

Halting at Nobel, the train was met by two more gunmen who tried to force open the door to the baggage car. Mail clerk John McClintock refused to open the door until the gang leader put a large bundle of dynamite under the car and yelled, "If you don't open up, we'll blow the car and you clear to hell!" With the car door opened, the robbers climbed on board and tossed down all the sacks of registered mail, estimated to have contained over $60,000 in negotiable checks. The loot quickly was transferred to a waiting auto, and the robbers jumped in and sped off.

As soon as word of the robbery had been received, Alameda County Sheriff M.B. Driver and District Attorney Earl Warren undertook a massive manhunt. A reward of $10,000 was posted for information leading to the conviction of the robbers. The case was broken when a trap was sprung at the Oakland post office by police late in the afternoon of November 30. Frank Smith, later identified as the gang leader, came out of the post office and after a confrontation, was shot and killed by Police Inspector Walter Garrett. Following a tip, police then arrested Smith's wife at their home in East Oakland. The other three members of the gang subsequently were apprehended in Seattle.

DWARFED by the dimensions of the great bridge the electric auto ferry *Fresno* passes beneath the abuilding structure on a run to Oakland Pier.
R.S. Ford Collection

CHAPTER 15

In the Shadow of the Bridge

IN THE YEARS prior to 1930, many plans had been put forward for some sort of a Bay bridge. Crossings had been proposed by many different groups and had received acclaim and backing by many others. But still, a concerted effort was lacking to win agreement as to the location and type of crossing as well as a commitment for the many millions of dollars that such a crossing would cost.

During all this time, a young civil engineer named Charles Henry Purcell was practicing his profession at various locations throughout the country. In time, Purcell, who had been graduated from the University of Nebraska, was named Bridge Engineer for the state of Oregon. This appointment was followed a few years later with a position with the United States Bureau of Roads. In February 1928, Purcell was selected for the position of state highway engineer for the State of California. In this capacity, he was head of the organization responsible for the construction of the growing net of state highways.

In appraising the state highway system, Purcell was amazed at the total absence of any direct state highway connection between San Francisco and the cities of the East Bay. To him, it seemed totally unrealistic that motorists should either have to drive the circuitous route around the south end of the Bay or be at the mercy of the Southern Pacific-Golden Gate Ferries.

Studying the many plans for a Bay bridge, Purcell came to the conclusion that a bridge was engineeringly feasible and that the only real difficulties lay in the fields of politics and financing. After being named in 1929 to the Hoover-Young San Francisco-Oakland Bay Bridge Commission, Purcell pushed for the construction of a Bay bridge in what must have appeared almost a personal crusade. The results of his tireless efforts came to fruition with the commitment by the State of California for the construction of the San Francisco-Oakland Bay Bridge. Because of his background as an expert in highway bridges, Purcell was named in January 1931 as chief engineer of the Bay bridge, a position that he held throughout the entire construction period.

Within a short time, barges were moored in midbay to serve as platforms for core drilling equipment which probed deep into Bay-bottom rock. It was not long until commuters began to keep track of the progress of the exploratory drilling. About a year later, as the ferries continued to ply back and forth, the exploratory work was completed, and to the casual observer, all work on the bridge seemed to have ceased. But elsewhere teams of design engineers were busily preparing the reams of specifications for this, the start of the greatest bridge project ever undertaken on the West Coast.

Soon, initial contracts were let for the construction of caissons and piers that would serve as foundations for the bridge. Day by day, as the work progressed, the concrete piers slowly took shape. Ferry riders could watch a line of piers under construction stretching from near the Key System pier over to Yerba Buena Island and then on to San Francisco. Careful observers also could spot the beginnings of construction of the two-level tunnel through Yerba Buena Island.

At about this time, a contract was let to Columbia Steel Company for $23,600,000 for the design and construction of the steel superstructure of the bridge. Soon, design engineers

THE BRIDGE GOES UP: Beneath cloudy skies, the *Oakland* (top) approaches Alameda Pier. Naked bridge towers in the background indicate the year as 1935. By February 1936, cable spinning and deck construction was under way; this view (middle), taken from the ferry *Oakland,* looks toward the concrete massif of the midbay cable anchorage.
**Louis L. Stein Jr. Collection;
R.S. Ford Collection**

UNCOMPLETED Bay Bridge forms backdrop for San Francisco-bound *Lake Tahoe.* Within a few years, auto traffic was crossing the bay high above the water, and the *Lake Tahoe* (as well as the *Fresno,* page 194) would be working routes on Puget Sound.
R.S. Ford Collection

n Chicago, Gary, and Ambridge, Pennsylvania, were busily preparing the thousands of working drawings for this immense undertaking. To make the steel beams for the bridge, iron ore was mined in northern Michigan and shipped to the mills of the Carnegie-Illinois Steel Company at Gary and Pittsburgh. Here, it was milled to the strictest of specifications and subsequently shipped to a large mobilization yard at the edge of the Bay.

On Thursday, March 1, 1934, the first steel for the bridge was delivered to one of the concrete piers west of Yerba Buena Island, where erection of the bridge was begun by the American Bridge Company. Soon, steel began inching skyward to form the towers for the bridge, the tallest of which was 519 feet above mean lower low water. With the completion of the towers, a more exciting phase of bridge-building began: the spinning of cables for the suspension portion of the bridge, the hanging of the deck below the cables, and the building of the cantilever section.

West of Yerba Buena Island, the great bridge crossed over the ferry lanes. Here, riders could crane their necks so as to gaze hundreds of feet upward to see men, appearing as mere specks, crawling about the spidery cables as the spinning wheels went back and forth stranding the 17,446 separate wires into solid cables.

Excitement heightened on board the ferries as the bridge neared completion. Finally, the two-level deck was completed save for one section of the San Francisco approach. This last portion, bearing a large American flag, was raised into place on Friday, August 28, 1936, amid cheers and whistles. The engineering marvel of the century was completed, and soon the dream of driving an auto across the Bay would become a reality. Yes, everyone agreed, we certainly were living in a world of remarkable progress. There were others, however, who realized with sadness that the days of the ferries were numbered. They knew that since the bridge soon would be opened to vehicular traffic, it would be only a matter of time until life as a ferry commuter would be a thing of the past.

During the years of construction of the Bay Bridge, three of the older ferries were retired. The first to go, in 1931, was the venerable old *Melrose*, the first auto ferry on the Bay. She was followed in 1934 by the *Transit*, which ended a 58-year career of transporting freight cars across the Bay. In 1935, the *Thoroughfare* was retired and for a time it was rumored that she would be converted into a floating nightclub on the Bay. However, she eventually found a much less glamorous fate, as a fish reduction plant at Benicia. Through the years, the old ferry slowly deteriorated; she finally was towed over to McNears Beach, near San Rafael, and abandoned. The remains of the ferry finally were put to the torch on April 10, 1957, when she was burned for scrap.

The Red Spot

One of the better known Southern Pacific ferries was the *Sierra Nevada*, which originally had been built for the Western Pacific Railroad in 1913. Launched as the *Edward T. Jeffery*, the ferry later carried the name *Feather River* until she was purchased by the Southern Pacific in 1933 and renamed the *Sierra Nevada*. This many-named ferry was the only boat on the Bay to have been operated by four different companies:

HULK OF THE *Thoroughfare* slowly crumbles on the mud at McNears Point in Marin County. She finally burned in 1957.
Robert W. Parkinson

Western Pacific Railroad, Southern Pacific Company, Key System, and Richmond-San Rafael Ferry. Furthermore, she was the only ferry to have been painted in three different colors. As a Western Pacific ferry, she originally was painted a dark red, hence the nickname "Red Spot." In later years, when rechristened the *Feather River*, she was painted the gleaming white of most ferries. Still later, while operated by Key System, she was painted the bright orange of that company's ferry fleet.

When the Western Pacific arrived in the East Bay in 1912, that railroad built a ferry pier a short distance south of Oakland Pier. After using the single-ended ferry *Telephone* for a short while, the railroad contracted with Moore and Scott Iron Works in Oakland for the construction of a large double-ended ferry for transbay service. This magnificent steel-hulled ferry, which cost $300,000 to build, was launched at 2:15 p.m. on July 19, 1913. She was christened the *Edward T. Jeffery* by Miss Flora C. Levey, daughter of C.M. Levey, vice president and general manager of the Western Pacific. On the following August 11, the new ferry was taken for a trial run around the Bay under the command of Captain John Richardson. On board the ferry for the trial run were Levey and other railroad officials as well as R.S. Moore and John T. Scott of the shipyard.

WITH THE BRIDGE which will put her in eclipse looming in the background, the *Sierra Nevada* makes her way from Alameda Pier to San Francisco. **R.S. Ford Collection**

AS TOWERS of the big bridge rises in the background, the *Piedmont* enters the slip at Alameda Pier. Now, the ferries are still in command, five of them can be seen in this photo.
Louis L. Stein Jr. Collection

After completion of the test run and acceptance of the craft by the railroad, she was placed in service between the Western Pacific mole and the Ferry Building. In May 1933, Western Pacific abandoned its passenger ferry operations in favor of using the Southern Pacific facilities at Oakland Pier. At that time, the ferry, now named the *Feather River,* was purchased by the Southern Pacific, who renamed her the *Sierra Nevada* and placed her on the run to Alameda Pier.

Fog Schedules

When the decade of the 1930s began, the ferry business was near its zenith with some 20 passenger and auto ferries plying the lines of the four companies using the Ferry Building. As most of the boats operated on frequencies of 20 minutes or less, there were some 20 ferry arrivals and a like number of departures each hour. All of this traffic helped to create a highly congested area near the Ferry Building and was particularly conducive to collisions during inclement weather. Storms also were factors affecting the operation of the ferries, requiring captain and crew to use all of their seamanship skills in order to navigate the Bay. Instead of crossing the Bay smoothly and routinely, boats would roll and pitch in perilous battle with pounding waves and buffeting winds.

One of the more notable stormy crossings took place on a black night in January 1932. The auto ferry *Fresno* was tied up at the south end of the Ferry Building. In her wheelhouse Captain W.S. Carson peered across the Bay, but because of the blowing rain, the lights of Oakland Pier were completely obscured. At 8:00 p.m., he sounded a blast on the air horn and signaled the deck crew to cast off. Because of the storm that night, few people had ventured out, and there were only 11 autos and 25 passengers on board the big ferry.

With her diesel engines throbbing, the *Fresno* moved out into the teeth of the gale. The south wind shrieked around the wheelhouse as the captain looked out into the inky blackness and set his course for Oakland Pier. Five minutes out from the Ferry Building, the rolling and pitching ferry was caught by a giant wave which crashed on board and spilled tons of water into the engine room. The torrent of water shorted out the electrical control panel and the giant diesel engines suddenly stopped dead. Chief Engineer Charles Scholl tried repeatedly to get them started, but to no avail. Captain Carson began sounding distress signals on the air horn and sending up flares. All of the while, a south wind was blowing the disabled ferry northward at an alarming rate.

As the ferry neared Alcatraz Island, the lights of a tug could be seen approaching through the gloom. Soon the *Williams* hove to, and there ensued a hectic two hours during which tow lines were put on board the ferry only to part because of the strain caused by the heavy seas. Brave crewmen worked on slippery decks while frightened passengers watched through rain-drenched windows. Finally, after the arrival of a second tug, the *Sea Rover,* two tow lines were placed and the *Fresno* was towed to Oakland Pier, arriving there at 10:15 p.m.

The following summer, a dense fog lying off the Ferry Building caused another in a long list of foggy collisions. On August 14, 1933, ferries were operating on what was called the "fog schedule." This operation reduced the number of boats by about one-third, and thus reduced the possibility of collisions. For example, during normal operating hours, the Oakland Pier passenger run operated at 20-minute headways, but during "fog schedules," headway was increased to 40 minutes.

On that particular foggy morning, the *Oakland,* under the command of Captain Albert Anderson, departed for Alameda on the 7:15 a.m. crossing. The fog was so dense that Captain Anderson stationed a lookout at the bow to listen for sounds of other ferries and ships. A scant three minutes out of the Ferry Building, the lookout yelled a warning on hearing the air horn of an approaching auto ferry. But too late! Out of the fog came the *Lake Tahoe,* and before either captain could get his boat stopped, the two came together with a splintering crash.

In fact, there was no serious damage other than a smashed fantail on the *Oakland.* After backing off, each ferry was able to creep slowly to its respective destination. On reaching Alameda Pier, the *Oakland* experienced difficulty in making port because of damage from the collision. Seeing the problem, many of the men on board lent hands on pulling lines so that the ferry could be moored. After the passengers had debarked, the *Oakland* went over to the shipyard for repairs. The temporary loss of this ferry resulted in the annulment of the 7:50 boat from Alameda Pier, as it was not until nearly 9 o'clock that a relief boat could be brought to Alameda to fill the *Oakland's* schedule.

One of the last notable ferry collisions on the Bay occurred in dense fog beneath the new Bay Bridge on the morning of November 30, 1936. As was usually the case in such weather, the ferries were creeping slowly across the Bay, while above on the bridge, cars and buses were going across at only slightly reduced speeds. On that morning, Captain James C. Susan was taking the *Berkeley* from Alameda Pier to the Ferry Building. Nearing the midbay cable anchorage, Captain Susan sensed more than saw an approaching ferry. Suddenly, the auto ferry *El Paso* emerged out of the fog and struck the *Berkeley* a glancing blow on her bow. Momentum carried the two ferries forward, and before Captain J.M. Gaynor, on the *El Paso,* could get his ferry stopped, she slammed into the *Berkeley* a second time.

After stopping, both captains surveyed their ferries and found only negligible structural damage. Fortunately only 13 passengers had been injured, and after all had received first aid, the two ferries got underway again and continued to their berths.

Battling the Bridge

During the years prior to the opening of the Bay Bridge, Southern Pacific-Golden Gate Ferries experienced a steady growth in traffic and a corresponding growth in earnings. By the end of 1930, earnings were paid $2.01 per share of common stock and $27.07 per share of preferred stock. By 1934, the annual number of autos carried had risen to 4,975,237 and the number of passengers to 13,011,112. Gross revenues during that year were $4,700,485, and net revenues were $600,057.

In October 1934, the management of the ferry company announced that all further dividends would be suspended because the soon-to-be-opened Bay Bridge had forced the value of ferry stock to a very low level. During that month, quotations on S.P.-G.G. "A" stock went as low as 3½, while that of "B" stock went down to 1-3/8. A.D. McDonald, chairman of the board of directors of the ferry company, instituted a financial belt-tightening program so that the firm would be able to pay its bonded indebtedness and be ready to compete with the Bay Bridge, once that facility was opened to traffic. As a part of its bridge-battling strategy, the ferry company increased its depreciation schedules so that by the end of the decade, all ferries and other properties would be fully depreciated. This increase is illustrated by noting that in 1933 the depreciation was set at $668,863, while for the following year, the depreciation was put at $1,157,318.

NEARLY COMPLETE but not yet open, the Bay Bridge provides backdrop for the *New Orleans,* on her way from Oakland Pier to San Francisco in March 1936. Doomsday was nearing.   **R.S. Ford Collection**

THE *OAKLAND* leaves Oakland Pier. To the right, suburban electric cars sit on tail track to west of trainshed. **Southern Pacific**

In an effort to cut costs, S.P.-G.G. applied to the State Railroad Commission on January 14, 1935, for permission to abandon the Richmond auto ferry line. The company pointed out that during both 1933 and 1934 the line had suffered losses of more than $25,000. The commission denied the abandonment request, but it granted the company the right to reduce service to only two daily trips, one round trip in the morning and one in the late afternoon. The commission allowed the company to discontinue all trips on Sundays and holidays.

Shortly before the Bay Bridge was opened to vehicular traffic, the ferry company announced a new fare schedule to take effect on November 12, 1936, the opening day of the Bay Bridge. The new fares were essentially the same as the tolls that would be charged by the bridge and were designed to meet the competition.

If fares were to be competitive with the bridge, so were schedules. All-night ferry service was stressed. E.H. Maggard, vice president of the company, stated that with the opening of the bridge, ferries would be run between the Ferry Building and Oakland Pier on a 7½-minute headway until 9:00 p.m., then at 9:15, 9:30, 9:45, 10:00, and hourly until 6:00 a.m., when the 7½-minute headway would be resumed. Similar all-night service would be operated on the Berkeley line, with boats leaving the Hyde Street wharf every 20 minutes until 8:30 p.m., then at 9:00, 9:30, 10:00, 10:30 and hourly until 6:30 a.m. when the 20-minute service would start again. There was, however, no all-night service on either the Alameda Pier line or the Creek Route.

With the approach of 1937, the effect of the Bay Bridge on the auto ferry system was making itself felt. Losses were mounting on all lines except the still heavily patronized Oakland Pier route. To offset losses on the Creek Route—the "Nickel Ferry" of years gone by—one-way fares were raised from five cents to 10 cents on December 27, 1936, but still the losses mounted.

On June 4, 1937, Southern Pacific-Golden Gate Ferries applied to the State Railroad Commission for permission to abandon three lines: the former Monticello Steamship Company route to Vallejo, the Richmond ferry, and the Creek Route. The application also requested suspension of all-night service on the Berkeley line as well as the introduction of a special reduced fare on the Oakland Pier line. Fares on this latter line would be further reduced to meet the challenge of the Bay Bridge. One-way fares were proposed to be 30 cents for car and driver and 50 cents for a round-trip ticket.

At the hearings on these applications, Dr. Ford K. Edwards

TABLE 6 -- *Auto Ferry Tariff, November 12, 1936*

BETWEEN Oakland Pier or Alameda Pier AND San Francisco:

Auto, driver, and 4 passengers	$ 0.65
Auto with trailer and driver	1.15
Truck with driver	0.75
Truck with trailer and driver	1.50
Bus with driver	0.75
Motorcycle with driver	0.20
Motorcycle with sidecar and driver	0.30
Extra passengers, each	0.05
Monthly commute (50 trips) for auto, driver, and 4 passengers	22.50

THE CAPTAIN is all business as he pilots the *Oakland* out of the slip at Alameda Pier on one of the last days of passenger ferry service on this line. Capt. William Elsasser typified the highly professional S.P. ferrymen. **R.S. Ford Collection**

DOING BATTLE with the new bridge, the *El Paso* departs from Oakland with a full load of autos while, to left, the *San Mateo* makes her approach. Due to frequent service, low fares, the auto ferries managed to retain good patronage for a while after bridge opened.
R.S. Ford Collection

presented testimony that the ferry company was losing $23,000 annually on the Berkeley line, $20,000 annually on the Oakland Pier line, and $2,400 annually on the Creek Route. Dr. Edwards concluded his presentation with the opinion that because the ferry company could not operate economically with the existing fares, lower fares would only cause the company to lose more money, and hence the fare reduction should be denied. Following this testimony, Oakland City Attorney Bert Fernhoff vigorously protested the proposed abandonment of the Creek Route. He stated that this line was a vital link between downtown Oakland and downtown San Francisco. With the loss of this line, he said, citizens of Oakland would have to rely on train service and then a transfer to ferries to get across the Bay. He admitted that the 10-cent fare was a real transportation bargain, as one could make the round trip for 20 cents, which was less than the one-way fare by train and ferry.

One week after the hearings had been concluded, the ferry company returned to the commission with an amended application asking to end all service on the Hyde Street-Berkeley line. This was approved together with the original applications, and service ceased on the affected lines on October 16, 1937.

Abandonment of the three lines left Southern Pacific-Golden Gate Ferries with only three remaining routes: San Francisco to Oakland Pier, San Francisco to Alameda Pier, and Hyde Street to Sausalito. The abandonments also left the ferry company with a surplus of ferries. The *Golden Coast, Golden Dawn,* and *Golden Way* subsequently were beached and dismantled; the *Golden Gate,* moored at Oakland Outer Harbor, sank and later was dismantled. The *Golden Era* was tied up for several years until sold in February 1939 to the Sacramento Speedboat Association and towed to Sacramento to be used as a clubhouse. Also surplus were the *City of Sacramento, Napa Valley,* and *Calistoga.* The *City of Sacramento* was tied up on the Estuary to be available for relief service; the other two boats were tied up at the company wharf in Vallejo.

The ferry company now felt itself in a position to throw its entire strength into a battle for survival with both the Bay Bridge and the Golden Gate Bridge. Up to this time, the California Toll Bridge Authority had gone on the assumption that once the Bay Bridge had been opened for traffic, the ferry company would routinely go out of business without so much as a struggle. When it became evident that this would not be

HURRY! The main floor Southern Pacific waiting room at the Ferry Building could be a madhouse of people scurrying for the ferry. Key System and Northwestern Pacific had like facilities on the same floor. In mid-1970s area was utilized as office space for the California Department of Conservation. **Southern Pacific**

ON MORNING TRIPS to The City (above), commuters took seats to read of the morning news in the *San Francisco Chronicle* or, perhaps, the Hearst competition, the *Examiner*. The trip home in the evening (below) was a more relaxed affair, with many gathering on the rear deck to smoke, chat, or reflect on the events of the day. Alas, a comparable decompression chamber does not exist in this day and age.

Both Southern Pacific

DINING AFLOAT: Restaurant crew on the *Oakland* awaits the arrival of the next boatload of hungry commuters (above). There was hardly time for a leisurely repast, however. Breakfast is in full swing (below) on board the *Sierra Nevada* as commuters grab a quick bite during the 18-minute crossing.
Both Southern Pacific

the case, the Authority began discussions on ways to clear the Bay from the competing auto ferries.

One of the first suggestions was that the Toll Bridge Authority should buy up all the properties of Southern Pacific-Golden Gate Ferries. In reply, the ferry company said it would sell to the Authority 10 ferries and the facilities at Oakland Pier and Alameda Pier for $6 million. But attorneys for the Authority said that body had no legal right to purchase any competing ferry system. Assemblyman Ken B. Dawson of San Francisco authored a bill during the 1937 session of the legislature authorizing the Toll Bridge Authority to purchase the ferry system for the quoted figure. The bill died.

On November 3, 1937, Earl Lee Kelly, State Director of Public Works, requested Governor Culbert L. Olsen to call a special session of the legislature in order to solve the problem of state purchase of the ferry system. Kelly maintained the state could save $16 million over a period of 30 years if the Bay Bridge had no ferry competition. With publication of Kelly's statement, the San Francisco Board of Supervisors voted nine to two favoring state purchase of the auto ferries; in contrast, the cities of the East Bay were mostly opposed.

On June 27, 1938, the State Railroad Commission ordered Southern Pacific-Golden Gate Ferries to suspend all service on the Hyde Street-Sausalito line in favor of the Golden Gate Bridge. At the same time, the commission refused to act on a petition from the State Toll Bridge Authority asking for either forced abandonment of the lines to the East Bay or the forced increase of fares from 35 cents to that of the one-way toll of 50 cents charged on the Bay Bridge. In denying the petition, the commission noted that ferry service to the East Bay was now a profitable operation, citing a company report showing a net profit of $56,286.29 during the six-month period from August 1937 to February 1938.

Abandonment of service to Marin County again left the company with a surplus of boats. It was decided to keep the six steel electric ferries, the three ferries of the *San Mateo* class, and the three Monticello boats. All others would be sold or scrapped. The first to be sold were the three boats of the

San Francisco - Oakland Pier
(Mission Street Terminal)

Leave San Francisco South End of Ferry Building	Crossing Time 18 Minutes	Leave Oakland Pier Foot of 7th Street
6 00 AM		6 00 AM
6 30 AM		*6 30 AM
7 00 AM		6 45 AM
then every	Foot Passengers Not Carried	then every
15 minutes until		15 minutes until
7 30 PM		**7 00 PM**
7 40 PM		**7 10 PM**
then every	Extra Service When Traffic Demands	then every
20 minutes until		20 minutes until
10 00 PM		**9 30 PM**
10 30 PM		**10 00 PM**
11 00 PM		**10 30 PM**
then hourly until		then hourly until
6 00 AM		5 30 AM

San Francisco - Sausalito
(Hyde Street Terminal)

Leave San Francisco foot of Hyde Street	Crossing Time 20 Minutes	Leave Sausalito Water Street Slip
Every		Every
20 Minutes		20 Minutes
6 00 AM		5 30 AM
to		to
7 00 PM	Foot Passengers One Way 15c Round Trip 25c	6 30 PM
then every		then every
30 minutes until		30 minutes until
9 00 PM		**8 30 PM**
then hourly until		then hourly until
4 00 AM		3 30 AM
then every		then every
30 minutes until		30 minutes until
6 00 AM		5 30 AM

TRUCKS:
Highway Load Limits Carried.

TIME TABLE
ROAD MAP
FARES

AUTO FERRY
SERVICE
SAN FRANCISCO BAY

Southern Pacific Golden Gate Ferries, Ltd.

"O. 43 50M 10-17-37

San Francisco - Alameda

Monday to Saturday

Leave San Francisco South End of Ferry Building		Leave Alameda Foot of Pacific Avenue	
6 15 AM	then every	6 15 AM	**7 06 PM**
6 45 AM	30 min. until	6 50 AM	**8 06 PM**
7 15 AM	**4 45 PM**	8 50 AM	**9 06 PM**
7 45 AM	x **5 15 PM**	then every	**10 06 PM**
8 15 AM	x **5 45 PM**	30 min. until	**11 06 PM**
then every	**6 15 PM**	**6 20 PM**	12 06 AM
30 min. until	**6 45 PM**	then	1 06 AM
12 15 PM		**Sundays & Holidays only**	
* **12 45 PM**	then every	Leave San Francisco	Leave Alameda
* **1 15 PM**	hour until	6 45 AM	6 15 AM
1 45 PM	12 45 AM	then every hour until 12 45 AM	7 06 AM then hourly till 1 06 AM

* Daily except Saturday.
x Saturday only.
Crossing Time 20 Minutes.

Foot Passengers Not Carried
Note: Trucks weighing over 25,000 lbs. gross or exceeding 9 ft. 8 in. in height not carried.

Restaurant Prices Reduced

Special Chef Breakfast	20c - 25c - 30c - 45c
Snail, Butterhorn or Danish rolls and Coffee	15c
Plate Luncheon (11:00 a. m. to 3:00 p. m.)	35c
Choice of Soup or Pudding - Choice of Seven Entrees - Tea, Coffee or Milk.	
(Salad Bowl and Above Luncheons - 50c)	
The Salad Bowl	25c
Cheese Chunk and Crackers with Beer	25c
Beer or Ale with Crackers	15c
Coca Cola or Soda Pop	5c
Sherry, Port, Red or White Wine with Meals	10c

SAVE TIME :: EAT ON THE BOAT
RESTAURANT : WASHROOMS : NEWS STANDS
BOOTBLACK SMOKING ROOMS ON ALL BOATS

TIME TABLE - - CITY MAPS

SAVE MONEY—USE THE AUTO FERRIES

Cheapest Way to Cross the Bay

30c ONE WAY
Auto and Party of Five

50 TRIP TICKET—$10	ROUND TRIP—50c
20¢ A TRIP	**25¢** A TRIP
car and driver good for 6 months	car and party of 5 return limit 30 days

Auto Trailer 30c one way - 50c round trip

Southern Pacific Golden Gate Ferries, Ltd.

C. F. Fennema, General Manager — **G. E. Collins, Traffic Agent**
65 Market Street, San Francisco, Calif.
No. 45-10M 7-39

Auto Ferry Service

CREEK ROUTE
FERRY
SAN FRANCISCO · OAKLAND

Convenient Route for Automobiles and Trucks

Leave San Francisco South End of Ferry Building	Crossing time between San Francisco and Broadway 35 min., except crossing time is 50 min. when boat stops at Alameda.	Leave Oakland foot of Broadway
8 25 AM		9 15 AM
10 10 AM	**No Service Sundays and Holidays**	11 00 AM
11 45 AM		12 30 PM
1 50 PM		2 40 PM
3 30 PM	* Stops at Alameda Pier daily except Saturday for Vehicles only.	* 4 20 PM
* 5 20 PM		6 15 PM

Sausalito, Berkeley and Oakland Pier Auto Ferries Operate All Night.

Southern Pacific Golden Gate Ferries, Ltd.

No. 61 50M Effective Jan. 1st 1937

SAN FRANCISCO-OAKLAND
Vehicles only—foot passengers not carried

Leave San Francisco South end Ferry Bldg.	Leave Oakland Pier Foot of 7th Street
MONDAYS TO SATURDAYS, Incl.	
Every **15** minutes	
6 30 AM to **8 00 PM**	6 30 AM to **7 00 PM**
Every **20** minutes	
8 00 PM to **10 PM**	**7 10 PM** to **9 30 PM**
Every **30** minutes	
10 00 PM to **12 midnite**	**9 30 PM** to **11 30 PM**
Every HOUR	
12 midnite to 6 AM then 6 30 AM	**11 30 PM** to 5 30 AM then 6 AM, 6 30 AM
SATURDAY NIGHTS	
Every **20** minutes	
8 00 PM to 3 00 AM	**7 10 PM** to 3 00 AM
Every HOUR	
3 00 AM to 6 AM then 6 30 AM	3 30 AM to 5 30 AM then 6 AM, 6 30 AM
SUNDAYS & HOLIDAYS	
Every **30** minutes	
6 00 AM to 8 00 AM	6 00 AM to 7 30 AM
Every **20** minutes	
8 00 AM to 10 00 AM	7 30 AM to 9 50 AM
Every **15** minutes	
10 00 AM to **12 midnite** then 12 30 AM	10 00 AM to **12 midnite** then 12 30 AM
Every HOUR	
1 00 AM to 6 AM then 6 30 AM	12 30 AM to 5 30 AM then 6 AM

SAN FRANCISCO - ALAMEDA
Leave San Francisco **9 10 PM** and Alameda **9 30 PM**
Daily except Saturdays, Sundays and Holidays.
Restaurant, Newsstand & Bootblack on all boats

TRUCKS: Highway load limits carried. Crossing time 18 minutes. EXTRA SERVICE: during periods of heavy traffic a boat leaves terminals San Francisco and Oakland as often as every 9 or 10 minutes. HOLIDAY SERVICE will be operated New Year's, Washington's Birthday, Decoration Day, July 4th, Labor Day, Thanksgiving and Christmas.

Collection of R. S. Ford

S.P.- GOLDEN GATE FERRIES SCHEDULES 1937-1939

WAITING PATIENTLY for its passengers, the *Alameda* lies berthed in the Oakland slip at the San Francisco Ferry Building. The Alameda slip is to the left, the Key System slip to the right. Large building in left background is the headquarters of the vast Southern Pacific empire.
R.S. Ford Collection

New Orleans class. These were bought by the Richmond-San Rafael Ferry and Transportation Company in the latter part of 1938 for use on their route from Point Richmond to Point San Quentin.

Five of the "Golden Boats," the *Golden Age, Golden Bear, Golden Poppy, Golden Shore,* and *Golden State,* were sold to the Puget Sound Navigation Company and its subsidiary, Kitsap County Transportation Company. All five boats were towed northward in the latter part of 1937. The *Golden West,* after initially being sold to the Puget Sound Navigation Company, was resold to the San Diego-Coronado Ferry Company before departing from San Francisco Bay. There were no takers for the *Golden Gate,* and she was dismantled.

When the State Railroad Commission issued its order calling for the abandonment of ferry service to Sausalito but refusing to order the abandonment of auto ferry service to the East Bay, Bay Bridge Chief Purcell was decidedly unhappy. With only the lines to the East Bay in operation, he argued, the ferry company could throw its entire financial resources into competition with the Bay Bridge. Thus, it would take much longer to retire the bonds on the bridge and would cost the taxpayers of the state more money.

In rebuttal to Purcell's statement, Wallace Ware, president of the State Railroad Commission, commented:

> "The Commission cannot deny a common carrier the right to exist. It can, and did order the abandonment of unprofitable lines. But, the decision as to whether to stay in or go out of business is beyond the purview of the Commission and is strictly up to the common carrier involved."

It soon became apparent that a showdown was approaching between the Bay Bridge (and the Toll Bridge Authority) and Southern Pacific-Golden Gate Ferries. This fact became even more evident as the time approached for the end of passenger ferry operations across the Bay in favor of electric train operation across the Bay Bridge. Late in 1938, Southern Pacific announced its plan to abandon Alameda Pier with the opening of train service across the bridge. Concomitant with this announcement came word from the ferry company that auto ferry service to Alameda Pier would be abandoned on January 15, 1939.

This latter announcement evoked a storm of protest from both sides of the Bay. Both the cities of San Francisco and Alameda went on record as being opposed to the abandonment proposal. At a hearing before the State Railroad Commission on the matter, Reginald L. Vaughn, special counsel to the city of Alameda, suggested that auto ferry service might be curtailed to only two trips per day. The Civic League of Improvement Clubs of Alameda cited the need for direct auto ferry service from Alameda to San Francisco, and for direct transportation from San Francisco to the Alameda Naval Air Base. In reply to all of this opposition, Evan Foulds, counsel for the ferry company, argued that minimal service in the form of but two trips per day would not even meet operating expenses. He pointed out that even with capacity loads on both trips, the gross revenue would be only $42 per day while operating costs would be $162 per day.

In a decision that pleased no one, the Railroad Commission ruled that beginning January 15, 1939, Southern Pacific-Golden Gate Ferries should provide a minimum of one crossing each way daily except Sundays and holidays. This minimal service subsequently was performed by a boat which left the Ferry Building at 9:10 p.m. and departed from Alameda Pier 20 minutes later.

For all intents and purposes, Southern Pacific-Golden Gate Ferries was reduced to only one line, that between San Francisco and Oakland Pier. Even though this line was well patronized, time was fast running out for the auto ferries; within another 18 months, triumph of bridge over boat would be complete.

A Ferry Christmas

In the early part of this century, commuter clubs developed on the various westbound ferry trips. They evolved as people habitually took the same trains each morning which connected with the same boats. This consistency was heightened by the fact that over the years schedules changed but little. For example, in 1910, one of the most heavily traveled commute ferries departed from Oakland Pier at 7:30 each morning. Twenty years later, a 7:30 boat still departed from Oakland Pier and carried substantially the same numbers of people.

With the same faces seen six mornings a week—in those days everyone worked at least a half day on Saturday—it was natural that informal clubs would form for each morning crossing. There were commuter clubs on the morning runs from Oakland Pier and also on the parallel runs on the Key System ferries.

Commuter clubs also were present on the ferries from Alameda Pier, and it was here that the most famous of all commuter clubs flourished. This was the Alameda 7:30 S.P. Commuters Club which convened six mornings a week on the boat which departed from Alameda Pier at 7:51 and arrived at the Ferry Building at 8:11 a.m. This ferry was the connection for three heavily traveled trains: the Encinal Avenue train which left South High Street at 7:27 a.m., the Lincoln Avenue train which left North Park Street at the same time, and the express train from Dutton Avenue which departed from that station at 7:13 a.m.

The Alameda 7:30 S.P. Commuters Club was one of the more active clubs on the Bay. The group had some sort of program planned at least once a month. In summertime, it would be a bevy of lovely secretaries who would be lined up for a bathing beauty contest. The first day of fall always was celebrated with "Straw Hat Day," when many a commuter would ceremoniously toss his "Sailer" straw hat far out into the Bay. During the fall there were football rallies on Saturdays, and the biggest rally of the year took place on the third Saturday of November. This was the day that a certain form of madness gripped the entire Bay Area; this was Big Game Day. In those days, the most important football game of the year occurred when the Golden Bears of the University of California met the

NOTHING COULD BE FINER than to enjoy the view of the Bay from the upper deck of a ferry. In this photo, the *Oakland* is heading beneath the Bay Bridge.
R.S. Ford Collection

Indians of Stanford University. It mattered not what the win-loss record of either team was; the game usually was so packed with emotion that past records did not count. On Big Game Day, the Old Blues from Cal and the Old Reds from Stanford would sing their school songs and talk about the famous plays of yesteryear.

Perhaps the most important tradition of any of the commuter clubs was the annual Christmas parties celebrated on the morning of the last working day before that holiday. Ever since the days of the old *Bay City* which always had been decorated with boughs of evergreens, Christmas parties were held annually. Commuters on the Oakland Pier ferries boasted that their parties were better than those on the rival Key System boats. But, members of the Alameda 7:30 S.P. Commuters Club *knew* that their parties were bigger and better than on any other boat on the Bay.

Each year, the parties got bigger, decorations became brighter, and the music, food, and drink more lavish. Finally, Christmas 1938 arrived and everyone knew that this would be the last Ferry Christmas. Next year there would be no more ferries, and commuters would be whisked to their jobs on the swift trains crossing the great Bay Bridge. The members of the Alameda 7:30 S.P. Commuters Club were determined to make the Ferry Christmas of 1938 the greatest of all since the tradition began back in 1908.

As he had been since 1925, Walter D. Miracle was named master of ceremonies for the occasion. The celebration took place on board the *Piedmont* on her morning crossing of Friday, December 23. Admission to the Christmas party, as always, was by way of a donation of canned goods to be given to families in need. By the time the ferry was ready to cast off, many thousands of cans of food had been collected, enabling Miracle and his group to provide many "miracles" for needy families who otherwise may have gone hungry during the holidays.

In the Main Saloon of the ferry there was a huge glittering Christmas tree, and as the ferry crossed the Bay there were carols, music, gifts, and much camaraderie. Almost everyone on board was on a first name basis with everyone else, passengers and crew alike, as most had been making this same trip six days per week for many years.

By the time the ferry approached the Ferry Building, liquid Christmas cheer was flowing like water. Everyone was living for just this one bittersweet moment that soon would be over. In remembering that very last Ferry Christmas, Walter Miracle commented some time later,

> "The *Piedmont* drifted over to Treasure Island and arrived later at the Ferry Building, but nobody cared. After we docked, commuters shook hands with the crew, looked away quickly, blinked, and went ashore. The Ferry Christmas party was over . . . forever."

The Death of an Institution

With the arrival of New Year's Day 1939, East Bay commuters began to look forward in earnest to the start of train operation across the Bay Bridge. Most realized, of course, that in only a few weeks a tradition would be ending. With the advent of a more modern mode of crossing the Bay, the era of the faithful ferries would be ending.

Gone would be the commuter clubs, the happy times, and the leisurely crossings during which a man had time to meditate. Gone would be the ferry breakfasts on the way to work and the multitude of other things that gave the ferries their charm and glamor. As the number of days grew fewer, more and more people began making special trips across the Bay to savor for one last time the thrill of going to San Francisco by ferry. Families came with their children clutching bags of bread crumbs to toss to the wheeling and crying gulls that followed every ferry as it went back and forth across the Bay.

At night, with the gentle golden arch of the Bay Bridge's sodium vapor lights soaring overhead, one could enjoy the sparkle of lights on both sides of the dark waters. Looking west, one could see the glow of Market Street behind the illuminated tower of the Ferry Building. To the north, with letters large enough for all the world to see, was a red neon sign spelling out *WELLMAN COFFEE*. To the east, one could identify the Key System pier by its huge red neon sign. Beyond was, to many a small fry, the most wondrous sign of all, the giant Sherwin-Williams animated neon sign spelling out *IT COVERS THE EARTH* as a flood of red neon paint spilled over a green globe. As a backdrop to these signs were the sparkling lights of the East Bay, looking like a blanket of diamonds tossed on the dark shape of the Berkeley Hills. To all of these was added the special tang and scent of the Bay, the fragrance of salt air and the ships that one would never forget.

In anticipation of the last day of Southern Pacific commuter ferry service, the railroad announced early in January the details of the service changes. All train-service to and from Alameda Pier would be discontinued as would the San Francisco to Alameda Pier passenger ferries. This discontinuance would result in the retiring of the *Oakland, Piedmont,* and *Sierra Nevada* as well as the laying off of all ferry crews operating from that facility. The pier trainshed and Alameda Pier Tower also would be abandoned. For the time being, the auto ferry service performed by Southern Pacific-Golden Gate Ferries would continue, but at a greatly reduced level.

At Oakland Pier, electric train service would no longer be performed, although mainline steam train service would continue without interruption. At that facility, the ferries *Alameda, Santa Clara,* and *Berkeley* would be retained with full crews. The *Sacramento* would be tied up for standby service, although she would have no regular crew. In all, it was estimated that about 100 ferrymen would be retired or laid off due to the change.

On the last full day of operation, January 14, all of the various commuter clubs held some sort of memorial services. The most publicized was that held by the Alameda 7:30 S.P. Commuters Club on board the *Piedmont.* The previous morning, the *San Francisco Chronicle* carried a story by staff writer Earle Ennis telling of the plans for the last day celebration. The story ended with the following comment,

> "Funeral services for the dying ferry system will be held on the S.P. ferryboat *Piedmont,* beginning at 7:50 o'clock tomorrow morning by the Alameda 7:30 Commuters Club. The service will mark the passing of the old familiar ferries."

The next morning, as 2,000 or more commuters went on board the *Piedmont,* each was handed a Commuters Crying Towel. This was a section of paper toweling on which had been printed the funeral program and the words to a number of songs, all enclosed within a black border. After almost everyone was on board, Walter D. Miracle, acting as chief undertaker, led a procession of silk-hatted pallbearers made up of longtime commuters Gustav Horst, Otto Shearer, Frank Thornton, and Frank Kelly. The pallbearers carried a model of

RADIATING THE CHARM of another age, the ferry and station building at Alameda Pier (above) basks in the sunlight of a Fall, 1938, day; in foreground is ticket office for the auto ferry. Looking bayward, one might have seen the *Sierra Nevada* churning up foam (below) as her forward propeller is reversed for entering the slip at Alameda Pier. Outline of the big Bay Bridge, still under construction, can be seen dimly in the distance.
Both R.S. Ford Collection

the *Sacramento* on board and were followed by others carrying placards bearing names of historic ferries. After everyone had boarded the *Piedmont,* Captain Enos Fouratt sounded a sonorous blast on the whistle, and the ferry began her very last 7:50 departure for San Francisco.

Everyone soon assembled on the afterdeck, and Miracle introduced Robert Lowenstein, who at that time was 71 and had been making this morning trip each working day since 1882. Because he was the oldest regular commuter, Lowenstein was named Honorary Captain of Commuter Ferries. Lowenstein was then asked if he had any particular memories of his many years of crossing San Francisco Bay by ferry. He recalled that during one evening trip in the 1890s, he was watching the lights of San Francisco from the deck when he noticed a woman jump overboard. With a yell, he tossed a life preserver overboard. With horror, he saw that she could not reach it, and as he watched, she was sucked under the churning paddle wheels. After the ferry had stopped, one of the mates got a lifeboat into the water and retrieved the body.

Back on board, the mate called out, "Who threw the life preserver to her?"

Lowenstein replied, "I did. Why do you ask?"

END OF AN ERA: Led by Walter D. Miracle, the "pallbearers" of the Alameda 7:30 S.P. Commuters Club carry a model of the *Sacramento* on board the *Piedmont* for the final morning commute run from Alameda Pier on January 14, 1939.
Vernon J. Sappers Collection

To this, the mate replied with a great deal of profanity, "Why you should be made to pay for it because we couldn't find it!"

At midbay, almost in the shadow of the Bay Bridge, the assembled group broke into song, ending with a rendition of "Auld Lang Syne." The pallbearers then picked up the bier and brought it to the rail. Miracle then intoned,

> "And now comes our painful duty, dear old ferryboat, to give you up to Father Neptune."

With that blessing, the model splashed overboard, and those lining the rail tossed marigold blossoms after it.

Ironically, instead of sinking, the model of the *Sacramento* soon bobbed to the surface and floated off. It was retrieved some two hours later by the Coast Guard as it was passing beneath the Golden Gate Bridge on the ebb tide. Returned to the Commuters Club, the model later was presented to the Alameda Historical Society.

With the ceremony over, a few bottles were passed about and the ferry made its way to the Ferry Building. After nearly colliding with an eastbound Key System boat, the *Piedmont* docked at 8:30, nearly 20 minutes late.

All that day and into the night, people rode the faithful ferries back and forth across the Bay. Finally it was time for the last trips of the commuter ferries. At Oakland Pier, the last electric trains came in shortly past 1:30 Sunday morning, connecting with the 1:40 boat for San Francisco. This last ferry, the *Alameda,* with Captain William A. Elsasser at the helm, made the last commuter run from Oakland Pier to San Francisco, arriving there at 2:05 a.m. The *Alameda* then returned to Oakland Pier, where she tied up for the night.

Unlike Oakland Pier where there would be early morning ferry departures as usual, patrons and employees at Alameda Pier knew that there would be no tomorrow. During normal operating procedures, the *Oakland* was called the "long boat," that is, she was used from the first morning run until the last run at night. Assisting the *Oakland* usually would be the *Sierra Nevada,* running as the "short boat" and tying up in early eve-

MAN IN GRAY: S.P. Passenger representative P.J. Hagerty typified the pleasant personality of the "men in gray" who assisted railroad and ferry passengers. Wharfinger's office was at Oakland Pier. Such public servants became scarce in later years.
R.S. Ford Collection

TWIN-STACKER *Santa Clara* churns her way toward Oakland Pier. This ferry and her sister, the *Alameda*, were large and fast and were used almost exclusively on the run to Oakland Pier.

R.S. Ford Collection

FIGURE 8

COMMUTERS FAREWELL TO SANTA CLAUS

TOMORROW, DECEMBER 23, 7:30 A.M. BOAT

44th (and last) XMAS PARTY

FUN • MUSIC • MERRIMENT
SERPENTINE • BALLOONS • NOISEMAKERS

HEAR SANTA'S FAREWELL SPEECH

MUSIC ON UPPER DECK (Soft and Sweet)
MUSIC ON LOWER DECK (Loud and Sour)
HAVE THE FOLKS AT HOME HEAR
THE PROGRAM OVER KPO 8:00 A. M.

As usual all this for a can of food for the needy
(BOY SCOUTS WILL ASSIST)

7:30 A. M. COMMUTERS CLUB

COMMUTER'S CRYING TOWEL

Farewell Ferry Boat Party
of
ALAMEDA 7:30 S. P. COMMUTERS CLUB
Friday, January 13, 1939

1. Funeral Procession
2. Installing Honorary Captain - - - Upper Deck
3. Musical Selections - - - Upper Deck
4. Strange Interlude - - - Passing Around the Bier
5. Burial Service - - - Lower Deck
6. Musical Selections - - - Lower Deck

1
Gee, but I'd give the world to see
That old gang of mine
I can't forget the old quartette
That sang "Sweet Adeline"
Goodbye forever old fellows and gals.
Goodbye forever old sweethearts and pals,
God bless them
Gee, but I'd give the world to see
That old gang of mine.

2
My Bonnie lies over the ocean
My Bonnie lies over the sea
My Bonnie lies over the ocean
Oh bring back my Bonnie to me, to me.

Bring back, bring back,
Oh bring back my Bonnie to me, to me
Bring back, bring back,
Oh bring back my Bonnie to me.

Last night as I lay on my pillow
Last night as I lay on my bed
Last night as I lay on my pillow
I dream't that my Bonnie was dead.

3
Memories, memories,
Dreams of love so true
O'er the sea of memory
Drifting back to you.
Childhood days, wildwood days
Among the birds and bees
You left me alone but
Still you're my own
In my beautiful memories.

4
Should auld acquaintance be forgot?
And never brought to mind?
Should auld acquaintance be forgot
And days of auld lang syne?

Chorus
For auld lang syne, my dear
For auld lang syne,
We'll take a cup o'kindness yet.
For the days of Auld Lang Syne.

And here's a hand, my trusty friend
And gie's a hand O'thine,
We'll take a richt-gude willie-waught
For the days of Auld Lang Syne.

STATION Ala. Pier — TRAIN REGISTER Jan. 14-1939 A.D. 19— Last and Final Sheet — WESTWARD

TRAIN	SIGNALS DISPLAYED	CONDUCTOR	ENGINEER	ENGINE	ARRIVED	DEPARTED	LOADS	EMPTIES	MS	CONDUCTOR	ENGINEER
Steamer	P.M.	Arrived	Departed	Capt.	Enr.	Line.	Autos	To	From	S.F.	
Oakland		3.10	3.28	Susan	3.26	3.25	5	6			
Piedmont		3.43	3.58	Fouratt	3.56	3.55	9	9			
Oakland		4.09	4.32	Susan	4.30	4.28	7	6			
Piedmont		4.45	4.56	Fouratt	4.54	4.53	6	6			
Oakland		5.14	5.33	Susan	5.30	5.31	8	4			
Piedmont		5.41	6.00	Fouratt	5.58	5.55	5	9			
Oakland		6.15	6.29	Susan	6.27½	6.25½	3	4			
Piedmont		6.47	Tie up Boat	Last Trips this schedule			X	6			
Oakland		7.11	7.15	Susan	7.02	7.04	6	1			
✓		8.07	8.10	✓	8.03	8.02	8	6			
✓		9.05	9.10	✓	9.07	9.03	9	6			
✓		10.06	10.08	✓	10.04	10.03	3	2			
✓		11.06	11.12	✓	11.07	11.09	8	9			
✓	A.M.	12.06	12.10	✓	12.06	12.07	11	6			
✓		1.10	1.23	✓	1.11	1.10	?	?			

Last boat to operate in Passenger service to Ala Pier

Collection of R. S. Ford

FAREWELL TO THE FERRIES

For the last two days of operation to Alameda Pier, the *Piedmont* was used with the *Oakland*. On the final night of operation, the *Piedmont* arrived at Alameda Pier on the last trip of her "short boat" schedule. On board the ferry, which was under the command of Captain Fouratt, were the usual complement of homeward-bound commuters and six automobiles. After discharging her passengers and cars, the *Piedmont* pulled out from the slip on her way to the shipyard and the final tie up, never to return. This left only the *Oakland*, with Captain James C. Susan, to provide the seven final departures from Alameda Pier.

The last trains into Alameda Pier arrived from the Lincoln Avenue line at 1:01 a.m., Sunday morning, and from the Encinal Avenue line one minute later. A short time later, at 1:10 a.m., the *Oakland* arrived in the slip with a large complement of well-wishers on board. The last trains departed from the train platform at 1:15, and the *Oakland* cast off at 1:23 a.m. The ferry made her way over to San Francisco, arriving there at 1:42 a.m. Instead of returning to Alameda Pier to tie up as was usually the case, Captain Susan then took the *Oakland* over to the shipyard, where she was tied up alongside the *Piedmont* and *Sierra Nevada*.

At Alameda Pier, after the last ferry and train had departed, a small group of employees gathered. One said, "Well, I guess that's it." The misty-eyed crewmen knew that a tradition was dead. Come Monday morning, the train platform, waiting room, and slip would stand deserted and silent. Never again would the stream of commuters flow onto the ferries in the morning and move homeward through the great building at nightfall. Finally, the building lights were put out, the towerman came down from his perch at Alameda Pier Tower, and the small, silent group walked slowly to their autos to go home.

But, the old Alameda Pier was not yet quite dead. True, there would be no more red trains, and the gleaming white ferries would no longer nose into the ornate covered slip. But, the auto ferry service provided by Southern Pacific-Golden Gate Ferries survived a few weeks longer. In spite of advertisements placed in the local newspapers encouraging patronage of the auto ferries, overwhelming losses and an almost total lack of use prompted the service to be withdrawn with little public notice by early February 1939.

ning when the schedule changed from 30-minute to 60-minute headways. The spare boat on the Alameda Pier run ordinarily was the *Piedmont*, which would be brought over whenever one of the regular boats was out of service. These three boats were used on the Alameda Pier run because all were capable of carrying automobiles. This auto service, although not generally publicized, provided Alamedans with 15-minute auto ferry service to San Francisco when considered in combination with the Southern Pacific-Golden Gate ferries.

During the last week of operation at Alameda Pier, the *Oakland* and *Sierra Nevada* alternated in their runs. The *Sierra Nevada* tied up for the last time on Thursday, January 12, when Captain Albert Anderson brought her into the slip at 6:41 p.m. After discharging her passengers and nine autos, the ferry proceeded to the Peralta Street shipyard, where she was docked and her fires banked.

NEWSSTAND on the *Oakland* (above) and sister boats did a brisk business. Snacks and smokes were available, too. As the big bridge came into use, last ferry runs were made. Below is the *Sierra Nevada* as she approaches Alameda Pier on her last commute run from San Francisco on January 12, 1939. Two days later, Alameda Pier was shut down.
Both R.S. Ford Collection

IT WAS THE SAD DUTY of Capt. James C. Susan to pilot the *Oakland* on the last trip from San Francisco to Alameda Pier. It was at 1:23 a.m. on January 15, 1939, that Susan nudged the *Oakland's* bow into the slip at Alameda, closing the books on a great era. **R.S. Ford Collection**

With the demise of Alameda Pier, Oakland Pier became the only remaining transbay ferry terminal on the east side of San Francisco Bay. Service was provided by the four remaining Southern Pacific passenger ferries as well as the six steel electric auto ferries of the Southern Pacific-Golden Gate line. All of the other auto ferries had been removed from service and offered for sale.

After the three Alameda passenger ferries had become surplus, they were leased to the Key System to provide additional ferry service to the Golden Gate International Exposition on Treasure Island. After being repainted in the orange livery of Key System, the three ferries worked with the four Key System boats during the fair seasons of 1939 and 1940. The *Oakland* and *Piedmont* usually were seen on the run from the Ferry Building to the main entrance to Treasure Island. The *Sierra Nevada* most often was used on the run from the Key System pier to the east entrance to Treasure Island. With the closing of the fair, all three ferries were returned to the Southern Pacific. The *Sierra Nevada* was repainted white and was used as an extra boat at Oakland Pier. Both the *Oakland* and *Piedmont* were retired and scheduled for dismantling.

In commenting on the pending disposal of the two older ferries, one W.R. Hogarty wrote a letter to the editor of the *San Francisco Chronicle* urging the preservation of at least one of them. He urged that one of the boats be converted into a maritime museum depicting the nautical history of San Francisco Bay. Hogarty ended his letter by noting,

"Unless something is done to save these boats, they soon will be only memories in the minds of countless commuters."

In the fall of 1940, the *Oakland* was towed to the old Broadway Wharf, where she was tied up for dismantling. While there, she caught fire and was nearly destroyed by a blaze that sent up a pillar of smoke that could be seen for miles around. After the fire was put out, the hulk of the ferry was towed to the Alameda mud flats and beached. Vandals soon stripped the once-proud ferry and she disappeared from view. The venerable old *Piedmont* slipped away almost unnoticed. She was taken to the Sacramento-San Joaquin Delta and beached on one of the islands where she disintegrated after being stripped and vandalized.

The Last Auto Ferry

In the latter part of 1939, it was announced that the *Yosemite* had been bought by the Argentina-Uruguayan Navigation Touring Co. for $70,000. This firm planned to use the ferry on the 30-mile crossing of the Rio de la Plata between Buenos Aires and Colonia, located at the south end of the highway for Montevideo. So that the ferry could make the 9,000-mile sea voyage under her own power, she was taken to the Bethlehem Shipbuilding Corporation yard for a thorough rebuilding. Included in the $35,000 job was the installation of crew quarters, interior I-beam bracing, two additional keels for increased stability, and extra fuel and water tanks. The ferry also was converted to single-end operation, and the aft wheelhouse was made into a radio room complete with a 50-watt Heintz and Kauffman transmitter.

The crew for the ferry, rechristened the *Argentina,* arrived from Uruguay in January 1940. Headed by Captain Eduardo M. Saez, who formerly was with the Uruguayan Navy, the crew consisted of 21 men and a small dog named Peyke. Captain Saez planned to sail from San Francisco on or about January 21. He said that he hoped to get to Buenos Aires in about 50 days, trusting that the ferry could maintain a speed of about 10 knots. Planned ports of call included San Pedro, Manzanillo, Trinidad, Pará, and Pernambuco. Home port for the ferry would be Montevideo.

It took much longer to outfit the *Argentina* than originally contemplated, and it was not until the first of April that the rebuilding job was completed. Finally, on the afternoon of April 16, 1940, the ferry was ready to cast off from the Hyde Street pier on what probably would be the longest sea journey of any ferry in history. On hand to bid the ferry good-by was retired Captain Michael H. Skibinski, who had been captain of the *Yosemite* while she had been on the San Francisco to Richmond run during the years 1926 to 1928. Finally, at 4:00 p.m., Captain Saez pulled the whistle cord and the deckhands

Alameda Pier Finale

NAPOLEON would have been at home in the upper floor waiting room at Alameda Pier, S.P.'s most ornate ferry facility (left). Exterior view taken in last months (below) showed red trains and auto ferry toll booth.
**Louis L. Stein Collection;
R.S. Ford Collection**

ALAMEDA PIER from the air was an impressive sight. There were separate slips for train ferries (above) and auto boats. Western Pacific railroad yards were across Estuary, at top of photo. On the last night of service, January 14, 1939, two apron-tenders and two inspectors pose glumly for the camera (below). Note fare register for foot passengers.
Both R.S. Ford Collection

cast off. The *Argentina* backed into the Bay, turned, and headed out to sea beneath the Golden Gate Bridge.

By the beginning of 1940, Southern Pacific-Golden Gate Ferries recognized that with lowered tolls on the Bay Bridge, the ferries had little or no chance of economic competition. Even with the prevailing 30-cent fare, the operation had become only marginal at best. With the prospect of having to lower fares even farther, the situation became impossible. With no financial resources left, the ferry company filed for bankruptcy on April 1, 1940, and Sterling Carr was named as Trustee. At the same time, the company applied for the abandonment of the only remaining auto ferry line.

At the subsequent abandonment hearing, opposition statements were heard from bondholders and employees. These two groups proposed that a new company be formed to take over the operation of the Oakland Pier auto ferry line. It was proposed that the new company be formed as a combination of bondholders and employees. Because of this proposal, the State Railroad Commission deferred any ruling on the abandonment until the Southern Pacific Company, sole holder of Southern Pacific-Golden Gate Ferry stock, had time to study the proposition. Carr announced that the Oakland Pier auto ferry would meantime continue to operate on a day-to-day basis.

In mid-May 1940, Southern Pacific rejected the proposal for a new operating company. Representatives of the railroad stated that they were interested neither in relinquishing their control of the ferry company nor in continuing the operation. Having no other recourse, Burton J. Wyman, Referee in Bankruptcy, ordered the ferries stopped. His order was issued late

BOOMER BOATS: Key Route fell heir to two S.P. ferries to carry pier heavy traffic to the 1939 Golden Gate International Exposition. *Piedmont* (above) and *Sierra Nevada* (below) shuttled between Key Route pier and Treasure Island for two seasons, repainted in Key's orange livery.
Both Bert H. Ward

in the afternoon of Thursday, May 16, 1940; the order became effective at 9 o'clock that night.

When Captain Edward Hallin stepped into the wheelhouse of the ferry *Lake Tahoe* at 9:20 p.m. that night, he knew that this was to be the last crossing of an auto ferry on San Francisco Bay. At departure time, he sounded his air horn and the deckhands cast off. In an adjacent slip, one of the Southern Pacific passenger ferries sat with lights aglow. From her stack came an answering triple blast, which in maritime parlance meant, "Good-by, good luck." After an uneventful trip across the Bay, the *Lake Tahoe* arrived at Oakland Pier at 9:40. After the few autos had driven off the ferry, Captain Hallin made his final entry in the log book of the *Lake Tahoe* and closed the cover on 31 years of history of auto ferries running between San Francisco and the East Bay.

With the end of auto ferry service, the electric ferries were taken to the Estuary where they were tied up next to the other remaining auto ferries. All boats initially were offered for sale to the Toll Bridge Authority with the suggestion that they be held in reserve for use during a national emergency. In reply to this offer, Morgan Keaton, deputy director of the State Department of Public Works, stated that the Toll Bridge Authority had no legal right to purchase or operate the boats. In addition, he noted that the state would be unable to maintain the ferries from revenues received from the existing 25-cent tolls.

On July 8, 1940, Laurence Tharp, who represented the Anglo-California National Bank, reported that the six electric ferries *(Fresno, Lake Tahoe, Mendocino, Redwood Empire, Santa Rosa,* and *Stockton)* had been purchased by a Brazilian firm for $330,000. A week later, on June 17, Tharp held a public auction on the steps of the San Francisco City Hall for the five remaining ferries. Present were a group of newsmen, several idle bystanders, and three secretaries who were on their lunch break. Holding up his hand, Tharp announced in a loud voice:

> "This is the public sale of the Golden Gate ferries *Calistoga, Napa Valley, City of Sacramento, San Mateo,* and *Shasta.* Does anyone here wish to make a bid?"
>
> Silence.
>
> "Doesn't anyone here wish to make a bid on even one boat?"
>
> More silence.
>
> "I take it that there are no bidders present."
>
> Continued silence.

Because of the total lack of response, Tharp scheduled another auction three weeks hence at the old Broadway Wharf in Oakland. That same day, he announced that the Brazilian firm had defaulted on its bid to buy the electric ferries because they had failed to post the necessary deposit.

The next day, Tharp announced that a second bid had been received for the six electric ferries. This bid was by Puget Sound Navigation Company and was in the amount of $330,001. Because the bid was accompanied by a certified check covering the required deposit, the bid was accepted by the bankruptcy court and the trustee of the ferry company. Accompanying this bid was a second bid from the same company for the ferries *Shasta* and *San Mateo.*

One by one, the ex-Southern Pacific-Golden Gate ferries began leaving San Francisco Bay. Two of the last to leave were the *Lake Tahoe* and *Redwood Empire.* These ferries were towed through the Golden Gate on August 10, 1940, by the sea tug *Commissioner,* bound for Puget Sound.

With the sale of eight ferries, the Southern Pacific-Golden Gate fleet was reduced to but three boats, the *Calistoga, City of Sacramento,* and *Napa Valley.* The *Calistoga* was acquired by the U.S. Government and although the latter two were purchased by Puget Sound Navigation Company, they were requisitioned by the Maritime Commission for wartime service on San Francisco Bay.

During the war, the *Calistoga* was repainted Navy gray and renamed *YFB-21*; she spent most of the war years moored at Mare Island and at Port Chicago. After the war, she was declared surplus and sold to Moore Drydock Company; she was burned for scrap near the former site of Alameda Pier on January 11, 1948. The *Napa Valley* fared somewhat better; after being released by the Maritime Commission, she was towed to Puget Sound for service on the Black Ball ferry routes in 1942. Two years later, the *City of Sacramento* also was acquired by Puget Sound Navigation Company and the last of the once-great Monticello Steamship fleet left the Bay.

After the abandonment of auto ferry service, passenger ferries continued to be operated by Southern Pacific between Oakland Pier and the Ferry Building. This service initially was operated on a 20-minute headway during the day and a 40-minute headway at night. Thus it still was possible for persons bound for San Francisco from the East Bay to use the Southern Pacific ferries.

To get to Oakland Pier, however, one had to board mainline trains at suburban stations such as Richmond and Fruitvale or use a city bus. With the cessation of electric suburban train service to the pier, East Bay Transit Company extended its No. 88-Market Street bus from downtown Oakland to the pier. Admittedly, using mainline trains or a bus to the pier was much less convenient than the defunct direct electric train service. Time would show, however, that the preservation of this remnant of the ferry system would prove a blessing to many thousands of commuters a number of years later.

RACING PAST the West Oakland roundhouse with its stable of steam locomotives, a two-car Shattuck Avenue red train heads for Oakland Pier. At left distance is a westbound Seventh Street train; along this multi-tracked section, Shattuck Ave. and Seventh Street trains had their own separate sets of double track. **R.S. Ford Collection**

CHAPTER 16

Last Trains to the Pier

During the period of construction of the Bay Bridge, Southern Pacific suburban electric trains continued to operate to Oakland Pier and Alameda Pier as they had done for many years. Since the decade of the 1920s, when the system experienced a general decline in traffic and a gradual increase in labor costs, the railroad began a program of service reductions in an attempt to get costs in line with income.

The first abandonment of track of the Oakland, Alameda and Berkeley Lines took place in the early part of 1931 as a consequence of the expansion of the University of California campus in Berkeley. During that year, the University acquired a two-block area west of Dana Street and south of Allston Way. The property was planned as the site of Harmon Gymnasium and Edwards Field. Bisecting the area was Ellsworth Street, running along which were the tracks of the Berkeley-Ellsworth Street Line.

An agreement was worked out among the University, the city of Berkeley, and the Southern Pacific, whereby Ellsworth Street would be abandoned north of Bancroft Way. This required the railroad to relocate its University Station two blocks south to the southwest corner of Bancroft Way and

THREE S.P. LINES tied up at Thousand Oaks, where train and crew (left) take some spot time. North Berkeley substation is to left. A train from the Shattuck Ave. line (lower left) rolls downgrade from the Northbrae tunnel toward Solano Ave. and Thousand Oaks. **Louis L. Stein Jr. Collection; W.C. Whittaker**

Ellsworth Street. After the change, which went into effect on May 10, 1931, Southern Pacific trains terminated just short of the Key System-East Bay Street Railways streetcar tracks on Bancroft Way.

In the early part of 1932, a major service reduction was jointly announced by Southern Pacific and Key System. The reduction which took place February 28 called for a 40-minute headway on all lines in Oakland and Berkeley all day on Sundays and holidays and after 7:00 p.m. on weekdays. A similar lengthened headway was proposed for the Alameda lines; however, prior to the effective date, a petition bearing the signatures of 4,200 Alameda residents protesting the service reduction was filed with the State Railroad Commission.

After a series of hearings, during which many Alameda residents spoke against any service reductions, the commission ruled on April 5, 1932 that beginning April 14, Southern Pacific could operate the Alameda lines on an hourly headway on Sundays and holidays as well as on weekdays after 7:00 p.m. The city of Alameda immediately applied for a rehearing, but in vain.

The Non-Competitive Era

The Depression year 1933 saw a plan evolve which had striking similarities to the Composite Equivalent plan of 15 years earlier. In the early part of that year, Southern Pacific and Key System jointly approached the Railroad Commission with a proposal which would eliminate all duplicate lines and would result in two intertwined but non-competitive transbay interurban systems.

The plan, which was approved by the commission on March 16, 1933, divided the East Bay into territories which were defined by which railroad had the prior line. For example, at that time, Berkeley was served by four Southern Pacific and three Key System transbay lines. The new plan called for Southern Pacific to abandon its Ellsworth Street line in favor of the Key System Alcatraz Avenue line. The terminal of this latter line, in turn, would be cut back from Bancroft Way and Shattuck Avenue to Bancroft Way and Telegraph Avenue, thus favoring the S.P. Shattuck Avenue line. Along Shattuck Avenue, Key System would cut its Berkeley line back to South Berkeley, leaving Southern Pacific as the sole operator of transbay service in downtown Berkeley. Key System, however, would be allowed to keep its Berkeley line tracks in place for special movements during football season.

The closely competitive California Street and Sacramento Street lines would be merged into one route, with Key System being the survivor. The outer portion of the Key System Sacramento Street line, which ran along Hopkins Street from Rose Street to Northbrae, would be abandoned. In return, that portion of the Southern Pacific California Street line between Rose Street and Monterey Avenue would be turned over to Key System to form the outer end of the surviving Sacramento Street line. All remaining trackage of the California Street line would be abandoned. This complex arrangement would give Southern Pacific exclusive right to the Northbrae area of

RED TRAINS AT WORK: A three-car Shattuck Ave. train accelerates across the Eunice Street overpass, with Berryman Yard to left behind train (above). Red train at Berkeley station (below) sits above what four decades later became a BART subway station. **Both W.C. Whittaker**

THE APPURTENANCES of a multi-tracked, heavy-duty railroad were everywhere in evidence as this two-car Shattuck Ave. train glides beneath S.P. signal bridge. Oakland Pier is in right distance. Electric trains used tracks 3, 4, 5 and 6; mainline steam trains used tracks

Berkeley while Key System would have exclusive rights to the Sacramento Street corridor.

In Oakland, the Southern Pacific 18th Street line would be abandoned in favor of the parallel Key System 22nd Street line. Service formerly operated along Webster Street would be replaced by a Southern Pacific motorcoach line running along Franklin Street. With the announcement of these changes, the Railroad Commission noted that there would be an annual savings of more than $128,000 to Southern Pacific and more than $182,000 to Key System. As a condition to the proposed changes, the commission ruled that all March commutation tickets would be valid on trains of either railroad from the date of changeover, March 26, to the end of the month.

Two days before the sweeping changes were to go into effect, the city of Berkeley filed a protest with the Railroad Commission arguing that elimination of the Ellsworth and California Street lines would force patrons to walk too far in order to reach their closest station. In reply, the Commission noted that under the new plan, stations were so located that it would be no more than a half-mile walk from nearly any point in Berkeley to the nearest station. The commission concluded that this distance would not be too far to expect the average commuter to walk each morning and evening.

With the arrival of Sunday morning, March 26, 1933, the Southern Pacific electric suburban system was reduced to but five lines: Seventh Street, Shattuck Avenue, Ninth Street, Encinal Avenue, and Lincoln Avenue. Abandonment of the other three lines resulted in savings not only from reduced train miles and crew hours but also from the closing of five interlocking towers. Closed in Berkeley were Woolsey Tower, which controlled movements of trains through Ellsworth Junction, and Rose Street Tower, which controlled the crossing of the Key System Sacramento Street line and the S.P. California Street line. Three interlocking towers on the 18th Street line were closed: Poplar Street Tower, controlling the crossing with the Key System 12th Street Line; Seventh and Webster Tower, controlling the crossing with the S.P. Seventh Street line; and Third and Webster Tower, controlling the crossing with the Western Pacific main line.

The Franklin St. Bus Line

With the abandonment of rail service along Webster Street, Southern Pacific inaugurated a motorcoach line connecting the

Oak Street Station on the Seventh Street line and Broadway and 20th Street in downtown Oakland. This coach line was an outgrowth of continued agitation by East Oakland interests for direct Southern Pacific service between downtown Oakland and points on the Seventh Street line. Service along this bus line was operated at 20-minute intervals daily; there was no service after 6:00 p.m.

The bus line was intended to provide service only between downtown Oakland and East Oakland points; it was not intended for use by transbay patrons. Thus, transfers issued on the bus were accepted only on eastbound trains, and transfers were accepted on the bus only from westbound trains. If, however, a patron desired to use the bus in order to go to San Francisco, he had to pay a local fare as far as Oak Street and then an additional transbay fare from that point.

Equipment for the bus line consisted of a former Los Angeles Railway bus of indeterminate make and vintage. This bus, No. 72, was painted blue and white and carried no identification other than a destination sign. Drivers for the line were provided by Southern Pacific Motor Transport Company. It is interesting to note that whenever the regular bus was laid up for repairs, the run usually was taken over by an old double-decked Pickwick Nite-Coach that had been converted to commuter service.

On April 1, 1937, the operation of this bus line was turned over to East Bay Transit Company on a contract basis and coach No. 72 was retired. East Bay Transit designated the line as No. 87-Oak Street, and operated small Twin Coaches in the 400 series on it. Passengers on this bus line had to be explicit when asking for transfers. Drivers issued transfers good on connecting East Bay Transit lines, but not good on S.P. trains.

S.P.'s LONE motor bus, No. 72, waits at the Oak Street station on the Seventh Street line, 1937 (above) as replacement service for the Webster Street trains. Other end of this bus line (left) was at Broadway and 20th with one of the East Bay Transit coaches which were used after April 1, 1937, at work.
Both Robert A. Burrowes

THOSE BIG RED TRAINS really dominated any street they happened to be running on! Here, a pier-bound train pauses at Oakland Station, on Seventh between Broadway and Washington streets. Automatic switching equipment, activated by the brush hanging astride the trolley wire just before the crossing, allowed these 1,200-volt trains to operate at full power when crossing 600-volt streetcar lines.

R.S. Ford Collection

For those traveling to East Oakland, an operator's check would be issued. This was valid on 7th Street trains at Oak Street, but would not be honored on any connecting E.B.T. line.

The contract with East Bay Transit Company to provide bus service to the Oak Street Station continued until rail service on the Seventh Street line was withdrawn in 1941. Concurrent with the abandonment of rail service, motorcoach service on the 87-Oak Street line was terminated.

Two other bus lines, both independent operations, made connections with the red trains at Melrose at various times. The earlier of these two was operated by a real estate developer and ran from Melrose Station to what is now Sequoyah Road and Fairway Avenue by way of East 14th Street, 90th Avenue, Thermal Street, 98th Avenue, and Mountain Boulevard. The service was begun about 1926 and was withdrawn in 1932; no fares were charged. The second bus line began operation about 1928 and ran from Melrose to the Oakland Airport by way of East 14th Street and 98th Avenue. The fare on this bus was 15 cents and the equipment consisted of a seven-passenger Lincoln sedan. Service on the line to the airport was discontinued in 1937 at about the time that Key System extended its Bay Farm Island bus line to the Oakland Airport.

On the night of Saturday, May 6, 1933, a disastrous fire swept the outer end of the Key System pier, destroying the entire trainshed, many interurban cars, and the ferry *Peralta*. Because of the fire, Key System was forced to suspend direct service to San Francisco. As an emergency measure, it was announced that Key System commutation tickets would be honored on Southern Pacific trains during the emergency. In addition, temporary transfer privileges were established between Key System streetcars on the K-Alcatraz Avenue line and Southern Pacific trains at South Berkeley. These special measures continued in effect until Key System was able to resume normal operations one week later.

In Oakland, a special service was operated during this emergency by Southern Pacific along the tracks of the former 18th Street line as far as 18th and Poplar Streets. This special service was operated only for one day, Monday, May 8, as a Southern Pacific connection with streetcars run on the 12th Street and 22nd Street lines of Key System.

On February 7, 1935, Southern Pacific and Key System jointly petitioned the State Railroad Commission for permission to interchange monthly commutation tickets. This idea had long been sought by commuter groups and was supported

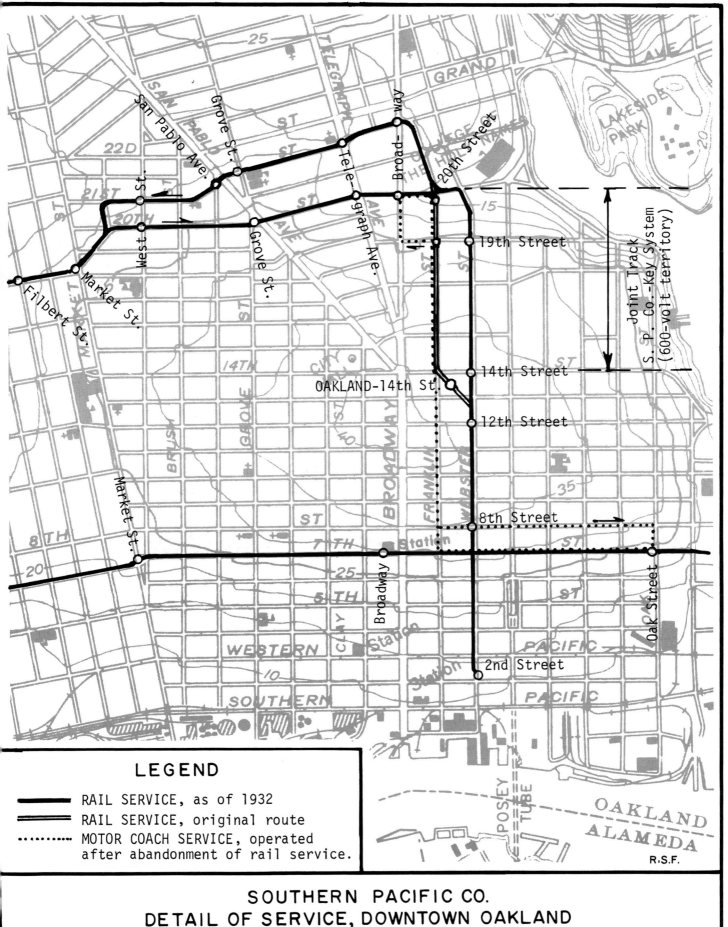

COMBOS were a common sight on Seventh Street trains. This one is at Melrose.
Charles D. Savage

by C.C. Boynton, President of the Trans-Bay Commuters League. It was proposed that the agreement become effective on April 1, 1935.

The plan, which was approved by the commission on February 18, contained a clause stating that it would be terminated if it was denied by the Interstate Commerce Commission, if it resulted in excessive costs to either railroad, or if either railroad experienced excessive ticket sales. The plan contained the following three features:

    1. Any eastbound Key System commute ticket could be exchanged at the Ferry Building for a first-zone eastbound Southern Pacific ticket.

    2. Any first-zone eastbound Southern Pacific ticket could be exchanged at the Ferry Building for an eastbound Key System ticket.

    3. Westbound Southern Pacific commute tickets would be honored on westbound Key System trains of the Sacramento Street line if boarded east of Parker Street Station.

In addition to the exchange of tickets plan, one other ticket collection feature also went into effect on April 1, 1935. No longer would a passenger be issued refund coupons on payment of a cash fare in lieu of a commute ticket. This brought to an end the practice of many commuters who "forgot" their commute books, paid cash fares, and received refund coupons. At a later date, these same commuters would submit both their refund coupons and their unused commute tickets for cash refunds, thus in effect obtaining free transportation across the Bay.

Difficulties With Alameda

Over the years, the city of Alameda repeatedly complained to the State Railroad Commission about the train service performed in that city by Southern Pacific. One of the more trivial matters brought before the commission by the city was that of available seats on the ferries from Alameda Pier. On December 9, 1933, the city filed a brief with the commission asking that the Dutton Avenue Express be rescheduled because the passengers arriving on that train usually boarded the ferry before those arriving on the Encinal Avenue and Lincoln Avenue trains. This situation forced many Alameda patrons to stand up all of the way across the Bay, a condition that seemed outrageous to the Alameda City Council. The brief asked that the offending train be rescheduled to arrive at Alameda Pier after the passengers from the Alameda trains had had a chance to board the ferry and take their seats.

In reply to the brief, G.E. Gaylord, Superintendent of the Southern Pacific, explained that the schedule of the Dutton

WITH A HANDFUL of hat checks, brakeman Jess Ginger works his way down the aisle of a pier-bound train in a scene typical of commuter trains everywhere. **R.S. Ford Collection**

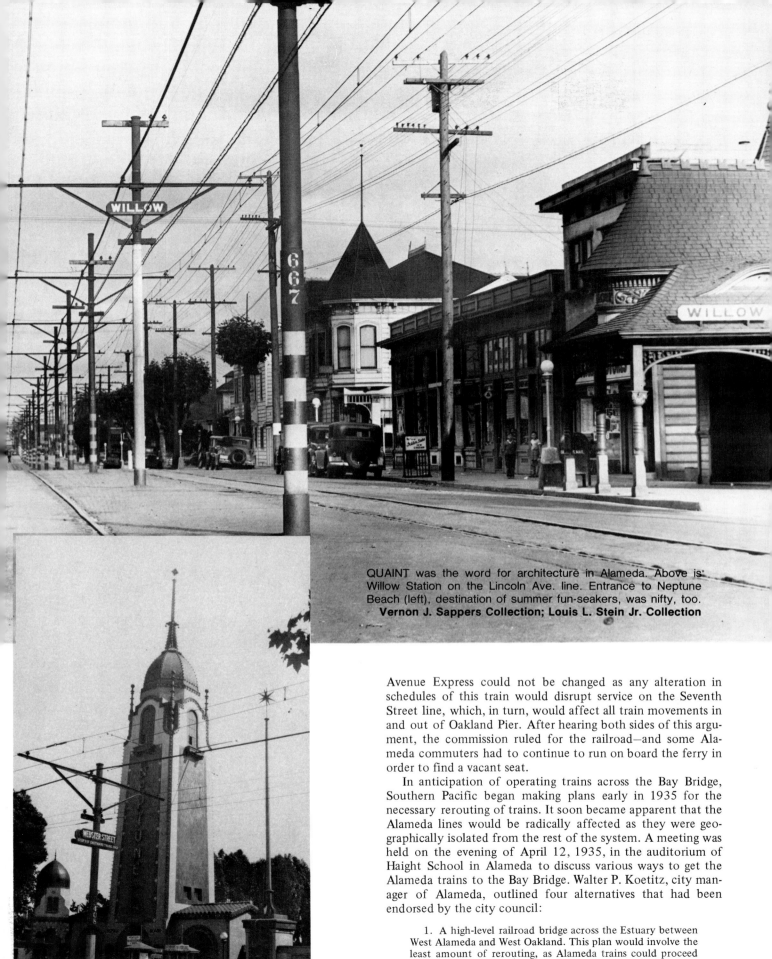

QUAINT was the word for architecture in Alameda. Above is Willow Station on the Lincoln Ave. line. Entrance to Neptune Beach (left), destination of summer fun-seakers, was nifty, too.
Vernon J. Sappers Collection; Louis L. Stein Jr. Collection

Avenue Express could not be changed as any alteration in schedules of this train would disrupt service on the Seventh Street line, which, in turn, would affect all train movements in and out of Oakland Pier. After hearing both sides of this argument, the commission ruled for the railroad—and some Alameda commuters had to continue to run on board the ferry in order to find a vacant seat.

In anticipation of operating trains across the Bay Bridge, Southern Pacific began making plans early in 1935 for the necessary rerouting of trains. It soon became apparent that the Alameda lines would be radically affected as they were geographically isolated from the rest of the system. A meeting was held on the evening of April 12, 1935, in the auditorium of Haight School in Alameda to discuss various ways to get the Alameda trains to the Bay Bridge. Walter P. Koetitz, city manager of Alameda, outlined four alternatives that had been endorsed by the city council:

1. A high-level railroad bridge across the Estuary between West Alameda and West Oakland. This plan would involve the least amount of rerouting, as Alameda trains could proceed

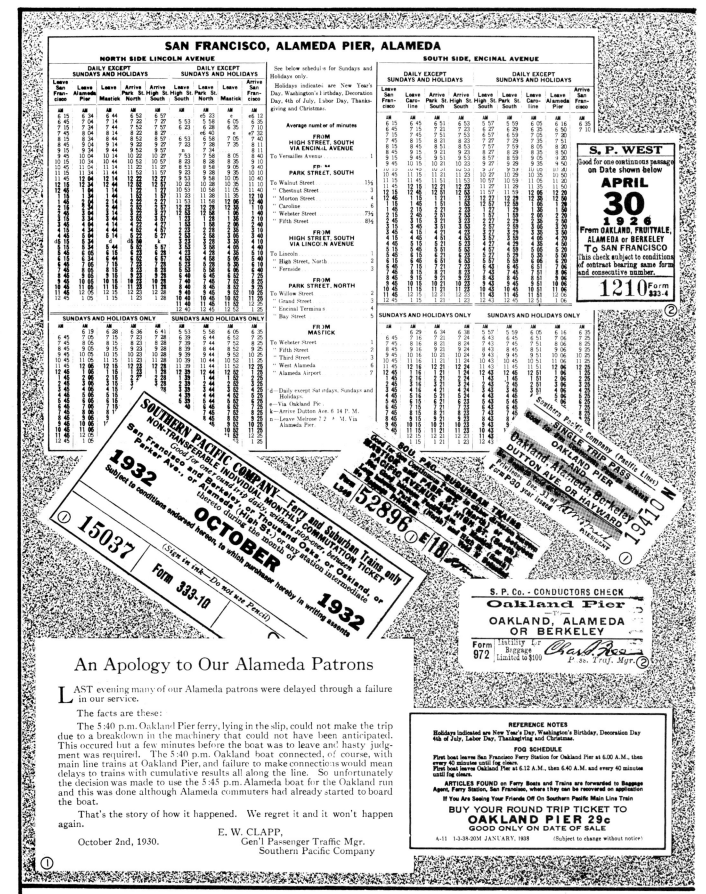

S.P. SCHEDULES 1926-

FIGURE 9

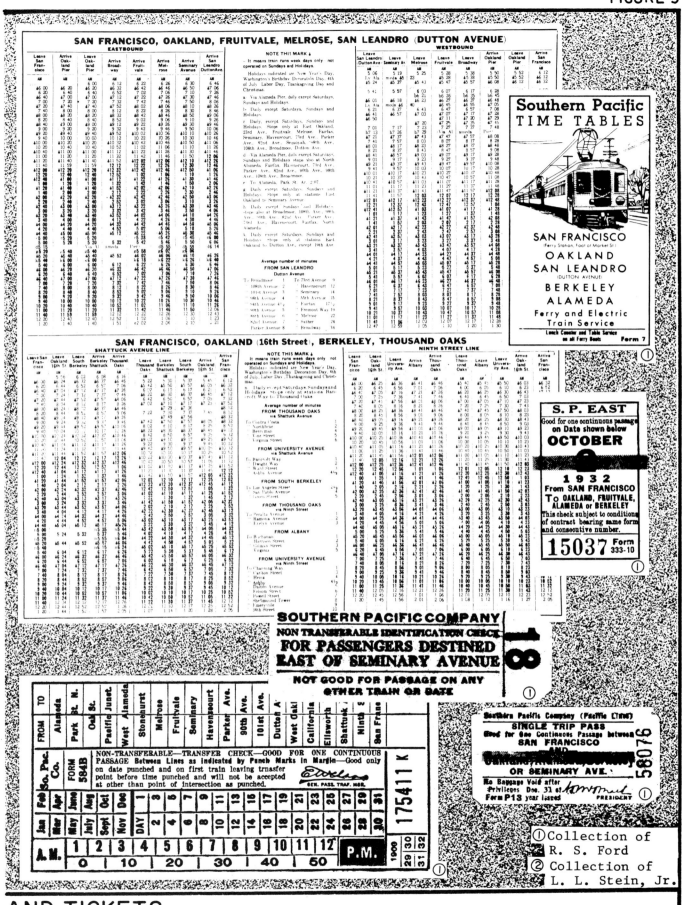

AND TICKETS
-1938

ELEGANT ALAMEDA pier (above) trainyard is full of red electrics, awaiting the homeward rush of transbay commuters. **R.S. Ford Collection**

PIER-BOUND train at Alameda-North Park Street, is approaching from Fernside Blvd. and Lincoln Junction. **Charles D. Savage**

by way of their present routes to West Alameda and thence to West Oakland and the Bay Bridge.

2. A less costly low-level bascule bridge at the same location. It was conceded by the City that this plan probably would not be approved by the War Department on the ground that it would be a hazard to navigation.

3. An underwater railroad tube at the West Alameda location.

4. An underwater combination railroad and highway tube at the West Alameda location. The City noted that the two tube plans were very costly and probably had the least chance of being built.

After presentation of the four plans by the city manager, F.L. Burkhalter, Vice President of the Southern Pacific, presented the railroad's plan to route the trains to the Bay Bridge. This plan envisioned the reversal of the present two lines, with trains originating at West Alameda, traveling eastward through Alameda to the Fruitvale Avenue Bridge, and then using the Seventh Street line to get to the Bay Bridge. The railroad favored this plan because it involved the fewest physical improvements; the fact was, the two Alameda lines were operating at a loss. Burkhalter said this plan already had been endorsed by the State Railroad Commission.

Expectedly, the city of Alameda filed a protest on December 13, 1935, against the Southern Pacific proposal to reverse the direction of the two Alameda lines. The protest reiterated the city's preference for an Estuary crossing at West Alameda, estimated to cost about $2,500,000. As an alternative, the city suggested that trains could be operated as far as Webster Street, where they could connect with buses using the Posey Tube and Harrison Street to get to the Bay Bridge.

On April 16, 1936, the State Railroad Commission gave formal approval to the rerouting of Alameda trains by way of the Fruitvale Avenue bridge. At the same time, the commission approved a request by the South Pacific Coast Railway, owner of Alameda Pier, to abandon that facility on the day that trains became operational across the Bay Bridge.

Unhappy with all this, Alameda City Manager B. Ray Fritz filed a protest with the Interstate Commerce Commission on June 6, 1936. The protest noted that abandonment of Alameda Pier and the rerouting of trains would inconvenience many commuters residing in Alameda. But the I.C.C. approved the abandonment proposal on October 2, with the formal date of the abandonment of Alameda Pier to take place "any time on or after October 14, 1936." After receipt of the I.C.C. order, Southern Pacific made assurances that Alameda Pier would be kept in operation until train service was begun across the Bay Bridge in 1939.

On February 11, 1937, James Eschen, Mayor of Alameda, sent applications to the California Toll Bridge Authority, the California Division of Highways, and the U.S. Public Works Administration requesting funds to construct a $5,500,000 high-level railroad and highway bridge over the Estuary from West Alameda to West Oakland. Mayor Eschen pleaded that without such a crossing, Alameda forever would be isolated from San Francisco. He claimed that the Southern Pacific plan to reroute trains was poorly conceived and would cause such inconveniences to the traveling public that the Alameda lines would suffer additional losses in patronage.

The application for funds for a new bridge got nowhere, and the city of Alameda was forced to accept the fact that a poorer level of service was inevitable once the trains began operating across the Bay Bridge. Thus rebuffed, the city, on April 6, 1938, refused to renew the S.P.'s franchise for the Encinal Avenue line. Instead, Alameda issued a revokable license to the railroad in hopes that threats of revocation might ensure a tolerable level of service along this line.

QUITE A CROWD has gathered to see the aftermath of this wreck at San Pablo and Stanford Aves. on July 24, 1936. Motorman of the streetcar was killed and four passengers seriously injured.
Vernon J. Sappers Collection

THE WRECK AT Pacific Junction, 1934. Middle car of Lincoln Ave. train split a switch, and the resultant mess tied up both lines. **R.S. Ford Collection**

AS BIG CHANGES loomed for the red trains, the Berkeley mail train continued its daily rounds. Here motor 701 heads for Oakland Pier with viaduct in background soon to be used by Bay Bridge-bound trains. **Charles D. Savage**

End of S.P. Operations

The decade of the 1930s was relatively free of serious wrecks or other mishaps. Only a few such occurrences have been documented. For example, in the summer of 1934, the middle car of an eastbound Lincoln Avenue train split the switch at Pacific Junction with calamitous results. The rear of the middle car, trailer No. 404, was dumped on the ground, and the rear car was hit by a steel pole that had been sheared off at the ground. Service on both Alameda lines was completely tied up for several hours until crews could clear the tracks and get the rails back in operating condition.

Two years later, on the afternoon of Friday, July 24, 1936, an accident at the intersection of San Pablo and Stanford Avenues killed a motorman and disrupted service on the Shattuck Avenue line for nearly an hour. That afternoon, East Bay Street Railways Motorman James E. McDowell was operating his streetcar along San Pablo Avenue on a trip from downtown Oakland to the terminus at Ashby Avenue; the car was E.B.S.R. 350. After stopping at the Stanford Avenue crossing so that several passengers could alight, Motorman McDowell, apparently unaware of an approaching red train, started through the crossing.

According to Crossing Gateman Daniel J. Eachen, the warning bells were ringing and the red signal lights were flashing; in fact, he said, one crossing gate had already come down, and the gate which would have blocked the streetcar came down just behind it.

With a thunderous crash, the speeding eastward Southern Pacific train struck the streetcar at its left front corner. The

WEST SIDE of Oakland Pier trainshed usually not seen by patrons. Here car 321 pokes its head into the sunlight between runs.
R.S. Ford Collection

BY LATE 1938, trains were identified by route numerals although still operating to the pier. This is Oakland Pier, looking east with a Shattuck Ave. train ready for boardings.
W.C. Whittaker

MASS MOVEMENTS were a specialty of the red electrics. A 10-car consist rolls down Central Ave. past Caroline Station in Alameda;

IF YOU GOT HERE just now, you missed this Encinal Ave. train disappearing toward the Alameda Pier. **Vernon J. Sappers Collection**

AT ALAMEDA PIER, trains displaying "6" disc ran eastward on the Lincoln Ave. line and westward on Encinal Ave.; "4" disc meant just the reverse. **W.C. Whittaker**

UPSTAGED: Brand-new streamliner *City of San Francisco* occupies adjacent track to red car 308 at West Alameda Shops in August 1936. Trainmaster F.E. Sullivan is on platform of the electric. All servicing of early-day diesel steamliners was done here.

R.S. Ford Collection

force of the impact was so great that the trolley was jarred off the track and into a position parallel with the S.P. train. Motorman McDowell was hurled through a window and under the wheels of the train; he was killed instantly. Four passengers on board the streetcar were injured when they were tossed from their seats. Engineer Joseph J. Taylor and Conductor J.W. Bronner, on the S.P. train, escaped injury.

During the post-accident investigation, Southern Pacific officials noted that their agreement with East Bay Street Railways gave the S.P. trains the absolute right-of-way at this crossing regardless of any signals.

The next year, on the morning of May 3, a two-car Shattuck Avenue train was involved in a collision at the intersection of Shattuck and University Avenues. At 6:08 that morning, Engineer James E. Gualco started his train from Berkeley Station and slowly notched the controller, accelerating for the grade beyond University Avenue. With a green traffic light showing, Engineer Gualco sounded his bell and approached the intersection. Suddenly, he saw a University Avenue streetcar move onto the crossing.

Sounding his whistle, Engineer Gualco threw his brakes into full emergency, but the heavy train rolled into the intersection and slammed into the side of the streetcar. The impact knocked the car, East Bay Street Railways No. 941, off the track and nearly tipped it over. Fortunately, because of the early hour, there were no passengers on board the streetcar.

Shaken but uninjured, Motorman Wallace H. Steir climbed off his car in a somewhat dazed condition. A subsequent investigation of the accident placed the blame on Motorman Steir for attempting to cross Shattuck Avenue against the red light.

In early 1937, Southern Pacific applied to the Interstate Commerce Commission for permission to absorb all assets and properties of the South Pacific Coast Railway. At the time of the application, the South Pacific Coast owned 32.8 miles of mainline track, 45.0 miles of secondary track, the property and structures at Alameda Pier, and a number of the electric suburban cars used on the Oakland, Alameda, and Berkeley lines. All of this trackage, property, and equipment had a total book value of $9,841,000. On November 26, 1937, the I.C.C. approved this merger, and on that date all remnants of Jim Fair's railroad ceased to exist as a separate entity.

Also in 1937, Southern Pacific embarked on a program of closing nearly all of its agency stations on the East Bay suburban electric lines. One of the first to go was the agency station at South Berkeley, the old Lorin Station of years before. This station was closed on November 3, 1937, leaving the South Berkeley area with only two adjacent center-of-the-street station areas, one for Southern Pacific trains and the other for Key System trains.

Four months later, on March 29, 1938, Southern Pacific received permission from the State Railroad Commission to close the downtown Berkeley Station and dispose of the property, estimated to have a value of more than $100,000. After being closed, the imposing station building was razed, erasing a Berkeley landmark that had stood since the days of the steam locals. In its place, Southern Pacific opened a small city ticket office in the building constructed on the station site. This office, located at 137 Shattuck Square, was equipped with an outside bench to serve as a waiting area. Today, this ticket office site is occupied by a barber shop, and the yellow tiled bench on the west side of the shop serves as a nearly forgotten reminder of the days when Southern Pacific trains served downtown Berkeley.

During the year 1938, all of the O.A. & B. cars received certain modifications to enable them to be operated across the Bay Bridge. In addition, track changes were made in Alameda and West Oakland connecting the Southern Pacific suburban system with the rails leading to the bridge. The last day of Southern Pacific-operated suburban trains was Wednesday, November 30, 1938. On the following morning, all electric suburban train operation was taken over by the Interurban Electric Railway Company.

The only change in train operation occurring on that date was the discontinuance of the Berkeley Mail Train service on the Shattuck Avenue line. This mail train service had begun during the early years of electric operation, and in 1938 consisted of some 12 runs with a baggage motor between the mail dock at Oakland Pier and the "mail spur" in downtown Berkeley. These runs were supplemented by several additional runs which terminated at 16th Street Station. The mail train service was utilized by the Berkeley and Oakland Post Offices as part of the transcontinental mail and parcel post service.

Interurban Electric operated the local trains to Oakland Pier and Alameda Pier during the month of December 1938 and the first half of January 1939. Shortly after 1 o'clock on the morning of Sunday, January 15, 1939, the final train runs were made to and from Alameda Pier. This was followed at 1:33 a.m. with the last arrivals of electric trains at Oakland Pier. After connecting with the ferry for the last time, the trains of the Seventh Street, Shattuck Avenue, and Ninth Street lines made their final departures at 1:40 a.m.

Unlike the ferries, where the last commuter runs already had been made, these trains ran to their respective terminals and then tied up for the night. The following morning, these same trains would be starting their runs on brand new schedules across the Bay Bridge and into a brand new San Francisco Terminal.

FINIS FOR ALAMEDA PIER: Conductor Al Butler, right, and Brakeman Charles Smith stand by the last Dutton Ave. Express to leave from Alameda Pier on Friday, January 13, 1939. Note marker lamps which were used on all trains at night until modification for Bay Bridge service brought the installation of red bullseye marker lights. **R.S. Ford Collection**

BIG RED MAKES IT TO THE CITY: On December 18, 1938 cars 357 and 375 covered all brand-new Bay Bridge trackage which would be used by Interurban Electric. Train is entering East Bay Terminal on tract that will, in revenue service, be the outbound track.
R.S. Ford Collection

CHAPTER 17

The Interurban Electric

THE OPERATION of trains across the Bay Bridge and into a terminal in downtown San Francisco involved a great deal of corporate, financial, and engineering planning. The first significant step toward this operation was taken by the Southern Pacific on November 14, 1934, when the Interurban Electric Railway Company was formed as a wholly-owned subsidiary. The new company, capitalized at $200,000, was set up solely as a passenger carrier to operate the existing Oakland, Alameda and Berkeley Lines across the Bay Bridge.

In order to formalize operations across the bridge, Interurban Electric entered into an agreement with the State Toll Bridge Authority on March 6, 1936. The agreement, which was similar to those entered into between the Authority and Key System and with Sacramento Northern Railway, provided for certain modifications to rolling stock and lines.

The agreement stipulated that Interurban Electric would maintain its share of the Bridge Railway and would have exclusive rights to the 52 Southern Pacific cars deeded to the Toll Bridge Authority in return for funds advanced to make the necessary changes to lines and rolling stock. The agreement concluded with the provision that in the event that Interurban

BAY SEASCAPE was altered forever by the new transbay bridge. Aerial view looks eastward; Bridge Railway terminal loop and terminal building foreground. Treasure Island, site of the 1939 Golden Gate International Exposition, is at left center, off Yerba Buena Island. Five S.P. and two Key System ferries can also be seen. **R.S. Ford Collection**

Electric should abandon passenger service, the Toll Bridge Authority would have the right to take over any and all track in order to continue operation of the system.

After the agreement had been signed, Interurban Electric applied to the State Railroad Commission for a Certificate of Public Convenience and Necessity. Concurrently, Southern Pacific applied to that body for permission to abandon all suburban service between San Francisco and East Bay points and to transfer this operation to its subsidiary. On March 23, 1936, the commission issued the Certificate of Public Convenience and approved the Southern Pacific abandonment petition subject to the following conditions:

> 1. All rail facilities and ferry service to and from Alameda Pier shall be transferred to ownership and operation by Interurban Electric.
>
> 2. All rail facilities and ferry service to and from Oakland Pier shall be retained by Southern Pacific.
>
> 3. The facilities at Oakland Pier shall be used by Interurban Electric until such time that service is begun across the Bay Bridge.
>
> 4. The ownership of certain cars shall be transferred to Interurban Electric, while the remainder shall be deeded to the Toll Bridge Authority in compensation for funds advanced to Southern Pacific to make track and equipment modifications.

The Bridge Railway

When the San Francisco-Oakland Bay Bridge was designed, space was provided on the south half of the lower deck for a double-tracked interurban railway. With the completion of the vehicular portion of the bridge, work was begun on the design and construction of the railway facilities. These facilities were financed through the sale of $15 million in Reconstruction Finance Corporation bonds. The Bridge Railway, which was owned by the California Toll Bridge Authority, extended from the east side of San Francisco Bay 6.89 miles to the terminal loop in San Francisco. It was designed to accommodate the trains of three electric railways: Interurban Electric, Key System, and Sacramento Northern.

From the beginning, it was recognized that the equipment of the three railways that would use the facilities were not completely compatible. Whereas Interurban Electric operated its equipment at 1,200 volts, Key System equipment was designed to operate at 600 volts. Sacramento Northern equipment was multi-voltage, being able to operate at 600, 1,200, and 1,500 volts. Because of these differences of operating voltages, the first obstacle to overcome was the design of a multi-voltage electrical distribution system that would be compatible to all three railways. Four such systems ultimately were proposed:

> 1. A catenary trolley system at +600 volts potential to the running rails. Although Interurban Electric cars 362 to

QUITE LITERALLY overshadowing the faithful ferries was the Bay Bridge, as workmen put finishing touches on the lower deck rails of the Bridge Railway. Below can be seen the ferries *Santa Clara* and *Mendocino*. **Southern Pacific**

367 were equipped with dual-voltage equipment and thus could operate at 600 volts, none of the other cars was so equipped. The principal modification to the other cars would consist of change-over switches to connect the series-connected traction motors to parallel connection. No modification would be required for either Key System or Sacramento Northern equipment.

> 2. A catenary trolley system at +1200 volts potential to the running rails. Dual-voltage equipment, consisting of in-

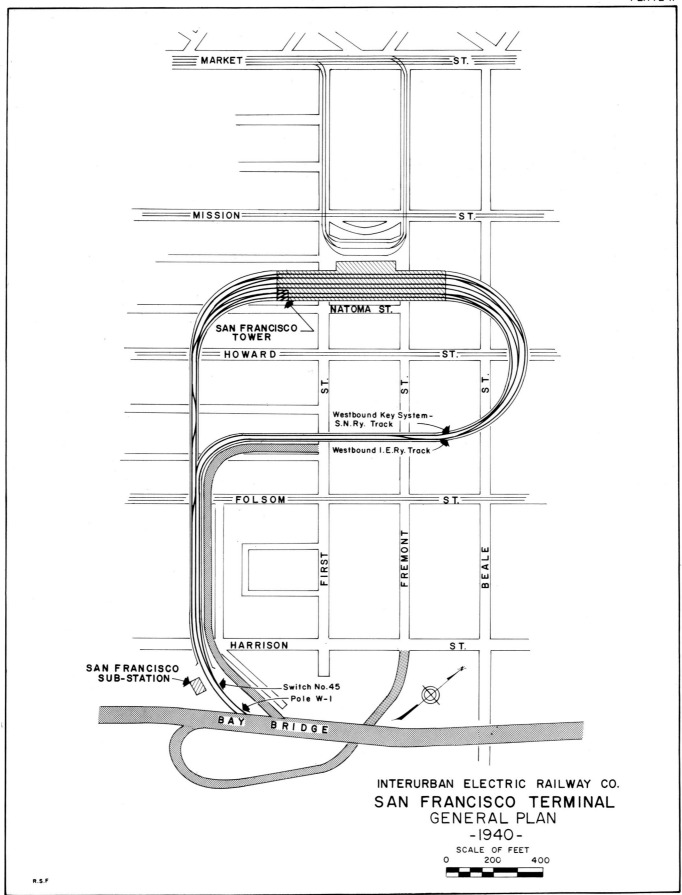

CONTRACTOR'S work train was this rolling woodpile, shown here near east entrance to terminal building during construction of the Bridge Railway.
R.S. Ford Collection

creased insulation, change-over switches, new controls, and other items would be required on all Key System cars. No modification would be required on Interurban Electric or Sacramento Northern equipment.

3. **A catenary trolley system at +1200 volts potential to the running rails and a third-rail system at +600 volts potential to the running rails.** This system would allow the three railways to operate their respective equipment at the same voltage as used on their home tracks. The only equipment modifications would be to Key System cars where third-rail pickup shoes would be installed.

4. **A balanced "three-wire" system using a catenary trolley system at +600 volts potential to the running rails and a third-rail system at -600 volts potential to the running rails.** This system would provide 600 volts between either the trolley wire or the third rail and the running rails; it also would provide 1,200 volts between the trolley wire and the third rail. Equipment modifications would include third-rail shoes and change-over equipment on all cars using the Bridge Railway. Trains of both Interurban Electric and Sacramento Northern would operate across the Bridge with pantographs in contact with the catenary trolley wire and third-rail shoes in contact with the third rail, thus obtaining 1200 volts power. Key System would operate one-half of its trains with pantographs in contact with the catenary trolley wire only and one-half with pantographs dropped and third-rail shoes in contact with the third rail only, thus obtaining only 600 volts power.

After a lengthy engineering and economic study, it was decided that the catenary-third rail system outlined in plan No. 3 was the most feasible. The study showed that this system would be about $185,000 cheaper to build than the other systems, and would cost $10,000 less annually to operate. This system also would allow for a simplified division of power costs, as Key System could be billed for power used from the third rail system; Interurban Electric and Sacramento Northern would be jointly billed for power used from the catenary system.

Planning for a San Francisco terminal was begun in 1932 by the State Department of Public Works in cooperation with Southern Pacific and Key System. All plans for terminals envisioned some type of elevated operation, and more than 20 plans were prepared. Of the three final plans espoused by the railroads, one sited a six-track terminal between Minna and Natoma Streets and spanning First and Fremont Streets. The unique feature of this plan was that after using Tracks 1 to 4 for discharging passengers, trains would leave the terminal, negotiate a balloon track, and reenter the terminal on Tracks 3 to 6 to receive passengers.

A nearly identical plan had the six-track terminal located between Third and Fourth Streets, parallel to Minna and Natoma Streets. The balloon track would be located in the area between Fourth and Fifth Streets. The most ambitious plan called for two elevated six-track stations in downtown San Francisco. Trains would leave the Bay Bridge by way of a curving viaduct to the first station, located at the Fremont-First Streets site. Trains then would go by way of an elevated alignment roughly along Tehama Street to the terminal, which spanned Sixth Street between Minna and Natoma Streets. The balloon track for this terminal would be located near the northeast corner of Seventh and Howard Streets.

An entirely different concept was proposed with the "stub-station" plan. This plan showed an elevated viaduct leading from the Bay Bridge to a two-level stub-track terminal along the east side of Third Street and spanning Howard and Mission Streets. The two-level structure would have five tracks on each level; the two track levels would merge near Folsom Street. To the north of the terminal would be a multi-level arcade leading to the main entrance on Market Street just west of the Palace Hotel.

In contrast to the several railroad plans, the state-sponsored plan proposed a terminal loop with a somewhat smaller four-track elevated station placed on the loop near Mission Street. A two-track elevated viaduct would lead to the terminal, looping by way of Clementina and Fremont Streets. Trains would leave the terminal and return directly to the bridge by way of a single-track viaduct running from Second and Howard Streets to Essex and Folsom Streets, where a junction would be made with the main two-track viaduct from the bridge. The terminal building in this scheme would be located between First and Second Streets, slightly west of the location of the structure that ultimately was built.

After cost estimates for the various plans had been analyzed, the state-sponsored plan, with some modifications, was adopted. The resulting terminal building, which cost $2,228,000 to construct, was located facing Mission Street between First and Fremont Streets. It was located astride the terminal loop, which at this location was divided into six tracks.

The three-story reinforced concrete building contained a large waiting room with shops and restaurants on the ground level. The second level, which was even with the level of the three-track streetcar loop in front of the building, contained ticket offices for the three railways, a newsstand, train schedule boards, and a small waiting area. The upper, or track level, contained four loading platforms, each 700 feet long. These platforms, which could accommodate a 10-car train, could handle 1,600 passengers per train loading.

On the Oakland side of the Bay Bridge, the mole leading to the Key System pier had been widened for the vehicular approach to the Bridge. This mole was made the site of the Bridge Railway storage and maintenance yards. Two separate yards were built. The one on the west was under a 1,200-volt catenary trolley wire to provide storage and maintenance of 123 Interurban Electric cars. The yard to the east was similar and under a 600-volt catenary trolley wire to provide storage

POINT OF DIVERGENCE of the San Francisco terminal loop. Westward I.E. trains used right-hand track; second track curving to right was for westward Key System and Sacramento Northern trains. All eastward trains used track at far left. All this is now paved for buses.
R.S. Ford Collection

INTERURBAN ELECTRIC built a new shop building at Bridge Yard, at east end of bridge. This construction view looks east; bridge tollgate is in background visible through steel framework.
R.S. Ford Collection

and maintenance for 88 Key System articulated units and 27 Sacramento Northern cars. Each of the two yards had car washing tracks, an inspection building, oil houses, and other facilities for the routine servicing of equipment.

A number of different routing schemes were proposed for the East Bay as it would be necessary to bring Interurban Electric, Key System, and Sacramento Northern trains together onto one lead through the Bridge Yards and onto the Bay Bridge. The rerouting of Key System trains (and Sacramento Northern trains, which used Key System tracks) was the simplest as their approach to the Key System Pier led through the proposed area of the Bridge Yards. Bringing the Interurban Electric trains over to the area of the Key System mole was another matter.

In December 1932, Southern Pacific proposed to route the I.E. trains from the Bridge Yards directly to 16th Street Station. Here, the track would rise on a viaduct and diverge while crossing over the S.P. mainline tracks. Seventh Street and Alameda trains would swing southward and join the existing elevated structure at 14th Street; Berkeley District trains would swing northward and join the elevated structure near 18th Street Junction. In place of the Suburban Elevation Station, which would be removed, two curving elevated stations would be built, one on each leg of the viaduct.

Two years later, Southern Pacific and Key System jointly sponsored a novel proposal which involved both railroads. In this plan, Key System Berkeley, Claremont, and Piedmont trains, as well as Sacramento Northern trains, would use their existing route to Yerba Buena Avenue. Interurban Electric Berkeley District trains would use a set of adjacent tracks as far as the Key System undercrossing with the S.P. mainline tracks. Here, the I.E. tracks would go by way of a long, curving, elevated alignment over the Key System and S.P. tracks and join the existing tracks at the foot of Park Street in Emeryville.

Key System 12th Street and 22nd Street trains and I.E. 7th Street and Alameda trains would use joint trackage from the Bridge Yard to near the foot of 22nd Street. Here, an elevated, diverging viaduct would carry the trains of both railroads over the S.P. mainline tracks as well as putting them onto their home rails. Key System trains would continue up 22nd Street, with 12th Street trains using a new curved connection at 22nd and Poplar Streets. A curved elevated alignment would carry Interurban Electric trains onto the viaduct leading to the Suburban Elevation at 16th Street Station.

As in San Francisco, there was a state-sponsored plan which was the least complicated and which ultimately was adopted. This plan utilized a minimal of rerouting of Key System trains; Interurban Electric trains used a double-tracked lead from the Bridge Yards to a Y-shaped viaduct near the foot of 26th Street. In an eastward direction, the tracks diverged while passing over the S.P. main line; the point of divergence was named 26th Street Junction. One pair of tracks, used by Seventh Street and Alameda trains, curved southward and descended to ground level, where they merged with the former Berkeley main line at 22nd Street Junction. The other pair of tracks, used by Berkeley District trains, curved northward and joined the Berkeley main line at 32nd Street Junction.

One other track modification was necessary so that Interurban Electric trains could enter the Bridge Railway. A new double-tracked curve was built extending from Seventh and Cedar Streets to Bay and Shorey Streets. This connection would bring trains of the Seventh Street and Alameda Lines onto the former Berkeley main line just west of 16th Street Station.

Westward Interurban Electric trains entered the Bridge Yard area by using a flyover to avoid a level crossing with the eastward main line of the Key System and Sacramento Northern. The westward I.E. main line then went past the north side of the I.E. shop building and joined the westward Key System-Sacramento Northern tracks at West Junction. Coming off the bridge, Interurban Electric trains used the joint track around the south side of the I.E. yard as far as East Junction. Here, the eastward I.E. track diverged while the Key System-Sacramento Northern track curved left beneath the I.E. flyover.

One of the more difficult problems facing the designers of the Bridge Railway was that of handling large volumes of traffic during morning and evening commute periods. It was anticipated that upwards of 17,000 people would be traveling across the Bridge by train during any given 20-minute rush period. With all passengers seated, this volume of patronage would require 19 separate 10-car trains operating on an average headway of 63½ seconds. Traffic problems were further complicated by ascending and descending grades of up to three percent, 20-degree curves, the threading of trains through terminal loop switches, and periods of fog which could reduce visibility to but a few feet. To meet these exacting conditions, an automatic train control and electrical interlocking system was designed by General Railway Signal Company.

The train control system was based on cab signal indicator lights which informed the engineer of his maximum permissible speed. Cab signal equipment manufactured by General Railway Signal Company was installed on all Key System and Sacramento Northern equipment. Interurban Electric equipment received compatible equipment manufactured by Union Switch and Signal Division of Westinghouse Air Brake Company.

In each cab there was a signal panel which indicated, through the use of illuminated numerals, the maximum speed on any particular section of track. On a clear track, a green

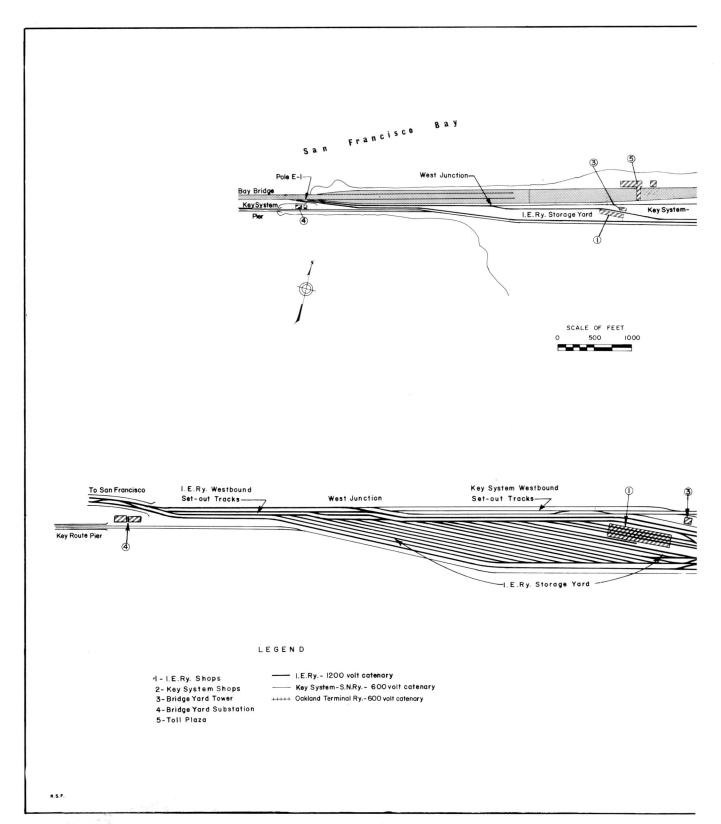

"35" would be displayed. Slower speeds were indicated by a green and yellow "25" or a yellow "17". Very slow speeds, such as that required on entering the Terminal Building, were indicated by a red "11".

Near the bottom of the panel was a violet "NS", which was illuminated whenever the train was being operated beyond the limits of the train control territory. Below the "NS" indicator was a white light which was illuminated when the train was being operated equal to or in excess of the indicated maximum permissible speed.

In practice, when running under a green "35" aspect, the white light came on when a speed of 35 miles per hour was attained. If the train continued to accelerate to a speed of 36 miles per hour, a low-pitched speed warning whistle (General

PLATE 12

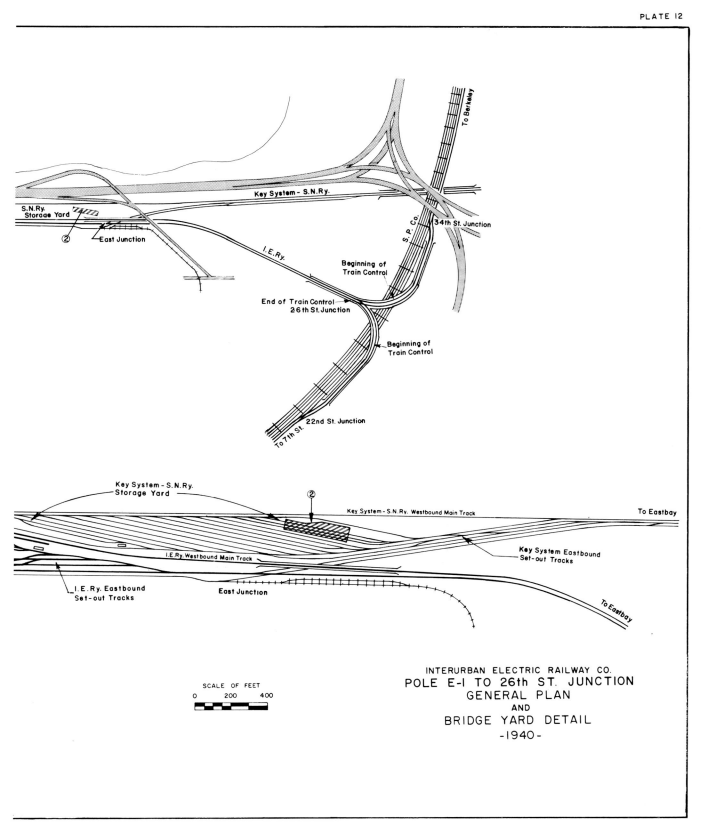

INTERURBAN ELECTRIC RAILWAY CO.
POLE E-1 TO 26th ST. JUNCTION
GENERAL PLAN
AND
BRIDGE YARD DETAIL
-1940-

THE NEW BRIDGE YARD. The I.E. 1,200 volt storage yard is empty while Key System 600 volt tracks at right hold a rake of Key's new articulated units. Shop building is in distance.
R.S. Ford Collection

FLYING LOW: Westward I.E. trains entered the Bridge Yard on a flyover to avoid a level crossing with the eastward Key System-S.N. main line. The flyover is seen here with a westward Berkeley No. 3 train. An eastward Alameda No. 4 train has just passed over the switch at East Junction and is crossing the Key System 600 volt lead from the Key Route pier. Track with third rail is Key eastward main line; end of third rail is a few yards beyond the flyover. Track at far right is Oakland Terminal Ry. 600 volt switching line.
Thomas Gray Collection

Railway Signal Equipment utilized a bell) would sound and the power to the traction motors would be cut off. As soon as the speed dropped below 36 miles per hour, the speed warning whistle would be silenced and the power could be applied to the traction motors once again.

With a yellow-green "25" aspect, the white light would appear at 25 miles per hour and the speed warning whistle would sound at 26 miles per hour. With a yellow "17" aspect, the white light would appear at 17 miles per hour and the speed warning whistle would sound at 17½ miles per hour. When the red "11" aspect appeared, the white light would be illuminated at 11 miles per hour and the speed warning whistle would sound at 11½ miles per hour. In addition, a high-pitched acknowledgment warning whistle (G.R.S. equipment utilized a buzzer) would sound until the engineer depressed the acknowledgment lever and placed the brake valve handle in full service position.

In all cases, failure to respond to the speed warning whistle within 2½ seconds resulted in an automatic emergency brake application unless the engineer had moved the brake valve handle to the full service position.

The nucleus of the speed control system was a series of train sensors placed at regular intervals between the rails. This equipment detected passing trains and fed coded signals into the rails. Each car was equipped with a pair of receiver coils placed ahead of the wheels near track level. These coils picked up the coded signals carried in the rails and transmitted them to train control equipment in the car. The system governed all train movements in and out of the San Francisco terminal as well as across the Bay Bridge and through the Bridge Yards. In addition, on Interurban Electric tracks, train movements were governed as far east as 26th Street Junction.

To supplement the speed control system, operators at interlocking plants at each end of the bridge controlled the routings of trains within their respective territories. Using the "Entrance-Exit," or "N-X" system designed by General Railway Signal Company, an operator merely had to press buttons at each end of the desired routing shown on the track layout panel, thereby activating all signals and switches along the desired route. If, however, any portion of the route was occupied or otherwise unavailable, an alternative route automatically would be selected. Use of this system made for quick and efficient routings of all trains through congested yard and terminal areas.

Another feature of the "N-X" system was the automatic train describer. This feature automatically identified the destination of all approaching trains. For example, when a train departed from San Francisco, its route designation would be transmitted to the Bridge Yard Interlocking Tower. Here, the train designation would be displayed by route letter or number on the track layout panel, and the operator knew that there would be about 10 minutes of elapsed time before that particular train entered the limits of the interlocking plant.

The train describer had the ability of showing the destinations of the first three approaching trains and indicating the presence of seven following trains by illuminated lights. The interlocking plant operator could tell at a glance of the presence of up to 10 trains crossing the bridge and could plan their routes accordingly.

Because of the train describer, it was necessary that all trains using the Bridge Railway be identified by either a route letter or number. Key System, during the days of the commuter ferries, had adopted letter designations for all its transbay train lines. Interurban Electric adopted a numeral system

CAB SHOT of car 378 shows Union Switch and Signal cab signal installation. Lever for train control cut-in is located between controller and brake valve; train control acknowledgement lever is on floor at left side of cab. When not in use, compact cab equipment was protected by a door. **R.S. Ford Collection**

of route designation in the latter part of 1938. When train service was begun across the Bay Bridge in January 1939, Interurban Electric used only the numerals 2 through 6 as route designations. Express train designations 7 and 9 were added a short time later. It is interesting to note that on the train describer board, Key System was assigned a route "G". This designation was never used for transbay trains, although the G-Westbrae streetcar line connected with "H" trains at University Avenue and Sacramento Street in Berkeley.

An interesting feature of the train describer was the automatic sorting of trains which took place at Switch 45 at the west end of the bridge. Here, Interurban Electric trains were sorted from Key System and Sacramento Northern trains. This was done because I.E. trains used the right-hand terminal lead and the other trains used the left-hand lead. Because the head end of trains might be only a minute apart, there was very little time to activate this switch, especially when trains were

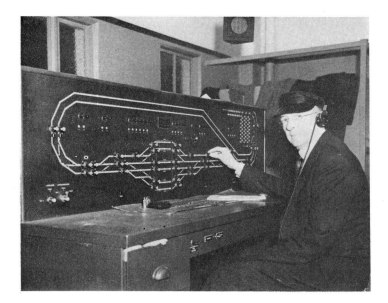

All 86 motor cars and 15 control trailers also received window wipers, new draft sills, rebuilt underframes, additional braking equipment, and track sanders. Furthermore, an emergency lighting system with motor-generators and 32-volt batteries was added to each car.

As mentioned previously, a major departure from traditional practice was the identification of routes by numbers and the use of illuminated destination signs. Heretofore, routes and destinations had been identified through the use of variously

TABLE 7 -- *Bridge Railway Route Designations*

INTERURBAN ELECTRIC	2 - Oakland-Dutton Ave. : 7th St. 3 - Berkeley-Shattuck Avenue [1] 4 - Alameda-Encinal Avenue [1] 5 - Berkeley-9th Street 6 - Alameda-Lincoln Avenue [1] 7 - Dutton Avenue Express [2] 9 - Shattuck Avenue Express [2]
KEY SYSTEM	A - Oakland-12th Street B - Oakland-22nd Street C - Piedmont-40th Street E - Claremont-55th Street F - Berkeley-Adeline Street G - (not used) H - Berkeley-Sacramento Street
SACRAMENTO NORTHERN	N - All trains

[1] Eastward designation; westward designation dependent on eastward routing
[2] Express trains used "2" and "3" designations, respectively, until 2/01/39

long, cutting to but a few seconds the elapsed time between the tail of one train and the head end of the following train. Hence, the sequence of westward trains carried by the train describer was used at Switch 45 to sort trains. In many instances, the switch automatically would be thrown only seconds after the first train had cleared it.

So that Interurban Electric trains could operate across the bridge, all cars received certain modifications in addition to the Bridge Railway signaling equipment. Modifications consisted of full-length roller-bearing gates in place of those that covered only the lower half of the platform door opening. In addition, Westinghouse fully automatic Tight-Lock couplers were placed on all cars with the exception of the baggage motors. The new couplers allowed for the rapid adding and cutting off of equipment at the Bridge Yards set-out tracks. Previously, coupling had been accomplished through the use of Janney couplers, with separate connections of air hoses and electrical jumper cables.

colored metal disc signs mounted on the left front of each train. The new identification system utilized a yellow metal disc bearing a large black numeral for route identification. Above this disc, which was placed on the left front of each car, was an illuminated roller destination sign. Similar roller destination signs were installed in the upper sash of side windows near each end of each car.

DISPATCHER E.W. Arnold (above) sits before Terminal layout panel at the San Francisco interlocking tower. The May 17 test trip (right) saw this five-car train operated on every line of the East Bay system. Here the train is seen at Harrison Street on the Ninth Street line.
Both R.S. Ford Collection

MAJOR LINE relocation included building the new 26th Street Viaduct shown as trolley wire installation was underway on September 16, 1938. This view was taken from front platform of car 378.
R.S. Ford Collection

Test Trains Across the Bridge

Construction of the Bridge Railway began with the driving of the first spike at Span E-22 on Tuesday, February 1, 1938. Construction then proceeded at a rapid pace until by the end of the year, most rail and electrical appurtenances were in place.

All during the period of construction, the West Alameda Shops were modifying cars for Bridge Railway service. On May 17, 1938, a five-car test train of rebuilt cars was taken from West Alameda for a trial run on the East Bay lines. The train was headed by motorized car No. 378, which had come out of the shops after being rebuilt from trailer car No. 435.

By early September, track construction for the Interurban Electric lead to the Bridge Yard had been nearly completed, and the 1,200-volt catenary trolley wire extended as far west as the shop building, then under construction. On September 16, 1938, the first trial run was made across the 26th Street viaduct using car No. 378. Leaving Oakland Pier, this one-car train ran out the Berkeley main line as far as 32nd Street Junction. After changing ends, the car was switched onto the new track leading to the viaduct. The car then was run up to the top of the viaduct, where it stalled due to its pantograph losing touch with a too-high trolley wire.

After surveying the situation, Trainmaster F.E. Sullivan decided to have everyone aboard help push the car down the west side to a section with, hopefully, lower trolley wire. With everyone pushing, heaving, and shoving, the car was rolled far enough to make contact with the trolley wire again. In recalling the incident, photographer Jack Gutte commented,

> "I sure caught hell from Sullivan for not helping to push that car. But, I did get my pictures!"

Under power again, the car was run to the end of the 1,200-volt trolley section, and then returned to Oakland Pier on the eastward track with no difficulties.

A week later, on September 23, a group of Southern Pacific and Interurban Electric officials boarded a special train at Oakland Pier as part of the run of the first train to be operated across the Bay Bridge. Carrying white flags, this special train ran by way of 22nd Street Junction and the 26th Street viaduct as far as the Bridge Yard. Here, at the end of the track, the party transferred to a waiting Key System articulated unit for the trip across the Bridge. Use of the Key System train was necessary because rail facilities across the Bay Bridge had been energized at only 600 volts. This was because the Key System main line to the Key Route Pier crossed the area of the Bridge Yard, and it had not been feasible to extend, prematurely, the 1,200-volt trolley west of the I.E. shop building.

HOSTLER connects jumper cables between two cars; in this 1936 view train line and other hoses can be clearly seen. Installation of Westinghouse tightlock couplers eliminated this time-consuming step in making up trains.

N.B. Eddlestone Collection

After Key System, S.P. and I.E. officials had boarded, the Key System train headed west. At West Junction, where the bridge track diverged from the Key System main line, the switch was lined for the bridge. The train then headed west, onto the bridge, and up the long grade toward the Yerba Buena Island tunnel. This crossing was one of the few times that a Key train ran on the Bridge Railway with its pantograph raised and drawing power from the catenary trolley wire; the third rail had not yet been energized. At Pole W-1, on the west side of the Bay, the train stopped, and after changing ends returned to the Bridge Yard along the same track. Use of only the westward track was necessary because the eastward track still had a gap where the Key System main line crossed it.

The first run of a red train across the bridge was made on Saturday, October 8, using combination baggage coaches Nos. 601 and 602. Because there still was no physical connection between the Southern Pacific and Key System, the train was forced to use a circuitous routing. After leaving Oakland Pier, the train ran to the interchange with the Oakland Terminal Railway. Here, locomotive No. 4, a 2-6-2 built by Baldwin in 1923, coupled onto the train and took it over to the Bridge Yard. Near East Junction, Key System freight motor No. 1000

SLIGHTLY EMBARASSING incident occurred when car 378, on inspection trip, stalled at top of viaduct when its pantograph lost touch with newly installed trolley wire. With everyone (but the photographer) pushing, the car was slowly rolled downhill until pan once again touched the wire. Wire at top of grade was immediately lowered.

R.S. Ford Collection

TRIAL TRIP of October 6, 1938, required push by Oakland Terminal Railway steamer No. 4. Catenary above is 600-volt; train required 1,200 volts.
R.S. Ford Collection

took the train and pulled it through the 600-volt territory as far as Pole E-1 at the east end of the bridge.

After posing for photographs of this rare occasion of a Key System freight motor coupled to a Southern Pacific train, the motor was uncoupled and ran back to the Yard. The power in the catenary west of Pole E-1 then was increased to 1,200 volts and the train ran across the bridge as far as Pole W-1. After returning to Pole E-1, the pantographs were lowered, the voltage was reduced to 600, and Key System Motor No. 1000 took the train to the Oakland Terminal Railway, where the steam engine was waiting for the trip back to the O.T.-S.P. interchange.

On November 30, a second test trip was made across the Bay Bridge with the same two combination baggage cars. This time, car No. 602 contained special radio remote equipment installed by the National Broadcasting Company. On board the train were NBC Radio Engineers George B. McElwain and E.C. Callahan, who broadcast the event on the short wave 10-meter band to a receiver station located on the roof of the 111 Sutter Building in San Francisco.

Like the previous test train, this one had to be taken to the Bridge Yard by way of the Oakland Terminal Railway, and then pulled as far as Pole E-1 by Key System freight motor No. 1000. Once on the bridge, the train ran under its own power as far as the Yerba Buena Island Tunnel before returning to the Bridge Yards and Oakland Pier. This same equipment was used on a third test run across the Bay Bridge on December 5.

On December 18, a trial run using cars 357 and 375 became the first red train to be run through the San Francisco terminal building. Five days later, car No. 378 made this same trip. The final trial trip to San Francisco was made on Friday, January 6, 1939. Because the third rail had been energized the day before, Key System made a trial run across the bridge with an articulated unit drawing power from the 600-volt third rail. A trial run also was made that same day with a Sacramento Northern train which utilized the 1,200-volt catenary while crossing the bridge.

On Thursday, December 1, 1938, Interurban Electric Railway Company took over all operations of the former Oakland, Alameda and Berkeley lines of the Southern Pacific at an annual rental of $50,000. With the beginning of Interurban Electric service, a number of administrative changes went into effect. Previously, under the aegis of the Western Division-Electric Lines, G.E. Gaylord had been superintendent, C.A. Veale, assistant superintendent, F.E. Sullivan, trainmaster, and S.L. Dolan, assistant trainmaster.

The new operations were divided into two closely related entities. The Interurban Electric Railway, with offices at Oakland Pier, was headed by R.E. Hallawell, who was named manager. Hallawell was assisted by Dolan, trainmaster, H. Dieckman, assistant trainmaster, and N.B. Eddlestone, inspector.

The operations of the Bridge Railway, which was headquartered in the San Francisco terminal building, was headed by Superintendent Sullivan and Assistant Superintendent E.E. Stearns. In April 1939, the position of assistant superintendent, Bridge Railway, was abolished and was replaced by two trainmasters, Stearns and Eddlestone.

By the middle part of January 1939, America's newest suburban electric railway was completed and ready for trains and commuters. On the morning of Saturday, January 14, three special trains arrived at the San Francisco Bridge Terminal for the dedication of the new facilities. The first two were Key System trains operating from 22nd and Broadway in Oakland. Each of these trains consisted of seven articulated units, on board which were many East Bay dignitaries as well as Alfred J. Lundberg, president of Key System, A.T. Mercier, president of Interurban Electric, and Charles H. Purcell, chief engineer of the Bay Bridge.

The other special was a six-car Sacramento Northern train which had come nonstop from Sacramento. The two trains arrived at the terminal shortly before 11 o'clock and were greeted by Mayor Angelo J. Rossi of San Francisco.

In front of the terminal building, at First and Mission Streets, a crowd of several thousand persons had gathered for the ceremonies. After the welcoming address by Mayor Rossi, words of enthusiasm were spoken by Mayors Edward N. Ament of Berkeley, Henry A. Weichert of Alameda, Oliver Ellsworth of Piedmont, and Frank W. Clark, director of the California Department of Public Works. Purcell then addressed the crowd on the accomplishments achieved by the building of the Bridge Railway. He closed by saying that he was pleased to turn the entire Bay Bridge facilities over to the people of the State of California. Lieutenant Governor Ellis E. Patterson then accepted the bridge on behalf of the citizens of the state.

With the ceremonies concluded, the guests made their way up to the track level and reboarded their trains. Today, the specials had the Bridge Railway tracks to themselves. Tomorrow, revenue service would begin.

HELP FROM A FRIEND: Key System freight motor 1000 (above and below) was the prime mover for this test train, consisting of S.P. combos 601, 602. Use of the 600-volt loco was required between the Oakland Terminal Railway and Pole E-1 for each trial run with a 1,200-volt red train at this stage of construction. **Both R.S. Ford Collection**

Trying Out the New Bridge

TRAINMASTER F.E. Sullivan is at controls of car 602 as it makes first trial run of a red train across the Bay Bridge on October 8, 1938. **R.S. Ford Collection**

NBC RADIO BROADCAST was a feature of test run. Radio engineer George B. McElwain adjusts short-wave transmitter in baggage compartment of 602 on November 30, 1938. **R.S. Ford Collection**

RETURN TRIP of November 30 saw use of the eastward main track on the bridge for the first time. Train and crew is near the west end of the cantilever section.
R.S. Ford Collection

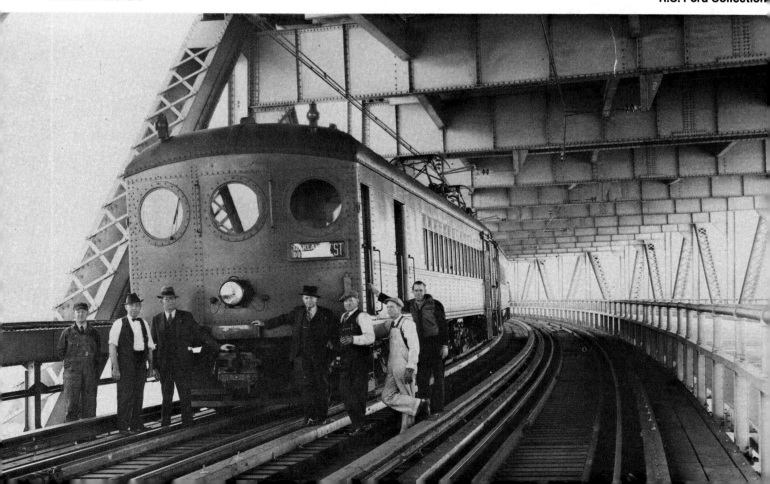

TRIALS CONTINUE as opening day for bridge service nears. Two crewmen of car 378 pose with Trainmaster Sullivan (center) in the East Bay Terminal on December 23, 1938.
R.S. Ford Collection

ANOTHER TEST RUN brought out this group of S.P. workers and officials, again including Trainmaster Sullivan who must not have spent much time in his office during this period. Magnificent new bridge railway, but same old rattan seats awaited the public.
R.S. Ford Collection

CHECKING OUT the Key System's new articulated equipment was Sullivan, left, and Foreman of Engines Walter Marlin, on December 18, 1938. Key's new cars gave its service a brand new image, something S.P. was unable to accomplish with its same old red electrics.
R.S. Ford Collection

THE BIG DAY ARRIVES: Crowd of thousands gathers on the morning of Saturday, January 14, 1939, for dedication of the Bridge Railway and East Bay Terminal. Mission Street is in left foreground; three-track street car loop passes in front of building. As of 1977, streetcars still looped here, but the terminal itself handled only buses.
R.S. Ford Collection

The Bridge Railway Opens

The last Seventh Street train from Oakland Pier arrived at Dutton Avenue at 2:21 a.m., Sunday, January 15, 1939. This train ordinarily would have returned to Melrose to tie up at 2:40 a.m. Instead, the 10-car train was parked at the end of track and kept lighted and heated for the benefit of the hundreds of people on board. This crowd had boarded the train after it left Oakland Pier and was waiting to ride the first scheduled train across the Bay Bridge.

Finally, the great moment arrived. Promptly at 4:48 a.m., conductor E.A. Wosnak gave two hard pulls on the signal cord and engineer E. Truchard sounded the gong and released the air brakes. Amid a chorus of cheers, Interurban Electric train No. 1001 left Dutton Avenue on the very first revenue run across the Bay Bridge. A stop was made at Broadmoor to pick up the members of the Broadmoor Men's Club, who boarded the train carrying a large banner reading *HANDS ACROSS THE BAY*. Because the train now was filled to capacity, it ran nonstop to San Francisco, much to the disappointment of crowds waiting to board at other stations.

The train arrived at the San Francisco Terminal at 5:50 a.m., and was followed at 6:10 and 6:11 by trains from the Shattuck Avenue and Ninth Street lines. A few minutes later, at 6:17 a.m., the first Key System train arrived from the A-Oakland-12th Street line. The first I.E. train from Alameda, running by way of the Lincoln Avenue line, was due to leave West Alameda at 5:43 a.m. Because of switching difficulties, it was not able to depart until 6:35.

This delay forced the annulment of the first Encinal Avenue train, which was scheduled to leave at 6:18. The first Lincoln Avenue train finally arrived in San Francisco at 7:25, well past its 6:31 scheduled arrival time. The first Sacramento Northern train into the terminal was train No. 15, a local from Concord, which arrived at 7:44 a.m.

All that Sunday, crowds rode the trains and marveled at the view of San Francisco Bay as seen from a train crossing the great bridge. However, the real test of the railway came the

FIGURE 10

No. 14

Please Admit

Mr. F. E. Sullivan

To

FIRST ELECTRIC TEST TRAIN
San Francisco-Oakland Bay Bridge
Railway System

10:00 a.m.
Friday, September 23, 1938
Oakland Mole

BIG NEWS
for trans-bay travelers

INTERURBAN ELECTRIC RAILWAY COMPANY

Starting January 15th

All the way across the Bay on

"THE BIG RED CARS"

Sunday morning, January 15th, the BIG RED CARS of the Interurban Electric Railway Company will flash across the great 8¼-mile San Francisco-Oakland Bay Bridge to inaugurate the first trans-bay rail service between San Francisco and Oakland, Berkeley, Alameda, Albany, Emeryville and San Leandro!

On this and all the days to follow, foraging seagulls, puzzling in vain the strange new ways of the world, will wheel in frantic flight as the BIG RED CARS rush by, spanning the Bay by rail!

High above, in broad-windowed, comfortable cars, you and thousands of other passengers will thrill anew each day to an exciting, unforgettable experience—a sail by rail across San Francisco Bay. And as you look down at the water and boats below, you'll hear that faint, familiar refrain of whirling wheels coursing their swift way along the smoothest, safest highway in the world—steel rails!

Ride the BIG RED CARS *all the way and both ways* across the Bay. No changing en route. No change in fares. All Eastbay lines of the IER will cross the Bridge and converge on the brand new San Francisco-Oakland Terminal building at Mission between First and Fremont streets (one block south of Market).

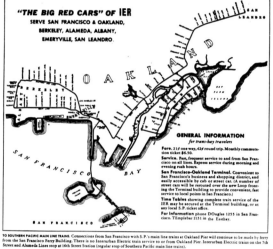

"THE BIG RED CARS" OF IER
SERVE SAN FRANCISCO & OAKLAND,
BERKELEY, ALAMEDA, ALBANY,
EMERYVILLE, SAN LEANDRO.

GENERAL INFORMATION
for trans-bay travelers

Fare. 21¢ one way, 42¢ round trip. Monthly commutation ticket $6.50.

Service. Fast, frequent service to and from San Francisco on all lines. Express service during morning and evening rush hours.

San Francisco-Oakland Terminal. Convenient to San Francisco's business and shopping district, and easily accessible by cab or street car. (A number of street cars will be rerouted over the new Loop fronting the Terminal building to provide convenient, fast service to local points in San Francisco.)

Time Tables showing complete train service of the IER may be secured at the Terminal building, or at any local S.P. ticket office.

For Information phone DOuglas 1255 in San Francisco, TEmplebar 2151 in the Eastbay.

TO SOUTHERN PACIFIC MAIN LINE TRAINS. Connections from San Francisco with S.P.'s main line trains at Oakland Pier will continue to be made by ferry from the San Francisco Ferry Building. There is no Interurban Electric train service to or from Oakland Pier. Interurban Electric trains on the 7th Street and Alameda Lines stop at 16th Street Station (regular stop of Southern Pacific main line trains).

INTERURBAN ELECTRIC RAILWAY COMPANY

OUR REGRETS AND THANKS

TO OUR PATRONS:

We sincerely regret the delays and interruptions in schedules since the inauguration of electric train service over the Bay Bridge, January 15th, and we want you to know that we appreciate the patience and consideration patrons have shown us in the face of these inconveniences to them.

Inauguration of train service over the bridge involved a very radical change in operations with a great many more difficulties to meet and overcome than were involved in the previous operation of these trains when connections were made with the ferries. On the inauguration of the bridge service, problems developed that could not have been foreseen and in addition several failures occurred in mechanism which could not have been anticipated plus several traffic accidents that blocked service on several lines. Thus the service was not only delayed but also trains in the rush hours have been overcrowded.

Everything is being done to the limit of our abilities to remedy the situation. Difficulties are being ironed out, service is improving and we believe that within a few days we will be providing normal service on regular schedules—the kind of service all officers and employes of this company earnestly desire to give.

R. E. HALLAWELL, Manager,
Interurban Electric Railway.

Collection of R. S. Ford

BRIDGE RAILWAY INAUGURATION

INSIDE THE TERMINAL, most I.E. trains used tracks 2 and 3; track 1, behind train at left, was used by I.E. expresses. Key System and Sacramento Northern used tracks at far right. Track areas are now paved and used by buses of Alameda-Contra Costa Transit District and Greyhound Lines. **Southern Pacific**

next morning, Monday, January 16. It was then that the new system was strained to the limit as thousands of commuters crowded on board the San Francisco-bound trains.

Although the new railway functioned adequately, a serious problem developed at First and Market Streets, where the Bridge Terminal-bound streetcars of both the Municipal Railway and the Market Street Railway were switched from the lines running down Market Street. Here, a tie-up of historic proportions developed, backing streetcars up along the two inbound tracks on Market Street for many blocks. Because no cars were able to use the new loop in front of the terminal, thousands of commuters were forced to walk from the terminal to their places of business, making many up to one hour late for work. That afternoon, the homeward-bound crowd flowed a little smoother, but still there were many delays and minor problems, prompting comments such as, "It was never like this on the ferries!"

During the first few weeks of operation across the Bay Bridge, a number of difficulties arose, caused mostly by inexperience on the part of trainmen, although some were due to engineering or technological flaws. Of the latter, one of the more serious problems was the periodic derailment of I.E. cars as they rounded the curve leading into the Bridge Terminal building. It soon was found that because of the slow speed, the flanges of the wheels would ride up and over the switch frogs, thus derailing the car. Installation of frog guards eliminated most of the derailments; however, derailments still occasionally happened, usually at most inopportune times.

Another source of trouble was that of malfunctioning cab signal equipment while trains were being operated across the bridge. Many of the older engineers had not yet become accustomed to relying completely on the cab signals. Thus, with a clear track ahead, they would not react fast enough to a "red 11" when it was displayed due to a malfunction. With both a high-pitched and a low-pitched whistle blowing in his ear, the engineer would be stamping his foot around trying to find the acknowledgment pedal. All too soon, the 2½-second time limit would be up, and the train would come to a shuddering and screeching stop.

Getting the train started again wasn't a simple matter, either. At first, the rules said that only Herman Engelhart of the State Railroad Commission could break the seal and cut

ELEVATED LINES served San Francisco for the first time, as the Bridge Railway looped above streets to enter and leave the terminal. Berkeley-Shattuck Ave. train (above) heads east (to right) over First Street. Approaching bridge (below), an eastbound Seventh Street local passes a terminal-bound Key System C-Piedmont train.

Both Thomas Gray Collection

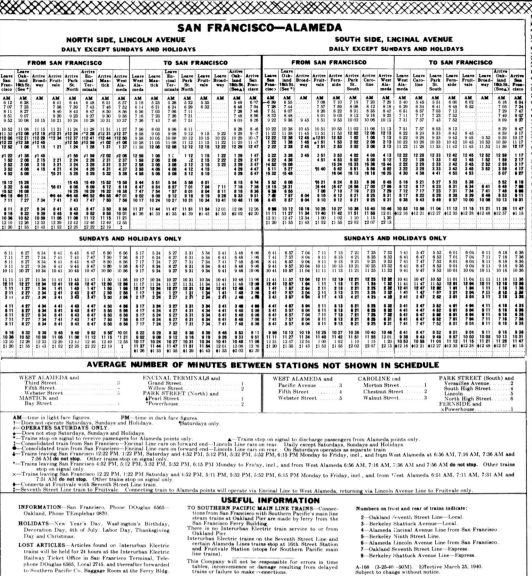

FIGURE II

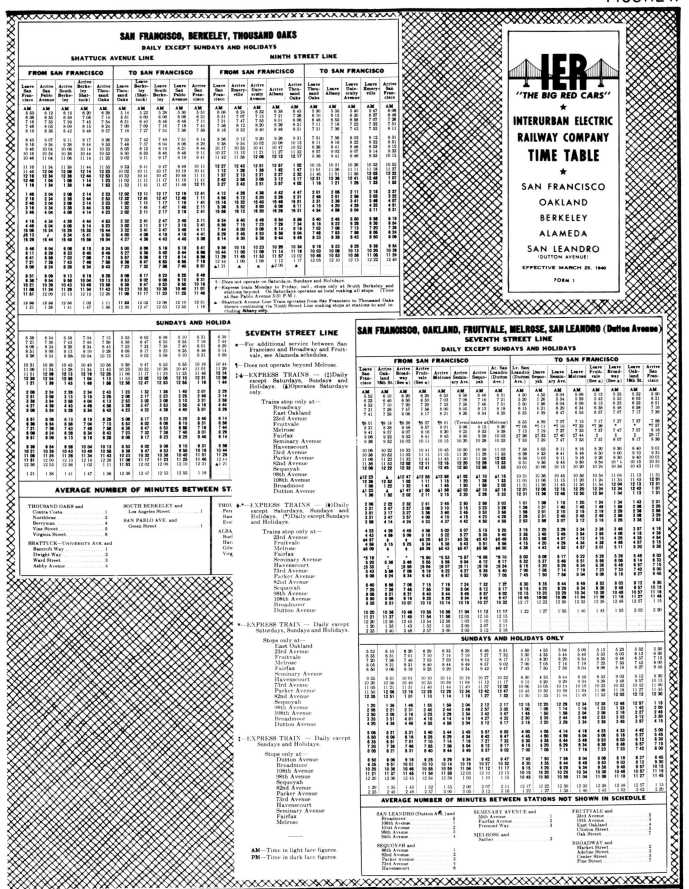

TIME TABLES

AFTER COMING off the 26th Street viaduct at 22nd Street Junction, this eastward Seventh Street train runs parallel to S.P. mainline.
Charles D. Savage

EASTBOUND Seventh Street train stops at Suburban Elevation of Oakland-16th Street Station. Short viaduct section was Oakland's only 'el'. During the days of the ferries, this would have been a westbound train from Berkeley.
Thomas Gray Collection

SUBURBAN ELEVATION tracks at Oakland 16th Street Station as seen from ground level mainline tracks.
Charles D. Savage

OUTWARD CHANGES in appearance of the red trains after inauguration of the Bridge Railway were few—mainly automatic couplers, dome markers and numeric disc signs. Here, a three-car Dutton Ave. train pauses at Melrose. **Charles D. Savage**

out the train control equipment, thus releasing the brakes and restoring the power. The first few times that this happened, the entire Bridge Railway was tied up while a search was made for this responsible official. Later, this rule was relaxed, with the responsibility being delegated to the manager of the Bridge Railway.

From the beginning, the San Francisco terminal was a busy interurban station, with 519 scheduled departures each weekday. Trains of Interurban Electric used Tracks 1, 2, and 3; those of Key System and Sacramento Northern used Tracks 4, 5, and 6. With the great number of trains entering and leaving the terminal, it frequently was possible to see as many as six trains in the terminal at one time. Because of signaling and other requirements, arrivals and departures initially were timed to the quarter minute. However, running trains on 75-second headways proved impractical, and schedules were modified three months later to reflect arrivals and departures on the full minute only.

With the beginning of train service across the Bay Bridge, rail travel through Alameda was reversed. Whereas during ferry operations trains traveled west through town toward the pier, with the start of bridge service both Alameda lines started at West Alameda and proceeded east through the city to the Fruitvale Avenue bridge where trains doubled back along the Seventh Street line to the Bay Bridge. Because of this "going around the horn" type of routing, the running time from West Alameda to San Francisco was increased from the previous 25 minutes to 53 minutes. This was offset by shortened running times from stations in the eastern part of Alameda which experienced a reduced time to San Francisco on the order of five minutes.

Alameda greeted this reversal of operation with somewhat less than wholehearted enthusiasm. In the latter part of March 1939, the Alameda Municipal Transportation League proposed that a survey be taken of commuters to determine what stations they used, what train they took, and what they thought of the new service. At that same time, the League retained the service of J. Ragmar Montin, a transportation engineer, to prepare a report which contended that the City of Alameda was now receiving a level of S.P. service far inferior to that during the last full year of ferry operation.

During the time that the League was making its study, the City of Alameda, represented by City Manager Charles R. Schwanenberg and City Attorney H. Albert George, filed a petition with the State Toll Bridge Authority seeking assistance in securing a more direct service to San Francisco. The petition stressed the inferiority of service performed by Interurban Electric and asked that an investigation be made of the feasibility of constructing an Estuary crossing at West Alameda.

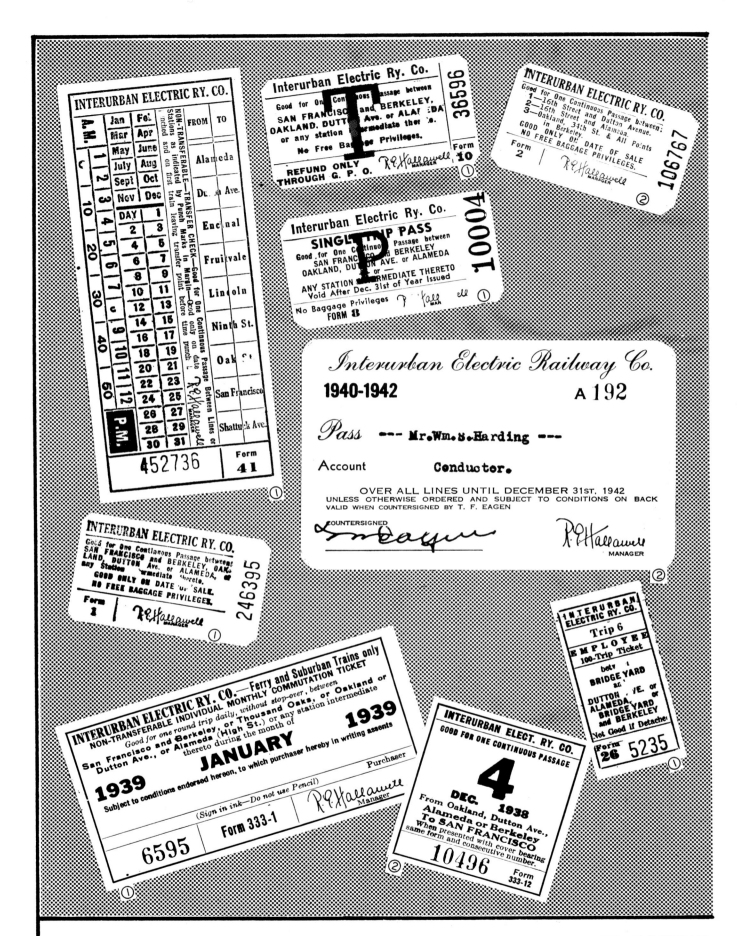

INTERURBAN ELECTRIC

FIGURE 12

① Collection of R. S. Ford
② Collection of L. L. Stein, Jr.

TRANSPORTATION

TABLE 8 -- Station Schedule of Train Movements, San Francisco Terminal, Tuesday, February 7, 1939, 4:00 p.m. to 6:00 p.m.

Arriving Westward				Departing Eastward				Arriving Westward				Departing Eastward			
Time	Track	Route Designation	Line	Time	Track	Route Designation	Line	Time	Track	Route Designation	Line	Time	Track	Route Designation	Line
4:00:00	2	3	Berk-Shattuck	4:00:00	3	2	Dutton-7th St	5:00:00	2	9*	Shatt.Express	5:01:15	4	B	Oakland-22nd
01:15	2	5	Berk-9th St.	01:15	4	B	Oakland-22nd	01:15	2	3-5	Shatt.-9th St	02:30	6	A	Oakland-12th
02:30	5	H	Berk-Sacto St	02:30	4	A	Oakland-12th	02:30	5	H	Berk-Sacto St	05:00	2	9	Shatt.Express
03:45	5	F	Berk-Adeline	07:30	5	H	Berk-Shattuck	03:45	6	F	Berk-Adeline	06:15	5	3-5	Shatt.-9th St
07:30	4	E	Claremnt-55th	08:45	5	F	Berk-Adeline	05:00	1	7*	Dutton Exprss	07:30	6	H	Berk-Sacto St
08:45	4	C	Piedmont-40th	12:30	4	E	Claremnt-55th	07:30	4	E	Claremnt-55th	08:45	1	F	Berk-Adeline
10:00	3	2	Dutton-7th St	13:45	4	C	Piedmont-40th	08:45	6	C	Piedmont-40th	10:00	4	7	Dutton Exprss
11:15	2	6	Ala.-Lincoln	15:00	2	3	Berk-Shattuck	10:00	2	6*	Ala.-Lincoln	12:30	6	E	Claremnt-55th
16:15	4	B	Oakland-22nd	16:15	2	5	Berk-9th St.	11:15	3	4*	Ala.-Encinal	13:45	4	C	Piedmont-40th
17:30	4	A	Oakland-12th	17:30	2	4	Ala.-Encinal	12:30	1	2	Dutton-7th St	15:00	1	6	Ala.-Lincoln
20:00	2	3	Berk-Shattuck	18:45	3	2	Dutton-7th St	13:45	2	4	Ala.-Encinal	16:15	3	4	Ala.-Encinal
21:15	2	5	Berk-9th St.	21:15	4	B	Oakland-22nd	16:15	4	B	Oakland-22nd	17:30	1	7	Dutton Exprss
22:30	5	H	Berk-Sacto St	22:30	4	A	Oakland-12th	17:30	6	A	Oakland-12th	18:45	2	2	Dutton-7th St
23:45	5	F	Berk-Adeline	27:30	5	H	Berk-Shattuck	18:45	6	#27	Sacto.Nor.Ry	21:15	4	B	Oakland-22nd
27:30	4	E	Claremnt-55th	28:45	5	F	Berk-Adeline	20:00	3	9*	Shatt.Express	22:30	6	A	Oakland-12th
28:45	4	C	Piedmont-40th	32:30	4	E	Claremnt-55th	21:15	2	3-5	Shatt.-9th St	23:45	6	#32	Sacto.Nor.Ry
30:00	3	2	Dutton-7th St	33:45	4	C	Piedmont-40th	22:30	5	H	Berk-Sacto St	25:00	3	9	Shatt.Express
31:15	2	4	Ala.-Encinal	35:00	4	3	Berk-Shattuck	23:45	6	F	Berk-Adeline	26:15	2	3-5	Shatt.-9th St
36:15	4	B	Oakland-22nd	36:15	2	5	Berk-9th St.	27:30	4	E	Claremnt-55th	27:30	5	H	Berk-Sacto St
37:30	4	A	Oakland-12th	37:30	2	6	Ala.-Lincoln	28:45	6	C	Piedmont-40th	28:45	6	F	Berk-Adeline
38:45	6	DH-8*	Sacto.Nor.Ry	38:45	3	2	Dutton-7th St	30:00	2	4-6*	Encinl-Lincln	32:30	4	E	Claremnt-55th
40:00	2	3	Berk-Shattuck	41:15	4	B	Oakland-22nd	31:15	1	2	Dutton-7th St	33:45	6	C	Piedmont-40th
41:15	2	5	Berk-9th St.	42:30	4	A	Oakland-12th	32:30	2	6	Ala.-Lincoln	35:00	2	4-6	Encinl-Lincln
42:30	5	H	Berk-Sacto St	43:45	6	#8	Sacto.Nor.Ry	36:15	4	B	Oakland-22nd	36:15	1	7	Dutton Exprss
43:45	5	F	Berk-Adeline	47:30	5	H	Berk-Sacto St	37:30	6	A	Oakland-12th	37:30	2	2	Dutton-7th St
47:30	4	E	Claremnt-55th	48:45	5	F	Berk-Adeline	40:00	2	3	Berk-Shattuck	41:15	4	B	Oakland-22nd
48:45	4	C	Piedmont-40th	50:00	2	3-5	Shatt.-9th St	41:15	2	5	Berk-9th St.	42:30	6	A	Oakland-12th
50:00	2	4*	Ala.-Encinal	52:30	4	E	Claremnt-55th	42:30	5	H	Berk-Sacto St	45:00	2	3	Berk-Shattuck
51:15	1	2	Dutton-7th St	53:45	4	C	Piedmont-40th	43:45	5	F	Berk-Adeline	46:15	2	5	Berk-9th St.
52:30	3	6	Ala.-Lincoln	55:00	2	4	Ala.-Encinal	47:30	4	E	Claremnt-55th	47:30	5	H	Berk-Sacto St
56:15	4	B	Oakland-22nd	56:15	1	7	Dutton Exprss	48:45	4	C	Piedmont-40th	48:45	5	F	Berk-Adeline
57:30	6	A	Oakland-12th	57:30	3	2	Dutton-7th St	50:00	3	2	Dutton-7th St	52:30	4	E	Claremnt-55th
								51:15	2	4	Ala.-Encinal	53:45	4	C	Piedmont-40th
								56:15	4	B	Oakland-22nd	55:00	2	6	Ala.-Lincoln
								57:30	4	A	Oakland-12th	56:15	3	2	Dutton-7th St
								58:45	6	#7	Sacto.Nor.Ry				

* - Deadhead run from Bridge Yard
Sacramento Northern trains:
#7 - *The Comet* - From Chico, Yuba City, Marysville, and Sacramento
#8 - *The Meteor* - To Sacramento, Marysville, Yuba City, and Chico
#27 - **From Concord**, Walnut Creek, Lafayette, and Oakland
#32 - To Oakland, Lafayette, Walnut Creek, and Concord

END OF TRACK at Dutton Ave. is shared by No. 2 Seventh Street local and No. 7 Dutton Ave. Express — **Thomas Gray Collection**

The Montin report, and the city's petition seemed to have the I.E. on the defensive. Railway officials issued a statement pointing out that the company was providing the best possible service under the circumstances. Passenger traffic on the two Alameda lines had been declining for a number of years, the statement said, adding that both Interurban Electric and Key System had lost the use of about $10 million worth of ferries, piers, and other facilities rendered useless by the opening of the Bridge Railway.

Early in April, agitation for better transbay transportation in Alameda reached the level that there was serious talk of getting rid of the red trains and substituting a municipal bus line connecting with a municipal ferry running between Alameda Pier and San Francisco. City Attorney George pointed out that even if the city should begin such a municipal service, the city could not prevent either Interurban Electric or Key System from also serving Alameda. He also noted that although the city could easily terminate the license covering operation of the Encinal Avenue line, the Lincoln Avenue line was covered by a franchise, and the city was powerless to terminate it as it still had a number of years remaining.

Mayor Henry A. Weichhart cautioned the city not to undertake a project that could cost millions of dollars but would shorten the travel time to San Francisco by only a few minutes. The Alameda Municipal Transportation League in early April secured the signatures of more than 4,000 Alameda residents on a petition requesting resumption of ferry service from Alameda Pier to San Francisco. At the same time, Ben F. Lamborn, President of the League, sent letters to the Reconstruction Finance Corporation, the Toll Bridge Authority, and the State Railroad Commission complaining that Alameda had received little consideration from any public body in the planning of the Bridge Railway system. Lamborn concluded his letters with pleas for financial assistance to get a better level of transbay service for the people of Alameda.

On April 26, 1939, City Manager Schwanenberg announced the results of a passenger traffic survey made on the red trains by the city on the sixth of that month. The survey showed that there were only 2,561 westbound riders on that particular day. Schwanenberg concluded that the small number of riders demonstrated the absurdity of any continued agitation for renewed ferry service from Alameda Pier or the formation of a municipal bus system.

Undaunted, the Alameda Municipal Transportation League presented a report to the Alameda City Council on June 9 outlining a plan for a $557,700 municipal ferry and bus system. The plan envisioned the purchase of three former Southern Pacific-Golden Gate auto ferries and 25 buses. Included in the estimated cost would be funds for the modernization of the Alameda Pier facilities, which had been abandoned six months previously. The report, which was prefaced by the statement that Alameda was facing a potential loss of population because of a paucity of direct transportation across the Bay, stated that the system could gross $447,000 annually and have net earnings of $33,000. These figures were based on a 21-cent one-way bus fare from Alameda to San Francisco or an auto ferry fare of 25 cents for car and driver. The report included sample schedules, which indicated that the buses and ferries would operate on a 22½-minute headway throughout the day and hourly at night and on weekends.

In rebuttal to this proposal, City Manager Schwanenberg presented his own report on a municipal ferry system, but without the bus portion. The city report showed that with similar fares and headways, the ferry system would suffer a monthly deficit of $9,917.

THOUGH RED INK was mounting, I.E. trains went about their daily duties. Encinal Ave. train (above) approaches Morton Street station in Alameda. Single-car Shattuck Ave. run (below) negotiates 26th Street viaduct on a beautifully-clear day. **Both Charles D. Savage**

The Transportation League proposal was further discussed at the July 28 meeting of the city council. At this meeting, the League proposed that because of an expected annual profit, the city should give consideration to collecting transbay fares only during morning and evening commute hours; free transbay transportation could be provided city residents between the hours of 8:30 a.m. and 4:00 p.m. The League also claimed that the system could be financed through a low-interest loan from the Reconstruction Finance Corporation or from a loan from the Alameda Municipal Lighting System, which showed an average annual profit of $200,000.

Finally, on August 16, the City of Alameda announced that after an exhaustive study of a municipal transbay transportation system, it had concluded that any such system would lose about $125,000 per year. On that note, all further talk of a city-operated transit system was laid to rest, and the citizens of the island city were forced to rely on the faithful red trains —at least for the time being.

NINTH STREET LINE was one of I.E.'s weaker performers, but had its own scenic attractions. Two-car train (above) rolls downgrade along Solano Ave., while (below) a single-car train stops at Shellmound Station. Shellmound Tower and the S.P. mainline are at left.
Charles D. Savage; W.C. Whittaker

STEAM-POWERED local freight paces Seventh Street I.E. train in East Oakland. Choo-choo was bound for the First Street route.
W.C. Whittaker

The Beginning of the End

When Interurban Electric began operating across the Bay Bridge, headways on all lines were essentially the same as during the days of ferry operations. Daytime service on the lines to Oakland and Berkeley were operated on a 20-minute headway. Each of the two Alameda lines operated on a 40-minute headway, thus affording 20-minute service to that city. Unfortunately, the steady decline of patronage which had begun in 1925 had accelerated since the opening of the Bay Bridge to vehicular traffic in 1936, and it was time to face realities and consider retrenchments.

In spite of adjusted train schedules, the expected number of transbay passengers never was realized by either Interurban Electric or Key System. Although one-way fares were held at the 21-cent level charged during the days of the ferries, both railroads actually received less per passenger after the start of Bridge Railway service because of a 2½-cent toll imposed by the Toll Bridge Authority for each transbay passenger carried. Furthermore, much of the decline in patronage could actually be attributed to the expanding metropolitan area of the East Bay.

For example, what had been open fields along the outer portion of the Seventh Street line in 1912 had, by 1920, become the site of choice residential tracts. In turn, transbay commuters who lived there eventually moved farther out, and by 1940, these areas were populated mostly by people who worked in Oakland or San Leandro and got to their jobs by auto or local transit. Perhaps the most striking change was that experienced along West Seventh Street. Here, in the 1880s, were grand old homes built in close proximity to the "local" stations at Market Street and Pine Street. Commuters by the hundreds lived in the area and used the steam locals as a way to get to and from work. Sixty years later, the locale had become a depressed area, with few if any persons commuting to San Francisco from those stations.

The overall effect of rising costs and declining patronage forced both Interurban Electric and Key System to make a study of operating economies. One proposal considered by the Interurban would be the substitution of buses for trains on both Alameda lines as well as on the Berkeley-Ninth Street line. In the case of the Alameda lines, the buses could use the Posey Tube to cross the Estuary, thus avoiding the more circuitous route used by the trains.

Ultimately, it was decided to retain rail service on all lines but on lengthened headways to reduce costs. To this end, Interurban Electric and Key System applied to the State Railroad Commission in December 1939 for permission to reduce the frequency of service on all lines. During the hearings on the applications, testimony pointed out that Interurban Electric was suffering an annual loss of about $1 million and Key System was losing about $200,000 annually.

One of the reasons given for the far greater losses by I.E. was the fact that all trainmen were members of the railroad brotherhoods and hence, all trains, like those of the Southern Pacific, were operated with a minimum of three men. In contrast, employees of Key System were members of the street railway union, and consequently, their trains could be operated with a minimum of two men. After hearing this testimony, the Railroad Commission allowed both railroads to reduce off-peak service beginning February 26, 1940.

With the reduced schedules in effect, for the first time in nearly 30 years electric trains no longer operated at 20-minute intervals along Shattuck Avenue or Seventh Street. The basic headway for these two lines was lengthened to 30 minutes; Sunday and holiday service was changed from 40-minute to 45-minute headways. Service on the Ninth Street line was drastically reduced, with headways being lengthened from 20 minutes to 45 minutes daily including Sundays. Service to Alameda was changed to hourly on each line, thus giving that

TABLE 9 -- *Annual Passenger Traffic, 1919 to 1940*

Year	Number	Year	Number	Year	Number
1919	29,764,571	1926	21,406,086	1933	14,373,519
1920	22,657,418	1927	20,450,885	1934	14,030,135
1921	22,465,237	1928	20,058,403	1935	14,169,108
1922	21,388,908	1929	19,204,289	1936	14,286,025
1923	22,252,342	1930	18,155,805	1937	12,450,526
1924	21,949,058	1931	16,589,806	1938	10,482,071
1925	22,602,246	1932	14,682,516	1939	9,937,000 e/
				1940	9,600,000 e/

e/- Estimate

city 30-minute service throughout the day. These lengthened headways reduced the total daily number of Interurban Electric departures from San Francisco from 210 to 162 during the week and from 128 to 114 on Sundays and holidays.

And then came the bombshell. On the same date that service was reduced, Interurban Electric petitioned the State Railroad Commission for permission to abandon all rail service on the grounds that the service was losing too much money and that any further continuation of operation would threaten the financial condition of the parent corporation, Southern Pacific. Concurrent with the filing of that petition, Key System applied to provide substitute service for all abandoned Interurban Electric lines.

Because the proposed abandonment involved a considerable portion of the use of the Bridge Railway facilities, the State Railroad Commission directed its staff to make a traffic survey of the Interurban Electric lines as well as those of Key System. Based on the data developed by the survey and passenger traf-

TABLE 10 -- *Bridge Railway Daily Passenger Traffic, April 24, 1940*

INTERURBAN ELECTRIC	Westward	Eastward	Total
Seventh Street	5,900	6,077	11,977
Encinal Avenue	2,081	2,006	4,087
Lincoln Avenue	1,454	1,387	2,841
Shattuck Avenue	4,389	4,494	8,883
Ninth Street	1,619	1,666	3,285
Total ..	15,443	15,630	31,073
KEY SYSTEM	**Westward**	**Eastward**	**Total**
Oakland-12th Street	2,751	2,617	5,368
Oakland-22nd Street	3,217	3,277	6,494
Piedmont-40th Street	2,236	2,290	4,526
Claremont-55th Street	2,013	2,059	4,072
Berkeley-Adeline Street	2,464	2,468	4,932
Berkeley-Sacramento Street	1,854	1,718	3,572
Total ..	14,535	14,429	28,964

fic statistics provided by the railroad for the years 1919 to 1939, it was concluded by the commission that continued operation of the Interurban Electric red trains was indeed not economically justified.

During the hearings, opposition to total abandonment was heard from many East Bay cities and commuter groups. In addition, the Toll Bridge Authority protested the abandonment on the grounds that Interurban Electric provided a necessary service that could not be duplicated by Key System. Although the Toll Bridge Authority had the legal right under the agreement of March 6, 1933, to take over all Interurban

FOOTBALL SPECIALS were a feature of the Shattuck Ave. line, which passed near the University of California Memorial Stadium. This one is headed by a combo; marked "C", it is the third special of the day.
Charles D. Savage

MAGNIFICENT HOLDOVER from the days of the Central Pacific, the Oakland-Seventh and Broadway station was marked by ornate gable emblem. This historic building was still standing in 1977—in use as a grocery and delicatessen. Ticket agent in the days of the red trains was Miss Edna Colson (below).

W.C. Whittaker; R.S. Ford Collection

Electric service, their abandonment protest stopped short of offering to do so.

Because of the bleak economic picture, the Railroad Commission had little alternative other than to authorize the abandonment of the system as sought; this they did on August 26, 1940. The fate of the red trains was permanently sealed with the concurrence of abandonment by the Interstate Commerce Commission on November 9, 1940.

In April 1940, there was a major reorganization of both the Interurban Electric and Bridge Railway management. R.E. Hallawell remained as manager of I.E.; Elliot Pope was named Trainmaster and S.L. Dolan took the post of Assistant Trainmaster of I.E. and Superintendent of the Bridge Railway. F.E. Sullivan, named Assistant Superintendent of the Bridge Railway at this time, died a few weeks thereafter.

Four months later, in August, many in the management positions of Interurban Electric and the Bridge Railway were rotated to other positions. The new management lineup was Dolan as Manager of I.E. and Assistant Superintendent of the Bridge Railway, Hallawell as Assistant Manager of I.E., Pope continued as Trainmaster of I.E., N.B. Eddlestone as Superintendent of the Bridge Railway, and Paul Stapp, Trainmaster of the Bridge Railway.

In June of the following year, the management was reorganized for the last time. Eddlestone was named Manager of the I.E. and Assistant Superintendent of the Bridge Railway, Dolan was shuffled to Assistant Manager of I.E., Pope remained as Trainmaster of I.E., Stapp was Superintendent and Assistant Trainmaster of the Bridge Railway, and J. Walker was Trainmaster of the Bridge Railway.

In recalling his days as the last manager of the Interurban Electric, Eddlestone commented,

"We ran the railroad during its last days, and I was on board the last train to Berkeley. The next morning, I was out of a job."

Like other Southern Pacific men, however, Eddlestone was absorbed into the parent company and continued his railroading career.

MID-DAY ALAMEDA trains shrank to one-car affairs toward the last; typical was Lincoln Ave. train (above). Seventh Street line, on the other hand, carried bigger crowds, as witness four-car train (below) at Parker Ave. station. Local freight with one of the new diesels is bound for Chevrolet plant.

Charles D. Savage; W.C. Whittaker

DOWNTOWN BERKELEY'S main street, Shattuck Ave., carried two pairs of electric railway tracks. East Bay Transit tracks were at right; I.E. tracks on left were later used by Key System bridge units.
Bay Area Electric Railroad Assn. Collection

The Last Red Trains

Because they were the greatest money losers and the easiest to replace, the Alameda lines were the first to go. At 12:10 a.m. on January 18, 1941, the last Lincoln Avenue train left the Bridge Terminal. It was followed at 12:31 a.m. by the last Encinal Avenue train. The last Interurban Electric revenue service to Alameda was performed by the "owl" connection at Fruitvale, which left that station at 1:53 a.m. after connecting with a Seventh Street train. This "owl" train went by way of the Encinal Avenue line to West Alameda and then returned to Fruitvale by way of the Lincoln Avenue line, tying up there at 2:28 a.m., bringing to a close nearly 40 years of electric train service to the island city.

Early that same morning, Key System inaugurated its trio of Alameda to San Francisco bus lines, which operated by way of the shorter Posey Tube route. At the beginning, the three coach routes, the O-Santa Clara Avenue, T-Lincoln Avenue, and W-Encinal Avenue lines operated throughout the day. Within a number of years, however, only the Santa Clara Avenue coach line remained in full-time operation. Today, both Lincoln Avenue and Encinal Avenue are essentially devoid of any form of public transportation.

In order to replace the Seventh Street line, Key System proposed an extension of its A-Oakland-12th Street rail line. This replacement was accomplished in two stages. The last full day of red train operation along Seventh Street was March 21, 1941. The following morning, at 2:25 a.m., the last Seventh Street train departed from the San Francisco Terminal Building, arriving at the Dutton Avenue terminus at 3:16 a.m. A few hours later, Key System began operating its "A" trains along the route of the East 14th Street local car line to a temporary terminal at 105th Avenue.

With the discontinuance of the Seventh Street line, Southern Pacific Company, owner of the tracks and right-of-way, deeded that portion of the line between Melrose and Havenscourt to the City of Oakland. The city, in turn, leased this trackage to Key System, and after the necessary track connections had been made at East 14th Street, "A" trains began operating to a new terminal at Havenscourt on April 14, 1941. This was three miles short of the old I.E. outer terminal at Dutton Ave.

Also with the abandonment of the I.E. Seventh Street line, the shops at West Alameda were closed. Thereafter, all routine maintenance of cars was performed at the Bridge Yards. When the last Seventh Street train had completed its run, Southern Pacific immediately took down the catenary trolley wire over this line, thus precluding any further electric train movements. Cars stranded at West Alameda and other

FIGURE 13

```
        INTERURBAN ELECTRIC RAILWAY COMPANY
                          Bridge Yard, March 12, 1941
              SPECIAL NOTICE NO. 299


ALL CONCERNED:

        In accordance with authority of Railroad Commission,
Key System will commence transbay service between San Leandro,
Oakland and San Francisco March 22, 1941, and Interurban Elec-
tric service will be discontinued, the last trains to be oper-
ated will be as follows:

        Arrive San Francisco 2:20 AM, Saturday, March 22, 1941
        Leave San Francisco  2:25 AM, Saturday, March 22, 1941

        Key System will not accept on their services any form
of Southern Pacific or Interurban transportation, other than
the Interurban commutation ticket sold for $6.50.  Employes
holding reduced rate transportation desiring to use Key System
service will, of necessity, have to acquire Key System transpor-
tation.


                                        S. L. DOLAN
                                          Manager
```

```
        INTERURBAN ELECTRIC RAILWAY COMPANY
                          Bridge Yard, March 18, 1941.

                      BULLETIN NO. 58
                      TIMETABLE NO. 3
CONDUCTORS
ENGINEERS
BRAKEMEN
YARDMEN
HOSTLERS
OTHERS CONCERNED:

  1.  Effective 4:01 AM, Saturday, March 22, 1941,
      operation of Interurban Electric Railway trains
      for carrying passengers on the Seventh Street
      Line between San Francisco and Dutton Avenue,
      San Leandro, will be abandoned.

  2.  Effective at 4:01 AM, Saturday, March 22, 1941,
      all Interurban Electric Railway operations be-
      tween Fruitvale and Dutton Avenue, San Leandro,
      will be abandoned.

  3.  Effective 4:01 AM, Saturday, March 22, 1941, the
      schedules shown on Pages 10, 11, 12, 13, 22 and
      23 of timetable No. 3 are cancelled.

  4.  Effective 4:01 AM, Saturday, March 22, 1941,
      Conductors' and Engineers' runs 1 to 14 inclusive,
      as shown on roster, Pages 2 and 3 of timetable
      No. 3, also bulletins Nos. 12, 48 and 56 are
      cancelled.


                                        S. L. DOLAN
                                          Manager
```

NOTICE TO THE PUBLIC

The KEY SYSTEM transbay service between Berkeley and San Francisco will be commenced Saturday, July 26, 1941, at which time under authority of California Railroad Commission Decision No. 34389, dated July 3, 1941, INTERURBAN ELECTRIC RAILWAY COMPANY will discontinue service between San Francisco and Berkeley via the Shattuck Ave. and Ninth St. Lines.

The last trains to be operated by INTERURBAN ELECTRIC RAILWAY to and from Berkeley will be the trains---

ARRIVING SAN FRANCISCO:
  via Ninth St. Line   12:40 a.m., Saturday, July 26, 1941
  via Shattuck Ave Line   1:16 a.m., Saturday, July 26, 1941
LEAVING SAN FRANCISCO:
  via Ninth St. Line   12:44 a.m., Saturday, July 26, 1941
  via Shattuck Ave. Line 1:21 a.m., Saturday, July 26, 1941

Thereafter no passenger train service will be operated by INTERURBAN ELECTRIC RAILWAY, and all applicable schedules and tariffs will be cancelled.

INTERURBAN ELECTRIC RAILWAY CO.

INDIVIDUAL MONTHLY COMMUTATION TICKET
Good For One Round-Trip Daily, Without
Stopover, Between DUTTON AVE., ALAMEDA
BERKELEY, AND BERTONI'S RESTAURANT

DURING MONTH OF **JULY, 1941**

Form 21-5   (Sign in Ink)   (Purchaser)

INTERRUPTED ELECTRIC RAILWAY CO.

You Owe Crew Clerk A Damn Good Drink

Collection of R. S. Ford

INTERURBAN ELECTRIC ABANDONMENT

MIND-BOGGLING choice of three electric railway modes was available to the lucky passenger in South Berkeley. From left to right, we behold East Bay Transit streetcar on the 3-Grove Street line, an I.E. 3-Shattuck Ave. train bound for San Francisco, and a Key System F-Adeline Street train also bound for The City. Just out of picture to right, we are assured, was a Key K-Alcatraz Ave. local car.
Addison H. Laflin Jr.

locations subsequently were brought to West Oakland for dead storage by steam engines.

After the closing of the Seventh Street line, Interurban Electric was left with only the two lines running to Berkeley. These originally had been slated for abandonment on March 1, 1940. But the date was postponed to April 1, as Key System said it was not ready to assume the substitute service. For one thing, Key System did not have enough cars. During March, State Director of Public Works Frank W. Clark contacted William P. St. Sure, Vice President and General Manager of Key System, offering the lease of the state-owned red trains to that company. Clark mentioned that the state would be willing to provide Key System with whatever assistance it could in providing transportation service to Berkeley.

However, before the April 1 deadline for Interurban Electric abandonment was reached, Clark again contacted St. Sure and notified him that the state would be unable to lease any red trains as legal counsel felt that such a lease would jeopardize the right of the Toll Bridge Authority to take legal action against Interurban Electric for breach of contract. Thus, Key System was forced to look elsewhere for the needed equipment to operate the extended F-Berkeley-Adeline Street train line.

Because the April 1 deadline was fast approaching, the Berkeley City Council became alarmed that Interurban Electric might give up the service before Key System could get its own trains in operation. To quiet Berkeley's fears, State Railroad Commissioner Ray L. Riley quoted a letter that he had received from A.T. Mercier, President of the Interurban Electric. The letter said in part,

> "Officers of Key System today have advised us of the difficulties they are experiencing in inaugurating their Berkeley service and from complications resulting from the attitude of the Toll Bridge Authority in declining to allow them to use the State-owned equipment now leased to us. The Key System, we are informed, has had to make other arrangements to provide adequate transportation facilities between the Metropolitan Oakland area and San Francisco.
>
> "In view of the complications referred to and the delays encountered by the Key System, Interurban Electric will be willing to continue operation of its Berkeley Ninth and Shattuck lines beyond April 1 for a reasonable period providing all parties make every effort possible to make the Key substitute service in Berkeley effective at the earliest date."

Riley also called the attention of the Berkeley City Council to the fact that due to the National Defense Program, Key System had found it extremely difficult to obtain the necessary materials and equipment with which to build and operate the new service to Berkeley. Because of all of these factors, Riley concluded, Interurban Electric would not be allowed to abandon either of the two Berkeley lines until such time that Key System was ready to provide the substitute service.

And so for the next four months, red trains continued to rumble through the streets of Berkeley. All the while, Key System was involved in the construction of a single-track connection from South Berkeley along the grade of their former line to downtown Berkeley. After preparing several times for the last day of operation, only to see the date postponed, I.E.R. finally announced that under no circumstances would trains be operated beyond August 1, regardless of any lack of capability on the part of Key System.

Finally, with crews working day and night, Key System completed the new extension for its F-Berkeley-Adeline Street rail line, and by the middle of July, definite plans could be made to abandon the last two Interurban Electric train lines and substitute Key System service.

And so finally it arrived—the last full day of operation of the Interurban Electric red trains—Friday, July 25, 1941. All that day, many rode and photographed the trains that had for so long been a familiar sight in downtown Berkeley. Ultimately, at 12:44 a.m. Saturday morning, the last Ninth Street train left the San Francisco Terminal for Thousand Oaks, arriving there at 1:17 a.m. This train then continued by way of the Shattuck Avenue line to Berryman Yard for the final tieup.

The last Shattuck Avenue train departed from Thousand Oaks at 12:38 a.m., made the last westward revenue run along Shattuck and arrived in San Francisco at 1:16 a.m. During the five-minute layover, flashbulbs popped to record this scene for posterity. At 1:21 a.m. a final "Bo-o-o-oard!" was heard and Conductor Charles Moisan sounded two bleeps on the train signal. The two-car train then moved slowly out of the Terminal Building and up the grade toward the Bay Bridge. Picking up speed, the train crossed the Bridge and wound its way through the East Bay. On board were a great many railfans and well-wishers as well as Bridge Railway Manager Eddlestone and Key System President Alfred J. Lundberg.

The train arrived at Thousand Oaks at 1:56 a.m. and as was the custom for the last night run of Shattuck trains, continued to Albany. After changing ends, the train returned to Berryman Yard where, at 2:10, the two cars from the other Shattuck train and the one car from the last Ninth Street train were coupled. The five-car train then proceeded down Shattuck Avenue.

After making a stop at 34th Street, where the last of the faithful railfans got off, the equipment was taken to West Oakland and placed in dead storage. That same night, the Southern Pacific-owned cars at the Bridge Yard were sorted from those owned by the Toll Bridge Authority and were brought to West Oakland also for dead storage. Thus ended some 80 years of Southern Pacific and Interurban Electric suburban service in the East Bay.

Two days after the last red train had tied up, a farewell party was held for all employees at Bellini's Restaurant on Telegraph Avenue in Oakland. All of the former trainmen, dispatchers, agents, and everyone else who had worked for the railway were invited. Souvenir admission tickets were distributed for the party and were a facsimile of an I.E. commute ticket, but in place of the name of the railway, was the name "Interrupted Electric Railway Co."

Key System, meanwhile, did not have its equipment shortage solved. Absorbing parts of the I.E. Seventh Street and Berkeley lines added mileage and passengers. After being denied the lease of 30 of the red trains for use on the extended "F" line, Key System was forced to abandon the H-Berkeley-Sacramento Street rail line in order to release the necessary equipment. This was done concurrent with the abandonment of Interurban Electric service. Abandonment of the "H" trains also forced the abandonment of the connecting G-Westbrae streetcar line.

On the morning of Saturday, July 26, 1941, Key System inaugurated the G-Albany motorcoach line to provide service to the territory formerly served by the Ninth Street line. On that same date, "F" trains began running to a temporary terminal at University and Shattuck Avenues in downtown Berkeley. A bus connection was provided between that point and Northbrae. By August 6, the necessary track work had been completed at Shattuck Avenue and Dwight Way, and "F" trains began operating all of the way to Northbrae, eliminating the need of the connecting bus.

At this same time, streetcars of the 4-Shattuck Avenue line began using the former Interurban Electric tracks as far as University Avenue. Key System subsequently extended the "F" train line through the Northbrae Tunnel to a new Thousand Oaks station at Solano Avenue and The Alameda.

After the abandonment of Interurban Electric service, Southern Pacific retained certain portions of the system for industrial switching purposes. These were the tracks of the former Shattuck Avenue line from Emeryville to Dwight Way, the former Ninth Street line from Shellmound to Heinz Street, the former Seventh Street line from East Oakland to Melrose and from Havenscourt to 103rd Avenue, and the former Lincoln Avenue line from Fruitvale to West Alameda by way of Tynan. All other trackage was abandoned.

The portion of the viaduct over the Southern Pacific main-

RONALD COLMAN was starring in "Lost Horizon" at the Oaks Theater in 1940, and you could get there via this Shattuck Ave. local train, taking the curve into the Thousand Oaks wye. **W.C. Whittaker**

BOWING OUT: Shattuck Ave. express rolls eastward at Stanford Ave. on last day of operation; this was last No. 9 to operate.
Robert A. Burrowes

MELANCHOLY MOMENT has arrived as Bridge Railway manager N.B. Eddlestone, left, and Key System President Alfred J. Lundberg stand in front of the last Interurban Electric train. Photo was taken at Thousand Oaks shortly before 2:00 a.m. on Saturday, July 26, 1941. Time had run out for the red trains in the East Bay.
Vernon J. Sappers Collection

line tracks between 34th Street Junction and the connection with the Bridge Railway tracks became the property of the Oakland Terminal Railway for use as a rail access to the Oakland Army Base. The south half of this viaduct was converted to vehicular use. Both portions of this viaduct continue in use today.

After abandonment of service, all cars owned by the Southern Pacific were moved to a spur near Decoto. Most subsequently were sent to Los Angeles for service on the Pacific Electric Railway, with the remainder being scrapped. Those cars owned by the Toll Bridge Authority were stored at the Bridge Yards until sold to the Houston Shop Corporation. Many of these latter cars subsequently were sent to other parts of the nation for use during World War II.

At the beginning of World War II, the State Railroad Commission realized that some form of public transportation between East Bay points and the various shipyards would have to be developed. One of the first suggestions was the utilization of some of the recently abandoned Interurban Electric trackage. This idea, which was contained in a Railroad Commission "Plan One" Report, envisaged a line running from Dutton Avenue by way of Melrose, Seventh Street, Oakland-16th Street Station, and the former Ninth Street line to Albany. Here, 5.5 miles of new track would be built along the center of Panhandle Boulevard and Cutting Boulevard to a terminal at Garrard Avenue near the Richmond Shipyards.

The route of the extension from Albany to Richmond bore a striking resemblance to the Richmond line proposed by Southern Pacific some 30 years previously. In fact, the new proposal had an undercrossing beneath the Southern Pacific tracks at Stege Station, much the same as the proposed Richmond line did. The Railroad Commission estimated that this "Belt Line" would cost about $1 million to construct and equip; it was proposed that Key System be the operator.

Although this Richmond "Belt Line" never came to fruition, two segments of the former Interurban Electric system were utilized for shipyard service. One was a portion of the abandoned Seventh Street line between Broadway and Pine Street. This track was rehabilitated and used as part of the 1-East 14th Street and 3-Grove Street car lines to serve the

THE REPLACEMENT: Key System built a new Thousand Oaks station just east of The Alameda, in space once occupied by the S.P. westbound track. Bumper and curved derail were installed to prevent trains coming downgrade from over-running end of track. After abandonment of Key System train service in 1958 trackway and station were removed as part of the Solano Ave. extension project and nearby rail tunnel was thrown open to autos. **R.S. Ford**

Moore Dry Dock shipyard. Another portion was that part of the former Ninth Street line between Heinz Street and Buchanan Street. This portion became a part of the Richmond Shipyard Railway, which ran between 40th Street and San Pablo Avenue, in Emeryville, and the Richmond Shipyards.

The Richmond Shipyard Railway was built during the early years of World War II, and at the time it was considered a great feat of engineering. After being told that "it can't be done," Key System Vice President and General Manager William P. St. Sure, assisted by the various departments of Key System, combed the entire nation for parts, pieces, and equipment with which to build and operate the line. What St. Sure and his men wound up with was an improbable railway indeed.

To begin with, the rolling stock consisted of strange-looking former New York elevated cars. All of the rail was second-hand, with much of it coming from the former Interurban Electric Encinal Avenue line in Alameda. The catenary trolley wire, too, was from the former I.E. lines, including much of the trolley wire installed on the Bay Bridge for the red trains. For power transmission, two of the I.E. substations were moved to new locations on the Shipyard Railway.

Finally, as the former elevated cars were designed to draw power from a third rail, a number of them were equipped in the Key System shops with pantographs which had been removed from the Interurban Electric cars prior to their being sold or scrapped. Thus, even after the last red train rolled through the streets of Berkeley, parts and pieces of the Interurban Electric survived for a few more years to serve the nation during World War II.

With all train service abandoned and much of the track and equipment disposed of, the Interurban Electric Railway Company went about the task of closing up shop and going out of business. This took nearly eight years because of a number of lawsuits and legal liabilities. The largest litigation against the company was a suit filed by the California Toll Bridge Authority on March 15, 1944. The suit charged a breach of contract and asked damages amounting to $15,794,257.43. After a number of hearings, the suit finally was settled in December of the following year with a payment to the Toll Bridge Authority of $750,000.

After all litigation had been settled and all outstanding debts had been paid, the board of directors of the Interurban Electric Railway Company met for the last time on August 3, 1949. On that date, a Certificate of Dissolution was filed with the California Secretary of State. This document certified that all company business had been completed, the company had no assets or liabilities, and there was no further business to transact. With the filing of the certificate, the Interurban Electric Railway Company ceased to exist.

NEARLY BEREFT OF PAYING CUSTOMERS, the *Eureka* steams east from the Ferry Building. During the last decade of operation. S.P. ferries operated only as mainline train connections, with business dropping off year by year. **Southern Pacific**

CHAPTER 18

Finished With Engines

WHEN THE TRANSBAY trains of Interurban Electric and Key System began operating across the Bay Bridge, the waters of San Francisco Bay no longer were churned into white wakes by the many ferries plying back and forth between San Francisco and the East Bay. Instead, only an occasional white trail was produced by the remnants of the Southern Pacific fleet operating between the Ferry Building and Oakland Pier.

Needing at most only three boats to maintain regular service, Southern Pacific retired the *Alameda* and *Santa Clara*; ferry service was provided by the *Sacramento* and *Berkeley,* assisted by the *Eureka,* which had been transferred to the East Bay operation after Northwestern Pacific ferry service between the Ferry Building and Sausalito was abandoned in 1941.

The *Oakland, Piedmont,* and *Sierra Nevada* were leased to Key System, which operated 10-cent ferries between the Ferry Building and the west entrance to Treasure Island, site of the Golden Gate International Exposition during 1939 and 1940. During the first year of the fair, the orange-painted *Sierra Nevada* also worked a ferry route between the east entrance to Treasure Island and the Key Route pier, where connections were made with trains on the Line X-Exposition route. Exposition ferry service lasted only until the 1940 fair closed on September 29th. After that, S.P.'s "old white ladies" had the bay to themselves.

283

A NEARLY EMPTY *Sacramento* approaches Oakland Pier in the fall of 1939. With the red trains now using the Bay Bridge, the ferries were no longer a major transbay carrier.
R.S. Ford Collection

Shipyard Ferries

With the advent of World War II, three shipyards were put into operation in Richmond and one just north of Sausalito, in Marin County. To get the thousands of yard workers to and from their jobs, the United States Maritime Commission established a shipyard ferry system on San Francisco Bay. Operator of the system, under a contract in effect on July 30, 1942, was the Wilmington Transportation Company, which had run ships between Wilmington and Avalon, on Santa Catalina Island.

For the service, the government requisitioned five bay ferries, the *Alameda, Santa Clara,* and *Sierra Nevada* from the Southern Pacific, the *City of Sacramento* from the Southern Pacific-Golden Gate Ferries, and the *Yerba Buena* from the Key System. Also requisitioned from the Key System were the *San Leandro* and *Hayward,* which were assigned to the Portland shipyard operation also run by the Wilmington company.

The first ferry line placed in operation was the run from San Francisco to Richmond Yard No. 3; service was begun on this route with the *Yerba Buena* on September 18, 1942. Service to the Marinship Yard was begun on November 1, with the *Santa Clara* plying this route. Ferry service to Richmond Yard No. 1 began on November 15 using the *Sierra Nevada,* and the route to Yard No. 2 started on December 1st using the *City of Sacramento.* The *Alameda* initially was assigned the role of relief boat.

Service to the yards left San Francisco from the Transport Building, which was the former auto ferry terminal at the foot of Mission Street. Boats arrived at each yard one-half hour before each shift change and left one-half hour after the change. The ferries to Yards Nos. 1 and 2 shared a slip at Richmond and alternated their service, i.e., a boat would arrive in Richmond with employees for Yard No. 1 and leave with those from Yard No. 2, and vice versa. Initially, ferry service was run directly to Marinship Yard, but beginning on January 1, 1943, a stop was made in both directions at the old auto ferry slip at the foot of Hyde Street.

Taking the ferry to the shipyards reminded many of the days before the bridges. Seen were familiar faces of officers and crewmen, many of whom had come out of retirement to operate the boats. Usually the crossings were uneventful, and for those going on shift, the crossing time could be taken up in the restaurant or snack bar. Going home, particularly at the end of the swing shift or graveyard shift, the 500 or so shipyard personnel on the ferry usually used the time to rest and relax.

The *Sierra Nevada* frequently was used on the run to Marinship Yard. One night in December 1942, the ferry cast off from the Transport Building just before midnight. After crossing the dark waters of San Francisco Bay, it approached the entrance buoys at the mouth of Richardson Bay. Because of the wartime blackout, the captain misjudged the dimly illuminated buoys and missed the channel. With a sudden lurch and heave, the *Sierra Nevada* shuddered to a stop on a mudbar. After making repeated efforts to back off, the captain informed the passengers that they would have several hours to wait until the tide came in far enough to lift the ferry off the mud. Finally, at 3:30 a.m., there was sufficient water depth, and the ferry was able to resume the trip to Marinship.

That same month, the very last Ferry Christmas was celebrated on San Francisco Bay. The event was the idea of Edward O'Gaffney, a local bandleader who remembered the Ferry Christmases of old. With the assistance of the *San Francisco Chronicle* and the San Francisco Junior Chamber of Commerce, O'Gaffney made arrangements to have a gala party on board the *Santa Clara*.

When the graveyard shift from Richmond Yard No. 2 boarded the ferry at 7:30 on the morning of December 24, they were greeted with music and refreshments. The main deck of the ferry had been festooned with ribbons, tinsel, and evergreens, giving the entire boat a holiday spirit. The party quickly got into full swing once the ferry cast off from Richmond, and the events of the crossing were broadcast over radio station KGO.

Similar Christmas parties also were held that day on other ferries for workers from the other shifts at Richmond Yard No. 2 as well as for those that worked at Richmond Yards Nos. 1 and 3 and Marinship Yard.

On more than one occasion, the former Northwestern Pacific ferry *Eureka,* at that time a Southern Pacific boat, was called upon to provide relief service on the shipyard ferries. On one of her trips to Richmond Yard No. 3 on a particularly foggy morning in January 1943, she was struck in the foredeck by the bow of a freighter. The collision resulted in a huge notch being cleaved into the ferry and which caused an estimated $25,000 worth of damage.

On January 1, 1945, alternating ferry service to Richmond Yards Nos. 1 and 2 was consolidated into a single run; ferry service on this route was completely withdrawn on the first of the following March. The last day of that same month saw the final runs of the ferries to Richmond Yard No. 3 and Marinship Yard.

During the period of operation of the shipyard ferries, from September 18, 1942 to March 31, 1945, a total of 11,105,655 passengers were carried. This passenger count was divided as follows: San Francisco to/from Richmond Yard No. 1, 2,223,002; to/from Yard No. 2, 1,903,272; to/from Yard No. 3, 4,561,071; to/from Marinship Yard, 2,418,310.

Because of the termination of the Portland shipyard service on September 22, 1943, the *San Leandro* and *Hayward* were transferred back to the San Francisco Bay operations. The *Hayward* entered service on the run to Richmond Yards Nos. 1 and 2 on October 9, 1943, and the *San Leandro* entered service on the same run on the following February 13. Arrival of these two boats allowed the *City of Sacramento* to be returned to the War Shipping Administration on May 18, 1944; this ferry subsequently was redelivered to the Puget Sound Navigation Company. The *Alameda* was declared surplus and released to the Navy, who renamed her the *YHB-25* and used her for housing purposes.

The *Yerba Buena* was delivered to the War Shipping Administration on April 5, 1945, and subsequently redelivered to the Army Transportation Service. The ferry was renamed the *Ernie Pyle* to commemorate the famous war correspondent, but she regained her original name a short time later. The *San Leandro* also became the property of the Army Transportation Service. Both ferries were used to transport troops between San Francisco and Camp Stoneman, near Pittsburg. In later years, the *San Leandro* usually was docked at the old passenger ferry slip on the east side of Treasure Island.

The *Sierra Nevada, Hayward,* and *Santa Clara* were delivered to the War Shipping Administration at the termination of the contract with the Wilmington Transportation Company on April 30, 1945. The *Sierra Nevada* was purchased by the Sierra

NOW OWNED by the U.S. Navy and "renamed" *YHB-25*, the aging *Alameda* is moored at the south side of the Oakland Pier.

Thomas Gray Collection

Steamship Company, operator of the 4,486-ton freighter *Sierra*. The ferry subsequently was tied up and removed from documentation. She was redocumented after being sold in May 1947 to the Richmond-San Rafael Ferry and Transportation Company who rebuilt her as an auto ferry for service between Point Richmond and Point San Quentin.

In November 1947, the *Santa Clara* and the aging *Tamalpais,* formerly operated by the Northwestern Pacific, were towed to a mudbar near the former site of Alameda Pier. Stripped of everything usable, the *Tamalpais* was burned first, followed by the *Santa Clara*, which was put to the torch by employees of Moore Dry Dock Company on December 10, 1947.

As the smoke billowed a hundred or so feet skyward, a spokesman for the company told a reporter from the *Oakland Tribune* that this method of scrapping was the most economical way to salvage the 1,800 tons of steel in each boat. Following these two ferries, the *Calistoga* and then the *Hayward* met the same fate. The *Alameda* was the last to go; she was set ablaze on January 28, 1948.

BUSY AGAIN! The *Sacramento* comes into Oakland Pier crowded with commuters during the Key System strike of 1947. It was just like the old days, with boats jammed to capacity. But it didn't last long. **Southern Pacific**

The Last Ferry Tale

With the cessation of hostilities, activity at Oakland Pier went into a slow decline as passenger traffic on steam trains began to taper off. Boats left Oakland Pier and San Francisco on the hour and half hour, with two ferries being used. There was a brief revival of activity during June 1947, when the employees of Key System Transit Lines went on strike.

With all streetcar, bus, and transbay train service halted, commuters were forced to find other means of transportation across the bay. Many took Southern Pacific trains from Berkeley, Oakland-16th Street, or other East Bay stations. Others drove to Oakland Pier, causing traffic jams and parking problems of historic proportions. In time, the strike was settled, and once again the ferries resumed their usually lonely trips back and forth across the bay.

By the early 1950s, the *Sacramento* and *Eureka* were used as the regular boats, with the *Berkeley* being tied up in standby status. However, time was fast running out for the *Sacramento*. On Sunday, November 28, 1954, while crossing the bay, the spring beam of the *Sacramento* broke, rendering her inoperable. Because of this and the fact that Southern Pacific had just purchased the ferry *San Leandro* from the Army Transportation Corps, the decision was made to retire the *Sacramento*.

The ferry later was sold to the Pacific Shipwrecking and Salvage Company. After all of her machinery had been removed, the ferry was disposed of to the Redondo Sport Fishing Company. This latter concern had her lower deck opened up and had bait tanks installed. The *Sacramento* then was towed to Southern California waters, where she was moored two miles west of Redondo Beach, becoming a familiar sight as she was used by countless people angling for salt water fish.

Amid high winds and heavy seas, the *Sacramento* sank in 200 feet of water on Sunday, December 1, 1964. Debris from the ferry subsequently washed up on the beach, where treasure hunters claimed such items as life boats, pieces of railing, and timbers. But the *Sacramento* was gone.

When the *San Leandro* was purchased from the Army, she was taken to the Moore Dry Dock yard for a thorough overhaul, installation of rolling steel doors on each end, improved lower deck clearance, and a coat of paint. After making a number of test runs between Oakland Pier and the Ferry Building during the month of December 1954, she was placed in revenue service on Wednesday, January 5, 1955.

Four months after the *San Leandro* was placed in service, a spectacular fire broke out at the Ferry Building on the afternoon of April 1, 1955. The fire was first noticed by a janitor who saw smoke curling from some exposed timbers in the roof of the carpenter shop. Before long, flames were licking at the roof, and they quickly spread to the adjacent creosoted pilings. The fire, which caused an estimated $750,000 in damage, was answered by over 40 pieces of fire equipment as well as the fireboat *Phoenix,* assisted by three military tugs with fire hoses.

As the black smoke billowed skyward, the four-alarm fire attracted a great many spectators who lined the far side of The Embarcadero. The flames quickly ate into the finger pier sepa-

LAST FERRY acquired by S.P. was the former Key System boat *San Leandro*, a turbo-electric boat seen here en route to Oakland Pier.
Southern Pacific

rating Slips 3 and 4, the former Key System slips. Many feared that the entire Ferry Building would become engulfed in flames. Others, knowing that the structure rested on concrete pilings, feared that the building might collapse into the bay.

During the height of the fire, the *San Leandro* approached from Oakland Pier. Seeing the extent of the blaze, Captain Richard Thomas stopped his ferry. Realizing that "she's a big one," Captain Thomas turned his ferry around and headed back to the safety of Oakland Pier. Passengers on board the ferry were then transferred to buses which took them across the Bay Bridge. All further ferry schedules were annulled for that day and not resumed until the following morning.

It took some seven hours after the first alarm was turned in at 5:17 p.m. to put the fire out. Even after midnight, there were still 14 pieces of fire equipment standing by to quench the still smoldering embers. Destroyed was the carpenter shop, the machine shop, the boiler room, and a large part of the

ON HER LAST DAY OF SERVICE, the *San Leandro* awaits departure time at Oakland Pier. During the nearly 77 years that Oakland Pier was in service, this ferry slip witnessed some 1.5 million departures.
R.S. Ford

upper ramps formerly used by Key System patrons. Also a casualty was the multi-tiered white bell tower which had the appearance of a Grecian temple and which had stood at the end of the center dolphin for many years to guide the ferries through the fog. This bell tower probably is best remembered as the abode of "Eddie the One-Legged Seagull" of Earle Ennis fame.

The same month as the disastrous Ferry Building fire, the Southern Pacific received permission to increase the one-way fare, Oakland Pier to San Francisco, from 29 cents to 50 cents. This increase was accomplished by changing the tariff rate from coach to first class. The fare increase was designed to put the transbay fare on a par with that charged by Key System Transit Lines trains and buses. Not taken into account, however, was the fact that while the Key System fare applied from any point within Zone 1 of the East Bay, the Southern Pacific fare was applicable only from Oakland Pier.

In the latter part of 1956, Southern Pacific announced that the *Eureka* would be retired at the end of the year. However, New Year's Day 1957 came and went and the grand old ferry continued to ply the Bay. In February 1957, after her main shaft broke, it was decided that it would be too expensive to repair the ferry. The *Eureka* eventually was presented to the San Francisco Maritime Museum for display as a monument to the doughty ferries which once criss-crossed the Bay.

At the meeting of January 16, 1959, the California State Park Commission formally accepted the *Eureka* on behalf of the Maritime Museum. The commission then appropriated $27,500 for the maintenance and repair of the ferry. The following month, the *Eureka* was taken from Oakland Pier to the former Richmond-San Rafael ferry slip at Point Richmond where she sat idle for the next three years.

In 1962, the ferry was taken to the Oakland Dock and Warehouse Company pier on the Estuary where she was tied up for over a year while undergoing repairs and repainting. Finally, on September 30, 1963, the *Eureka* was towed across the Bay to the Hyde Street Wharf where she was placed on permanent display.

The handwriting had long been on the wall, and during the latter part of 1957, Southern Pacific applied to the Public Utilities Commission to abandon the ferry service between Oakland Pier and San Francisco. In place of this service, it proposed to operate motor coaches between Oakland-16th Street Station and downtown San Francisco.

In opposition to the abandonment application, Charles Ertola, a member of the San Francisco Board of Supervisors, presented a resolution asking the commission to deny the request and suggesting that the City and County of San Francisco acquire and operate the ferries. The resolution was passed by the board of supervisors, but without the support of the San Francisco Public Utilities Commission. This latter body, after hearing a statement by Charles D. Miller, Manager of the San Francisco Municipal Railway, backed away from support of a municipal ferry system which was estimated to cost about $50,000 per month to operate.

The petition for abandonment of the ferries then was approved by the P.U.C., and the final day of operation was scheduled to be July 29, 1958. With the imminent demise of the ferries, word got around that the two remaining boats, the *Berkeley* and the *San Leandro,* soon would be for sale. This prompted Kenneth Morris, Deputy Premier of the State of Queensland, Australia, to investigate the possibility of purchasing the two ferries for service on the 30-mile run from Brisbane to Stradbroke Island. The offer of purchase was withdrawn, however, as the cost of preparing the ferries for a 7,000-mile ocean voyage was substantial.

During the final year of ferry operations, the *San Leandro* was used in daily service, with the *Berkeley* tied up in semi-retired status. Schedules called for the *San Leandro* to depart from Oakland Pier about every 70 minutes, from 4:30 a.m. until 11:20 a.m. Service was resumed at 3:25 p.m., with the ferry again leaving about every 70 minutes until 11:10 p.m. In all, 14 crossings were made each day. The suspension of service during midday was due to a lack of mainline train arrivals and departures during that period.

In April of the last year of operation, another transbay transportation system made preparations to bow out. This was the Bridge Railway, which by now was operated solely by Key System Transit Lines. At 4:04 on the morning of Sunday, April 20, 1958, the last Key System train left the San Francisco Terminal. As this train, packed to capacity with railfans and regulars, crossed the Bridge with bells ringing and whistles blaring, an era of transbay transportation came to a close. Below, docked at Oakland Pier was the *San Leandro,* the last remaining non-bus form of transbay transportation in existence.

Only too soon, the end of July 1958 arrived and with it the end of passenger ferry service across San Francisco Bay. The last weekend of operation saw many thousands of people coming to Oakland Pier to ride the ferry across the Bay. So great were the crowds that Southern Pacific had to operate continuous service throughout the day. In so doing, the railroad was forced to find an extra crew to operate the ferry between the hours of 11:30 a.m. and 3:25 p.m.

On its last scheduled revenue trip, the *San Leandro* was slated to leave Oakland Pier at 11:10 p.m. after making a connection with train No. 9, the *Shasta Daylight.* Promptly at departure time, Captain Frank Diaz sounded the whistle, and the crew of the *San Leandro* cast off with some 1,600 exuberant people on board. Scarcely anyone noticed that the *Shasta Daylight* had not yet arrived, foretelling another "last trip" in about an hour.

All of the way over to the Ferry Building, the strains of "Auld Lang Syne" and other songs were heard as many a bottle was passed among the revelers. Also on board the ferry were about 60 more sober members of the Bay Area Electric Railroad Association. These railfans were on hand to tape-record, photograph and to emotionally experience this, the last ferry operation on San Francisco Bay.

On the trip across the Bay, a reporter from the *San Francisco Chronicle* interviewed a number of the passengers and crew. Among those he talked to was janitor Harry Davidson, who had worked on the ferries for 26 years. He remarked,

> "It's the same as taking your home away. I hear that they are going to take her to Australia. I sure would be glad to go along if they do."

Also interviewed was Captain Diaz, who commented,

> "I guess it's just one of those things. I'm sorry it had to happen, but now that it has, I'm going to retire."

Arriving at the Ferry Building at 11:30, almost everyone on board trooped off. However, the ever-faithful railfans knew that an extra trip would be run, so they stayed on board and had the ferry to themselves on the trip back to Oakland Pier. There, the passengers from the *Daylight* boarded the ferry, and again Captain Diaz blew the whistle for the "last, last trip." On arriving at the Ferry Building, Captain Diaz walked to the other wheelhouse and made preparations for the very last revenue trip from San Francisco to Oakland Pier.

As the ferry slid out of the slip, from across the waters came the triple blasts from numerous ship whistles, signifying goodby to the ferries. Each of these whistles was dutifully answered by a single blast on the whistle of the *San Leandro.* Finally, the end came as the *San Leandro* moved into the Oakland Pier slip, where she tied up for the last time.

The following morning, there was much activity on board the ferry as a ceremonial final trip was scheduled to depart from Oakland Pier at 10 o'clock. By departure time, more than 500 officials, old commuters, ferryboat buffs, railfans, historians, and others had come on board. As the ferry cast off, a group of middle-aged "boys and girls," all former members of the South of Market Boys and Girls Club, sang a medley of old songs.

Near midbay, the ferry was stopped and the mayors from seven Bay Area cities gathered on the deck for a tribute to the ferries. At the close of the ceremony, Mayor Clifford Rishell of Oakland, and Acting Mayor Henry Rolph of San Francisco, heaved a large wreath overboard on which was inscribed

LAST OF A LONG LINE of ferry skippers, Capt. Richard Thomas pilots the *Eureka* out of the slip at Oakland Pier. The end of a splendid calling was not far off. **R.S. Ford**

LAST HURRAH: With capacity crowd on board, the *San Leandro* (left) leaves Oakland Pier on last day of operation; so great were the crowds that an extra crew had to be called. Upper deck of the *San Leandro* (below, left) had only a sprinkling of passengers several days before the end.
Both R.S. Ford

GOOD-BYE OLD FRIEND. Continuing on to the Ferry Building, the ferry was met by the fireboat *Phoenix,* displaying plumes of water which shot many tens of feet into the air. As the *San Leandro* entered the slip, the San Francisco Municipal Band, under the guest direction of Arthur Fiedler, struck up a rousing rendition of "Stars and Stripes Forever."

With the "last, last, last trip" completed, the ferry returned to Oakland Pier, arriving there at 11:20 a.m. As the passengers slowly walked off the ferry, Captain Patrick McGarrigle gathered his things and walked to the west wheelhouse for the last movement of the ferry. After casting off, the ferry steamed out into the Bay, made a wide turn, and entered the old auto ferry slip next to the *Berkeley*. When the crew had tied up, Captain McGarrigle rang "Finished With Engines" on the engine telegraph, ending some 105 years of ferry service across the Bay.

Down in the engine room, as the ferry grew silent, Chief Engineer Frederic F. Small unscrewed the brass plate which read *STR. SAN LEANDRO—1923.* He remarked,

"I'm going to set this in concrete in front of my home. It's about all I've got to show for these 47 years on the ferries."

The two ferries sat silent and cold, side by side, for some time after abandonment of service. However, the days were numbered for the Oakland Pier, as even then plans were being drafted for another use for this valuable waterfront property.

Aftermath and Rebirth

In July 1959, the *Berkeley* was sold to the Golden Gate Fish Company for an undisclosed sum. The fish company had plans to convert the ferry to a fish reduction plant to be moored along the Estuary. A month later, Luther W. Conover came to the rescue of this ferry and purchased her for his Trade Fair at Sausalito. The ferry was taken across the Bay to the old Northwestern Pacific ferry slip at Sausalito on August 13, 1959.

After being outfitted with shops on her lower deck, the ferry was opened to the public. Patrons were invited to roam the ferry and inspect her upper deck which remained intact with parquet flooring and stained-glass windows. The *Berkeley* remained tied up at Sausalito for nearly 14 years. In the early part of 1973, she was purchased by the San Diego Maritime Museum. After being repaired at the Bethlehem Shipbuilding Corporation yard, the same yard which built her nearly 75 years previously, the *Berkeley* was towed to Southern California where she is now on permanent display.

The *San Leandro* was not as fortunate as either the *Eureka* or the *Berkeley*. At first it was rumored that she had been purchased by a Mexican group, the Fomento Turistico Maritino. This organization had plans to remodel the ferry as a floating casino and moor her off the coast at Acapulco. However, the ferry was purchased by Empire Shipping Corporation and taken to San Francisco, where she was docked at Pier 14.

After being refurbished and repainted, the ferry was maintained in serviceable condition by Franklin Machine Works.

REBIRTH: A sleek Bay Area Rapid Transit District train approaches Oakland West Station from San Francisco, 1977. To right is Seventh Street along which the red trains had rolled 40 years previously. **R.S. Ford**

The owners announced that they were planning to operate the ferry in passenger service in the near future, and that she was available for lease. However, this use of the ferry never materialized, and she sat tied up for over 10 years.

On July 3, 1963, Empire sold the *San Leandro* to restaurateurs Frank Parisi and Orval D. Ogle, both of Sacramento. With this sale, it was rumored that the ferry would be cut into pieces and trucked to Lake Tahoe. Reassembled, she was to be converted to a casino and moored on the Nevada side of the lake, but this plan, too, died aborning. In July 1967, it was discovered that vandals had been methodically stripping the interior of the *San Leandro* of all brass, copper, and anything else of value. Personnel of the Franklin Machine Works had boarded the ferry on a tip and had found a man removing tubing in the engine room. Although they startled him, he dropped his tools and got away. After surveying the situation, it was found that most of the working parts of the ferry were missing.

The end of the *San Leandro* nearly came on the night of September 8, 1969, when a fire broke out at Pier 14. The condemned, worm-eaten pier had stood vacant for many years, and before firemen could quell the flames, the fire had spread to the *San Leandro.* By the time the fire was extinguished, the once-proud ferry, although still afloat, had been reduced to a tangle of twisted metal and smoldering ruins.

The ferry was rebuilt with two upper decks with a new plan to make her into a floating office building. In the interim, she was towed to a new mooring at Pier 37. Once again, however, the ferry was nearly destroyed by fire when Pier 37 went up in smoke on September 21, 1975. The remains of the ferry were then towed to old Pier 42, out toward China Basin, where in 1977 she awaited an uncertain future.

With the abandonment of ferry service from Oakland Pier in 1958, the facility continued to be a train terminal for another two years. Although trains transferred their passengers to buses at Oakland-16th Street Station, all runs began and ended at Oakland Pier. Finally, on the night of Saturday, May 14, 1960, train No. 20, *The Klamath,* made the final departure from Oakland Pier. Thereafter, trains originated and terminated at West Oakland; all mail and express was handled by a new terminal facility at Oakland-16th Street Station. A few months later, the division offices were moved from the pier to a new office building located near the Oakland-16th Street Station.

On November 23, 1960, the 50-year lease of the Oakland Pier property expired, and the facilities and all buildings thereon passed to the ownership of the Port of Oakland. With the tracks removed, the buildings at Oakland Pier stood vacant until 1966 when the entire area was razed to make way for the new Seventh Street Marine Terminal.

Way back in 1851, when Rodman Gibbons and his Gibbons' Folly were the topics of conversation, no one could have foreseen the growth of the waterfront centered about the Oakland Pier area. That Oakland Point was the logical place to locate the eastern terminal of a transbay ferry operation was demonstrated with the construction of the various piers and wharves which culminated with Oakland Pier. The foresight of Rodman Gibbons again was proven in 1967 when the old Oakland Pier area was chosen by the Bay Area Rapid Transit District as the location of the eastern portal of the Trans-Bay Tube.

The modern electric suburban trains of the Bay Area Rapid Transit District began operation from East Bay points through the former Oakland Pier area on their way to San Francisco through the Trans-Bay Tube on September 16, 1974. Outwardly, these sleek silver trains bear little resemblance to the red trains of years ago, but the principle of their design, construction, and operation is essentially the same as that which was developed nearly 70 years ago.

The Southern Pacific-Interurban Electric red trains and the Key System orange trains are gone these many years. They were abandoned because government and management alike decided that trains were an outmoded and old-fashioned form of transportation. But that wisdom has been replaced with a new realization that the old electric railway, brought up to date technologically and esthetically, can serve again to move the Bay Area's masses quickly, safely and efficiently. With the inauguration of transbay rail service by the Bay Area Rapid Transit District in 1974, rail rapid transit returned to the San Francisco Bay Area.

And, to bring our story to complete full circle, new ferry boats are once again plying the deep, blue waters of San Francisco Bay between The City and Marin County. So we have the start, perhaps, of a brand-new Ferry Tale.

CLASS 58-EMC-1: Car 329 is seen at Oakland Pier during the first years of operation. Car at that time had steel-sash windows and General Electric S-164-D pantograph; color was Pullman green with gold lettering. **Southern Pacific**

CLASS 58-EMC-1: Car 302 at West Alameda shows rebuilding with porthole end windows, wood sash windows, new cherry red color, and application of Westinghouse S-522 pantographs. **R.S. Ford Collection**

APPENDIX A

Electric Railway Equipment

THE ELECTRIC CARS of the Oakland, Alameda and Berkeley Lines were designed for one purpose alone: to transport a large number of commuters efficiently and economically. The cars were built with double-width platforms for rapid entraining and detraining and had a 3 and 2 seating arrangement to achieve the highest possible seating capacity per car. The cars were of spartan interior arrangements, with rattan walkover seats, a lack of interior sheathing on ceilings and walls, and all but one class had only bare light globes for illumination. The cars were initially without any form of heat, but heaters finally were installed after the cars had been in service some 10 years. To simplify maintenance, the cars from all three builders were nearly identical in dimensions and appearance.

Southern Pacific numbered the cars on the East Bay and the Portland electric railway properties on one equipment roster. Cars were assigned to either the Oakland, Alameda and Berkeley Lines (O.A. & B.) or to the Oregon and California Lines (O. & C.), better known as the "Red Electrics." The cars of the O.A. & B. Lines were assigned to 10 classes, depending on car length, builder, type, year, and equipment. All motor cars originally were equipped with a roller pantograph manufactured by General Electric Company. In the early 1920s, these pantographs were replaced with more efficient slider types manufactured by Westinghouse Electric and Manufacturing Company.

At one time, all 29 combination passenger-baggage cars contained lavatories. These cars were designed for newspaper and baggage service on the projected (but never built) long-haul lines to Richmond and San Jose. In time, 21 of the cars were rebuilt as coaches, and the lavatories were removed from the remaining cars of this type.

The cars of the East Bay system originally were divided between three ownerships for accounting purposes. Each owner was identified by its initials carried above the car number: S.P. for Southern Pacific,

TABLE 11 -- *Electric Railway Numbering Series*[1]

Car numbers	Type	System[2]
100-102	Freight motor	O&C
200-220	Coach, motor	O&C
300-387	" "	OA&B
400-437	Coach, trailer, non-control	OA&B
438-461	" " , control	OA&B
470-486	" " "	O&C
500-516	Baggage-coach, motor	O&C
600-628	" " "	OA&B
700-701	Baggage, motor	OA&B
750-754	" "	O&C
770-772	Railway Post Office, motor	O&C
800-819	Street car	OA&B
850-883	" "	O&C

1/ After 1914
2/ OA&B: Oakland, Alameda and Berkeley Lines
  O&C: Oregon and California Lines
NOTE: Numbering system adopted after freight motor CP 200 delivered to Pacific Electric Railway

C.P. for Central Pacific, and S.P.C. for South Pacific Coast. In 1937, all cars received an S.P. numeral prefix. This prefix was eliminated when cars were re-lettered for the Interurban Electric Railway.

The affiliated Northwestern Pacific Railroad, which once served Marin County—north of San Francisco Bay—with a third-rail rapid transit system, operated cars similar to those of the Oakland, Alameda and Berkeley Lines. The railroad purchased 18 cars in 1929 of a design nearly identical to Southern Pacific's Class 58-EMC-3. Aside from being operated from a third rail, the only outward difference was the color; N.W.P. cars were painted a deep orange.

INTERIORS of the East Bay suburban cars were utilitarian, but you could certainly pack in the crowds! Trainman W.C. Tornell demonstrates use of Ohmer Fare Register.
R.S. Ford Collection

CLASS 58-EMC-1: Car 312 (left) in builder's photo taken at A.C. & F. factory. Cars were shipped west minus electrical equipment. By 1925 (below), cars had been rebuilt with porthole end windows and painted red. Note the "S.P.C." ownership over the car number.
Leo Mitchell Collection; Vernon J. Sappers Collection

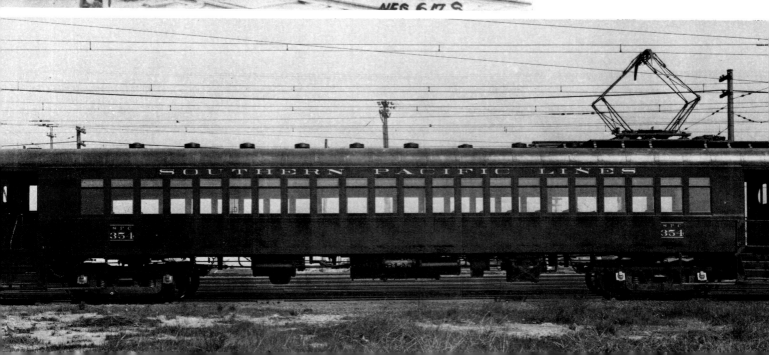

CLASS 58-EMC-2: Car 348 and train passes Key System portion of Bridge Yard. Except for high gates, roller destination signs and a modern slider pantograph, car was little changed from original delivery.   **Charles D. Savage**

CLASS 58-EMC-3: Car 362 and class was built by St. Louis, and had one blanked-off window which was the location of the partition between smoking, non-smoking section.   **Vernon J. Sappers Collection**

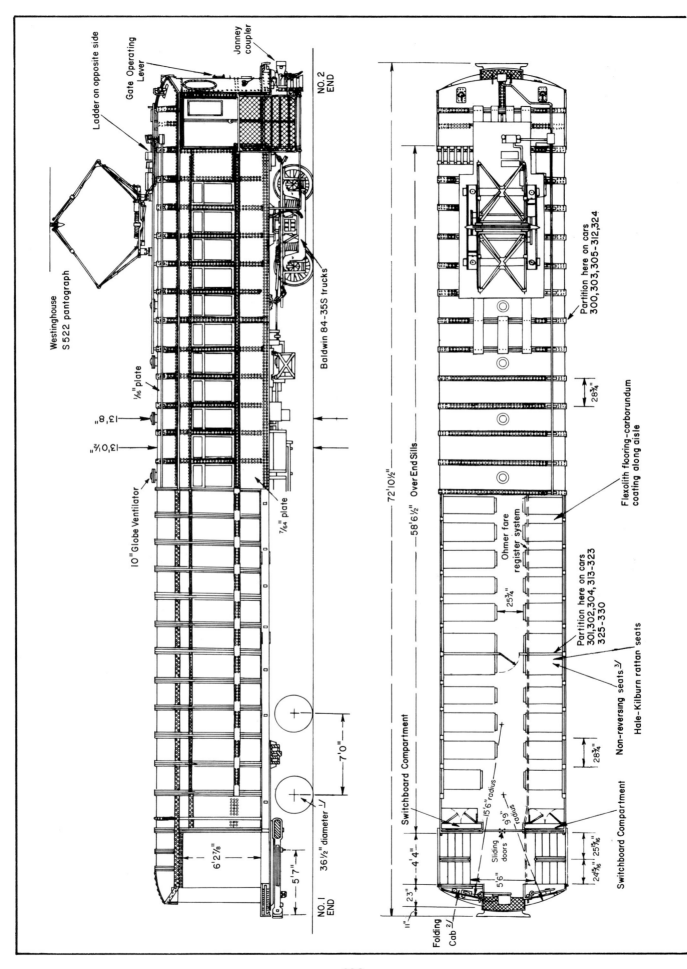

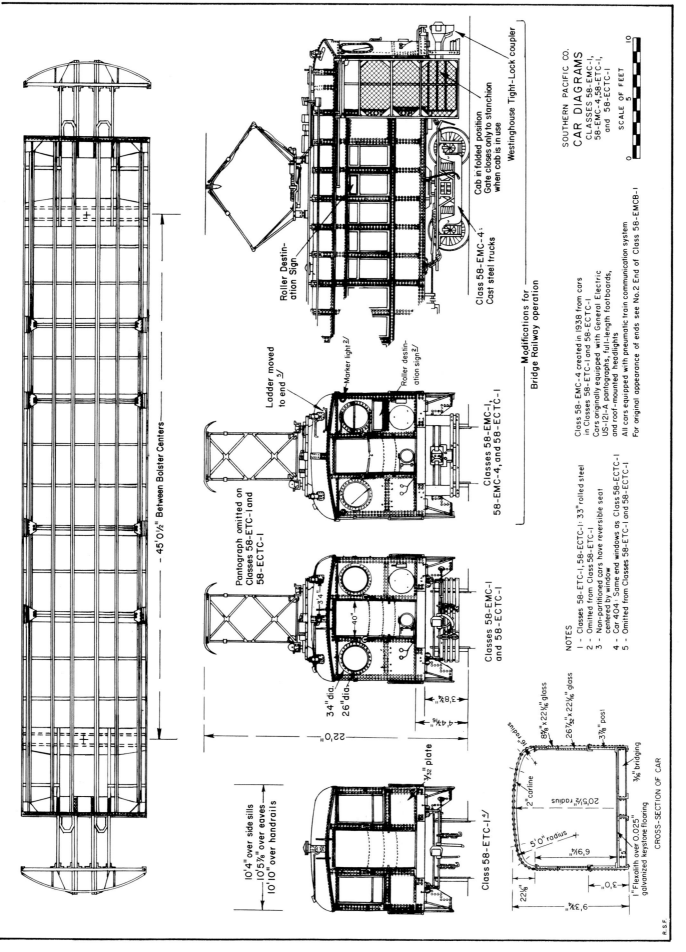

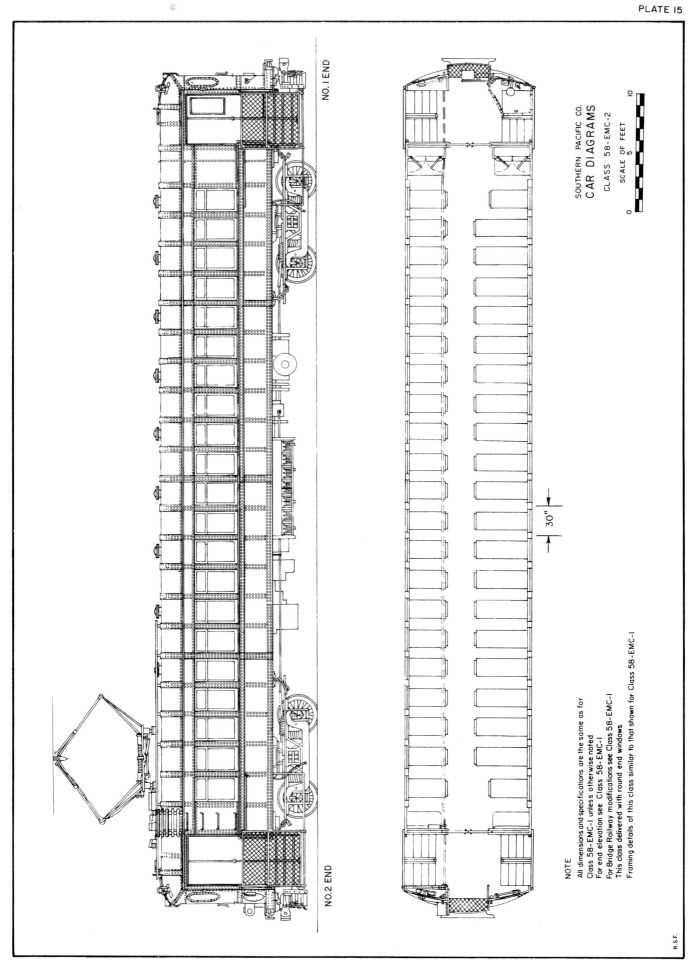

CLASS 58-EMC-4: Brand-new 378 has just emerged from the West Alameda Shops. Car was built as non-control trailer 435 (Class 58-ETC-1), rebuilt as a motor in 1938. Main differences from 58-EMC-1 class were cast-steel trucks and Type PC controls. Below, a five-car train of the new 58-EMC-4 class stops at Blanding Junction on a 1938 test run.

Both R.S. Ford Collection

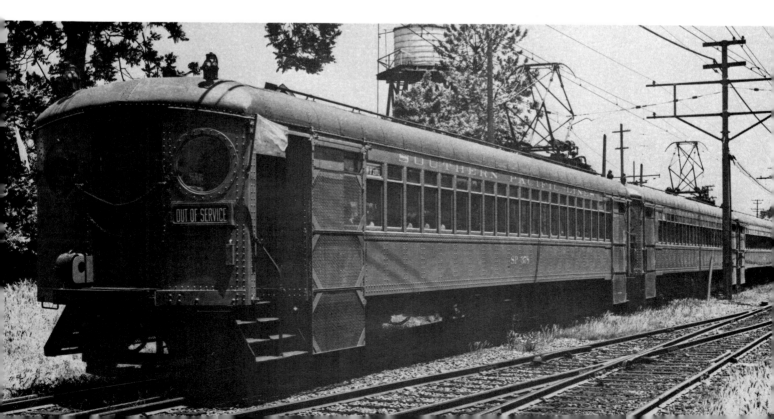

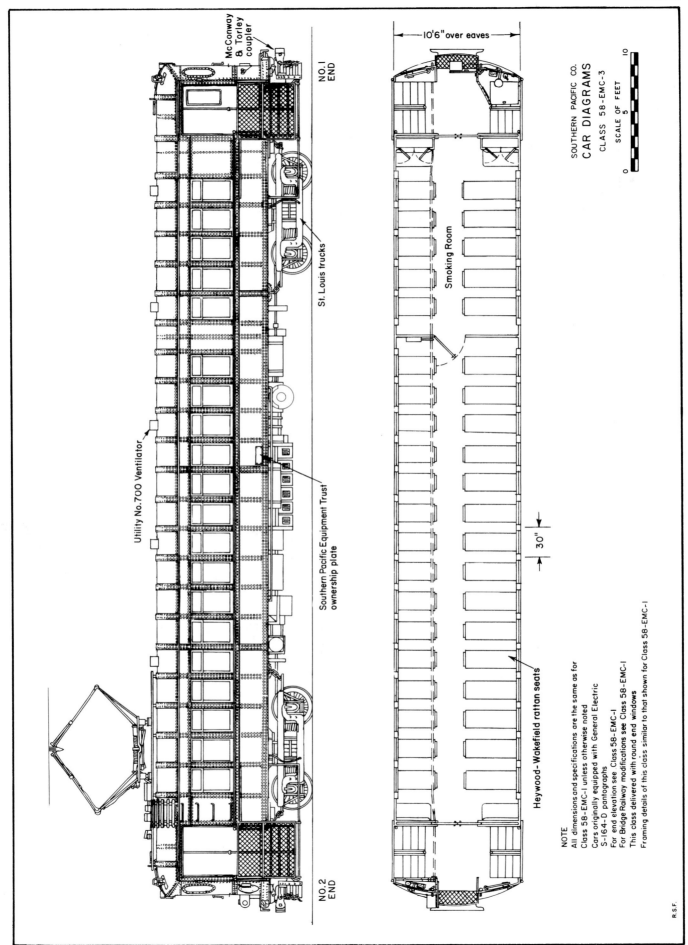

CLASS 58-ETC-1: Car 420 (above) in a builder's photo was one of 45 original non-control trailers on the O.A. & B lines; none of them was equipped with pilots, marker lights or route signs. Only one car of this class (404) was rebuilt with porthole end windows. Car 427 (below) is at Alameda Pier.

Leo Mitchell Collection; R.S. Ford Collection

CLASS 58-ECTC-1: Except for lack of pantograph and motor equipment, the contol trailers (called "mulies" by trainmen) were like cars of Class 58-EMC-1. Car 455 is shown after a wreck during squared-off end window days.
Vernon J. Sappers Collection

INTERIORS of trailers were identical to those of Class 58-EMC-1; this view shows interior of trailer 400 on 1911 trial run. Three-and-two seating was the norm.
Vernon J. Sappers Collection

CONVERTED from class 58-ETC-1 to 58-ECTC-1, car 442 was one of a group (438-446) getting controls in 1915 and 1916.
Charles D. Savage

CLASS 58-EMCB-1: Car 617 (left), shown in 1911 builder's photo, was rebuilt in 1938 to coach 370. Mechanically, cars of class 58-EMCB-1 were identical to those of class 58-EMC-1. Car 608 (below) lays over at Oakland Pier in early years; this car also was rebuilt in 1938 to coach 353. **Both Leo Mitchell Collection**

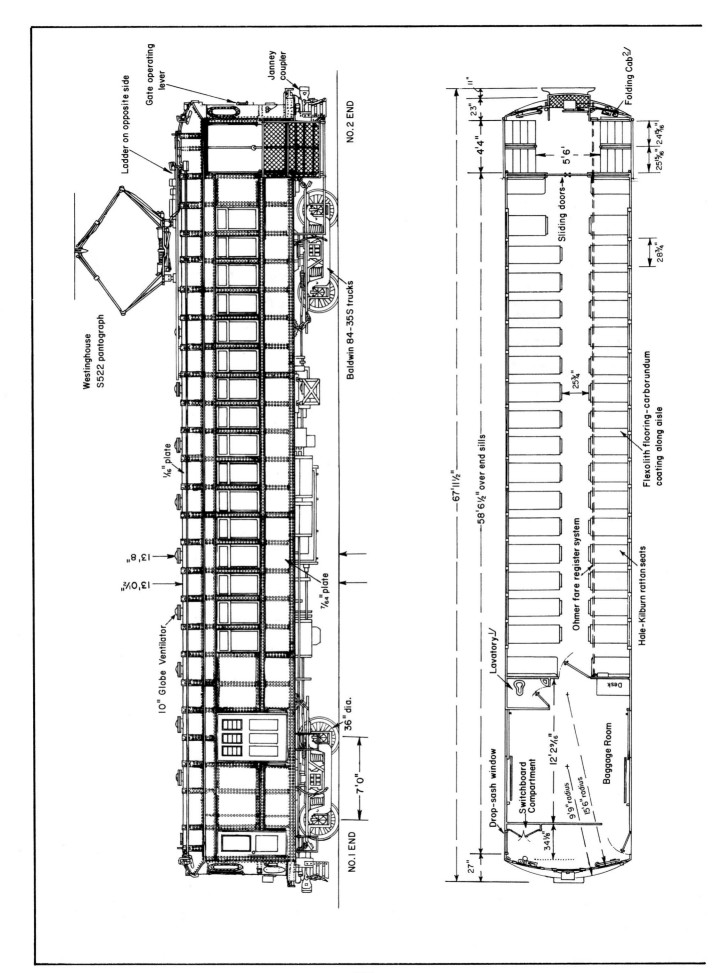

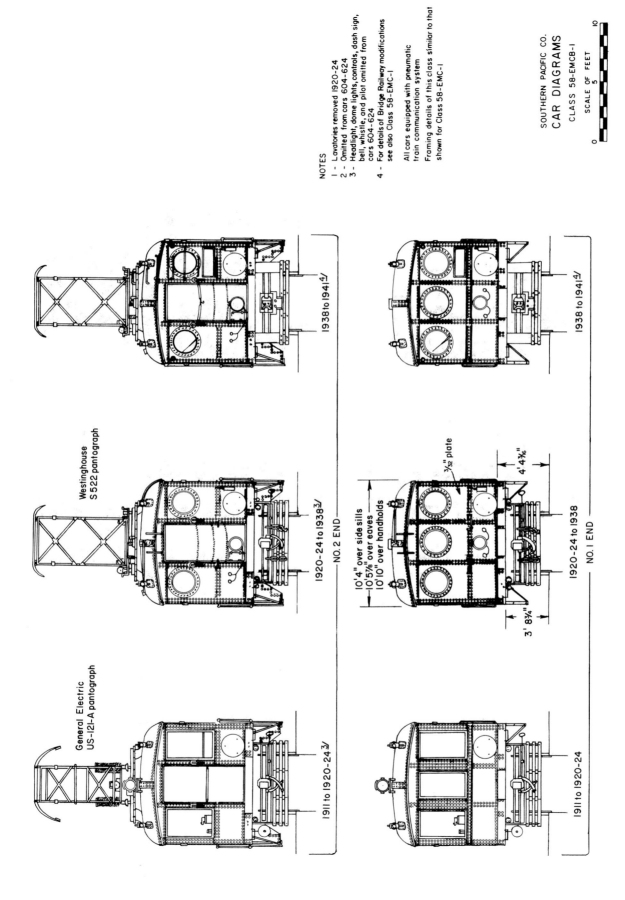

CLASS 58-EMCB-2: New cherry-red paint job on combo 628 (below) fairly glistens as car awaits assignment at Oakland Pier; trailer 400 is at right. Interior view (left) looks toward baggage section of car 625. **Collection of Vernon J. Sappers; Collection of R.S. Ford**

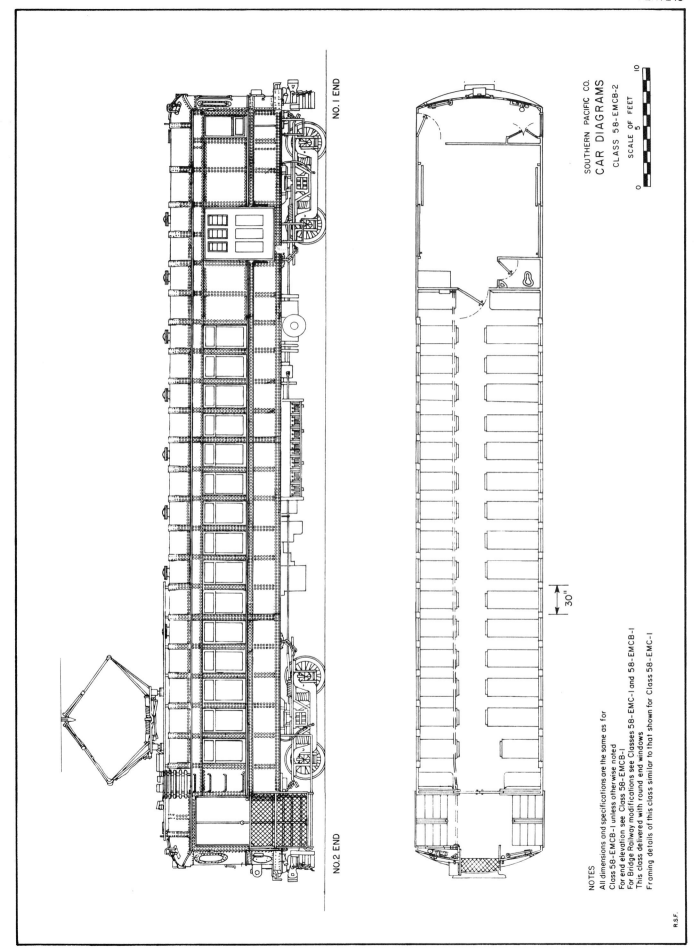

CLASS 58-EMB-1: S.P. baggage motors were a common sight at Oakland Pier and on the Berkeley line; car 701 (right) has a roller pantograph. **Leo Mitchell Collection**

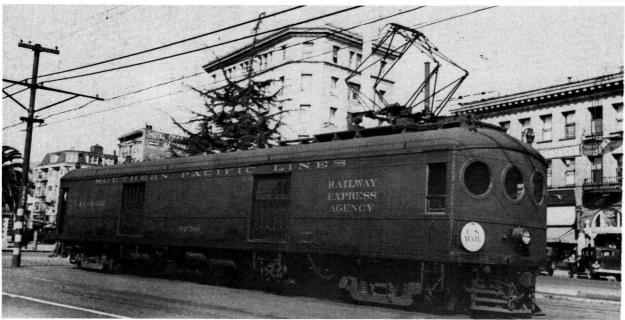

BAGGAGE MOTOR 700 carried U.S. mail, baggage and Railway Express Agency parcels out to Berkeley and back; she is seen here in downtown Berkeley (above). Interior of the baggage motor (left) was spacious. **Charles D. Savage; Vernon J. Sappers Collection**

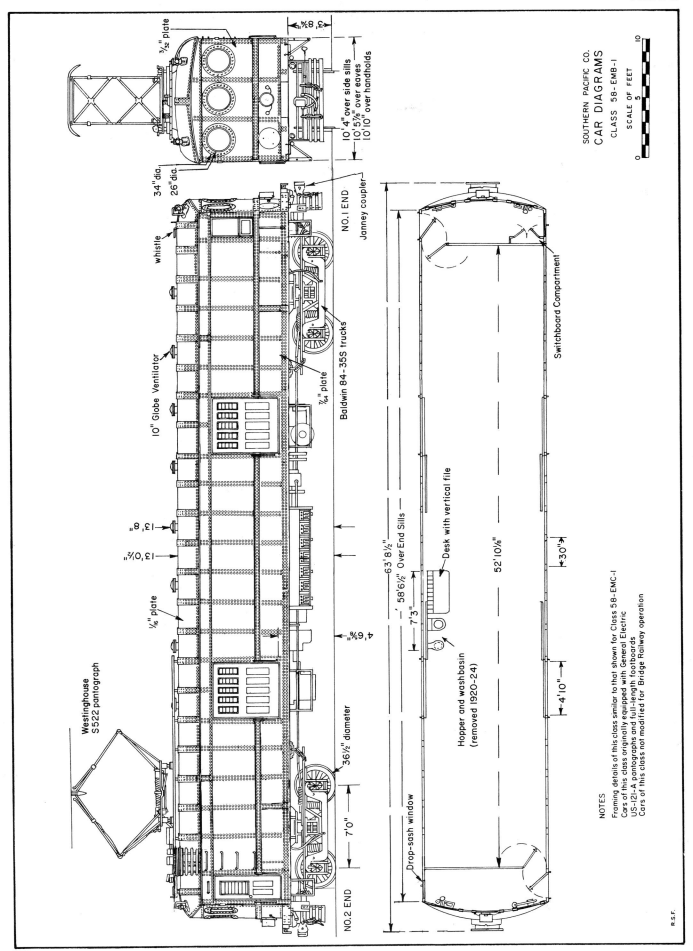

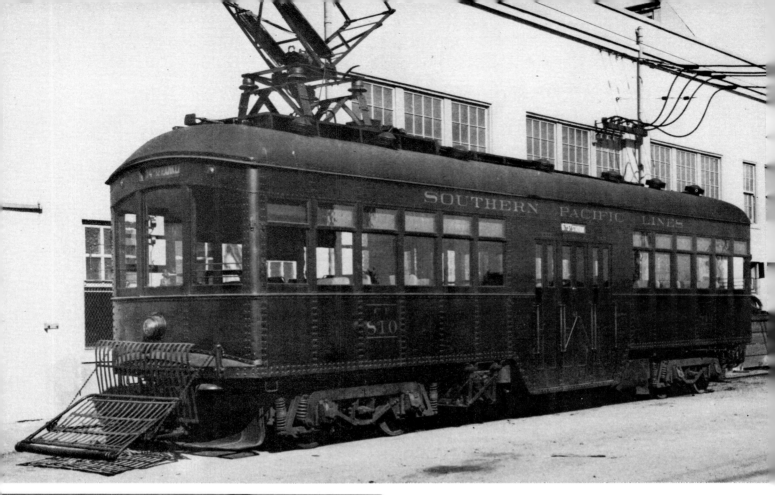

CLASS 45-ES-1: S.P. "dinkies" shuttled for years between Oakland and Alameda, but were the first victims of buses and autos. Car 810 (above) was one of two widely traveled cars in series. In 1913 car was sent to Los Angeles to become Pacific Electric 170; it was returned in 1919. Interior (left) of car 801 was photographed before lights and electrical equipment had been installed. **Southern Pacific; Vernon J. Sappers Collection**

CLASS ES-36½: Locomotive 200 was sole member of this class, and didn't last long.
Vernon J. Sappers Collection

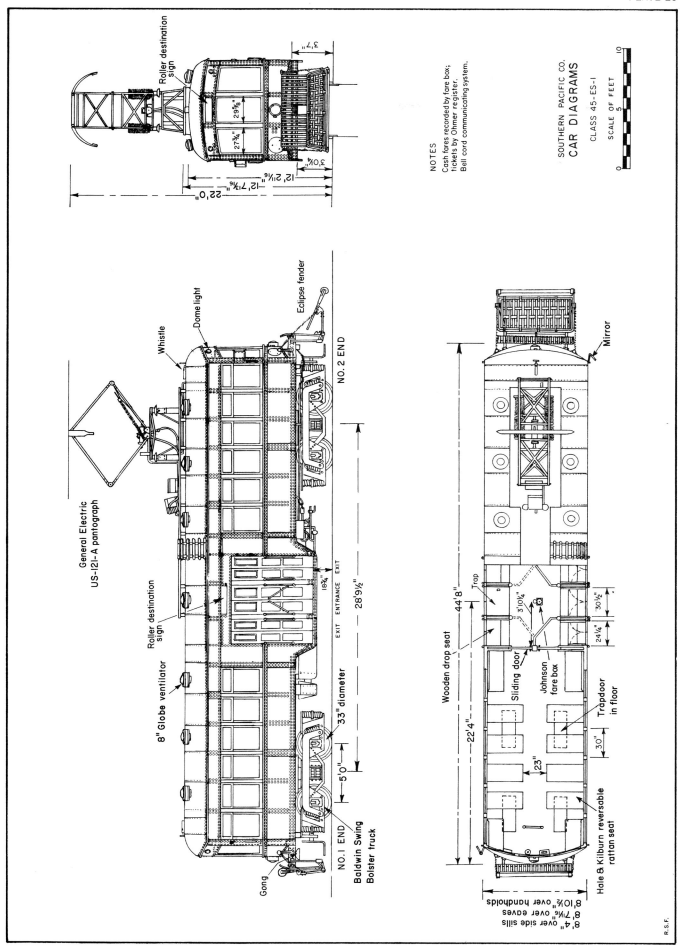

TABLE 12 -- *General Specifications*

Car numbers[2]		Class	Builder	Year	Seating capacity	Weight (pounds)	Brake system	Brake cylinders		Journals	Motors[3]
Original	Rebuilt							No.	Size		
200		ES-36½	Baldwin-Westinghouse	1912	...	124,200	14-EL [6]	1	16x12	5½x10	WH 308D3
300-302		58-EMC-1	American Car & Foundry	1911	116	123,380	AML [6]	1	"	5x9	GE 207A
303-310		"	" " " "	"	"	"	"	1	"	"	"
311-312		"	" " " "	"	"	"	"	1	"	"	"
313-318		"	" " " "	"	"	"	"	1	"	"	"
319-330		"	" " " "	"	"	"	"	1	"	"	"
331-335		"	" " " "	"	"	"	"	1	"	"	"
336		"	" " " "	"	"	"	"	1	"	"	"
337-339		"	" " " "	"	"	122,620	"	1	"	"	"
340-346		58-EMC-2	Pullman-Standard	1912	111	125,660	"	1	"	"	"
347-349		"	" "	"	"	"	"	1	"	"	"
	350	58-EMC-1	American Car & Foundry	1911	116	122,620	"	1	"	"	"
	351	"	" " " "	"	"	"	"	1	"	"	"
	352	"	" " " "	"	"	"	"	1	"	"	"
	353-361	"	" " " "	"	"	"	"	1	16x12 [5]	"	"
362-367		58-EMC-3	St. Louis Car Co.	1924	108	125,160	AMU [6]	2	12x12 [5]	"	"
	368	58-EMC-1	American Car & Foundry	1911	116	123,380	AML [6]	1	16x12 [5]	"	"
	369	"	" " " "	"	"	"	"	1	16x12	"	"
	370-377	"	" " " "	"	"	"	"	1	"	"	"
	378-380	58-EMC-4	" " " "	"	"	122,820	"	2	12x12	"	"
	381	"	" " " "	"	"	"	"	2	"	"	"
	382	"	" " " "	"	"	"	"	2	"	"	"
	383-385	"	" " " "	"	"	"	"	2	"	"	"
	386	"	" " " "	"	"	"	"	2	"	"	"
	387	"	" " " "	"	"	"	"	2	"	"	"
400-406		58-ETC-1	" " " "	"	"	70,860	ATL [7]	1	"	4¼x8	None
407		"	" " " "	"	"	"	"	1	"	"	"
408-414		"	" " " "	"	"	"	"	1	"	"	"
415		"	" " " "	"	"	"	"	1	"	"	"
416		"	" " " "	"	"	"	"	1	"	"	"
417		"	" " " "	"	"	"	"	1	"	"	"
418-419		"	" " " "	"	"	"	"	1	"	"	"
420		"	" " " "	"	"	"	"	1	"	"	"
421-424		"	" " " "	"	"	"	"	1	"	"	"
425-426		"	" " " "	"	"	"	"	1	"	"	"
427-434		"	" " " "	"	"	"	"	1	"	"	"
435-437		"	" " " "	"	"	"	"	1	"	"	"
438-439		58-ECTC-1	" " " "	"	"	79,800	AML [6]	1	"	"	"
440-444		"	" " " "	"	"	"	"	1	"	"	"
445		58-ETC-1	" " " "	"	"	70,860	ATL [7] [6]	1	"	"	"
446-455		58-ECTC-1	" " " "	"	"	79,800	AML [6]	1	"	"	"
456-458		"	" " " "	"	"	"	"	1	"	"	"
459		"	" " " "	"	"	"	"	1	"	"	"
	460	"	" " " "	"	"	"	"	1	"	"	"
	461	"	" " " "	"	"	"	"	1	"	"	"
600-603		58-EMCB-1	" " " "	"	88	119,640	"	1	16x12	5x9	GE 207A
604-605		"	" " " "	"	"	"	"	1	"	"	"
606		"	" " " "	"	"	"	"	1	"	"	"
607		"	" " " "	"	"	"	"	1	"	"	"
608-616		"	" " " "	"	"	"	"	1	"	"	"
617-624		"	" " " "	"	"	"	"	1	"	"	"
625-628		58-EMCB-2	Pullman-Standard	1912	83	122,220	"	1	"	"	"
700-701		58-EMB-1	" "	"	..	106,080	"	1	"	"	"
800-819		45-ES-1	" "	"	54	61,780	AMM	1	12x12	4¼x8	WH 327C

1/ For dimensions, see Car Diagrams.
2/ Cars listed under rebuilt number are also listed under original number.
3/ All motorized equipment have four motors
4/ Ownership: C.P. : Central Pacific; S.P. : Southern Pacific
    S.P.C. : South Pacific Coast
    T.B.A. : California Toll Bridge Authority

of Electric Railway Equipment[1]

Total Horse-power	Gear ratio	Controls	Partitioned	Owner[4]		Rebuilt		Remarks
				Original	Bridge Ry.	From	To	
1,000	16:57	WH Type HL	....	C.P.	...			
500	17:64	GE Type M	Yes	S.P.C.	T.B.A.			
"	"	"	"	"	"			Received two 12x12 cylinders, 1939
"	"	"	"	C.P.	S.P.			
"	"	"	"	S.P.	"			
"	"	"	No	"	"			
"	"	"	"	"	...		460	Rebuilt 1922
"	"	"	"	"	S.P.			
"	"	"	"	"	"			
"	"	"	"	C.P.	"			
"	"	"	"	S.P.	"	459		
"	"	"	"	C.P.	"	439		
"	"	"	Yes	S.P.C.	T.B.A.	606		
"	"	"	"	"	"	608-616		
"	"	GE Type PC101	"	"	"			
"	"	GE Type M	"	"	S.P.	604		
"	"	"	"	"	"	605		
"	"	"	"	C.P.	"	617-624		
"	"	GE Type PC103	No	"	"	435-437		
"	"	"	"	S.P.	"	445		
"	"	"	"	C.P.	"	438		
"	"	"	"	S.P.	"	456-458		
"	"	"	"	"	"	460		
"	"	"	"	S.P.C.	T.B.A.	461		
...	.....	None	"	"	"			
...	.....	"	"	"	"			Wrecked
...	.....	"	"	"	"			
...	.....	"	"	"	"			To T.B.A., replacement for 407
...	.....	"	"	"	S.P.			
...	.....	"	"	"	T.B.A.			
...	.....	"	"	"	S.P.			
...	.....	"	"	"	T.B.A.			
...	.....	"	"	"	S.P.			
...	.....	"	"	C.P.	"			
...	.....	"	"	"	...		378-380	Rebuilt 1938
...	.....	GE Type M	"	"	...		382,351	" "
...	.....	"	"	S.P.	S.P.			
...	.....	None	"	"	...		381	Rebuilt 1938
...	.....	GE Type M	"	"	S.P.			
...	.....	"	"	"	...		383-385	Rebuilt 1938
...	.....	"	"	"	...		350	" "
...	.....	"	"	"	...	336	386	Rebuilt 1922, 1938
...	.....	"	"	S.P.C.	...	607	387	" " "
500	17:64	"	Yes	"	S.P.			
"	"	"	"	"	...		368,369	Rebuilt 1938
"	"	"	"	"	...		352	" "
"	"	"	"	"	...		461	Rebuilt 1922
"	"	"	"	"	...		353-361	Rebuilt 1938
"	"	"	"	C.P.	...		370-377	" "
"	"	"	"	S.P.C.	S.P.			
"	"	GE Type HL	"	C.P.	...			

5/ Equipped with Brake Lever Stops
6/ Equipped with Westinghouse L3G brake valve
7/ Equipped with Westinghouse L2G brake valve

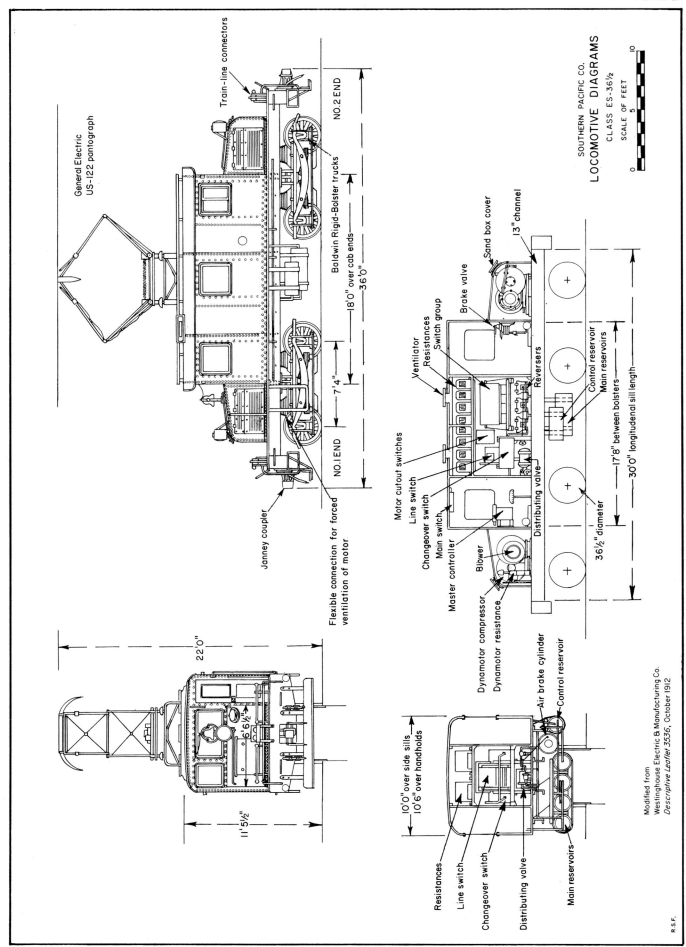

Final Disposition of Equipment

Locomotive CP 200

In 1912, Southern Pacific placed an order with Baldwin Locomotive Works for 15 62-ton Class D steeple-cab electric locomotives. Outshopped as a typical Baldwin-Westinghouse product, 10 of the 750-volt/1500-volt freight motors went to the Pacific Electric Railway, where they became PE 1601 to PE 1610. Three locomotives went to the Southern Pacific "Red Electric" system in Oregon, where they were numbered 100 to 102. Another locomotive went to the Peninsular Railway, in San Jose, where it became No. 4.

The final locomotive of this order was delivered to the O.A. & B. Lines, where it was numbered CP 200. The locomotive was used at West Alameda for only a short while because railroad brotherhood contracts then in effect precluded its use in switching service. The locomotive was leased to the Pacific Electric on October 15, 1914, and renumbered PE 1611; Pacific Electric purchased the locomotive on August 1, 1915. Of the locomotives of this order which were operated by Pacific Electric, the former CP 200 was the last to be scrapped; it was cut up at National Metals Company in January 1956.

Streetcars

Of the 160 pieces of passenger equipment assigned to the Oakland, Alameda and Berkeley Lines, streetcars CP 810 to CP 819 were the first to leave the property. The cars were transferred to the Pacific Electric Railway on March 1, 1913, for local service in Southern California.

TABLE 13 -- *Final Disposition Of Street Cars*

Original number	Subsequent number	Disposition
CP 800	EBSR 601	Scrapped 1933
CP 801	EBSR 602	" "
CP 802	EBSR 603	" "
CP 803	EBSR 604	" "
CP 804	1/	" "
CP 805	1/	" "
CP 806	1/	" "
CP 807	1/	" "
CP 808	1/	" "
CP 809	1/	" "
CP 810	PE 170, CP 810, 1/	" "
CP 811 I	PE 176	Body sold 1934
CP 812	PE 172	" " "
CP 813	PE 173	" " "
CP 814	PE 174	" " "
CP 815	PE 175	" " "
CP 816	PE 171, CP 811 II, 1/	Scrapped 1933
CP 817	PE 177	Body sold 1934
CP 818	PE 178	" " "
CP 819	PE 179	" " " 2/

1/ Sold to East Bay Street Railways, Ltd. but not used.
2/ Body acquired by Orange Empire Trolley Museum 1974

Initially used in Pasadena, the cars also saw service in San Bernardino, Long Beach, and other communities. In 1919, Pacific Electric cars 170 and 171 were returned to Oakland, where they were renumbered CP 810 and CP 811, respectively.

When the O.A. & B. streetcar service was abandoned on March 20, 1926, all 12 remaining streetcars were purchased by the Key System-owned East Bay Street Railways, Ltd., for use on the 32-Adeline Street and 33-Sacramento Street local lines. Cars CP 800 to CP 803 were rebuilt by E.B.S.R.; the other cars were placed in storage. Rebuilding consisted of modifying the cars to operate on 600 volts, replacing center folding doors with sliding doors, installing steel pilots, replacing the US-121-A pantographs with Westinghouse S-529 slider-type pantographs, repainting the cars in the green and cream livery of the street railway company, and renumbering them 601 to 604. When E.B.S.R. abandoned its Adeline Street and Sacramento Street local lines on February 28, 1932, these four cars were withdrawn from service. All former Southern Pacific streetcars were scrapped in 1933.

The cars that went to Pacific Electric lasted only a short while longer. Five had been retired by 1928 and the remaining three, which had been used in Long Beach, were retired in 1934. After being retired, Pacific Electric sold the bodies of the cars for use as summer homes, four of which are known to be still in existence as of this writing. One of these latter, PE 179 (CP 819) has been acquired by Orange Empire Railway Museum at Perris.

Suburban Cars Owned by California Toll Bridge Authority

In 1936, Southern Pacific transferred ownership of 30 motors and 22 trailers to the California Toll Bridge Authority in return for funds for its share of the Bridge Railway. On abandonment of service, the Toll Bridge Authority-owned cars were taken from the Bridge Yard and placed in storage on the unused trestle leading to the out-of-service Key System ferry terminal. Most of these cars were sold to the Houston Shop Corporation for redelivery to other users. Before redelivery, all motorized cars had their electrical equipment removed, and cars were sent to their ultimate destination on their own wheels.

One group of 10 cars went to the Aberdeen Proving Grounds of the U.S. Army Ordnance Corps. Renumbered USA 8000 to 8002, 8004, 8007 to 8009, and 8065 to 8067, the cars were placed in service to provide transportation between the Proving Grounds and Aberdeen, Md. The cars usually were towed by gas-electric motor PM-75. In 1954, the cars were declared surplus and were sold for scrap.

Another group of seven cars went to the Ogden Army Depot. The demotorized coaches were renumbered USA 102 to 105 and the demotorized combination baggage-coach was renumbered USA 8036. Two trailers also were a part of this group; they kept their old numbers (O.A. & B. 409 and 414) and were never used. The cars were placed in service for transportation of depot employees to and from Salt Lake City. An Army diesel would take a train to the interchange with the Bamberger Railroad, and an electric car or locomotive would take the train from that point. The former O.A. & B. cars never proved very popular as they lacked insulation to protect riders from the cold Utah winters. In 1947, the cars were declared surplus and taken to Pueblo, Colorado, for scrapping.

Another group of 20 cars went to the Red River Army Depot at Texarkana, Texas. The cars were used to transport workers between the parking area and the ammunition storage areas, some several miles distant. The train was hauled by a diesel switcher and began operation in 1943. During the height of operations, the train carried a daily total of 5,600 passengers and was operated around-the-clock to accommodate the three shifts. The last day of operation was December 31, 1954, after which the cars were sold for scrap.

A group of 10 former motor cars were purchased by the Gulf Shipbuilding Corporation for use on a shipyard train between Mobile and Chickasaw, Alabama. The cars were lettered THE GULF ARROW, and were numbered 1 to 10. In service, the cars were pulled by a steam locomotive. Service was terminated in 1945, after which the cars were sold. One was used as a kitchen car on a Frisco wrecking train; the car, SL-SF 102292, was scrapped in 1970. It has been reported that some of the cars also were barged to Cuba in 1946.

Six trailers were sold to the Santa Fe Railway for use with other former O.A. & B. cars at that time owned by the U.S. Maritime Commission. The cars were repainted green and were lettered A.T.S.F. Five of the former non-control trailers were renumbered into the 435-439 series. Car 437 was wrecked in 1945 and was not returned to service. At the conclusion of the service in 1947, all remaining cars were sold for scrap.

CAR USA 8004 at Aberdeen (Md.) Proving Grounds, March 1954, shortly before scrapping. This was reportedly once O.A. & B. 304. **Robert Townley**

Of the 52 cars owned by the Toll Bridge Authority, only three did not see further use after the system was abandoned. These three, O.A. & B. 355, 363, and one other from Class 58-EMC-3, were sold to Hyman-Michaels Company of South San Francisco. The cars were scrapped at that company's yard in 1941.

Suburban Cars Owned by Southern Pacific Company

After the abandonment of Interurban Electric service, Southern Pacific stored its 94 cars near the West Oakland roundhouse on the formerly electrified mainline tracks leading to Oakland Pier. These cars later were moved to Halvern, a long spur near Decoto. All but eight of the cars later were requisitioned by the United States Maritime Commission for use on shipyard trains in Los Angeles and Portland and also for the transportation of military personnel between San Diego and Los Angeles.

One group of 15 trailers was sent north to Portland for shipyard train service. After being relettered *UNITED STATES MARITIME COMMISSION,* the still-red cars, bearing their O.A. & B. numbers entered service between downtown Portland and the shipyards at Vancouver, Washington. Among those used for this service were cars 417, 420, 425, 427, 430, 440, 444, 447, 449, 450, 451, 454, and 455. The service was operated by the Spokane, Portland & Seattle Railway and ran from a terminal on the west side of the Willamette River just south of Steel Bridge. Shipyard trains bypassed the Portland Union Station and then used the S.P. & S. Astoria Line as far as Willbridge Junction. At this point, the shipyard trains turned north on the main line to Seattle as far as the Vancouver, Washington, station where they swung east on a viaduct to the shipyard. One intermediate stop was made at East St. Johns. After the war, the service was terminated, and most of the cars were cut up for scrap. The body of one car, painted yellow, served as a flower stand near Linneman Junction for a number of years. Another car body was taken to eastern Oregon, near Hermiston, where it sat derelict for some time.

A group of 18 trailers was sent to San Diego to work with ex-O.A. & B. cars owned by Santa Fe in the transportation of military personnel between San Diego and Los Angeles. The total of 24 cars was divided into two cuts of nine cars and one of six cars. Cars within a cut were permanently coupled and the end car on each cut was equipped with A.A.R. couplers. One end car on each cut also was outfitted with a lavatory. Trains of either 15, 18, or 24 cars were common. The trains usually were pulled by a 3700-class 4-8-2 locomotive; either a standard baggage car or combination baggage-coach was placed between the engine's tender and the first car to act as a buffer. Among the cars assigned to this service were the 429, 441, and 448. The service was operated until 1947, after which time both the USMC and Santa Fe owned cars were sold for scrap. The three cuts of cars were taken to Pueblo, Colorado, for scrapping.

Cars 433 and 434, owned by the Maritime Commission, were sent to Los Angeles. The cars were never used on the Pacific Electric, and they were stored at the Torrance shops until 1944. No. 433 eventually went to Fort McClellan, Alabama, where it became USA 255; No. 434 reportedly went to the Bremerton (Washington) Navy Yard the following year.

The bodies of control trailers 446 and 452 were retained by Southern Pacific and used as temporary offices at the 5th & Kirkham Streets Freight Yard. After the war, the two car bodies were sold to an Oakland yacht harbor where one was used as a restaurant and the other as a marine storage supply room; both car bodies were sold for scrap in the early part of 1969.

TABLE 14 -- *Equipment Histories : O. A. & B. Lines-Pacific Electric-Los Angeles Metropolitan Transit Authority*

Oakland Alameda & Berkeley Lines	U.S. Maritime Commission	Pacific Electric Railway (1944)	Pacific Electric Railway (1947)	Los Angeles Metropolitan Transit Authority	Year Scrapped
313	400	4660	...	....	1947
314	314	4600	414	....	1957
315	315	4601 I	...	....	1/
316	401	401	...	....	1947
317	317	4602	424	1531	1961
318	318	4603	406	....	1957
319	319	4604	417	1527	1959
320	402	402	...	....	1947
321	403	4601 II	407	1519	1961
322	322	4630	455	1705	1961
323	323	4631	451	1701	1961
324	404	404	...	....	1947
325	405	4662	...	....	1947
326	406	4661	...	....	1947
327	327	4632	430	....	1953
328	328	4633	452	1702	1961
329	329	4634	453	1703	1961
330	330	4635	432	1540	1961
331	331	4636	434	1542	1961
332	332	4637	457	1707	2/
333	333	4605	423	1532	1958
334	334	4638	404	....	1958
335	335	4606	419	1529	1961
337	337	4607	425	1534	1958
338	338	4608	401	....	1954
339	339	4609	426	1535	1961
340	340	4610	410	1521	1959
341	341	4611	412	1523	1961
342	342	4612	415	1525	1961
343	343	4613	416	1526	1959
344	344	4614	418	1528	3/
345	345	4615	409	1520	1961
346	346	4616	427	1536	1961
347	347	4617	413	1524	1961
348	348	4618	403	1516	1961
349	349	4619	402	1515	1961
350	350	4620	421	....	1953
351	351	4621	422	....	1958
368	368	4622	400	....	1953
369	369	4623	408	....	1955
370	370	4624	420	1530	1961
371	371	4625	411	1522	1961
372	372	4626	456	1706	1961
373	373	4627	459	1708	1961
374	374	4628	436	1544	1961
375	375	4629	428	1537	1961
378	378	4639	437	1545	1961
379	379	4640	435	1543	4/
380	380	4641	433	1541	1961
381	381	4642	454	....	1959
382	382	4643	429	1538	1961
383	383	4644	458	....	1953
384	384	4645	431	1539	1959
385	385	4646	450	1700	1961
386	386	4647	405	1518	1961
625	25 300	4700	496,499 II 5/	1547	1961
626	26 301	4701	497	....	1953
627	27 302	4702	498	1546	3/
628	28 303	4703, 4599 6/	499 I	....	1954 7/
700	...	1465 8/	...	....	1953
701	...	1466 8/	...	....	1954 9/

1/ Wrecked, October 1946
2/ At California Railway Museum
3/ At Orange Empire Trolley Museum
4/ At Travel Town, Griffith Park, Los Angeles
5/ Renumbered early 1958
6/ Renumbered early 1947
7/ Cannibalized 1954, scrapped 1958
8/ 1941 number
9/ Body to Bakersfield Shops, 1954

BEHIND STEAM, four-car "Gulf Arrow" awaits another run to shipyard at Chickasaw, Alabama, in 1942 on the Gulf, Mobile & Ohio Railroad at Beauregard Street Station, Mobile.
Marvin Maynard Collection

FORMER O.A. & B. TRAILERS were used by Maritime Commission in Portland, Ore., shipyard service. Trailer 425 and mates is at the Guild Lake Yards of the S.P. & S. Railroad.
B.H. Ward

Combination baggage-coaches 600 to 603 were sold to the Houston Shop Corporation and were added to the group of Toll Bridge Authority-owned cars that went to the U.S. Army Ordinance Corps.

The two baggage motors, Nos. 700 and 701, were taken to the PE shops at Torrance; they were converted to 600-volt operation, had their baggage doors enlarged, were equipped with footboards in place of pilots, had pneumatic-based trolley poles installed in place of pantographs, and were numbered PE 1465 and 1466. Called box motors on the P.E., these two cars were used throughout the vast Pacific Electric system until retired in 1953. The body of PE 1465 (SP 700) was taken to Bakersfield for use as a store room at the Southern Pacific shop; the PE 1466 (SP 701) was cut up for scrap.

The group of cars acquired by the Maritime Commission for shipyard service in Los Angeles included cars 315-335, 337-351, 368-375, 378-386, and 625-628. After being delivered to the Pacific Electric shops, they were modified to 600-volt operation and were equipped with spring-base trolley poles. The cars entered service between Los Angeles and the Cal-Ship yards on March 19, 1943. Other than being lettered *UNITED STATES MARITIME COMMISSION,* they appeared little changed from the days when they operated across the Bay Bridge. All but seven of the cars kept their original numbers. These seven, the 313, 316, 320, 321, 324, 325, and 326, were demotorized and were renumbered 400 to 406, respectively. The electrical equipment from these cars was used to motorize seven former Northwestern Pacific trailers of similar design.

In April 1944, Pacific Electric acquired 30 of the ex-I.E. cars for $167,580; these cars subsequently became PE 4600-4629. After the war, the remaining 18 coaches were purchased; they became PE 4630-4647. At the same time, the four combination passenger-baggage cars were purchased. On the Southern Pacific, these cars had been numbered 625-628, but after being purchased by the Maritime Commission, they were renumbered 25-28 so as not to confuse them with the Pacific Electric 600-class suburban cars. In April 1944, these cars were renumbered to USMC 300-303. When acquired by Pacific Electric, they became PE 4700-4703. Combo 4703 was given U-5-A brake valve equipment in the early part of 1947 to enable it to work in train service with the former Northwestern Pacific cars, PE 4500-4518. At that time, this car was renumbered PE 4599.

In 1945, the seven ex-motors, USMC 400-406, were assigned to the Union Pacific Railroad for use in troop trains in the Los Angeles area. In 1947, Pacific Electric bought these cars for parts. Trailers 400, 405, and 406 subsequently were renumbered PE 4660, 4662, and 4661, respectively. Trailer 403 (O.A. & B. 320) was re-motorized and numbered 4601 to replace the first car of that number (O.A. & B. 315) which had been wrecked in a collision with a freight train in October 1946. The three trailers 4660-4662 were used on race track specials to and from Santa Anita in 1947 and were retired shortly thereafter. The three cars, along with unused USMC trailers 401, 402, and 404 (O.A. & B. 316, 320, and 324) were scrapped at Torrance in 1947.

That same year, Pacific Electric began a modernization program for its former Southern Pacific and Northwestern Pacific cars. At a cost of more than $7,500 per car, each unit received enclosed platforms with doors and traps replacing open platforms with sliding gates, additional windows on each side where gates formerly hung, new green plush

STRUNG OUT behind Santa Fe locomotive 3750, ex-O.A. & B. cars bring a load of Navy and Marine personnel back to San Diego from Los Angeles.
R.P. Middlebrook

WHOLE NEW LEGEND was written about the former O.A. & B. cars on the Pacific Electric, where the huge cars were affectionately dubbed "Blimps". Lead car of this San Pedro train was once Pullman-built O.A. & B. 348, class 58-EMC-2. **R.S. Ford**

tubular-frame seats replacing rattan walkover seats, aluminum ceiling lining, bull's-eye interior lights, and new flooring. Interiors of cars were painted a two-toned green with an ivory ceiling; exteriors received a coat of bright red paint with orange trim and letterboard.

All cars again were renumbered, with cars having replacement Westinghouse U-5-A brake equipment being numbered 400-447, and those with the original L-3-G equipment being numbered 450-459. The combination cars were renumbered 496-499. After the rebuilding, cars 400-447 could operate in train service with the former Northwestern Pacific cars, now numbered 300-317, as well with the combos, numbers 496-499. Cars 450 to 459 formed their own small class and could not be operated in multiple unit with any other car type. With the emergence of these 80 cars from the Torrance Shops, all former standard Pacific Electric cars were displaced from the heavily traveled Southern District lines. In time, these cars, affectionately called "blimps" due to their large size, became the standard for traction in the Los Angeles area.

In 1953, Pacific Electric sold its passenger system to Metropolitan Coach Lines. The new operator continued the operation of the "blimps" with little change other than placing a new emblem on the sides of the cars. On March 3, 1958, the Los Angeles Metropolitan Transit Authority took over all operations of the Metropolitan Coach Lines. The "blimps" soon were renumbered again. The remaining cars of the 400-447 class were numbered 1515-1545; those of the 450-459 class were renumbered 1731-1739. The two remaining passenger-baggage cars were renumbered 1546 and 1547. With the renumbering, car No. 1543 (O.A. & B. 379) was painted in the new LAMTA colors, light and dark green with a white roof.

Early in 1961, it was announced that Los Angeles Metropolitan Transit Authority would abandon all remaining interurban rail service between Los Angeles and Long Beach. Early on the morning of Sunday, April 9, 1961, the final runs to Long Beach were made. The last revenue train left the Sixth and Main Streets station in downtown Los Angeles at 3:44 a.m. and consisted of cars Nos. 1525 (O.A. & B. 342) and 1522 (O.A. & B. 371). This train was followed at 3:49 by a second section consisting of Nos. 1543 (O.A. & B. 379) and 1524 (O.A. & B. 347). Following these two trains was a two-car special chartered by the Electric Railway Historical Society of Southern California. The special

EXCEPT FOR trolley pole in place of pantograph, U.S. Maritime Commission 329 is little changed from O.A. & B. days. Shipyard train has stopped at Watts on the P.E. four-track trunk line.
Bay Area Electric Railroad Assn. Collection

ONE OF A KIND: The only "green blimp," LAMTA 1543, approaches Compton on a Bay Area Electric Railroad Assn. charter in 1961, shortly before abandonment. By this time, this 1911-vintage car had carried seven different identifications: SP 379, IER 379, USMC 379, PE 4640, PE 435, MCL 435 and finally LAMTA 1543. **Addison H. Laflin Jr.**

consisted of cars 1519 (O.A. & B. 321) and 1502 (formerly Northwestern Pacific No. 254). The special pulled into Morgan Yard, near Long Beach, at 4:53 a.m., bringing to a close multiple-unit electric traction in Southern California.

All but four of the "blimps" finally were scrapped by National Metals Company. The green blimp, No. 1543 (O.A. & B. 379), is now on display at Travel Town in Griffith Park, Los Angeles. Coach No. 1528 (O.A. & B. 344) and passenger-baggage No. 1546 (O.A. & B. 627) are preserved in operating condition at Orange Empire Railway Museum near Riverside. These two cars are operated on an irregular basis and are retained with their Pacific Electric modifications. The fourth car is at the California Railway Museum at Rio Vista Junction. This car is O.A. & B. 332, formerly L.A.M.T.A. No. 1707; when restored to its original appearance, it will be the sole survivor of the "Big Red Trains" of Southern Pacific and Interurban Electric.

Big Red Comes Home

During the apex of the development of electric railways in central California, there were no fewer than 14 separate companies operating 17 different systems, ranging from metropolitan street railways to small-town car lines, from side-of-the-road trolley lines to long-haul interurbans and heavy-duty commuter-oriented suburban systems. Each of these 17 systems had its own character, equipment, and operating peculiarities; there was little duplication from one system to another. One by one, the systems faded and ultimately were abandoned due to mounting competition from buses, bridges, and the private automobile. Today, the San Francisco Municipal Railway stands as the lone survivor of this one-time proliferation of electric traction.

In 1943, nine electric railway enthusiasts informally organized the Bay Area Railfans Association to share their common interests in electric traction and also to acquire a car from the former San Francisco and Napa Valley Railroad. Attracting other railfans, this group reorganized as the Bay Area Electric Railroad Association in December 1946, an organization dedicated to the preservation of the electric railway as an integral part of American transportation history.

This organization, in addition to holding meetings and excursions, began acquiring electric railway equipment representative of the different systems in California. As more and more systems were abandoned, more cars became available for preservation. In addition, other cars from long-abandoned lines were purchased from owners who had used them as chicken coops, sheds, and the like. By the late 1950s, it became clear to the group that a site must be found to store and to operate this valuable collection of equipment. The necessity of a site was emphasized by the loss through fire set by vandals of the Napa Valley coach acquired 16 years previously.

In 1960, a museum site was purchased at Rio Vista Junction, located on State Route 12, about halfway between Fairfield and Rio Vista. That this site should be the home of the California Railway Museum was more than appropriate. Years previously, Rio Vista Junction was a station on the main line of the Sacramento Northern Railway. Here, passengers destined to Rio Vista and Isleton transferred from electric trains to the motor bus of the Rio Vista Transit Company. In 1960, this former main line was still in service as the Montezuma Branch, and it would be possible to receive shipments of cars and materials by rail at the museum.

Upon acquisition of the site, the long task of constructing an operating railway museum began. To be developed by the members were 22 acres of grassland and a few buildings. With the diligent labor of members and the contributions from friends, the museum slowly took shape. Today, there is a four-track car barn, a one-half-mile loop of track, a shop building, bookstore, picnic grounds, and a myriad of other improvements marking an operating railway museum.

All during the time of construction of the museum, the collection of cars and equipment continued to grow. Ultimately there were more than 30 electric cars and locomotives on the property. Represented was equipment from such railways as Key System, Sacramento Northern, San Francisco Municipal Railway, and other Bay Area systems. More distant lines, such as Salt Lake and Utah Railroad and Indiana Railroad also were represented. However, it was long felt by the members that the collection never could be complete without the inclusion of a "Big Red Car" from the Southern Pacific-Interurban Electric system.

In the latter part of 1969, the body of former S.P. coach 332 was located at the Fellows Shipyard at Terminal Island, near Long Beach. Unfortunately, during its eight-year stay on Terminal Island, all of the underbody equipment had been removed from this car, although seats, controls, and the remainder of the car was intact. After donors had raised sufficient funds, the car was shipped to Rio Vista Junction, arriving there on May 21, 1970.

Restoration of the car to its condition when it was operated by Southern Pacific began with the removal of platform doors and other

THE STORY OF CAR 332: Working as lead car of a Seventh Street local in the days of operation to Oakland Pier, car 332 was as typical a red electric as one could find.

R.S. Ford Collection

items installed by the Pacific Electric in 1944. Ultimately, trucks, a pantograph, and other equipment will be secured and the car will be returned to operating condition. One day in the future, the pantograph will be raised, the air will be pumped up, and one of the museum members, acting as conductor, will give two pulls on the signal cord. The engineer, another museum member, then will release the brakes, notch up the controller, and ease Southern Pacific No. 332 through the switches and onto the main line of the California Railway Museum. When this happens, the SP's Big Red Trains will have achieved their proper place in the annals of California traction history.

HOMECOMING: Car 332 was still typical of the red electrics after restoration at California Railway Museum, Rio Vista Junction, Calif., in 1973. Yet to come: reinstallation of gates, pantograph, motor trucks, running gear and new window sashes. Big Red was home again.

R.S. Ford

APPENDIX B

Railway Operations

WHEREAS KEY SYSTEM was essentially a street railway, the Southern Pacific (and later Interurban Electric) was in every respect a *railroad* operation. Trains were dispatched and operated in a railroad-like manner, operating timetables were published, ticket agents manned stations, and uniformed trainmen wearing S.P., and later I.E.R., insignia ran the trains.

In a fashion similar to the heavy-duty commuter railroads on the East Coast, the Oakland, Alameda and Berkeley lines possessed a number of operating characteristics that proclaimed its railroad parentage. One of these was in the identification of routes through the use of variously colored metal disc signs and illuminated dome lights. By day, the routing of the suburban trains was identified by a 22-inch diameter colored metal disc sign mounted on the left front of each train. Streetcars boasted a 16-inch diameter colored disc sign mounted on the right front of each car. Streetcars and suburban cars (except non-control trailers) each had a pair of roof-mounted dome lights at each end. The dome lights contained changeable lenses which could display a red, yellow, green, or white aspect. Although not all combinations were used, 10 were available.

The colored disc and dome signals were used primarily for route identification by interlocking plant operators. By day, the operators identified the route of approaching trains and streetcars by their colored disc signs. At night, trains and streetcars were readily identified by a pair of colored lights on the roof.

Crew assignments on the red trains were based on runs. Runs for each line were placed in a pool and were posted on a rotating basis, and crews making a particular run changed to the next lower run number the following day. For example, in 1932, the Ellsworth Street line posted six runs, Numbers 117 to 122. The crew standing for Run 122 started at 4:38 p.m. and was released at 1:13 a.m. The next day, this same crew would be on Run 121 which started at 3:18 p.m. and ended at 12:33 a.m. Continuing to change to the next lower run number each day, this crew ended four days later on Run 117, which began at 5:30 a.m. and was released at 1:38 p.m. The following day, this crew again

TABLE 15 -- *Disc, Dome, And Whistle Signals*

STEAM LOCALS

Route	Whistle Signal
Berryman	— o —
West Berkeley (to 2/19/12)	o o —
" " (after 2/19/12)	— o —
Melrose	o o — o
Alameda Loop (Pier Suburban)	o — — o
" " (Swing Suburban)	— — — o
High Street	o — o —
14th Street	o o — —
Stonehurst	— — — o
Main line trains	o o

O.A. & B. LINES

Route	Disc and Dome Signal	Whistle Signal
Shattuck Avenue (to 2/27/24)	Red & red	— o —
" " (after 2/27/24)	" "	o — —
Shattuck Express	Yellow & yellow	o — —
Ellsworth Street	Red & yellow	o — — o o
California Street (to 2/27/24)	White & white	— — — o
" " (after 2/27/24)	" "	o — — o
Ninth Street	Red & white	o — o —
Berkeley Mail Train	Green & white	o o o — —
18th Street	Green & green	o o — —
7th Street	Green & green	o o — — o
Dutton Express	Yellow & yellow	— — o o o
Horseshoe (to 2/27/24)	Red & green	— o —
" " (after 2/27/24)	" "	— — — o
Lincoln Avenue	Green & white	o — o — o
Encinal Avenue	Red & white	o — — o —
Webster Street	Green & green 1/	o o —
Street cars (to 8/01/13)	Red & red 1/	o o — o o —
" " (after 8/01/13)	" " 1/	o o — — o o

INTERURBAN ELECTRIC

Route	Disc and Dome Signal	Whistle Signal
Shattuck Avenue	Red & red	o — —
Shattuck Express	Yellow & yellow	o — —
Ninth Street	Red & white	o — o —
Seventh Street	Green & green	o o — — o
Dutton Express	Yellow & yellow	o o — — o
Lincoln Avenue	Green & red	o — o — o
Encinal Avenue	Green & yellow	— o — o

1/ Red & red dome signals; street cars used the following disc sign colors:
   White: Peninsular line cars
   Red : Crosstown line cars to or from Encinal Avenue
   Green: Crosstown line cars to or from Lincoln Avenue

TABLE 16 -- *Storage Yards*

Yard	Distance from S.F.	Lines served	Capacity[1]	Date Opened	Date Closed
Oakland Pier	3.5	All lines	5 spurs, 3 sidings (85 cars)	1/22/82	1/14/39
Alameda Pier	3.0	Alameda lines	3 spurs, 3 sidings (65 cars)	3/15/84	1/14/39
Berryman I	10.7	Berryman	3 spurs, 1 siding (22 cars)	7/01/78	12/29/11
Berryman II	10.9	Shattuck Ave, Ellsworth St, California St., 9th Street	6 spurs (30 cars)	12/30/11	7/25/41
Berkeley Freight Yard	9.3	Ellsworth St.	1 spur (6 cars)	12/31/11	2/18/12[2]
Shellmound [3]	6.8	California St., 9th Street	1 spur (5 cars)	9/12/21	1/14/28
West Berkeley	9.4	West Berkeley	1 spur, House and Depot tracks (8 cars)	3/01/77	7/04/17
East Oakland I	8.2	Melrose, Alameda, Stonehurst	4 spurs (57 cars)	4/30/83	12/11/11
East Oakland II	8.2	7th Street, Horseshoe, Stonehurst	1 spur (5 cars)	12/12/11	2/25/40
Fruitvale	9.0	Lincoln Ave., Encinal Ave.	2 spurs (8 cars)	2/26/40	1/18/41
Melrose	10.8	7th Street, Horseshoe, Suburban Connection	3 spurs, 1 lead, Depot tracks (15 cars)	12/12/11	3/21/41
14th Street I	7.1	14th Street	Depot tracks (4 cars)	3/30/81	6/19/11
14th Street II	7.1	18th Street, Webster St., Street cars	3 spurs, Depot tracks (12 cars)	6/20/11	11/07/26
2nd & Webster	8.4	18th Street	2 spurs (7 cars)	11/08/26	3/25/33
High Street I	9.7	High Street	3 spurs (9 cars)	7/01/78	5/31/11
High Street II	9.7	Encinal Ave., Lincoln Ave., Street cars	2 spurs (10 cars)	6/01/11	2/25/40
West Alameda	5.2	All lines	6 sidings (160 cars)	2/01/11	3/21/41
Bridge Yard	5.2	All lines	13 sidings (115 cars)	1/15/39	7/25/41[4]

1/ Yard capacity not necessarily the same as shown during entire time that yard was in operation.

2/ Ellsworth Street line assigned to Berkeley Freight Yard on 12/31/11 but could not use yard until early January as trolley wire had not yet been installed; used Berryman Yard temporarily. Ellsworth Street line reassigned to Berryman Yard on 2/18/12. Berkeley Freight Yard used only for freight loading/unloading movements thereafter.

3/ Not a tie-up yard; used only during layover time for California Street and 9th Street lines.

4/ Yard continued in operation for Key System trains.

would be on Run 122. The Run Roster called for Runs 117 and 120 to be off duty on Sundays, which allowed Ellsworth line crews to have one Sunday off every three weeks. This day off was augmented during the cyclic switch from Run 117 to 122, which allowed the crew 27 hours off between runs.

Not all runs were maintained in a line pool, as runs standing for express trains, mail trains, shop trains, and other movements usually either held the same run number daily or were paired, with crews alternating runs each day. One unusual run was Run 90, an "Owl Run" which went on duty at Melrose each night except Saturday at 11:23 p.m. This run worked the late night trains on the Seventh Street line and was released at Melrose after tieing up the last train at 2:20 a.m. The run was recalled at 4:48 a.m. for the first train on the Seventh Street line, and the run was released for the day at 9:17 a.m. Another unusual run was operated by inspectors during the early years of operation. This run made several trips between Melrose and East Oakland between 2:00 and 4:00 a.m., stopping at Fruitvale and 23rd Avenue. The run was operated solely for the benefit of employes living near those stations.

From the later years of the steam locals to the final year that the electric trains connected with the ferries, schedules changed but little. For example, steam-local timetable No. 23 (August 1, 1911) showed Berryman Line train No. 422 leaving Oakland Pier at 9:20 a.m. as part of Run 19. Twenty-eight years later, the same train with the same run number still departed at 9:20 a.m., although it now was an electric train running on the Shattuck Avenue line.

There were only two significant schedule changes during the many years that the steam locals and the electric trains met the ferries. The first was a reduction (on June 1, 1905) of the basic headway on the lines from Oakland Pier from 30 minutes to 20 minutes. The second change concerned night and Sunday service. During and immediately after the transition from steam to electric service, 20-minute service was the rule until 8 o'clock, after which trains ran on 40-minute headways. On weekends, additional service was provided, allowing for 20-minute service until midnight. The lines from Alameda Pier operated on a 30-minute daytime and 45-minute evening headway; however, 20-minute service periodically was operated under authority of Special Occasion Time Table Supplement "X". By 1930, the increasing use of automobiles had cut severely into night and Sunday patronage. So, beginning on February 28, 1932, daytime frequencies (i.e., 20 minutes on trains from Oakland Pier) was operated only until 7:00 p.m., with 40-minute service being performed thereafter and all day on Sundays.

The consistency of operation was drastically changed during the short years of Interurban Electric operation across the Bay Bridge. At first, the new company made an attempt to maintain the traditional 20-minute headways during daytime hours and 40-minute headways during nights and Sundays on all but the Alameda lines. These latter lines operated during the day on an alternating 40-minute headway, effectively giving that city 20-minute service; night and Sunday service was every 80 minutes on each of the two lines.

Within a year, it was evident that declining patronage and soaring costs dictated longer headways on all lines. With the adoption of Time Table No. 3 on February 26, 1940, daytime headways on the Shattuck Avenue and Seventh Street lines was set at 30 minutes; night and Sunday headways were 45 minutes. Headways on the two Alameda lines were lengthened to hourly during the day (providing half-hourly service to Alameda) and 75 minutes at night and on Sundays. The Ninth Street line was affected the most, as daytime headways were lengthened from 20 minutes to 40 minutes, and night and Sunday service going from 40 minutes to 45 minutes.

Mail Trains

The Oakland, Alameda and Berkeley Lines was unique among Bay Area electric railroads in that scheduled mail trains were operated. The trains were not railway post office runs, as on the Pacific Electric and the Napa Valley Route, but were operated for the transportation of sacked mail between Oakland Pier and Oakland-16th Street and also Berkeley. Scheduled mail service was inaugurated on December 1, 1923, and trains usually consisted of one baggage motor. On occasion, until January 15, 1928, an American Express Company car would be coupled behind the baggage motor. Unloading and loading of sacked mail and express would be accomplished at Oakland-16th Street while holding the eastward main line of the Suburban Elevation opposite the baggage elevator. With the short headways, crews had to work fast so that the car also could be turned and take the westward track without delaying any suburban trains. From March 26, 1933, to August 1, 1937, the first morning eastward trip used the ground level track in front of the station. Access to the track was by way of the ramp formerly used by 18th Street line trains. In Berkeley, unloading and loading was accomplished in front of the station while holding the eastward track. After the station building was razed, mail trains were spotted on the mail spur immediately west of the former station site. Sacked mail service also was operated between Oakland Pier and Alameda; in this case, mail was transported on scheduled shop trains. All mail train service was discontinued on November 30, 1938.

Freight Operations

The Oakland, Alameda and Berkeley Lines was considered a valuable freight switching feeder to the vast Southern Pacific system. From the time of the steam locals, freight switching service was provided to the many lumber yards, industries, and manufacturing plants that were located adjacent to the tracks. With the electrification of 1912, it was proposed to utilize electric freight motor No. 200. In preparation, the Chevrolet plant near 73rd Avenue, the Pacific Coast Borax plant at Pacific Junction, and a number of other locations were provided with electrified yard and team tracks.

In addition, freight stations were maintained at three locations: Berkeley (Ward Street), Melrose, and Alameda (Park Street North). By 1914, the use of the electric freight motor had proven impractical, and thereafter most local switching was performed by the ubiquitous 0-6-0 steam switchers. On occasion, switching of freight cars would be handled by a pair of passenger motors. Beginning in 1940, an increasing number of switching chores were taken over by diesel locomotives, although 1200-class steam switchers were in use until after cessation of electric operations.

Storage Yards

Southern Pacific operated storage yards at Oakland Pier, Alameda Pier, and at various times at 12 other locations throughout the system. Maintaining yards at outlying locations reduced to a minimum the need for non-revenue deadhead trips. Thus, early morning starts could originate at or near their outer terminals, and late-night trains did not have to make a long deadhead run in order to tie up. The yards located at the two piers, and in later years the Bridge Yard, were used chiefly for midday storage of rush-hour equipment.

Interlocking Facilities

All movements through junctions, drawbridges, and crossings with other railways were controlled either by switchtenders or interlocking plants. During the early years of the steam locals, interlocking towers were located only at Oakland Pier and 1st and Harrison Streets. In time, switchtenders at the other locations were replaced by interlocking towers until there were a total of 22 towers in operation. The last switchtenders were stationed at Pacific Junction and Thousand Oaks. Those at Pacific Junction remained until Pacific Junction Tower was activated in 1932. Although a tower was built at Thousand Oaks, it was never activated and eventually was razed. Switchtenders continued to serve that location until the California Street line was discontinued in 1933, after which trainmen handled switches there.

All original interlocking plants on the East Bay suburban lines were of the mechanical type and contained Taylor-Armstrong equipment. Beginning in 1911, electropneumatic and electric plants were constructed. Electropneumatic plants contained Union Switch and Signal Company equipment; switches were activated from a 6½"x8½" cylinder using air at a pressure of 80 pounds per square inch. Valves for each cylinder were operated by magnets controlled by a 14-volt direct current line from the tower. Signals were moved by a 4-inch single-action air cylinder controlled by a 14-volt DC magnet. The plants at Poplar Street and 1st and Webster were variations of the basic electropneumatic type. That at Poplar Street was operated at 110 volts alternating current; air was piped from 16th Street Tower. The tower at 1st and Webster Streets operated at 55 volts AC.

Electric plants contained General Railway Signal Company equipment. Switches controlled by these plants were operated by one horsepower, 110-volt DC motors through either a gear and cam or a switch and lock arrangement. Signals were activated from a ¼-hp, 110-volt DC motor.

Movements to and across the Fruitvale and the Harrison Street drawbridges were controlled by towers on each side of each span. Bridgetenders were used to coordinate bridge openings with water traffic.

TABLE 17 -- Interlocking Facilities

Name of Tower	Controls	Type[1]	Date Opened	Date Closed	Name of Tower	Controls	Type[1]	Date Opened	Date Closed
Oakland Pier	All movements in and out of Oakland Pier.	EP[2]	1/22/82	1/14/39[3]	Kirkham Street	Movement between Oakland Pier and West Oakland Yard via 1st Street.	EP	8/23/06	12/29/12
16th Street[4]	All movements through 16th Street Station; junction of Berkeley District and 18th Street line.	EP	8/23/06	3/21/41[3]	Magnolia St.	Movement between Oakland Pier and West Oakland Yard via 1st Street; crossing of 1st St. and W.P.R.R.	EP	12/29/12	3/
Shell Mound	Junction of Berkeley District and 9th Street line.	EP	8/01/13	7/25/41	Alameda Pier	All movements in and out of Alameda Pier.	E	11/01/14	1/14/39
Golden Gate[5]	Junction of Berkeley District and California Street line; crossing with Key System and A.T.&S.F.Ry.	E	1/18/04	7/25/41	Pacific Jct.	Junction of Encinal Ave. line and Lincoln Ave. line.	E	12/28/32	1/18/41
Woolsey	Junction of Berkeley District and Ellsworth St. line; crossing with Key System.	E	8/01/13	3/25/33	Encinal Jct.[8]	Junction of Encinal Ave. line and 8th St.-Webster Jct. route.	E	8/01/13	12/26/23
Masonic	Movement over single track, Albany to Thousand Oaks; crossing of 9th St. line and A.T.&S.F.Ry.	E	8/01/13	7/25/41	Mastick Jct.	Junction of Lincoln Ave. line and 8th St.-Webster Jct. route.	EP	8/01/13	12/26/23
Rose Street	Crossing of California Street line and Key System.	E	8/01/13	3/25/33	Blanding Jct.	Junction of Lincoln Ave. line and Alameda-Fruitvale route; approach to Fruitvale Bridge.	E	8/01/13	1/18/41
Thousand Oaks	Junction of Shattuck Ave., California St., and 9th St. lines.	...	6/	.....	Webster Jct.	Junction of Webster St. line and 8th St.-Webster Jct. route; approach to Harrison St. Bridge.	EP	8/23/06	12/26/23
West Oakland	Crossing of 7th St. line and Cedar St. freight route.	EP	8/23/06	3/21/41	1st & Harrison	Junction of Alameda Loop and 1st St. route; crossing of Webster St. line and 1st St. route; approach to Harrison St. Bridge.	M	9/28/98	12/29/12
Clinton	Crossing of 7th St. line and Western Pacific R.R.	M	12/29/12	3/21/41	1st & Webster	Junction-crossing of Webster St. line and 1st St. route; approach to Harrison St. Bridge.	EP	12/29/12	12/26/23
East Oakland	Junction of 7th St. line and 1st Street route.	E	8/23/06	12/18/11	3rd & Webster	Crossing of Webster St. line and Western Pacific R.R.	EP	12/29/12	3/25/33
Fruitvale[7]	Junction of 7th St. line and Alameda line; approach to Fruitvale Bridge.	EP	8/23/06	1/18/41[3]	7th & Webster[9]	Crossing of 7th St. line and Webster Street line.	EP	1/18/04	3/25/33
Melrose	Crossing of 7th St. line and Western Pacific R.R.	M	12/29/12	3/21/41	San Francisco	All movements across Bay Bridge and in and out of Trans-Bay Terminal.	E	1/15/39	7/25/41[10]
Poplar Street	Crossing of 18th St. line and Key System.	EP	11/01/14	3/25/33	Bridge Yard	All movements between east end of Bay Bridge and east end of train control territory.	E	1/15/39	7/25/41[10]

1. M : Mechanical; E : Electric; EP : Electropneumatic.
2. Original tower had mechanical equipment. Reconstructed December 1912; switch tenders used during reconstruction.
3. Closed for suburban trains; continued in operation for main line trains.
4. Original tower was at 14th Street. Present tower constructed in December 1913; dwarf signals used during construction.
5. Reconstructed December 1911 to August 1913; switch tenders used during reconstruction.
6. Tower constructed but never activated; switch tenders used.
7. Original tower was on north side of tracks; new tower was built on south side of tracks in 1912. Original tower building moved to Encinal Junction.
8. After deactivation, tower building moved to Pacific Junction.
9. All interlocking towers except 7th & Webster Tower were side-of-the-track structures. This tower was located on signal bridge spanning Webster Street at north curb line of 7th Street.
10. Closed for Interurban Electric trains; continued in operation for Key System trains.

Crossing Watchmen

Crossing watchmen, with their ever-present watchmen's shanty, were a colorful and necessary part of the East Bay suburban lines. Some 32 street crossings, many with Key System streetcar lines, were thus protected. In later years, some crossings, such as 23rd Avenue, received automatic crossing gates. At other crossings, particularly in downtown Oakland and Berkeley, traffic lights replaced crossing watchmen. However, even during the final years of service, there were a few crossings that were still protected by a man with a hand-held "STOP" sign by day and a red lantern by night.

Trackage Ownership

Ownership of the trackage over which trains of the O.A. & B. Lines operated was divided between four distinct, although related corporations. Ownership of the various segments of the system was divided as follows:

CENTRAL PACIFIC RAILWAY
1. **Seventh Street Line:** Oakland Pier to Dutton Avenue.
2. **Horseshoe Line:** Fruitvale to San Antonio Junction via Lincoln Avenue and Mastick Junction.
3. **Pacific Avenue Extension:** Pacific Junction to foot of Pacific Avenue.
4. **Total Track Miles:** Main Line–18.450; Second Track–17.797; Sidings–11.665.

SOUTH PACIFIC COAST RAILWAY
1. **Webster Street Line:** Alameda Pier to Oakland-14th Street.
2. **Encinal Avenue Line:** Alameda Pier to High Street.
3. **West Alameda:** All yard, wye, and shop trackage.
4. **Total Track Miles:** Main Line–10.995; Second Track–10.495; Sidings–10.187.

SOUTHERN PACIFIC RAILROAD
1. **Shattuck Avenue Line:** Oakland Pier to Thousand Oaks.
2. **Ellsworth Street Line:** Ellsworth Junction to University Campus.
3. **California Street Line:** California Junction to Thousand Oaks.
4. **Ninth Street Line:** Ninth Street Junction to Thousand Oaks.
5. **18th Street Line:** Oakland-16th Street to Oakland-14th Street including balloon track in front of 16th Street Station.
6. **Total Track Miles:** Main Line–18.450; Second Track–19.380; Sidings–4.192.

SOUTHERN PACIFIC COMPANY
1. **Lincoln Avenue Line:** Pacific Junction to Mastick Junction.
2. **Fernside Loop:** Encinal Avenue and High Street to Lincoln Junction.
3. **Cross-Town Line:** On 8th Street between Mastick Junction and Encinal Junction.
4. **Total Track Miles:** Main Line–1.431; Second Track–1.431; Sidings–1.539.

Automatic Block Signal System

Various portions of the O.A. & B. Lines were protected by automatic block signals manufactured by Union Switch & Signal Company. Power for the signal system was generated at the Fruitvale power house. The three substations stepped the voltage down to 2,300 volts for distribution to the signal system. Block signal protection was provided as follows:

1. **Seventh Street Line:** Two-blade lower-quadrant semaphores were installed on signal bridges from Oakland Pier to Bay Street and from Fallon Street to Melrose. Dwarf two-blade semaphores were mounted on center poles from Melrose to Dutton Avenue (these were replaced by three-position signal lights in 1938). No signal protection along 7th Street between Bay and Fallon Streets.
2. **Shattuck Avenue Line:** Two-blade lower-quadrant semaphores were installed on signal bridges from Oakland Pier to Shellmound. Dwarf two-blade semaphores were mounted on center poles from Shellmound to University Avenue and from Vine Street to Thousand Oaks. Dwarf two-blade semaphores were mounted on curb poles from University Avenue to Vine Street.
3. **Horseshoe Line:** Two-blade lower-quadrant semaphores were installed on signal bridges from Fruitvale to Fruitvale Bridge. Two-blade lower-quadrant semaphores were mounted on masts from Fruitvale Bridge to Lincoln Junction.
4. **Alameda Loop Lines:** Two-blade lower-quadrant semaphores were installed on signal bridges from Alameda Pier to West Alameda. Dwarf two-blade semaphores were mounted on center poles from West Alameda to Lincoln Park via both routes.
5. **Ellsworth Street Line:** A signal light mounted on a curb pole protected the single track section between Derby and University Campus.

East Bay Lines Through the Years

Steam Locals

BERRYMAN LINE

August 16, 1876: First day of service. Trains operated on one to two hour intervals until 7 p.m. by Central Pacific between Berkeley and West Oakland, where connection is made with Seventh Street trains for ferry.
July 1, 1878: Service extended from Berkeley north to Berryman (located at Shattuck and Vine Street).
April 30, 1883: Inner terminal shifted from West Oakland to Oakland Pier. Daytime frequency changed to 30 minutes; hourly at night.
August 22, 1897: Operation of trains taken over by Southern Pacific.
June 1, 1905: Daytime frequency changed to 20 minutes; 40 minutes at night.
August 1, 1908: Inaugurate two evening express trains, Oakland Pier to Berryman. Operate daily except Saturday and Sunday, making first stop at Dwight Way.
March 1, 1910: No baggage handled on eastward trains during evening commute period.
February 20, 1911: Headway reduced from 40 minutes to 20 minutes between 8 p.m. and midnight on Saturdays and Sundays.
December 23, 1911: Steam trains alternate with electric trains during daytime hours.
December 30, 1911: Last day of steam local service.

Stations	Type[1]/ Local trains	Type[1]/ Express trains	Distance from S.F.	Remarks
OAKLAND PIER	T	T	3.0	
Oakland	s	-	5.5	
B Street	c	-	6.2	
Emery	c	-	6.6	Originally called Emory's
Shell Mound	c	-	6.8	
Richmond Junction	-	-	*7.0*	
San Pablo Avenue	s	-	7.5	Originally called Golden Gate
Alcatraz Avenue	s	-	8.5	Originally called Lorin
Ashby Avenue	s	-	8.8	
Dwight Way	s	s	9.5	
Berkeley	s	s	10.0	Terminal before 7/01/78
BERRYMAN	T	T	10.7	

1/ Station types: T : Terminal station
    s : All trains stop
    c : Conditional station, only certain trains stop.

WEST BERKELEY LINE

March 1, 1877: First day of service. Trains operated by Central Pacific between West Oakland and Berkeley (Delaware Street). Five trips operated between 7:30 a.m. and 6:00 p.m.
April 30, 1883: Inner terminal shifted to Shell Mound. Inaugurate 30-minute headways during morning and evening hours, about hourly at other times; trains operate from 6:30 a.m. to 7:30 p.m.
August 12, 1893: Operation of line taken over by Southern Pacific.
August 12, 1893: Midday headways reduced to 30 minutes on Sundays; trains operate from 6:30 a.m. to 12:30 a.m.
January 18, 1904: Service extended eastward from Berkeley to Corbin; inner terminal shifted to Oakland Pier. Headways changed to 30 minutes all day.
June 1, 1905: Inner terminal shifted from Oakland Pier to Oakland-16th Street. Morning and evening headways are 20 minutes; hourly at other times.
March 1, 1910: Sunday and holiday headways are 20 minutes all day.
February 20, 1911: Service extended eastward from Corbin to Richmond for five trains.
January 11, 1912: Inner terminal shifted from Oakland-16th Street to Shell Mound. One midday trip runs Corbin to Oakland Pier and return to change engines.
February 19, 1912: Discontinue all but two trips, Shellmound to Corbin. Six trains operate daily, Shell Mound to Richmond.
July 4, 1917: Last day of service. Service between Oakland Pier and Berkeley (University Ave.), Fleming, Vigorit, Stege, and Richmond taken over by local trains to Port Costa and Avon.

Stations	Type[1]/	Distance from S.F.	Remarks
OAKLAND PIER	T	3.5	
Oakland-16th Street	s	5.5	
B Street	s	6.2	
Emery	s	6.6	Originally called Emory's
Shell Mound	s	6.8	
Richmond Junction	-	*7.0*	
Stockyards	s	7.8	
Potter	s	8.2	
Carlton	s	8.5	Station opened 8/01/08
Posen	s	9.0	
Berkeley (University Ave.)	s	9.2	Station opened 8/16/13
Berkeley (Delaware St.)	s	9.4	Station closed 8/15/13
Corbin	s	10.2	
Fleming	f	10.7	
Nobel	f	11.2	
Vigorit	f	11.6	
Stege	s	13.1	
Pullman Shops	f	13.9	
RICHMOND	T	15.0	

1/ Station types: T : Terminal station
    s : All trains stop
    f : Flag stop

MELROSE LINE

September 2, 1862: First day of service; operated by San Francisco and Oakland Railroad between Oakland Point and Broadway. Trains operate about once every two hours from 6 a.m. to 6 p.m.
September 28, 1864: Service extended from Broadway eastward to San Antonio (later called Brooklyn and East Oakland).
November 8, 1869: Operation of line taken over by Central Pacific. Trains operated hourly from 6 a.m. to 6 p.m. plus one extra train at midnight.
June 29, 1870: SF&O merged with San Francisco and Alameda R.R. to form San Francisco, Oakland and Alameda R.R.
August 22, 1870: SF, O&A merged into Central Pacific.
January 16, 1871: Service to Oakland Point Pier abandoned; trains operated to Oakland Long Wharf.
January 22, 1882: First day of service into Oakland Pier; service to Oakland Long Wharf discontinued. Begin left-hand operation along Seventh Street.
April 30, 1883: Service extended eastward to Fruitvale during morning and afternoon hours. Trains operate on 30-minute headways during daytime and hourly at night.
April 1, 1885: Operation of line taken over by Southern Pacific.
August 12, 1893: Begin full service to Fruitvale; Oak Street local service inaugurated.
February 28, 1901: Discontinue Oak Street local.
June 1, 1905: Headways changed to 20 minutes during daytime and 40 minutes at night.
February 14, 1906: Service extended eastward to Austin (later called Melrose).
March 1, 1910: No baggage carried on eastward evening trains.
February 20, 1911: 20-minute headway on Saturday and Sunday extended from 8 p.m. to midnight.
August 1, 1911: Inaugurate two evening express trains, Oakland Pier to Melrose via First Street. Trains operate daily except Saturdays and Sundays; first stop is Fruitvale.
December 1, 1911: Steam trains alternate with electric trains during daytime hours.
December 12, 1911: Last day of steam local service.

Stations	Type[1]/ Local trains	Type[1]/ Express trains	Distance from S.F.	Remarks
OAKLAND PIER	T	T	3.5	
West Oakland Jct.	-	-	*4.7*	
Pine	s	+	5.0	Called West Oakland before 8/01/08
Center Street	s	+	5.4	
Adeline Street	s	+	5.8	
Market Street	s	+	6.2	
Broadway	s	+	6.6	
Oak Street	s	+	7.2	
Clinton	s	+	7.8	
East Oakland	s	-	8.2	Called San Antonio before 5/16/70; called Brooklyn from 5/16/70 to 4/30/83.
23rd Avenue	s	-	9.0	
Fruitvale	s	s	9.6	
Sather	s	s	10.2	
MELROSE	T	T	10.8	Called Austin before 8/23/06

1/ Station types: T : Terminal station
    s : All trains stop
    + : Express trains operate via 1st Street route.

STONEHURST LINE

October 10, 1909: First day of service. Trains operated about hourly during morning and afternoon-evening hours daily except Sundays, and from late morning to early evening on Sundays. Six trips operate to/from Oakland Pier via First Street route; all others operate only to/from Fruitvale, connecting there with trains of Melrose Line.
December 19, 1911: Reduce number of trips to/from Oakland Pier from six to one.
September 23, 1930: Last day of service.

Stations	Type[1]/	Distance from S.F.	Remarks
OAKLAND PIER	T	3.5	
West Oakland Junction	-	*4.7*	
1st and Broadway	s	6.7	
East Oakland	s	8.2	
23rd Avenue	s	9.0	
Fruitvale	s	9.6	Terminal station for most trains
Seminary Avenue	f	11.1	Station opened 12/19/11
Kohler	f	11.5	
Fitchburg	f	12.1	
Elmhurst	s	13.4	
STONEHURST	T	14.3	

1/ Station types: T : Terminal station
    s : All trains stop
    f : Flag stop

ALAMEDA LINE

August 25, 1864: First day of service. Trains operated by San Francisco and Alameda R.R. from Alameda Wharf to Alameda via Railroad Avenue (now called Lincoln Avenue). Trains run every one to two hours from 4:45 a.m. to 7:15 p.m.
March 1, 1865: Service extended from Alameda to San Leandro.
August 26, 1865: Service extended from San Leandro to Hayward.
May 16, 1870: Three additional trips added between Alameda Wharf and Alameda.
June 29, 1870: Combined with San Francisco and Oakland R.R. to form San Francisco, Oakland and Alameda R.R.
August 22, 1870: Operation of line taken over by Central Pacific.
November 28, 1870: Short-trip runs extended from Alameda to Fruitvale.
November 3, 1873: Service cut back from Hayward to Fruitvale. Service discontinued to Alameda Wharf. Trains run from Oakland Long Wharf via 7th Street, Alice Street bridge, Alameda, and to Fruitvale. Trains operate hourly, 8 a.m. to 7 p.m.; most trains terminate at Alameda.
January 22, 1882: First day of service into Oakland Pier; service to Oakland Long Wharf discontinued.
April 30, 1883: Headways changed to 30 minutes; trains operate 6 a.m. to midnight. Only two trains operate through to Fruitvale; all others terminate at Alameda.
July 1, 1887: Operation of line taken over by Southern Pacific.
September 28, 1898: Service rerouted from Alice St. Bridge and 7th Street to Harrison St. Bridge and First St.
June 1, 1905: Inaugurate Alameda loop service. Trains operate from Oakland Pier via 1st Street to Fruitvale; return via Alameda, Harrison St. bridge, and 1st Street. Certain trains operate via reverse route or to/from Alameda only. During daytime, trains operate every 40 minutes, with 20-minute service during morning and afternoon hours; 40-minute service operated at night.
August 23, 1906: Inaugurate service from Oakland Pier to Alameda Pier via Fruitvale (designated Swing Suburban Service); also operate loop trains as previously (designated Pier Suburban Service).
August 1, 1908: Route designated as Horseshoe Line.
August 1, 1911: Route designated as Steam Loop. Swing Suburban service to Alameda Pier discontinued. Pier Suburban trains operate from Oakland Pier via Harrison Street bridge, Alameda, and Fruitvale until midmorning; operate via reverse route thereafter.
December 18, 1911: Last day of service of steam locals.

Stations	Type1/	Distance from S.F.	Remarks
OPERATED : August 25, 1864 to November 2, 1873			
ALAMEDA WHARF	T	3.5	
Alameda Station	s	6.5	
Fruit Vale	s	7.5	
Simpson's	s	9.5	
San Leandro	s	13.5	
HAYWARD'S	T	19.5	
OPERATED : November 3, 1873 to May 31, 1905			
OAKLAND PIER	T	3.5	
West Oakland Junction	-	4.7	
Oakland, 1st Street	s	6.7	
Webster St. Crossing	-	6.8	
Webster Junction	-	7.2	
Mastick	s	8.2	
Bay Street	s	8.6	
Grand Street	s	9.1	
Willow Street	s	9.5	
Alameda	s	10.0	Terminal station for most trains.
Fernside	f	10.5	
FRUITVALE	T	11.1	
OPERATED : June 1, 1905 to December 18, 1911			
OAKLAND PIER	T	3.5	
West Oakland Junction	-	4.7	
Oakland, 1st Street	s	6.7	
Webster St. Crossing	-	6.8	
East Oakland	s	8.2	
23rd Avenue	s	9.0	
Fruitvale	s	9.6	
Fernside	f	10.1	
Blanding Junction	-	10.8	
Alameda, Park Street	s	10.0	
Willow Street	s	9.5	
Grand Street	s	9.1	
Bay Street	s	8.6	
Mastick	s	8.2	
Webster Junction	-	7.2	
Webster St. Crossing	-	6.8	
Oakland, 1st Street	s	6.7	
West Oakland Junction	-	4.7	
OAKLAND PIER	T	3.5	21.2 miles from initial station.
Alameda Point	c	5.2	
Alameda Junction	-	5.0	
ALAMEDA PIER	T	3.0	16.9 miles from initial station.

1/ Station types: T : Terminal station
s : All trains stop
f : Flag stop
c : Conditional station, only certain trains stop

14th STREET LINE

May 30, 1881: First day of service. Narrow gauge trains operated by South Pacific Coast Railroad between original Alameda Pier and 14th Street by way of Webster Street bridge. Trains operate hourly between 6 a.m. and 10 p.m.
July 16, 1883: Trains operate 6 a.m. to midnight.
March 15, 1884: First day of service into new Alameda Mole Terminal.
May 31, 1884: Trains operate on 30-minute headways, 7 a.m. to 7:30 p.m.; then hourly until 11:45 p.m.
July 1, 1887: Operation of line taken over by Southern Pacific. Trains operate from 6 a.m. to 12:20 a.m.
September 28, 1898: Service rerouted from Webster Street bridge to Harrison Street bridge. Most local runs taken over by standard gauge equipment.
August 23, 1906: Operation of line transferred from Coast Division to Western Division.
June 19, 1911: Last day of service of steam locals.

Station	Type1/	Distance from S.F.	Remarks
ALAMEDA PIER	T	3.0	
Alameda Junction	-	5.0	
Webster Junction	-	5.9	
7th & Webster Streets	s	6.6	
14th STREET	T	7.0	

1/ Station types: T : Terminal station
s : All trains stop

HIGH STREET LINE

June 1, 1878: First day of service. South Pacific Coast operated three main line narrow gauge trains between original Alameda Pier, Park Street, and points south. One additional train operated only as Park Street.
July 1, 1878: Hourly service inaugurated between San Francisco and Park Street. Trains operate from 5:45 a.m. to 12:25 a.m.
June 16, 1883: Service extended eastward to High Street.
March 15, 1884: First day of service into new Alameda Mole Terminal.
May 31, 1886: Trains operate on 30-minute headways from 6:45 a.m. to 7:15 p.m., then hourly until 11:30 p.m.
July 1, 1887: Operation of line taken over by Southern Pacific. Trains operate from 6:45 a.m. to 12:45 a.m.
November 20, 1902: First day of operation of standard gauge trains. Track continues as dual gauge for narrow gauge trains destined for San Jose and points south.
April 17, 1906: Last narrow gauge train operatd.
August 23, 1906: Operation of line transferred from Coast Division to Western Division.
May 31, 1911: Last day of service of steam locals.

Stations	Type1/	Distance from S.F.	Remarks
ALAMEDA PIER	T	3.0	
Alameda Junction	f	5.0	
West Alameda	s	5.2	
5th Street	s	6.8	
Webster Street	s	7.1	Originally called 7th Street
Encinal Park	s	7.5	
Morton Street	s	7.9	
Chestnut Street	s	8.4	
Park Street	s	9.0	
Versailles Avenue	s	9.4	
HIGH STREET	T	9.7	

1/ Station types: T : Terminal station
s : All trains stop
f : Flag stop

The Red Trains

SHATTUCK AVENUE LINE

December 23, 1911: Initiate partial electric service, with electric trains alternating runs with steam trains. No electric train service during morning or evening hours. Eastern terminal is Berryman.
December 31, 1911: Initiate full electric train service between Oakland Pier and Thousand Oaks.
November 1, 1914: Change Oakland-16th Street station from ground level to Suburban Elevation.
September 12, 1921: Change Saturday and Sunday evening headway from 20 minutes to 40 minutes.
September 4, 1923: Establish two evening express trains, Oakland Pier to Thousand Oaks; make first stop at Berkeley.
January 15, 1928: Trackage from Contra Costa to Thousand Oaks changed from double track to single track.
February 28, 1932: Change daytime Sunday headway from 20 minutes to 40 minutes.
February 1, 1934: Establish three morning express trains, Berkeley to Oakland Pier. Stop only at stations to and including South Berkeley, then at San Pablo Avenue. Add third evening express train, Oakland Pier to Thousand Oaks. Eastward express trains make first stop at Bancroft Way.
January 27, 1935: Change one morning express train to run from Berryman instead of from Berkeley.
December 1, 1938: Operation of line taken over by Interurban Electric Railway.
January 14, 1939: Last day of operation to/from Oakland Pier.
January 15, 1939: Begin operation to San Francisco via Bay Bridge. Establish one westward morning express train; last stop is Bancroft Way. Establish two eastward evening express trains; first stop is Bancroft Way. Local trains and express trains display "3" disc.
March 26, 1939: Discontinue evening express service. Reduce evening express service to one train. Local trains display "3" disc; express trains display "9" disc.
February 26, 1940: Change daytime headway from 20 minutes to 30 minutes; change night and Sunday headway from 40 minuts to 45 minutes.
July 25, 1941: Last day of service.

Stations	Type[1]/ Local trains	Type[1]/ Express trains	Station no. and distance from S.F.	Remarks
OPERATED: December 23, 1911 to January 14, 1939				
OAKLAND PIER	T	T	3.5	
Oakland-16th Street	s	-	A5.5	
Shellmound Tower	c	-	A7.0	Called Richmond Jct. until 12/31/13; called Shellmound Jct. 1/01/14 to 9/12/21; station closed for this line 1/14/28
Ninth St. Junc.	-	-	K7.1	Called Shellmound Junc. until 5/31/13
Green Street	f	-	K7.2	Station opened for this line as conditional stop 1/15/28; made flag stop 3/26/33
San Pablo Avenue	s	-	K7.5	Station opened for this line 1/12/21: Trains stop only when California St. trains not operating to Pier; station closed for this line 1/14/28. Station reopened 3/26/33.
Los Angeles Street	f	-	K7.8	" " " " " "
California Junc.	-	-	K8.0	
South Berkeley****	s	-	K8.5	
Ellsworth Junc.	-	-	K8.6	Called Woolsey Junc. before 6/01/13
Ashby Avenue	s	-	K8.8	
Ward St.(north side)***	s	-	K9.2	
Berkeley Freight Yard			K9.3	
Dwight Way	s	-	K9.5	
Bancroft Way**	s	-	K9.8	Station opened 5/20/14
Berkeley	s	s	K10.0	
Virginia Street*	s	s	K10.4	
Vine Street*	s	s	K10.7	Called Berryman before 5/31/13
Berryman	s	s	K10.9	Called Eunice Street before 5/31/13
Northbrae	s	s	K11.3	
Contra Costa	f	f	K11.5	Station opened 9/12/21
THOUSAND OAKS	T	T	K11.8	
OPERATED: January 15, 1939 to July 25, 1941				
SAN FRANCISCO	T	T	0.00	
West Junction	-	-	K5.20	
Bridge Yard	f	-	K5.75	
East Junction	-	-	K6.11	
26th St. Junc.	-	-	K6.89	
34th St. Junc.	-	-	K7.25	
9th St. Junc.	-	-	K8.07	
Green Street	f	-	K8.17	
San Pablo Avenue	s	-	K8.51	
Los Angeles Street	f	-	K8.75	
South Berkeley****	s	s	K9.41	Express stop after 2/26/40
Ashby Avenue	s	s	K9.79	" " " " "
Ward St.(north side)***	s	s	K10.17	" " " " "
Dwight Way	s	s	K10.46	" " " " "
Bancroft Way**	s	s	K10.72	
Berkeley	s	s	K10.95	Express trains stop head end at University Avenue
Virginia Street*	s	s	K11.34	
Vine Street*	s	s	K11.59	
Berryman	s	s	K11.89	
Northbrae	s	s	K12.23	
Contra Costa	s	s	K12.48	Eastward trains only stop before 2/26/40; thereafter all trains stop
THOUSAND OAKS*****	T	T	K12.70	

[1]/ Station types: T : Terminal station
    s : All trains stop
    f : Flag stop
    c : Conditional station, only certain trains stop.
* Station stop is on near side of intersection in direction moving; at other stations, stop is on far side unless noted.
** Trains make safety stop before crossing intersection.
*** With 3 cars or less, train must clear Ward St. crossing.
**** Trains must clear Alcatraz Avenue; with 5 or more cars, train may block Alcatraz Avenue but must clear Grove Street at all times.
***** Trains must stop with west end clear of Fresno Street. When east end blocks Colusa Street, trainman must be posted at all times at east end to prevent accidents.

ELLSWORTH STREET LINE

December 31, 1911: First day of service.
June 1, 1913: Change tie-up location from Berkeley Freight Yard to Berryman Yard.
November 1, 1914: Change Oakland-16th Street station from ground level to Suburban Elevation..
September 12, 1921: Provide off-peak connecting service between Oakland Pier and Shellmound Park for Ninth Street and California Street trains. Change Saturday and Sunday evening headway from 20 minutes to 40 minutes.
January 15, 1928: Discontinue off-peak connecting service account Ninth Street and California Street trains operate through to Oakland Pier at all hours.
May 10, 1931: Service cut back from University Campus to Bancroft Way.
February 1, 1932: Change daytime Sunday headway from 20 minutes to 40 minutes.
March 25, 1933: Last day of service.

Stations	Type[1]/	Station no. and distance from S.F.	Remarks
OAKLAND PIER	T	3.5	
Oakland-16th Street	s	A5.5	
34th Street	c	A6.2	Off-peak hours, 9/12/21 to 1/14/28
Emeryville	c	A6.6	" " " 9/12/21 to 1/14/28
Shellmound Park	s	A7.0	Transfer to California St. and 9th St. trains, 9/12/21 to 1/14/28
Ninth Street Junction	-	K7.1	Called Shellmound Jct., 2/19/12 to 5/31/13
California Junction	-	K8.0	
Ellsworth Junction	-	K8.6	Called Woolsey Jct. before 6/01/13
Tremont Street	s	KC8.8	Replaced by Woolsey, 1/15/28
Woolsey (Shattuck Ave.)**	s	KC8.9	Station opened 1/15/28
Wheeler Street	s	KC9.0	Replaced by Woolsey, 1/15/28
Prince Street (north side)	s	KC9.2	
Russell Street*	s	KC9.5	Station opened 6/01/13
Derby Street (south side)	s	KC9.7	
Dwight Way**	s	KC10.0	
Bancroft Way***	s	KC10.2	Station opened 6/01/13; Terminal station after 5/10/31
UNIVERSITY CAMPUS	T	KC10.3	Called Allston, 12/31/11 to 5/31/13 Station closed 5/09/31

[1]/ Station types: T : Terminal station
    s : All trains stop
    c : Conditional station, only certain trains stop.
* Station stop is on near side of intersection in direction moving; at all other stations, stop is on far side unless noted.
** Trains make safety stop before crossing intersection.
*** Bancroft Way as Terminal station: Stop with east end of train on south property line to clear wigwag circuit.

CALIFORNIA STREET LINE

January 4, 1912: Begin partial service with 80-minute headway. Trains through-routed with Shattuck Avenue line.
January 11, 1912: Inaugurate full service with 20-minute headways.
February 19, 1912: Trains through-routed with Ninth Street line, forming Berkeley Loop operation.
September 12, 1921: Off-peak service operates only to Shellmound Park; patrons transfer to/from Ellsworth Street trains.
February 17, 1924: Midday service on Saturdays and Sundays operated through to Oakland Pier.
February 1, 1925: Resume full service between Thousand Oaks and Oakland Pier.
March 25, 1933: Last day of service.

Stations	Type[1]/	Station no. and distance from S.F.	Remarks
OAKLAND PIER	T	3.5	
Oakland-16th Street	s	A5.5	
B Street	s	A6.2	Closed for this line 2/18/12
Emery	s	A6.6	" " " " 2/18/12
Shellmound Park	s	K6.8	Off-peak terminal station 9/12/21 to 1/31/25
Ninth Street Junction	-	K7.1	Called Shellmound Jct, 2/19/12 to 5/31/13
Green Street	f	K7.2	Station opened 2/28/32
San Pablo Avenue	s	K7.5	
Los Angeles Street	f	K7.8	
California Junction	-	K8.0	
61st Street (north side)	s	KB8.1	Called Felton Street before 6/01/13
Alcatraz*	s	KB8.3	Station opened 1/15/28
Harmon Street	s	KB8.4	Replaced by Alcatraz 1/15/28
Ashby Avenue**	s	KB8.7	
Ward Street*	s	KB9.0	
Dwight Way**	s	KB9.3	
Bancroft Way**	s	KB9.6	
University Avenue**	s	KB9.9	Also called University (East)
Francisco*	f	KB10.1	Station opened 11/01/14
Cedar Street*	s	KB10.3	
Hopkins Street (north side)	s	KB10.7	
Posen	f	KB10.9	Station opened 9/12/21
Monterey Avenue	s	KB11.1	
THOUSAND OAKS	T	K11.8	11.5 miles from S.F.

[1]/ Station types: T : Terminal station
    s : All trains stop
    f : Flag stop
* Station stop is on near side of intersection in direction moving; at all other stations, stop is on far side unless noted.
** Trains make safety stop before crossing intersection.

NINTH STREET LINE

February 3, 1912: Begin partial service. One trip daily in each direction through-routed with Shattuck Avenue line.
February 19, 1912: First day of full service with 20-minute headways. Trains are through-routed with California Street line, forming Berkeley Loop operation.
September 12, 1921: Off-peak service operates only to Shellmound Park. Patrons transfer to/from Ellsworth Street trains.
February 17, 1924: Midday service on Saturdays and Sundays operated through to Oakland Pier.

February 1, 1925: Resume full service between Thousand Oaks and Oakland Pier.
March 25, 1933: Last day of service of Ninth Street-California Street loop operation.
December 1, 1938: Operation of line taken over by Interurban Electric Railway.
January 14, 1939: Last day of operation to Oakland Pier.
January 15, 1939: Begin operation to San Francisco via Bay Bridge. All trains display "5" disc.
February 26, 1940: Change daytime headway from 20 minutes to 40 minutes; change night and Sunday headway from 40 minutes to 45 minutes.
July 25, 1941: Last day of service.

Stations	Type[1]	Station no. and distance from S.F.	Remarks
OPERATED: February 3, 1912 to January 14, 1939			
OAKLAND PIER	T	3.5	
Oakland-16th Street	s	A5.5	
34th Street	f	A6.2	Called B St. before 11/01/14
Emeryville	s	A6.6	Called Emery before 9/12/21
Shellmound Park	s	K6.8	Regular stop until 9/12/21; off-peak terminal station 9/12/21 to 1/31/25
Shellmound Tower	f	A7.0	Called Richmond Junction until 1/01/14; called Shellmound Jct. 1/01/14 to 9/12/21
Ninth Street Junction	-	K7.1	Called Shellmound Jct. before 5/31/13
9th & Powell*	f	KA7.3	Station opened 8/01/13
Folsom (south side)	s	KA7.5	
Dalton Avenue	s	KA7.8	Also called 65th Street
Murray	f	KA8.1	Station opened 8/01/13
Heinz	s	KA8.2	Called Hawthorne before 1/15/28
Carlton Street*	s	KA8.5	
Channing Way (north side)	s	KA9.0	
University Avenue**	s	KA9.3	Also called University (West)
Virginia	s	KA9.6	
Gilman (south side)	s	KA10.0	
Harrison	f	KA10.2	Station opened 11/01/14
Buchanan*	f	KA10.7	Station opened 1/15/28
Albany**	s	KA10.9	
Evelyn Avenue	f	KA11.2	Station opened 11/01/14
Ramona Avenue	s	KA11.4	
Peralta Avenue*	s	KA11.7	Station opened 8/01/13
THOUSAND OAKS	T	K11.8	12.0 miles from San Francisco
OPERATED: January 15, 1939 to July 25, 1941			
SAN FRANCISCO	T	0.00	
West Junction	-	*K5.20*	
Bridge Yard	f	*K5.75*	
East Junction	-	*K6.11*	
26th Street Junction	-	*K6.89*	
34th Street Junction	-	*K7.25*	
34th Street	s	A7.26	
Emeryville	s	A7.52	
Shellmound Tower	f	A8.06	
9th Street Junction	-	*K8.07*	
9th & Powell	s	KA8.22	
Folsom (south side)	s	KA8.49	
Dalton Avenue*	s	KA8.75	
Ashby**	s	KA9.06	
Heinz (north side)	s	KA9.21	
Carlton Street*	s	KA9.47	
Channing Way (north side)	s	KA9.91	
University Avenue**	s	KA10.27	
Virginia Street*	s	KA10.58	
Gilman (south side)	s	KA10.94	
Harrison	f	KA11.20	
Buchanan*	f	KA11.65	
Albany**	s	KA11.90	
Evelyn Avenue	f	KA12.12	
Ramona Avenue	s	KA12.39	
Peralta Avenue*	s	KA12.64	
THOUSAND OAKS	T	K12.98	

[1]/ Station types: T : Terminal station
  s : All trains stop
  f : Flag stop
* Station stop is on near side of intersection in direction moving; at all other stations, stop is on far side unless noted.
** Trains make safety stop before crossing intersection.

18th STREET LINE

November 1, 1914: First day of service.
December 27, 1923: Inaugurate late evening franchise trip between 14th Street and 2nd and Webster Streets, using westerly track on Webster Street, to hold franchise of recently abandoned Webster Street line.
February 27, 1924: Inaugurate two morning tripper runs, except Sundays, from 19th Street to Oakland Pier. Inaugurate three evening tripper runs, except Saturdays and Sundays, from Oakland Pier to 14th Street.
November 8, 1926: Service rerouted by way of joint Key System-SP tracks on Webster Street between 20th and 14th Streets. All service on Franklin Street discontinued. Full service inaugurated to new terminal at 2nd and Webster Streets. Operate one morning tripper, except Sundays, from 19th and Webster to Oakland Pier. Operate three evening tripper runs, except Saturdays and Sundays, from Oakland Pier to 2nd and Webster.
February 1, 1930: Reduce evening trippers to two runs.
February 28, 1932: Discontinue operation of morning tripper runs between 19th Street and Oakland Pier. Inaugurate one midday, Saturdays only, tripper run between Oakland Pier and 2nd and Webster. Reduce evening tripper to one run. Evening tripper may turn at 12th Street if all passengers are discharged.
March 25, 1933: Last day of service.

Stations	Type[1]	Station no. and distance from S.F.	Remarks
OPERATED: November 1, 1914 to November 7, 1926			
OAKLAND PIER	T	3.5	
Oakland-16th Street	-	A5.5	
Wood Street	f	J5.6	
Peralta Street*	f	J5.8	
Adeline Street*	f	J6.3	
Filbert Street	f	J6.4	
Eastbound Single Track via 20th Street			
Market Street, south	s	J6.5	
West Street, south*	s	J6.7	
San Pablo Avenue	s	J6.9	
Telegraph Avenue, south	s	J7.1	
Broadway, south	s	J7.2	
Westbound Single Track via 21st Street[2]			
Market Street, north	s	JA6.6	
West Street, north*	s	JA6.8	
Grove Street	s	JA7.0	
Telegraph Avenue, north	s	JA7.2	
Broadway, north	s	JA7.3	
Double Track via Franklin Street			
20th Street	s	J7.3	0.2 mile from Broadway, north
19th Street	s	J7.4	
14th STREET	T	M7.1	7.6 miles from San Francisco
OPERATED: November 8, 1926 to March 25, 1933			
OAKLAND PIER	T	3.5	
Oakland-16th Street	-	A5.5	
Wood Street	f	J5.6	
Peralta Street*	f	J5.8	
Adeline Street*	f	J6.3	
Filbert Street	f	J6.4	
Eastbound Single Track via 20th Street			
Market Street, south	s	J6.5	
West Street, south*	s	J6.7	
Grove Street, south	s	J6.9	
Telegraph Avenue, south	s	J7.1	
Broadway, south	s	J7.2	
Westbound Single Track via 21st Street[2]			
Market Street, north	s	JA6.6	
West Street, north*	s	JA6.8	
San Pablo Avenue	s	JA6.9	
Grove Street, north	s	JA7.0	
Telegraph Avenue, north	s	JA7.2	
Broadway, north	s	JA7.3	
Double Track via Webster Street			
19th & Webster*	s	J7.4	0.3 mile from Broadway, north
14th & Webster**	s	J7.7	
12th & Webster	s	J7.9	
8th & Webster**	s	J8.1	
2nd & WEBSTER	T	J8.4	

[1]/ Station types: T : Terminal station
  s : All trains stop
  f : Flag stop
[2]/ Now called 22nd Street.
* Station stop is on near side of intersection in direction moving; at all other stations, stop is on far side.
** Trains make safety stop before crossing intersection.

SEVENTH STREET LINE

December 1, 1911: Initiate partial electric train service; trains alternate runs with steam locals. No electric train service operated during morning or evening hours.
December 13, 1911: Initiate full electric train service between Oakland Pier and Melrose. Initiate two evening express trains to Melrose; first stop is 23rd Avenue.
April 11, 1912: Alternate trains operate through to 55th Avenue.
December 29, 1912: Full service extended to Hillsdale.
October 1, 1913: Service extended from Hillsdale to Havenscourt where trains connect with Suburban Connection for Dutton Avenue.
September 12, 1921: Initiate morning express, Dutton Avenue to Oakland Pier. Train operates as part of Horseshoe Line; last stop is Seminary Avenue, then Fruitvale and all Horseshoe Line stops west thereof. Initiate two evening trains, Oakland Pier to Dutton Avenue, making all stops. Initiate one late night train, Oakland Pier to Dutton Avenue, making all stops.
February 17, 1924: Regular service extended from Havenscourt to Dutton Avenue. Initiate one morning express train, Dutton Avenue to Alameda Pier; last stop is Sather, then Alameda, North Park. Initiate one evening express train, Alameda Pier to Dutton Avenue; first stop is Alameda-North Park, then Sather and all stations east thereof. Inaugurate two evening express trains originating at Oakland Pier; operates to Melrose, the other to Havenscourt. First stop is East Oakland, then 23rd Avenue and all stations east thereof.
February 1, 1934: Add one evening eastward express train, Oakland Pier to Dutton Avenue. First stop is East Oakland, then 23rd Avenue, Fruitvale, Melrose, Seminary Ave., Havenscourt, 73rd Ave., Parker Ave., 82nd Ave., Sequoyah, 98th Ave., 108th Ave., Broadmoor, and Dutton Avenue.
December 1, 1938: Operation of line taken over by Interurban Electric Railway.
January 14, 1939: Last day of service to Oakland Pier.
January 15, 1939: Begin operation to San Francisco via Bay Bridge. Establish two morning westward express trains; last stop for earlier train is 23rd Avenue, that for later train is Melrose. Establish four eastward evening express trains; three make first stop 23rd Avenue, the other operates nonstop to Melrose. All express trains omit Sather, Fremont Way, 55th Ave., 86th Ave., 94th Ave., 101st Ave. Local and express trains display "2" disc.
March 26, 1939: Discontinue practice of separation of equipment eastward and consolidation of equipment westward at Seminary Avenue. All equipment operates through/from Dutton Avenue. Local trains display "2" disc; express trains display "7" disc.
February 26, 1940: Change daytime headways from 20 minutes to 30 minutes; change night and Sunday headways from 40 minutes to 45 minutes. Establish one morning local short trip to Melrose only. Establish two Saturday midday express trains, San Francisco to Dutton Avenue. Make first stop at Broadway, then East Oakland, 23rd Avenue and all express stops east thereof. One evening express train makes first stop at Broadwy; first stop for another is East Oakland; first stop for remaining two is 23rd Avenue.
March 21, 1941: Last day of service..

Stations	Type[1/]		Station no. and distance from S.F.	Remarks
	Local trains	Express trains		

OPERATED: December 1, 1911 to January 14, 1939

Stations	Local	Express	Station no.	Remarks
OAKLAND PIER	T	T	3.5	
West Oakland Jct.	-	-	*D4.7*	
Pine	s	-	G5.0	
Center Street	s	-	G5.4	
Adeline Street	s	-	G5.8	
Market Street	s	-	G6.2	
Broadway	s	-	G6.6	
Oak Street	s	-	G7.2	
Clinton	s	-	G7.8	
East Oakland	s	s	D8.2	
19th Avenue	c	-	D8.7	Station opened 1/15/28
23rd Avenue**	s	s	D9.0	
Fruitvale	s	s	D9.6	
Sather	s	s	D10.2	
Melrose	s	s	G10.8	
Fremont Way	s	s	G11.1	
Fairfax	s	s	G11.5	Called Bellvue until 12/29/12
55th Avenue	s	s	G11.7	Station closed 12/29/12; reopened 1/15/28
Seminary Ave.(west side)	s	s	G12.0	
Hillsdale Avenue	s	-	G12.2	Station closed 12/29/12
Havenscourt	s	s	G12.5	Station closed 12/30/12
Church Street	c	-	G12.7	Station opened 9/12/21, closed 1/15/28; also called Chevrolet.
73rd Avenue	f	f	G13.0	Also called Yoakum Ave.
Parker Avenue	s	s	G13.2	
82nd Avenue*	f	f	G13.5	
86th Avenue*	f	f	G13.7	Also called Oakland Ave.
Sequoyah*	s	s	G14.0	Also called Grand Ave.
94th Avenue*	f	f	G14.2	
98th Avenue*	f	f	G14.4	Also called Jones St.
101st Avenue	f	f	G14.6	
103rd Ave. Junc.	-	-	*G14.7*	
108th Avenue	f	f	G15.1	
Broadmoor	s	s	G15.3	
DUTTON AVENUE***	T	T	G15.5	

OPERATED: January 15, 1939 to March 21, 1941

Stations	Local	Express	Station no.	Remarks
SAN FRANCISCO	T	T	0.00	
West Junction	-	-	*K5.20*	
Bridge Yard	f	-	K5.75	
East Junction	-	-	*K6.11*	
26th St. Junc.	-	-	*K6.89*	
22nd St. Junc.	-	-	*A7.23*	
Oakland-16th Street	s	-	A7.53	
Pine	s	-	G8.45	
Center Street	s	-	G8.85	
Adeline Street	s	-	G9.22	
Market Street	s	-	G9.57	
Broadway	s	c	G10.09	Express stop after 2/26/40
Oak Street	s	-	G10.60	
Clinton	s	-	G11.18	
East Oakland	s	c	D11.67	Express stop after 2/26/40
19th Avenue	s	-	D12.15	Flag stop before 2/26/40
23rd Avenue**	s	c	D12.53	
Fruitvale	s	s	D13.20	
Sather	s	-	D13.67	
Melrose	s	s	G14.27	
Fremont Way	s	-	G14.59	
Fairfax	s	s	G14.92	
55th Avenue	s	-	G15.14	
Seminary Ave.(west side)	s	s	G15.39	
Havenscourt	s	s	G16.01	
73rd Avenue	f	f	G16.41	
Parker Avenue	s	-	G16.67	
82nd Avenue*	f	f	G16.94	
86th Avenue*	f	-	G17.18	
Sequoyah*	s	s	G17.47	Also called 90th Avenue
94th Avenue*	f	-	G17.63	
98th Avenue*	f	f	G17.87	
101st Avenue	f	-	G18.15	
103rd Ave. Junc.	-	-	*G18.26*	
108th Avenue	f	-	G18.50	
Broadmoor	s	-	G18.78	
DUTTON AVENUE***	T	T	G19.03	

1/ Station types: T : Terminal station
　　　　　　　　s : All trains stop
　　　　　　　　f : Flag stop
　　　　　　　　c : Conditional station, only certain trains stop.
* Station stop is on near side of intersection in direction moving; at other stations, stop is on far side unless noted.
** Trains make safety stop before crossing intersection.
*** Stop 50 feet west of west curb line, Dutton Avenue.

SUBURBAN CONNECTION

October 1, 1913: First day of service. Trains operate on 40-minute headway, connecting at Havenscourt with Seventh Street line trains from Oakland Pier.

February 16, 1924: Last day of service. Trains of Seventh Street line operate over this line beginning February 17, 1924.

Stations	Type[1/]	Station no. and distance from S.F.	Remarks
MELROSE	T	G10.8	
Fremont Way	s	G11.1	
Fairfax	s	G11.5	
Seminary Avenue (west side)	s	G12.0	
Havenscourt	s	G12.5	Terminal station for most trains before 9:00 p.m.
73rd Avenue	f	G13.0	Also known as Yoakum Ave.
82nd Avenue*	f	G13.5	
86th Avenue*	f	G13.7	Also known as Oakland Ave.
Sequoyah*	s	G14.0	Called 90th Ave. before 11/01/14; called Sequoia 11/01/14 to 9/12/21
98th Avenue*	f	G14.4	Also known as Jones St.
103rd Avenue Junction	-	*G14.7*	
105th Avenue	f	G14.9	
108th Avenue	f	G15.1	Station opened 9/12/21
Broadmoor	s	G15.3	
DUTTON AVENUE**	T	G15.5	

1/ Station types: T : Terminal station
　　　　　　　　s : All trains stop
　　　　　　　　f : Flag stop
* Station stop is on near side of intersection in direction moving; at all other stations, stop is on far side.
** Stop 50 feet west of west curb line of Dutton Avenue.

HORSESHOE LINE
OAKLAND PIER, ALAMEDA AND MELROSE LINE

December 19, 1911: First day of service. Trains operate between Oakland Pier and Alameda Pier via Fruitvale between 7:59 a.m. and 4:47 p.m. At other times, trains turn at Mastick. Certain trains make franchise trip on 8th Street between Mastick Jct. and Encinal Jct.

August 1, 1913: Discontinue all service on this line between 10 a.m. and 4 p.m. and also after 8 p.m. All service to Alameda Pier discontinued except for one early-morning trip from Melrose to Alameda Pier and return to Oakland Pier. All remaining trains of this line turn at Pacific Jct., Mastick, or Alameda. Inaugurate two non-revenue shop trains between Oakland Pier and West Alameda.

October 1, 1913: Inaugurate midday and night service between Fruitvale and Alameda-North Park designated as Alameda Swing Service line. Trains connect at Fruitvale with Seventh Street trains. Morning and afternoon service on Horseshoe line is unchanged.

December 1, 1913: Reestablish separate midday and late-night service between Oakland Pier and Pacific Jct., designated as the Oakland Pier-Alameda and Pacific Junction line. Discontinue all service on the Alameda Swing Service line. Morning and afternoon service on the Horseshoe line is unchanged.

November 1, 1914: Combine all runs between Oakland Pier and Alameda and Pacific Jct. into Horseshoe line.

September 12, 1921: Initiate one early morning run from Melrose to Dutton Avenue and return to Oakland Pier. Make no stops eastward; last westward stop is Seminary Avenue, then stop at Fruitvale and all regular Horseshoe stations west thereof.

February 16, 1924: Last day of operation of early morning run from Melrose to Dutton Avenue and return to Oakland Pier.

January 15, 1928: Change designation of line to Oakland Pier, Alameda and Melrose line. Discontinue all regularly scheduled revenue runs between Oakland Pier and Alameda points. Establish early morning connecting service between Fruitvale and Pacific Jct. Establish two morning trains, daily except Sunday, to Oakland Pier from Melrose, one from Alameda, North Park, and one from Fruitvale. Establish one Saturday only midday train, Oakland Pier to Melrose. Establish one daily except Saturday and Sunday afternoon train from Oakland Pier to Alameda, North Park. Establish several non-revenue runs (tie-up of equipment, shop trains, etc.) between Oakland Pier, East Oakland, Fruitvale, and West Alameda.

February 28, 1932: Extend run of afternoon train from Alameda, North Park to Melrose.

February 1, 1934: Discontinue one morning train from Melrose to Oakland Pier. Discontinue afternoon Alameda, North Park, and Melrose train.

December 1, 1938: Operation of line taken over by Interurban Electric Railway.

January 14, 1939: Last day of service.

Special Note:

The Horseshoe Line, and its later designation, Oakland Pier, Alameda, and Melrose Line, was a complex assortment of at least 29 separate routings and sub-routings during the 28 years that the line was operated. In the beginning, the line was designed to take Alameda patrons to and from main line trains at Oakland Pier. After 1928, however, revenue trains of this line were operated only during morning and evening peak hours between Oakland Pier and Fruitvale, Alameda (North Park), or Melrose.

Initially, service on this line operated from Oakland Pier to Alameda Pier via Fruitvale Bridge. This routing resulted, prior to 1914, in trains traveling in two directions while on a single run (i.e., eastward from Oakland Pier to Lincoln Junction and westward beyond) and thus having double train numbers (i.e., Train No. 308-2215). This practice was discarded on November 1, 1914, and thereafter, trains from Oakland Pier carried even train numbers, regardless of direction traveled, and trains toward Oakland Pier carried odd train numbers.

After January 14, 1928, most trains on the Oakland Pier, Alameda, and Melrose Line were deadheads, shop trains, and other non-revenue runs. The few revenue runs that continued were limited to peak hour service. These were: westward morning trips (odd-numbered trains), eastward midday Saturday trips (even-numbered trains), and eastward late afternoon trips, except Saturdays and Sundays (even-numbered trains). No revenue trips were operated on Sundays.

In addition to revenue trains operating from Oakland Pier, the Horseshoe Line (and its later equivalent) carried a number of connecting revenue runs. (These included early morning trains from Melrose or Fruitvale to Pacific Junction and return and the "owl" service performed by the Alameda Loop trains to and from their Seventh Street train connection at Fruitvale.

There were still other special routings for Horseshoe trains. These are described individually below:

Shop Trains. Regularly scheduled trains between Oakland Pier and the West Alameda shops were operated from August 1, 1913 to January 14, 1939. The trains were operated for the purpose of transporting employes, cars, and materials (brake shoes, etc.) between the two terminals. At first, the service consisted of two trains daily in each direction. Service was changed on January 15, 1928, to two trains from Oakland Pier and one returning. Service was further reduced to only one trip in each direction on March 26, 1933. From February 17, 1924, to January 14, 1928, the two eastward shop trains carried U.S. Mail between Oakland Pier and Alameda-North Park. Two eastward shop trains made franchise runs on the "Sather leg" of the Fruitvale wye from September 12, 1921, to February 16, 1924. One eastward shop train made a franchise run on 8th Street from the time that the streetcar service was abandoned (December 27, 1923) until the track was removed.

Special Occasion Train. Like trains of other lines operating in Alameda, trains of the Horseshoe Line periodically were governed by Supplement "X" to Time Table No. 2. When this supplement was in effect, Horseshoe trains operated on a 20-minute headway between Oakland Pier and Alameda Pier until 6:59 p.m.; thereafter, trains operated to Alameda (N. Park) or Melrose until 2:03 a.m.

Alameda Swing Service. On August 1, 1913, service on the Horseshoe Line was reduced to only morning and evening rush hours. Trains of this line operated only between Oakland Pier and Pacific Junction, except for one early-morning run from Alameda Pier to Oakland Pier. To fulfill midday and evening service, operation of the Alameda Swing Service was begun on October 1, 1913. Trains on this latter line connected with those of the Seventh Street Line at Fruitvale and operated only to Alameda (N. Park). On December 1, 1913, the Alameda Swing Service was extended on both ends so that it operated between Oakland Pier and Pacific Junction, as did the Horseshoe trains. Even though there was all-day service between Oakland Pier and Pacific Junction, there were actually two lines operating. Horseshoe trains continued to be operated only during morning and evening rush hours. Trains on the Oakland Pier-Alameda and Pacific Junction Line operated during other hours. This mode of operation continued in effect until November 1, 1914, when Horseshoe trains again operated at all hours.

18th Street Service. From December 8 to 17, 1914, the Fruitvale Bridge was closed for repairs. This closure resulted in the Horseshoe Line being split into two separate operations. One portion operated during peak hours between Oakland Pier and Melrose via the Seventh Street Line, and a total of 15 trips was made on this portion each day.

To provide service to Alameda, a most interesting routing was used. Trains operated from Oakland Pier via Oakland-16th Street, the 18th Street Line, 14th Street station, Webster Street, Harrison Bridge, and Lincoln Avenue to Alameda (N. Park). Tie-ups were at High Street, and the first morning run made a round trip between High Street and Alameda Pier, operating via Alameda (N. Park). The last night trip on this line went from Alameda Pier to Alameda (N. Park) and then continued around the Fernside Loop to High Street. The service was operated on a 90-minute headway throughout the day. Stops were made at Oakland-16th St., 14th St., 2nd and Webster, and all suburban stations in Alameda. Eastward trains also stopped at stations along the 18th St. Line to receive passengers for Alameda; westward trains stopped at these stations to discharge passengers.

Stations	Type[1/]	Station no. and distance from S.F.	Remarks
OAKLAND PIER	T	3.5	
West Oakland Junction	-	D4.7	
Cedar Street	c	G4.8	Station closed 5/31/13
Pine	c	G5.0	Station opened for this line 5/12/21
Adeline Street	c	G5.8	" " " " "
Broadway	s	G6.6	
East Oakland	s	D8.2	
19th Avenue	f	D8.7	Station opened 9/12/21
23rd Avenue	s	D9.0	Station opened for this line 8/01/13
Fruitvale	s	D9.6	
Sather	s	D10.2	
MELROSE[2/]	T	G10.8	
Fruitvale Power House	f	HA9.7	Also called Fernside Power House
Pearl Street	c	HA9.4	Station opened 2/28/32
Lincoln Junction	-	H9.3	Called Blanding Junction before 6/01/13
Alameda, North Park	s	H9.0	Called Alameda before 9/12/21; Terminal station after 1/15/28
Willow Street	s	H8.5	
Grand Street	s	H8.1	
Stanton	s	H7.9	
Bay Street	s	H7.6	
Mastick	s	H7.2	
Mastick Junction	-	H7.1	
Webster Street	s	H6.9	
Fifth Street	s	H6.6	
Third Street	s	H6.2	
Pacific Junction	-	MA6.0	Terminal station 8/01/13 to 1/14/28
West Alameda	f	MA5.2	
Alameda Junction	-	M5.0	
ALAMEDA PIER	T	3.0	19.7 miles from Oakland Pier

1/ Station types: T : Terminal station
    s : All trains stop
    f : Flag stop
    c : Conditional station, only certain trains stop.
2/ Trains of this line operating east of Melrose stop at regular stations of Seventh Street and Suburban Connection lines.

WEBSTER STREET LINE

June 20, 1911: First day of service.
December 26, 1923: Last day of service.

Stations	Type[1/]	Station no. and distance from S.F.	Remarks
ALAMEDA PIER	T	3.0	
Alameda Junction	-	M5.0	
West Alameda	f	M5.2	Station opened 8/01/13
Webster Street	f	M6.0	" " 8/01/13, also known as United Engineering Co.
San Antonio Junction	-	I8.7	
7th & Webster Streets	s	M6.7	
14th STREET	T	M7.1	

1/ Station types: T : Terminal station
    s : All trains stop
    f : Flag stop

ENCINAL AVENUE LINE

June 1, 1911: First day of service between Alameda Pier and High Street.
August 1, 1911: Begin operation of Alameda loop service in conjunction with Lincoln Avenue line.
December 1, 1938: Operation of line taken over by Interurban Electric Railway.
January 14, 1939: Last day of service to Alameda Pier.
January 15, 1939: Begin operation to San Francisco via Bay Bridge. Establish daytime headway of 40 minutes, alternating with trains of Lioncoln Avenue line, thus providing Alameda with 20-minute service. Establish night and Sunday headways of 80 minutes, alternating with trains of Lincoln Avenue line. Operate two morning westward (daily except Sundays) and one evening eastward (daily except Saturdays and Sundays) train consolidated with Lincoln Avenue train between Fruitvale and San Francisco. All trains display "4" disc.
February 12, 1939: Change Sunday headway from 80 minutes to 60 minutes; no change in night headways.
March 26, 1939: Discontinue morning consolidated Encinal-Lincoln Avenue trains. Add one evening eastward (daily except Saturdays and Sundays) consolidated Encinal-Lincoln Avenue train. Eastward trains display "4" disc; westward trains display "6" disc.
February 26, 1940: Change daytime headway from 40 minutes to 60 minutes; no change in night or Sunday headways. Change tie-up location from High Street to Fruitvale. Establish one eastward midday (Saturday only) consolidated Encinal-Lincoln Avenue trains. Add one evening eastward (daily except Saturdays and Sundays) consolidated Encinal-Lincoln Avenue train. Eastward trains display "4" disc; westward trains display disc to correspond to next eastward trip.
January 18, 1941: Last day of service.

Stations	Type[1/]	Station no. and distance from S.F.	Remarks
OPERATED: June 1, 1911 to January 14, 1939			
ALAMEDA PIER	T	3.0	
Alameda Junction	-	M5.0	
West Alameda	c	MA5.2	
Pacific Junction	-	MA6.0	
Pacific Avenue	c	MA6.1	Station opened 8/01/13
5th Street	s	MA6.8	
Webster Street*	s	MA7.1	
Encinal Junction	-	MA7.4	
Caroline	s	MA7.5	Called Encinal Park before 1/15/28
Morton Street	s	MA7.9	
Chestnut Street	s	MA8.4	
Walnut Street	s	MA8.7	
Park Street, south	s	MA9.0	
Versailles Avenue	s	MA9.4	
HIGH STREET, SOUTH**	T	MA9.7	
OPERATED: January 15, 1939 to January 18, 1941			
SAN FRANCISCO	T	0.00	
West Junction	-	K5.20	
Bridge Yard	f	K5.75	
East Junction	-	K6.11	
26th Street Junction	-	K6.89	
22nd Street Junction	-	A7.23	
Oakland-16th Street	f	A7.53	Westward trains detrain; eastward trains entrain. Conditional stop only after 2/26/40
7th & Broadway	c	G10.09	" " " " "
Fruitvale	c	D13.20	
Fernside Power House	f	H13.60	
Blanding Junction	-	H13.72	
Fernside	s	MA13.88	
North High Street**	s	MA14.29	
Lincoln	s	MA14.78	
South High Street**	s	MA15.22	
Versailles Avenue	s	MA15.58	
South Park Street**	s	MA15.91	
Walnut Street	s	MA16.21	
Chestnut Street	s	MA16.57	
Morton Street	s	MA17.03	
Caroline	s	MA17.47	
Webster Street*	s	MA17.88	
5th Street	s	MA18.17	
Pacific Avenue	s	MA18.84	
Pacific Junction	-	MA18.92	
WEST ALAMEDA***	T	H18.02	19.76 miles from San Francisco

1/ Station types: T : Terminal station
    s : All trains stop
    f : Flag stop
    c : Conditional station, only certain trains stop.
  * Station stop is on near side of intersection in direction moving; at all other stations, stop is on far side.
 ** Trains make safety stop before crossing intersection.
*** Stop clear of shop crossing.

LINCOLN AVENUE LINE

August 1, 1911: First day of service. Operated from Alameda Pier to Alameda and Fernside Loop via Webster Junction. Runs combined with Encinal Avenue line.
August 1, 1913: Rerouted via Pacific Junction.
September 12, 1921: Establish two eastward morning trains via Webster Junction and stopping at Tynan daily except Sunday. On Sundays, operate via Pacific Jct. Establish one midday train on Saturdays operating from Alameda to pier via Webster Jct. and stopping at Tynan; on other days operates via Pacific Jct. Establish one evening train, daily except Saturday and Sunday, operating from Alameda to pier via Webster Junction and stopping at Tynan. On other days, operate via Pacific Jct.
January 15, 1928: Discontinue all service via Webster Junction.
December 1, 1938: Operation of line taken over by Interurban Electric Railway.
January 14, 1939: Last day of operation to Alameda Pier.
January 15, 1939: Begin operation to San Francisco via Bay Bridge. Establish daytime headway of 40 minutes, alternating with trains of Encinal Avenue line, thus providing Alameda with 20-minute service. Establish night and Sunday headway of 80 minutes, alternating with trains of Encinal Avenue

line. Operate two morning westward (daily except Sundays) and one evening eastward (daily except Saturdays and Sundays) train consolidated with Encinal Avenue train between Fruitvale and San Francisco. All trains display "4" disc.

February 12, 1939: Change Sunday headway from 80 minutes to 60 minutes; no change in night headways.

March 26, 1939: Discontinue morning consolidated Lincoln-Encinal Avenue trains. Add one evening eastward (daily except Saturdays and Sundays) consolidated Lincoln-Encinal Avenue train. Eastward trains display "6" disc; westward trains display disc to correspond to next eastward trip.

February 26, 1940: Change daytime headway from 40 minutes to 60 minutes; no change in night or Sunday headways. Change tie-up location from High Street to Fruitvale. Establish two eastward midday (Saturday only) consolidated Lincoln-Encinal Avenue trains. Add one evening eastward (daily except Saturdays and Sundays) consolidated Lincoln Encinal Avenue train. Eastward trains display "6" disc; westward trains display disc to correspond to next eastward trip.

January 18, 1941: Last day of service.

Stations	Type[1]	Station no. and distance from S.F.	Remarks
OPERATED: August 1, 1911 to July 31, 1913 for all trains and September 12, 1921 to January 14, 1928 for certain trains			
ALAMEDA PIER	T	3.0	
Alameda Junction	-	M5.0	
West Alameda	f	M5.2	Closed for this line 7/31/13
Webster Street	s	M6.0	" " " " 7/31/13
San Antonio Junction	-	I8.7	
Tynan	s	I8.3	Station opened 9/12/21; station closed 1/14/28
Mastick Junction	-	H7.1	
Mastick	s	H7.2	
Bay Street	s	H7.6	
Grand Street	s	H8.1	
Willow Street	s	H8.5	
Alameda, Park Street North	s	H9.0	
Lincoln Junction	-	H9.3	Called Blanding Junction before 6/01/13
Fernside**	f	H9.5	
High Street, north**	f	H9.9	
Lincoln Park	s	H10.4	
HIGH STREET	T	MA9.7	
OPERATED: August 1, 1913 to January 14, 1939			
ALAMEDA PIER	T	3.0	
Alameda Airport	f	MA3.7	Station opened 2/28/32
Alameda Junction	-	M5.0	
West Alameda	f	MA5.2	
Pacific Junction	-	MA6.0	
Third Street	s	H6.2	Station opened 11/01/14
Fifth Street	s	H6.6	
Webster Street**	s	H6.9	
Mastick Junction	-	H7.1	
Mastick	s	H7.2	
Bay Street	s	H7.6	
Encinal Terminals	s	H7.9	Station opened 11/01/14; called Stanton before 1/15/28
Grand Street	s	H8.1	
Willow Street	s	H8.5	
North Park	s	H9.0	Called Alameda before 9/12/21
Lincoln Junction	-	H9.3	
Fernside**	s	H9.5	
North High Street**	s	H9.9	
Lincoln	s	H10.4	Called Lincoln Park before 1/15/28
HIGH STREET	T	MA9.7	
OPERATED: January 15, 1939 to January 18, 1941			
SAN FRANCISCO	T	0.00	
West Junction	-	K5.20	
Bridge Yard	f	K5.75	
East Junction	-	K6.11	
26th St. Junction	-	K6.89	
22nd St. Junction	-	A7.23	
Oakland-16th Street	f	A7.53	Westward trains detrain; eastward trains entrain
Broadway	c	G10.09	Station opened for this line 2/26/40
Fruitvale	c	D13.20	" " " " " "
Fernside Power House	f	H13.60	
Blanding Junction	-	H13.72	
Pearl Street	f	H13.81	
North Park*	s	H14.21	
Willow	s	H14.75	
Grand	s	H15.14	
Encinal Terminals	s	H15.40	
Bay	s	H15.69	
Mastick	s	H16.09	
Webster Street**	s	H16.34	
Fifth Street	s	H16.71	
Third Street	s	H16.99	
Pacific Junction	-	H17.18	
WEST ALAMEDA***	T	H18.02	

[1] Station types: T : Terminal station
s : All trains stop
f : Flag stop
c : Conditional station, only certain trains stop.
* Stop clear of Park Street
** Trains make safety stop before crossing intersection
*** Stop clear of shop crossing

Streetcars

PENINSULAR LINE

March 27, 1912: First day of service; operated between Oakland-16th Street and 14th and Franklin Streets. Suburban cars used on this line; trains operate as Second Class.

June 1, 1913: Trains of this line changed to First Class.

August 1, 1913: First day of service to Alameda. Streetcars replace suburban cars. Streetcars operated between Oakland-16th Street and 14th and Franklin Streets and also Oakland-16th Street and Alameda. Alameda loop operated only in clockwise direction, viz.: from Mastick via Lincoln Ave., Fernside Blvd., Encinal Ave., 8th St. and to Mastick.

September 1, 1913: Begin operation of Alameda loop in both directions. Alternate cars take different loop directions.

September 12, 1921: Begin operation of late-night franchise car along Webster Street from 12th to 14th Streets.

December 26, 1923: Last day of service to Alameda.

March 20, 1926: Last day of service between Oakland-16th St. and 14th and Franklin Streets.

Route:
Peninsular Line cars operate between Oakland-16th Street Station and 14th Street Station via 18th Street line, Oakland-Alameda streetcars operate from Oakland-16th Street Station to Lincoln Park, Alameda, via trackage of the 18th Street line, and Webster Street line to Webster Junction and thence to Mastick and Alameda loop via 8th Street, Encinal Avenue line, and Lincoln Avenue line. Streetcars stop at all SP Co. stations, at near side of all intersections, and at other locations where "Car Stop" signs are displayed.

Specials

BERKELEY MAIL TRAINS

December 1, 1923: First day of service. Operate 11 trips, Oakland Pier to Berkeley and return; 2 trips, Oakland Pier to Oakland-16th St. and return.

January 15, 1928: Discontinue taking American Express Company cars to and from Berkeley.

March 26, 1933: First morning eastward mail train routed to ground level track at Oakland-16th St. via ramp and balloon track formerly used by 18th St. line trains and streetcars.

August 1, 1937: Discontinue use of ground level facilities at Oakland-16th Street.

November 30, 1938: Last day of service.

Route:
From Oakland Pier to Oakland-16th Street and Berkeley via Shattuck Avenue line. Mail trains do not carry passengers. Mail trains depart Oakland Pier between California and Ninth Street line trains (after May 26, 1933: ahead of Ninth Street train). Mail trains arrive Oakland Pier following Ninth Street train.

Rules, Notices, and Special Instructions

Included at the back of most railroad operating timetables is a section entitled "Special Instructions." The Oakland, Alameda and Berkeley Lines and the Interurban Electric were no exception to this practice. This section contained various rules and other pertinent information relating to the operation of the system. Information contained therein ranged from Rule 30, which said that the gong must be sounded before equipment is moved, to data on interlocking plants, drawbridges, normal position of switches, and speed restrictions. Also included were rules for making air brake tests and use of main tracks as well as a host of miscellaneous instructions.

The following section contains some "Special Instructions" excerpted from two typical operating timetables. The first, representative of the years of Southern Pacific operation, is dated February 28, 1932. At that time, each line was operating with its own numbered timetable. For example, the timetable issued for that date for the Ellsworth Street line was No. 7, while that for the Shattuck Avenue line was No. 8, and the one for the 18th Street line was No. 9. The second excerpt is from Interurban Electric Time Table No. 1, dated January 15, 1939. It presents detailed instructions for operating trains across the Bay Bridge. Handling the Big Red trains was a highly technical job demanding a thorough knowledge of hundreds of rules, regulations and operating procedures. A glance at these instructions will help the reader gain an appreciation of the complexity of the system.

SOUTHERN PACIFIC COMPANY : WESTERN DIVISION ELECTRIC LINES
Time Table Nos. 7, 8, and 9
February 28, 1932

RULE 17 (c). Westward trains approaching Alameda Pier dim headlights to avoid interference with Ferry Boats.

RULE 19. Except in foggy weather, markers will not be used on electric trains during daylight hours.

RULE 33. When crossing flagmen find it necessary to leave their post of duty for a short time and no special device is provided, they will display a yellow flag by day and a yellow light by night, which will indicate to train and enginemen that crossing is temporarily protected by flagman, and train and enginemen will be governed accordingly.

RULE 83 (a). Only trains terminating at Oakland Pier and Alameda Pier will register.

RULE 91. Outside of block signal limits, trains in the same direction must keep not less than 1200 feet apart, except when closing up at stations.

RULE 93. All Electric Lines are within Yard Limits.

RULE 98. Railroad crossings not interlocked: (a) Parker Street on Ninth Street Line between Carlton and Channing Way, Berkeley. Steam trains or engines must be protected before crossing Ninth St. Line.
(b) Key System Line at Ward Street, Berkeley. Trains and yard engines using Ward Street Spur must be protected before crossing Key System track.
Drawbridge Interlocked: Fruitvale Ave. between Fruitvale and Lincoln Junction.

RULE 99. At points specified below, FIRST CLASS TRAINS need not comply with Rule 99, except in foggy weather; responsibility for collision rests with following train.

(a) Shattuck Ave. Line—Between University Ave. and Bancroft Way.
(b) Shattuck Ave. Line—Oakland Sixteenth St., mail trains only.
(c) Seventh St. Line—Between Washington and Broadway.
(d) Seventh St. Line—1000 feet east and west of Seminary Ave.
(e) Lincoln Ave. Line—Between North Park St. and Foley St., Alameda.
(f) Encinal Ave. Line—Between High St. and Pole 535, 220 feet east of High Street.

RULE 104. THE NORMAL POSITION OF SWITCHES AT THE END OF DOUBLE TRACK AND AT JUNCTIONS WILL BE AS FOLLOWS:

Location	Normal Position
Alameda—Mastick, Junction	
Oakland—103rd Ave., Junction	For Lincoln Ave. Main Track.
Oakland—2nd & Webster, end double track	For Dutton Ave. Main Track.
Oakland—20th & Webster, Junction eastward track	For westward movement.
Oakland—20th & Webster, Junction westward track	Loose point.
Oakland—14th & Webster, Junction eastward track	Trolley selection.
Oakland—14th & Webster, Junction westward track	Trolley selection.
	Loose point.

OIL BUFFER SPRING SWITCHES ARE LOCATED AT THE FOLLOWING POINTS:

Location	Normal Position
(a) East end crossover Seminary Ave., Seventh St. Line	Crossover movement
(b) End double track Derby, Ellsworth Line	Westward movement
(c) East end of Siding Ramona, Ninth St. Line	Westward movement
(d) West end of Siding Ramona, Ninth St. Line	Eastward movement
(e) End of double track Albany, Ninth St. Line	Westward movement
(f) End of double track, Thousand Oaks, Ninth St. Line	Eastward movement
(g) End of double track, Contra Costa, Shattuck Ave. Line	Westward movement

These switches should only be split by electric equipment and only when lined in their normal position as they are equipped with single-acting oil buffers.

CROSSOVERS AND SWITCHES EQUIPPED WITH SPRINGS

Location	Normal Position
(a) West end of crossover Pole 3590, Addison St., Berkeley, Shattuck Ave. Line	Main track
(b) Junction switch, westward track Thousand Oaks, Berkeley, California St. Line	Main track
(c) West end of crossover, Melrose, Seventh St. Line	Main track
(d) West end of crossover, Seminary Ave., Seventh St. Line	Crossover movement
(e) West end of crossover, West of Havenscourt, Seventh St. Line	Main track
(f) West end of crossover, Broadmoor, Seventh St. Line	Crossover movement
(g) East end of crossover, Oak St., Alameda, Lincoln Ave. Line	Main track
(h) East end of crossover, 3rd and Pacific, Lincoln Ave. Line Alameda	Main track

USE OF MAIN TRACKS.

Main tracks between Oakland Pier and Westerly end of the elevated tracks approaching 16th St. Station, and between Oakland Pier and Bay Street (West Oakland), numbering from north, are designated 1, 2, 3, 4, 5, 6, 7, 8, 9 and 10, and used as follows:

No. 3—Westward electric trains, via Oakland (Sixteenth Street).
No. 4—Eastward electric trains, via Oakland (Sixteenth Street).
No. 5—Westward electric trains of Seventh Street line.
No. 6—Eastward electric trains of Seventh Street line.

Main tracks between Oakland (Sixteenth Street) and Shell Mound Tower, numbering from the Bay, are designated as 1, 2, 3, 4, 5 and 6, and used as follows:

No. 5—Westward electric trains, via Oakland (Sixteenth Street).
No. 6—Eastward electric trains, via Oakland (Sixteenth Street).

Main tracks between East Oakland and Sather numbering from north are designated 1, 2, 3 and 4.

No. 1—Westward electric trains Seventh Street line.
No. 2—Eastward electric trains Seventh Street line.

Main tracks between Alameda Pier and West Alameda, numbering from the north, are designated as 1, 2, 3 and 4, and used as follows:

No. 1—Westward trains Trolley deenergized between bridges 6 and 8 and 60 feet east of bridge 37.
No. 2—Eastward trains Trolley deenergized between bridges 6 and 8 and 60 feet east of bridge 37.

No. 3—Westward trains via Pacific and Encinal Avenue.
No. 4—Eastward trains Pacific and Encinal Avenues.

On lines of light travel, except Seventh Street line west of Havenscourt in non-peak periods, train and enginemen will treat all stations as flag stops. Trainmen must announce stations in ample time to avoid carrying passengers by.

In case of power interruption signal operator may display "S" sign in which case trains must not exceed series position of controller. When signs are removed, normal speed may be resumed.

Station stops should be made with middle of train under or opposite station sign unless instructions on schedule page indicate otherwise.

Headlights of motors standing at end of wharf at Oakland Pier and Alameda Pier must be dimmed when steamer is entering slip. Headlights of eastward trains must be out while standing at Oakland Pier and dimmed when ready to leave.

INTERURBAN ELECTRIC RAILWAY COMPANY
Time Table No. 1
January 15, 1939

Except as the Rules and Regulations of the Transportation Department, Southern Pacific Company, (Pacific Lines), effective June 15, 1930, Rules and Regulations governing Care and Operation of Air Brake and Air Signal Apparatus, Southern Pacific Company, (Pacific Lines), effective May 1, 1926 and Rules and Regulations for the Operation of Trains under Continuous Automatic Cab Signal and Speed Control System, Interurban Electric Ry. Co., effective January 1, 1939, may be modified, supplemented or superseded, those Rules and Regulations remain in full force and effect for the government of the railroad operated by the Interurban Electric Railway Company.

The operation of that portion of the railroad comprising the westward main track from West Junction to San Francisco, the eastward main track from San Francisco to East Junction, crossovers between main tracks within those limits, and all tracks within San Francisco Terminal is assigned to the supervision of the Superintendent—Bridge Railway at San Francisco.

RULE 17 (C). When the rules require headlights to be displayed, they will be dimmed in the following territory:

(a) On the San Francisco-Oakland Bay Bridge (except through the tunnel on Yerba Buena Island), westward from West Junction to San Francisco and eastward from San Francisco to east end of Bridge at catenary bridge No. 1.

(b) Seventh Street Line—between Pine Street and Fallon Street.

(c) Shattuck Avenue Line—between Ward Street and Vine Street.

(d) Ninth Street Line—between Albany and Thousand Oaks.

RULE 19. Electric cars are equipped with red bulls-eye lights on ends of car. They will serve as markers and, except in foggy weather, will not be lighted during daylight hours.

RULE 30. The gong must be sounded before equipment is moved. Enginemen must, at all times, place themselves in a position in the cab which will assure them the best vision of the track ahead and the approach of pedestrians and vehicles, and must assume a standing position before moving equipment and remain standing until equipment has moved at least 30 feet.

RULE 83 (A). Only trains terminating at San Francisco will register and then only on the initial trip of each run.

RULE 91. Outside of block system limits or train control territory, trains in the same direction must keep not less than 1200 feet apart, except when closing up at stations.

RULE 93. Will not apply.
All tracks of Interurban Electric Ry. Co., are within yard limits.
Within yard limits main track may be used, protecting as prescribed by Rule 99.

RULE 98. RAILROAD CROSSINGS AT GRADE NOT INTERLOCKED.

Southern Pacific Company at Parker Street on Ninth Street Line between Carlton Street and Channing Way. Southern Pacific trains and engines using crossing will protect.

Southern Pacific Company at Pacific Avenue on Encinal Avenue Line at Pacific Junction. Southern Pacific trains and engines using crossing will protect.

DRAWBRIDGES INTERLOCKED

Fruitvale Ave., Drawbridge—Tidal Canal, Oakland Inner Harbor.

RULE 99. At points specified below, FIRST-CLASS TRAINS need not comply with Rule 99, except in foggy weather. All trains will move with caution between these points.

(a) Shattuck Avenue Line—Between University Avenue and Bancroft Way.
(b) Seventh Street Line—Between Broadway and Washington.
(c) Seventh Street Line—1000 feet east and west of Seminary Avenue.
(d) Lincoln Avenue Line—Between North Park Street and Foley Street.
(e) Encinal Avenue Line—Between High Street and Pole 540 east of High Street crossover.
(f) Encinal Avenue Line—Between West Alameda and crossover 1150 feet west.

RULE 104. THE NORMAL POSITION OF SWITCHES AT THE END OF DOUBLE TRACK AND AT JUNCTIONS WILL BE AS FOLLOWS:

Location	Normal Position
Alameda-Mastick Junction	For Lincoln Avenue Main Track
Alameda-Pacific Junction	For Lincoln Avenue Main Track
Oakland-103rd Avenue Junction	For Dutton Avenue Main Track

RULE 107. When a train is at a station, trains on the other track must not enter the station until the first named train and the approaching train.

Westward trains have preference to stations between 12:01 A.M. and 12:01 P.M., and eastward trains have preference between 12:01 P.M. and 12:01 A.M.

On the Seventh Street Line an ordinance prohibits two trains occupying tracks at the same time between a point 100 feet east of Broadway and a point 100 feet west of Washington Street. If necessary for two trains to occupy this territory simultaneously, only one train should be moving.

Electric trains have preference over Southern Pacific trains at Fruitvale.

RULE 206 (A). Will not apply.
First class schedules will be assumed at initial point by trainmen and enginemen in accordance with Rosters, as shown on Pages 2 and 3, or as amended.

RULE 880. Engineers who have had less than 610 days actual experience in freight service, and less than 60 days experience on Western Division, Southern Pacific Co., and who have not qualified in the handling of trains in Continuous Automatic Cab Signal and Speed Control System, must not be used in passenger service of Interurban Electric Ry. Co.

RULE 1007 (Cab Signal Rules). Rule 99 will not apply to trains moving with the current of traffic within train control territory, except:

(a) Westward trains within that portion of train control territory extending from its initial point on the 26th Street elevated structure to the west end of that structure at catenary bridge No. 65 must be protected as prescribed by Rule 99.

(b) In event of derailment within train control territory the train must be protected as prescribed by Rule 99.

(c) Motors or engines not equipped with Cab Signal and Speed Control apparatus must be protected as prescribed by Rule 99 at all times while operating within limits of train control territory and will enter and operate through train control territory with caution, not exceeding eleven miles per hour.

RULE 1008 (Cab Signal Rules). Movement against current of traffic within that portion of train control territory assigned to supervision of Superintendent—Bridge Railway must not be made except on receipt of written instructions, on prescribed form, issued by authority and over the signature of Superintendent—Bridge Railway; this form to be made in triplicate, copy to be given to conductor and engineer of each train so authorized to move against current of traffic, third copy to be returned to Superintendent—Bridge Railway by the employe issuing same.

RULE 1014 (Cab Signal Rules). Limits of train control territory on westward main tracks extend from fixed signal on 7th Street Line 600 feet east of 26th Street Junction, and from fixed signal on Shattuck Avenue Line 520 feet east of 26th Street Junction to 26th Street Junction, thence via Tracks "F," "C," and "A" to San Francisco.

Limits of train control territory on eastward main track extends from San Francisco via Track "B" to fixed signal 65 feet west of 26th Street Junction.

Limits of train control territory include all tracks in San Francisco Terminal, westbound set-out tracks "A" and "D" and eastbound set-out tracks "H" and "I".

Entrance to train control territory, via reverse traffic route on 7th Street Line, is at dwarf signal 14La 320 feet east of 26th Street Junction and, on Shattuck Avenue Line, at dwarf signal 14Lb 434 feet east of 26th Street Junction.

AUTOMATIC BLOCK SYSTEM

RULE 509. Following block signals equipped with a triangular number plate include in their control limits a special protective device. When these signals indicate "STOP," careful inspection must be made of track or structure, as indicated below, and it must be known that it is safe for passage of trains before proceeding:

No. 3755: Protection for oil buffer switch at end of double track at Contra Costa.

No. 4291: Protection for oil buffer switch at end of double track at Albany.

RULE 511. When one switch of a crossover is equipped with spring, the rigid switch must be left lined for crossover movement until movement is completed.

CROSSOVERS ON THE SAN FRANCISCO–OAKLAND BAY BRIDGE

There are five pairs of emergency crossovers on the Bridge structure. Each pair consists of one left and one right hand turnout. They are identified and located as follows:

(a) **Rincon**   Located at the west end of the Bridge where it passes over Rincon Hill.

(b) **Anchorage**   Located immediately east and west of the Center Anchorage.

(c) **Island**   Located on Yerba Buena Island.

(d) **Cantilever**   Located on the East Bay crossing approximately 1500 feet east of the Cantilever Span.

(e) **Mole**   Located at the east end of Bridge.

Switches of these crossovers are manually operated and must not be thrown, or the crossovers used except under direction of the Superintendent—Bridge Railway.

If it becomes necessary to use these crossovers, flag protection, in both directions, as prescribed by Rule 99, must first be provided on the main track to be used; and the switch taking out of track upon which the train to be crossed over is standing must then be thrown, and at least one minute elapse before switch in the opposite track is thrown and crossover movement commenced.

CROSSOVERS AND SWITCHES EQUIPPED WITH SPRINGS

Location	Normal Position
West end of crossover Addison Street, Berkeley, Shattuck Avenue Line	Main track
West end of crossover, Melrose, Seventh Street Line	Main track
West end of crossover, Seminary Avenue, Seventh Street Line	Crossover movement
West end of crossover, Broadmoor, Seventh Street Line	Crossover movement
West end of crossover, 3rd and Pacific Avenue, Alameda Lincoln Avenue Line	Main track

OIL BUFFER SPRING SWITCHES

When a block signal in advance of a facing point oil buffer spring switch indicates "STOP," careful examination must be made before passing over it. When making trailing point movement and train is stopped on switch, a reverse movement must not be made, nor the slack taken until the switch has been thrown by hand. When movement has been completed through switch, reverse movement must not be made until point closes.

Running switches are prohibited and sand must not be used while passing over these switches.

Switches are located as follows and speed indicated must not be exceeded when passing over such switches:

Location	Normal Position	M.P.H.
East end of crossover, Seminary Ave. Seventh Street Line	Crossover movement	East 15 / West 15
East end of siding, Ramona, Ninth Street Line	Westward Movement	East 15
West end of siding, Ramona, Ninth Street Line	Eastward movement	West 15
End of double track, Albany, Ninth Street	Westward movement	East 15
End of double track, Thousand Oaks, Ninth Street Line	Eastward movement	West 15
End of double track, Contra Costa, Shattuck Avenue Line	Westward movement	East 15 / West 15

These switches should be split only by electric equipment and only when lined in their normal position, as they are equipped with single acting buffers.

SPECIAL SIGNALS

Two indication dwarf signals are located between main tracks at each end of each pair of crossovers comprising Rincon, Island, and Cantilever crossovers, and at each end of each crossover comprising the Anchorage and Mole crossovers. The signals indicate the position of crossover switches.

A Proceed indication will be displayed when all switches in both main tracks located between each pair of signals are lined for movement on main track.

A Stop indication will be displayed when one or more switches in either or both main tracks is lined for crossover movement, or some other condition exists which might affect safe movement on main track.

A train, operating either with or against the current of traffic and finding a signal displaying a Stop indication, unless otherwise provided, must stop before passing the signal and careful inspection made of crossover switches. It must be known that they are lined for proper route and safe for passage of trains before proceeding.

When the light fails in a signal, train may proceed without stopping provided cab signal indication is more favorable than "Red 11", but report must be made from first convenient point of communication. If cab signal indication is "Red 11", the special signal must be regarded as displaying its most restrictive indication.

INTERURBAN ELECTRIC RAILWAY COMPANY
Time Table No. 1 (Continued)

USE OF MAIN TRACKS

(a) Main tracks between Oakland (Sixteenth Street) and 22nd Street Junction, numbering from the Bay, are designated as 1, 2, 3, 4, 5 and 6 and used as follows:
  No. 5.—Eastward trains of Interurban Electric Ry. Co., via Oakland (Sixteenth Street).
  No. 6—Westward trains of Interurban Electric Ry. Co., via Oakland (Sixteenth Street).

(b) Main tracks between 34th Street Junction and Shellmound Tower numbering from the Bay, are designated as 1, 2, 3, 4, 5 and 6 and used as follows:
  No. 5—Westward trains of Interurban Electric Ry. Co., via Shellmound.
  No. 6—Eastward trains of Interurban Electric Ry. Co., via Shellmound.

(c) Main tracks between East Oakland and Sather, numbering from north, are designated 1, 2, 3, and 4 and used as follows:
  No. 1—Westward trains of Interurban Electric Ry. Co.
  No. 2—Eastward trains of Interurban Electric Ry. Co.

(d) Main tracks between West Alameda and Alameda Airport, numbering from north, are designated 1, 2, 3 and 4 and used as follows:
  No. 3—Eastward trains of Interurban Electric Ry. Co.
  No. 4—Westward trains of Interurban Electric Ry. Co.

(e) Main tracks between 26th Street Junction and San Francisco are lettered and used as follows:
  Track "F"—Westward trains 26th Street Junction to West Junction.
  Track "C"—Westward trains West Junction to west switch of westbound set-out tracks. Used jointly with Key System and Sacramento Northern.
  Track "A"—Westward trains west switch of westbound set-out tracks to San Francisco. Used jointly with Key System and Sacramento Northern.
  Track "B"—Eastward trains San Francisco to 26th Street Junction. Used jointly with Key System and Sacramento Northern, San Francisco to East Junction.

(f) Tracks in San Francisco Terminal, numbering from the north (Mission Street) are designated 1, 2, 3, 4, 5 and 6 and used as follows:
  Nos. 1, 2 and 3—Trains of Interurban Electric Ry. Co.
  Nos. 4, 5 and 6—Trains of Key System and Sacramento Northern.

SET-OUT TRACKS—BRIDGE YARD

(a) Westbound Set-Out Tracks are lettered and, from the north, are designated "A" and "D".

(b) Eastbound Set-Out Tracks are lettered and, from the south, are designated "H" and "I".

MISCELLANEOUS

1. In case of power interruption signal operator may display "S" sign, in which case trains must not exceed series position of controller. When signs are removed, normal speed may be resumed.

2. Station stops should be made with middle of train under or opposite station sign, unless instructions on schedule page indicate otherwise.

3. In addition to those telephones located as shown on schedule pages, others are installed at each set of crossovers on the Bridge, at both ends of Eastbound and Westbound Set-Out Tracks, and in crotch of wye at top of elevated structure at 26th Street Junction.

4. Push button located on side of relay case on east side of Twelfth Street Melrose should be used to operate wigwags while switching.

5. Train gates must be kept closed at all times while train is moving on San Francisco-Oakland Bay Bridge. If, for any reason, it becomes necessary to open gates while train is standing on the Bridge, they must be opened only by the conductor or under his direction, and the following will govern:

  (a) Gates must not be opened to permit detraining between tracks, except in case of accident or other cause which would make it impossible to do otherwise. Should it become necessary to permit detraining between tracks, flag protection must first be provided and train movements on the opposite track stopped short of the point of detraining.

  (b) Under all other conditions, except as specified in paragraph (a), gates on trains standing on eastward track must be opened on the south side only and, when standing on westward track, on the north side only. In the case of a train standing on either track, employes may detrain over the end of car through the vestibule at head end or rear end of train, but in doing so must alight on the track upon which train is standing.

  (c) If a gate is opened to permit detraining of an employe, it must be closed promptly after he has alighted to prevent detraining of passengers.

6. During non-peak periods, trainmen and enginemen will treat all stations on the following lines as flag stops:
  (a) Ninth Street Line—except at Ashby, University Avenue, and Albany Stations, at which stops must be made;
  (b) Shattuck Avenue Line—east of University Avenue;
  (c) Seventh Street Line—east of Havenscourt.

7. When opposing trains approach on double track on a public street, speed of both must be reduced and gongs must be sounded until the head end of each passes the rear end of the other.

8. On Shattuck Ave. Line between University Ave. and Ward St. at all times, and in residential districts during night hours, the use of crossing warning whistle signals should be avoided as much as possible consistent with safe operation.

9. At the following places vehicles parked at curb will not clear passing trains:
  Stanford Ave., east of Shellmound Tower on both tracks.
  Central Ave., Alameda, between Fourth St. and Pacific Junction on eastward track. Between Alameda Belt Line Crossing and Pacific Junction on westward track.
  Encinal Ave., between South High St. and Briggs Ave. on westward track.
  Shattuck Ave., eastward track between Addison and University Avenue.
  Trains will approach with caution when vehicles are parked at these locations, and engineers must assure themselves that such automobiles are clear of train.

10. Controller must never be locked while train is in motion. When an emergency stop is made by use of the pilot valve, brake valve handle should immediately be placed in emergency position and remain there until train has stopped. With "UC" valve allow 8 seconds before making release.

11. The following motor cars are equipped with two brake cylinders or with brake lever stops:
  Nos. 352 to 367, inclusive.   Nos. 378 to 387, inclusive.
  Motor cars which are not equipped with two brake cylinders or with brake lever stops must not be operated single on the San Francisco-Oakland Bay Bridge.

12. In case of delay to eastward trains enroute, they may turn back short of outside terminals, if necessary to do so to protect return schedule.

13. **(a) ROUTE SIGNS**—(displayed over side windows)

Position on Roll	Wording	To Be Displayed
1	SAN FRANCISCO	Not to be used.
2	SAN FRANCISCO EXPRESS	On westward express trains destined San Francisco.
3	OAKLAND, DUTTON AVE., 7'ST	All eastward and westward locals via 7th St. Line.
4	FRUITVALE, 7'ST	Not to be used.
5	MELROSE, 7'ST	Not to be used.
6	DUTTON AVE. EXPRESS	On eastward express trains via 7th St. Line destined Dutton Avenue.
7	SEMINARY AVE., 7'ST	Not to be used.
8	SPECIAL SERVICE	On special movements.
9	BERKELEY, SHATTUCK AVE	On all eastward and westward locals via Shattuck Ave. Line.
10	SHATTUCK AVE. EXPRESS	On eastward express trains via Shattuck Ave. Line.
11	BERKELEY, 9'ST	On all eastward and westward locals via 9th St. Line.
12	NINTH STREET EXPRESS	Not to be used.
13	ALAMEDA	Not to be used.
14	ALAMEDA, LINCOLN AVE	On all eastward and westward Alameda trains via Lincoln Ave. Line.
15	ALAMEDA, ENCINAL AVE	On all eastward and westward Alameda trains via Encinal Ave. Line.
16	OUT OF SERVICE	On cars which are out of service.
17	FOOTBALL SPECIAL	Football service.

(b) DESTINATION SIGNS—(displayed on ends of cars)

Position on Roll	Wording	To Be Displayed
1	SAN FRANCISCO	On all westward trains destined San Francisco except express trains.
2	SAN FRANCISCO EXPRESS	On westward express trains destined San Francisco.
3	OAKLAND, DUTTON AVE., 7'ST	All eastward locals via 7th Street Line.
4	FRUITVALE, 7'ST	Not to be used.
5	MELROSE, 7'ST	Not to be used.
6	DUTTON AVE. EXPRESS	On eastward express trains via 7th Street Line destined Dutton Ave.
7	SEMINARY AVENUE, 7'ST	Not to be used.
8	SPECIAL SERVICE	On special movements.
9	BERKELEY, SHATTUCK AVE	On all eastward locals via Shattuck Avenue Line.
10	SHATTUCK AVE. EXPRESS	On eastward express trains via Shattuck Avenue Line.
11	BERKELEY, 9'ST	On all eastward locals via 9th Street Line.
12	NINTH ST. EXPRESS	Not to be used.
13	ALAMEDA	Not to be used.
14	ALAMEDA, LINCOLN AVE	On all eastward Alameda trains via Lincoln Avenue Line.
15	ALAMEDA, ENCINAL AVE	On all eastward Alameda trains via Encinal Avenue Line.
16	OUT OF SERVICE	On cars which are out of service.
17	FOOTBALL SPECIAL	Football service.

(c) Proper route and destination signs must be displayed on all westward trains before departure from east terminal. Route and destination signs on westward trains approaching San Francisco must be changed to the correct wording for the eastward move while train is passing over the Bridge and before arrival San Francisco. Trainmen and train gatemen will see that signs in cars to which they are assigned are properly displayed. Conductors should see that their crews understand the proper handling of signs.

14. **DISC SIGNS, DOME LIGHTS AND WHISTLE SIGNALS**

	Disc No.	Dome Signals	Whistle Signals
(a) Seventh Street Line			
(1) Local Trains	2	Green and Green	o o — — o
(2) Express Trains	2	Yellow and Yellow	o o — — o
(b) Shattuck Avenue Line			
(1) Local Trains	3	Red and Red	o — — — o
(2) Express Trains	3	Yellow and Yellow	o — — — o o
(c) Encinal Avenue Line	4	Green and Yellow	— — o o o
(d) Lincoln Avenue Line	4	Green and Red	o o — o o
(e) Ninth Street Line	5	Red and White	o — o o o

Trainmen and enginemen must see that the proper disc signs and dome lights are displayed and that alarm whistle signals are sounded for information of signal men when necessary.

15. All concerned are warned that insufficient clearance exists on the San Francisco-Oakland Bay Bridge to clear a man between the side of train on westward track and the collision wall separating the railroad right-of-way from the vehicular roadway. Under no condition should a person attempt to stand between the collision wall and the westward train to permit passage of train on that track. Engineers operating westward trains and observing a person standing between collision wall and the westward track must bring train to stop before reaching the point where the person is standing. Persons whose duties require their working on or about the railroad or attendant facilities on the Bridge must take position on planked walk at the south side of the Bridge, standing close against girders during passage of train on either track.

16. Traffic light signals 7th and Harrison Streets, Oakland, governing movements on Seventh St., will be operated by track circuit approach. Eastward circuit starts at Webster St., westward at Alice St. Trains will not exceed ten (10) miles per hour crossing Webster St., and will approach and pass over Harrison St. with caution, not exceeding ten (10) miles per hour. Enginemen keep a careful watch for vehicular and pedestrian traffic. Eastward trains may increase speed after head end of train passes Harrison St. In case of failure traffic light signals, trains will stop before crossing Harrison St. and proceed over crossing with caution.

17. Steam engines are permitted to operate over portions of the Interurban Electric Railway Lines as shown below. Movements outside of these limits must not be made with steam engines.

Encinal Avenue Line:
Lincoln Avenue Line: Both tracks South High to Alameda Airport. Both tracks Fruitvale to Mastick Junction. Eastward track 5th and Lincoln to Pacific Junction. Westward track Pacific Junction to crossover Pole 780.

Seventh Street Line: 103rd Ave., Junction to 68th Ave., Havenscourt. Fallon Street to Melrose. Both tracks east end of 16th Street elevated structure to 22nd Street Junction.

Shattuck Avenue Line: Both tracks 34th Street Junction to University Ave. Eastward track University Ave. to Vine Street.

Ninth Street Line: Both tracks Ninth Street Junction to a point 500 feet east of north line of Heinz Avenue.

INTERURBAN ELECTRIC RAILWAY COMPANY
Time Table No. 1 (Continued)

18. Three position light type signal located opposite Pole 836 Mastick, governs eastward movements from Tynan. Semaphore type indicator near this signal is for information of yardmen and will indicate trains approaching from the west as far as Pole 796, and from the east Pole 716. Both derailer and junction switch must be reversed before starting a movement from Tynan route.

19. To prevent obstructing view of auto drivers of approaching trains, cars must not be left within 300 feet of eastward Encinal Ave. track at Pacific Ave., Pacific Junction.

20. A clock equipped with sweep hand registering seconds, a push button type electric switch and a telephone, all mounted together, are located at the west end of each platform and at approximately the mid-point of each platform in the train shed at San Francisco. These facilities are for the purpose of starting trains from the Terminal and will be referred to as "Starting Stations". The push button switches, when depressed, illuminate an indicator light in the Interlocking Tower. On platform serving Track 1 there is one push button switch at each location. On platform serving Tracks 2 and 3 there are two push button switches at each location, the one nearest Track 2 applying to trains on that track, and the one nearest Track 3 applying to trains on that track. The telephone is for communicating with the Interlocking Tower.

    At least one minute before scheduled departure time of a train, conductor will station himself at Starting Station nearest the head end of his train and, when the sweep hand on clock at that location indicates fifteen seconds in advance of departure time, he will depress the proper push button switch and at the same time raise his hand vertically over his head. Brakemen and gatemen will station themselves on station platform immediately adjacent to steps of car platform to which assigned, and when conductor raises his hand, brakeman or gateman nearest him will repeat the signal which will be relayed by each succeeding employe toward the rear of train. Immediately the signal has been relayed, each succeeding brakeman or gateman, except the first, will board train and close train gates. After gates have once closed they must not again be opened except on direction of conductor. After having depressed push button switch, conductor will board train at first opening and gates will be closed. When gates on rear car have been closed, the usual starting hand signal will be initiated by employe assigned to that car and this signal will be relayed through the train toward the conductor who, when he receives it will sound communicating signal 16(a). Upon receipt of communicating signal 16(a) engineer will proceed, provided indication of interlocking signal governing movement out of train shed is other than "Stop". Lamp signal, given by holding lamp at arm's length above the head, may be used instead of corresponding hand signal, if necessary.

    Success of the operation on close headways out of San Francisco during peak periods depends upon utmost alertness of all concerned. During periods when schedules provide a five minute lay-over in San Francisco, enginemen and trainmen must not leave their trains while standing in the Terminal. At other times they must be at their proper stations on or about the train at least two minutes before its scheduled departure time. Every effort must be made to depart San Francisco exactly on time.

21. Westward trains and engines, including switching movements, must not exceed eight (8) miles per hour between Pole 2674 and 12th St. crossing, Melrose, to provide proper time interval for operation of wigwag signals. Westward trains five cars or less making Melrose station stop, stop with west end of train just east of Pole 2674.

22. On all trains engineer's cab at rear of train must be folded and gate closed.

23. (a) Tonnage of electric work trains operated by one motor car must not exceed 600 Ms on all lines, except:

    (1) Between Fernside or Lincoln Junction Alameda and Fruitvale, including east and west legs of wye at Fruitvale. 450 Ms
    (2) Between 9th Street Junction and University Ave., Shattuck Avenue Line.
    (3) Between University Ave. and Thousand Oaks, Shattuck Avenue Line. 150 Ms
    (4) Between Albany and Thousand Oaks, Ninth Street Line.
    (5) Over elevated structures at 16th Street, 26th Street, in Bridge Yard and on the San Francisco-Oakland Bay Bridge. One motor car work trains must not be operated.

    (b) Electric work trains working on or over elevated structures at 16th Street, 26th Street, in Bridge Yard or the San Francisco-Oakland Bay Bridge must include two motors per 160 Ms, or fraction thereof, handled.

    (c) When handling loaded cars, controller must not be moved beyond the series position. In switching loads under no circumstances must controller be moved beyond the switching point or HELD IN THAT POSITION LONGER THAN TEN SECONDS at a time so that the grids will not be damaged.

    (d) WHEN PLOWING BALLAST USE TWO (2) MOTORS.
    Gross weights of cars vary, depending upon commodity therein. As a general average see below:
    Gross weight loaded Rodger Ballast Car average.................. 80,000 lbs.
    "Hart Convertible" Cars loaded average.......................... 150,000 "
    Gondolas loaded with gravel..................................... 160,000 "
    Box cars and flats loaded with steel............................ 165,000 "

24. Eastward trains of four cars or less making safety or station stop at Melrose stop at marker located between Poles 2676 and 2675, and not exceed eight (8) miles per hour from the stop until head end of train is across 14th St. Eastward trains of five or more cars will make station or safety stop at Pole 2677 near 14th St., and move with caution not exceeding eight (8) miles per hour until head end of train is across 14th St. Westward movement over this crossing to be made with caution not exceeding eight (8) miles per hour.

25. Eastward Seventh St. trains with four or less cars scheduled to stop at Sather will stop with head end of train west of Pole 2627. Those not scheduled to stop, use not less than twenty (20) seconds between Pole 2627 and High St.

INTERLOCKING

(a) Movements governed by short-arm or dwarf signals must be made with caution and position of switches observed, as such signals govern movements for various routes.

(b) On double track within yard limits, except within Train Control Territory, signal operator may arrange to move trains from one tower to another against the current of traffic, after having an understanding by telephone for each movement. Before moving trains against the current of traffic signal operator must know that track to be used is clear of opposing engines and trains.

SPEED RESTRICTIONS

City	Limits of Restriction	Speed M.P.H.
All	Through crossovers and turnouts	10
All	Through all spring switches	15
All	Through all facing point girder rail switches	8
All	Passing schools, during school hours	With caution
All	Around all curves, unless further restricted	25
All	Through interlocking limits	With caution
All	Passing station when no stop is made	15
Oakland	Between West Oakland Junction and Pine	15
Oakland	Crossing Cypress Street	With caution
Oakland	Crossing Washington, Broadway and Franklin	15
Oakland	Crossing Webster St. and Harrison St.	10
Oakland	23rd Ave.—Westward trains not scheduled to stop	10
Oakland	Crossing 29th Ave.	20
Oakland	Approaching Melrose	With caution
Oakland	Between Pole 2674, Melrose and 12th Street Westward	8
Oakland	Crossing 14th St., Melrose	8
Oakland	Crossing 46th Ave., 47th Ave., 48th Ave., and 50th Ave.	20
Oakland	Approaching Seminary Avenue	With caution
Oakland	Crossing Seminary Ave. and 60th Ave. westward	8
Oakland	Approaching Havenscourt	With caution
Oakland	Between Church St. and 73rd Ave.	15
Oakland	Crossing 73rd Ave. (make safety stop when moving against current traffic if no flagman on crossing)	8
Oakland	Crossing 94th Ave.	15
Oakland	Approaching Dutton Ave.	With caution
Emeryville	Crossing Park Ave.—Eastward trains only	15
Emeryville	Around curve Shellmound tower	20
Oakland	Crossing San Pablo Ave. at Stanford	15
Berkeley	Crossing Ward St. (beginning 60 ft. from near side)	15
Berkeley	Between Ward St. and University Ave.	25
Berkeley	Crossing Addison St.	8
Berkeley	Approaching University Ave. (between Pole 3590 and University Ave. crossing eastward trains use 20 seconds)	15
Berkeley	Vine and Shattuck—passing fire house	15

SPEED RESTRICTIONS—Continued

City	Limits of Restriction	Speed M.P.H.
Berkeley	Berryman—approaching crossover between Poles 3687-3688	With caution
Berkeley	Through Northbrae tunnel	15
Berkeley	Crossing The Alameda	15
Berkeley	Crossing Dwight Way (Ninth St. Line)	15
Berkeley	Crossing 9th and Cedar	With caution
Albany	Crossing San Pablo Ave.	15
Berkeley	Through girder rail switch end of double track Ninth St. Line, Thousand Oaks	8
Oakland	Crossing Fruitvale Ave. Drawbridge	8
Alameda	Around curve east leg wye Fruitvale	15
Alameda	Around curve between Fernside Junction and Blanding Junction	8
Alameda	Around curve, Lincoln Ave. Line, Pacific Jct.	15
Alameda	Crossing Pacific Ave. between Mastick-Tynan	6
Alameda	Crossing Buena Vista between Mastick-Tynan	6
Alameda	Crossing Willow St. and Park St. on Lincoln Ave.	15
Alameda	Crossing Park St. on Encinal Ave.	15
Alameda	Around curve Encinal Ave. Line east of Pacific Jct.	20
Alameda	Crossing steam tracks Encinal Line Pacific Jct. team track	25
Alameda	Yard engines on Lincoln Ave. between Park and Pacific Jct. (make safety stop Lincoln and Webster)	15
Alameda	During season beaches open, operate with caution between 4th St. and 8th St.	With caution
Alameda	South High St., approaching crossover between Poles 537 and 539	With caution

The speed of all trains and engines is restricted to fifteen (15) miles per hour beginning at a point not less than sixty (60) feet from the nearest rail of the following street railway crossings to and until the head end of train shall have reached and passed over the crossing.

Seventh St. Line:
Washington St.
Broadway

Shattuck Ave. Line:
San Pablo and Stanford
(Also watch carefully for fire apparatus.)
Grove and Adeline
University Avenue

S. L. DOLAN,
Trainmaster

F. E. SULLIVAN,
Superintendent—Bridge Railway

H. DIECKMAN,
Asst. Trainmaster

APPENDIX C

Ferry Steamer Operations

OPERATION OF THE Southern Pacific passenger ferries, although entirely separate, was closely coordinated with the railway system. Schedules of the passenger ferries were shown on the railway operating timetables, and those ferries operating from Oakland Pier were considered a part of the Seventh Street rail line. In fact, for many years, the first westward crossing on Sunday mornings carried a Seventh Street train number even though there was no rail connection; the ferry run was identified with the notation "Steamer Trip."

Three boats were used on the run from Oakland Pier. The first boat for each day would depart from the pier just before 6 o'clock in the morning; it would finally tie up over in San Francisco about 7 p.m. The second boat of any particular day would leave San Francisco also about 6 a.m. and would tie up in Oakland shortly after midnight. The third boat for that day would leave Oakland Pier shortly after the first boat and would finally tie up at Oakland Pier shortly after 1 a.m. the next morning. Schedules were arranged so that the three boats continually rotated their runs, i.e., the first boat would take the second boat's run the following day and the third boat's run the next day.

In a similar manner, the two boats working out of Alameda Pier would alternate their runs daily. The first boat would start at about 6 a.m. from Alameda Pier and tie up in San Francisco about midnight. The second boat would make its early morning departure from San Francisco and tie up at Alameda Pier in the late evening.

The Creek Route used two boats daily except Sundays and holidays; on Sundays and holidays, a third boat would be used as traffic demanded. One boat worked out of Oakland, and operated from early morning until late evening. The other boat worked out of San Francisco and had a similar schedule except that it tied up some hours earlier.

Auto ferry service to Oakland Pier in later years utilized four boats on a 15-minute headway. On Sundays and holidays, additional vessels would be used as traffic warranted. The four boats in base service would be in operation from early morning until late evening. After 11 o'clock at night, one boat would be used in hourly "owl" service until 6 o'clock the next morning. Similarly, three boats would be used during the day on the Hyde Street-Berkeley line, and a single "owl" boat would operate hourly throughout the night. The auto ferry lines to Alameda and to Richmond both utilized two boats. Both lines operated only from early morning until midnight; no "owl" service was operated.

The many ferries used over the years by Southern Pacific varied as much in their construction and mechanical characteristics as they did in appearance. Initially, most ferries were of wooden construction with hulls receiving a sheathing of copper plate so as to withstand the effects of a salt-water environment. Beginning with the launching of the *Berkeley* in 1898, boats of steel construction began making their appearance on the bay. The second *Thoroughfare*, built in 1912, was the last new wooden ferry turned out by the Southern Pacific shipyard, although the *Sacramento* and the *Eureka*, commissioned some 10 years later, were rebuilt from older, wooden-hulled ferries. The newest wooden ferries on the combined Southern Pacific system were those of the *Golden Poppy* class which had been built in 1927 for the Golden Gate Ferry Company. These auto ferries were built the same year as the steel auto ferries of the *Lake Tahoe* class and were among the newest ferries on the bay.

Ferry propulsion was of two basic types, paddle wheel and screw propeller. Paddle-wheel boats were noted for their extreme beam, with some having as much as 78 feet of deck width over a hull width of 42 feet. Hence, there would be an overhang, or sponson, of about 15 to 17 feet on each side to allow for the paddle wheels. Sponsons on propeller boats were much less, being on the order of eight to 10 feet.

Most paddle-wheel boats were powered by a simple beam engine. All but one of these had an engine which transmitted its power to the paddle wheel through a walking beam on the texas deck. The theory of the walking beam engine was simplicity itself. In the engine room, a huge single-cylinder, low-pressure steam engine was mounted vertically. The cylinder rod was connected to the walking beam, which was slung in trunions at the top of a giant A-frame anchored to the hull of the boat. The opposite end of the walking beam was connected to a push rod which, being attached to the paddle crank rod, turned the paddle wheels. The connecting rods, from engine to walking beam and back to

WHEELHOUSE of the auto ferry *Thoroughfare* (top) was dominated by the ship's wheel. The captain stood at right near the ship's telegraph and under the whistle cord; note spittoon on floor. Engine room of the Bay City (above) was compact and efficient. Scotch Marine Boilers are at left. **Both Vernon J. Sappers Collection**

SPACIOUSNESS of the upper deck of the Santa Clara is apparent (below). Lower deck of the ferry (bottom) was more utilitarian.
Both Vernon J. Sappers Collection

the paddle wheels, occupied space in the fidley, which was the vertical section in the center of the boat enclosing boiler uptakes, stack, escape pipes, and a host of other tubing and equipment. Many paddle-wheel ferries had windows in the fidley where passengers could watch the giant rod with its pendulum-like upward and downward movement. Of all the beam ferries, only the *Piedmont* lacked a walking beam. In that ferry, the engine was mounted horizontally and connected directly to the paddle-wheel crank. This engine had a cylinder diameter only a few inches less than the very largest, but the stroke was a whopping 168 inches.

The four paddle-wheel boats built after 1900 were equipped with compound engines rather than beam engines. The engines in these latter boats were paired, with one for each paddle wheel. This design gave the boat greater manueverability as each paddle wheel could be turned independently.

Screw-propelled boats had as much variety, although not as much character, as the paddle-wheel boats. Compound engines were found on the three auto ferries that had been rebuilt from Key System passenger ferries *(Golden Dawn, Golden Era,* and *Golden Way)* as well as on the *Sierra Nevada.*

The *Berkeley* was the first bay ferry to be equipped with a three-cylinder triple expansion engine. Seven other boats, mostly auto ferries, also had this type of engine. Two boats, the *Napa Valley* and the *City of Sacramento,* had four-cylinder triple expansion engines. The former was equipped with a single engine while the latter had twin engines. The engines were similar to other triple expansion engines with the addition of a second tertiary, or low-pressure cylinder.

An entirely different type of steam engine was found on the *San Leandro,* formerly a Key System boat. Like most other vessels of the Key System fleet, the *San Leandro* was equipped with a steam turbine that provided power to operate the electrically driven propeller shaft. In many respects, the steam turbine-electric propulsion was more similar to the diesel-electric propulsion found in the newer auto ferries than it was to the other steam-powered ferries.

The newest auto ferries, those of the *Lake Tahoe* and *Golden Age* classes, were of diesel-electric propulsion. The steel ferries, those of the *Lake Tahoe* class, were powered by four New London diesel engines which provided power to the electrically driven propeller shafts. The wooden diesel ferries were of two basic types. The *Golden Gate* and *Golden West* were equipped with two Werkspoor diesel engines; the *Golden State* had three engines of this type. The *Golden Age, Golden Bear, Golden Poppy,* and *Golden Shore* were equipped with three Ingersoll-Rand diesel engines. All of the diesel-electric ferries were equipped with two electric motors.

Boilers used on the ferries were of two basic types, fire-tube and water-tube. The concept of the fire-tube boiler is much older than that of the water-tube boiler and hence was the type used on most ferries built prior to 1900. Fire-tube boilers produce steam efficiently, but they have limitations on size and operating pressure. Early boilers of this type also were prone to unexpected explosions. Early day ferries, such as the *El Capitan* which was built in 1868, used fire-tube boilers. Similar boilers were placed in boats until 1910.

A modified type of fire-tube boiler was the Scotch Marine, which was noted for its compactness and efficiency. This type was installed in the three South Pacific Coast ferries as well as in the second *Thoroughfare.* The dryback boiler, on board the *Eureka,* was a similar type.

Water-tube boilers were of more recent design, having been in use since 1903 when nine of this type were installed in the *Asbury Park,* which later was renamed the *City of Sacramento.* Boilers of this type can operate at much higher pressures than can fire-tube boilers. Furthermore, super-heaters can be used to raise the temperature of the steam far above its saturation temperature. All steam-powered ferries built after 1913 utilized water-tube boilers.

Boats built prior to 1898 were fired with coal. This fact is easily recognizable in noting early day photos which show a ferry with a jet-black plume of coal smoke. With the advent of fuel oil (Bunker C oil used in steam locomotives), boats were modernized, and by 1920, there were no longer any coal burners operating on the bay.

New Life for the Auto Ferries

Of the 28 auto ferries operated by Southern Pacific-Golden Gate Ferries, 20 saw service on other ferry operations. Operations ranged from the close-by Richmond-San Rafael Ferry to distant operations in San Diego Bay, Puget Sound, Canada, and Argentina.

The most distant operation was that of the Argentina-Uruguayan Navigation Touring Company. This corporation acquired the *Yosemite,* and after renaming her the *Argentina,* sailed her to South America where she saw service on the 30-mile crossing of the Rio de la Plata.

Unfortunately, the ferry company ceased operations within a few years, and the *Argentina* was converted to a barge. She eventually was abandoned and sunk.

The Richmond-San Rafael Ferry and Transportation Company acquired the three boats of the *New Orleans* class in 1938. The *New Orleans* was renamed the *Russian River;* the other two boats, the *El Paso* and *Klamath,* were not renamed. These three boats provided the mainstay of service between Point Richmond and Point San Quentin until 1947, when the *Sierra Nevada,* rebuilt as an auto ferry, was added to the fleet.

Ferry service on this line continued until September 1, 1956, when the Richmond-San Rafael Bridge was opened for vehicular traffic. The *El Paso* and *Russian River* were subsequently dismantled; the *Klamath* was rebuilt as a floating office building and is now docked near the Ferry Building in San Francisco. The *Sierra Nevada* was taken to San Pedro, where she is now a part of the Ports of Call Trade Center.

Two former bay ferries ended their days working the San Diego-Coronado ferry route. The *Golden West,* after being sold to the Puget Sound Navigation Company, was resold to the San Diego-Coronado Ferry Company before departing from San Francisco Bay in 1937. Renamed the *North Island,* the ferry worked on San Diego Bay until displaced by the San Diego-Coronado Bridge, which was opened to traffic on August 3, 1969. Like the other four ferries of this system, the *North Island* was sold at public auction. After lying idle for many years, the old ferry was scrapped in 1974.

The *Golden Shore* was purchased by the Puget Sound Navigation Company and worked the ferry routes on Puget Sound (as the *Elwha*) until 1944 when she was purchased by the Coronado Ferry and towed to San Diego Bay. Renamed the *Silver Strand,* the ferry was in service until displaced by the San Diego-Coronado Bridge. She was then sold at auction to the City of Chula Vista which had planned to convert her into a center for the theater arts. When this plan fell through, the ferry again was sold at public auction. Her new owners towed her to Los Angeles Harbor for conversion into a restaurant. In December 1970, a major storm blew in from the sea and ran the ferry aground where winds and high waters demolished her.

Fifteen auto ferries of the Southern Pacific-Golden Gate Ferries fleet were purchased by Puget Sound Navigation Company (the "Black Ball Line") and its subsidiary, Kitsap County Transportation Company. Beginning with their first purchase in 1937 of five "Golden Boats" and culminating with the purchase of the last two Montecello boats, the former bay fleet formed the nucleus of the Puget Sound ferry system in the period from 1940 to the mid-1950s.

The *Golden Age, Golden Bear, Golden Poppy, Golden Shore,* and *Golden State* were the first bay ferries to be taken to Puget Sound; they left San Francisco Bay during the latter part of 1937. Only four completed the tow trip north.

Amid high seas and howling winds, the 1½-inch diameter steel tow line between the sea tug *Active* and the ferry *Golden Bear* parted at about 4:00 p.m. on November 15, 1937, while west of Coos Bay, Oregon. After drifting for some 20 hours, during which time its crew of 20 worked steadily to keep the ferry from foundering, the *Active,* assisted by the U.S. Coast Guard cutter *Pulaski,* succeeded in recapturing the craft. When a new tow line was made fast on board the ferry, its crew was transferred to the *Pulaski,* and the damage to the ferry was surveyed. There wasn't much left.

The remains of the ferry wallowed low in the water with a 45-degree list to starboard. Drift bolts, which had held the superstructure together, had worked loose during the heavy seas, and most of the above-deck construction had collapsed; only one wheelhouse was left intact. After being towed to the nearby coastal town of Empire, the *Golden Bear* was tied up. Because it would cost at least $30,000 to make her seaworthy again, company officials ordered her engines and equipment removed for use on other P.S.N. ferries. The hull of the ferry subsequently was converted to a barge; she ended her life by being sunk to form part of a breakwater.

The same stormy period of weather also nearly wrecked the *Golden State.* A week later, while off the Oregon coast, this ferry, too, became storm battered. However, her tow line did not part and the tug *Commissioner* was able to get her to safety. She was tied up for several days at Astoria until better weather returned and she could continue her trip northward. Even so, the *Golden State* suffered major storm damage.

After arrival on Puget Sound, the four surviving ferries were refurbished and given Indian names. The *Golden Age* became the *Klahanie* (Great Out-of-doors), the *Golden Poppy* became the *Chetzemoka* (the name of a Clallan Indian chief), and the *Golden State* became the *Kehloken* (Swan). The *Golden Shore* was renamed the *Elwha* (Elk) and served until 1944 when she was sold to the San Diego-Coronado Ferry Company. The *Kehloken* was retired in 1973, and two years later the

TABLE 18 -- *Specifications of Ferry Steamers*

Name	Documentation Number	Type[1]	Tonnage		Dimensions[2] (feet)			No. in crew	Year built	Builder	Location	Indicated Horsepower
			Gross	Net	Length	Breadth	Depth					
Alameda *(I)*	1216	P,s.w.	813	621	193.0	38.8	11.3		1866	Patrick Tiernan	San Francisco	350
ALAMEDA *(II)*	211868	"	2302	1320	273.0 293.0	42.3 76.0	15.3	18	1913	Southern Pacific	Oakland	2500
Alvira	106687	P,st.w	469	443	144.5[4]	33.6	6.0	30	1889	Alexander Hay	San Francisco	200
Amador	1953	P,s.w.	985	756	199.0	39.0	10.6	11	1869	Patrick Tiernan[5]	"	300
Bay City	3068	"	1283	933	230.0 247.0	36.8 66.1	13.6	13	1878	William Collyer	"	800
BERKELEY	3770	P,s.sc	1945[6]	1245[6]	261.4 279.0	40.2	14.1	28[6]	1898	Union Iron Works	"	1450
CALISTOGA	204629	A,s.sc	2680[8]	1516[8]	298.0 308.4	45.0 65.0	16.1	16	1907	Maryland Steel Co.[8]	Sparrows Pt.,Md.	2600
Capital	5181	P,s.w.	1989	1522	277.3	47.0	10.9		1865	John G. North[9]	San Francisco	900
CITY OF SACRAMENTO	107848	A,t.sc	3016	1829	297.2 308.0	50.4 67.3	15.4	70	1903	W. Cramp & Sons[10]	Philadelphia	5900
Clinton	5177	P,s.w.	194		170.0				1853	Domingo Marucci	San Francisco	125
Contra Costa	5180	"	449[12]						1857	John G. North	"	150
El Capitan	8230	"	982	669	194.0	33.6 62.6	14.5	14	1868	Patrick Tiernan	"	250
EL PASO	224327	A,s.sc	1953	926	234.0 246.0	45.0 63.5	17.0	13	1924	Bethlehem Steel	"	1400
Encinal	135972	P,s.w.	2014	1633	245.0 274.0	40.4 72.6	14.5	15[14]	1888	Austin Hills[13]	"	1000
Eureka	25279	"	2420	1500	277.0 299.6	42.7 78.6	15.7	15	1922	Southern Pacific[15]	Oakland	1500
FRESNO	226344	A,s.sc	2468	1604	242.5 256.0	46.2 66.0	17.3	14	1927	Bethlehem Steel	San Francisco	1800(b)
Garden City	85592	P,s.w.	1080	730	208.0 243.0	37.0 66.5	13.6	19	1879	William Collyer	"	625
Golden Age	227249	A,s.sc	779	480	226.8 240.0	44.0 60.0	15.9	12	1928	General Eng.& Dry Dock	Alameda	1200(b)
Golden Bear	226605	"	779	479	226.8 240.0	44.0 60.0	15.9	12	1927	" " "	"	1200(b)
Golden Coast	200207	"	616	385	175.4 200.0	38.0 60.0	17.0	15	1903	John Dickie	"	1200
Golden Dawn	201830	"	612	395	180.0 202.0	38.0 60.0	18.0	15	1905	" "	"	2000
Golden Era	204736	"	673	435	194.3 200.0	38.1 60.0	19.2	15	1908	" "	"	2000
Golden Gate	222308	"	598	387	206.5 220.0	37.3 60.0	15.9	10	1922	J. Robertson	"	1300(b)
Golden Poppy	226687	"	779	479	226.8 240.0	44.0 60.0	15.9	12	1927	General Eng.& Dry Dock	"	1200(b)
Golden Shore	226767	"	779	479	226.8 240.0	44.0 60.0	15.9	12	1927	" " "	"	1200(b)
Golden State	225772	"	780	481	226.8 240.0	44.0 60.0	15.9	12	1926	" " "	"	1200(b)
Golden Way	203912	"	1138	774	189.0 200.0	38.0 60.0	19.0	15	1907	John Dickie	"	2000
Golden West	222833	"	594	379	214.1 220.0	44.4 60.0	15.2	9	1923	J. Robertson	"	1300(b)

343

TABLE 18 -- Specifications of Ferry Steamers (Continued)

Grace Barton	86082	P,st.w	194	160	100.0		26.0	6.5	10[16]	1890	George Damon	San Francisco	60
KLAMATH	224401	A,s.sc	1952	925	234.0	246.0	45.0 63.5	17.0	13	1924	Bethlehem Steel	"	1300
LAKE TAHOE	226588	"	2468	1604	242.5	256.0	46.2 66.0	17.3	14	1927	Moore Dry Dock Co.	Oakland	1800(b)
Louise	15222	P,s.w.	368		148.0		30.0	9.1		1864	E. M. Birdsall	San Francisco	125
Mare Island	90428	"	338	295	124.0		28.2	7.6		1870	Patrick Tiernan	"	125
Melrose	205918	A,s.w.	2662	1677	273.0	294.0	43.0 77.0	17.9	8[17]	1908	Southern Pacific	Oakland	1340
MENDOCINO	226712	A,s.sc	2467	1603	242.5	256.0	46.2 66.0	17.3	14	1927	Bethlehem Steel	San Francisco	1800(b)
NAPA VALLEY	207420	"	2185[18]	1289[18]	231.2	242.0	48.7 62.4	15.3	34[19]	1910	Union Iron Works[18]	"	2600
Newark	130118	P,s.w.	1783[20]	1345[20]	268.0	294.0	42.0 78.0	12.8 20	30[21]	1877	William Collyer	"	1200
NEW ORLEANS	224347	A,s.sc	1952	925	234.0	246.0	45.0 63.5	17.0	13	1924	Bethlehem Steel	"	1400
Oakland (I)	19141	P,s.w.	418[22]							1859	Patrick Tiernan		200
Oakland (II)	19447	"	1672	1108	265.0	283.0	41.5 72.6	16.0	19[23]	1875	"	Oakland	200
Piedmont	150313	"	1854	1169	257.1	273.0	39.5 74.1	15.6	23[24]	1883	"	"	257
REDWOOD EMPIRE	226738	A,s.sc	2470	1605	242.5	256.0	46.2 66.0	17.3	14	1927	Moore Dry Dock Co.	"	1800(b)
Ranger		P,s.sc	29							1853		San Francisco	
Rosalie	111022	"	318	226	136.5		27.0	10.0	28	1893	Charles G. White	Alameda Point	350
Sacramento	130118	P,s.w.	2254	1378	268.0	295.0	42.0 78.0	18.6	18	1923	Southern Pacific[25]	Oakland	1400
San Antonio	23218	"	659							1858	Captain Lockwood	San Antonio	
SAN LEANDRO	222781	P,s.sc	1653	1048	225.0	240.0	42.1 62.6	17.1	16	1923	L.A. Shipbuilding Co.	San Pedro	1325(s)
SAN MATEO	222386	A,s.sc	1782	1120	216.7	230.0	42.1 63.5	17.3	14	1922	Bethlehem Steel	San Francisco	1400
SANTA CLARA	213389	P,s.w.	2282	1308	273.0	293.0	42.3 76.0	15.3	18	1915	Southern Pacific	Oakland	2500
SANTA ROSA	226599	A,s.sc	2465	1602	242.5	251.0	46.2 66.0	17.3	14	1927	General Eng.& Dry Dock	Alameda	1800(b)
SHASTA	222598	"	1782	1120	216.7	230.0	42.1 63.5	17.3	13	1922	Bethlehem Steel	San Francisco	1400
SIERRA NEVADA	211506	P,s.sc	1578	1025	218.0	230.0	42.0 62.5	16.6	20	1913	Moore & Scott	Oakland	2500
Sophie MacLane		P,s.w.	242			148.0	29.0	9.0		1858	Patrick Tiernan	San Francisco	
STOCKTON	226567	A,s.sc	2467	1603	242.5	256.0	46.2 66.0	17.3	14	1927	Bethlehem Steel	"	1800(b)
Thoroughfare (I)	24855	F,s.w.	1012	667	248.0		38.4	12.7	13	1871	Patrick Tiernan	"	400
Thoroughfare (II)	209734	A,s.w.	2604	1731	273.0	294.0	42.6 77.0	17.4	15	1912	Southern Pacific	Oakland	1300
Transit	145079	F,s.w.	1566	1079	313.5	338.0	40.5 75.0	15.7	27[26]	1875	Patrick Tiernan	"	500
Washoe	26797	P,s.w.	580							1864	Henry Owens	San Francisco	250
YOSEMITE	222722	A,s.sc	1782	1120	216.7	230.0	42.1 63.5	17.3	13	1923	Bethlehem Steel	"	1400

See explanations and footnotes at end of table.

TABLE 18 -- *Specifications of Ferry Steamers* (Continued)

Name	Engines			Boilers			Former Name(s)	Subsequent Name(s)	Status
	No.	Type	Size (inches)	No.	Type				
Alameda (I)	1	Vertical beam	42x120	1	Fire tube				Dismantled 1898
ALAMEDA (II)	2	2-cyl.compound	20x40x96	4	Water tube			YHB-25	Burned 1/28/48
Alvira	1	Reciprocating		1	Fire tube				Abandoned 1916
Amador	1	"		1	"				Destroyed 5/26/15
Bay City	1	Vertical beam	52x144	2	Scotch marine				Dismantled 1929
BERKELEY	1	3-cyl.triple exp.	22x34x56x36	2	"	7/			Docked at San Diego
CALISTOGA	1	4-cyl.triple exp.	24½x40x47x47x42	4	Single end		FLORIDA	YFB-21	Burned 3/08/48
Capital	1	Vertical beam			Fire tube				Burned 1896
CITY OF SACRAMENTO	2	4-cyl.triple exp.	23x37½x43x43x30	9	Water tube	10/	ASBURY PARK	KAHLOKE,LANGDALE QUEEN	Docked at Vancouver,B.C.
Clinton	1	Vertical beam	27x96	2	Fire tube	11/			Sunk 10/27/1877
Contra Costa	1	"	29x108	4	"				Dismantled 1885
El Capitan	1	"	36x144	4	"				Sold 6/14/25
EL PASO	1	3-cyl.triple exp.	19x32x56x36	3	Water tube				Dismantled 1956
Encinal	1	Vertical beam	52x144	4	Scotch marine				Sold 1935; burned 1959
Eureka	1	"	65x144	4	Dryback		Ukiah		Docked at Hyde St. Wharf
FRESNO	4	Diesel*			..None..			WILLAPA, FRESNO	Docked at Martinez
Garden City	1	Vertical beam	46x144	2	Scotch marine				Beached near Port Costa
Golden Age	3	Diesel*			..None..			Klahanie	Retired 1975
Golden Bear	3	Diesel*			..None..				Wrecked 11/15/37
Golden Coast	1	3-cyl.triple exp.	17x26x42½x28	2	Water tube		Yerba Buena,Harry E. Speas		Dismantled 1939
Golden Dawn	1	Double compound	(2)20x(2)40x28	2	"		San Francisco		" 1939
"	1	"	"	2	"		Fernwood		Beached,Sacramento,1939
Golden Gate	2	Diesel*			..None..				Sunk 1937
Golden Poppy	3	Diesel*			..None..			Chetzemoka	Sunk 5/31/77
Golden Shore	3	Diesel*			..None..			Elwha,Silver Strand	Wrecked 1970
Golden State	3	Diesel*			..None..			Kehloken	Retired 1973
Golden Way	1	Double compound	(2)20x(2)40x28	2	Water tube		Claremont		Dismantled 1939
Golden West	2	Diesel*			..None..			North Island	Dismantled 1974

TABLE 18 -- *Specifications of Ferry Steamers* (Continued)

Grace Barton	1	Reciprocating	19x32x56x36		Fire tube	Burned 1916
KLAMATH	1	2-cyl.triple exp.	19x32x56x36	3	Water tube	Docked in San Francisco
LAKE TAHOE	4	Diesel*	......		..None..	In service, Puget Sound
Louise	1	Compound	18x40x30	2	Fire tube	Dismantled 1878
Mare Island	1	Reciprocating				Dismantled 1898, Alaska
Melrose	2	Inclined compound	23½x38½x96	4	Scotch marine	Dismantled 1931
MENDOCINO	4	Diesel*	......		..None..	In service, Puget Sound
NAPA VALLEY	1	4-cyl.triple exp.	25x41x48x48x24	4	Single end	Burned 1956
Newark	1	Vertical beam	65x144	2	" "	Rebuilt 1923
NEW ORLEANS	1	3-cyl.triple exp.	19x32x56x36	3	Water tube	Dismantled 1956
Oakland (I)	2	Reciprocating		2	Fire tube	Dismantled 1874
Oakland (II)	1	Vertical beam	60x144	2	Single end	Burned 1940
Piedmont	1	Horizontal beam	57x168	2	" "	Beached 1940
REDWOOD EMPIRE	4	Diesel*	......		..None..	In service, Puget Sound
Ranger					Fire tube	Blew up 1854
Rosalie	1	2-cyl. compound	15x34x24	2	Single end	Sunk 1964, Redondo Beach
Sacramento	1	Vertical beam	65x144	2	"	Rebuilt to barge, ca. 1871
San Antonio	1	"				Burned 1975 27/
SAN LEANDRO	1	Steam turbine*	......	2	Water tube	Retired 1973
SAN MATEO	1	3-cyl.triple exp.	19x32x54x36	3	" "	Burned 12/10/47
SANTA CLARA	2	2-cyl. compound	20x40x96	4	" "	Docked at Oakland
SANTA ROSA	4	Diesel*	......		..None..	Docked at Portland
SHASTA	1	3-cyl.triple exp.	19x32x54x36	3	Water tube	Docked at San Pedro
SIERRA NEVADA	2	2-cyl. compound	20x42x28	4	" "	Blew up 1864
Sophie MacLane	2	Reciprocating	20x60		..None..	In service, Puget Sound
STOCKTON	4	Diesel*	......		Fire tube	Dismantled 1909
Thoroughfare (I)	1	Reciprocating				Burned 1957, McNears Point
Thoroughfare (II)	2	2-cyl. compound	22½x38½x96	2	Scotch marine	Dismantled 1934
Transit	1	Vertical beam	60x132	2	Single end	Dismantled 1878
Washoe						Sunk 1948, South America
YOSEMITE	1	3-cyl.triple exp.	19x32x54x36	3	Water tube	

Additional names column (right of steam data):
- LAKE TAHOE → ILLAHEE
- MENDOCINO → NISQUALLY
- NAPA VALLEY → MALAHAT
- Newark → Sacramento
- NEW ORLEANS → RUSSIAN RIVER
- Oakland (II) → Chrysopolis
- REDWOOD EMPIRE → QUINAULT
- Sacramento → Newark
- SANTA ROSA → ENETAI, SANTA ROSA
- SHASTA → EDWARD T. JEFFEREY 28/
- STOCKTON → KLICKITAT
- YOSEMITE → ARGENTINA

See explanations and footnotes at end of table.

TABLE 18 -- *Specifications of Ferry Steamers* (Continued)

Explanations and footnotes

Ferry names shown in CAPS are of steel construction, all others are of wood construction.

1. Ferry types: A : Auto ferry; F : Freight car ferry; P : Passenger ferry.
   s.w. : Side wheel; st.w. : Stern wheel; s.sc. : Single screw propeller; t.sc. : Twin screw propeller.
2. First length and beam dimension is hull dimension; *italics* indicate deck dimensions.
3. Indicated horsepower: (b) braking horsepower; (s) shaft horsepower.
4. 1903 length : 144.0
5. Rebuilt from single-ender to specifications shown by Central Pacific at Oakland in 1878.
6. Tonnage changed in 1926 to 1883 gross and 1168 net; crew reduced to 20.
7. Rebuilt with 4 water tube boilers.
8. Rebuilt to auto ferry with specifications shown by Monticello Steamship Co. in 1927; original tonnage was 2312 gross and 1270 net.
9. Rebuilt from single-ender to specifications shown by Patrick Tiernan at Oakland Point in 1876.
10. Rebuilt to auto ferry with specifications shown by Monticello Steamship Co. in 1927. Reboilered with 6 water tube boilers after 1930.
11. One boiler until 1866.
12. Tonnage shown is after being rebuilt and lengthened to 30 feet in 1865.
13. Associated with William Collyer and Charles G. White.
14. Crew increased to 25 in 1912.
15. Rebuilt to specifications shown from ferry Ukiah which had been built by Northwestern Pacific R.R. in Tiburon in 1890.
16. Crew reduced to 5 in 1912.
17. Crew increased to 16 in 1915.
18. Rebuilt to auto ferry with specifications shown by Monticello Steamship Co. in 1927; original tonnage was 1500 gross and 884 net. Tonnage reduced to 1490 gross and 814 net in 1923.
19. Crew reduced to 24 in 1927.
20. Rebuilt in 1903; tonnage increased to 2197 gross and 1758 net. Depth increased to 18.8 feet.
21. Crew reduced to 18 in 1915.
22. Tonnage reduced to 285 in 1870.
23. Crew reduced to 13 in 1912.
24. Crew reduced to 18 in 1909 and to 17 in 1912.
25. Rebuilt from ferry Newark.
26. Crew reduced to 13 in 1912.
27. Hulk docked in San Francisco.
28. and FEATHER RIVER.
* plus electric motors.

Chetzemoka and *Klahanie,* the last of the wooden diesel-electric ferries, were removed from service.

The *Chetzemoka* subsequently was purchased by Arnold Gridley, who invested over $60,000 to make the ferry serviceable for a journey back to San Francisco Bay. Gridley planned to dock the ferry in San Francisco, where she would be the location of exclusive shops and boutiques. On the night of May 28, 1977, the sea tug *Express,* with the *Chetzemoka* in tow, left the Todd Shipyard in Seattle. Two nights later, while off the coast of Washington, the ferry began taking excessive amounts of water; she sank the following day.

In the latter part of 1940, Puget Sound Navigation Company purchased the six steel diesel-electric ferries and the steam ferries *Shasta* and *San Mateo.* All were towed to Puget Sound. Seven boats made the trip with no difficulty, but the *Lake Tahoe* was nearly lost when heavy seas broke the tow line while she was off Trinidad Head in northern California. After drifting for 36 hours, during which time a skeleton crew kept her pumps going, the ferry was rescued. She then was brought into Humboldt Bay where emergency repairs were made before resuming the journey northward.

Like the former "Golden Boats" four years previously, the eight ferries were refurbished by Puget Sound Navigation Company. The electric ferries were given Indian names: the *Fresno* became the *Willapa* (name of an Indian tribe), the *Lake Tahoe* became the *Illahee* (land, place), the *Mendocino* became the *Nisqually* (name of an Indian tribe), the *Redwood Empire* became the *Quinault* (name of a river), the *Santa Rosa* became the *Enetai* (on the other side), and the *Stockton* became the *Klickitat* (name of an Indian tribe). Before entering service, the *Willapa* and *Enetai* were rebuilt as single-end, direct-drive diesel ferries. The *Shasta* and *San Mateo* were neither rebuilt nor renamed. All these ferries became a part of the Washington State Ferry System in 1951.

In the latter part of 1968, the *Enetai* and *Willapa* were declared surplus. The former was purchased by Donald V. Clair, renamed *Santa Rosa,* and returned to San Francisco Bay; she is now docked at Oakland. Likewise, the *Willapa* was purchased by Tom Gentry, renamed *Fresno,* and also returned to the bay; this ferry is now docked at Martinez. The *Shasta* was retired in 1959, and she was towed to Portland and converted into a restaurant. The *San Mateo* finished out her years as the sole remaining steam ferry on Puget Sound. Unable to maintain her because of mounting costs of repairs, Washington State Ferries was forced to retire her in 1969. As of this writing, the four remaining steel diesel-electric ferries, although now nearly 50 years old, are still in service. The *Quinault* (nee *Redwood Empire*) is operated daily on the Fauntleroy-Vashon-Southworth route, a run this ferry has been on for some 30 years. The *Illahee* (nee *Lake Tahoe*) provides supplementary service on the Edmonds-Kingston route. The *Nisqually* (nee *Mendocino*) and the *Klickitat* (nee *Stockton*) provide scheduled service during summer months and supplementary service during winter months on the Anacortes-San Juan Islands route.

As a Puget Sound boat, the *Napa Valley,* by then renamed the *Malahat,* saw little service. She experienced a disastrous fire in 1943 after which she was extensively rebuilt. Even then, however, she was used mostly as an extra boat. In 1956, she was towed to Portland for dismantling, but during scrapping, she again caught fire; this time she was destroyed.

The most illustrious career of the ferries which journeyed north belongs to the *City of Sacramento.* Like the *Napa Valley,* this boat was taken to Puget Sound in 1944, but she kept her bay name when she entered service on the Seattle-Bremerton run in December 1945. In April 1952, she was transferred to Canadian registry, being owned by that time by Black Ball Transport, Ltd., the Canadian counterpart of Puget Sound Navigation Company. That same year, the ferry was completely rebuilt and equipped with diesel-electric drive in place of her steam engines. The once-renowned *Asbury Park* soon emerged as the *Kahloke* (white swan) and entered service on June 27, 1953, on the North Vancouver (Horseshoe Bay) to Nanaimo (Departure Bay) run, an open-water crossing of the Gulf of Georgia requiring some two hours for each trip.

In 1961, the Province of British Columbia purchased the Black Ball ferries, and the big ferry again was renamed, this time to *Langdale Queen.* That same year, the ferry was assigned to the one-hour crossing from Horseshoe Bay to Langdale, on the Sechelt Peninsula. In 1972, the ferry was relegated to auxiliary service, being used daily during summer months and only on weekends at other times. In 1976, the *Langdale Queen* was taken out of service, having been replaced by a newly constructed ferry. The former *City of Sacramento* then was taken to Deas Dock in Vancouver, where she was laid up awaiting an uncertain future.

Bibliography

Books and Other Publications

Adams, Edson F. *Oakland's Early History*. Anonymous. 1932.
Anonymous. *Cast-Steel Motor Trucks for the S.P. Co.* Electric Railway Journal. Volume 37, Number 11. March 18, 1911.
_____*Signalling for a Train a Minute on the San Francisco Bay Bridge*. Railway Age. Volume 106, Number 19. May 13, 1939.
_____*Southern Pacific Company Entertains A.I.E.E.* Electric Railway Journal. Volume 37, Number 22. June 3, 1911.
_____*Southern Pacific Electrification at Oakland: Fruitvale Power and Substation*. Electric Railway Journal. Volume 37, Number 5. February 4, 1911.
_____*Southern Pacific Electrification at Oakland: Rolling Stock and Repair Shops*. Electric Railway Journal. Volume 37, Number 24. June 17, 1911. (Reprinted in Traction Heritage, Volume 2, Number 1, January 1969.)
_____*The Big Red Cars*. Western Railroader. Volume 19, Number 7. May 1956.
_____*The Fruitvale Power Plant*. Journal of Electricity, Power and Gas. Volume 26, Number 22. June 3, 1911.
_____*Ye Olden Oakland Days*. Tribune Publishing Company. 1922.
Beckman, Roy C. *The Romance of Oakland*. Landes and Kelsey. 1932.
Beebe, Lucius. *The Central Pacific and the Southern Pacific Railroads*. Howell-North. 1963.
Best, Gerald M. *Iron Horses to Promontory*. Golden West. 1969.
Best, Gerald M. and Joslyn, David L. *Locomotives of the Southern Pacific Company*. The Railway and Locomotive Historical Society. Bulletin 94. March 1956.
Bronson, William. *The Earth Shook and the Sky Burned*. Doubleday and Company. 1959.
Buckingham, Fisher A. *Origins and Early Economic Developments of Oakland*. University of California, Berkeley. Unpublished M.A. thesis. 1947.
Cummings, G.A. and Pladwell, E.S. *Oakland—A History*. Grant Miller. 1942.
Daggett, Stuart. *Chapters on the History of the Southern Pacific*. Ronald Press. 1922.
Demoro, Harre. *The Evergreen Fleet*. Golden West. 1971.
Dickinson, A. Bray. *Narrow Gauge to the Redwoods*. Trans-Anglo. 1967.
Dodge, Richard V. *Rails of the Silver Gate*. Pacific Railway Journal. 1960.
Dunsomb, Guy L. *A Century of Southern Pacific Steam Locomotives*. Published by the author, 2nd edition. 1967.
Ferrier, William W. *Berkeley, California*. Anonymous. 1933.
General Railway Signal Company. *Railway Signalling on the San Francisco-Oakland Bay Bridge*. Bulletin 173. July 1939.
Guppy, R.T. *Electrification of the Oakland Suburban Lines*. Railway Age Gazette. Volume 53, Number 11. September 13, 1912.
Harlan, George H. and Fisher, Clement, Jr. *Of Walking Beams and Paddle Wheels*. Bay Books. 1951.
Harlan, George H. *San Francisco Bay Ferryboats*. Howell-North. 1967.
Heath, Erle. *Seventy-five Years of Progress—A Historical Sketch of the Southern Pacific*. Southern Pacific Company. 1945.
Hedene, Phil. *The Red Electrics of Portland, Oregon*. Interurbans. Special No. 8. November 1949.
Hinkle, Edgar J. and McCann, William E. *Oakland, 1852-1938*. Oakland Public Library. 1939.
Houston, Mary R. *Early History of Berkeley, California*. University of California, Berkeley. Unpublished M.A. thesis. 1925.
Howarth, Fred. *Interurbans of Utah*. Interurbans. Special No. 15. August 1954.
Interurban Electric Railway Company. *Rules and Regulations for the Operationn of Trains under Continuous Automatic Cab Signal and Speed Control System*. January 1, 1939.
Jenevein, Richard G. *Transportation in the East Bay*. Central Trade School. 1944.
Kraus, George. *High Road to Promontory*. American West. 1969.
Lane, Carl D. *American Paddle Steamboats*. Coward-McCann. 1943.
Leale, Marion. *Captain John Leale: Recollections of a Tule Sailor*. George Fields. 1939.
MacGregor, Bruce A. *South Pacific Coast*. Howell-North. 1968.
MacMullen, Jerry. *Paddle-Wheel Days in California*. Stanford University Press. 3rd edition. 1945.
Newell, Gordon and Williamson, Joe. *Pacific Steamboats*. Superior Press. 1958.
Oakland City Planning Commission. *Report on East Bay Mass Transportation Survey*. City of Oakland. 1935.
Parkinson, Robert W. *Notes on Steam Train Predecessors of East Bay Electric Lines of the Southern Pacific*. California-Nevada Railroad Historical Society. Bulletin, Volume 5, Number 1. January 1941.
_____*Southern Pacific's East Bay Steam Suburban Service*. Western Railroader. Volume 35, Number 10, Issue No. 392. November-December 1972.
Reisenberg, Felix, Jr. *Golden Gate: The Story of San Francisco Harbor*. Tudor. 1940.
Russell, H.A. *Lighting Equipment of Ferry Steamer "Thoroughfare."* Journal of Electricity, Power and Gas. Volume 29, Number 6. August 10, 1912.
Sandoval, John. *Transcontinental Railroad Comes to the East Bay*. Western Railroader. Volume 32, Number 9, Issue No. 355. September 1969.
Sappers, Vernon J. and others. *From Shore to Shore—The Key Route*. Peralta Associates. 1948.
Shaw, Frederick and others. *Oil Lamps and Iron Ponies: A Chronicle of the Narrow Gauges*. Bay Books. 1949.
Southern Pacific Company. *Rules and Regulations for the Government of Employees in the Operation of the Oakland, Alameda and Berkeley Electric Power and Power Distributing Systems*. June 1, 1911.
_____*Diagrams: Common Standard Electric Train Cars*. Motive Power Department. 1924.
Stindt, Fred and Dunscomb, Guy L. *The Northwestern Pacific Railroad*. Published by the authors. 1964.
Stuart, Reginald R. *San Leandro—A History*. First Methodist Church. 1951.
Swett, Ira L. *Pacific Electric All-Time Roster*. Interurbans. Special No. 3. March 1946.
_____*Bamberger Railroad*. Interurbans. Special No. 4. September 1946.
_____*Cars of Pacific Electric—Volume I: City and Suburban Cars*. Interurbans. Special No. 28. Volume 22, Number 2. Summer 1964.
_____*Cars of Pacific Electric—Volume II: Interurban and Deluxe Cars*. Interurbans. Special No. 36. Volume 23, Number 1. Spring 1965.
_____*Cars of Pacific Electric—Volume III: Combos, RPOs, Box Motors, Work Motors, Locomotives, Tower Cars, Service Cars*. Interurbans. Special No. 37. Volume 23, Number 2. Summer 1965.
Swett, Ira L. and Aitken, Harry C. *Napa Valley Route*. Interurbans. Special No. 47. 1975.
Tufveson, Ray. *A History of the Interurban Electric Railway*. California-Nevada Railroad Historical Society. Bulletin. October 1940.
Turner, Robert D. *Vancouver Island Railroads*. Golden West. 1973.
United States Department of Commerce. *List of Merchant Vessels of the United States*. Government Printing Office. Published annually, 1868 to 1925.
_____*Merchant Vessels of the United States*. Government Printing Office. Published annually, 1926 to 1958.
Vigness, Paul G. *History of Alameda*. Anonymous. 1939.
Westinghouse Electric and Manufacturing Company. *600-1200-1500 Volt Locomotives for Southern Pacific Railroad Company*. Descriptive Leaflet 3536. October 1912.
Wilson, Neill and Taylor, Frank. *Southern Pacific*. McGraw-Hill. 1952.

Newspapers

Alameda County Gazette: 1859 to 1866
Alameda Daily Encinal: 1901 to 1902
Alameda Argus: 1905 to 1912
Alameda Times-Star: 1911 to 1939
Bay Area Electric Railroad Review: 1948 to 1973
Berkeley Advocate: 1877
Berkeley Daily Gazette: 1911 to 1941
California Chronicle: 1853
Oakland Daily News: 1861 to 1879
Oakland Daily Transcript: 1868 to 1876
Oakland Enquirer: 1902 to 1916
Oakland Post-Enquirer: 1920 to 1941
Oakland Times: 1878 to 1882
Oakland Tribune: 1873 to 1958
Oakland Tribune Yearbook: 1911 to 1925
Richmond Independent: 1925
San Francisco Daily Alta California: 1852 to 1888
San Francisco Bulletin: 1857 to 1906
San Francisco Call: 1894 to 1920
San Francisco Call-Bulletin: 1921 to 1941
San Francisco Chronicle: 1869 to 1973
San Francisco Examiner: 1868 to 1939
San Francisco Herald: 1853
Southern Pacific Bulletin: 1915 to 1941
West End (Alameda) *News:* 1881

Index

ACTIVE	342	
Adam's Point	54	
AJAX	134	
Alameda	29	
ALAMEDA (I)	32	
ALAMEDA (II)	134	
Alameda Loop Line	113	
Alameda Municipal Transportation League	265	
Alameda, Oakland & Piedmont R.R.	55	
Alameda Pier	29	
Alameda Pier Auto Ferry	174	
Alameda Pier Fire	81	
Alameda Point	52	
Alameda 7:30 S.P. Commuters Club	206	
Alameda Valley R.R.	29	
ALCISCO	173	
ALERT	173	
Alice St. Bridge	44	
ALVIRA	74	
AMADOR	67	
American Bridge Co.	197	
American Railroad Union	75	
ANASHA	64	
Andrus, Mayor W.R.	55	
ARGENTINA	213	
Argentina-Uruguayan Navigation Co.	213	
ASBURY PARK	342	
Athens Athletic Club	183	
Athens Terminal Bldg.	183	
Bay & Coast R.R.	52	
Bay Area Electric Railroad Association	289	
Bay Area Railfans Assn.	319	
Bay Area Rapid Transit District	291	
BAY CITY	52	
Berkeley	47	
BERKELEY	80	
Berkeley Auto Ferry	174	
Berkeley Branch R.R.	49	
Berkeley Land & Improvement Association	48	
Berkeley Railroad & Ferry Co.	48	
Berryman	49	
BIDDLE	138	
Black Ball Transport, Ltd.	217	
BOSTON	18	
Bridge Railway	241	
Bridge Yard	244	
British Columbia Ferries	348	
Brotherhood of Locomotive Firemen	75	
Brotherhood of Railway Trainmen	144	
Brown News Co.	141	
CALEB COPE	18	
California Pacific R.R.	35	
California Railway Museum	319	
California Street Line	120	
California Toll Bridge Authority	203	
CALISTOGA	201	
CAPITAL	62	
Carpenter, E.R.	19	
Carpenter, Horace	19	
Carpenter's Wharf	62	
Central Pacific R.R.	26	
CHETZEMOKA	342	
Chipman & Aughinbaugh	19	
CHRYSOPOLIS	62	
CITY OF SACRAMENTO	201	
Clark, Frank W.	253	
Clinton	23	
CLINTON	19	
Cohen, Alfred A.	26	
College of California	47	
Commerce St. Wharf	19	
COMMISSIONER	217	
CONFIDENCE	20	
CONTRA COSTA	19	
Contra Costa Ferry	19	
Contra Costa R.R.	32	
Contra Costa Steam Navigation Co.	19	
Creek Route	63	
Crocker, Charles	35	
Crosstown Line	99	
Davie, John L.	74	
Davie Transportation Co.	74	
Davis, A.E. "Hog"	51	
Davis Street Wharf	20	
"Death Curve"	128	
Debs, Eugene V.	75	
Decoration Day Disaster	70	
Dietz, A.C.	53	
Donahue, Peter	36	
Dumbarton Point	52	
Durant, Henry	48	
Earthquake (1868)	26	
Earthquake (1906)	87	
East Bay Street Railways	186	
East Bay Transit Co.	217	
East Oakland Protective League	142	
E.B. MASTICK	29	
EDWARD T. JEFFEREY	164	
18th Street Line	125	
EL CAPITAN	27	
Ellsworth Street Line	123	
EL PASO	166	
Elsey, Charles	54	
ELWHA	342	
Emory's	49	
EMPIRE	19	
Encinal	20	
ENCINAL	69	
Encinal Avenue Line (steam)	81	
Encinal Avenue Line (electric)	106	
ENETAI	348	
ERASTUS CORNING	18	
EUREKA	283	
F.A. DOUTY	173	
Fair, Sen. James G.	51	
FEATHER RIVER	197	
F.D. ATHERTON	32	
Felton, John B.	23	
FERNWOOD	136	
Ferryboatmen's Union	159	
Ferry Building (1875)	62	
Ferry Building (1898)	77	
Flood Building	147	
Franklin Street Bus Line	223	
Freight Operations	323	
FRESNO	173	
Fruitvale Avenue Bridge	94	
Fruitvale Powerhouse	101	
GARDEN CITY	53	
General Railway Signal Co.	246	
GENERAL SUTTER	18	
Gibbons, Rodman	18	
Goat Island	23	
GOLDEN AGE	205	
GOLDEN BEAR	205	
GOLDEN COAST	201	
GOLDEN DAWN	201	
GOLDEN ERA	201	
GOLDEN GATE	201	
GOLDEN POPPY	205	
GOLDEN SHORE	205	
GOLDEN STATE	205	
GOLDEN WAY	201	
GOLDEN WEST	205	
Golden Gate Ferry Co.	170	
Golden Gate Bridge	203	
GOLIAH	22	
Gompers, Samuel	77	
Goss, George	23	
GOVERNOR IRWIN	82	
GRACE BARTON	74	
Graves, Hiram T.	48	
Harriman, E.H.	98	
Harrison Street Bridge	79	
Harte, Bret	38	
Hayward	26	
HAYWARD	284	
HECTOR	18	
Hibbard's Encinal Wharf	24	
Hoover-Young Bay Bridge Commission	195	
Hopkins, Mark	35	
Horseshoe Line	87	
Huntington, Collis P.	26	
ILLAHEE	348	
Indian Creek Slough	24	
Interlocking Facilities	323	
Interrupted Electric Railway Company	279	
IRISBANK	174	
Jackson Street Wharf	19	
Jacob's Landing	48	
JENNY LIND	18	
J.G. KELLOGG	30	
JUANITA	71	
KANGAROO	18	
KATE HAYES	19	
KEHLOKEN	342	
Key Route	85	
Key Route Pier	86	
Key Route Pier Fire	224	
Key System Transit Co.	169	
Key System Transit Lines	287	
Kitsap County Transportation Company	205	
K.J. LUCKENBACH	164	
KLAHANIE	342	
KLAMATH	166	
KLICKITAT	348	
KORRIGAN III	138	
Krutschnitt, Julius	99	
Lake Merritt	24	
Lake Merritt Railway	54	
LAKE TAHOE	173	
LANGDALE QUEEN	348	
Larue, James B.	20	
LIBERTY	24	
Lincoln Avenue Line (steam)	99	
Lincoln Avenue Line (electric)	111	
Los Angeles & San Pedro R.R.	30	
Los Angeles Metropolitan Transit Authority	318	
Los Gatos	52	
LOUISE	24	
Low, Governor Frederick F.	32	
Lundberg, Alfred J.	190	
Mail Trains	323	
MALAHAT	348	
MARE ISLAND	49	
Mare Island-Vallejo Ferry Co.	49	
Marinship Yard	284	
Marion	36	
MARIPOSA	38	
Market Street R.R.	24	
Martinez-Benicia Ferry	179	
Masters, Mates and Pilots Association	159	
Mastick, E.B.	29	
McAdoo, William Gibbs	151	
Meetz, Thomas	55	
MELROSE	90	
Melrose Extension	114	
MENDOCINO	173	
Mercier, A.T.	253	
Merritt, Dr. Samuel	38	
Metropolitan Coach Lines	318	
Minturn, Charles	18	
Miracle, Walter D.	207	
Monticello Steamship Co.	200	
Moon and Adams Landing	19	
Mott, Frank K.	143	
NAPA VALLEY	201	
National Broadcasting Co.	253	
Newark	52	
NEWARK	52	
NEW ORLEANS	166	
Nickel Ferry	135	
Ninth Street Line	122	
NISQUALLY	348	
North Boat Works	22	
Northbrae Tunnel	120	
NORTH ISLAND	342	
North, John G.	19	
North Pacific Coast R.R.	36	
Northern Railway	49	
Northwestern Pacific R.R.	144	
OAKLAND (Locomotive)	27	
OAKLAND (Ferry—I)	20	
OAKLAND (Ferry—II)	62	
Oakland Bar	19	
Oakland Long Wharf	43	
Oakland Pier	64	

Oakland Point		43
Oakland Point Pier		27
Oakland Terminal Ry.		252
Oakland Township R.R.		57
Ocean View		48
O'Farrell, Jasper		61
OLD BETSY		24
Olsen, Governor Culbert L.		203
Opposition Line		20
Orange Empire Railway Museum		315
Order of Railway Conductors		146
Oregon and California Lines		293
Otis, Frank		143
Pacific Electric Ry.		144
Pacific Junction		106
Pacific Wharf		19
Panama-Pacific International Exposition		135
Patterson, Lt.Gov. Ellis E.		253
Peninsular Railway		115
PENNSYLVANIAN		174
PERALTA (I)		20
PERALTA (II)		224
Peralta Landing		20
PHOENIX		94
PIEDMONT		67
Point Richmond		123
Puget Sound Navigation Co.		205
Purcell, Charles H.		195
QUEEN CITY		20
QUINAULT		348
Railroad Strike (1894)		75
RANGER		19
RED JACKET		19
Redondo Sport Fishing Co.		287
REDWOOD EMPIRE		173
REINDEER		43
RESTLESS		164
Richmond Auto Ferry Line		166
Richmond Line		123
Richmond-San Francisco Transportation Co.		166
Richmond-San Rafael Ferry & Transportation Co.		286
Richmond Shipyards		284
Rolph, James, Jr.		162
ROSALIE		74
Rossi, Angelo J.		253
RUSSIAN RIVER		342
SACRAMENTO		166
Sacramento Northern Ry.		153
Sacramento St. Line		120
SAN ANTONIO		20
San Antonio Creek		19
San Antonio Creek Freight Piers		52
San Antonio Steam Navigation Company		20
San Diego-Coronado Ferry Co.		205
San Francisco & Alameda R.R.		26
San Francisco & Colorado River R.R.		59
San Francisco & Oakland Railroad & Ferry Co.		23
San Francisco Bay R.R.		36
San Francisco Maritime Museum		288
San Francisco, Oakland and Alameda R.R.		33
San Francisco, Oakland and San Jose R.R.		85
San Francisco-Oakland Bay Bridge		190
San Francisco-Oakland Terminal Railways		111
San Francisco-Sacramento R.R.		153
San Francisco Terminal Bldg.		243
SAN GABRIEL		30
SAN JOSE		95
San Jose & Stockton R.R.		29
San Leandro		30
SAN LEANDRO		173
SAN MATEO (I)		134
SAN MATEO (II)		163
SANTA CLARA		134
SANTA ROSA		173
SEA ROVER		198
Seventh Street Line (electric)		101
Seventh Street Line (steam)		27
Seventh Street Parade		115
Seventh Street Underpass		171
SHASTA		163
Shattuck Ave. Line (electric)		120
Shattuck Ave. Line (Key Route)		86
Shattuck Ave. Line (steam)		49
Shaw's Wharf		22
Shipyard Railway		280
Shoup, Paul		144
SIERRA NEVADA		197
SILVER STRAND		342
Simpson's		39
Six Minute Ferry		163
Smith, Francis M.		85
SONOMA		39
SOPHIE MacLANE		30
South Pacific Coast R.R.		51
South Pacific Coast Ry.		59
Southern Pacific-Golden Gate Company		177
Southern Pacific-Golden Gate Ferries, Ltd.		179
Southern Pacific R.R.		49
Speas, Harry E.		174
Sproule, William		137
Stanford, Leland		26
Stanford, Leland, Mrs.		75
Stations:		
Berkeley (I)		122
Berkeley (II)		126
Berkeley (III)		237
Berkeley-Delaware Street		128
Berkeley-3rd and University		129
Dutton Avenue		190
First & Broadway		126
14th & Franklin		182
Havenscourt		276
Oakland-16th St.		127
South Berkeley		236
Suburban Elevation		128
Stewart, A.O.		175
STOCKTON		173
Stockton & Copperopolis R.R.		27
Stonehurst		115
St. Sure, William P.		278
Sullivan, F.E.		253
TAMALPAIS		286
TAMPICO		94
Taylor's Wharf		27
TELEPHONE		197
THEODORE JUDAH		49
THOROUGHFARE (I)		44
THOROUGHFARE (II)		132
Thousand Oaks		99
TIBURON		70
TRANSIT		63
Transport Building		284
26th Street Viaduct		245
UNDERWRITER		62
Union Switch & Signal Div.		246
U.S. Maritime Commission		316
U.S. Railroad Administration		151
Vallejo Street Wharf		22
Vallejo's Mills		29
Vulcan Iron Works		24
Washington State Ferries		348
WASHOE		26
Webster Street		56
Webster Street Bridge		55
Webster Street Line (electric)		111
Webster Street Line (steam)		57
West Alameda Shops		106
Western Pacific R.R. (first)		27
Whitney Ferry & Transportation Company		74
WILLAPA		348
WILLIAMS		198
Wilmington Transportation Co.		284
Woodstock		29
YERBA BUENA (I)		96
YERBA BUENA (II)		284
YOSEMITE		163

REFERENCE LIST OF FERRY CAPTAINS

Name	Ferry	Company[1]	Page
Anderson, Albert	OAKLAND	S.P.	199
	SIERRA NEVADA	S.P.	212
Anderson, C.J.	GARDEN CITY	S.P.	164
	SANTA CLARA	S.P.	135
Blaker, Charles H.	PIEDMONT	S.P.	96
Blaker, James	BERKELEY	S.P.	97
Carson, Charles	SANTA CLARA	S.P.	135
Carson, W.S.	FRESNO	S.P.-G.G.	198
Chamberlin, J.B.	MELROSE	S.P.	174
Crowdace, Charles	ENCINAL	S.P.	138
Curley, J.	MELROSE	S.P.	90
Diaz, Frank	SAN LEANDRO	S.P.	289
Elsasser, William A.	ALAMEDA	S.P.	209
Forsberg, Samuel	MELROSE	S.P.	138
Fouratt, Enos	PIEDMONT	S.P.	209
Fouratt, George	SACRAMENTO	S.P.	166
Fouratt, John R.	KANGAROO	———	18
Gaynor, J.M.	EL PASO	S.P.-G.G.	199
Gray, Thomas	GENERAL SUTTER	———	18
Hackett, Edward	EL CAPITAN	C.P.	44
Hackett, John	THOROUGHFARE	C.P.	44
Hallin, Edward	LAKE TAHOE	S.P.-G.G.	217
Hickey, John	MELROSE	S.P.	132
Holmes, H.H.	MELROSE	S.P.	164
Jacobsen, Nils A.	ENCINAL	S.P.	138
Jones, E.A.	BERKELEY	S.P.	95
Leale, John	NEWARK	S.P.C.	52
	ALAMEDA	C.P.	76
	OAKLAND	S.P.	81
Lewis, John	CONTRA COSTA	C.C.S.N.	22
Lewis, John	FERNWOOD	Key Route	137
McGarrigle, Patrick	SAN LEANDRO	S.P.	290
McKechnie, Donald	BAY CITY	S.P.	136
McKenzie, William	THOROUGHFARE	S.P.	132
McLean, James	THOROUGHFARE	S.P.	133
Murphy, William	ENCINAL	S.P.C.	97
Patterson, Carlisle P.	SAN ANTONIO	S.A.S.N.	20
Ramsdall, B.H.	ERASTUS CORNING	C.C.S.N.	18
Richardson, John	EDWARD T. JEFFEREY	W.P.R.R.	197
Richter, William	MELROSE	S.P.	138
Rogers, William	BAY CITY	S.P.	132
Saez, Eduardo M.	ARGENTINA	A.-U.N.T.	213
Skibinski, Michael H.	YOSEMITE	S.P.	213
Souza, James	SANTA CLARA	S.P.	174
Susan, James C.	BERKELEY	S.P.	199
	OAKLAND	S.P.	212
Susan, W.J.	PIEDMONT	S.P.	174
Talbot, T.E.	SANTA CLARA	S.P.	135
Thomas, Richard	SAN LEANDRO	S.P.	287
Wall, Peter	BAY CITY	S.P.	132
Webster, George W.	RANGER	———	20
Wold, P.F.	ALAMEDA	S.P.	134

1. S.P.—Southern Pacific
  S.P.-G.G.—Southern Pacific-Golden Gate Ferries
  C.P.—Central Pacific
  S.P.C.—South Pacific Coast
  C.C.S.N.—Contra Costa Steam Navigation Co.
  S.A.S.N.—San Antonio Steam Navigation Co.
  W.P.R.R.—Wester Pacific Railroad
  A.-U.N.T.—Argentina-Uruguayan Navigation Touring Co.

EASTWARD BERKELEY DISTRICT TRAINS

- BERKELEY SHATTUCK AVENUE
- SHATTUCK EXPRESS
- BERKELEY 9TH STREET
- BERKELEY CALIFORNIA STREET
- BERKELEY ELLSWORTH STREET
- OAKLAND 14TH & FRANKLIN STS VIA 18TH STREET — DOES NOT STOP AT 16TH ST. STATION

STRE

- ENCINAL AVE ALAMEDA
- LINCOLN AVE ALAMEDA

NOTE - Westward trains carry disc signs reading "SAN FRANCISCO VIA OAKLAND PIER" or "SAN FRANCISCO VIA ALAMEDA PIER" using appropriate color and design for route used.

O.A.&B. LINES